CONOR CRUISE O'BRIEN
by Mick O'Dea RHA

TRINITY COLLEGE DUBLIN
THE COLLEGE HISTORICAL SOCIETY

TRINITY COLLEGE DUBLIN

The College Historical Society
Oratory and Debate

1770–2020

PATRICK GEOGHEGAN

Hinds

The Lilliput Press

Published by
THE LILLIPUT PRESS
62-63 Sitric Road, Arbour Hill,
Dublin 7, Ireland
www.lilliputpress.ie

and

HINDS
13 Carlisle Avenue
Dublin 4
Ireland
www.hinds.ie
mail@hinds.ie

First published 2020

ISBN-13 978-1-843517-77-1

The endpapers contain a selection of the portraits of Hist members by Mick O'Dea RHA, which were commissioned in celebration of the 250th Anniversary of the founding of the Society.

Typeset in 11pt on 13pt Adobe Garamond
Design by Susan Waine
Printed in Ireland by Walsh Colour Print, Castleisland, Co. Kerry

CONTENTS

The illustrations have been placed together in one section between page 236 and 237. The first page of this section contains the Table of Illustrations.

FOREWORD

IT IS A GREAT PRIVILEGE to write the Foreword to this history of The College Historical Society by Dr Patrick Geoghegan, published to mark the 250th anniversary of the oldest student debating society. It is a splendid scholarly piece of work written by a leading academic historian with the elegance and ease that Dr Geoghegan has brought to his major studies of Robert Emmet and Daniel O'Connell, to his lectures, and indeed to his popular radio programmes. When the project was mooted it was clear that he was by far the best qualified person to write a professional history of 250 years of a society whose members have contributed so much to Trinity College, to Ireland and indeed worldwide. It was obvious that Dr Geoghegan would bring great skills and experience to the task, and that the book would entertain as much as inform. He is an eminent authority on the eighteenth and nineteenth centuries with the consequent ability to set the Hist in its political, social and intellectual context – it was founded in the eighteenth century and arguably it had its greatest impact in the nineteenth century.

Three revolutions were powerfully influenced by former members of the Hist, 1798 (Wolfe Tone), 1803 (Robert Emmet) and 1848 (Thomas Davis). The Irish Parliamentary Party (1874) was founded by Isaac Butt, the Gaelic League by Douglas Hyde (1893) and the first signatory to the Ulster Covenant in 1912 was Edward Carson. Dr Geoghegan describes the careers of its most remarkable members as undergraduates and graduates, taking us from one extraordinary episode to another. Readers will find that the story of the Hist is intricately intertwined with the changes in the island of Ireland and the relationship with the United Kingdom – great figures of the day spoke at the Society while some among the members who debated with them went on to replace them. Hist members spoke and later acted on opposite sides of big matters – Robert Emmet was defended by one Hist lawyer and prosecuted by another. Carson defended the Marquis of Queensberry when he was accused of libel by Oscar Wilde, who had been a fellow member of the Hist.

Dr Geoghegan, a Fellow of Trinity College, has been a loyal supporter of the Society, speaking often and chairing debates – he is a fine orator and the members were honoured when he accepted the invitation to be elected a Vice-President. We value the fact that he was a student member of the Literary and Historical Society, the 'L&H' of UCD – he did not see the Hist as an insider; likewise this history shows a perspective that comes from a person who started as an outsider. We will never know how Dr Geoghegan managed to produce such a detailed account of the Hist while holding his appointment as a special adviser (2017–20) to the Taoiseach, Leo Varadkar TD, during the Brexit crisis. We are deeply grateful to Dr Geoghegan – he has opened up so many new associations for the Hist, with many surprises, for example connecting with James Joyce who was never a member and may never have spoken at the Society, and Sir Robert Anderson, an ex-Auditor who became famous for his work in Scotland Yard. These are sidelights on an otherwise extraordinary story of a Society that was usually focused on great questions of the day – though punctuated with humorous motions that tested the wit of the members.

The Trinity Trust made an important and generous grant to support publication including research assistance for Dr Geoghegan. The manuscript was skilfully and knowledgeably edited by Ross Hinds, Vice-President of the Hist, and published jointly by Hinds and by The Lilliput Press.

The Hist was founded by students with the permission of the Board of Trinity College Dublin in March 1770, just at the time when many ideas of the Enlightenment were coming to a head. Baroque music was giving way to Classical – Ludwig van Beethoven was born in December 1770. The European world, adapting to the Reformation and invigorated by Isaac Newton's science, was reacting to the ideas of Francis Bacon, Voltaire, Jean-Jacques Rousseau and Adam Smith, the philosophy of René Descartes, Baruch Spinoza, John Locke, David Hume and Immanuel Kant, and a host of other great thinkers. The Marquis de Condorcet and others were arguing for equality of men and women, and for the abolition of slavery. The last of the thirty-five volumes of the *Encyclopédie* on science and philosophy, compiled by 150 authorities under the leadership of Denis Diderot, were about to be published. James Hutton and others were arguing how the shape of the Earth had been and was continuing to be changed inexorably by great forces of nature over millions of years. Biologists were astonished by the discovery of monstrous fossils leading the Compte de Buffon, Jean-Baptiste Lamarck and Erasmus Darwin to argue that evolution had occurred. Joseph Black, the Irishman who discovered carbon dioxide, Henry Cavendish (hydrogen), Joseph Priestly and Antoine Lavoisier (oxygen) were laying the basis for modern chemistry. James Watt, a friend of both Smith and Black at Glasgow, radically modified the steam engine providing the power needed to give the industrial revolution its name – engines before Watt were so inefficient they could only be used beside coal mines. The world was alight with discoveries, debates and discussions, and books to match, of a significance that we can now recognize had never been seen before. Within a few years, the American Revolution (1776) and the French Revolution (1789) would transform the legal basis of government and set us slowly and steadily on the paths to secular liberal democracy – the nation state as we know it today was being defined in those few decades at the end of the eighteenth century. These times can be seen as the most concentrated, most pervasive and significant revolutionary period in modern history. Even if today the transitions are far from complete, the writing was on the wall: faith was being challenged by reason, monarchy by democracy and edicts were being replaced by laws made by increasingly representative assemblies.

We can see that those thirteen students who founded the Hist, had set up a debating society devoted to historical analysis and diligent exploration of the facts of any matter, where they could develop skills that encouraged them in revolutionary thinking at a time of revolution. The College, set beautifully in the magnificent buildings of Parliament and Library Squares, was tiny, with 400–500 students – incidentally the numbers were about the same at Cambridge, which did not have a debating society until forty-five years later (McDowell and Webb).

The case for founding the Hist was made to the Board of the College by Michael Kearney, one of the seven Senior Fellows who were in those days *ex-officio* members of the Board. It is more than a curiosity that he was the seven times great grand-uncle of Barack Obama. Kearney was a friend of Edmund Burke from whom he had obtained the Minute Book of Burke's Club of 1747. It was probably expected that the Hist would be influenced by Burke, as it has been. The Minute Book of the Club is the most prized possession of the Society; the Hist participated in raising funds towards the statue of Burke that was unveiled at Front Gate in 1868; in 1897 it initiated the celebrations of the centenary of Burke's death; the minutes of the first meeting of Burke's Club were read in 1920 to celebrate 150 years of the Hist; the text of the Minute Book, edited by A.P.I. Samuels, ex-Auditor, was published posthumously in 1923. College and the Hist celebrated the Bicentenary of Burke's birth in 1928 when the Burke Bicentenary Commemoration Fund was established to support the Hist. In 1947 Harold Laski gave a major address on Edmund Burke commemorating the bicentenary of Burke's Club – there was enough in Burke to be admired across the political spectrum. The occasion is brilliantly described by Dr Geoghegan.

The Society prospered. Membership increased to fifty by the end of 1770, and to over 700 in the next twenty years – most of the members were graduates (*The College Historical Society*, R.B. McDowell. Dublin University Press, 1932). The Society met in what is today the magnificent Senior Common Room, which came to be known as the 'Historical Room'; the Board felt it had to ask permission to use the Hist rooms on the occasion of the visit of the Lord Lieutenant in 1783. This was a year after substantial political independence had been conceded to Grattan's Parliament. Some members of the Society were MPs. Laurence Parsons, later 2nd Earl of Rosse, was an MP when he was elected Auditor of the Society (for the second time) in 1781.

Patrick Geoghegan builds on the earliest record of the Society so lovingly produced by T.S.C. Dagg (*College Historical Society: A History (1770-1920).* Tralee 1969) and the valuable anthology edited by Budd and Hinds (*The Hist and Edmund Burke's Club*, Lilliput 1997) after the Society had celebrated its bicentenary in 1970. Geoghegan tells how students in the Hist, who were later to play leading roles in the transformation of Ireland, North and South, first tested their ideas in the Society. It took its name from the its initial focus on historical questions, at first restricted to British history. This may have seemed a benign and constructive objective to the Board, but it did not last long. In 1782, reacting no doubt to the new status of the Irish Parliament, the Board lifted this restriction, and the Society gained confidence as it developed its long and sometimes tempestuous relationship with College. Students joined in demands for Catholic emancipation and, as McDowell and Webb record, 'liberalism soon came close to treason'. Tensions arose and by 1794 the Board moved to confine membership to students of the College, which would have disbarred 500 members. The Board forced the issue and decided to exclude the Society from its magnificent rooms unless it agreed to this new rule. This caused a split in the Society between those who accepted it, the Intern Society, and the rest who formed the first Extern Society. The schism was finally ended in 1806 when the records and property of the Extern Society were presented to the Intern Society. By 1815 the Society had left College again, reviving once more outside College where it remained until 1843.

As Geoghegan recounts, many great figures first made their reputations in the Hist. Tone, Emmet, Thomas Moore, Davis, John Blake Dillon, Butt, Hyde and Carson are more or less household names in Ireland, having made such lasting contributions to modern Ireland and are held high in various pantheons. Davis, who was Auditor (1839) and President (1840), made the mistake of being a thinker, a poet and a writer who did not die for his country, but he left the most generous and constructive ideas for a new Ireland. The Young Irelanders grew out of the Hist, as did their paper the *Nation* with its call 'educate that you may be free'. It took our country more than a century to take Davis's advice – one might wish that he would have had a larger influence had he not died of scarlet fever when he was thirty, but perhaps not. I cannot see that some of those who say they followed his ideas could have properly understood him. It is less well known that the Society's members included many notable novelists, from Charles Maturin, Sheridan Le Fanu and Bram Stoker to Oscar Wilde and Samuel Beckett.

Edward Carson, the leader of Unionism, was a friend of his contemporary, John Redmond, the last important leader of the Home Rule movement; Carson attended Redmond's funeral Mass. It is not clear whether Redmond was in the Hist with Carson but there is no doubt that many friendships were made in the Hist that endured in spite of significant political differences. Many Hist people had leading roles in the legal and political administration of Ireland, and in the Church of Ireland, between the Union and independence, including Lord Ashbourne, Lord Chancellor of Ireland, and William Connor Magee, Archbishop of York – Dr Geoghegan has ensured they are not forgotten. Some played important parts in the transition from British rule to the new regimes, North and South. Lord Glenavy, ex-Auditor and President of the Society, became the Chair of the Seanad of the Free State frustrating – for a while – Mr de Valera's impatience with the Upper House. Sir Donnell Deeny, Vice-President, formerly Lord Justice of Appeal in Northern Ireland, has recently made the case that Sir James Andrews, ex-Auditor, and other Hist lawyers, helped to establish and maintain the independence of the judiciary of Northern Ireland at a difficult time.

In the nineteenth century there were 'few among the leaders of public opinion in Ireland who did not pass through *The Historical*' [1] but that could not last. Competition came from the graduates of four new universities founded in the nineteenth century, each with its debating society (led in three out of the four cases by an *Auditor*), each contributing leaders in politics and the law and other walks of life, North and South.

Hist members largely missed out on the revolutions that led to the partition of Ireland, and indeed Trinity was somewhat disconnected from the newly formed Free State – though many senior political figures spoke at the Hist and Hist people went on to the law more or less as before independence. But no one would have said that Trinity or the Hist was fully engaged in the new Ireland – partly because some wanted to isolate the College.

Joining the Hist in 1962, I found a society that was completely different from all others in Ireland. The infamous 'Ban' by which Archbishop John Charles McQuaid prohibited Catholic parents from sending their children to Trinity on pain of 'mortal sin', was too widely complied with, and vigorously enforced when challenged. One result was that many students came to Trinity from Great Britain to fill the

1 William Macneile Dixon, *Trinity College Dublin* (London, 2002)

available places. About one third of the students came from the Republic, and the same from Northern Ireland (almost all Protestants) and from Great Britain. There were a few students from the Commonwealth following in the footsteps of Jaja Wachuku, first Foreign Minister of Nigeria. The UK students had a different schooling, wider experiences and good grants, so they set the pace in many respects, which was good for us all. The membership of the Hist reflected the student body. This made for a great variety of personalities and ideas, ranging from members of the Cumann Gaelach and the Fabian Society, to the entire membership of the '1964 Committee', an active group of young Tories, led by Patrick Evershed CBE. Of the few Irish Catholics many had been students at Clongowes Wood College which had a reputation for encouraging independence of mind. British Catholics, including Michael Newcombe, Auditor 1962-63, made distinctive contributions. Women were excluded from the Society.

You could not have made it up! But when all was said and done the Hist, with all its weaknesses, was thoroughly cosmopolitan, a contrast with almost everything else in Ireland. It provided a rich intellectual and social formation. What it lacked in 'Irishness' was compensated for by its diversity in membership and ideas. Moreover it was a superb debating society, ruled by laws that owed much to curious traditions and governed by Private Business – which often went on into the early hours of the morning. It fulfilled the role that Davis envisaged when he spoke to the Society on *The Utility of Debating Societies in Remedying the Defects of a University Education.*

The College Board had a way of regulating the Society; motions for discussion had to be approved by the Board before the beginning of term. In 1957 the Hist debated the motion 'That this house disapproves of Birth Control', which was debated in camera, that is in private, 'at the request of the Board'. In 1958 the Hist decided to debate divorce. The Auditor, Michael Knight, suggested that the Correspondence Secretary, Ian Simons, invite Archbishop John Charles McQuaid, which he did. The Archbishop is believed to have spoken with Provost A.J. McConnell, who summoned Knight and Simons and instructed the Society not to debate the subject. Later in the session the Hist debated a motion 'That A.I.D. should be accepted by Society' with Bethel Solomons, the famous Jewish gynaecologist, in the Chair. Perhaps few people knew what A.I.D. was. In 1959 he was again in the chair when the Society debated homosexuality. In 1962–63 motions still had to be seen by the Board. One motion in Newcombe's year, 'That Abortion be made Legal' on 27 February 1963, had to be held in camera. The Hist was pushing at boundaries that were only fully breached fifty years later.

Elected Auditor for 1964–65 at a time when there was hope for reconciliation between North and South, and for the modernization of both, I wanted to explore in my Inaugural Address what lay ahead for Ireland. The population of the Republic of Ireland had fallen below three million. The policy that our past should be our future was failing. I loved my country and yet I despaired of it – much as I do today, though the balance has shifted very much for the better – the Enlightenment is winning out in the end even if it taking a bit longer than I expected.

I hoped to have Brian Faulkner and Charles Haughey, the two rising powers in Irish politics, among the speakers. Faulkner declined, Haughey accepted, ducking out at the last minute and 'sending' Brian Lenihan in his stead – an early example of their relationship. As mentioned by Patrick Geoghegan, my invitation to speak to Father James McDyer, the dedicated social reformer, perhaps the most powerful orator in Ireland, was not approved by his authorities. He was confined as much as possible as curate in the remote village of Glencolumbkille in County Donegal, where I had spent three weeks at a student workcamp. Remarkably he was not even allowed to accept my separate invitation to attend the meeting. Peadar O'Donnell, 'the grand old man of the left', and McDyer's great supporter took his place. Lieutenant General Michael Costello, the innovative manager of the Irish Sugar Company, spoke. He was also supporting Father McDyer by running a vegetable processing industry in Glencolumbkille. Costello had made a grant to Trinity leading to the foundation of the Department of Genetics by George Dawson and represented my interest in modernizing Ireland through science and technology. Senator Owen Sheehy Skeffington, a nearly lone liberal voice, who had taught me how to debate at non-denominational Sandford Park School, took up the theme of modernisation in politics and society. He had been banned from speaking at the L&H in UCD in 1949 by President Michael Tierney.

Skeff had by some distance the greatest influence on the students of the College in the 1960s and was highly regarded throughout the country. As Garret FitzGerald wrote: 'Although avowedly agnostic, his behaviour was of the kind commonly called Christian, although not universal amongst people of that faith.'[2] The Trinity Christians recognized his qualities by electing him to Seanad Éireann on four occasions between 1951 and 1969. Sean O'Faoláin in his funeral oration called him 'the inspiration, and very often the conscience, of all who knew him'.[3]

I have always thought myself fortunate to have spent more time in the Hist than anywhere else in College. Ideas flowed freely, speeches were often brilliant. Most of us had serious interests in the affairs of the world. Every student in College could become a member for a few shillings – between 100 and 200 students attended debates from time to time and came from throughout the College. A few hundred more read the papers and magazines in the Conversation Room, played snooker and billiards for a small charge that helped to pay for the Society, or studied in the workrooms at the top of the GMB. My officers included three scientists (Michael Cameron, David Wagstaff and myself), one mathematician (Cian Ó hÉigeartaigh), one medical student (Hugh O'Neill) and one historian (Edward Liddle). Ó hÉigeartaigh, as Record Secretary, once read the minutes in Irish (an Entrance Scholar in mathematics, he was elected a Scholar of the House in Irish) but had to recant when faced with impeachment. A brilliant speaker, he was nominated as the 'Committee' candidate for Auditor, with the surprise support of a Tory, Brian [now Sir Brian] Williamson. Shortly afterwards, in a packed chamber, with standing room only, a motion to admit women was defeated. In an unforgettable moment Ó hÉigeartaigh rose to his feet, shaking with emotion, and declared that he was withdrawing from the election for Auditor. He was a candidate in the election – the Committee insisted that it would not withdraw *its* nomination. In the event Michael Cameron, who had also advocated the

2 Garret FitzGerald, *All in a Life: an Autobiography* (Dublin, 1991), p. 48
3 Andrée Sheehy Skeffington, *Skeff: A Life of Owen Sheehy Skeffington,* (Dublin, 1991), p. 240

admission of women, was elected. A great admirer of India, where he had lived for a while, he went on to succeed in business in the United States, becoming a generous and loyal supporter of the Society.

Competing with students from the Literary and Debating Society in NUI Galway, the Philosophical Society in University College Cork, the Literary and Historical Society in University College Dublin and the Literary and Scientific Society at Queen's University Belfast at university interdebates, and in The Irish Times Debating Competition, broadened my experiences in ways that could not otherwise have been fulfilled. Anthony Clare, Patrick Cosgrave and John Cooke were prominent in the L&H, which met in the Physics Theatre in Earlsfort Terrace on a Saturday night: it was the greatest challenge, a bear pit, in which weak speakers were cheerfully destroyed by Edward McParland and other wits. While Cosgrave (later the biographer of Margaret Thatcher) and others there seemed to believe the sun rose and set in London, we in Trinity, at least those of us who were Irish, thought Ireland was more important. Michael D. Higgins, Seán Ó hUiginn and Gearóid Ó Tuathaigh were prominent in Galway; Belfast had Eamonn McCann and Michael Farrell.

The influence of the Hist showed itself over and over again, on no occasion more so than in 1970 when we celebrated the Bicentenary with a week of celebrations, which are fully described by Geoghegan. Senator Edward Kennedy pleased us all by quoting Macneile Dixon's accolade: the Hist 'may fairly be described as the greatest of all the schools of orators'.

The Hist was remembered by Roy Jenkins, Chancellor of Oxford, speaking at the Quatercentenary Dinner of Trinity in the House of Commons in 1992. He vividly described his participation in a debate followed by a meal and 'blind' in the GMB – compared to this event he said, Oxford and Cambridge were decidedly red brick. In the late 1990s, Eric Lowry, ex-Auditor and Vice-President, organized a meeting in the rooms of the Oxford Union, at which many former members of the Hist and other Trinity graduates heard a brilliant exposition of the Peace Process by the former Taoiseach, Albert Reynolds. Edward Heath was in the Chair. Afterwards Reynolds told a few of us over coffee that the IRA would never disarm – they would put the guns 'under the thatch'. Reynolds was due to speak at the Inaugural of Tim Smyth in 2007 but was too ill to attend. Sir John

Major took the opportunity to speak of Reynold's contribution to the Peace Process in the most generous terms, leaving no one in any doubt that Reynolds did his country great service.

Now as the Hist heads past 250 years we can say that it has been of some service. Not only has it provided Trinity students with a vigorous forum in which to argue their ideas, where they learned how to run a democratic organization, it also ensured that they could listen to and challenge leading figures from all walks of society. We may have been more polite than the L&H but we were no less a challenge. 'Dangerous ideas positively encouraged', a headline claim of Trinity College today has been at the heart of the Hist for 250 years.

As students few of us knew that William Rowan Hamilton, one of the greatest mathematical physicists of the nineteenth century, participated keenly in the Hist while he was a Fellow. His status was illustrated by being the first person elected a foreign member of the National Academy of Sciences in Washington. Three generations of the Churchill family spoke at the Society. The Hist has been addressed by every leader of the Free State and the Republic of Ireland and by many leaders from Northern Ireland. In 1934 Éamon de Valera, then President of the Executive Council, who was as wary of Trinity as it was of him, chose to speak at the Inaugural Meeting of the Society; his address could have been seen as an overture to Trinity, which was not taken up for many years. The Society can be proud of its more recent graduates, none more so than Mary Harney. The first woman to be elected Auditor, co-founder and leader of the Progressive Democrats, she became the first woman to be Tánaiste (Deputy Prime Minister). We mourned the early passing in 2011 of Brian Lenihan, an officer in the late 1970s who became a Fianna Fáil TD and then Minister for Finance during the deep crisis of 2008 – he had a brilliant future. David Ford, ex-Auditor, Scholar in Classics, became the first non-ordained holder of the Regius Chair of Divinity at Cambridge.

The Hist has long had links with the Department of Foreign Affairs, numbering Frederick Boland – always remembered as a wise Chancellor of the University – and Conor Cruise O'Brien among our members, both of whom served as Presidents of the Society. It can be argued that O'Brien had the most formidable and wide-ranging intellect of twentieth-century Ireland – who else can match the author of books on Albert Camus, Thomas Jefferson and Edmund Burke – who also held many senior offices. He was Minister for Post and Telegraphs with responsibility for policy on Northern Ireland, he was special representative in the Congo of the Secretary-General of the United Nations, he was the founding Vice-Chancellor of the University of Ghana and he was Editor-in-Chief of *The Observer*, just some of his other achievements in a radical career fizzing with controversy. Recent graduates include David O'Sullivan, Ambassador of the EU to the United States, and Rory Montgomery, Irish Ambassador to the EU. Dr Geoghegan tells the role of the Hist in the career of Taoiseach Leo Varadkar – he was a member but was not elected to the Committee of the Hist in the same week as he was elected Chair of Young Fine Gael – many will agree, some grudgingly no doubt, that this was a good week for Irish politics. Recent members have welcomed him to the Hist stand in Freshers' Week when he has been known to renew his membership.

Micheal O'Siadhail, one of those renegades from Clongowes, started in the Hist where his powerful oratory dominated debates even as a Freshman. Although Calliope, his muse, called him away he has remained close to the Hist and the many friends he first met there. He stood apart then and has continued to be a *different* poet, now more international than Irish, which is mightily seen in his courageous exploration of the Holocaust in *The Gossamer Wall* and his startling history of civilization in *The Five Quintets.* He has honoured the Hist by readily agreeing to celebrate the Society in verse. 'Hist' portrays the Society as it was in the 1960s. No one should ever expect the Hist to remain the same but it is pleasing to dream about the time when you were there and have it written up with such affection by one its most remarkable members.

DAVID MCCONNELL
Ex-Auditor
President

HIST

In Celebration of 250 years of
The College Historical Society,
Trinity College Dublin

Let two hundred years, two score and ten
Echo through this chamber of debate:
That this house.... A motion passed again,
Ayes and *no's* such arguments create.
Emmet, Davis, Goldsmith, Moore and Tone,
Solemn names of those who surely spoke,
Whose prestige and eloquence we loan,
Ghosting orators to still evoke.
Sometimes loggerheaded either-ors,
Yielding to the win-lose logic of debate;
Yet those times we spark more light than heat,
Dared nuances someone's speech explores.
Now from both sides of the floor we fête,
This arena where we found our feet.

On a point of order! someone calls —
Order we more honour in the breach —
Still for novices a silence falls,
Soft deflowering of a maiden speech.
Broken in, you face the taunting few,
Brazen out the wag and heckler's jeer,
Grasp the ballot box to steady you,
Trusting to a countering *Hear! Hear!*
Confident, keep learning ploys and tricks,
Play then to the house, outwit with guile,
Driving home an argument that sticks,
Score your point to swing the rank and file.
Ordinary members' aye or no
Sway a balanced motion's touch and go.

On a point of information! Youth
Parallels the universe and we're
Cocksure of the black and white of truth,
Members aren't ordinary here!
Finding what in turn we might become,
We both pose and posture as needs be;
Left or right we beat our callow drum,
This or that of burning certainty.
Through the chair! Do we then slowly grow
Into all those argued views we hold,
Taking every stance to heart as though
Roles we play will shape how we unfold?
Full of green and youthful self-esteem,
Gravitas and swaggered futures dream.

Lessons in the politics of power,
Ballots and electoral upsets,
Private business till the witching hour,
Late cabal intrigues, impeachment threats.
Laws and rules and learned formality,
Proper modes and manners of address,
Earned marked thanks of the Society,
All in earnest — yet a playfulness.
Although sincere we somehow still all know
How the Hist is our first practice run,
Our tongue-in-cheek careers in embryo,
Mixing both what's serious and fun.
In rules and arguments our lives gestate,
Interns in the hothouse of debate.

Those who stood before this membership
Never will now suffer from stage fright,
Or in mid-speech begin to lose the grip,
Letting belly butterflies take flight.
Through our lives if we are called to speak
Or to marshal arguments at speed;
Schooled in oratorical technique,
Everyone who hears us will take heed.
In debate's seedbed a sureness bloomed,
More a confidence than simply skill,
Self-belief with which we were imbued.
Fluency and presence now assumed,
Unbeknownst to us we're moving still
Motions of a lifelong gratitude.

MICHEAL O'SIADHAIL

INTRODUCTION

THIS BOOK is a study of oratory and debate over 250 years, exploring the contribution of the College Historical Society to Ireland and to the world. The records of the Society, held in the Manuscripts and Archives Research Library in Trinity, are extensive, if stronger for some decades than others, and cover the membership, laws, financial reports, prizes and medals, as well as the minutes and journals of the weekly meetings. Given the depth of material, supplemented by memoirs and correspondence, and the detailed coverage of some debates in the national newspapers, it would be possible to write an entire book about any single decade of the Society's history. Instead this book seeks to give a high-level overview of the entire history, examining how the Society provided a forum for members from different backgrounds and beliefs to come together, test their ideas, be challenged, and develop their oratorical styles, and it provides snapshots of the national (and sometimes international) careers of some of the most prominent.

The Society was also a place where guests came to present their ideas, often reported in the media, and some of the most significant of these visits are explored. This it is not a book about the laws and rules of Society, or some of the more arcane procedural elements, even though learning to navigate these very laws and procedures was invaluable training for those who had later careers in the law courts or in parliament. Rather it is a study of orators and oratory, debaters and debates, and the ideas that were articulated in the Society over two-and-a-half centuries.

The precursor to the Society was Edmund Burke's Club in 1747, followed by the Historical Society from 1770 to 1815, the societies which kept the flame alive outside of the walls of Trinity after the Society was suppressed, and finally the College Historical Society from 1843 to the present. With these (sometimes overlapping) incarnations we see a continuity in terms of laws and traditions, records and journals, and, in some cases, memberships. The Society was an ideal as well as a reality, and it survived significant challenges to its existence without ever losing its identity.

The Society has changed considerably over the past 250 years. Oratorical styles haves gone through many fashions, motions for debate have changed considerably, and even the format of meetings and events has evolved significantly. None the less, there is a remarkable continuity. For example, every generation suspects that its successors are not as serious, not as impressive, not as good. This attitude was there from the beginning. At the start of the sixth session, in 1775, the chair criticised the Society for already being in decline, and regretted that it was no longer producing 'wits and poets and orators'. Similar criticisms have been made in later generations, and yet wits, and poets and orators, and more besides, continue to come through its ranks.

Trinity, too, has changed significantly in this period. From being a small university, restricted in who it could admit, it has grown into a much larger, global university, open to students with talent and ability. And, of course, Ireland itself has changed. The story of the Society traces the development of Ireland from being an outpost and colony of the British Empire, through to the winning of independence, and then to taking its place among the nations of the earth. Members of the Society did more than study this history; they helped make it.

By studying the debaters and the debates, the book provides an insight into the changes we see happening in Ireland and across the world over 250 years. Sometimes the Society was an agent of change, sometimes an observer, but whether it was the question of self-determination in Ireland, the rise of totalitarianism in Europe, apartheid in South Africa, injustice in the world, or on many other issues, the Society provided a space to challenge orthodoxies and confront the *status quo* and helped drive change.

For far too long, the biggest weakness undermining the Society was the exclusion of women. It will surprise many people to learn that women sometimes attended meetings of the Society in its early years, although this was a controversial issue over much of its history. In 1931 the Society voted to admit women but unfortunately the change was never implemented. This had profound consequences, and it continued to be a divisive issue until the policy of exclusion became untenable and was dropped in 1968. The book details the controversy over the different decades and the role women and men played in making it happen, and the controversy stands in contrast to the Society's role as a catalyst for change in so many other areas.

Over 250 years the Society has been a sphere of ideas, championing free debate and democratic principles. It was where thousands of students saw the democratic ideal in action, the belief that ideas should be contested in a public sphere, debated by speakers on different sides, and then put to a public vote. Of course, not all the speeches, nor everything that happened, was idealistic and high-minded. This was a cauldron where personalities and egos sometimes clashed, and where youthful exuberance could easily be confused with showboating and histrionics. For some, the Society was an arena of ambition where they tested themselves against their contemporaries and honed the skills that would serve them later in life, in politics, in the law, in the media, in business, in the arts, in academia, and in a range of other careers. For others, it was about the opportunity to meet people from different backgrounds and beliefs, in a place where opposing viewpoints were treated with respect and could be argued and debated.

The legacy of the Society is the way it has provided a peaceful forum to speakers representing every shade of opinion, where great ideas have been contested, minds informed and character and identity formed. Today, in the twenty-first century, it still serves the same vital function.

PATRICK GEOGHEGAN
Trinity College Dublin
4 February 2020

ACKNOWLEDGMENTS

IT WAS AN HONOUR to have been asked by the College Historical Society to write its history. My thanks to the President of the Society, Dr David McConnell, for the invitation and to the many Auditors and Record Secretaries I have worked with over the course of this project.

There is a remarkable amount of archival material in the Manuscripts' Room of Trinity and I am grateful to Ellen O'Flaherty, the Archivist, for her advice, guidance and support. I am also indebted to my research assistant, Dr Timothy Murtagh, who did extraordinary work going through an enormous amount of material and to the Trinity Trust who provided generous funding for the project. My thanks also to Dr Sean O'Reilly, who helped with material relating to the international careers of former members of the Society.

A number of people provided information on their time in the Society, filling in gaps, and providing unique insights and perspectives. There are too many to mention all of them by name, by I am especially grateful to Ivana Bacik, Ursula Quill, Gully Stanford, Timothy Smyth, Niamh Ní Mhaoileoin, Donnell Deeny, Ted Smyth, Cathal McCann, Sallyanne Godson, Doreen Shivnen, Paul Gleeson, Leo Varadkar, Paul Geaney, Huw Duffy, Thomas Kinsella, Hannah McCarthy, Julia McCarthy, and Jamie Walsh. Over the time I have been working on this project I have had many conversations with Adrian Langan, and he was generous enough to read and provide extensive commentary on the first two-thirds of the book. His insights and encouragement were invaluable and I am indebted to him for the enormous impact he has had on the direction of the book.

Ross Hinds was one of the best editors I have ever worked with and brought his own expertise on the Hist to the project. My thanks to him and also the team at Lilliput, especially Antony Farrell and Professor David Dickson.

Finally, my thanks to my wife, Olivia, and our daughter, Ellie, for providing the greatest happiness of all.

ABBREVIATIONS

Dagg, *CHS*	T.S.C. Dagg. *College Historical Society: A History (1770-1920).* Tralee, 1969.
DIB	James McGuire and James Quinn (eds). *Dictionary of Irish Biography.* 11 volumes. Cambridge, 2009-2019. dib.cambridge.org.
FTCD	Fellow of Trinity College Dublin
McDowell and Webb	R.B. McDowell and D.A. Webb. *Trinity College Dublin, 1592-1952: an academic history,* Cambridge, 1982.
ODNB	Colin Matthew and Brian Harrison (eds). *Oxford Dictionary of National Biography.* 60 volumes. Oxford, 2004. www.oxforddnb.com
TCD	Trinity College Dublin.

IMAGE CREDITS

Some of the Archives of the College Historical Society have been moved to the Library of Trinity College Dublin, where they receive professional care. The images of these documents are used in this book with acknowledgment to the Board of Trinity College Dublin. The images were created by Gillian Whelan, Digital Collections, Library of Trinity College Dublin. The photographs are from the Archives remaining with the College Historical Society.

EDMUND BURKE'S CLUB AND THE ORIGINS OF THE HISTORICAL SOCIETY, 1747-1769

1

THE COLLEGE HISTORICAL SOCIETY was not founded by Edmund Burke. This idea became part of the creation myth of the Society, with future generations of members eager to trace a direct line to the great political theorist and statesman. The reality is that Edmund Burke was the driving force behind a different Club, a small gathering of students that met thirty-two times in 1747 before dwindling away at the end of the academic year. Nevertheless, it cast a long shadow and its legacy includes the College Historical Society. The records of the Club, in Burke's own hand, were carefully preserved and they helped inform and shape a new student society founded in College in 1770. Its ambitions, its rules, and its central belief in the potential of oratory to be a force for good was passed down to a new generation and directly influenced those who followed in its path. Burke was not there in 1770 when the Historical Society was founded, but he played a key role its genesis. From the beginning, the emphasis was on the power of the word, and the first words came from Burke.

The short-lived club was a formative experience for Burke, as he studied how to construct an argument, defend a position against attack, and think on his feet. He learned the art of oratory as well as the skill of debating, and the training served him well for the rest of his life as he went on to become one of the great orators and thinkers in the British House of Commons.

Recognising the influence of the Club, Burke's great biographer, F. P. Lock, has sagely noted, 'play-acting and role-playing, a delight in impersonation, a taste for the dramatic and the melodramatic;

these anticipate the histrionic qualities that characterise some of Burke's parliamentary performances'.[1] Burke's legacy as an orator and writer was far-reaching. For the great nineteenth-century essayist, William Hazlitt, he was 'the greatest man since Milton', for the great nineteenth-century statesman, William Ewart Gladstone, he was the source of timeless political wisdom, 'applicable to the circumstances of today, and full of the deepest and most valuable lessons to guide the policy of a country'. Today in the twenty-first century Burke is hailed, to quote a profile in *The Guardian*, as 'one of the most gifted, original and complex people ever to sit in the House of Commons'.[2]

The Club founded by Edmund Burke and some of his friends met for the first time on Tuesday 21 April 1747 at a house on George's Lane in Dublin. Grandly styling itself 'Academy of Belles Lettres', it was more commonly called simply 'The Club'. At its second meeting, on Friday 25 April, the rules and laws of the Club were agreed and it was formally established to provide opportunities for 'correcting our taste, regulating and enriching our judgment, brightening our wit, and enlarging our judgment'.[3] Considering that language was the 'cement' of society, it set out that 'the business of the Club is speeching, reading, writing, and arguing in Morality, History, Criticism, Politics, and all the useful braches of Philosophy'.

The Club met twice a week, on Tuesdays and Fridays, from 5 p.m. to 9 p.m. At the Tuesday meeting a speech was given, and a paper on another subject circulated with 'the Author passing his word and Honour he wrote it originally for that time and purpose'. At the Friday meeting an historical speech was 'spoken off with proper emphasis and action', and a written paper on some aspect of a moral question was delivered. The rest of the meetings were spent 'in reading, speeching' and whatever else the chairman decided. As F. P. Lock has analysed, 'the Club's main activity was the practice of rhetoric. Members made extempore speeches on given subjects, or delivered orations carefully prepared in advance. Sometimes model

---

1 F.P. Lock, *Edmund Burke, Volume* 1, *1730-1784* (Oxford, 1999), p. 51.

2 David Marquand, 'My hero: Edmund Burke', *The Guardian,* 11 September 2010.

3 TCD MUN/SOC/HIST 81; Dagg, *CHS,* p.2.

speeches from famous authors would be rehearsed, at others a subject would be debated in parliamentary manner'.[4]

The meetings were chaired by the President, an office which was elected weekly, and while in office the President could not propose a motion or take part in a debate. The office of Censor was also created to examine the conduct of members and award thanks or censure. We know from the minute book of the Club that it met 32 times, and Burke sat six times as President, and twice as Censor, and he has been described as 'the moving spirit' who was never once absent from the meetings'.[5]

At the meeting on Tuesday 28 April 1747, the first formal debate took place and Burke delivered a speech and was awarded 'thanks for the matter of his oration, but not for his delivery of it'.[6] A debate on Irish manufacturing proved controversial, as there were criticisms of British Government, and a law was proposed on 8 May prohibiting the discussion of any question 'relating to the Gov-ernment of our country which may possibly affect our loyalty'. Burke opposed this vehemently, believing it a restraint on 'considering what would be more useful to our country' that would 'take away a most considerable part of our improvement'. Although in a minority, he argued that 'there is no danger of our showing any disloyalty to His Majesty'. However he was not successful and the new rule was passed.

Burke was in the chair as President on 14 May, but his behaviour was criticised by one student Joseph Hamilton, who attacked him for being 'damn'd absolute', and this was supported by Matthew Mohun, one of the original founders. As a result, Hamilton and Mohun were accused of 'indecency and contempt of the President'. Found guilty, Hamilton was fined, while Mohun was censured, admonished and fined, and had his forthcoming presidency removed. On 18 May, there was a Lustrum, a review of all the members. At this Mohun was put on trial for his conduct. Considered to have behaved 'still worse' at this trial, and he was

---

4 Lock, *Edmund Burke,* p. 49.

5 Dagg, *CHS,* p. 3.

6 TCD MUN/SOC/HIST 81.

'formally expelled [from] the Society forever' for his 'ill-conduct and neglect'.[7]

It is not clear from the minutes how much of this was role play and how much was genuine. Lock has suggested that 'a strongly marked parodic element pervades its activities, and especially the formal structures which regulated them'.[8] Certainly some of elements of the system of fines, thanks and censures was designed to mirror and parody the existing system in Trinity. That said, some of these disputes seem to have been taken very seriously by its members and there could be severe repercussions, as we see when Mohun was expelled from the Club.

The Censor at this time was William Dennis, one of Burke's closest friends. Even though he had supported Burke in expelling Mohun, he soon found himself the next target. As he lamented in a letter to a mutual friend, 'for my good services, I am now threatened with expulsion by Burke, who is a terrible fellow'. Dennis claimed Burke was accusing him for 'a design of destroying the Club, when, alas, no one has a greater desire to preserve it'. And he reproached Burke for being 'very active' at trying to get him punished. It is not clear whether this clash was playful, or whether tempers had indeed become heated at the meeting on 26 May 1747. It seems there was some kind of breach, but it was not long lasting, and the friendship continued afterwards. As Lock notes, 'the trial itself, on the 30th , was a model of due process. For Burke at least, the experience was a valuable preparation for the ritualised aggression of public life'.[9]

In the debates over the following weeks, Dennis spoke in favour of leniency to the Jacobite rebels, with Burke opposed. There was also a motion on piracy, which Burke opposed, while he spoke in defence of the actions of General John Huske, who had been defeated at the battle of Falkirk in 1745. Burke also delivered an oration on Lucius Junius Brutus, the founder of the Roman Republic. Some debates were chosen from classical history or mythology, others from modern day politics. They ranged from a discussion of whether Alcibiades or Coriolanus was the greater man,

7 TCD MUN/SOC/HIST 8; Dagg, *CHS,* pp. 5-6.

8 Lock, *Edmund Burke,* p. 49-50.

9 Ibid., p. 50.

to the War of the Austrian Succession, which was coming to an end.

Burke had been scheduled to give a lecture on oratory at the meeting of Tuesday 7 July 1747, but he had not finished it, and was forced to apologise claiming that he expected the Society to be prorogued. As a result, Burke was charged with 'disrespect' in 'talking of prorogation as a point already agreed, when it was not even moved in the Society'.[10] Urged to hand the speech in, Burke promised to do so the following Tuesday. The last meeting of the Club, however, appears to have taken place that Friday, 10 July 1747, when Burke delivered an oration on the character of Ulysses as he discussed in 'The Embassy of Ulysses and Menelaus to recover Helen'. With the College term ending, this seems to have brought the Club's activities to a conclusion. As far as the records show, it never reconvened.

Its legacy, however was a long one. Burke kept possession of the Minute Book and in 1770 he gave it to his friend, Professor Michael Kearney, a Fellow of the University who was attempting to persuade the Board that a student society should be founded within the College. The records of the Club thus helped shape the formation of the Historical Society and was given pride of place within the Society's library. Burke's role in the creation myth of the Society was itself created much later, in the nineteenth century, when Burke was hailed to have a position in the political world as 'Shakespeare was in the moral world'.[11] This perhaps explains why the minute book was not always guarded carefully. It was lost when the Society left College in 1815, until Walter Berwick, the treasurer of the External Society, spotted it in a bookstore on the quays and purchased it for a few pence.[12] When Berwick died in a railway accident in 1868 the book was sold again, and it was only in 1877 that Walter Fitzwilliam Starkie, the Record Secretary, saw it in a second-hand bookshop and purchased it, restoring it to the Society's library.

When tracing the origins of the Society it must be noted that a second club also had a strong influence. On 24 October 1753 a 'Historical Club' was established to cultivate historical knowledge,

---

10 TCD MUN/SOC/HIST 8; Dagg, *CHS,* p. 8.

11 H. Reeve (ed.), *The Greville Memoirs* (3 vols., London, 1875), iii, 209.

12 Dagg, *CHS,* p. 9.

and a monthly debate soon became part of its features. This too met outside of the walls of College. Christopher Temple Emmet, the brother of Thomas and Robert, referenced this Club in a speech in 1780 when he discussed how the Historical Society had risen like a Phoenix from 'the embers of another institution' and had grown into 'a purer flame', noting how the members of the original club had 'long feared that their blaze like the short-lived meteor would glitter for a moment to decay for ever'.[13]

Some of the finest orators of the Irish parliament in the second half of the eighteenth century were members of this Club, including Barry Yelverton (later Lord Avonmore) who was a founding member. It also included Henry Grattan, Walter Hussey (later Walter Hussey Burgh), and John Scott (later Lord Clonmel).[14] However, as time went on it declined in popularity, fading into irrelevance. In 1770 it was decided to establish a new debating society in Trinity. Burke's Club was taken as an inspiration, the Historical Club served as a guide, and the Historical Society was created.

13 Dagg, *CHS,* p. 11.
14 Ibid., pp. 10-11.

THE FOUNDATION OF THE HISTORICAL SOCIETY, 1770-1778

2

IN 1770 some students believed that the time was right for a new body to discuss and debate and they were encouraged in their ambition by Dr Michael Kearney and the Revd Dr John Forsayeth (in the years ahead both men served as Regius Professor of Law in Trinity). The driving force, however, was Henry Duquery, a young student who had been elected a Scholar, and who deserves recognition for his leadership in persuading the Board to support the creation of a new Society and to allow it to meet on the grounds of College.

And so, the Historical Society met for the first time on Wednesday 21 March 1770 when thirteen Senior Sophister students gathered in the Common Room in College. Michael Truell took the chair, Richard Cary was elected Treasurer, and Michael Cahill was elected Secretary. A resolution was passed thanking Dr Kearney 'for his kindness in exerting his influence at the Board in favour of this Society and for his generous promise of assisting them in their historical proceedings'.[1] The Revd Dr Forsayeth was also thanked 'for his patronage of and attention to this Society'. Finally, 'Our worthy member' Henry Duquery was also praised, 'for his zealous promotion of the interests of this Society during its infancy'.

Several laws were passed concerning the regulation of the Society, including the rule that only final year students and graduates could be members, a portion of history was then assigned for discussion at the next meeting, before the meeting was adjourned. The Society made the decision that only British history would be studied, and

1 TCD MUN/SOC/HIST 1; Dagg, *CHS*, p. 16.

this reflected a certain insularity and insecurity about the position of Ireland that reflected the wider political outlook at the time. The change of this rule in 1782 likewise reflected the new political self-confidence following legislative independence.

From the beginning the Society was concerned with resolutions and laws and they served a valuable function, even if they did add an extra level of formality to proceedings.[2] Members learned about how formal proceedings operated, they learned what could be done within the regulations, and what could be challenged, as well as how to campaign to change rules they opposed or indeed block changes. Given that the most likely careers for members afterwards were in politics, the law, the church or academic life this was training which served them well and taught them how to navigate complex sets of sometimes arcane rules and traditions and achieve results.

At the second meeting, on Wednesday 28 March 1770, there was an examination on the piece of history assigned the previous week, and a motion was passed allowing the Secretary 'sufficient time' to reduce and reorder the resolutions that had to be passed. A poem by James Whitelaw was read out loud addressed to Joseph Stock FTCD, who was in charge of maintaining student discipline, who was praised for keeping order and indulging the Society, without being too severe. It was agreed that meetings would begin at 6 p.m. and resolutions were passed detailing the punishment of members who were absent.[3]

The first debate proper took place at the third meeting, on Wednesday 4 April 1770, when the motion, 'Whether that Egyptian Law which Ordained the Perpetuation of Professions from Father to Son was a Beneficial Institution' was debated.[4] Eleven students were present and the motion was defeated by eight votes to three. At this meeting there was a proposal to allow Junior Sophisters to join, but it was narrowly defeated by six votes to five. The first session of the Society concluded on 13 June 1770.

The second session of the Society began on Wednesday 24 October 1770 with the focus on History, Composition and Oratory. From the beginning the Society also had an external dimension, and

2 TCD MUN/SOC/HIST 43.

3 TCD MUN/SOC/HIST 1.

4 TCD MUN/SOC/HIST 1; Dagg, *CHS*, p. 17.

was determined to attempt to ameliorate some of the problems in society. And so a committee was established 'to collect subscriptions for the relief of the poor at this period of distress and misery'. The key figure here was James Whitelaw and he sat on a committee of three 'to enquire into the state of the Four Courts Marshalsea', a debtors' prison in Dublin. Its report was hard-hitting on the condition of the prisoners, and on 22 April 1771 the Society resolved to raise funds to help release some of the debtors.[5]

This marked the beginning of Whitelaw's extraordinary contribution to helping the poor. After leaving Trinity he became a clergyman and in 1798 he set out to compile a census of the population of Dublin, supported by the Government, with the object 'to encourage improvement in policing, social conditions, industry and education'.[6] The census was carried out at his own expense, and Whitelaw and his assistants visited every house in the poorer sections of the city to ensure accurate returns. It took five months of work, ten hours a day, to gather the information, and a further five years to tabulate the results, and it is considered 'an early example of a systematic scientific approach to demography'. Rosemary Richey, in the Royal Irish Academy's monumental, multi-volume, *Dictionary of Irish Biography*, notes that Whitelaw 'argued that overcrowding, poverty and general wretchedness were very much in evidence', blaming high rents and recommending that 'the worst homes be pulled down and factories and commercial buildings be removed from residential areas'.

In the laws of the Society, which were codified in 1771, members were required to attend in their academic gowns. When a member was speaking the others were required to 'sit quietly, and hearken attentively to his speech, permitting him to conclude without interruption unless he transgresseth order'. Members who did not live in College were allowed leave at 11 p.m. without permission, but anyone else had to receive the approval of the Society. It was also determined that 'if from the warmth of any debate, or any other cause, personal disputes shall happen between any of the members when assembled', the dispute would be submitted to the Society for

5 Dagg, *CHS*, p. 24.

6 Rosemary Richey, 'James Whitelaw', DIB.

resolution, 'and its award abided by, under penalty of expulsion to the refusing party'.

Permission was received from the Board for the meetings to take place in the Common Room, in the rooms over the Dining Hall.[7] The meetings of the Historical Society took place on Wednesdays, and began at 6 p.m. The first part of the evening was an examination on certain parts of history, and medals were awarded at different points in the year. The meeting then adjourned for refreshments, chiefly tea and coffee, where the members would discuss the events of the previous meeting and the speakers who were due to debate that evening. The experienced speakers, rivals for the oratory prizes, usually brought friends with them, and would run through the order of proceedings with them. Also in attendance were the 'untried' men, who were there to see how things worked, and 'in whose countenance you could read the most determined resolution to eclipse the glories of all modern names'.[8]

The Chairman for each debate was selected by seniority and held office for one evening only. Once the chair was taken the motion was proposed, and two speakers, who had been appointed to speak three weeks earlier, were invited to debate on either side. The debate was then opened to the floor, and there could be a sharp contrast between the quality of the different speeches. The debate part having concluded, the doors were closed, and the business of the Society was only then conducted. This was known as 'the after debate' and the reports of the committees were received, the conduct of officers was discussed, new laws and regulations were proposed, and honours were considered for various candidates.

The office of Auditor was created on 24 April 1771 and in doing so established the tradition, common across most student societies in Ireland today, of calling the elected student head by that title. As Thomas Dagg notes in his history of the Society, 'It has always been regarded as one of much distinction both inside and outside the University, and election to this office is, perhaps, the highest honour that can be conferred upon a student by his fellow students.'[9] The

7 W.B.S. Taylor, *History of the University of Dublin* (Dublin, 1819). p. 202.

8 [Mortimer O'Sullivan], *College Recollections* (Dublin, 1825), p. 225.

9 TCD MUN/SOC/HIST 1; Dagg, *CHS,* p. 19.

idea was Henry Duquery's and he proposed the motion, which was seconded by Michael Truell, calling for the creation of an officer 'who shall have the inspection of the records, journals and accounts, together with a general control of the several officers of this Society committed to his care'. The Auditor was to be elected by ballot every four months, the Treasurer and Librarian for three months, and the Secretary was held by members for one month. James Reid, later headmaster of Midleton College in Cork, was unanimously elected the first Auditor of the Society. Henry Duquery succeeded him as Auditor, followed by John Robert Scott.

In the first meeting of the 1771–72 session James Whitelaw was in the chair and he praised the members for having shown 'a spirit of unanimity and concord that silenced envy and frustrated every attempt at malice'.[10] At this meeting nine students were proposed for membership, but five were rejected. One of those rejected was John Philpot Curran, who went on to become one of the greatest lawyers and one of the greatest parliamentary orators of the late-eighteenth century. At the closing meeting of this session William Preston was in the chair and he devoted his speech to discussing the benefits of speaking at the Society, even for those who did not intend to pursue a career where speaking was required. He believed that members would 'be freed from that faulty diffidence, that painful embarrassment, and bashful timidity, that too often attend sensibility, and throw a shade on genius'.[11] Preston argued that a fear of speaking in public kept 'modest merit in obscurity, and make the wise man appear in the company of fools as the fool ought to appear in the company of wise men'. Preston went on to become a successful lawyer, poet and dramatist and was a founding member of the Royal Irish Academy in 1785, serving as its first Secretary.[12] A supporter of Catholic emancipation, he contributed to *The Press,* the journal of the United Irishmen, in 1797-8, and was the author of a play *Democratic Rage,* which attempted to capture the tragedy of the French revolution.

Richard Frankland and William Day were the Auditors for the

10 Ibid.

11 Dagg, *CHS,* p. 25.

12 Sinéad Sturgeon, 'William Preston', *DIB.*

1772-73 session and the Committee included some figures who would achieve eminence in the law and politics. A Senior Sophister, William Downes, served as Treasurer and went on to have a successful career as a barrister. He was appointed Lord Chief Justice in 1803 after Lord Kilwarden was killed during Robert Emmet's rebellion. Considered the most able candidate, in the poem 'The Metropolis', published in 1806, Downes is praised as 'the acknowledged father of the laws'.[13] Another student in his final year, Isaac Corry, served as Secretary for part of the session and became MP for Newry in 1776 (succeeding his father) and sat in parliament until 1800. Described by a contemporary as a 'forceful, compact and methodical debater', he avoided oratorical flourishes and was considered one of the most effective Opposition speakers in the 1780s.[14] A supporter of the Act of Union, he was appointed Chancellor of the Exchequer in 1799 and engaged in increasingly heated debates with Henry Grattan. After Grattan called Corry 'a half-bred lawyer, a half-bred statesman, a mock patriot, a swaggering bully... and a liar', the two men fought a duel at Ballsbridge and Corry was wounded in the arm. In his lifetime 'some regarded him as an accomplished parliamentarian, others as an unscrupulously ambitious political adventurer'.[15]

'The highest compliment' that the Society bestowed, as future Auditor, Theobald Wolfe Tone later recalled, was to invite one of its medallists to deliver the closing speech at the final meeting of a session.[16] Richard Archdall concluded the session on 3 March 1773 with a speech that paid tribute to 'this school of Classic Literature and Oratorical Competition'.[17] Predicting that some of its members might end up taking a part 'in his country's cause', guiding her councils, and protecting her rights, he said they would be grateful for the training they had received in the Society and would 'reflect on the hours which are past and shall not regret them'. Archdall

13 Patrick M. Geoghegan, 'William Downes', *DIB*.

14 James Quinn, 'Isaac Corry', *DIB*.

15 Ibid.

16 William Theobald Wolfe Tone (ed.), *Memoirs of Theobald Wolfe Tone* (London, 1827), p. 18.

17 TCD MUN/SOC/HIST 1; Dagg, *CHS,* p. 26.

suggested that the Society encouraged 'knowledge, eloquence and principles' and 'promoted happiness' by encouraging people 'to be useful'. The speech concluded with a prophecy that in centuries to come 'unanimous senates and a happy people shall do honour to the memory of the Historical Society'.

In December 1773 the Society agreed to create two silver medals, one for prose and one for verse, with the winners awarded the privilege of being able to select a Junior Sophister student to become a member. Richard Archdall and John Wolfe won the first of these medals, and immediately proposed two Junior Sophister students for membership. Elected Auditor of the Society in 1774, Archdall had a successful session and it marked the beginning of an eminent career in the law and politics. Elected an MP in 1790, he supported the Act of Union in 1799 and 1800, and afterwards became an MP in the British House of Commons.[18]

In 1774 John Hely-Hutchinson became Provost, an appointment that horrified the vast majority of the Fellows because he was a career politician, married, and 'widely deemed unfit'.[19] There began a campaign of resistance to his provostship and this featured in some of the meetings of the Society. He had one strong defender in the Society, Henry Duquery, who was married to Hely-Hutchinson's sister, and who was still attending meetings. At its second meeting of the session, on Wednesday 2 November 1774, Archdall proposed a resolution to send an address to the new Provost 'requesting to be honoured with his general protection'. This was furiously opposed by some members, and there followed a heated discussion, and a final vote was postponed. One of the most influential members in this discussion was Duquery, who eloquently made the case for supporting the new Provost.

At the next meeting, the resolution was modified slightly, and the debate resumed, and was tied 12-12, and only settled in the end by the casting vote of the chair. The new Auditor, Edward Beaty, together with Duquery and Archdall, were appointed to bring the message to the Provost. In the years ahead Hely-Hutchinson was to

18 Edith Mary Johnston-Liik, *History of the Irish Parliament, 1692-1800* (6 volumes, Belfast, 2002), iii, 108.

19 James Kelly, 'John Hely-Hutchinson', *DIB*.

be a good friend to the Society and provided help whenever requested.

In every generation members or former members have lamented the glories of former years. Such exercises in nostalgia were evident from the very beginning. At the close of the 6th session in 1775, William Ball was in the chair and he used the opportunity to criticise the members for skipping the History portion of the evening, while the five or six who did attend were 'very ill prepared, attempting at awkward, broken answers from half-hearted whispers of a scarce better prepared neighbour'.[20] Ball was mournful that 'the soil which reared a Burke, the soil which produced a Hussey' was no longer producing 'wits and poets and orators'. The speech concluded by urging the members to throw off the shackles of indolence and emulate the virtues of its earlier members.

Encouraging oratory was an objective from the beginning and in October 1776 a committee was established to examine how best to encourage it. It was agreed that the Auditor, Treasurer and Librarian would examine the votes for the best speeches of those who had spoken three times during the session and award the unanimous thanks of the Society to those who had excelled.

Attendance at meetings could sometimes be a problem. Speaking at the opening meeting of the 1777-78 session, the new Auditor, Edward Mayne, a recent graduate who went on to become a successful lawyer and Judge of the Court of the King's Bench, urged the members to abandon 'the company of ladies', 'the pleasure of seeing and being seen', and even 'the delights of the bottle', to take part in the debates.[21] He believed that the meetings enabled members to benefit from 'the conversations of persons of sense' leading to 'the improvement of the manners' and 'instruction and experience in the most noble of sciences and in the scarcest of excellent arts'.

William Saurin succeeded Mayne as Auditor that session. He went on to become a successful barrister and opposed the Act of Union in 1799, attacking it as 'dangerous and improper' and calling on the yeomanry 'to take into their consideration a question of the

20 TCD MUN/SOC/HIST 2; Dagg, *CHS*, p. 30.
21 TCD MUN/SOC/HIST 2; Dagg, *CHS*, p. 35.

greatest national importance'.[22] Entering parliament in 1800 to oppose the measure, he claimed that popular resistance to it would be justified. However, afterwards he came to terms with the new political reality, and served as Attorney General (1807–21), where his opposition to the Catholic Board made him the enemy of Daniel O'Connell, who threatened to horse-whip him during the Magee Trial in 1813.[23]

So what happened to Henry Duquery, the founding father of the Society, and one of its first Auditors? He pursued first a career in the law, and then entered political life, and big things were predicted of him, given that he was 'a great orator at the bar'.[24] Friends with Barry Yelverton, after leaving Trinity Duquery joined the newly formed Monks of the Order of St Patrick ('the Monks of the Screw') in 1779, a forum for political debate that met every Saturday and had a significant overlap in terms of membership with the Society. Famed for his ability with words, it was said that he had 'the elegance of [Joseph] Addison', the writer and poet.[25]

Appointed surveyor of customs for Dublin, Duquery became second serjeant in 1791, serving with ability until his resignation in 1793. He also embarked on a political career. Returned for Armagh Borough in 1790, he served as MP for Rathcormac, Co. Cork, between 1790 and 1797. In parliament he supported the legislation giving Catholics the right to vote in 1793, though he argued the Government should have gone further. This was the theme of one of his finest speeches in the House of Commons on 10 January 1793 during the debate on Catholic relief. Knowing that Britain was on the verge of going to war with revolutionary France, Duquery suggested that 'we found her formidable in a state of slavery, we cannot expect to find her less powerful in what she conceives at least to be a state of freedom'.[26] Ireland faced invasion and, worse, it could

---

22 Desmond McCabe, 'William Saurin', *DIB*.

23 See P.M. Geoghegan, *King Dan: the rise of Daniel O'Connell* (Dublin, 2008), Chapter six.

24 Oliver J. Burke, *Anecdotes of the Connaught Circuit* (Dublin, 1885), p. 182.

25 Rosemary Richey, 'Henry Duquery', *DIB*,

26 *Parliamentary register of Ireland* (Dublin, 1793), vol. 13, col. 23.

not rely on the loyalty of the majority of the popularity. Security and victory, he believed, would require enlisting Catholics in the struggle, which would mean the Irish parliament had 'to make atonement for the error and oppression of those who have gone before them'.[27] This was an opportunity, he argued, to 'prove to our Catholic brethren that we have minds superior to bigotry, and that whatever may be the extent of their sufferings, our justice is equal to their wrongs'.

It was an eloquent plea for toleration, recognising that the strength and security of the empire depended on giving Irish Catholics a share in the struggle. 'Against the same enemy are the British and Irish soldiers going now to march', he reminded his listeners, 'upon the same field they must conquer or perish. There is no distinction in the day of battle and there should be none in the hour of peace'.[28] In a stirring conclusion, he suggested that if emancipation was passed, 'you shall behold Ireland taking her place in the great rank of nations'.[29] Supported by the British Government, equally anxious to secure Irish loyalty, a Catholic Relief Act was passed on 9 April 1793, giving Catholics the right to vote, as well as serve in the army and practice as barristers, and it also removed the prohibition on taking degrees, thus opening up Trinity and the Historical Society to Catholics. It was a major act of political reform, forged in the fires of international war, and Duquery played his part in making it a reality.

In his memoir of Lord Charlemont, Francis Hardy praised Duquery's 'perspicuity of intellect', and called him a man of 'higher honour'.[30] Tragedy, however, struck in the summer of 1793. On a tour of the Holy Land, and taking notes for a book he was never able to write, he became seriously unwell. At the time it was called 'sunstroke', but in reality it was something far more damaging and debilitating. He never fully recovered, and he was never as sharp or as able after that. In 1795 Duquery proposed an amendment condemning the war with France and the British Prime Minister's

27 Ibid., col. 25.

28 Ibid., col. 26.

29 Ibid., col. 27.

30 Francis Hardy, *Memoirs of the political and private life of James Caulfield, Earl of Charlemont* (2 volumes, London, 1810), ii, 346.

refusal to negotiate for peace. One later account suggested he was 'dying from the head down', suffering from dementia in his final years. Declining to seek re-election in 1797, he is believed to have opposed the Act of Union, before his death in 1804. In the nineteenth century a leading legal expert suggested that 'had he retained his intellect, his fame would have rivalled, probably, that of Plunket, Burke, Burrowes, O'Connell or Sheil'.[31] Instead Duquery faded from public memory, with his work as a lawyer and a politician largely forgotten. However, even for those who do not celebrate his name, his legacy lives on in the weekly meetings of a student Society which was infused with his spirit of public service and which argued, influenced and helped transform some of the biggest debates of the day for 250 years and beyond.

31 Burke, *Anecdotes of the Connaught Circuit*, p. 182.

3 'A THEATRE OF WAR AND OF TUMULT': THE FIRST GOLDEN AGE OF ORATORY, 1779-1789

THE PERIOD 1779 TO 1789 was a golden age of oratory in the Society, bringing together speakers who went on to achieve national and international fame for the quality of their speaking and their contribution to public life. The vigour in the Society reflected what was happening outside of the walls of Trinity, with the American War of Independence leading to demands for free trade, greater parliamentary independence, and a growing self-confidence about the Irish nation, however defined. For the first time Irish politics was being debated in the Society, Irish history studied, and the proximity to the House of Commons on College Green meant that members were at the centre of the great political discussions taking place at that time. As Theobald Wolfe Tone later recounted, this was a time in the Society when 'the laws of the country were insulted, the discipline of the university condemned, and disorder, and misrule and anarchy' let loose.[1]

Contributing to the Society's success in this period was the fateful decision to include Irish political questions as subjects for debate, and this had the effect of creating a new energy, with members inspired to tackle the very questions that were dominating public debate. The Society became something more than a training ground for future politicians and lawyers. It became the crucible where ideas where challenged and tested and where the political thinking as well as the oratorical style of its members were forged. The Society was neither radical nor moderate, attracting members of all political

1 Speech of Tone, quoted in Dagg, *CHS*, p. 62; TCD MUN/HIST/6.

beliefs who would express at different times radical, moderate and other beliefs. This was where ambitious young men looked to make their mark. As Marianne Elliott writes in her masterful biography of Wolfe Tone, 'it was not through scholastic attainment that the young men of Trinity prepared their future reputations... No, in Ireland those reputations, and the friendships and connections to sustain them, were first made in the Historical Society.'[2] As she notes, 'it was the first college debating society in the British Isles and was the training ground for almost all the leading political figures in the age of Grattan's Parliament'.

As a result of this new energy, the debates began to be attended by more students than ever before. This was partly because of the new direction of the Society, partly because more students were attending Trinity, and partly because the Society opened its membership to Junior Sophisters in October 1780, further increasing its ranks.[3] Originally this was a trial run for a year, but it success encouraged the Society to make the rule permanent.

This was a time of controversy outside of Trinity, and often the heat of those battles seeped into the student debates, especially in the second half of the decade. Many of the most notable members of the Society were critical of this new direction, and some of the most savage criticisms come from this time. Speaking from the chair on 24 June 1789 Theobald Wolfe Tone attacked the Society for turning into 'a mob of gladiators', and others similarly condemned the debates for becoming a place where 'those scenes of party violence' occurred.[4] So there is a contradiction and tension here. This was the era of Laurence Parsons and Charles Kendal Bushe, Peter Burrowes and William Plunket, Thomas Goold and George Miller, Standish O'Grady and Christopher Temple Emmet, Thomas Addis Emmet, and, of course, Theobald Wolfe Tone. Yet few at the time would have considered it a golden age for oratory, precisely because it requires the benefit of hindsight to assess these things. Without themselves being aware of it, a golden generation of orators came together to debate the greatest issues of the day. As Tone

2 Marianne Elliott, *Wolfe Tone*, (2nd edition Liverpool, 2012), p. 31.

3 Dagg, *CHS*, p. 35.

4 TCD MUN/HIST/6; Dagg, *CHS*, p. 62 and p. 59.

himself suggested in June 1789, the Society appeared to be 'breaking our order, and shooting wildly across the system, glaring and fiery and portentous'. [5] The debates reflected this tension and were enhanced by it, with a new energy generated by a youthful generation of future leaders finding their voice.

The first debate on an Irish political question took place on 6 January 1779 on the motion, 'Whether an Union with Great Britain would be of Advantage to Ireland'. The motion was defeated by 8 votes to 6, with Christopher Temple Emmet opposing the motion. The religious restrictions in Ireland formed the backdrop for the debate on the motion, 'Whether Universal Toleration should be Encouraged by a Wise Legislature', and the motion was passed by 17 votes to 4.[6]

Emmet chaired the final debate of the session on 30 June 1779 and used his speech to call for a return to more fundraising in the Society for charities. He noted that the members had 'hitherto parted with the orphan's prayer, the captive's praise, and the widow's blessing', but that these were absent that session.[7] Urging greater benevolence, he suggested it would ensure that its 'blessings like the dew of heaven through long revolving ages [would] distinguish the Historical Society'.

On the opening night of the new session in October 1779 a new law was passed creating honorary membership, thus allowing members who had graduated the opportunity to return and debate in the Society without being subjected to further expenses.[8] This helped strengthen the links with the House of Commons across the road on College Green, and some graduates who had entered parliament 'gladly availed themselves of such an opportunity for the practice of public speaking'.[9] On some occasions, honorary members who had been scheduled to speak were excused on the grounds of 'compulsory attendance in the House of Commons'.

---

5 Speech of Tone, quoted in Dagg, *CHS*, p. 62; TCD MUN/HIST/6.

6 TCD MUN/HIST/3.

7 TCD MUN/HIST/3; Dagg, *CHS*, p. 36.

8 TCD MUN/HIST/3; Dagg, *CHS*, p. 38.

9 David Plunket (ed.), *Life, letters and speeches of Lord Plunket* (2 vols, London, 1867), i, 33.

It was noted that 'The Historical Society derived much dignity and importance from the intimate relations that existed between it and the Irish House of Commons.'[10] The relationship was reciprocal. The House of Commons created a special gallery for Trinity students to attend wearing their gowns, 'where they might imbibe a love of eloquence and of liberty, and learn the principles of a just and proud ambition, the details of public business, and the rudiments of constitutional law'. This relationship continued until 1795, when the students broke into 'a boisterous tumult' after a speech of Henry Grattan attacking the British Government for recalling Lord Fitzwilliam.[11] The Speaker, John Foster, ordered the students' gallery to be cleared and the students were forcibly removed and 'were never again suffered to enter as privileged persons'.

The motions debated in the period 1779–80 reflected the political turmoil of the time. It also reveals the sympathies of the members. It is notable that there was unanimous support for the motion that 'America was Justifiable in her Secession from Great Britain'. On the subject of the future of Ireland there was more division. On the subject of 'Whether Ireland could possibly subsist independent of any other Nation', the motion was defeated by 14 votes to 7, with two-thirds in favour of continuing the existing connection with Britain in some form. The use of pensions by the Irish administration to control the parliament was heavily criticised, and the motion 'Whether the Power which the King Possesses of Bestowing Pensions is Dangerous to the Constitution', passed by 17 votes to 4.

A motion of 'Whether the Power of Impressing Seamen ought to be allowed in a Free Country' was defeated by 12 votes to 5. The role of the Volunteers, which had been formed to defend Ireland from French invasion and which became an extra-parliamentary force agitating for political and economic reform, was also debated. The motion, 'Whether the Volunteers or Standing Army are the most Effectual', was decided in favour of the Volunteers by 13 votes to 6, with Laurence Parsons on the winning side.

---

10 Ibid.

11 John Edward Walsh, *Sketches of Ireland sixty years ago* (Dublin, 1847), p. 175.

Peter Burrowes, who had served as Auditor during the session, closed the debate for the 1779-80 session when he delivered an eloquent speech from the chair, paying tribute to the Society for bringing in many reforms, including the creation of honorary membership, and widening the questions for debate. Calling on the members to have the courage to serve the public good, he suggested that Ireland was entering a critical phase of its history when they would achieve 'political glory... civil liberty', marking the beginning of a 'blessed era of their country's emancipation'.[12] It was stirring stuff, with Burrowes arguing that each member had the capacity to serve 'his country in the most exalted station'. Emphasising the power of oratory to change the world, he claimed it could 'fix the dissipated, fire the indolent, convert the prejudiced, and charm even the invidious'. The speech concluded with a prediction that when future historians looked back on this period they would trace 'the rapid yet clear stream' of collected eloquence 'to its distinguished source, the Historical Society'.

The debates in the 1780-81 session continued to reflect the wider debates in society. A motion suggesting that the Volunteers should 'interfere in parliamentary measures' was defeated by 19 votes to 5, while one supporting the admission of Catholics of property to the Volunteers was passed by 14 votes to 4.

Laurence Parsons was elected Auditor of the Society on 10 January 1781. Regarded as one of the finest orators of the day, he had won the medal for oratory, and had played a leading role in the business of the Society. In January 1780 he had presented the Society with a ceremonial gown to be worn by the chair, and as a result he was praised by the Society for his 'distinguished merit'.[13] In February 1781 the Society met in Parson's rooms in College, because the Common Room was required by the Board for another purpose.[14]

In April 1781 Richard Crosbie was expelled from the Society by a unanimous vote, after an order had been issued requiring all members to attend a meeting. Part scientist, part showman, Crosbie would go on to achieve fame as Ireland's first aeronaut. Inspired by

12 TCD MUN/HIST/3; Dagg, *CHS*, p. 42.

13 TCD MUN/HIST/3.

14 TCD MUN/HIST/3.

balloon experiments in France, he attempted to fly across the Irish Sea in 1785 after constructing his own hydrogen balloon. In January 1785 he travelled from Ranelagh Gardens to Clontarf, in a trip that was viewed by over 20,000 people.[15] In May 1785 he attempted a second journey across the Irish Sea, but found he was too heavy for the balloon and so Richard McGwire, a twenty-one-year old Trinity student volunteered to take his place. The journey ended in near disaster, with the balloon crashing into the sea a few miles off the coast of Howth, where he was rescued. Heralded as a hero upon his return, McGwire was awarded a knighthood and a commission in the army, and the Historical Society debated whether it should present him with a medal or make him an honorary member.

During this session it was proposed to make all MPs eligible for membership of the Society, but this was rejected by the Board. The influence of Parsons was evident in the design of the proposal.

Parsons chaired the final meeting of the following session, on 13 June 1781, and spoke of how the students at Trinity had a singular advantage compared to those at Oxford or Cambridge. Being right beside the house of parliament and the law courts enabled them to hear 'some of the most finished orators of the present age'.[16] They could learn this art by example, 'while the youth of the English universities can only learn it by precept'. Political life in Dublin also gave the students the opportunity 'of exercising and thereby strengthening and improving your growing abilities'.

Parsons concluded by predicting great things for his fellow members. He said that he often flattered himself 'with the pleasing reflection that many of my juvenile acquaintances may on a future day be found as able and honest advocates for their country as they have been sincere and warm friends to him'.[17]

William Plunket became a member of the Society on 6 March 1782 and immediately established himself as one of its finest members. As a later portrait described him, he had 'the readiest, the

---

15 Bryan McMahon, *Ascend or die: Richard Crosbie, pioneer of balloon flight* (Dublin, 2010), p. 89.

16 TCD MUN/HIST/3; Dagg, *CHS*, p. 46.

17 TCD MUN/HIST/3.

keenest, and the most polished satire'.[18] In parliament he was 'distinguished as a profound and accurate and eloquent orator, as a debater he was ready, well informed and dauntless'.

Taking advantage of the political turmoil in Britain following the collapse of Lord North's government, legislative independence was secured by the Irish parliament on 16 April 1782. Although the significance of this victory would be debated by historians for many years to come, with differing opinions about whether the achievement was real or symbolic, it was clear that this marked the beginning of a new period of political self-confidence in the country. This was reflected in the Society, with the decision taken to repeal the resolution ordaining that only British history could be studied. It was agreed that in 'this era of Liberty, when Ireland has extorted her rights, it is the business and indispensable duty of every Irishman to be acquainted with the laws and constitution of his native country'.[19] One of the first texts prescribed for study was William Molyneux's seminal text, *The Case of Ireland Stated.* The Society also arranged the purchase of ten copies of Grattan's speech to the Irish parliament on 16 April 1782 'in which the rights of Ireland are so ably asserted'.[20]

Laurence Parsons stood for election to parliament for the University of Dublin in a by-election in July 1782 and was successful, defeating his opponent by 41 votes to 33.[21] His biographer, N. D. Atkinson, attributes this in a large part to the prestige he had won for his work in the Historical Society, suggesting that 'The victory belonged mainly to the Historical Society'.[22] A remarkable and unique honour followed. Parsons was elected Auditor of the Society for a second time in December 1782, thus becoming the only person to ever hold the office while also serving as a member of parliament.

In this session motions debated included a number on American politics, for example, 'Whether America would be Wise in accepting

18 TCD MUN/HIST/4; Dagg, *CHS*, p. 374.

19 TCD MUN/HIST/4; Dagg, *CHS*, p. 46.

20 TCD MUN/HIST/4; Dagg, *CHS*, p. 48.

21 N.D. Atkinson, 'Sir Laurence Parsons, 2nd Earl of Rosse, 1758–1841' (unpublished Ph.D. thesis, University of Dublin, 1961). p. 63.

22 Ibid., p. 64.

the same Constitution that Ireland at Present Enjoys', which was defeated by 24 votes to 2, and 'Whether the Independence of North America would be of service to the Continental Powers of Europe', which passed by 20 votes to 5. Irish history also featured. A motion on 'Whether the Attempt of the Irish in 1641 to Expel the English ought to be termed Rebellion?' was defeated by 32 votes to 5, with Thomas Addis Emmet on the side of the opposition. There was near unanimity for an interesting motion on whether 'the establishment of a Catholic University [would] be of advantage to Ireland?' and it passed by 22 votes to 2. The motion asking whether 'It is likely that the Independence of America will be Injurious to England?' was passed by 14 votes to 10, with Thomas Addis Emmet again with the opposition.

Thomas Addis Emmet's oratorical style in Trinity was later analysed by R. R. Madden who gathered first-hand accounts of what he had been like. Madden described him as having 'an impressive earnestness of manner, an honesty of purpose, and sincerity of conviction in the delivery of his sentiments, a strict adherence to truth... [and] a closeness of reasoning that never deviated from its essential line of argument'.[23]

At the close of the session a formal connection was established between the Historical Society and the Speculative Society in Edinburgh, with Thomas Addis Emmet central to the discussion. At this time, Emmet was a medical student in Edinburgh and he was keen to establish close links, and he served on the sub-committee which worked out the terms. It was agreed that members of the Speculative Society would be admitted as members of the Historical Society and be entitled to speak and compete for awards.

There was controversy at the meeting on 19 November 1783 when four poems were read. The first, 'A defence of the age', by William Plunket, was awarded a medal, as was one by Standish O'Grady.[24] O'Grady was elected Auditor later that session. However, a poem entitled, 'The Incognitos, a Northern Tale', signed Borealis, provoked angry reactions, as it attacked the Volunteers and various

23 R. R. Madden, *The United Irishmen: their lives and times* (2nd series, 2 vols, London, 1843), ii, 14.

24 TCD MUN/HIST/4; Dagg, *CHS*, p. 52.

named individuals. The usual vote of thanks was defeated and instead a resolution was passed by 37 votes to 12 condemning the poem for its 'very unjust and scandalous abuse of the Volunteers' as well as for its 'unjust calumny of several respectable private characters'. It was resolved that the poem should be 'burned by the hands of the porter, Samuel Bilson, in presence of the Society'. Bilson was called in and, as the records note, 'the said poem was burned accordingly'.[25]

This was the same meeting where Theobald Wolfe Tone was elected a member, his membership proposed by George Miller and seconded by William Plunket. He attended his first meeting on 3 December. Writing a decade later, Tone reminisced about his days in the Society, 'a most admirable institution', and was proud of the three medals he had won, the fact that he had been elected Auditor, and had been invited to speak at the close of a session.[26]

Fifty new members joined that session, and new seats had to be added to the room. The average attendance was fifty-seven and debates generated much more interest among the students.[27] Motions included the question, 'Should this Kingdom keep a Standing Army' (defeated by 20 votes to 8), and 'Should Universal Toleration be Encouraged by a Wise Legislature?' (passed by 28 votes to 16). A debate on whether the new United States should expel royalists from the country was defeated by 29 votes to 14. During this period the porter, Samuel Bilson, was killed after he fell from the top of the Society room's stairs. Tone chaired a committee to aid Bilson's distressed children.[28]

The earliest example of the Society taking an interest in celebrity culture occurred in June 1784. Sarah Siddons, a twenty-eight-year old British performer who was on her way to becoming the most famous tragic actress of the eighteenth century, was visiting Dublin, and the Society proposed a motion to present her with a copy of the Oxford edition of Shakespeare's works.[29] Others however disagreed,

25 TCD MUN/HIST/4; Dagg, *CHS*, p. 53.
26 Tone, *Memoirs*, p. 18.
27 TCD MUN/HIST/4; Dagg, *CHS*, p. 54.
28 Elliott, *Wolfe Tone,* p. 32.
29 TCD MUN/HIST/5; Dagg, *CHS*, p. 55.

wanting to go further, and proposed presenting her with a gold medal. There was no agreement before midnight, when the meeting was adjourned, and it does not appear from the records that the proposal ever went any further.

Charles Kendal Bushe was elected a member on 26 October 1784, the first meeting of the 1784–85 session. He soon marked himself out as one of the finest orators in the Society and was awarded a medal for oratory a few months later on 5 January 1785. He was on the opposition side when the question was debated, 'Whether we are more Indebted for the Constitutional Liberty of Great Britain to Bad than Good Princes?' (19 December 1784). He was praised for his conduct in the chair during a particularly heated debate in January 1785, and a vote of thanks was passed afterwards praising 'his very proper, steady and polite conduct in the chair... when spirited exertions were necessary'.[30] Thomas Dagg rightly considers Bushe 'undoubtedly one of the greatest of the orators who received their early training in the Historical Society'.[31]

Another of the great speakers was Thomas Goold, a remarkable student from Cork, who was also awarded a medal for oratory. Goold had inherited £10,000 following the death of his father and was determined to spend it neither wisely nor well. He spent most of it on various entertainments, as well as on singing, dancing and fencing lessons.[32]

Tone was a proposer of the question 'Is an Absentee Tax Admissible in a Free State?' on 9 June 1784 and the motion was carried.[33] At the close of the session Tone was awarded the remarkable thanks for the Society for his contribution during the year. In January 1785 he was one of four candidates proposed for Auditor, but was not elected. He was again one of four candidates nominated on 27 April 1785, and was again unsuccessful, this time losing out to George Miller. Miller was the outstanding orator of the session, and when the returns were calculated for the period to 30 March he came first on 315, with Goold second on 210, Tone third

30 TCD MUN/HIST/5; Dagg, *CHS*, p. 55.

31 TCD MUN/HIST/5; Dagg, *CHS*, p. 382.

32 P.M. Geoghegan, 'Thomas Goold', *DIB*.

33 TCD MUN/HIST/5; Dagg, *CHS*, p. 56.

on 209, and Bushe fourth on 142. Medals were awarded to Miller and Goold, and it was afterwards agreed unanimously 'that an extra medal be presented to Mr Tone for his exertions in oratory during the last period'.[34]

Tone soon established himself at the centre of the life of the Society. After his death, the *Freeman's Journal* noted that when he was at Trinity 'his company was courted by every student of taste in the university, and so attractive was his conversation that many young men of the first rank and fortune solicited his acquaintance'.[35] It was said that when it came to oratory he overcame 'a weak voice and ungraceful manner' and 'succeeded in a wonderful degree'. When it came to history he displayed 'penetrating judgement and powerful memory'. And when it came to composition his works 'stood unrivalled in the collection of that Society'.

Charles Kendal Bushe opened the 1785–76 session on 26 October 1785 with a speech on the importance of studying oratory. At the next meeting, on 3 November, George Miller received permission to resign as Auditor. Tone, Bushe and two others were nominated to succeed him. Third time lucky, Tone was elected as Auditor. On 4 January 1786 he was awarded another medal for oratory, and later in the month a medal for history. He resigned as Auditor on 8 February. Motions debated that session included, 'Was the Union of Advantage to Scotland?' (defeated by 44 votes to 6), and 'Would it have been politic for America to accept the Constitution Ireland at Present Enjoys?' (defeated by 34 votes to 12).[36] It is a measure of Tone's popularity in the Society that when his three medals were stolen on 1 November 1786 the Society voted to make him three replacements 'to perpetuate those proofs of our discernment' and to 'testify our respect for so valuable a member'.[37] The motion was passed unanimously.

John Radcliffe served as Auditor for part of this session, and together with his friends, Richard Jebb and Wolfe Tone, went on to write a satirical novel, *Belmont Castle, or Suffering Sensibility,* in

34 TCD MUN/HIST/5; Dagg, *CHS*, p. 57.

35 Elliott, *Wolfe Tone,* p. 34.

36 TCD MUN/HIST/5; Dagg, *CHS*, p. 58.

37 TCD MUN/HIST/5; Dagg, *CHS*, p. 59.

1787.[38] The novel was a *roman-à-clef* in epistolary form and made fun of various figures they knew. Jebb's section focused on their contemporary in the Society, Thomas Goold, who was satirised for his foppish appearance and behaviour.[39] Radcliffe later became a successful lawyer and was appointed a judge of the prerogative court in 1816. Jebb opposed the Union, writing an influential pamphlet against it, and was appointed a judge in 1818.

On 24 January 1787 Tone called in to the Society on his return from London, where he was doing a bad job of studying to be a barrister. He returned to the Society in December 1788 and Elliott considers strong evidence of 'his attachment to the Society that it was his first port of call on his return to Ireland'.[40]

George Miller had been elected to give the speech to close the session, but he found himself overwhelmed with preparing for the Fellowship examination and was forced to back out. In his place, Pemberton Rudd was chosen, and he delivered a speech critical of the Society, commenting on the way history was being neglected, compositions were being 'read with wrong stops, false cadence and ill-intended pronunciation', and too much time was being devoted to private business. He also suggested that throughout the year, and especially in the second half of the session, the debates were 'marked by the most careless apathy and indifference', with some members behaving in an intemperate and disorderly way. These criticisms seem to have merit, and the problems continued the following year. At the opening meeting of the 1787-88 session Jonas Green reflected on the previous session and launched a vehement attack on the members for not attending for the history portion of the evening, a 'desertion' which he believed 'outraged all decency'.[41] He also criticised members for allowing the Society to become the scene of 'party violence and illiberal resentment' he considered 'marked and disgraced your proceedings'. Treasurer for part of this session was Robert Ross, who went on to become a Major-General in the British army, and achieved infamy when he ordered the burning of the

38 Rosemary Richey, 'John Radcliffe', *DIB*.

39 Desmond McCabe and Linde Lunney, 'Richard Jebb', *DIB*.

40 Elliott, *Wolfe Tone,* p. 39.

41 TCD MUN/HIST/5; Dagg, *CHS*, p. 59.

White House, the Capitol Building, and other public buildings in Washington DC in 1814. He was killed by American sharpshooters when attempting to capture Baltimore a few weeks later.[42]

When Christopher Temple Emmet died suddenly in March 1788 he was honoured by the Society which offered a gold medal for the best elegy on his death. Speaking at the close of the session, George Miller noted that 'even now the well-earned applause of this assembly is not confined within these walls. We have seen it give an early celebrity to the abilities of a man who in his short but honourable life adorned the profession of an advocate with the brilliancy of genius and the varied erudition of a scholar.'[43]

Tone was an active participant in the debates of the Society in the 1788–89 session. On 15 April 1789 he proposed the award of a silver medal to the author of the best poem celebrating the recovery of King George III from illness, and this passed. He also introduced a rule preventing members from publishing poems that had been awarded medals unless they received the permission of the Society. The question 'Should Foreign Troops be Admitted into this Country for its Defence in Case of Actual Invasion or Declared Rebellion?' was defeated without a division. Likewise the question 'Whether an Union with Great Britain would be of Advantage to Ireland' was unanimously rejected. The views of the members were also evident in the defeat of the question on 'Whether Great Britain had a Right to Tax the American Colonies?'[44]

Miller won his Fellowship in 1789 and the Society presented him with an address of congratulation on 24 June. It was at this meeting that Tone spoke from the chair, delivering the closing address for the session. He began dramatically by announcing, 'At the close of a troublesome and tempestuous session, which has been marked by a variety of important incidents, I have the high honour to meet you in the situation to which your goodness has raised me.'[45]

Tone announced that his role was to tell the truth no matter whom it offended, and that he was determined to 'boldly tell you of

42 David Murphy, 'Robert Ross', *DIB*.

43 TCD MUN/HIST/6; Dagg, *CHS*, pp 59-60.

44 TCD MUN/HIST/; Dagg, *CHS*, p. 61.

45 TCD MUN/HIST/6; Dagg, *CHS*, p. 62.

your faults' even though it would lead to 'the certain forfeiture of your favour'. Listing their 'follies and faults', he argued that a 'vindictive spirit of sanguinary personal resentment' had pervaded the meetings, and 'disgraced your proceedings'. Suggesting that the Society was being turned into 'a theatre of war and of tumult', he complained that 'the seat of science' was being turned into 'a field of blood'.

With remarkable invective, Tone attacked them for not taking the history examination seriously, 'a wretched evasion of the spirit of your laws by a thin attendance of members not half prepared'. As for the debates, he complained that a 'clear and spirited investigation of the question' had been replaced 'into commonplace harangues or more ruinous contention and invective'. Speaking about the compositions, he had a withering put down: 'Silence is mercy – this is not your era for compositions!'[46] The speech ended, however, on an uplifting and inspiring note. Tone admitted that 'dark and gloomy as are our prospects, I do not yet despair of the republic'. Calling on them to be 'bold yet temperate in debate', he urged them to 'think of your past glories' and 'ye shall live!'

Given the coming together of so many extraordinary figures in the Society in this period, it is worth concluding this chapter with a look at some of their future glories. Laurence Parsons (Sir Laurence Parsons after 1791) was a leading figure in the Irish House of Commons in the 1790s, taking an independent line separate from both the Government and Henry Grattan, whom he despised. A vocal opponent of the Union, it was Parsons who proposed the 'crucial amendment' deleting a reference to it from the King's address on 24 January 1799.[47] Succeeding his uncle as 2nd Earl of Rosse in 1807, he became Irish Postmaster-General and has been described as 'attentive and reforming' in that role. His son, William, succeeded him and as 3rd Earl of Rosse became a celebrated astronomer, while a grandson, Laurence Knox, was the founder of *The Irish Times* in 1859.[48]

Charles Kendal Bushe pursued a career in the law, and entered

46 TCD MUN/HIST/6; Dagg, *CHS*, p. 63.
47 See James Kelly, 'Laurence Parsons', *ODNB.*
48 See P.M. Geoghegan, 'Laurence Knox, *DIB.*

the House of Commons in 1796 as MP for Callan, Co. Kilkenny. In parliament he defended his friend, Wolfe Tone, then in exile, from attacks, saying that he would 'ever lament his fate with compassion for his errors, admiration for his talents, and abhorrence for his political opinions'.[49] Fervently opposed to the union, he wrote one of the best pamphlets on the subject, a satirical attack on Government efforts entitled *Cease your Funning* in 1799. For his work, he was awarded the freedom of Dublin on 17 January 1800.[50] Appointed Solicitor General for Ireland in 1805, he became Lord Chief Justice in 1822. A sometimes harsh judge of characters, Jonah Barrington said that he was 'nearly devoid of public and private enemies as any man'.

Assessing his oratorical style, Lord Brougham said that Bushe's 'power of narration has not perhaps been equalled... Perfect simplicity, but united with elegance'.[51] When describing a scene, Brougham said that Bushe had the ability to make his listeners believe that they had 'witnessed the reality'. Henry Grattan noted that as an orator Bushe was 'graceful, fluent, plausible and zealous'. He suggested that Bushe had the ability to 'clothe his ideas in a garb of rich and overflowing eloquence, with a voice that charmed, he modulated its tones so as to fall upon the ear with softness and almost with the sweetness of melody'. When Bushe spoke, 'his eyes kindled, and a glow of fire animated his whole frame... Few were blessed by Providence with talents like those of Bushe'. In his novel, *Jack Hinton,* Charles Lever refers to 'the elegance of manner and classical perfection of wit that makes Bushe the Cicero of his nation'.[52]

Peter Burrowes was called to the bar in 1785 and built a successful practice, defending Theobald Wolfe Tone in 1798 and Robert Emmet in 1803. A firm supporter of Catholic emancipation (Laurence Parsons believed that his mother was a Catholic), he entered parliament in 1799 to oppose the Act of Union. After the Union passed he asked Parsons how it might be possible to

49 James Quinn, 'Charles Kendal Bushe', *DIB.*

50 James Quinn, 'Charles Kendal Bushe', *DIB.*

51 Dagg, *CHS*, p. 382.

52 Dagg, *CHS*, p. 383.

permanently unite the two countries if the Catholics of Ireland were 'permanently alienated'.[53]

William Plunket became a noted barrister in the 1790s, but his opposition to radical activities led to the severing of his friendships with Wolfe Tone and Thomas Addis Emmet.[54] Becoming MP for Charlemont in 1798, he opposed the Act of Union, and it has been said that 'the eloquence, passion and fury of his defence of the Constitution added fire to the debates'.[55] In 1803 he acted for the prosecution in the trial of Robert Emmet, leading to some accusations that he was betraying his former radical principles and friendships. Having served as Solicitor General and then Attorney General for Ireland, he entered the British House of Commons, and 'established himself as a formidable orator', in part through his speeches in favour of Catholic emancipation. Elevated to the peerage as Baron Plunket in 1827, he became Lord Chancellor for Ireland in 1831 and served (apart from a short break in 1838) until 1841. As Maeve Ryan has noted in the *Dictionary of Irish Biography*, 'his perceived prioritisation of careerist self-advancement over principle... did little for his reputation. His flagrant nepotism in distributing favours to members of his extended family finally destroyed any reputation for principle he had earned in his early career'.

Called to the bar in 1791, his inheritance almost completely squandered, Goold achieved the gratitude of Edmund Burke after writing a pamphlet defending *Reflections on the revolution in France* from its critics, and he was invited to visit him at Beaconsfield. Goold delivered one of the first speeches attacking the proposed legislative union on 9 December 1798, and he followed up with a pamphlet against the measure. He entered parliament in 1800 specifically to oppose the union and in his maiden speech on 14 February he attacked the principle of empire, declaring that it 'has deluged the world with blood and never was achieved but by the downfall of the liberties of mankind'.[56] Goold ended his career as a

53 C.J. Woods, 'Peter Burrowes', *DIB*.

54 Maeve Ryan, William Plunket', *DIB*.

55 Ibid.

56 Thomas Goold, *Speech of Thomas Goold on 14 February 1800* (Dublin, 1800), p. 38.

Master at the Court of Chancery. Henry Grattan once said that he would 'stake his existence' on Goold's integrity, insisting that 'if he is not to be trusted I know not who is to be trusted'.[57]

George Miller became a Fellow in 1789 and in that year headed the negotiations with College to help win for Fellows the right to elect future Provosts.[58] In the 1800s he prepared a series of 84 lectures on Irish, British and world history and when these were published in eight volumes between 1816 and 1828 they were considered his *magnum opus* and 'reached a wide Irish and British readership'. A clergyman, he became headmaster of Armagh Royal School in 1817, where he had to deal with a two-day riot, and in 1843 was made Vicar General of the diocese of Armagh.

Standish O'Grady was called to the bar in 1787 and became Attorney General in 1803, just in time to prosecute Robert Emmet for treason.[59] In 1805 he was created Lord Chief Baron, succeeding Lord Avonmore (Barry Yelverton). Considered 'one of the least dignified men to have ever sat on the bench', he was hugely popular, in part because of 'his tavern house humour' and the way he would exaggerate his strong Limerick accent for comic effect. Upon his retirement he was raised to the peerage as Baron O'Grady of Rockbarton and Viscount Guillamore of Cahir Guillamore.

Christopher Temple Emmet was called to the bar in 1781 and was regarded as 'perhaps the most talented young barrister of his day' becoming a king's counsel in 1787.[60] Tragedy hit in February 1788 when he was struck down by an illness and died suddenly. As a result, his younger brother, Thomas Addis Emmet, decided to abandon his medical studies and pursue a career in the law. Thomas Addis was called to the bar in 1790 and he became active in the political discussions of the day, joining the United Irishmen. A strong supporter of the rights of Catholics, Tone considered him 'the best of all the friends to Catholic emancipation'. Emmet had a flair for the theatrical. For example, when defending United Irish prisoners in 1796 he took the oath in court to test its legality. In 1798 he was

57 P.M. Geoghegan, 'Thomas Goold', *DIB*.

58 Desmond McCabe, 'George Miller', *DIB*.

59 P.M. Geoghegan, 'Standish O'Grady', *DIB*.

60 James Quinn, 'Thomas Addis Emmet', *DIB*.

part of a committee which gathered evidence of military atrocities against civilians and he presented this to his friend, Laurence Parsons. When the government moved against the United Irishmen in March 1798, Emmet was arrested and he was imprisoned in Newgate and later Kilmainham.

Following the failure of the 1798 rebellion, Emmet defended his belief that 'if Ireland were separated from England she would be the happiest spot on the face of the globe'.[61] Sent into exile to Fort George in Scotland, he was released in June 1802 and made his way to the Continent where he liaised with his brother, Robert, who was planning a new insurrection. Disillusioned with the regime of Napoleon Bonaparte, he emigrated to the United States in 1804 and established a legal practice in New York. In his first case, Emmet defended a fugitive slave, and he took many cases representing the New York Manumission Society, refusing to live in the South because of his opposition to slavery. James Quinn writes in the *Dictionary of Irish Biography* that Emmet 'soon built up a thriving practice and at the height of his career was one of New York's most celebrated lawyers, earning £15,000 a year'.[62] He was seized by a fit while in court on 14 November 1827 and died a few hours later at his home.

The final remarkable figure is, of course, Theobald Wolfe Tone himself. Tone's subsequent career is too well-known to need repeating here. A founding member of the United Irishmen, he wrote what has been called 'the most famous pamphlet in Irish history: *An argument on behalf of the Catholics of Ireland*, published in August 1791'.[63] Tone's political vision was set-out in what his biographer, Marianne Elliott, calls 'the most quoted passage in modern Irish history': 'To subvert the tyranny of our execrable Government, to break the connection with England, the never-failing source of all our political evils, and to assert the independence of my country.'[64] His mission: 'To unite the whole people of Ireland, to abolish the memory of all past dissensions, and to substitute the

61 Ibid.

62 Ibid.

63 Thomas Bartlett, 'Theobald Wolfe Tone', *DIB*.

64 Marianne Elliott, 'Theobald Wolfe Tone', *ODNB*.

common name of Irishman in the place of the denominations of Protestant, Catholic and Dissenter.'

Tone secured French military support for an invasion in the winter of 1796, which became the failed expedition to Bantry Bay. After the outbreak of the 1798 Rebellion Tone set-off with a French force to land in the north of Ireland, and was captured following 'a furious six hour sea battle' in which he distinguished himself.[65] Captured and brought to Dublin to be tried for high treason, Tone was found guilty and sentenced to death by hanging and beheading. To cheat the hangman, Tone committed suicide in prison by cutting his throat with a blade. His final words were 'What should I wish to live for?'

Considered the father of modern Irish republicanism, Tone became an inspiration to future generations. According to Sean O'Faolain, 'without him, republicanism in Ireland would virtually have no tradition'.[66] The Young Irelanders were inspired by his example, as were the Fenians, Patrick Pearse and the leaders of the 1916 Rising. As Thomas Bartlett concludes in the *Dictionary of the Irish Biography,* Tone 'had sought justice for the Catholics even though in doing so he had turned his back on the ascendancy. He had believed that the Irish government of the 1790s was wholly bereft of moral authority, and he had acted accordingly.'

---

65 Bartlett, 'Theobald Wolfe Tone', *DIB.*

66 Ibid.

THE AGE OF REBELLION, 1790-1800

4

THE SWIRLING TENSIONS within the Society came to a head in the 1790s and resulted in a rupture, with it splitting into two. One continued to meet inside College, with the approval of the authorities, one began meeting externally, with students threatened with expulsion if they attended.[1] The problems in the Society reflected what was happening politically in Ireland, with some fearful and some hopeful about developments in revolutionary France. It would be incorrect to say that one Society was the true continuation of the Society and the other an imitation. Both were drawn from the existing membership, both believed passionately in the rightness of their position, and both helped shape the Society which continued afterwards. One's view probably depends on how one regards the politics of the 1790s and whether conflict with the College and differing views on the future of the island should have been resolved through accommodation or defiance.

At the first meeting of the 1789–90 session the invited speaker was Edward Lysaght from Co. Clare, a recent graduate who had been called to the bar, and who had a reputation as a poet, a wit and a bon vivant.[2] Lysaght however failed to show and this is not, perhaps, surprising. As Patrick Fagan writes in the *Dictionary of Irish Biography*, 'he was a sot, a hard man, a ne'er-do-well who skulked for some time in Trinity College so as to be out of the way of bailiffs'. In his absence, Laurence Parsons took the chair as the most senior member present, with Wolfe Tone acting as secretary. Lysaght attended the next week, and spoke from the chair, but he appears to have been drunk and incoherent and in the records there are eight pages left blank.

1 *Freeman's Journal*, 13 June 1795.

2 Patrick Fagan, 'Edward Lysaght', *DIB*.

An anonymous poem signed 'Comhal' was submitted to the Society on 10 March 1790, and it was deliberately provocative and insulting. The Auditor proposed a motion, which was unanimously adopted, calling for it to be burned by the porter. A few nights later, an abusive anonymous letter was sent to the Society, containing what the Committee revealed were 'several groundless assertions on some respectable characters in the University and in this Society'.[3] This letter was also burned.

Attendance at some of the bigger political debates was impressive. There were 150 members present to debate the question, 'Whether an Union with England would be of Advantage to this Country?' Four Fellows attended this debate to see what was being said, and after a close-fought evening the motion was carried by 80 votes to 70. Some of the motions had a subversive sub-text. For example a debate on whether the people would be justified in turning out a corrupt parliament before a general election was carried by 41 votes to 4, and this was essentially a vindication of revolutionary activity if the circumstances warranted it. A motion suggesting that 'the Loss of America will Impair the Grandeur of the British Empire' was passed by 34 votes to 16.

At the start of the 1791–92 session, a former member, Thomas Prior, was presented with an address upon becoming a Fellow. In his response, he warned the Society to avoid becoming caught up in political controversy. Remembering his own experiences in the Society, where he 'experienced much entertainment, received much improvement, and frequently relieved an anxious mind', he described the Society as 'the brightest ornament of the Irish University'.[4] However, he warned that 'internal commotion may give serious alarm', and 'party spirit is the only demon of strength sufficient to shake your foundation'.

These words were echoed by Robert Orr at the close of the 1791–2 session when he urged the members to avoid debating modern politics. Warning that the name of the Society was not enough 'to give it celebrity', he reminded his listeners that 'its character must always depend on the exertions of its members'. The same message

3 TCD MUN/HIST/6; Dagg, *CHS*, p. 66.

4 TCD MUN/HIST/6; Dagg, *CHS*, pp. 66-7.

was delivered a year later at the close of the 1792–93 session, when John Schoales, a former Auditor, advised the members to listen to the heads of the University or else face 'destruction'.[5]

Richard Pennefather was elected Auditor for the first part of the 1792–3 session and even in a talented group of students he stood out for his piercing intellect. Awarded prizes in both mathematics and classics, he was later awarded the distinction of an *optime* when he graduated, which had only been awarded to seven students.[6] Although not a powerful speaker, he was a very good organiser, and Pennefather's year was notable for the focus on a wide range of questions, from philosophy to history to the classics.

Two radical students who played an important role in the Society in this decade were the brothers, Thomas and William Corbet, from Co. Cork. The elder brother, Thomas, became a Scholar in 1790 and graduated BA in 1791 but he only became closely involved in the Society as a graduate member. Elected Auditor for the 1793–94 session, he ran the Society effectively, and his Committee included Samuel Kyle as Treasurer, Robert Torrens as Librarian, and John Jebb, the younger brother of Richard Jebb. Described by a contemporary in Trinity as 'a low, smart little man', Corbet was a member of the United Irishmen, and was determined to break the connection between Britain and Ireland.[7] In 1795, during the crisis with College, Thomas Corbet was voted 'the remarkable thanks of this Society' for 'his attention to the interests of this Society in general, and his assiduity in preserving its records on the late critical occasion'.[8]

'Tall and delicate, of a mild disposition and very pleasing manners', his brother, William, became a Scholar in 1796 and graduated in 1797, and also became active in the Society, serving as a member of Committee and becoming friends with Thomas Moore and Robert Emmet.[9] He too joined the United Irishmen and was a strong supporter of Catholic emancipation.

The meeting on 2 April 1794 created a crisis in the Society.

5 TCD MUN/HIST/6; Dagg, *CHS*, p. 67.
6 Patrick Maume, 'Richard Pennefather', *DIB*.
7 James Quinn, 'Thomas Corbet', *DIB*.
8 TCD MUN/HIST/7; Dagg, *CHS*, p. 80.
9 James Quinn, 'William Corbet', *DIB*.

William Connor, a former member of the Society, had been expelled from College and forbidden from setting foot on the grounds. George Miller, the former medallist and Auditor, was now Junior Dean and was present at the meeting. Seeing Connor, he sent a message to the Auditor, Lewis Kerr, asking that Connor be instructed to leave the room or be ejected. It appears that Kerr refused to pass the message to the chair, Henry Adair, prompting Miller to contact him directly, but Adair declined to act. In the end, the Secretary was instructed to bring a message to Connor, who withdrew from the meeting.[10]

The next week, the Board sent a message to the Society instructing that anyone who was no longer on the College books could not continue as members. This was rejected by the Society, who argued of 'the great benefit which must result from the presence of members whose former exertions in the Society have gained the highest honours'.[11] Contributing to the crisis was the ill-health of the Provost, John Hely-Hutchinson, who was unable to attend these meetings of the Board, and who may have been a restraining influence on both sides.

At the next meeting of the Society, on 9 April 1794, 142 members attended. A message from the Board was read containing a list of criticisms and instructions. Chief among them was that 'the Board are much surprised and displeased' that the 'Historical Society should have continued on their books the name of a person prohibited by the Board from appearing in College' and insisting that the person was struck off from the books of the Society. A new rule was presented that only medallists of the Society would be able to continue as members after graduation, and the Board declared that it 'will not at present insist on any further regulations' in the hope that the Society 'will in future conduct themselves in such manner as shall gain the good opinion of the Governors of the College'.[12]

This message dominated the entire meeting. As midnight approached, a motion suspending the rule that the Society had to adjourn at midnight, was passed by 120 votes to 20. The Society came

10 TCD MUN/HIST/7; Dagg, *CHS*, p. 68.
11 TCD MUN/HIST/7; Dagg, *CHS*, p. 69.
12 TCD MUN/HIST/7; Dagg, *CHS*, p. 70.

close to a split on the night. The hardliners, a group which included Charles Kendal Bushe, refused to compromise and proposed taking the Society's property off College, so they could meet externally and continue in existence. A second group, which included Thomas Lefroy, looked for some arrangement with College, and developed a counter proposal which it sent to the Board. In this document it was agreed that in future anyone who had been expelled from the University would have their name removed as a member, but pleading for permission to allow external membership to continue.

On Saturday 12 April 1794 the Society met at the Exhibition Room, on the first floor of the Assembly House on William Street. This was the beginning of the Extern Society and 137 members attended, including Wolfe Tone and Thomas Lefroy, although some attended to try and put an end to this act of rebellion. At this meeting a resolution was passed asserting 'That it is the opinion of the present meeting that the Historical Society is now legally convened.'[13] This was carried by 114 votes to 10, with Lefroy opposing. Those who decided to break with College were not necessarily political radicals, although the majority were sympathetic to those demanding political reform. It revolved around whether College could impose conditions on the Society it viewed as draconian, and how the members should respond.

The response of the Vice Provost and the Board to the counter proposal was read at this meeting. Given what they called 'the impropriety of the proceedings of the Historical Society at their last meeting', they were not prepared to accept it and revealed that they had reclaimed the rooms which had been put at the disposal of the Society. Upon hearing this, the members decided to appeal directly to the Provost, and sent him a message regretting their exile from the University and thanking him for 'the kind protection with which you have so long honoured them'.[14] Unfortunately for them, Hely-Hutchinson was too unwell to intervene, and he died later that year.

On Wednesday 16 April the Society met for a second time outside College, and debated the question 'Is the Impressing of Seamen Consistent with the British Constitution?' The motion was defeated

13 TCD MUN/HIST/7; Dagg, *CHS*, p. 72.
14 TCD MUN/HIST/7; Dagg, *CHS*, p. 73.

by 40 votes to 21. Determined to put an end to this act of defiance, the Board threatened students with expulsion if they attended meetings, and carried through on their threats for anyone who was discovered to be a member.

Reflecting on this period in 1819 for a book entitled *Specimens of Irish eloquence*, Charles Phillips, a former member and barrister, suggested that Trinity 'never sustained such a loss as in the annihilation of the Historical Society'.[15] He believed there was not a single man in the church or at the bar 'who could not directly trace his success to the Historical Society', and he blamed the clash on 'some vulgar pretence' of a 'gang of bigotted monks'. 'The leading speech' which Philips chose for his volume, was the speech Charles Kendal Bushe gave at the close of this session. It is presented as the closing speech 'of the 24th session of the Historical Society of the University of Dublin, instituted in the year 1770'.

Bushe delivered this speech on 24 June 1794 and it is considered one of his finest speeches, as he defended the Society for its actions, while expressing a hope that some future agreement might be found with the Board. The speech was an eloquent defence of oratory, as Bushe declared that 'I shall tremble for my country when the practice of the study of oratory is cried down – its glory and its liberty will not long survive.'[16] Oratory, he proclaimed, was able to 'assert the independence of a nation, and adjust the unbalanced liberties of an empire', and the 'magic of a fire-touched tongue' could 'terrify a country into justice, and inspire another into freedom'.

According to tradition, Henry Grattan was at this meeting and pronounced afterwards that 'Bushe spoke with the lips of an angel'.[17] Richard Lalor Sheil later studied this speech and declared it 'a very eloquent oration ... remarkable for its purity and simplicity of style'.[18] Noting that 'in an assembly of insurgent students' some

---

15 Charles Phillips, *Specimens of Irish eloquence* (London, 1819), p. ccxii.

16 Ibid., p. 332.

17 Edith Somerville and Martin Ross, *An incorruptible Irishman: being an account of Chief Justice Charles Kendal Bushe and his wife, Nancy Crampton, and their times*, 1767-1843 (London, 1932), p. 26.

18 M. W. Savage (ed.), *Sketches, legal and political by the late Right Honourable Richard Lalor Sheil* (2 vols, 1855), i, 6.

hyperbole was unavoidable, but he believed it was 'the mature production of a vigorous mind, rather than the prolusion of a juvenile rhetorician'.

Edward Lawson chaired the first meeting of the new session, on 22 October 1794, where 80 members attended the Exhibition Room. In his speech he attacked the Board for its draconian decrees, and for refusing to compromise, urging the members to see this 'as the opening of a new campaign'.[19] He was also critical of the College for offering their 'inheritance to younger brethren' with 'colonists and culprits of all sorts and sizes' invited into their old rooms.

In the months ahead various resolutions were proposed in the Society in the attempt to find a solution to the impasse, but none went very far. In December 1794 the Society decided to send a deputation consisting of the Auditor, Lewis Kerr, and three other members to present an address to the Board and this seems to have brought the tensions in the Society to a head. In the event, Kerr's meeting with the Board, did not go well. He was examined by the Board in great detail before receiving 'a public admonition in the College Hall'.[20]

On 17 December 1794 a letter was delivered to the Auditor by Peter Burrowes. It revealed that 37 members of the Society, including Burrowes, William Plunket, Thomas Goold, Robert Torrens, Richard Jebb, and Thomas Lefroy, wished to withdraw their names from the membership of the Society, and they never attended the Extern Society again.[21] Two nights later, on 19 December 1794, a new Society was established within College, comprising some of the figures from this group, including Lefroy and Torrens. Twelve members were present, and they resolved unanimously to establish themselves as 'The Historical Society of the University of Dublin instituted for the cultivation of History, Oratory and Composition'.[22] The prescriptions of the Board were adopted. 'No question of modern politics shall be debated', Fellows were given the automatic right of being able to attend meetings, and no external

19 TCD MUN/HIST/7; Dagg, *CHS*, p. 74.

20 Dagg, *CHS*, p. 78.

21 TCD MUN/HIST/7; Dagg, *CHS*, p. 75.

22 TCD MUN/HIST/7; Dagg, *CHS*, p. 83.

members were to be allowed. It was also agreed that members of the 'late Society' would be eligible to join the new Society, provided they accepted the new regulations.

The second meeting of the Society took place on 24 December 1795 and was attended by sixteen members, including two future Provosts, Francis Sadleir and Samuel Kyle.[23] From January 1795 to sometime in 1797 the two Societies ran in parallel, often on the same evening. One was sometimes described as 'The Extern Society', the other as 'The Intern Society', including by those who attended their meetings. However, for the majority, the Society they attended was 'The Historical Society', and was the true heir of what had been established in 1770. For the purposes of distinguishing them here, I will use the terms 'The Extern Society' and 'The Intern Society', but the members themselves would have called their body 'The Historical Society'. Although they both followed the same format as before, with an examination on History followed by a debate, there were some noticeable differences between the two. 'The Extern Society' allowed non-students to attend meetings, opening it up to members of parliament and others, on payment of a fee of a guinea and a half to attend.[24] It was also not afraid to debate contemporary politics. Based in College, 'The Intern Society' was bound by the restrictions of the Board, on its membership and its subject matter. 'The Intern Society' considered itself a successor society, and so began numbering its sessions starting at one, but here there was much confusion and very often the numbering was interchangeable with members treating it as both a new society and a continuation of the old one.

Thomas Lefroy was unanimously elected Auditor of the new 'Intern Society', with Robert Torrens as Treasurer, and John Jebb as Secretary and Librarian. Described a year later by Jane Austen as a 'very gentlemanlike, good-looking, pleasant young man', Lefroy was a deeply conservative student, vehemently opposed to radicalism of any kind.[25]

---

23 Dagg, *CHS*, p. 85.

24 Arthur Houston (ed.), *Daniel O'Connell: his early life, and journal, 1795-1802* (London, 1906), p. 147.

25 David Murphy and Sylvie Kleinman, 'Thomas Langlois Lefroy', DIB.

An address was drawn up and sent to the Board confirming that they had constituted themselves under the regulations of College with 'full and perfect acquiescence' and had 'accepted the room in which the late Historical Society held their meetings'. In terms of format and practices, the Society followed the format of the older Historical Society, and the average attendance was 33 members. James Gerahty, a former member of the late Society, was invited to close the session on 24 June 1795.

'The Extern Society' also met weekly, and motions debated included one on the question, 'Was the interference of France in the dispute between Great Britain and her colonies justified?' (28 January 1795), passed by 36 votes to 16.[26] Seventy-three members attended the final meeting of the session on 24 June 1795. John Guthrie delivered a speech on the study of history, oratory and composition, and made reference to the pressure put on students to avoid attending the meetings.[27]

As far as the records go, this appears to have been the last meeting of the Society. However, there are some pieces of evidence which suggest the meetings continued, even though the records were not preserved. One is the way it continued to be attacked in meetings of 'The Intern Society'; the other is through the journals of people who attended, such as Daniel O'Connell.

When 'The Intern Society' met on 20 October 1795 at the start of the new session, the meeting was chaired by Thomas Lefroy, who delivered a speech outlining the need for the Society to follow a new curriculum of Modern History. Praising the College for its 'general support and parental kindness', he made a pointed reference to 'The Extern Society', dismissing them for continuing to meet 'by stealth in a suspected haunt'. Although the Society had started as if it were a new institution, with this the second session in its journals, others still made reference to this pre-existing history. When John William Reid delivered the speech at the close of the session in June 1796 he mentioned the honours that had been awarded over the previous twenty-six years. Robert Torrens was elected as Auditor for the part of the 1795–6 session, and John Jebb for part of 1796–7.

---

26 TCD MUN/HIST/11; Dagg, *CHS*, p. 81.

27 Dagg, *CHS*, p. 82.

In December 1796 Daniel O'Connell attended two meetings of 'The Extern Society', or as he described it in his journal simply 'The Historical Society'. At the time he was studying for the bar at the King's Inns as well as thinking about a political career and was determined to become a great orator. As a student in London this had meant attending the British House of Commons and watching the great orators, as well as the theatre, where he studied how actors projected their voice.[28] The motion for debate on Wednesday 14 December 1796 was whether elections for parliament every two years were better than elections every seven years. O'Connell prepared a speech, but when he arrived he discovered that the debate part of the evening had been cancelled.[29] He returned, two weeks later, on Wednesday 28 December where he spoke twice against the partition of Greece. O'Connell always analysed his performances afterwards and he noted that he 'spoke pretty well, better, indeed, than I expected'. He also took part in the history examination at the start of the evening, where the text was Blackstone's *Commentaries,* and he was proud that he answered 'I may safely say, better than any individual'.

It appears that 'The Extern Society' was unable to sustain its momentum, given the punitive measures being taken by the authorities against those who attended. During the 1796–97 session new members continued to join 'The Intern Society', with forty-nine new members elected, though there were also some defections to it, with seven members of 'The Extern Society' admitted as 'original members'. The Society seems to have stopped meeting sometime in 1797. Its final action took place nine years later, on 26 February 1806, when a resolution was passed requesting that its journals, library, and all other property should be collected and presented to 'The Intern Society of the University of Dublin'.[30]

The occasional barbs directed at 'The Extern Society' continued even after it stopped meeting. In his speech at the close of the 1796–97 session, George Moore exulted that 'You now stand unrivalled.'[31]

---

28 Geoghegan, *King Dan,* Chapter 2.

29 Houston, *Journal*, p. 147.

30 Dagg, *CHS*, p. 82.

31 Dagg, *CHS*, p. 88.

Observing that 'your former competitors rejected the protection of the University, you received it', he could barely conceal his delight that 'they have sunk into non-existence' while those in the Society had 'swelled into importance'.

In December 1796 Theobald Wolfe Tone was part of a French invasion force that attempted and failed to land at Bantry Bay. In the aftermath, there was panic given how close Ireland had come to being embroiled in war, and a major reorganisation of the military defences took place. Within Trinity, a new College Corps was established and it was given permission to meet in the rooms of the Historical Society, again associating the Society with loyalism.

On 6 December 1797 Robert Emmet joined the Society. The younger brother of Christopher Temple Emmet and Thomas Addis Emmet, he was nineteen years old, and a member of the United Irishmen, recruiting other students to the cause, which was a crime punishable by death if captured. Also joining the Society at this time was Thomas Moore, his great childhood friend who would later immortalise him in verse.

Moore, one of the first Catholics to attend Trinity since the restrictions were lifted, made his maiden speech on 10 January 1798 when he opposed the motion that 'the study of the Sciences [was] of more advantage than the study of the Belles Lettres'.[32] William Corbet also opposed the motion and it was defeated by 22 votes to 10. The same night, Emmet was appointed to chair a committee to decide on motions for debate in the weeks ahead. This was potentially controversial, with Ireland on the brink of open rebellion. Emmet was determined to find ways to evade the Board's prescription on debating modern-day politics and so began selecting motions that would enable speakers to draw parallels between ancient injustices and the present day.

The motion on 17 January 1798 was 'Whether the Discovery of America was of more Advantage than Injury to the Human Race?' based on the famous question posed by the French philosopher, the Abbé Guillaume Raynal. There was a heated exchange of views, but the 'advantage' side won by 21 votes to 10. At this meeting, Emmet presented his sixteen motions for the months ahead and these were

32 TCD MUN/HIST/12; Dagg, *CHS*, p. 91.

approved by 14 votes to 10. Delighted, Emmet and his friends (including Moore) left the meeting early and were fined for going before 11 o'clock.[33]

The two speakers who had been chosen to debate the motion 'Is Unlimited Freedom of Discussion the Best Means of Stopping the Progress of Erroneous Discussion?' on 7 February did not turn up and were fined, and the chair asked for names from the floor. Emmet volunteered to propose the motion and rose to speak. His maiden speech was a bravura performance, with even those opposed to his politics later praising 'the transcendent oratorical powers' he displayed at the Society.[34]

References to modern day politics was forbidden and Emmet 'adroitly kept within the terms of this rule', while still finding ways to evade it. A. C. Macartney, the future Vicar of Belfast, was present at the debate and he described it as follows. Emmet showed the necessity and advantage of liberty and why it should be encouraged by a good Government, and then 'proceeded to portray the evil effects of the despotism and tyranny of the Governments in antiquity, and most eloquently depicted those of the government of Greece and Rome'.[35]

Thomas Lefroy, now a rising barrister, opposed Emmet in the debate and rebutted the argument 'at considerable length'. Emmet delivered a speech in reply, 'evidently unpremeditated, and showed extraordinary ability in his answer to the objections stated by his opponent'. In his peroration he left his listeners in no doubt that he was referring to the present day, as he ended on a note of defiance: 'If a Government were vicious enough to put down the freedom of discussion, it would be the duty of the people to deliberate on the errors of their rulers, to consider well the wrongs they inflicted, and what the right course would be.'[36] The final line was both incendiary and electrifying: 'And having done so, it would then be their duty to draw practical conclusions.'

---

33 P.M. Geoghegan, *Robert Emmet: a life* (2nd edition, Dublin, 2003), p. 74.

34 Ibid., p. 75.

35 Madden, *United Irishmen* (3rd series, 3 volumes, Dublin, 1846), iii, 6.

36 Ibid.

As Macartney explained afterwards, it was impossible 'to give an idea of the eloquence or animation of the speaker'. The motion was carried by 27 votes to 20. Charles Phillips later gathered materials on Emmet for his study of John Philpot Curran and discovered that 'for his demeanour, his talents, and his virtue' Emmet had been 'admired, respected and beloved at university'.[37] His mind, it was said, 'was naturally melancholy and romantic' and having studied the classics intensely, he acted as if he 'lived, not as much in the scene around him, as in the society of the illustrious dead'.

An extraordinary meeting of the Society was held on Friday 9 February to overturn the recommendations for motions that Emmet had brought forward. 56 members were present and this time Emmet was defeated, with 34 voting for a more traditional approach, and 19 siding with him. The Society was beginning to split, and Moore described how there was a division evident between 'the supporters of power' on one side and Emmet and some others on the side of reform.

With Ireland on the brink of open rebellion, the College authorities began to worry about a contagion in the Historical Society corrupting the future leaders of Ireland. Emmet was the focal point for their concerns. He was the brother of a leading radical, and was suspected of being the head of one of the United Irishmen cells in the university, involved in the purchase and smuggling of guns. Led by the reactionary Bursar, Thomas Elrington, the Senior Fellows began attending the debates of the Society to monitor what was being said. On 21 February they were horrified to discover that the motion in two weeks' time was on the question, 'Is Duelling of Advantage to Society?' Another controversial motion was scheduled for the very next week, 'Ought a Soldier to Consider the Motives of War before he Engages in it?'

The Board decided to act. As Thomas Moore later recounted, they invited back a former member of the Society, 'a man of advanced standing and reputation for orator ... expressly for the purpose of answering Emmet' so they could 'neutralise the impressions of his fervid eloquence'.[38] This man was James Gerahty,

37 Charles Philips, *Curran and his contemporaries* (London, 1850), p. 277.

38 Geoghegan, *Emmet,* p. 77.

now 29 years old and a successful pro-Government barrister. The debate became a battle between 'the supporters of power' and the radical 'popular side' championed by Emmet.

The debate on the final day of February 1798 was eagerly awaited and the Common Room was packed. A delegation from the Board was also present, including Elrington himself. Emmet arrived shortly before 7 p.m. and spoke in favour of the motion, delivering a brilliant oration that electrified the audience. Posing the question of whether a soldier was obliged to follow orders he knew were wrong, Emmet insisted that such a proposition was dangerous to society and degrading to human nature. According to one observer, Emmet spoke with 'his back to the fire place, his hand moving backwards and forwards along the chimney piece'. It was said that Emmet spoke in a 'most impassioned manner' and 'gave utterance to language of singular force and beauty'. Emmet invited his listeners to imagine the example of a soldier who had fought bravely for an oppressor in war. He then described this man 'rushing, after death, into the presence of his creator, and exclaiming in an agony of remorse, whilst he holds forth his sword reeking still with the blood of the oppressed and the innocent, 'Oh God! I know not why I have done this'.

Writing years later, Thomas Moore, claimed that when Emmet was inspired by a subject then he was a man transformed, you could see 'his intellect in motion' and he 'rose above the level of ordinary men'.[39] Discussing his displays of oratory in the Historical Society, Moore described how 'he so often enchained the attention and sympathy of his young audience.' It was as if he was a different person when he rose to speak. 'No two individuals, indeed, could be much more unlike to each other than was the same youth to himself, *before* rising to speak, and *after*', wrote Moore. 'The brow that had appeared inanimate and almost dropping at once elevating itself in all the consciousness of power, and the whole countenance and figure of the speaker assuming a change as of one suddenly inspired.'[40]

Another direct contemporary wrote about how 'Emmet's fine, manly countenance glowed with an enthusiastic fervour as if he were addressing a numerous, but distracted assembly which he wished to

---

39 Dagg, *CHS*, p. 94.

40 Geoghegan, *Emmet*, p. 76.

persuade. His words flowed with a graceful fluency, and he combined his arguments with all the ease of a man accustomed to abstract discussions.'[41] Archibald Douglas, who was another close friend of Emmet in Trinity, suggested that 'so gifted a creature does not appear in a thousand years'.[42]

Gerahty and seven other speakers were lined up against Emmet; but Emmet was supported by just one other member. Invited to respond to some of the personalised attacks that had been made, Emmet rose to deliver his second speech of the evening, and it was here that everything went wrong. Gerahty began heckling and jeering and doing everything that he could to throw Emmet off balance. Unused to such tactics, Emmet began 'in the full career of his eloquence, to hesitate and repeat his words'. As Moore later recorded, he lost the thread of his argument, 'and then, after an effort or two to recover himself, sat down'. It was an embarrassing defeat. As Moore admitted, it 'left us deeply humiliated to see our hero, for the first time, inferior to himself'. When the question was put to the house and it was defeated by 21 votes to 16.

The debate on 7 March was meant to be about duelling, but Elrington was there to make sure it never happened. Emmet's tutor, Richard Graves, interrupted proceedings to request that the question 'be not agitated'. This demand was passed without a division. The Auditor suggested choosing another motion from Emmet's list, but here there was a rebellion, and the members voted against this by 30 votes to 10. There was no debate that night. Instead poems were read. Thomas Moore recited a humorous poem entitled 'Ode upon Nothing, with Notes by Trismegistus Rustifustius etc. etc.' The poem was well received, with much applause and laughter and Moore later won the medal for composition for it.[43]

Emmet stopped attending the debates of the Society as he prepared to withdraw from College. He was meant to speak at the debate on 7 April on the motion, 'Is Individual Happiness more Promoted by Matrimony or Celibacy?' but instead asked Thomas

41 Emmet and his contemporaries', *London and Dublin Magazine* (1825).

42 Geoghegan, *Emmet,* p. 69.

43 MUN/SOC/HIST/12; Dagg, *CHS*, p. 96.

Moore to take his place. This request was rejected by the Society and Emmet was fined. After this his name was erased from the membership list of the Society by order of the College authorities.[44]

Determined to eradicate radicalism in the Trinity, the University was subjected to a Visitation, where every single person who worked there, and every single student, was interrogated by the Lord Chancellor, the Earl of Clare. Emmet asked for permission to withdraw formally from College, but it was refused, as Clare revealed he wanted 'the pleasure of expelling young Emmet' himself.

Nineteen people were expelled, Catholics as well as Protestants, and they were a mixture of current students and recent graduates who were expelled from the College's yeomanry corps. In total eight members of the Historical Society were expelled, including one former Auditor: Robert Emmet, Peter McLoughlin, Thomas Corbet, William Corbet, Arthur Newport, John Browne, Michael Farrell, and Martin John Farrell.[45]

With the outbreak of the 1798 Rebellion on the night of 23 May 1798 the session came to an abrupt end. At the meeting on Wednesday 30 May only ten members attended, and the ordinary business of the meeting was suspended. John Sargant and the Auditor brought forward a motion to approve a pro-Government resolution and it was passed unanimously. It aligned the Historical Society with 'the common cause of their country, and resolved to join hand and defence of their liberties and laws', agreeing to suspend its meetings until 'the happy return of domestic tranquillity'.[46] With this, the Society adjourned for the summer.

With the rebellion crushed, the new session began on 24 October 1798. The turmoil of the year was referenced obliquely when an address of congratulation was issued to Samuel Kyle, which referenced how he had 'stood forward to oppose the fury of the frantic projectors' who had attempted to 'contaminate the vital principles' of the Society's existence by advocating a 'wild spirit of innovation'.[47] In Kyle's response he condemned the 'agitators' who

44 TCD MUN/SOC/HIST/12.

45 Dagg, *CHS*, p. 96.

46 Ibid., p. 97.

47 Ibid.

had tried to shake the stability of the Society, and denounced the 'wild projectors' who had threatened 'the calmness of our sober improvement'.

One of the 'most showy speakers' in this period was Hugh George Macklin, who was known as 'Hugo Grotius Braggadocio' because of his tendency to boast loudly on all subjects.[48] Moore was a close friend and later remembered that Macklin 'obtained a good deal of reputation both in his collegiate course and in the Historical Society'. Macklin delivered the closing speech in June 1800, and later went on to serve as Advocate-General in Bombay.

The characters dominant in the Society in this decade went on the achieve fame, success, and sometimes both. Richard Pennefather became a successful lawyer and served as a judge as Chief Baron of the Irish Exchequer from 1821 until 1859. During the famous Doneraile trial in 1829 he distinguished himself by intervening to help Daniel O'Connell and prevent a miscarriage of justice.[49] Considered by contemporaries as 'benevolent, humane and considerate', he was a popular figure and one tribute noted that he was 'respected by all the Irish bar'.[50]

Thomas Lefroy served as MP for the University of Dublin between 1830 and 1841 where it is noted in the *Dictionary of Irish Biography* that 'he supported the Tories and was a vocal critic of Catholic emancipation and Repeal'.[51] Appointed a judge, he presided over the trial of some of the Young Ireland leaders, including John Mitchel, whom he sentenced to fourteen years' transportation. In 1852 he became Lord Chief Justice of the Queen's Bench in Ireland, but questions were asked in parliament about his judicial capacity. In the film *Becoming Jane* in 2007, based on his youthful relationship with Jane Austen, he is played by James McAvoy, and some scholars have suggested that the character of Mr Darcy in *Pride and Prejudice* was inspired by him.

Lefroy's Treasurer, Robert Torrens, became a successful King's

48 Ibid., p. 99.

49 Richard Maume, 'Richard Pennefather', *DIB*, see Geoghegan, *King Dan,* Prologue.

50 Richard Maume, 'Richard Pennefather', *DIB*.

51 David Murphy and Sylvie Kleinman, 'Thomas Lefroy', *DIB*.

Counsel and was appointed a Judge of the Common Pleas in 1823.[52] The *Freeman's Journal* recorded that 'he took common-sense views of the questions and rarely ventured beyond his depth', which was fortunate as he was largely felt to be a mediocre judge.[53] O'Connell described him as 'quiet and gentlemanly' in 1824, and as a 'narrow-minded inveterate Orangeist' in 1843.

Thomas Corbet was part of the French expeditionary force to Ireland in September 1798, alongside Wolfe Tone, but his ship escaped to safety. Appointed a Captain in the Irish Legion in 1803, he fell out with some other members and was fatally wounded in a duel with one of them on 20 September 1804.[54]

William Corbet was arrested in Hamburg in 1798 by the English consul and transferred to Kilmainham Jail, where he escaped using a rope ladder in February 1801. Appointed a Captain in the Irish Legion in 1803, he served with the French 70th Regiment during the Peninsular War and fought at the battle of Leipzig in 1813. Promoted to Brigadier-General in 1831, he was Commander-in-Chief of the French forces in Greece in 1831. He died a Major-General in 1842, having received numerous military awards and awards, disappointed that they had not been 'gained in the cause of my native country'.[55]

John Jebb won medals for composition in 1793 and 1794 and went on to become a prominent theologian and Church of Ireland Bishop of Limerick.[56] Recognised as a great orator, he always acknowledged the influence of the Society in his development as a speaker.[57] As Dagg notes, 'it was said that when he was appointed Bishop of Limerick and took his seat in the House of Lords, his self-possession and the readiness of his replies, fully displayed the advantages of his early training'.[58] Jebb opposed Catholic emancipation in 1829, but nonetheless was considered 'a pacifying influence in the often bitter religious atmosphere of the 1820s in Ireland.'[59]

52 Desmond McCabe, 'Robert Torrens', *DIB*.
53 Ibid.
54 James Quinn, 'Thomas Corbet', *DIB*.
55 James Quinn, 'William Corbet', *DIB*.
56 Desmond McCabe, 'John Jebb', *DIB*.
57 Dagg, *CHS*, p. 98.
58 Ibid.
59 Desmond McCabe, 'John Jebb', *DIB*.

Thomas Moore went on to achieve fame as a writer and musician, and his collection of *Irish Melodies* published between 1808 and 1834 were hugely successful.[60] Moore also provided texts to what he described as 'our national music' and scholars have suggested that these reflected 'an unmistakeable intimation of dispossession and loss in the music itself'. *Lalla Rookh,* published in 1817, was a sequence of four long poems interspersed with songs, and in the *Dictionary of Irish Biography* it is hailed as having 'consolidated Moore's position as a romantic writer equal in standing to Byron and Shelley (if not Wordsworth)' and it was a huge success around Europe. Contemporary reviewers picked up on the allegorical references to Ireland in the swirling themes of rebellion and betrayal. His novel, *The Memoirs of Captain Rock*, published in 1824 has been called a 'sustained consideration of Ireland's subjugation' and contains the powerful line: 'in Ireland to be a Catholic was to be an outcast from the commonest privileges of humanity'.

In his lifetime Moore was considered a literary genius, famous as a political satirist and a writer of prose, poetry and history around the world. In later years he came to be dismissed unfairly as a Georgian sentimentalist, but as Harry White has shown 'he was among the most widely noticed and famous writers of the romantic generation not only in Britain and Ireland, but throughout Europe and the United States, and his published work was formative in many spheres of public opinion (notably Ireland, the Catholic question, and slavery).'[61] He helped politicise folk music and 'consolidated the notion that art music in Ireland should function exclusively as a vital but dependent intelligencer of verbal meaning'.

The story of perhaps the most famous member from this period, Robert Emmet, is well known. He led a failed rebellion against British rule on 23 July 1803 and afterwards was captured and put on trial where the Society was well represented. The prosecution was led by Standish O'Grady and William Plunket and his defence included Peter Burrowes. The official record of the trial was taken by William Ridgeway, a lawyer who was himself a former member of the Society. Found guilty and sentenced to death, Emmet

60 Harry White, 'Thomas Moore', *DIB*.
61 Ibid.

delivered his first major public speech since his humiliation at the Society in February 1798. He had learned from the experience and when the judge, Lord Norbury, tried to interrupt and mock Emmet, he was answered point by point. The speech is considered one of the greatest courtroom orations in history and has been studied ever since. The context in which it was delivered – a young man knowing he had failed and was about to face the scaffold the next day – elevates it above the ordinary and makes it a gripping display of courage under the greatest pressure. The legacy of the speech was enduring, both in Ireland and around the world. It was studied by a young Abraham Lincoln who, at the end of the American Civil War, pardoned a young Confederate spy sentenced to death because he made a speech 'which reminded me of young Emmet'.[62]

62 See Geoghegan, *Emmet,* p.1.

5

'A NURSERY OF INSUBORDINATION': THE DISSOLVING OF THE SOCIETY, 1801-1815

AFTER THE PASSING of the Act of Union the Society entered a period of turmoil and decline. Meetings were less well organized than before and sometimes there were no speeches at the opening of a session. Some students began to interrupt the meetings of the Society, determined to disrupt proceedings, causing mayhem and disorder. Infighting in the Society also became a problem, with meetings sometimes descending into acrimony, as a handful of members focused their energies on attacking other students. This served to draw the Society to the attention of the College authorities, and meetings were closely monitored, with the Board receiving detailed accounts of what was said. This period culminated in the dissolution of the Society in 1815, after the conflict with the Board came to breaking point.

Despite all of these problems, there were still some outstanding feats of oratory in the Society in these years, with a number of individuals developing the oratorical prowess that would later bring them greatness in the law, politics, literature, astronomy, poetry, journalism and the church. The Society continued to be the place where 'character was formed, information was acquired, style was cultivated, insight into character was quickened'.[1] As one participant in the debates later recalled, 'the little scenes of mimic wordy warfare in which we engaged were an admirable preparation for the more real conflict of reason and eloquence in which most of us were shortly to engage'.[2]

1 'A biographical sketch of the late John Sydney Taylor', *Dublin University Magazine* (1843), vol. 21, p. 237.

2 Ibid., p. 237.

'Is Toleration Hurtful to the Interests of Religion' was one of the motions debated in the 1801–02 session and it is notable that it was defeated unanimously.[3] Other motions debated that session included 'Should Nobility be Hereditary?' which passed by 30 votes to 16, and 'Are Tithes the Best Means of Supporting the Clergy?' which was defeated by 23 votes to 22. One of the new members was Michael Slattery, a law student who later studied for the Catholic priesthood and became Archbishop of Cashel and Emly. In the *Dictionary of Irish Biography* Slattery is praised as 'a churchman of ability' who 'opposed government attempts to interfere in church matters'.[4]

Disorganisation was a problem. There was no speech delivered at the opening of the 1803–04 session because the chair was unable to attend, nor was there any a year later, for the same reason.[5] Some students made their name in the Society with their writings and their speeches. Charles Robert Maturin was a leading debater during this period and won prizes for his compositions.[6] Although politically conservative he was in favour of Catholic emancipation, and later gave up on his ambition of acting to become a Church of Ireland clergyman and novelist. His novel, *The Wild Irish Boy* (1808) denounced the Union, while *The Milesian Chief* (1812) displayed a certain ambivalent attitude towards the United Irishmen.[7] His greatest novel, *Melmoth the Wanderer* (1820), was inspired by one of his own sermons, and was translated into many languages, influencing writers such as Baudelaire and James Clarence Mangan. Balzac hailed it as 'the greatest creation of one of the greatest geniuses of Europe'. Robert Miles in the *Oxford Dictionary of National Biography* has noted that 'with its Chinese box structure of tales within tales, and its obsessive elaboration of its Faustian theme, it constitutes a high-water mark in the Gothic genre'.[8] Oscar Wilde was related to Maturin and when he was released from Reading Gaol he took the name 'Sebastian Melmoth' as a tribute.[9] Writing in the

3 TCD HIST/MUN/SOC/14; Dagg, *CHS*, p. 102.
4 David Murphy, 'Michael Slattery', *DIB*.
5 TCD HIST/MUN/SOC/15; Dagg, *CHS*, pp 102-3.
6 Patrick Maume, 'Charles Robert Maturin', *DIB*; Dagg, *CHS*, p. 103.
7 Patrick Maume, 'Charles Robert Maturin', *DIB*.
8 Robert Miles, 'Charles Robert Maturin', *ODNB*.

Dictionary of Irish Biography, Patrick Maume has noted that 'Maturin's central concern as a novelist was the religious impulse and the exploration of extreme states of mind, with particular reference to evil and horror.'[10]

Many of meetings of the Society in the 1800s were disorderly and frequently disrupted. As Thomas Dagg notes, an entire meeting on 8 February 1804 was taken up with fines, before adjourning at midnight.[11] A report of the Committee dated 4 April expressed considerable concern at 'the unparalleled prevalence of disorder during the late period'.[12] Sometimes the troublemakers were not members, but other students who barged into the rooms, and the Junior Dean threatened 'academic sanctions' to curb the trouble.[13]

The problem, however, persisted. A report presented on 10 April 1805 referenced the 'disorder that has too frequently disgraced your meetings, and which if not checked will finally dissolve them'.[14] Motions debated that session included 'Should the Slave Trade be Abolished?' which was passed by 54 votes to 5 and 'Is the Civilisation of a Country Sufficient Recompense for the Loss of its Liberty?' which was defeated by 49 votes to 9.[15]

On 18 May 1805 a sub-committee was appointed to 'take such steps as may be consistent with the dignity of the present Society to procure the books of the library of the old Society'.[16] There was some success. Arthur Browne, the former Regius Professor of Civil and Canon Law, as well as sometime MP for the University of Dublin, and Prime Serjeant, died in June 1805. His widow left a considerable donation to the Society, including many of Browne's works and 'the original journal book of the old Society'.[17]

A number of figures in the Society at this time went on to have distinguished careers in the church. Joseph Henderson Singer was

---

9 Ibid.

10 Patrick Maume, 'Charles Robert Maturin', *DIB*.

11 Dagg, *CHS*, p. 103.

12 Ibid.

13 Ibid.

14 Ibid., pp 103-104; TCD HIST/MUN/SOC/16.

15 Ibid., p. 104.

16 Ibid., p. 101.

17 Ibid.

Auditor of the Society for part of the 1805–06 session, on his way to graduating BA with a gold medal. On 30 January 1805 he proposed the motion 'Is Luxury Beneficial to Society', and on 20 February 1805 opposed the motion, 'Was Elizabeth Justified in her Treatment of Mary Queen of Scots'.[18] Elected a Fellow in 1810, Singer twice served as Senior Lecturer in College in the 1840s and was also Professor of Modern History (1840–50) and Regius Professor of Divinity (1850-52) before becoming Bishop of Meath. Singer was noted for the quality of his preaching, and has been described as 'a leading figure in the evangelical section of the Church of Ireland'.[19]

In January 1807 the books and journals of 'The Extern Society' were formally handed over to the Society, and John Kinchella, Chairman of 'The Extern Society', was thanked for agreeing to hand them over. This marked the end of the tensions between the two groups.

Twice the College authorities had to intervene to try and put an end to the infighting in the Society. In the 1804-05 session the Auditor, Holwell Walshe, brought a charge against another member, Richard MacDonnell, although the details of the complaint do not appear in the records. This led to a motion being brought against Walshe in the following session. But on 22 January 1806 the Board issued an order preventing the discussion of the motion.[20]

More trouble was to follow. The Auditor, John Henry North, brought a charge against Walshe for publishing a poem that had been presented to the Society without having received permission first, 'a gross violation of the solemn declaration on his honour'.[21] This led Walshe to retaliate by announcing that he planned to bring forward a motion to impeach the Auditor 'for a groundless attack upon the honour of a member of this Society'. The Board was swift to intervene and it sent a detailed message to the Society that was read out at the meeting on 29 October 1806. There was criticism of North for wording his motion 'with an unnecessary asperity', while also recognising that Walshe should have received permission in advance.

18 TCD MUN/SOC/HIST 16.

19 Linde Lunney, 'Joseph Henderson Singer', *DIB*.

20 Dagg, *CHS*, p. 105.

21 Ibid.

The Board then ordered that all records of the proceedings connected with the controversy should be erased. In protest at this intervention, six members of the Society resigned. This included Francis Blackburne, who had graduated in 1803 and was still attending meetings, and who went on to twice serve as Lord Chancellor of Ireland (1852–53, and 1866–67).[22] Blackburne was noted for 'his clear and terse arguments and judgments' and, after his death, it was noted that 'no man ever filled so many high and judicial offices, and brought to the discharge of each such great and varied powers'.[23]

During this session Eaton Stannard Barrett was given permission to publish some of his poems that had been entered into the essay book. Barrett went on to achieve fame as a satirical writer, and his poem 'All the Talents' in 1807, published under the name *Polypus* and satirising the British Government, was a huge success.[24]

Despite the interventions of the Board, the acrimony in the Society continued. On 23 December 1807 an anonymous poem signed 'Marcus' was read that attacked various members of the Society. Instead of receiving the usual thanks, a motion was passed by 48 votes to 7 ordering 'that it be burned by the hands of the porter as scurrilous and malignant'.[25] Following-up on this, a motion was passed on 20 January 1808 expressing 'the utmost abhorrence at the practice of offering anonymous insults to members of the Society'.

The former Auditor, George Miller, now headmaster of Armagh Royal School, was back in Dublin to give lectures on history in the first part of 1808 and the Society issued a congratulatory address and offered him the use of its rooms.[26]

Henry Grattan Jnr., the son of the celebrated patriot, was a member of the Society in 1807–08 and won a medal for composition.[27] His father was delighted, telling him that he was 'happy to hear of your success'. Grattan Jnr. went on to have a distinguished career as an MP in the British parliament, and played

---

22 Dagg, *CHS*, p. 106; James Quinn, 'Francis Blackburne', *DIB*.

23 James Quinn, 'Francis Blackburne', *DIB*.

24 Richard Hawkins, 'Eaton Stannard Barrett' *DIB*.

25 TCD HIST/MUN/SOC/17; Dagg, *CHS*, p. 107.

26 Ibid.

27 Ibid.

a significant but largely neglected role in the campaign for Catholic emancipation in the 1820s.[28]

Thomas Romney Robinson was Auditor for part of the 1808–09 session. Robinson was something of a child prodigy and had entered Trinity in 1806 at the age of thirteen already the author of a published collection of poetry.[29] He was awarded the remarkable thanks of the Society for presenting a copy of his *Juvenile Poems* to the Society's Library.[30] 'A brilliant conversationalist and speaker', Robinson was a leading speaker in the Society and won a medal for some of his compositions.[31] Known as Romney Robinson during his Trinity days, he would often turn up to meetings of the Society after conducting some experiments, 'with the soil of the laboratory upon his face' and listen 'with a fervid and breathless attention to the first efforts of some young aspirant for oratorical reputation'.[32]

After graduation, Robinson was elected a Fellow in 1814 at the age of twenty-one and the Society sent him their congratulations, addressed to 'one of the most distinguished members our Society has ever produced'.[33] He was appointed astronomer to Armagh Observatory in 1823, a position he held for fifty-nine years, while also serving as Rector of Carrickmacross in Co. Monaghan. Robinson is credited in the *Dictionary of Irish Biography* with 'bringing the observatory to international prominence despite its limited resources, isolated location and poor observing conditions'. Through his friendship with William Parsons, the 3rd Earl of Rosse (the son of Laurence Parsons), he was involved in the construction of the great telescope at Birr Castle. Robinson's interest in meteorology led him to develop an instrument to measure wind speed and direction in 1846, and it became known as the Robinson cup-anemometer and is still used around the world.

William Hamilton Maxwell joined the Society on 1 November

28 Daniel Beaumont, 'Henry Grattan', *DIB*.

29 Patricia Byrne, 'Thomas Romney Robinson', *DIB*.

30 Dagg, *CHS*, p. 108.

31 Ibid., p. 103.

32 'A biographical sketch of the late John Sydney Taylor', *Dublin University Magazine* (1843), vol. 21, p. 240.

33 TCD HIST/MUN/SOC/22; Dagg, *CHS*, p. 126.

1809. Maxwell had 'a misspent college life', drinking heavily, although it has been suggested that this 'may have stood him in good stead later as a novelist and bon viveur'.[34] He went on to write eighteen novels and histories, while balancing his work as a clergyman (not always successfully), including 'his most celebrated and durable work', *Wild Sports of the West* (1832), an account of his 'day-to-day adventures as a sportsman in a hunting lodge'.[35]

The meeting on 1 November 1809 was also notable for electing Richard Sheil as a member. Shiel was one of the most remarkable orators in the history of the Society and he quickly established himself as one of the best speakers of his generation. He won medals for oratory, composition and history in his first year and medals for oratory and composition in his second.[36] A Catholic, educated at Stonyhurst in England, Sheil 'cultivated the art of public speaking and was particularly noted for his passionate delivery'.[37] Later, on 13 December 1809, Sheil spoke in favour of Catholic emancipation during the debate on the motion, 'Should Universal Toleration be a Part of the British Constitution?'[38] The motion passed by 36 votes to 24.

After graduation, Shiel was called to the bar in 1814, and he also wrote eight plays to supplement his income. He became involved in the campaign for Catholic emancipation, and spoke before the Catholic Board in 1813, winning the approval of Daniel O'Connell. He played a leading role in the Catholic Association in the 1820s and has been described as O'Connell's 'most effective lieutenant'. Elected an MP in 1830 he was 'a noted orator in the British parliament. His speeches were carefully prepared' but his rhetoric was considered 'elaborate' and by some 'artificial'.[39]

The Board continued to monitor closely the proceedings of the meetings, and summaries of the debates were reported back, including what was said by the speakers. Anything controversial was seized upon. During this session the Auditor was summoned to meet

---

34 Desmond McCabe, 'William Hamilton Maxwell', *DIB*.

35 Ibid.

36 Dagg, *CHS*, p. 109.

37 Sinéad Sturgeon, 'Richard Lalor Sheil', *DIB*.

38 TCD HIST/MUN/SOC/18.

39 Sinéad Sturgeon, 'Richard Lalor Sheil', *DIB*.

the Provost to explain 'certain inflammatory expressions said to have been used' by him during the debate on the question 'Should Universal Toleration be a Part of the British Constitution?'[40] There followed an 'exhaustive inquiry' before the charges were dropped.

Thomas Elrington became Provost in 1811 and this was bad news for the Society. As Bursar, Elrington had been the leading figure against the Society in the 1790s, and he was determined to control the activities of the Society. In an attempt to gain his favour, the Society sent him a letter of congratulation on his appointment. His response was read at the meeting on 11 December 1811 and in it he expressed his pleasure at receiving 'assurances of the Society's determination to observe those regulations which may be considered its charter; regulations... the result of deep reflection upon the relation which such a Society should bear to the College in which it is formed'.[41]

On 19 June 1810 Richard Sheil closed the 1809-10 session with a speech from the chair. At this meeting, his old school-friend, Thomas Wyse, a Catholic, was elected a member. Wyse was the other great orator of this period and over the next two years he was a dominant figure in the Society, winning medals in oratory, history and composition. Wyse first spoke at the meeting on 5 December 1810 and, based on the oratory marks for the evening, his biographer, James Auchmuty (a former Auditor of the Society) has called it 'one of the most brilliant maiden speeches the Society has ever heard'.[42] On 19 December 1810 he spoke in favour of having a universal diffusion of knowledge, and on 2 January 1811 in favour of universal tolerance. Other debates he spoke at include the one on 19 June 1811 when he defended early marriage as conducive to morality, and on 13 May 1812 when he argued that public discussion of affairs was of advantage to the nation.

Wyse won the medal for composition for his essay on 'A comparison between ancient and modern eloquence'. In it he hailed Cicero as 'the father of Roman eloquence', as well as Homer, 'who

---

40 Dagg, *CHS*, p. 109.

41 Ibid., p. 111.

42 James J. Auchmuty, *Sir Thomas Wyse, 1791-1862: the life and career of an educator* (London, 1939).

could have scaled heaven had it been practicable'.[43] James Auchmuty has noted that many of the causes Wyse later adopted were ones he spoke about at Trinity. For example, on 4 December 1811 Wyse supported the motion 'that Capital Punishment should be entirely Abolished'. Wyse was invited to give the closing speech of the 1811–12 session, although unfortunately no record of it was kept. However it was 'singled out for high praise from the ex-members who had established themselves in London'.[44]

Wyse went on to have an eminent career as a traveller, politician, educational reformer and diplomat.[45] Encouraged by Sheil to marry one of Napoleon's daughters to enhance his prospects of becoming a leader of the Irish Catholics, he married the sixteen-year-old Letitia Bonaparte, a niece of the former emperor, in 1821. The marriage was not a happy one and she left him after the second of their two sons was born. As C. J. Woods writes in the *Dictionary of Irish Biography*, his 'wife and two sons caused him much distress and expense, probably because, rigid in his views and ways, he placed little confidence in them, avoided them, kept them short of money, and engaged in legal action against them.'[46]

In 1826 Wyse played a leading role in encouraging Henry Villiers Stuart to stand against the Beresford interest in Co. Waterford in the general election, and the subsequent victory was a major turning point in the campaign for Catholic emancipation. Wyse stood for election in Co. Tipperary to the British House of Commons in 1830 and was one of five Catholics returned after the passing of the emancipation act. In parliament he focused on educational reform, and in 1836 he published *Educational Reform* arguing that it was necessary to educate the lower classes to prevent revolution. His work on education was considerable, and Auchmuty calls him 'one of the most considerable figures in the history of education in the nineteenth century' and 'the architect of Ireland's national system of education.'[47]

Wyse was not a supporter of Repeal and he fell out with

43 Ibid., p. 11.

44 Ibid., p. 13.

45 CJ Woods, 'Sir Thomas Wyse', *DIB*.

46 Ibid.

47 Auchmuty, *Sir Thomas Wyse,* p. 303.

O'Connell, whom he thought dishonest and unscrupulous. In later years he served as British minister plenipotentiary in Athens and was knighted in 1857. C. J. Woods has written that 'no other Irish Catholic rose so high and was so widely received in British ministerial circles', even being on good terms with Queen Victoria. He also recognises, however, that 'he had become more English than the English themselves' and, perhaps as a result, 'barely figures in Irish history'.

Although Catholics were able to attend Trinity since 1793 and take degrees there were still notable restrictions against them. A Catholic student was unable to put himself forward as a candidate for Scholarship, because this would make him part of the body corporate if successful. Nor were Catholics able to become Fellows. During this period there was not a single Auditor of the Historical Society who was Catholic. It is revealing that neither of the two best orators in the Society in this period – Richard Sheil and Thomas Wyse – served on Committee, much less were elected Auditor. This may have been their personal preference, but it also reflected the prevailing culture of the time and there was a strong loyalist element in the Society opposed to ever electing a Catholic. When John O'Brien, a leading debater in the Society, winner of the medal for oratory, and a Catholic, ran for Auditor in 1814, he lost narrowly. His defeat prompted one opponent to rejoice publicly that 'The Protestant Boys have carried the day'. Chants like that contributed to the febrile atmosphere in the Society at that time.[48] O'Brien later became MP for Limerick (1841–52), and his son, Peter, was Lord Chief Justice of Ireland.

When students returned from the long vacation in 1812 they discovered that the Provost and Senior Fellows had decided to restate the existing restrictions. No one was allowed attend the society unless they were a member, no one was allowed become a member unless they were a registered student, and no student could become a member until they were a Junior Sophister.[49] Further restrictions were also added. Every month the Society had to make a report of the motions debated, and the laws enacted, and present it to the

48 'Reminiscences of Dublin College life: The Historical Society in its decline', *Tait's Edinburgh Magazine* (1844), vol. 11, p. 24.

49 *The Dublin Inquisitor* (1821), vols 1-2, p. 443.

professor of modern history, to ensure that nothing inappropriate was being discussed or decided. In addition, any essay that was to be read in the Society had to be approved by another member who had to take responsibility for it in the event of any controversy.

These new rules had a disastrous effect on the Society. The restrictions on compositions were contrary to the Society's own rules and caused much disquiet, and there was much resentment about the level of oversight being introduced. Even worse, older members who had graduated from the College were no longer allowed join or attend the meetings, and the Society lost the benefit of their advice and experience. However, the Society acquiesced in the changes, and it was noted that 'a spirit of irregularity now began to pervade the meetings'.[50] A request was made to the Board for the new regulations to be lifted, but it was rejected. One member later wrote an account of this period, which was published anonymously, and he noted that no explanation for the changes was ever given to the students, and that the Provost and Senior Fellows had been unwilling to suffer 'the inconvenience arising from a momentary descent for their dignity'.

The Society made one final attempt to lessen the severity of these restrictions. A proposal was made to the Board that would allow the Auditor to invite distinguished speakers to chair the meetings, with the approval of the Provost, and that these occasions could be attended by all the students. The reasoning was clear and perfectly logical: 'the character of the Society depended on the excellence of the speeches delivered from the chair' and therefore the person selected must 'be recommended by talent, seniority on the books, and experience in public speaking', requisites that were in short supply among the limited numbers in the Society. The Board rejected this request as well. The Society continued on, 'in silent submission', although it attempted to evade some of the restrictions. For example, it began leaving the door open at meetings, to allow younger students to follow the debates from outside. This however was soon stopped as an order was issued that the doors were to be shut. The porter was also instructed to visit the meetings and check that everyone was wearing proper academic dress.

John Sydney Taylor, a descendant of Patrick Sarsfield through his

50 Ibid.

mother's side, achieved 'considerable notice' for his speeches at the Historical Society in 1813 and 1814.[51] Elected a Scholar in 1812, he overcame his natural shyness to great effect. It was later said that he 'completed his collegiate education' at the Historical Society, acquiring 'a fluency, a readiness, and an energy in debate' that served him well in later years.[52]

Taylor was able to inspire his listeners through a combination of humour and the quality of his language. During one debate on sensibility a number of speakers attempted to argue that it was an evil. Taylor compared the arguments to those of Sir Luke Lump who had attempted to prove that his wooden leg was better than a real one. Suggesting that poets could be happy because of their talents, not in spite of them, he concluded that even if a poet suffered calamities it was still worth it. He noted that 'His friends may forsake him, and the world may be a desert; and yet, even in such calamities, he finds a solace in his genius.'[53]

Invited to deliver the closing speech in June 1813, Taylor spoke about history and its significance. It was, he said, 'the great stimulant of genius' the gathering of information that 'receives the tribute of knowledge from every shore and diffuses it throughout the globe'.[54] The ending was both poignant and poetic as Taylor described the campaigns of Hannibal and the lessons that had been learnt from his failure, 'the surmounter of Alps, the thunderbolt of battle, the glory of one half of the world, and the terror of the other'.[55] The speech was awarded a gold medal by the Society and in April 1814 a motion was passed requesting Taylor to publish the speech.[56]

In 1813 the Erasmus Smith Chair of Oratory fell vacant and Taylor decided to apply for it, after studying the bequest and discovering that Scholars were eligible. Four candidates put themselves forward for the first day of examination, and Taylor made

51 'A biographical sketch of the late John Sydney Taylor', *Dublin University Magazine* (1843), vol. 21, p. 236.

52 Ibid., p. 237.

53 [Samuel O'Sullivan], *College Recollections* (London, 1825), p. 237.

54 'A biographical sketch of the late John Sydney Taylor', *Dublin University Magazine* (1843), vol. 21, p. 239.

55 Ibid., p. 240.

56 Dagg, *CHS*, p. 120.

it through to the final two. It was between him and Philip Cecil Crampton, a Fellow of the College, and in the end, not surprisingly, Crampton was appointed.[57]

After graduation, Taylor became a leading barrister and journalist. Editor of the *Morning Herald* in London in the 1820s and 1830s, he 'wrote several articles advocating a reform of the penal code and a review of the use of the death penalty for certain crimes'.[58] In 1840 he defended Edward Oxford who was charged with high treason after firing two pistols at Queen Victoria. The evidence was overwhelming, and everyone expected that Oxford would be found guilty and hanged, but Taylor led a skilful insanity defence and convinced the court. Oxford was sent to a lunatic asylum.

The Society had a high public profile in this period. Notices of the award of medals for History, Oratory, and Composition were published in the newspapers, and the Society paid for advertisements on the front page of the *Freeman's Journal*.[59] There was also some criticism of the Society. On 5 January 1814 a letter was published in the *Freeman's Journal* critising the Society for not having awarded a silver medal in poetry that had been established to honour the death of Dr Arthur George Orpen, a former Auditor (1807–08 session) who had died. A member of the Society responded with an unwise and sarcastic response two days later, suggesting that because 'extemporary eloquence' had become such an important feature of the Society, members spent more time on 'the fashionable exercise of scolding' and not on 'the minor accomplishments of verse and prose compositions'.[60] It was claimed that it was 'little wonder that the poor dead doctor should be forgotten among such confusion', and the Provost was mocked for writing three poems a week praising Orpen, which was dismissed as a 'childish' practice.

John Anster, a Catholic from Cork who became a Protestant while at Trinity allowing him to become a Scholar, made a strong impression in the Society. A poet, he won a medal for his speech

57 'A biographical sketch of the late John Sydney Taylor', *Dublin University Magazine* (1843), vol. 21, p. 243.

58 David Murphy, 'John Sydney Taylor', *DIB*.

59 See for example, *Freeman's Journal*, 6 July 1814.

60 *Freeman's Journal*, 5 January 1814; *Freeman's Journal*, 7 January 1814.

from the chair at the close of the 1813–14 session and medals for composition, including one for his poem 'An ode to fancy'.[61] After leaving Trinity he was called to the bar but found fame as a poet and translator. His translation of Goethe's *Faust* was the first in the English language, and the first part, published in 1835, was praised by Goethe himself. In 1850 he was appointed Regius Professor of Civil Law at Trinity and held the post until his death in 1867.

Mortimer O'Sullivan, a Catholic from Tipperary who became a Protestant before entering Trinity in 1811, became a Scholar in 1812 and was a leading member of the Society in the period 1814–15. In later years he became a Church of Ireland clergyman and polemicist, engaging in debates in print with Thomas Moore about the state of Ireland.[62] His younger brother, Samuel, entered Trinity a year later, became a Scholar in 1814 and a member of the Society, winning medals for his oratory.[63] Samuel also became a Church of Ireland clergyman after graduation and contributed to the *Dublin University Magazine,* where his anti-Catholic articles led Charles Gavan Duffy to attack him for his 'furious bigotry'. In 1825 Samuel O'Sullivan published anonymously a book entitled *College Recollections* which provided a detailed account of his time in the Historical Society, and especially of the events of 1815.

The Society, O'Sullivan argued, was a place where students who later achieved pre-eminence in the law, or politics, could test their abilities, and develop styles that later served them well in public life. For example, the future judge could be found 'fortifying himself in debate, amidst the forms of the society; and refusing to surrender to any summons from reasoning, unless authority were on its side'.[64] He also described the emotional and artistic speakers, who 'gave you images for argument, and attempted to win their way to your heart, not by a direct assault upon its barriers, but by sounding sweet music around them'.

O'Sullivan believed that no matter how fierce the debate, no

61 Linde Lunney, 'John Martin Anster', *DIB*; *Freeman's Journal*, 6 July 1814.

62 David Murphy and Sinéad Sturgeon, 'Mortimer O'Sullivan', *DIB.*

63 David Murphy, 'Samuel O'Sullivan', *DIB.*

64 Ibid., p. 227

matter how heated things became, there was an 'unbroken respect for established forms' and the authority of the chair was absolute. As he remembered it, the 'bitterest invectives were almost always free from the disgrace of personality, and the opponents of this hour could meet in the next without an angry or an uneasy feeling', but the records do not match his recollections.[65]

At this time a regular external criticism of the oratorical style developed at the Historical Society was that it was based on a 'flimsy style of composition', in which 'fancy and imagination' were used not to explain but to confuse 'and where reason is made their victim'.[66] This was certainly a feature of some of the speeches, but it was by no means dominant. The speeches that won distinction were the ones that cast aside ornament and provided 'a definite and substantial form'. It was only 'to speakers of this class' was praise and approbation given. 'The man who gave the most of *thought,* and who gave it in the best manner, was the man who was most respected, and ... possessed the power to attain distinction.'

O'Sullivan provides a vivid description of the oratorical styles at the time. One student, Francis Travers, 'looked like a man destitute of vital action'; there was mind and body, but no evidence of 'an energetic principle'.[67] However, when he spoke he was like 'an electric cloud highly charged' and once he was engaged by a subject his appearance totally changed. His half-closed eyes opened, and burned with a look of fire, and he delivered a remarkable oration. Afterwards he would resume his seat and relapse into his torpor, and could later be seen lounging in the Society room, 'with his eyes half-closed and his gait spiritless, as if he no longer retained power enough to give erectness to his figure or life to his motions'.

Controversy flared in 1813 and from a disputed auditorial election came the downfall of the Society. It began on 10 November 1813 with the election of the new Auditor. There were two candidates, Carrol Watson, a tall, athletic student from a wealthy Protestant family in Co. Tipperary, and Richard Stack, a Scholar from a Protestant family in Queen's County. It is not clear what the source of the enmity

65 [Samuel O'Sullivan], *College Recollections* (London, 1825), p. 227.

66 Ibid., p. 239.

67 Ibid., p. 231.

between the two candidates was but it was red hot.

On the night Watson won with 61 votes to 58, but the result was immediately contested with some of the votes disputed and he was prevented from discharging his duties when he tried to take the chair. The arguments continued until midnight when the meeting adjourned. The next morning, three former Auditors, including Romney Robinson (1808–09) and James Lendrick (1809–10), joined with John Smith, a supporter of Stack, to see the Provost to get a ruling on who was eligible to vote. Without knowing the circumstances of the disputed election, Elrington issued a paper supporting the delegation, setting out that graduates of the College had to reapply for membership and be balloted as a new member.

At the next meeting of the Society, on 17 November, the conflict resumed, and in the end it was agreed that three members who voted the week before were not eligible. A new election was called and both Watson and Stack were tied, receiving the same number of votes. James Lendrick was in the chair and had the casting vote and so Stack was elected in the most controversial of circumstances. Watson attempted to appeal to the Provost but with no success. Despite being unseated, Watson is still considered an Auditor of the Society, appearing in Trinity's own lists in the Calendar in the ninteenth century, as well as on the Society's own board in the twentieth.

The bitter infighting did not end there. At the next meeting, on 8 December, a motion was passed challenging the way Watson had written-up the records for 17 November, accusing him of falsifying them. An investigation was ordered, with Watson threatened with expulsion from the Society if the charges were proved. Watson had not tampered with the journals, but he had written into the records an account of the unruly conduct of his opponents from his own perspective.

Those who had been named by Watson wanted revenge and so a prosecution against him was arranged. When called to speak in his defence at the meeting, Watson realized the numbers were against him, so he proceeded to speak for hours until the bell rang for midnight and the meeting was adjourned. Employing long pauses, and speaking 'a jumble of facts and dates', he succeeded in counting down the time, and walked off at the striking of the bell for midnight 'with a glow of triumph on his cheek'.[68] Attempts to continue the prosecution the following weeks were met with the same tactics, and he obstructed things further by calling witnesses and asking them completely irrelevant questions. One student revealed that he never ate more than three eggs at breakfast, another that his favourite pasttime was playing his clarinet.

The affair dominated the meetings of the Society for weeks. On 12 January 1814 a witness was being examined and Romney Robinson intervened to prevent Watson from asking the question he wanted believing that it would lead to a quarrel. This prompted a heated exchange between Watson and another member, Hugh Dickson. 'Watson accused Dickson of lying, and Dickson called Watson a rascal' and both were fined by the chairman.[69] Dickson had his fine overturned later in the meeting when he apologised to the Society but not to Watson. At midnight the meeting adjourned, and Dickson went up to Watson and the conversation turned aggressive quickly with talk of a possible duel arising from it. Joseph Henderson Singer, former Auditor and now a Fellow, was at the meeting and witnessed the altercation. He told Dickson that if it was not resolved he would have to bring it before the Board. Another former member and Fellow, Francis Sadleir, brought the same message to Watson.

The next day Singer attempted to brook a compromise, but neither Watson nor Dickson was prepared to apologise first. Upon hearing what was going on, the Board decided to intervene and issued its own judgment. Both students had their names taken off the College roll.[70] Elrington also sent for Edward Hincks, a junior Fellow who was attending the meetings of the Society, to tell him that 'it would be better if he did not go to the Historical Society for a considerable time'.[71] As the dispute raged more and more students were blackballed when they applied for membership. Only two new members were admitted, with twenty-six rejected.[72] Ten members

68 'Reminiscences of Dublin College life: The Historical Society in its decline', *Tait's Edinburgh Magazine* (1844), vol. 11, p. 27.

69 Dagg, CHS, p. 123.

70 Ibid., p. 124.

71 Ibid.

72 Ibid.

were expelled on 29 December 1813 and thirty were expelled on 29 January 1814, ostensibly for not paying the money they owed.

The Board now took the opportunity provided by the controversy to press for further changes. By this time, it believed that the Society had become 'a nursery of insubordination'.[73] The debates were 'frequently disturbed by angry political discussion' and there was a fear that graduate members, who were engaged in active professional pursuits, were using the chamber to rehearse their arguments 'in those discussions which occupied the public attention'.[74] This was the same time that John Locke was being removed from the curriculum, a significant decision given that Trinity had been the first university to put Locke on the curriculum, back at the end of the seventeenth century. In the first part of the nineteenth century, however, Locke's ideas were now viewed by the Board as a threat to liberty instead of a defence of it.

The monthly reports frequently resulted in the Society being censured because of the motions that were being discussed. There was even criticism of the Society for discussing the first principles of the British Constitution, an area that had been debated from the earliest days. Elrington also objected to a range of motions, including 'Should Capital Punishment be Abolished?', 'Should Charles I have been Executed?', 'Should Brutus have slain Caesar?', and 'Was Cato's Suicide an Act of Heroism?' arguing that they might be 'productive of serious evils'.[75]

The absence of the senior figures from the Society was a huge blow. The order and decorum that had usually prevailed was now absent, as the members chafed against the new restrictions, while unable to articulate a clear strategy of resistance. The *Morning Chronicle* in London reported years later that the hostile restrictions of 'a determined and consistent foe' took its toll on the Society and 'it degenerated into an assembly of wrangling boys'.[76] Debates became more heated, with almost deliberate attempts by some to bring down the wrath of the authorities. Others responded with

73 *Freeman's Journal*, 10 March 1815.

74 [Samuel O'Sullivan], *College Recollections*, pp. 240-1.

75 *The Irish Quarterly Review*, 4, p. 520; *Freeman's Journal*, 10 March 1815.

76 *Morning Chronicle*, 25 January1838.

petulance and a 'puerility of conduct' that had not been present in the Society before.

The tensions in the Society reignited in June 1814. By this time William Brooke had succeeded Stack as Auditor, but the old quarrel was not too far below the surface. At the meeting on 1 June John O'Brien took offence at comments made by Stack who was in the chair and hit him. Immediately regretting what he did, he apologised to Stack and to the Society. The Junior Dean was soon made aware of the fight and worried that it might revive the old controversy. O'Brien threw himself at the mercy of the Board and apologised 'in the strongest manner'.[77] In a surprising act of restraint, the Board agreed not to punish him.

At the next meeting, on 8 June 1814, the Auditor moved that the voluntary apology offered to the Society by O'Brien should be considered perfectly satisfactory. However, Charles Wolfe intervened and moved an amendment suggesting that 'the Auditor's motion be considered useless' and this passed by 43 votes to 14.[78] Wolfe had won the medal for composition for one of his poems earlier in the session. Around this time he wrote 'The Burial of Sir John Moore after Corunna', published in 1815, which was hailed by Lord Byron as 'little inferior to the best ode that this prolific age had produced' and today it is considered 'to be among the best English-language poems of the nineteenth century'.[79]

Wolfe was invited to open the 1814–15 session with a speech, but he was unable to attend. A special meeting was arranged for Saturday 12 November where he delivered the oration and it was awarded a gold medal. Among the new members who joined that session was Henry Francis Lyte, who later became a clergyman and won fame for his hymns: 'Praise my soul the king of Heaven' (1834) and 'Abide with me' (1847).[80]

Tensions with the College continued to rise, and they came to a head when the Board attempted to make further demands on the Society in early 1815. A debate on 25 January 1815 proved to be a

77 Dagg, CHS, p. 127.

78 Ibid.

79 Rosemary Richey, 'Charles Wolfe', DIB.

80 P.M. Geoghegan, 'Henry Francis Lyte', DIB.

flashpoint. Two members, James Howlin and John Walker, took exception to things that the other was saying, and tempers flared. A challenge was issued, but before the duel took place the sheriff for Dublin received word and intervened, and upon hearing this the Board swooped to intervene. The two students were expelled as members of the Society, but that was only the start of things. Deliberate steps were taken to strangulate the Society. It was decided that Junior Sophisters would no longer be allowed attend the meetings, thus restricting the Society's membership even further, and the duration of meetings was reduced by an hour. Private business was also created. A committee of five was established to regulate the private business of the Society, without actually specifying what was meant by 'private business', and there could be no appeal against its decisions. An ultimatum was given to the Society. It must accept the new regulations 'by which you are in future to be governed' or 'we leave with the option... [of] dissolving your Society'.[81]

Fearing in their own words, the 'gradual annihilation' of the Society, the students fought to oppose these new restrictions.[82] Without the membership fees of the Junior Sophister students, the largest cohort of members, the Society would barely be able to function, and by restricting membership to just one year – Senior Sophisters – it reduced significantly the opportunity to develop oratorical skills. The committee also argued that the continuing exclusion of graduates only promoted disorder, rather than discouraging it. The creation of private business was also controversial. Effectively the Board was creating its own committee of five to run the Society and decide on all of its activities, so the Society decided to resist being controlled by 'an oligarchy of equals'. The committee argued that until then all business had been equally public to members, and equally private to strangers, so any change was unnecessary. The Committee sought clarification from the Board as to what it meant by 'private business' and was informed that it 'meant all business relating to the conduct of individuals in the Historical Society'.[83]

---

81 [Samuel O'Sullivan], *College Recollections* (London, 1825), p. 256.

82 *The Dublin Inquisitor* (1821), vols 1-2, p. 446.

83 Dagg, CHS, p. 132.

On 15 February 1815 the Historical Society met to vote itself out of existence. At a packed meeting of the Society, it debated how it should to respond to the College. The members all wore their medals, and the atmosphere was especially tense as the Auditor, Lundy Foote, read out the last communication from the Provost and Board. Bingham Walker Hamilton, a former Auditor (1812-13) and much-decorated veteran of the Society who was known as 'the independent member' rose to speak and argued that if the proposed restrictions were to be allowed 'the Historical Society could not exist'.[84] He proposed that 'under these circumstances there remains for us but one course – to dissolve our Society'. He therefore proposed to adjorn the meeting *sine die,* in other words with no appointed date for resumption.

Hamilton was considered one of the most talented speakers of his generation and his words carried enormous weight, especially because he usually avoided engaging in matters of controversy. Great things were expected of him, but his life was cut short when he was accidentally shot and killed at Laugharne in Wales on 12 October 1815. On this night Hamilton was in full strength and his words were 'elevated in the consciousness of worth, and in the remembrance of achieved distinction'.

The motion was opposed by a younger member of the Society, a man called Austin, who argued that the members should not indulge their 'irritated feelings' by adopting an 'extravagant notion'.[85] He appealed that the future generations of students should not be deprived of the benefits of the Society, and urged that the motion be defeated without dissent.

Travers was the next to speak and while he accepted that members should wait for 'indulgent governors' of the university, he warned that they should wait for them 'in the dignity of silence, not in the abjectness of ineffectual supplication'. When he denounced the 'degrading submission' of the College he was interrupted by several shouts of 'Order, order!' and the chair intervened to remind Travers that no submission from the Board could ever be degrading to students. Travers stood over his words, and argued with some

84 [Samuel O'Sullivan], *College Recollections*, p. 246.

85 Ibid., p. 254.

vehemence that the Society could not 'submit to regulations which must dishonour us'.[86] The arguments of Travers were ingenious. He argued that the Board had not demanded acceptance of the new regulations, in which case they would have to be accepted. Instead it had provided a choice, and therefore it allowed the regulations to be condemned and the Society to be dissolved. Travers concluded by suggesting that it was better for the Society to 'cease to exist' than it should continue in the way suggested, 'manacled – inglorious – abject'. He suggested that the past journals of the Society, and 'very walls of this place' would look reproachfully of them if they consented to it. And with a stirring piece of dramatic rhetoric, he called on the Society to dissolve 'before one shadow has fallen upon your reputation'. His final words were, 'Now dissolve, and choose rather that your Society shall live in the memories of admiring successors, than that it should waste away lingeringly and ingloriously before them.' There was sustained applause when he sat down, and it was some time before anyone else rose to speak. The mood was now turning very clearly in favour of dissolution.

The penultimate speaker spoke in a mock-heroic tone and called on the members to 'die all – die nobly – die like demigods'.[87] The ironic tone did not sit well with members, but Sykes continued on regardless, suggesting an amendment that the members should perish 'phoenix-like' by collecting 'all the benches, desks, and books into a large funeral pile' and setting themselves on fire with it all.

John Sydney Taylor was the final speaker of the night and closed the debate decisively. Answering the previous speaker, he criticised him for trying to make light of a very serious issue, reminding him that 'irony is not always a mark of superiority'. He proceeded to explain clearly why the new regulations could not be allowed stand, and why dissolution was better than disgrace. A message was given to future generations of students: 'You will leave behind you a spirit to animate the exertions of worthy successors, and a pure and perfect model according to which they may fashion the structure of a future Society.'[88]

86 Ibid., p. 256.

87 Ibid., p. 268.

88 Dagg, *CHS*, p. 136.

After he sat down the motion was put to the members, and it passed by 50 votes to 14, as it decided to 'resort to the only measure now left to them'.[89] Opposing this 'system of inquisitorial tyranny', it agreed on this 'voluntary dissolution' to avoid the unacceptable alternative: 'the ruin, the gradual ruin of the Society'. The hope was that by taking such a drastic step public attention would be drawn to the controversy and an outcry might lead to the revival of the Society. Five members of the Society were appointed as trustees to mind the records of the Society and, as the *Morning Chronicle* reported years later, 'in a moment of rash heroism the Society committed suicide by dissolving itself'.[90]

The so-called 'last night of the Historical Society' was much written about in the years ahead. In 1825 one member compared his emotional state to hearing that a close friend had died.[91] He noted that the College had lost 'its brightest ornament,' and for so many involved it left 'a feeling of bereavement'. He praised the Society as a place where 'the diligent came to enjoy a profitable relaxation, and the idle were brought into contact with educated minds' and where 'the superabundant spirit of first youth was attracted by the elegancies of literature, and engaged in the services of a purifying ambition'.[92]

The Provost received much criticism for his role in the suppression (which is what it effectively was) of the Society, and 'tyrant', 'bigot', and 'narrow minded' were some of the terms used to describe him.[93] In a series of public letters denouncing him, he was attacked for removing Locke from the curriculum ('You, Mr Provost, do you regret this?'), for allowing Orange societies to take root in College, and for what had happened to the Historical Society. 'Do you forget that you shut up the Historical Society?' one letter asked, noting the hypocrisy of an 'inestimable institution prohibiting in the very seat of science' the hearing of 'lectures, readings, and debates, oratory, history and composition'.[94] That year the Provost

89 *The Dublin Inquisitor* (1821), vols 1-2, p. 447.

90 *Morning Chronicle,* 25 January 1838.

91 [Samuel O'Sullivan], *College recollections*, p. 221.

92 Ibid., p. 223.

93 *Freeman's Journal*, 10 March 1815.

and Senior Fellows decided against the usual celebrations for Trinity, and so some sixty students decided to hold their own event in Morrison's Hotel. Among the toasts that evening was one to 'Mr. [Bingham Walker] Hamilton and the Historical Society' that 'the efforts of genius be crowned with success'.[95]

Following its dissolution, the books and other items belonging to the Society were confiscated by the College and placed into storage. A padlock was put on the door of the Society's rooms to prevent a return. To prevent an immediate reconstitution of the Society its rooms were redesignated and renamed as the 'Medical Society Room of Trinity College'.[96] When Samuel Kyle succeeded Elrington as Provost in 1820 there was new hope that he might allow the Society to be revived. After all, he had been a leading member of the Society in the 1790s and had served as Treasurer in 1793–94. But no change occurred. There was much criticism of the College for refusing to yield on the question. The decision to build a ball-court on the grounds, to discourage idleness among the students, was also criticised. It was noted in the *Dublin Inquisitor* that the same amount of care should have gone into 'reviving an institution which supplied so great a desideratum in collegiate education, and conferred such lustre on the establishment that supported it'.[97] It was also noted that within three months of the dissolution of the Society an Orange Lodge was established in the College, according to one account, 'without the slightest intimation of displeasure from the Provost or his obedient *Sanhedrin*'.[98]

The suppression of the Society was mourned as 'a grand error' and 'a great evil' in other newspapers at the time and in the years ahead.[99] According to the *Freeman's Journal* 'the character of the country rose with this institution' and it credited the creation of this

94 John Wilson Croker, *Crokeriana, or Familiar Epistles* (Dublin, 1818), p. 8.

95 *Freeman's Journal*, 30 May 1815.

96 *Freeman's Journal*, 22 March 1815.

97 *The Dublin Inquisitor* (1821), vols 1-2, 448.

98 'Reminiscences of Dublin College life: The Historical Society in its decline', *Tait's Edinburgh Magazine* (1844), vol 11, p. 21; *Morning Chronicle*, 25 January 1838.

99 *Freeman's Journal*, 6 December 1820.

'School of Oratory' with the reputation Ireland had earned for eloquence.[100] It suggested that William Plunket should raise the matter in parliament, claiming that it was 'nonsense to say it is not a subject of high national importance'.

The *Freeman's Journal* argued that 'a university in a capital city is a national evil', and suggested that 'the Historical Society was a preservative against that evil'.[101] It believed that ambition – intellectual ambition – was the best way of channelling 'that dangerous season of youth, when the judgment is weak and the passions are strong'. However, these pleas were ignored by the Board, both in 1815 and in the years ahead, and numerous requests to reconstitute the Society were rejected. It would be twenty-eight years before the Society would meet again in College.

100 *Freeman's Journal*, 18 February 1815.

101 *Freeman's Journal*, 6 December 1820.

6 IN THE SHADOW OF A GREAT NAME, 1816-1844

ALTHOUGH THE SOCIETY was dissolved – suppressed – destroyed – it was not dead. As a history of Trinity, published in the early nineteenth century made clear, the 'sacred fire' of the Society was 'kept alive – nourished, unquestionably, by the remembrance of "the mighty dead that rule us from their urns"'.[1] The history of the Society from 1816 to 1844 is the story of different and sometimes competing societies struggling to maintain the values and traditions of what had been lost. During this time there was sometimes tension and in-fighting, with occasional disputes about how to proceed. Some sought a resolution with College, others were opposed to a harsh compromise, and sometimes the conflict between conservative and liberal wings became public. It was also a time of innovation and inspiration, with women admitted as members of one of the successor societies, and orators of the calibre of Isaac Butt and Thomas Davis finding their voice and testing their ideas for the first time.

Following the suppression of the Society in 1815, some members decided to continue its activities outside of the walls of the University. John Sydney Taylor and some others met at Radley's Rooms on Dame Street in 1818, but the Society was to all intents in a state of suspension for five years. That changed in 1820 when six members met on 11 November to form a revived Society. In the official accounts of the Society this new incarnation is sometimes referred to as 'The Extern Society', to distinguish it from 'The Intern Society' that had existed

1 W.B.S. Taylor, *History of the University of Dublin* (Dublin, 1820) p. 307. Taylor was an older brother of John Sydney Taylor.

in College, but it called itself a variety of names, including 'The Historical Society', the 'Dublin Literary and Historical Society' and, after December 1832, 'The College Historical Society'. Looking back on this period, Joseph Napier, a leading member of the Society and later the President of the Society when it returned to College, quoted the Roman poet, Lucan, '*Stat magni nominis umbra*' and noted how the members had been 'occasionally refreshing it in our remembrance, by chanting a requiem over its grave'.[2]

The Oxford and Cambridge debating societies agreed to recognise the new Society, granting its members honorary status in their own, and this was interpreted by many as a recognition of their claim.[3] Its code of laws was essentially the same as in the original society before all the College regulations were inserted, and membership was restricted to students and graduates of Trinity, Oxford, and Cambridge. In this period there was no President of the Society, and the same people were involved year-on-year, with the majority graduates of the university.[4] Echlin Molyneux, a graduate, became the first Auditor, an office he occupied for eight years. The Society was essentially homeless and met at a variety of locations during this period, including the Rotunda, the Lecture Room of the Dublin Institute, John Milliken's premises on Grafton Street, and the Commercial Buildings on Dame Street, as it struggled to keep going.[5] Despite much opposition by the College, the Society managed to eke out an existence. The Society met at 8 p.m. on Friday evenings (later changing to Thursday) from the beginning of November to the end of June.[6] Party politics and religion were excluded from discussion, and strangers were allowed attend if they had written permission from a member.

A number of attempts were made to return to College. In the autumn of 1820, following the resignation of Thomas Elrington, who

2 Joseph Napier, *The Lectures, Essays and Letters* (Dublin, 1888), p. 252.

3 Dagg, *CHS*, p. 148.

4 Richard S.D. Campbell, *Ireland's Mission* (Dublin,1875), p. 52.

5 *Dublin Historical Record* (1952), vols 13-15, p. 62.

6 William Curry, *The Picture of Dublin, or Stranger's Guide to the Irish Metropolis* (Dublin, 1843), p. 322.

left to become a Bishop, and the election of Samuel Kyle as Provost, a petition was submitted to the Board of the University. This was signed by students and graduates, and supported by the majority of the Junior Fellows. Anxious to avoid giving any grounds for objecting to the petition, it offered to reconstitute the Society on any terms agreeable to the Board.[7] The Board responded with 'a laconic rejection', as the *Freeman's Journal* reported, and it declared that there was no time for the discussion of the matter.

In April 1825 the Society made another formal request to be reconstituted within College. A petition was created by the members and it was signed by 277 people, including one Fellow, sixty-two Scholars, and seventy-five graduates and presented to the Board.[8] Fifteen of the seventeen Junior Fellows offered to support the petition, but the Board responded with a peremptory dismissal claiming it had no time to discuss the matter and in any case did not consider it expedient to have a student debating society.

As the Society later recalled, during this period it was 'suffering under the ban of outlawry', reduced to making frequent petitions and seeing them rejected or ignored. The Society in this period was weak, and struggled to generate excitement. It was recognized that there was a prestige attached to the name of the 'Historical Society', but it was difficult to separate it from the university itself. No society formed outside of the walls of the College was able to generate the same level of interest among the students and graduates or capture the same spirit of excitement.

By 1826 the meetings were largely deserted, with frequently no more than five or six members present. Sometimes the debates had to be cancelled because of a lack of interest.[9] In the next session new measures were suggested as the Society became increasingly desperate. On 15 December 1827 it was proposed to admit 'members of the learned professions', and this was approved. A couple of weeks later it was proposed that the Society should merge with the Dublin Historical Society, and this was agreed, although the alliance proved

7 *Freeman's Journal*, 6 December 1820.

8 Dagg, *CHS*, p. 393.

9 Robert Walsh, *Address delivered in the dining hall of Trinity College on the 9 November 1864* (Dublin, 1864), p. 44.

a difficult and short-lived one. For six weeks there were good relations, but tensions quickly surfaced, and the older members of the Dublin Historical Society, who were in the minority, resented decisions being made by the younger Trinity men, and 'the novelty of the alliance' soon wore off.

Matters came to a head when at the close of the session. Joseph Napier, a recent graduate, was a leading member of the Society in this period, and he delivered a withering rebuke of the members of the Dublin Historical Society. In his speech from the chair at a meeting held at the Rotunda on Saturday 21 June 1828, Napier complained that 'the senior members treat us as a charitable institution that claims their annual subscription' and attacked them for attending infrequently and speaking with 'earnest exclamation' when they did. Despite shouts of 'Order!' he continued by criticising their lack of energy and industry, noting cruelly that even when they did speak their efforts were 'chilled and dampened by the frigid indifference of the hearers'.

The main subject of Napier's address was oratory, but he really used it as an opportunity to review the workings of the Society. He recognized that they only used a portion of the original title in their designation and this exposed a problem at the heart of the Society. In the recorded minute of the meeting it was designated as 'The Historical and Literary Society', in the pamphlet published immediately afterwards it was called 'The Dublin Historical and Literary Society', and at the start of his address he called the body the 'Historical Society'. Its identity was unclear. Celebrating the fact that the Society was free from the 'anxious solicitude of a cautious Dean' and the 'inquisitorial scissors' of the College authorities, Napier said he was glad that they were free from this 'paralysing protection'.[10] Referencing the attempts by some members to do a deal with College to return, he was dismissive of how they had 'prostrated themselves' before the authorities.

Napier was also critical of the apathy to be found in the Society, which he called 'a growing evil'. Therefore he suggested a number of new innovations, including a removal of the ban of the discussion

10 Joseph Napier, *Address delivered before the Dublin Historical and Literary Society on the evening of the 21st of June 1828* (Dublin, 1828).

of political questions and the formation of a library. However, at the end of the address, after it was agreed that the speech would be printed and distributed to members, an amendment was passed rejecting all the proposed innovations and distancing the Society from the sentiments expressed in it. At this point in his career Napier was a firm opponent of Catholic emancipation, and he became a secretary of one of the Brunswick Clubs established to oppose it, although his views later softened.[11]

One of the best speakers in the Society in this period was a friend of Napier called James Whiteside. Whiteside was hugely influenced by Peter Burrowes, whom he befriended at this time, and he was inspired by listening to stories of his political adventures with Henry Flood and his first-hand dealings with Robert Emmet, including defending him at his trial.[12]

Echlin Molyneux eventually stepped down, and Marmion Wilme Savage, another graduate became Auditor for the 1829–30 session, with James O'Brien succeeding him for the 1830-31 session. O'Brien, from Limerick, appears to have been the first Auditor of the Society who was a Roman Catholic, although the achievement was lessened by the fact that it was a much reduced Society struggling to stay in existence.

At the start of the next session, the Society decided to replace the title of Auditor with President and Joseph Pollack, a Scholar, became the first new President of the Society in 1831, serving for one year. A new member, Isaac Butt, who joined the Society in 1831 and became a Scholar in 1832, was the dominant orator in this period. Butt had entered Trinity at the age of fifteen, taking first place in the entrance examination, and was at this time of a strongly conservative mindset. At the debates he was frequently voted the best speaker on the night, for example after the debate on whether the constitution of Great Britain was more favourable to liberty than that of America.[13] On 9 April 1832 there was much discussion about whether the Society should petition the Provost and Senior Fellows once more to be readmitted,

---

11 Alexander Charles Ewald (ed.), *The Life and Letters of the Right Honorable. Sir Joseph Napier, Bart* (London, 1892), p.13.

12 Patrick Maume, 'James Whiteside', *DIB*.

13 TCD HIST/MUN/SOC/23; Dagg, *CHS*, p. 144.

although it did not go anywhere. On 14 June, Butt himself proposed the formation of a Committee to consider the most advisable method of returning to College, but the discussion of it and a counter motion was postponed and then deferred to the next session.

A young Catholic student, William Keogh, entered Trinity as a student in 1832 but, as his biographer notes, 'he threw himself enthusiastically' into the Historical Society and his studies in science suffered. He left in 1834 without taking a degree.[14] Deciding on a legal career, he was called to the bar in 1840, went on to become a successful lawyer, and was returned as an MP in 1847. He has been called 'the only Irish Catholic Tory in the Commons', and was made Solicitor General for Ireland in 1852, Attorney General for Ireland in 1855, and a judge in 1856. On the bench he was controversial, and enraged nationalist opinion with some of his judgments. For example, his handling of an agrarian murder trial was considered 'a brutal denial of justice' and 'many felt that his court management was disgracefully one-sided'.[15] His unpopularity meant that he required police protection from that point on and his mental health deteriorated. He committed suicide at a sanatorium in Germany in September 1878.

There was much turmoil in this period. For example, there was considerable debate about doing a deal with College, with some urging the Society to change to a new name. On 13 December 1832 it was put to a vote and the majority was in favour of the Society calling itself the 'College Historical Society'. William Torrens McCullough was President at the start of this session, and had been a hardliner opposed to a deal with College. He resigned as President later in this session, and was replaced by Butt. As President, Butt opened communications with College to see if an agreement about a return could be reached, but he faced opposition internally, and discovered huge opposition within Trinity. He later admitted to the Society that a return was 'hopeless'.[16] The Society also agreed to another merger, this time with the Athenaeum Society (a literary society largely comprised of Trinity graduates) and this went through

14 Desmond McCabe, 'William Keogh', *DIB*.

15 Ibid.

16 TCD HIST/MUN/SOC/23; Dagg, *CHS*, p. 148.

in early 1833, with the first meeting taking place at John Milliken's premises on Grafton Street on 21 February. However, Milliken was unhappy with the arrangement, and they were forced to look elsewhere as the challenge of finding a suitable venue to host the meetings continued.

Butt was awarded a gold medal for Oratory at the end of the session and it was no surprise to anyone. He had been voted best speaker when he opposed the question 'Ought Duelling to be Restricted by Legislative Enactment'? and again when he supported the suggestion that emigration could be a remedy for Irish distress. What is revealing is that he was often voted best speaker despite being on the losing side of the question when it was put to the members. It was later said that Butt's only serious competitor in the period was James O'Hea, a scholar of Trinity who later became President of the Society, who was said to be a cousin of Daniel O'Connell.[17] Unfortunately it appears that in later years O'Hea 'drank himself out of distinction'.

The issue of whether the Society should return to College continued to cause tension. When Butt delivered a presidential address at the end of the session on Oratory, he made reference to how the Society was 'now the legitimate successor' of the 'old Historical Society' and called on the members to 'prove the verity of our descent by the splendour of our achievements'.[18] He also addressed the 'difference of opinion' between members over whether further attempts should be made to return to College, and he expressed his own desire to meet in the rooms which had once 'echoed to the eloquence of a Curran and Bushe'. Admitting that 'freedom of independence' should never be forfeited, he explained that his 'ideal dream' was to one day see the Society return to Trinity, even though it looked impossible.

Butt discussed the nature of oratory, and suggested that 'Enthusiasm is the first attribute of the orator.'[19] He joked about one of the lecturers who had taught him logic in his Junior Freshman

---

17 See Terence de Vere White, *The Road of Excess* (Dublin, 1945), p. 23.

18 Isaac Butt, *An address delivered before the College Historical Society on the evening of Monday 24 June 1833* (Dublin, 1833), p. 30.

19 Ibid.

year who had declaimed against the 'degeneracy of the eloquence of this generation' and recommended that the students bought his own book. Defending the power of oratory, Butt argued that that because it appealed to the 'judgement of the many' it could never be 'employed in the maintenance of tyranny'.[20]

It was a stirring piece of oratory in its own right. Butt ended on an optimistic note, expressing his belief that better days were in store 'for my unhappy, but still my loved, my native land'. He explained it was 'the dream of an enthusiastic heart', that the time would come 'when faction shall flee away and dissention shall be forgotten; when Ireland's orators and Ireland's statesmen shall only seek their country's good; when laws shall be respected and yet liberty maintained'. And he predicted the rise of an orator 'whose voice shall teach her people wisdom, and whose efforts shall procure for him the epithet of the father of his country'.

At the end of the meeting Butt was re-elected President of the Society. During his term a decision was taken to restore the historic title of Auditor, alongside that of the President, and John Cochrane served as Auditor with Butt as President. This created more problems than it solved and caused considerable confusion over which was the most senior role, often depending on the personalities of those concerned. Butt stepped down as President to become Auditor of the Society for the 1834–35 session, but he resigned after a few months, and thereafter he stopped attending meetings. This was probably because he had taken over the editorship of the *Dublin University Magazine,* a periodical he himself had co-founded (alongside John Anster, William Archer Butler and others) in 1833.[21] Graduating in 1835, he was appointed the Whately Professor of Political Economy at Trinity in 1836, and held the chair until 1841.

During his time in Trinity Butt was a conservative and a unionist, and he was 'marked down as a champion of the Tories in the making'.[22] It was only in time that he came to believe in self-government, and became a leading figure of what became the Home Rule movement. Sergeant A.M. Sullivan described him as 'an

20 Ibid., p. 17.

21 Philip Bull, 'Isaac Butt', *DIB*.

22 Dagg, *CHS*, p. 394.

intellectual giant, who in one step had passed from studentship into a position of acknowledged leadership of the Irish Bar'.[23]

In this period the committee of the Society met in College on a Monday afternoon, usually in the rooms of the President or a Committee member, and the questions were chosen for debate, as well as the speakers and chairs, and the other organisational business was conducted.[24] Students and graduates were elected to the title of President, again serving for just one year, leading to some confusion about roles and responsibilities. On 4 November 1833 the Committee voted to remove entrance fees, so that anyone could attend, although a bar was to be placed across the room to separate visitors from members. Each month there was an extempore debate, with the motion chosen by ballot on the night of the meeting. In 1834 the decision was taken to move the Committee meetings to Fridays at 4 p.m.

A talented student and youthful orator, William Archer Butler, delivered the address at the opening of the 1834–35 session and he discussed the responsibility the Society had assumed by taking the name 'College Historical Society'.[25] It was, he said, 'a responsibility of unquestionable weight', and whether it would 'terminate in honour or degradation' was up to them. Butler supported the continuing prohibition on discussing modern day politics, arguing that it allowed the Society 'to soar above the corrupt atmosphere of faction, and to breathe a better and purer air'.

The restriction on discussing contemporary politics was frequently bypassed, and debates for the session included the repeal of the Corn Laws, the introduction of poor laws into Ireland, and whether England should go to war with Russia to preserve the independence of Turkey. The proceedings of the Society were followed with interest by newspapers and journals in Britain. For example, at this time the *Morning Chronicle* in London criticised the Society for indulging in modern day politics, and for choosing topics likely to irritate and provoke.[26] There was also criticism of the Society for discussing individuals who were still alive. The paper dismissed the

23 See White, *The Road of Excess.*

24 Dagg, *CHS*, p. 150.

25 Ibid., p. 151.

26 *Morning Chronicle*, 25 January 1838.

Society as 'a place of vain and factious display than of improvement – a place of garrulous impudence and not of oratory'. It was suggested that 'the glibbest talker' was sure of receiving the applause of the audience and the legitimacy of the Society was questioned.

Many of the debates were so popular that they continued at the next meeting, and some carried on for a third week. One of the extemporary debates was on whether women should be admitted to the debates of the Society. It was passed, and in the months ahead the attendance of women became a noted feature of the debates.[27] A debate about whether the policy of Charles James Fox was better than that of William Pitt was chaired by a young student who was beginning to make an impression, Thomas Davis. William Archer Butler delivered the closing address to the Society, on 26 June 1835. Discussing the sixty-five years of its 'often interrupted existence', he praised the Society for continuing to be 'the seminary of professional distinction'.

From this period we have a number of addresses to the Society which were published at the time. For example, John Cochrane, who served as President in 1835-36, published his address to the Society at the close of the session.[28] In it he hinted at some of the tensions that existed in the Society. It seems he had also wished to continue in some role in the Society for another year, but 'in that hope I have been disappointed'. However, he insisted that he left without 'any personal resentment' and left not 'a single foe'. He warned the Society to avoid allowing politics to destroy it from within, suggesting that if it went to the grave again this time there would be 'no second resurrection'.

Some Auditors and members in this period went on to achieve significant distinction. John Thomas Ball became a Member of Parliament and later Lord Chancellor for Ireland; R. Graves MacDonnell (Auditor in 1835–36), served as Governor of Gambia and later as Governor of Hong Kong; John Edward Walsh (Auditor in 1836–67) became Attorney General for Ireland and later Master of the Rolls; George Salmon was later Provost.

27 Ibid.

28 John Cochrane, *An address delivered before the College Historical Society on 24 June 1836* (Dublin, 1836).

One of the most illustrious members at this time was Joseph Sheridan Le Fanu, who served on the Committee alongside Thomas Davis and went on to achieve fame as a poet and writer. Le Fanu has been described as the leading ghost-story writer of the nineteenth century, and helped develop the genre in the Victorian era.[29] His vampire novella, *Carmilla,* published in 1872, influenced Bram Stoker, as well as cinematic representations of vampires in the twentieth century. Popularly known as Sheridan Le Fanu, he came from a respectable middle-class Protestant family. His maternal grandfather had attended to Robert Emmet on the scaffold.[30]

Le Fanu left detailed accounts of his time in the Society, taking pride in the fact that he had acquired, though his oratory, 'a character of being possessed of the most *imperturbable Brass'*, a reputation which he said he 'much coveted'.[31] Elected Treasurer of the Society, he was voted best speaker during the debate on an absentee tax in February 1837. He was awarded a silver medal at the end of the session.

The Society was comprised of members from all political backgrounds, but discussion of politics created tensions and clear conservative and radical wings soon became apparent. Different visions of the future direction of Ireland, and different ideas about what the Society should do next, started coming to the surface, and in the summer of 1837 became public. Controversy erupted over the organisation of the great end-of-year dinner which was to be held in Morrison's Hotel. The tension between the different factions in the Society erupted and the dinner was cancelled amidst much acrimony. On the conservative side, Le Fanu was regretful that 'the grand dinner of the Society has been blown up by the conduct of the radicals'. In its place, another dinner was arranged that Butt agreed to chair. Le Fanu was delighted to finally get to meet his hero and they soon became close friends.

The open conflict in the Society frequently attracted the criticism of the press. Believing that the Society had become too radical, on

29 Introduction to Joseph Sheridan Le Fanu, *A Debt of Honour* (London, 2012).

30 W.J. McCormack, 'Joseph Sheridan Le Fanu', *ODNB.*

31 Dagg, *CHS*, p. 155.

21 June 1837 the *Freeman's Journal* urged those concerned with their reputation to distance themselves from the Society. Referencing the controversial dinner, it described the Society as 'a rotten vessel' and the members were criticised for siding with the 'brilliant propagators of falsehood'.[32]

The Auditor for the session 1837-38 session was Thomas MacNevin and he became close friends in the Society with Thomas Davis, John Blake Dillon and others who would go to play prominent roles in the Young Ireland movement. A young Catholic from Galway, the son of a solicitor, MacNevin delivered a powerful speech to the Society in which he recommended going beyond battles and dynasties when studying history and searching instead for an understanding of their country, to prepare them for a time when 'all the genius, all the patriotism, all the feeling of Ireland, will be summoned to her aid in struggles great'.[33]

The tensions between the different factions in the Society resulted in a split. One contributing factor was the election of Dr Francis (Franc) Sadleir, the former member of the Society, as Provost on 22 December 1837. Sadleir was a reformer, and there were early indications that a deal might be possible. On 25 January 1838 the *Morning Chronicle* in London reported on a hope in Trinity that the Historical Society would shortly be revived.

In March 1838 the Board announced that it was willing to allow the return of the Society to College, provided the Junior Fellows agreed to chair the meetings, or arrange for someone suitable. There were also regulations about how the Society would be governed. Le Fanu railed against the 'most despotic system' being proposed and rejected the proposal. However, a significant minority was in favour of some compromise, and these pressures, combined with the disputes over contemporary politics, finally tore the revived Historical Society apart. It effectively collapsed after the final meeting of the session on 29 June 1838.

Attempts were made to form a new Society out of the ashes. On 14 March 1839 a committee of twenty met in College to discuss the formation of a new body, 'The Historical Society' for the promotion

32 *Freeman's Journal*, 21 June 1837.

33 James Quinn, *Young Ireland and the writing of history* (Dublin, 2015).

of eloquence and composition. Even though there was some continuation in membership, those involved were adamant that this was a new Society. This was something William Neilson Hancock, the Auditor for part of 1841–42, made clear in a letter to the *Freeman's Journal* in October 1843 when he discussed the paternity of the Society in response to something mischievous that had been written linking it with the older bodies. He was adamant that the Society founded in March 1839 'had no connection with any former historical society', even though he acknowledged the considerable overlap with the membership of the Historical Society that had ceased meeting.[34]

According to the new Society's minutes, 'ten conservatives and ten liberals' were elected 'to form the nucleus of such a Society' and they met in the rooms of Francis Kearney, a Fellow of Trinity, in House 27. Kearney was to have a huge influence on the development of Davis's thinking, and when he died suddenly Davis chose to dedicate his famous address in 1840 to him, recognising that he had concurred with most of the opinions in it.[35] Le Fanu and Davis were two of the twenty elected, and it was composed of members who had opposed the planned return to College. Membership was open to graduates or undergraduates of any university in the United Kingdom, those studying for the bar, or those at the Royal College of Surgeons. All applications were voted on, with one black bean in seven, or three black beans in total, sufficient to block a candidate. Davis was one of five members selected to draw up the code of laws for the Society and much time was spent trying to find a suitable location for meetings.

Daniel Owen Madden was an active member of the Society at this time and became close friends with Davis. In his later writings he praised him for his 'plain speech, his simplicity of manners, his aura of frankness and sincerity'.[36] Davis, he said, had a great love of books, and was full of 'good spirits and more joyous than he was later to be', and enjoyed the social side of the Society. A distinctly

---

34 *Freeman's Journal*, 4 October 1843.

35 Dagg, *CHS*, p. 396.

36 Helen Mulvey, *Thomas Davis and Ireland: a biographical study* (Washington D.C., 2003), p. 41.

average student, Davis was remembered as 'a steady, plodding student', and described as 'dreamy, self-absorbed and quickly emotional' by his biographer.[37] However, he loved reading, and was described as a 'book in breeches' by his classmates. But in the Historical Society he found his home, and it was the making of the man. It was in this period that Davis developed his interest in Irish affairs and the patriotic sentiments that would later win him national renown as a leading member of Young Ireland.

It has been said that 'Davis stands as one of the makers of modern Ireland' and his influence on subsequent Irish history can not be overestimated. Through the Young Ireland movement and the newspaper the *Nation* he helped create the idea of a new Irish nationality driven by a shared culture, a shared heritage, a shared language and a shared sense of community. It is worth noting that the connections between Young Ireland and the Historical Society were immediate and profound. Many of the figures who went on to play a prominent role in the movement met through the meetings of the debating society, and the friendships they forged in the Society were influential and enduring. A nexus was created between Thomas Davis, Thomas MacNevin, John Edward Pigot, John Blake Dillon, John O'Hagan, and others during this period when their world-view and their friendships were shaped in the debating society. As a leading scholar of the Young Ireland movement has noted, Davis later admitted that the Historical Society was the cradle of the Young Ireland movement. His speech on nationality, which was published by the Historical Society, 'was effectively Young Ireland's founding manifesto'.[38] It 'introduced the main themes that would appear again and again in their historical writings: Irishmen should study their country's history, appreciate her sufferings, learn from her mistakes, take pride in her achievements, honour her heroes, and use them as an inspiration to work for Ireland'. When the *Nation* was founded it was run almost like the Historical Society with regular meetings of the contributors where they 'thrashed out their ideas and differences in friendly discussion and argument'.[39]

---

37 Helen Mulvey, 'Thomas Davis', *ODNB*.

38 Quinn, *Young Ireland*.

39 Ibid.

The first regular meeting of the new Society took place on Tuesday 26 March 1839 at Leitrim House, on Upper Sackville Street. At this meeting Le Fanu was elected President of the Society, and Thomas Davis the Auditor. The first motion was in favour of the introduction of the secret ballot for general elections, and Davis proposed the motion, which was passed narrowly. Some members objected to the discussion of party politics or religion at the meetings, and a motion was proposed to block such topics in future, but Davis used a procedural loophole to avoid discussing the matter and the motion was withdrawn.

At the meeting on 16 April Le Fanu announced his intention to resign, because he did not want to have to deliver the usual address at the end of the year. However, Davis intervened to suggest that no address would be necessary and he agreed to remain on. Instead, Le Fanu entertained the members with a nationalist ballad he had written, 'Shamus O'Brien', which told the story of a 1798 rebel who was captured, put on trial, and escaped. It was later turned into an opera by Charles Villiers Stanford. One member exclaimed after the meeting, 'Shake hands! Le Fanu! Say what you like you must have some of the *right real feeling* in you or you could never have written that'.[40] There was no debate at the final meeting of the session, on 25 June 1839, and instead Davis read a paper on 'The Constitutions of England and America'.[41] At this meeting the new committee was elected, and Thomas Davis became President, with Charles Palmer Archer succeeding him as Auditor.

The following session, 1839–40, was a difficult one, and for some weeks there were no meetings because of insufficient attendance. Davis read another paper on 5 November 1839 on the United States constitution and received a unanimous vote of thanks. But apathy was a growing problem and the lack of a fixed meeting place was also inconvenient, with the Society using a number of different locations. However, there was good news on 19 June 1840 when the Cambridge Union announced that all members of the Historical Society had been elected honorary members, and Davis proposed a reciprocal arrangement that was passed.

40 Dagg, *CHS*, p. 157, and 161.

41 Ibid., p. 162.

It was at the final meeting of this session, 26 June 1840, that Thomas Davis delivered his famous presidential address. His subject was 'The Utility of Debating Societies in Remedying the Defects of a University Education', and it marked him out as a future national leader. Davis launched an attack on the curriculum at Trinity, and pleaded for the study of modern languages and broad educational reform.[42] He argued that the study of history and oratory was essential for a true education, and necessary to avoid democracy being contaminated by those who had no respect for history, tradition, or moral values.

In a stunning piece of rhetoric, Davis declared that 'on the shore of democracy is a monstrous danger – the violence and forwardness of selfish men ... ready to sacrifice ... the generous, the pious, the just – till general corruption, anarchy, despotism, and moral darkness shall re-barbarise the earth'. The message was that citizens had a moral obligation to act for the good of one's people. In the most quoted line he insisted, 'Gentlemen, you have a country'. And he called on them to use their power for good, insisting that 'Patriotism is human philosophy... Patriotism, once *felt* to be a duty, *becomes* one.'

The address was published as a pamphlet in October 1840 by the Society and Davis included a brief preface that included the challenge to his readers: 'How long will you sin against patriotism?' It urged them to put aside faction and act in union for the good 'of our common country'. The title page included a quote from Gotthold Ephraim Lessing: 'Think wrongly if you will, but think for yourself.' Davis sent the pamphlet to people he admired in Britain. Walter Savage Landor had written about oppressed nationalities across the world, and Davis had assumed that he would be sympathetic to the plight of Ireland. But he wrote back saying the pamphlet had given him great pain and that the new railways would make Ireland the richest country in the world.[43] Similarly, Davis was disappointed by the response of William Wordsworth, who warned him of the foolishness of the course he was pursuing and criticised his 'insular patriotism'.[44]

42 Mulvey, *Thomas Davis and Ireland*, p. 32.

43 *Freeman's Journal*, 25 October 1901.

The first attempt Davis made to put his ideas into practice came on 18 December 1840 when he proposed remodelling the Society, and creating a new off-shoot, the Dublin 'Lyceum', as a way of extending and 'increasing its utility'.[45] There were six sections to the Society, covering everything from History, Law, Literature, Ethics, to Classics and much more, with classes, readings and examinations held. There was much discussion over the following weeks, leading to a number of amendments, and the new Society met on 12 February 1841 in the upper part of No. 2 Marlborough Street under the name 'The Dublin Institute'. This building had been the home of the Dublin Savings Bank, popularly known as the Penny Bank, and the second floor had a large hall that could seat one hundred people.[46] It was here that the Society met. The building was renovated at the start of the twentieth century, and became the original home of the Abbey Theatre. However, it had only a limited success over the next few months, as Davis and other members became involved in national politics and turned their attentions elsewhere.

The new President of the Society for 1841–2 was John Blake Dillon. As his biographer, Brendan Ó Cathaoir, has noted, 'At Trinity he made the most important friendship of his political career, with Thomas Davis, whom he succeeded as President of the Historical Society.'[47] When Davis began putting his ideas on Irish nationality into action he found in Dillon 'his earliest confederate'. About 10 per cent of the students in Trinity at this time were Catholic, and Dillon and Thomas MacNevin were described as two young men who 'laughed at the pretensions of Protestant ascendancy' and considered themselves the equal of their fellow Protestant students.[48] Uniting 'a lofty enthusiasm with great lucidity of intellect and unvarying candour', Dillon delivered his presidential address on 8 November 1841 on the subject of 'Patriotism'. The speech referenced the 'long centuries of trial and affliction' in Ireland's history, and reminded the audience how sweet it was 'to gaze upon the flag that

44 Mulvey, *Thomas Davis and Ireland*, p. 37.

45 Dagg, *CHS*, p. 164.

46 Ibid., p. 400.

47 Brendan Ó Cathaoir, 'John Blake Dillon', *DIB*.

48 Quinn, *Young Ireland.*

waved above their heads in battle'.[49] Dillon suggested that 'it is sweet to hope that it shall wave again'. Answering the people who wanted to 'draw a veil over the past, and to obliterate it from their memory', Dillon argued that future prosperity and success depended on knowing your own country's history. John O'Hagan later claimed that before this speech he was a Whig, 'the next morning, and ever after I was a nationalist'.[50]

This was a legacy that was not apparent at the time. The Historical Society faced massive challenges in the early 1840s and its future hung in the balance. On a number of occasions the debates had to be cancelled, as the minutes say, 'in consequence of the thin attendance'.[51] John O'Hagan, a Catholic from Newry, was Auditor for the 1842–3 session. Some members from this period would go on to achieve eminence, including O'Hagan himself, John Edward Pigot, John Kells Ingram, Denis Caulfield Heron, and Charles Hemphill, but the Society was quickly losing its reputation. Even more damaging, a rival body, bearing the same name, and based in College was created, as a different group finally negotiated a deal with College. The agreement made in April 1843 enabled the Society to be reconstituted within Trinity, and it formally resumed activities in November 1843 with Provost Sadleir as the President. This was 'the Year of Repeal', with monster meetings taking place between March and October, and Trinity decided that some compromise was necessary to protect the students from being corrupted by radical ideas. The establishment of this new Society will be detailed in the next chapter, but its creation had a devastating effect on the external society. It had recruited nineteen undergraduates in 1842–43, but could only attract seven in 1843–44, and several members resigned to join the internal society.

Supported by its older members, the external society attempted to continue, but it faced haemorrhaging interest and support. David Richard Pigot, the son of the leading barrister of the same name and a brother of John Edward Pigot, was elected as Auditor of the external

49 Dagg, *CHS*, p. 170, Quinn, *Young Ireland.*

50 Quoted in Brendan Ó Caothair, *John Blake Dillon: Young Irelander* (Dublin, 1990), p. 8.

51 Dagg, *CHS*, p. 172.

Society for 1843–44, and his Committee included Ingram. Rooms were procured at Brunswick Street (now Pearse Street) but attendances were terrible, and meetings usually involved the resignation of committee members and others involved. The final meeting of the session, on 15 April 1844, ended in humiliation as the meeting was adjourned at 9 p.m. because of the lack of a quorum. It seems that only four people attended, and all were officers of the Society.

Ten people attended the first and final meeting of the new session of the Society on 4 November 1844. No new members had joined and it was clear that it was in crisis. It was discussed whether to seek a merger with the Law Debating Society and a sub-committee was appointed to investigate the practicability of such a coalition. The meeting was then adjourned, to meet again 'at such place and within such reasonable time as they [the sub-committee] shall think proper'. The Society never met again. It was an ignominious end to the Society, the heir of the many different incarnations who had persevered during the difficult years of exclusion from Trinity. However, its legacy was considerable. It – and the other successor societies – had ensured the survival and continuity of the Society in its darkest times, preserving its traditions, its values, and its history.

There were several different incarnations of the Historical Society in this period and many of the figures involved went on to achieve notable success. Joseph Napier became a successful lawyer and MP, arguing in parliament against Jewish emancipation and for maintaining the connection between church and state.[52] He was briefly Lord Chancellor for Ireland (1858–59) and was later made a Baronet and Vice-Chancellor of the University of Dublin.

James Whiteside, became a successful barrister and defended Charles Gavan Duffy at his state trial in 1844 and afterwards 'was recognized as the leading figure of the Irish bar'.[53] Considered one of the best speakers at the bar, he served as Solicitor General for Ireland and Attorney General for Ireland before becoming Chief Justice.

The longest serving Auditor of the Society, Echlin Molyneux, became a county judge and later Dean of the Law Faculty at Queen's College Belfast. An expert in equity, he is credited with raising the

52 Patrick Maume, Joseph Napier', *DIB*.

53 Patrick Maume, 'James Whiteside', *DIB*.

standards for legal practitioners in Ireland. His successor, Marmion Wilme Savage, became a successful novelist and journalist and his works included *The Falcon Family*, a satire on the Young Ireland movement.[54]

William Archer Butler later became a clergyman and Professor of Moral Philosophy at Trinity. A remarkable figure, he abandoned academic pursuits during the Famine so that he could look after those who were suffering. However, his life was brought to a tragic and premature end when he succumbed to fever in 1848.[55]

After the Famine, Isaac Butt took up the cause of Irish self-government and became the leader of the campaign for Home Rule in the 1870s. Writing in the *Dictionary of Irish Biography*, Philip Bull has recognized that: 'Butt's contribution to the development of Irish political life and, indeed, to British parliamentary institutions was a very significant one, pioneering new concepts and practical approaches.'[56]

William Torrens McCullough became a political and social reformer and served for many years in the British House of Commons. Among his successful campaigns was one to oblige local authorities to replace overcrowded slums with proper housing for working class families.[57]

Thomas Davis achieved fame through his co-founding of the *Nation* newspaper and involvement with what became known as the Young Ireland movement. The *Nation* set itself the mission 'To create and foster public opinion, and make it racy of the soil' so as to achieve 'the great end of Nationality'. It 'was decisive in its immediate effects, and its influence continued throughout the next century'.[58] Davis wrote many of the articles and in his ballads (for example, 'A nation once again') and articles he 'kept up an incessant flow of ideas, all aimed at developing Irish nationality and independence.'

Davis died on 16 September 1845 after contracting scarletina. Writing in the *Dictionary of Irish Biography*, John Molony has noted

54 Jessica March, 'Marmion Wilme Savage', *DIB*.

55 Linde Lunney, 'William Archer Butler, *DIB*.

56 Philip Bull, 'Isaac Butt', *DIB*.

57 Georgina Clinton and Sinéad Sturgeon, 'William Torrens McCullough', *DIB*.

58 John Molony, 'Thomas Davis', *DIB*.

that 'in his own lifetime Davis became a legend that was metamorphosed after his death. His influence on fellow Young Irelanders and on many of the nationalists that came after them was profound: Arthur Griffith, Patrick Pearse and Éamon de Valera all acknowledged a great debt to him.'

Thomas MacNevin became a leading Young Irelander and was one of the most prolific contributors to the *Nation*.[59] As James Quinn writes in the *Dictionary of Irish Biography*, he 'shared Davis's vision of national cultural regeneration, but had no interest in reviving the Irish language and believed that the Young Irelanders should avoid dwelling on the hazy recesses of ancient Irish history'. Devastated by Davis's death, he took it upon himself to write a single-volume history of Ireland as a sacred trust to his memory, but failed to complete it. It seems he had a mental breakdown as a result and withdrew from public life. He died in an asylum in Bristol in February 1848.

'A charismatic and handsome figure', John Edward Pigot contributed verse to the *Nation* and is credited with winning support for Young Ireland 'among fashionable society in Dublin'.[60] It is believed that he was the model for the protagonist of Marmion Wilme Savage's satire on the Young Ireland movement, *The Falcon Family*. In later years he advocated the establishment of a national art gallery in Ireland and was a founding member of the National Gallery of Ireland.

John O'Hagan became a prominent Young Irelander and wrote the poem, 'The Union' for the *Nation* on 22 April 1843 which began with the famous lines: 'How did they pass the Union? By perjury and fraud'.[61] He was not involved in the 1848 rebellion, but defended John Mitchel and Charles Gavan Duffy at their trials. In the 1870s he became a supporter of Home Rule and argued that Thomas Davis would have accepted it, because for 'the blind, levelling, envious, anarchic forces which are the awful menace of our time, he could feel nothing but repugnance'. He became a judge and was judicial commissioner of the court of the Irish Land Commission.

59 James Quinn, 'Thomas MacNevin', *DIB*.

60 Georgina Clinton and Sinéad Sturgeon, 'John Edward Pigot', *DIB*.

61 Sinéad Sturgeon and James Quinn, 'John O'Hagan', *DIB*.

John Blake Dillon was a founder of the *Nation* and was the driving force behind pushing the land tenure question in its pages. He supported the idea of a rebellion in 1848, and went into exile in the United States. In 1856 he took advantage of an amnesty to return to Ireland and was elected MP for Co. Tipperary in 1865. In parliament he brought forward a land bill that helped 'reverse the presumption in law that the tenant's improvements were his landlord's property' and this has been called 'a decisive contribution' that 'heralded the great era of Gladstonian reform'.[62]

The history of the Society – or rather the history of the different societies between 1820 and 1844 – is a confusing one. But there is a consistency and a pattern to it. The Historical Society was a palimpsest. Each new creation was superimposed on what had gone before and the earlier traces were obvious and distinct. Even though the different societies created after the dissolution were superseded by the new Society that was formed in College in 1843, and with whose existence they overlapped, they helped preserve the values and traditions of the Society until they could be passed on to a new generation. Despite their differences, despite the tensions, the members played their part in keeping the 'sacred flame' alive.

62 Brendan Ó Cathaoir, 'John Blake Dillon', *DIB*.

7

RESURRECTION AND RETURN, 1843-1857

THE LONG-AWAITED RETURN of the Society to Trinity took place in 1843. In April the Provost, Francis Sadleir, and the Board agreed to a request to allow it to be reformed within its walls, and plans began to restart the Society in the new academic year. Four students led negotiations for the Society: William Connor Magee, Hedges Eyre Chatterton (later Vice Chancellor of Ireland), John Cotter McDonnell (later Dean of Cashel), and Henry Jellett (later Dean of St Patrick's). They also had a powerful advocate at Board, the Bursar, Richard MacDonnell. A member of the Society in the early 1800s, MacDonnell was the father of Richard Graves MacDonnell, who had been Auditor of the external society in the 1830s. As the Society later recorded, MacDonnell was 'a friend to us at a time when our friends were few'.[1] Indeed it was noted that 'when some of those in high and exalted stations strongly condemned our objects' he 'came forward and supported us with all the influence at his command'. At the same time, a petition was signed by several hundred eminent people in the city asking the Board to allow the Society to return to College and this too was influential.[2] With Sadleir sympathetic, MacDonnell strongly supportive, notable public interest, and the students willing to compromise, a deal was finally agreed. The new College Historical Society, as it was named, described itself as having been founded in 1770, and revived in 1843, and numbered the session in 1843-44 as its first.

1 Dagg, *CHS*, 402. From address of James Clarke Lane at the 1867-68 session.

2 *The Irish Times*, 31 January 1969.

In many ways this was a victory for the College. The terms were very similar to those which had been rejected in 1815 and which had been such a grievance then. For example, Senior Sophisters were the only students who could become members and this put pressure on the Society from the beginning. As part of the deal the Provost was given the power to appoint a number of members to the Society, starting with the four students named above, and they were given the power of admitting others by ballot.[3] A committee of management was appointed that included the Junior Dean among its ranks. When the committee met on 13 May 1843 it approved the laws of the Society and elected its officers for the coming session. Magee had distinguished himself as a speaker in the external Society and the committee agreed that he should be appointed the first Auditor and deliver the address at the opening of the new session. A former Scholar and graduate, Magee faced a difficult challenge as Auditor, trying to establish the legitimacy of the new Society amidst doubt and suspicion. The Provost was elected President of the Society and four Vice-Presidents were chosen, included Francis Blackburne, the former Auditor from 1803–04 who was now Master of the Rolls. Afterwards seventy students joined the Society, and it quickly began to grow in numbers.

Not all students were happy with the announcement of the return. Some feared that the College should exert too great an influence and some were unwilling to surrender the freedom they had enjoyed outside of the walls.[4] The emphasis was placed on history, poetry and oratory, and there were examinations every quarter in the different areas, with the winning candidates receiving medals. Students presenting for the history had to complete a lengthy examination in ancient and modern history, and in poetry the compositions were carefully studied. For the oratory award the members voted on it by ballot.

Certain rules were prescribed by the Board, ensuring that a large measure of control was maintained over the Society. All twenty-nine

---

3 TCD HIST/MUN/SOC/26; Dagg, *CHS*, p. 177.

4 John Cotter MacDonell (ed.), *The Life and Correspondence of William Connor Magee Archbishop of York Bishop of Peterborough* (2 vols, London, 1896).

Fellows of the College were made *ex-officio* members. Only Senior Sophisters were allowed apply to join, except for fellow commoners (students who paid double fees who dined at high table) who were allowed apply in their third year. Graduates could continue as life members. Academic dress was required at all meetings, the meetings had to be chaired by someone senior (the President, a Vice-President, a Fellow, a Professor, or a Resident Master), and meetings had to conclude by midnight. At the end of each session the Society had to prepare a report on all the chairmen and motions debated and submit it to the Board for inspection. In addition, any member who incurred a College censure was automatically expelled.[5]

On Friday 16 November 1843 there was a huge gathering for the first public meeting of the Society in its old rooms, over the Dining Hall. The Provost took the chair at 8 p.m, thus conferring the Society with a mark of official approval after twenty-eight years in the wilderness.[6] Also in attendance was Lundy Foote, the final Auditor of the Society before it was dissolved, who was one of the trustees of that Society.

The opening address was read by Magee and it was considered 'the first of a long series of oratorical triumphs'.[7] Lasting more than an hour, it was described as holding its audience 'enchained in rapt attention', and it succeeded in silencing the opponents of the new Society. Magee criticised the defects of external societies, arguing that a 'magnitude' of evils was unavoidable in them. They were limited in nature and lacked restraint, and he claimed that this was why they had 'decided to restore the only Society which had ever been free from them for any length of time'.

Magee was one of the most eloquent speakers in the history of the Society, and already at this stage he was a 'tornado of a man', able to 'pour forth a brilliant series of sentences at the rate of more than two hundred words a minute'.[8] The effect was to sweep people along with the intensity of his arguments, and even seasoned observers later claimed that they would have placed him above 'any

5 Taylor, *History of the University of Dublin*, p. 305.

6 Ibid., p. 199.

7 MacDonnell, *Life and correspondence,* i, 9.

8 *The Sunday Times*, 2 September 1923.

one of the hundreds of great orators' they had heard. In his speech Magee addressed head-on the 'host of objections' that had been made when they had raised the possibility of reforming within College. They had been told any negotiation was 'hopeless, and even if it succeeded would be useless'. It had been predicted that the students would either oppose the move, or ignore it, and 'the scanty attendance or the listless indifference of our members would disgrace our meetings, and cause our efforts only to result in a mortification and confusion'. Despite these 'evil prophecies' the group had persevered, 'and the result is – we are here'.

A grandson of Archbishop William Magee, William Connor Magee was already making a name for himself in the world with his oratory, and it was a reputation that would only increase. Ordained a deacon in 1844, he became a Church of Ireland clergyman in 1845, and he won fame as a preacher when he served as minister of the Octagon chapel in Bath in the 1850s.[9] As rector of Enniskillen between 1860 and 1864 he fought a running battle with members of the Orange Order because of his determination to prevent them hanging flags and bunting from his church. Promoted to Dean of Cork, he delivered a powerful speech against the proposed disestablishment of the Church of Ireland in 1868 and it came to the attention of the Prime Minister, Benjamin Disraeli. Disraeli took the unusual step of appointing Magee as Bishop of Peterborough, and with it a seat in the House of Lords, and it was certainly the case that Magee's 'reputation for astounding brilliancy of speech' accounted for the 'daring innovation' of transferring a clergyman from Ireland to England.[10] Magee's maiden speech in 1869 was a powerful denunciation of Gladstone's measure. Attacking its 'hard' spirit, Magee claimed to be 'astonished at its intense shabbiness'. As David Murphy has noted in the Royal Irish Academy's *Dictionary of Irish Biography* 'he was soon recognized as one of the most polished parliamentary orators of the period'. His speech on the Intoxicating Liquor (Licensing) Bill in 1872 was for years quoted, and misquoted, in the press after he claimed that it was better for England to be free than compulsorily sober. Magee ended his career as Archbishop of

---

9 David Murphy, William Connor Magee', *DIB*.

10 *The Sunday Times*, 2 September 1923.

York, and but for his death some even predicted that he might have risen to become Archbishop of Canterbury.

In a powerful symbolic gesture, Lundy Foote was also invited to speak at the first meeting. From the beginning Foote struck a conciliatory tone. He gave a short history of the dissolution of the old Society and the read some letters from Elrington, in an attempt to show that the former Provost had not been against the Society, but had merely been trying to prevent the discussion of political topics. In a gesture recognising the legitimacy of the new body, he announced that he was giving to the committee of the new Society any of the property that was in his possession and he handed over whatever journals he had.

The new Society was a success from that point on and membership steadily increased. The first motion debated was whether the Americans were justified in putting the Revolutionary War spy, Major John Andre, to death, and it passed by seventeen votes to five. Over the next few months the Society debated the French revolution, the execution of Mary Queen of Scots, the abolition of capital punishment, and emigration. A motion was passed on 1 February 1844 establishing that the Auditor would sit beside the Chair of the meeting and advise him on keeping order and the management of business.[11] At the end of the session Charles Hare Hemphill, who had been a member of the external society, was elected the new Auditor. The legitimacy of the Society was now beyond doubt.

It was a recognition of the status and popularity of the new Society that the first meeting of the 1844–45 session, on 7 November 1844, was held in the Dining Hall, and was attended by many members of the old societies, both internal and external. Isaac Butt, now a King's Counsel, was present, and the Master of the Rolls, Blackburne, was in the chair. Fifteen new members of the Society were proposed, including John Kells Ingram, who had been a prominent figure in one of the external societies. The following week, sixteen new candidates were proposed.

Hemphill's opening address was dedicated to the surviving members of the 'Old Historical' and set out to critique the strengths

11 TCD HIST/MUN/SOC/26; Dagg, *CHS*, p. 184.

and weaknesses of the new Society. He praised the selection of subjects for debate in the previous year, and was relieved that 'all topics, religious or political, have been sedulously excluded'. But he was critical of the rooms the Society was using as they were not suitable for debates, and he regretted the absence of a good historical library.

There were also harsh criticisms of the members of the new Society for not taking their responsibilities seriously enough. Hemphill rebuked the members for neglecting the study of History, and noted that the debates the previous year had been too languid, and the responsibility for speaking had been repeatedly left to the same few people. The apathy of the members of College was also noted. It was a condition of the Society's existence that a Fellow, Professor, or Resident Master had to chair the meetings, and yet they had to draw 'largely on the patience of the *very few*' as others were unwilling to help out. Hemphill wanted membership of the Society to become 'the means of intellectual advancement', and also 'a harbour of friendship... in the stormy sea of life' and he suggested that their connection to the Historical Society should serve 'as a Masonic symbol' in the years ahead.

To address some of these concerns, the Society negotiated a deal with College to enable the debates to be held in the Dining Hall, and this was approved as the meeting on 21 November. The College returned 499 books to the Society, as well as some valuables, and a Librarian and sub-committee was established to investigate the creation of a proper library. Over the next decade a proper library was developed, largely thanks to the generosity of patrons, and it contained many works on current affairs as well as works of literature and history, and enabled the students to study 'what is going on in the world outside these walls'.[12] During this session a proposal was made to limit membership to 200, but this was rejected. On 6 March 1845 a decision was taken to move the night of meeting from Thursdays to Wednesdays, and the first meeting on the new day took place on 12 March 1845.

Edward Sullivan was Auditor for the 1845-46 session and the

12 Denis Caulfield Heron, *An Address Delivered Before the College Historical Society in the Dining Hall, Trinity College, on the First Night of the Fourth Session, 4 November 1846* (Dublin, 1846), p.10.

debates that year revealed a number of interesting student positions. A motion in favour of erecting a statue to Cromwell was narrowly defeated, and a motion confirming that a large city was the best location for a university was passed by a large majority. During this session the Society re-established its links with Oxford, and confirmed that honorary membership continued to exist, and the link with Cambridge was re-established the following year. After leaving Trinity Sullivan became a successful lawyer and as Solicitor General for Ireland in 1865 he is credited with being 'instrumental in plans to stamp out the Fenians'.[13] MP for Mallow (1865–70), he became Master of the Rolls in 1870 and Lord Chancellor of Ireland in 1883 and he moved decisively against the Invincibles.

Whenever a member of one of the external societies achieved distinction, the Society was quick to congratulate them, thus strengthening and reinforcing the connections between the groups. When John Kells Ingram was elected to Fellowship the Society sent him a letter of congratulations, and Ingram was greatly moved by the gesture. In an elegant response he noted that many people had doubted the Society would flourish when it was restored, but was delighted that they had been proven wrong, and he offered his full support promoting the interests of the Society in the future. William Neilson Hancock had been Auditor of the external society in the 1830s, and was appointed Professor of Political Economy at this time. Thanking the Society for their letter of congratulation, Hancock noted that he had 'watched with lively interest the great success' of the revival and promised to continue to support it.[14]

In the summer of 1846 a controversy erupted over one of the motions which had been debated in the previous session. On the surface it was innocuous enough, a motion inspired by Edmund Burke about whether a member of parliament should vote in accordance with the expressed opinions of the majority of his constituents, even when they differed from his own. However it provoked a furious reaction. The Church of Ireland Archbishop of Dublin, Richard Whately, one of the Visitors for the University, wrote a letter of complaint to the Provost. The controversy became public

13 Bridget Hourican, 'Sir Edward Sullivan', *DIB*.

14 Dagg, *CHS*, p. 190.

when he followed up by publishing a wider letter on the 'Danger of Debating Societies to Young Men' in the influential British journal, *Bentley's Miscellany* in June 1846.[15] Whately believed that the Burkean analysis of whether a member of parliament was a representative or a delegate was too deep a political question for students, and was more likely to 'generate a habit of talking without thinking'.

Whately extended his criticism to debating societies in general, with claims they were 'injurious to mental culture' and destructive to the interests of the students.[16] He levelled a number of charges, and made a number of strange recommendations. For example, he disliked having the debates decided by a majority of the students and wanted a moderator appointed to decide on the winning side, and he was also hugely critical of the value of extempore speeches. His greatest objection was to the questions being debated, and he argued that they were not suitable for a student intellect to understand. While recognising that the demand for regulations might force the students to establish their own society outside of the College walls, he argued that this would not necessarily be a bad thing, as it would at least not give 'the sanction of the University or College to a bad practice: the evil would be wholly at the door of the individuals concerned'.

The new Auditor decided to take on the Archbishop in his opening address, a courageous move in any circumstances, and even more so given that the Auditor was the first Catholic to be elected to the office in the history of the Society within the walls of Trinity. This was Denis Caulfield Heron, a remarkable young man who had just graduated from Trinity, and who had been a leading member of the final external society, before joining the new Society in 1844. Heron later recounted the excitement he had felt when he was elected by nine votes, and how it was taken as a sign that the students in Trinity were 'young men of ardent spirits who were possessed of no sectarian feelings towards their fellow students'.[17] For Heron it was a sign that 'a new era was about to dawn over Ireland', and

15 Richard Whately, 'Danger of Debating Societies to Young Men', *Bentley's Miscellany* (June 1846), vol. 19, pp 615-21.

16 Heron, *Address*, p. 4.

17 *Freeman's Journal*, 12 November 1868.

although he soon came to realize that sectarianism and exclusiveness had not been abolished, he still recognized his election as 'a most important matter'.

Heron had been prevented from becoming a Scholar in 1843, despite coming fifth out of all the students in the rigorous scholarship examination, because of his religion. Heron refused to attend the College Chapel and take Holy Communion or acquiesce in the religious requirements as other Catholics had done in the past.[18] Instead he appealed to the Visitors, and when they refused to hear his case he took it to court. The court ordered the Visitors to hear the case and what happened next became a part of College history. The Visitors, two Protestant Archbishops, decided against Heron, arguing that although Catholics could take degrees they couldn't become part of the body corporate. This led to a review and a Royal Commission in the 1850s resolved the issue of Catholics becoming scholars by creating a distinction between Foundation and non-Foundation Scholars. Heron, meanwhile, went on to become a successful lawyer and later Professor of Jurisprudence and Political Economy at Queen's College, Galway.

Heron's opening address was on the subject of self-education, and was a powerful defence of the functioning of the Society against the external attacks. It was delivered in the Dining Hall on 4 November 1846, 'the first night of the fourth session' according to the pamphlet published afterwards.[19] The Lord Chancellor Maziere Brady, was in the chair, and the gathering heard Heron celebrate the revival of the College Historical Society four years earlier. At the very start, Heron alluded to the question of his religion, and how in the past 'old prejudice' might have affected his election. But he took it was 'a marked token of the improved spirit of the age' that the election had not become 'a matter of misconstruction'.

Addressing the criticism of debating societies, Heron's response was respectful, and perfectly framed, as he rebutted the charges of the Archbishop of Dublin, and provided a robust defence of the Society and the value of debating in developing the intellect. Heron

---

18 Peter Boyle, *Trinity College Dublin: The Provosts, 1592-1927* (Dublin, 2015), p. 292.

19 Heron, *Address*, p. 4.

did not see a problem with extemporary speaking. He reassured the Archbishop that all speakers studied the subject in advance, and he suggested that there was nothing more valuable than being able to deploy his ideas, 'like a well-disciplined army, ready to turn and wheel, and assume every form, according to the mode of attack and the strength of the assailant'.[20] Someone with a pre-prepared speech risked marching 'like a column of undisciplined troops' straight ahead, no matter what, and could easily be picked off from the side.

For Heron the advantages of debating were three-fold: it provided 'a good manner, readiness of expression, and presence of mind'.[21] Addressing the suggestion that a moderator could choose the winning side, rather than a vote of the members, Heron argued that the whole point of debating was 'the cultivation of our powers of persuasion'.[22] He insisted if this was lost it was 'the end of oratory'. As for the charge that students did not have the intellect to understand the questions that were being debated, he asked where else would they be able to address the great questions of history if not at a university, 'When will we be old enough if we be not now?'

Another objection was that debating took students away from their studies. Heron denied this was the case, but argued that even if it was, then it was worth it because students needed a wider education, beyond what was learned in their college books. The narrow approach produced 'dry, chill, mechanical mere professional men'. But Heron argued that engagement in a society like theirs would augment 'our stores of language' and encourage 'a higher and more genial tone of character'.

Heron articulated what was one of the greatest strengths of the Society, then and into the future. It enabled students from different backgrounds and different political and religious viewpoints to mix with each other, exchange ideas, have their prejudices challenged, and their worldview transformed. As Heron explained, some students came to Trinity and only knew those 'who came from the same school, or county', becoming 'thus, one of a clique, his views all narrowed, his prejudices all confirmed). However, he insisted that

20 Ibid.

21 Ibid., p. 5.

22 Ibid., p.8.

the chief advantage of a university education was '*the enlarging of the mind to an enlightened sympathy with all*'.[23]

Heron felt that no real defence of the Society was necessary, as it was the heir to a system 'designed for us by the wisdom of ages', a system that had been 'tried by time, and which has stood the test'. 'We are the College Historical Society' he proudly declared. While Trinity was being dubbed 'the silent sister', the Society gave the College a voice 'full of melody and grandeur and destined to be heard'.

The Archbishop had also claimed that debating societies produced 'mere pleaders' who could appeal 'to the passions of illiterate jurymen'. Heron addressed that head on, referring to the great lawyers who had received their training in the Society, and referencing Charles Kendal Bushe. Discussing how the study of oratory produced some of the greatest figures in world history, from Demosthenes in Greece, to Cicero in Rome, he suggested that perseverance was the key to success, the ability to refuse to give in to failure, and to keep going no matter what.

Towards the close of the speech Heron made a reference to Emmet's rebellion in 1803, when 'bands of misguided peasants... with drunken shouts' marched on 'to horrid self-involving ruin'.[24] This was controversial, and afterwards some of Heron's friends challenged him for insulting 'poor Emmet's memory'.[25] But he explained that 'nothing could have been farther' from his intention, and he had merely been trying to contrast the 'horrors of war' in the age of rebellion, with 'the blessings of peace' in the age of railways.

Heron ended by delivering a powerful overview of how science was transforming the world, and urged the students to never lose sight of the patriotic spirit of wanting to improve their country. The final words were a tribute to the revived Society itself, calling on the students to 'win fame from the world, reflect honour on Ireland's university, and do good service for your native land', so that they could all say proudly in the future 'I too was a member of the College Historical Society'. Praising the speech afterwards, the Lord Chancellor declared that he had long attended many debating

---

23 Ibid., p. 10.

24 Ibid., p. 23.

25 Ibid., p. iv.

societies, 'but he had never heard a more impressive or a more eloquent and effective address delivered at any of them'.

We do not get much of a sense from the records of the impact of the Great Irish Famine on the Society or how it affected the tone and content of debates, but it does not appear to have changed things much. The Society, like Trinity itself, was cut-off and removed from the worst of what was happening across the country. As the Famine entered its worst year – 1847 – the Society passed a motion authorising the Treasurer to contribute ten pounds towards relief efforts in the city. This was a period when oratory became the dominant focus of the Society and away from history and poetry, as the Society re-established itself as primarily a debating Society.

Thomas Ebenezer Webb was Secretary of the Society in 1848-49. Ten years later, when he was appointed Professor of Moral Philosophy in Trinity, he revealed that nothing in his entire College career had given him as much pleasure as his connection with the Historical Society, insisting that the honours he had received there he regarded as 'the highest academic distinction I obtained'.[26] When he was starting out as a lawyer Webb displayed evidence of the training in eloquence and quick-thinking he had received in the Society. In one of his first cases he attempted to get a licence for a public house on Capel Street for his client, John McCarthy. However, there was an objection made claiming that McCarthy was too young. In a wonderful display of oratory, which settled the case in his favour, Webb reminded the court that Alexander the Great had crushed the Persian army by the age of twenty-two, Descartes had evolved a new system of philosophy by twenty-two, Pitt had become prime minister by twenty-four, Napoleon had scattered his enemies by twenty-four, and he ending his account by asking, 'at twenty-five is John McCarthy too young to manage a public house in Capel Street?' Webb went on to achieve distinction as a Judge and Regius Professor of Laws.

One of the greatest scientists in Ireland's history, William Rowan Hamilton, regretted that the Historical Society had not been around in College during his time as an undergraduate in the 1820s, so he enjoyed the opportunity to attend meetings and speak when he was

26 Dagg, *CHS*, p. 199.

a Professor in the 1840s. As a Fellow he was automatically an *ex-officio* member of the Society and he enjoyed the privileges that membership gave him. In November 1848 he was asked at short notice to second the motion of thanks to the Auditor at the inaugural meeting, and he did so without having had time to prepare anything in advance. In fact, he had not even time to change into academic dress, and he began his speech by apologising for not wearing a gown, which he insisted did not reflect 'the interest which he felt in this College Historical Society'.[27] Hamilton joked that he had entered Trinity at the wrong time – he had been too young to join the old Historical Society, and too old to join the new Society which had been readmitted in 1843. Listening to the speeches, he admitted, had brought back 'the emotions of youth', and he reminisced about how as a young man his heart had 'beat high with an ardour after fame' and how he valued his achievements more because of the support of 'generous rivals'.

In a poetic speech, Hamilton set out a vision of a more idealistic society, one where 'the useful, and even the utilitarian' were combined, 'as far as possible, with such idealism' as would advance the cause of Ireland. Praising the 'exuberant and lavish flow of Irish genius', which Hamilton noted sharply had even been acknowledged recently by *The Times,* he argued that this had the potential to change the world. This could be possible, he believed, by uniting the forces of 'reason and the imagination', and providing a car that would 'yoke the horses of the sun'.[28]

When attending the meetings of the Society, Hamilton enjoyed observing the cut-and-thrust of debate, and analysing how speakers constructed their arguments. He soon observed a trick some speakers used to make themselves appear more impressive. The artifice consisted of selecting the weakest arguments of an opponent and answering them at the beginning and end of a speech, and then leaving the most difficult points to rebut to the middle section where they could be dismissed 'with affected contempt'.[29]

---

27 Robert Perceval Graves, *Life of Sir William Rowan Hamilton* (3 vols, Dublin, 1882-89), vo. ii, 637.

28 Ibid., p. 638.

29 Ibid., p. 214.

A handful of the Auditors from this period achieved later distinction. The Auditor for the 1850–51 session was Hercules Henry Dickinson, and he became a Church of Ireland clergyman after his term ended. Vicar of St Ann's parish in Dublin for forty-seven years, he was a strong supporter of education for women. Together with Archbishop Richard Trench he helped found Alexandra College in 1866 and served as Warden and Chaplain.[30] The Provost, Francis Sadleir, died in December 1851. He was succeeded by Richard MacDonnell, who had done so much to restore the Society, and he became the new President of the Society on 4 February 1852.

The records for the Society in the years up to 1852 are not good, reflecting the way the Society went into a period of decline, with membership and attendance in decline, and debts increasing. This was addressed by the new Auditor of the Society, Frederick Graham Evelyn, at the start of the 1852–53 session, when he spoke of how 'apathy' was to blame for the 'declining state of our Society'.[31] He noted how many members did not attend the weekly meetings, choosing to go instead to other engagements, 'no matter how trifling'. An application for financial support was made to the Board in February 1853 and it received a positive response, in large part thanks to the support of the new Provost. £20 was given to the Society, and MacDonnell also sent a personal contribution of £2, but despite this support the Society remained in debt for five more years.

The opening of the 1853 session, on Wednesday 9 November 1853, was accompanied by some controversy when the Provost left the chair early, thus concluding the meeting. All had been going well as the new Auditor, Alexander George Richey, received the medal from the previous session, and delivered an impressive opening address. Ingram, now Professor of Oratory, was one of the respondents, and he gave a powerful tribute to Richey, who had been one of his former students. A hugely popular figure, Ingram was cheered loudly at the start and at the end of his speech. Isaac Butt was due to propose the traditional vote of thanks to the chairman, but the Provost seems to have been under some pressure and decided to end the meeting prematurely. The minutes tell part of the story, recording how 'the

30 David Murphy, 'Hercules Henry Dickinson', *DIB*.

31 Dagg, *CHS*, p. 192.

Provost *left the Chair* and *thereby* adjourned the meeting'. A student account records how the members kept shouting 'Butt! Butt!' as the Provost left the Dining Hall, just to annoy him. It was generally felt that the Provost 'behaved very shabbily'.[32] It seems MacDonnell had informed the Committee beforehand that he wanted to dispense with the traditional vote of thanks at the end, and Butt later admitted that 'as College men' they had taken his wishes as a command. MacDonnell's relations with the Society seem to have soured after this incident, and he resigned as President in 1855.

After leaving Trinity, Richey became a lawyer and historian and is considered to have broken 'new ground in the study of early Ireland'.[33] He became Deputy Regius Professor of Feudal and English Law at Trinity in 1871 and wrote a treatise on Irish land law that was quoted by Gladstone during the 1881 debate on the land bill.

The creation of a new student debating Society, the Undergraduate Philosophical Society, in 1853, posed a serious threat to the Historical Society. This other society, which was renamed the University Philosophical Society around 1870, was open to students in all years, and thus attracted the Freshman Students interested in debating who were unable to join the Historical Society until their final year. Lack of numbers had been a problem in the Society since its revival, and it was soon recognized that the other society was, in the words of the Provost, 'drafting off our men'.[34] The problem was that the majority of new students joined the Undergraduate Philosophical Society because it was the only one open to them, so that by the time they became Senior Sophisters they did not 'care to leave the place where they have won distinction and made friends to take the position of juniors in a rival society'.[35]

Changes needed to be made to the regulations or the Society risked being made redundant. Negotiations were opened with the Board to relax some of the regulations imposed on the Society. Following lengthy talks, it was agreed in November 1854 that Junior

---

32 G.B. Morgan to his mother, 10 November 1853, quoted in Dagg, *CHS*, p. 194.

33 Andrew O'Brien and Linde Lunney, 'Alexander George Richey', *DIB*.

34 See Dagg, *CHS*, p. 210.

35 Ibid.

Sophisters could be admitted for three years as an experiment. This proved a success, and in 1857 the rule was relaxed completely. It was also now permitted have a student chair the meetings if no senior person in College was able to do it.

At the opening of the 1854–55 session, the Auditor John Fox, urged members to remember the 'greatness of the "Old Historical"' but not to forget that there was an opportunity to 'emulate their triumphs'. Addressing the recent relaxation of the regulations, he insisted that the exclusion of Junior Sophisters had been a matter of complaint for many years and was considered 'justly obnoxious'. But he argued that the possibility of enrolling new members was meaningless unless the Society matched the potential increase in numbers with action, and he called on them to 'awake to exertion'.

In general the meetings that session were well-attended, although one debate had to be cancelled because of lack of interest. On 29 November 1854 the chairman spoke on the motion during the regular part of the debate from the chair, and this created some procedural concerns. It was afterwards agreed by the Society that in future the chairman would have to vacate the chair before speaking.

Joseph Napier, by this time a Member of Parliament, was elected as President of the Society following the resignation of the Provost and he was an inspired choice. He was a passionate supporter of the Society, and he delivered a major address at the close of meeting on Thursday 29 November 1855, reflecting on its history both within and outside of College. Napier addressed the role of the Society in the Trinity educational experience and he argued that it was 'not a supplemental part, it is integral'.[36] Suggesting that the Society 'must not be treated as an unwelcome intruder, only to be endured', he said it should be regarded 'as an established Institute which has a lawful claim to be generously encouraged' and which gave 'completeness to a liberal university education'. Napier insisted that an education would not be complete unless it contained an understanding of history, philosophy and poetry, and the context in which they were conceived.

In the vote of thanks, the Revd Dr W. D. Sadlier, a Senior Fellow,

36 Joseph Napier, *Address delivered at the close of the proceedings of the College Historical Society, 29 November 1855* (Dublin, 1855),p.3.

admitted that he had been seriously disturbed to hear the Provost had resigned as president, but he was reassured by the appointment of Napier. Despite being an MP, Napier chaired a number of the debates that session. Napier was President of the Society for the next twenty-eight years and despite all the pressures of work – including a brief period as Lord Chancellor– he continued to take an active role in the Society, and chaired its meetings frequently. It was noted that he took a special interest in encouraging members of the Society, and many 'young men of promise owed their first successful start in life to help or influence he exerted on their behalf'.[37]

Following a precedent established by the one of the external societies, women were allowed attend the final meeting of the 1856–57 session. The debate on Wednesday 10 June 1857, which closed the session, was long remembered for the eloquence on display. Chaired by Napier, a large number of students and visitors, men and women, gathered in the Dining Hall to hear a debate on whether Lord Grey's reform bill was framed in accordance with the wants of the country. Isaac Butt was one of the speakers on the proposition, with two young members, David Plunket and Edward Gibson, in opposition. The motion passed, and at the end Napier delivered an emotional address from the chair. He revealed that he had been going through his old papers and had discovered the closing address he had delivered to the Society in 1828. Noting that 'it was not delivered within the walls of the university', he spoke of how 'we were then exiled, we were obliged to take shelter outside in the city'. He then revealed that he written the address within the walls of Trinity, and admitted he had been unable to read it back without feeling 'deep and thrilling emotion'.[38] Napier was appointed Lord Chancellor of Ireland in March 1858 and received a congratulatory address from the Society.

Following on from the successful final meeting, the Society decided to issue invitations to allow women attend the opening meeting of the new session on 11 November 1857 in what was considered a bold move. This was, however, objected to by the

37 Alexander Charles Ewald (ed.), *The Life and Letters of the Right Honourable. Sir Joseph Napier, Bart* (London, 1892), p. 8.

38 Dagg, *CHS*, p. 198.

Provost at the last minute, and the cards were withdrawn on the evening of the meeting.[39] The innovation of allowing women to attend meetings of the Society was killed.

In this period new members of the Society were beginning to establish themselves in the Society. For example, a debate on the Act of Union ('That the Act of Union cannot be Defended on Grounds of Moral or Political Rectitude') was proposed by Edward Gibson, and opposed by a new member, John Pentland Mahaffy. Other notable speakers were W.E.H. Lecky and David Plunket. After years in the wilderness, it had taken over a decade for the Society to re-establish itself on firm grounds, and a new golden age of oratory was about to begin.

39 *Freeman's Journal*, 11 November 1857.

8 THE SECOND GOLDEN AGE OF ORATORY, 1858-1865

IT IS INVIDIOUS to describe any period of a Society's history as 'a golden age'; invariably every period has examples of genius and mediocrity, greatness and decline. But there was something particularly special about the energy in the Society in the late 1850s and early 1860s and for many years after people looked to that period of the Society's history when they talked about its greatness. Partly this was due to the quality of the oratory on display every week, partly it was due to the fame and distinction so many of the prominent individuals subsequently achieved. These were names which resonated in the late-nineteenth century: Edward Gibson, David Plunket, W.E.H. Lecky, Gerald FitzGibbon, as well as Robert Anderson, who was the lead police investigator during the Jack the Ripper murders.

This was also a period when the Society was at last on a stable financial footing. The Society had built up serious debts in the 1850s after a period of careless management, but these debts were finally discharged in the summer of 1858. In his opening address at the start of the 1858-59 session, the new Auditor, Edward Gibson, celebrated the liquidation of the debt 'bequeathed to us by the generosity of our predecessors'. The main argument in Gibson's address was how the study of oratory should be made compulsory in the university.

Gibson had been privately educated because of health problems, but these seem to have disappeared when he entered Trinity in 1853. A remarkable intellect, he graduated BA (1858) with a first in history, political science, and English literature and received a gold medal in each of the three subjects.[1] Considered an articulate and forceful

1 Patrick Maume, 'Edward Gibson', *DIB*.

orator, Gibson was one of the most dazzling speakers in the Society, but there was much competition, including from two of his closest friends, David Robert Plunket (a grandson of William Plunket on his father's side and Charles Kendal Bushe on his mother's) and William Edward Hartpole Lecky. All three received the gold medal for oratory from the Society (Gibson in 1857, Plunket in 1858, Lecky in 1859) and all three would go on to represent the University of Dublin constituency in the British House of Commons. In 1891 they were reunited for the annual Trinity alumni dinner in London, and it prompted them to reminisce about their time together in the Society. Lecky spoke after the dinner, and Plunket praised his speech for being 'so eloquent, so graceful, and in such perfect taste', and commented on how much it reminded him of 'the far-off hills of our old friendship.'

Lecky had developed a passion for oratory as a young boy and he found a home in the Historical Society. There he overcame his shyness and hesitancy and developed the confidence to embark on a career as a politician and a man of letters. Few would have predicted such things before he joined the Society. Many believed Lecky was destined to become a clergyman, and his poor academic performances (he graduated with a pass degree in 1859, and was relieved to do so) did not mark him out for greatness. But he mastered the art of oratory and Edward Gibson always spoke of how winning the gold medal 'had a considerable effect on his [Lecky's] character and future'.[2]

Lecky would prepare his speeches during long walks on the West Pier at Kingstown (now Dún Laoghaire), and he would then write a few notes on a slip of paper, about two inches long and one inch wide, which he would crumple up in his waistcoat pocket and take out whenever he needed reminding of his arguments.[3] The study of oratory became an obsession. His library was full of the speeches of the great Irish orators, and every Sunday he went to Trinity Church on Gardiner Street to hear Dr John Gregg ('Good John Gregg'), considered at the time the greatest pulpit orator in Dublin. Inspired

---

2 [Elisabeth Lecky] *A memoir of the Right Hon. William Edward Hartpole Lecky, by his wife* (London, 1903), p. 206.

3 Dagg, *CHS*, p. 206.

by this, in the evening, Lecky would practice delivering extempore speeches in his rooms in Trinity.

A former member of the Society, James Whiteside, was another favourite, and Lecky often attended the courts to see him in action. He was especially impressed by a humorous speech Whiteside delivered to the Society in May 1859, which he considered 'one of the most imposing I have ever heard'.[4] Although Whiteside 'spurned grammar, trampled on logic, and condemned consistency', he did it in such a brilliant way that Lecky could not help admiring the style. It was, he admitted, 'splendid nonsense'.

1858–59 was the most successful year in the Society since its revival, with membership increasing by 25 per cent, and debates in this session were wide-ranging. One motion was that the Ottoman conquests in Europe were beneficial to the progress of civilisation. Another was 'That the present mode of conducting capital punishment is objectionable'. Lecky spoke in favour of the motion on capital punishment, with Plunket against. The debate on whether England was bound to prevent the fall of Poland because of national self-interest was supported by Anthony Traill, a future Provost. John Kells Ingram was in the chair for the debate on 23 February 1859 on whether 'if Swift had never written, his silence ought not to be regretted'. Lecky spoke against the motion, and it was defeated by a large majority. Lecky and Plunket both spoke in favour of the motion that Carlyle's estimate of Cromwell is correct, but the motion was defeated heavily. During this session Lecky rose and delivered a speech that won enormous praise and was credited with raising 'the standard of debating rhetoric enormously'.[5] Thomas Snagge, who later became a distinguished judge, recorded how at the end of one evening, Lecky 'rose to his feet and, to the amazement of us all, poured forth a stream of mellifluous and finished eloquence that carried all before him. It was meteoric'. For Snagge it was not so much a speech as a recited essay, but no less brilliant for all of that. Another speaker who gained in reputation during the year was Gerald FitzGibbon, and Lecky predicted that he would be 'the star' of the following session.[6]

---

4 Ibid., p. 207.

5 Ibid., p. 206.

The debate on 6 April 1859 was a particularly heated one. The motion was 'That Pitt's Policy towards Ireland was Partial and Unjust' and it allowed for a rigorous critique of the Act of Union of 1800. The Lord Chancellor (and President of the Society) Napier was in the chair, and the debate was opened by Lecky who delivered a powerful speech in favour of the motion. After four members had spoken, Plunket proposed an amendment: 'that, while the general objects of Pitt's policy in carrying the union were good, the means adopted to effect it were impolitic and disgraceful'. This amendment was, however, defeated by fourteen votes to 8. The original motion was then put to the house and it passed by sixteen votes to 8. Napier addressed the Society from the chair and expressed his support for the majority decision.

The session closed on Wednesday 15 June 1859 with a debate on whether the growth of journalism is beneficial to Society. Close to four hundred people attended, and Lecky was given the task of opening the debate, and replying at the end. Lecky delivered an attack on political clergy and, although he was not satisfied with his performance afterwards, it was considered a great success. The next day *The Irish Times* called it 'a speech of considerable argumentative ability and extraordinary fluency'.[7] At the end of the meeting it was announced that Lecky had won the gold medal for oratory. Napier spoke from the chair and joked that the Presidency of the Society, unlike the Lord Chancellorship which was regularly under threat (and which he was about to lose), was something 'which no government could confer on him, and of which no opposition could deprive him'.

The *Daily Express* covered the meeting in detail, noting that 'if this were merely a discussion by an ordinary debating society it would scarcely deserve any special notice from the press'.[8] But it recognized that the College Historical Society was 'a society composed of the most distinguished students, and therefore deserved wider discussion'.

David Plunket won the gold medal for oratory at the end of that

6 Ibid., p. 205.

7 *The Irish Times*, 6 June 1859.

8 *Daily Express*, 16 June 1859.

session and he succeeded Gibson as Auditor. On 9 November 1859 he delivered a brilliant opening address to the Society at the start of the new session. It was delivered rather than read, and Lecky proclaimed that 'it was one of the finest addresses I ever heard', praising the delivery as 'finer than that of any speaker I know'.[9] *The Irish Times* reported how Plunket, 'in a very argumentative and able manner' was able to show 'that the exercise of eloquence on the platform was more important and influential now than at any former period'.[10] Plunket spoke on the importance of oratory, and warned students to avoid what he called 'the "artful dodges" of rhetoric'. He encouraged them to always speak on the side of the question they genuinely believed, and avoid affecting 'any excitement which you do not feel, or putting forward any argument in which you do not fully believe'.[11]

The speech ended with a rallying call for patriotism, reminding members that when the Society had been founded originally it had been at a time when 'the spirit of an awakening freedom and a new-born nationality began to breathe upon this land'. For ninety years, he declared, it had 'sent forth the best and greatest Irishmen', and the power of eloquence had raised the Irish from 'torpor and slavery' into being free. Eloquence had helped secure emancipation, and had provided hope and comfort during 'times of plague, of rebellion, of famine'. He ended by concluding that if potential new members were not 'roused by ambition – if you care not for friendship or good fellowship – if you are cold to patriotism' then he had 'no wish that you should become one of us'. Lecky believed that following this display of eloquence Plunket was 'pretty much at the head of the living speakers in Ireland'.

Two of the distinguished guests in attendance, Blackburne and Whiteside, moved votes of thanks, and Napier delivered a powerful defence of a broad university education from the chair, arguing that when it came to students' best long-term interests universities should not be 'cramming them, and hemming them for particular departments in life', but should allow him 'to cultivate all his faculties,

9 Dagg, *CHS*, p. 205.

10 *The Irish Times*, 10 November 1859.

11 Dagg, *CHS*, p. 203.

his genius, the feelings of his heart' and thus lay the foundations for wisdom, happiness, and citizenship. At this meeting Gibson was awarded the gold medal for composition, and, according to Lecky, his essay was 'praised to the skies' by Napier who awarded it.[12]

That session the debates were not as well attended as the previous year, but there were some standout meetings. On 14 December the motion was 'That the System of Flogging in Public Schools is Attended with Good Results'. Once again Pitt's policy towards Ireland was debated, and once again Lecky argued that the Union was impartial and unjust. This was the time when Lecky was working on the first edition of his *Leaders of Public Opinion,* which he published anonymously in 1861. It was reviewed in the *Cork Examiner* by someone who looked at the internal evidence and concluded that the author was connected with Trinity. Thinking of that debate, he guessed correctly that the author was 'perhaps one of that patriotic band who in 1860 introduced the question of the Union into the Historical Debating Society'.[13]

Present day politics was now the dominant focus of the debates, encouraged by the tacit approval of the Board. On 15 February 1860 the house debated whether the influence of *The Times* newspaper was detrimental to the interest of society, but it was not a popular motion and only Lecky spoke in favour. A motion on the Suez Canal scheme and whether it was desirable, was supported by Plunket and opposed by Lecky. The students were not warmly disposed to the total abstinence movement, and a motion claiming it deserved 'our warmest sympathy and support' was heavily defeated. There was a debate on the Opium trade, and even a motion on whether the Piedmontese government should have supported Garibaldi's expedition. The outbreak of the American Civil War promoted a special closing debate, 'That the Coercion of the Southern States of America was Neither Justifiable nor Expedient'. The motion was defeated and the Society would return to the subject over the course of the conflict.

Attempts were made to address the problem the Society had faced since its revival, the fact that it 'laboured under a truly deplorable

12 TCD HIST/MUN/SOC/29; Dagg, *CHS*, p. 205.

13 Dagg, *CHS*, p. 403. *Cork Examiner,* 7 February 1862.

deficiency of members'.[14] In March 1861 an attempt was made to approach the Board about allowing associate membership of the Society to Freshman students. There was a reasonable expectation that the approach would succeed, as the Provost had indicated his support for extending the membership, in part because the Undergraduate Philosophical Society was 'drafting off our men'.[15] However, the motion was opposed by an overwhelming majority, as the Society chose to maintain voluntarily the restriction which had been imposed on it arbitrarily. Enforced rules were protected as traditions, and Plunket, FitzGibbon and other leading members opposed the proposal.

The student who brought the motion forward, Henry John Wrixon, was elected Auditor for the new session, and in April 1862 he proposed it a second time, but again it was rejected. This time, following a procedural change, he was allowed include into the minutes a memorandum justifying a proposal and it outlined its merits. Associate membership would have allowed Freshmen attend and speak at the debates, though they would not have been allowed submit oratory returns or compete for prizes. Wrixon explained that the Undergraduate Philosophical Society recruited many of its potential members, and he noted that no one who had been a distinguished member of that Society for the past three years had gone on to become 'a working member of the College Historical Society'. One proposal which did succeed that session was one to create a new type of honorary membership, to ensure that members of the Society could continue to attend and be involved after graduation, without being able to serve as officers or compete for prizes.

Although born in Cork, Wrixon was raised in Australia, and he returned there after graduation, becoming a successful barrister. He served in the Victorian Legislative Assembly and as Solicitor General and Attorney General, and went to London in 1890 to represent Victoria in the Toy case, asserting the power of the colonies to refuse to admit people. His argumentation was impressive and he persuaded the Privy Council to reverse its judgement.[16] Wrixon ended his days

14 Dagg, *CHS*, p. 210.

15 Ibid.

16 Joseph McNabb, 'Sir Henry John Wrixon', *DIB*.

as President of the Victorian Legislative Council (1901-10) and Vice-Chancellor of the University of Melbourne (1897-1910).

On 13 March 1862 the Society voted on whether the office of Lord Lieutenant should be abolished, and the motion was carried. The meeting was chaired by Napier, and he admitted that he had once voted against abolition but had come to change his opinion after learning that so many of the Chief Secretaries had also come to share that view.[17]

Speeches were restricted to a maximum of thirty minutes, but on 9 December 1863 Maurice Hime proposed a motion to reduce the primary speakers to twenty-five, and the subsequent speakers to ten. This was prompted by his prejudice that the students 'must be rather stupid asses' because they were not distinguishing themselves academically.[18] The motion limiting speeches was written-out by Richard Ouseley Blake Lane, who posted and seconded the motion, but when it came to the discussion it was roundly destroyed. George Chadwick ridiculed Hime for thinking they were 'incapable of speaking because we do not get scholarship or honours', reminding him 'that an orator is born not made'. And he taunted him by suggesting that 'a man may win College honours and yet not know how to spell'. This was a reference to the text of the motion which Lane had written-out and spelled 'limitted' with two 't's. Chadwick suggested that the proposers might have limited the number of 't's when writing the motion and spelt 'limited' with one 't'. In the vote the proposal was, in Hime's own words, 'beaten hollow'.

The 1863–64 session was notable for having perhaps the worst Auditor in the history of the Society. Thomas Teignmouth Shore was only in office for the first two months of the session, but although he was a great friend of Lecky he took a detached approach to the Society. After delivering his opening address, and attending the first regular meeting of Society, he seems to have cut off his involvement completely. The Committee later decided that his conduct was 'deserving of the greatest censure of the Society' because of the way he never attended again, or arranged for a substitute, or 'attempted to offer any excuse for his absence'. Instead he 'entirely

17 *Cork Examiner*, 6 August 1866.

18 Dagg, *CHS*, p. 216.

disregarded the repeated remonstrances which were addressed to him' regarding his conduct.[19] After two months he stepped down to become a clergyman and was replaced by Robert Anderson, a Presbyterian. Anderson shared a similar reluctance to attend meetings of the Society, and in January 1865 a modification was made to the Society's laws requiring an Auditor to attend at least two-thirds of the meetings.

Anderson often reflected on his time in the Society afterwards. In his first memoir he noted that the question of his religion was of no more account in his dealings with the College authorities, or his fellow members in the Society, than 'whether I drank tea or coffee for breakfast'.[20] For him the great strength of the Society, and College in general, was that everyone met 'on perfectly even terms, and learned not only to hear, but to respect opinions and convictions which we did not share. Thought was free and sympathies were generous.'

The remarkable career of Anderson afterwards is worthy of mention. Engaged in secret service work shortly after leaving Trinity, Anderson became a key figure in the campaign against the Fenians, and went on to have a significant career at Scotland Yard. In 1909 he was praised in *The Strand Magazine* as someone who was 'for many years regarded as a terror to evil-doers and as the chief criminal expert in the country'.[21] 'Aggressive and dogmatic in his approach, he is described in the *Oxford Dictionary of National Biography* as a 'spymaster, detective chief, and author'.[22] In the middle of the Jack the Ripper murders he was put in charge of the Criminal Investigation Department (CID) but he was noticeably unsympathetic to the victims. He believed it was 'enough to say' that the women all belonged 'to a very small class of degraded women' and he later claimed to have stopped the murders by telling prostitutes the police would no longer be able to protect them.[23] Praised in his lifetime for

---

19 Dagg, *CHS*, p. 217.

20 Robert Anderson, *Sidelights on the Home Rule Movement* (New York, 1906), p. 29.

21 *The Strand Magazine* (November 1909), p. 535.

22 Bernard Porter, 'Robert Anderson', *ODNB*.

23 Robert Anderson, *The Lighter Side of My Official Life* (London, 1910), p. 136.

his scholarship, his books included *Crime and Criminals* and *Sidelights on the Home Rule Movement,* as well as theological studies where he argued that the Bible should be read literally.

In November 1909, now Sir Robert Anderson, he published a short account of his life in *The Strand Magazine,* and there followed further accounts in *Blackwood's Magazine* and these were soon put together into a book of reminiscences, *The Lighter Side of my Official Life* in 1910. In the book, Anderson celebrated the way he had developed as a speaker, despite his initial nerves and attributed 'any little capacity I have for public speaking' to his time in the College Historical Society.[24] He had good memories of his time at Trinity, but he said his fondest were of his time in the various clubs and societies, 'and first and chiefest to the famous College Historical'. He described the tension he had experienced before his maiden speech, and the confidence he had derived from it going well, and took this and his election as Auditor, as evidence 'that a man can do what he makes up his mind to do'.

The articles in *Blackwood's Magazine* and the subsequent book received huge attention at the time because of his admission that in May 1887 he had written the infamous series of articles on 'Parnellism and Crime' for *The Times,* published anonymously, which alleged that Charles Stewart Parnell was complicit in Irish terrorism.[25] The British Prime Minister, Herbert Asquith, in a response to a question in parliament from John Redmond, criticised Anderson for departing from 'the rules and traditions of the civil service', although Anderson was technically out of office at the time. Winston Churchill, then Home Secretary, criticised the 'spirit of great boastfulness' of Anderson's work and the 'spiteful' approach taken to his enemies. But Anderson was unapologetic.[26] Joseph Conrad later admitted that Anderson's accounts of his secret service activities in *Sidelights on the Home Rule Movement* was used as source material for his novel *The Secret Agent* (1907).

Robert Walsh, the Auditor of the 1864–65 session, delivered a superb history of the Society as his opening address in November

24 Anderson, *Lighter Side*, p. 6.

25 Ibid., appendix.

26 Bernard Porter, 'Robert Anderson', *ODNB.*

1864, and some chapters of this book have drawn on his work. During this session there was another debate on the American Civil War, on 8 February 1865 shortly before the war ended, and this time there was narrow support for the Confederacy, as the motion 'That the interests of humanity require the recognition of the Southern States of America' passed. A motion on giving women the franchise was soundly defeated. The following year, Richard O'Shaughnessy's opening address was on sociology, and this created a precedent where addresses covered a wide range of subjects and not the usual ones of oratory, history, and the Society itself.[27] As we will see in the next chapter, the decision by the next Auditor, Richard Ouseley Blake Lane, to discuss international politics in his inaugural would plunge the Society into one of its biggest controversies.

And what became of the golden generation and their leaders, Gibson, Plunket, Lecky and FitzGibbon? After graduation Edward Gibson became a barrister, but his real interest was politics. As we shall see in a later chapter, he became MP for the University of Dublin in 1875 and was appointed Attorney General for Ireland in 1877 in the Conservative Government. He is credited with rejuvenating the office and was 'more influential in determining Irish policy and defending it at Westminster than the Chief Secretary'.[28]

In the *Oxford Dictionary of National Biography*, Alvin Jackson writes that 'Gibson occupied a position of some prominence in the House of Commons, and he quickly built upon this through his informed and mellifluous speeches on Irish matters.... Unruffled by challenge, and persuasive in debate' he won the confidence of Disraeli, and became his principal adviser on Irish affairs in the 1880s.[29] After the death of Disraeli he worked with Sir Stafford Northcote, the Conservative leader in the House of Commons and 'one or two commentators even thought him a potential Prime Minister'.[30]

When Lord Salisbury became Prime Minister in 1885 he offered Gibson the job of Home Secretary. To the astonishment of many he turned this down to become Lord Chancellor of Ireland along with a

27 Dagg, *CHS*, p. 223.

28 Patrick Maume, 'Edward Gibson', *DIB*.

29 Alvin Jackson, 'Edward Gibson', *ODNB*.

30 Patrick Maume, 'Edward Gibson', *DIB*.

seat in Cabinet, and he became the only Lord Chancellor of Ireland to be given this honour. And so he went to the House of Lords as Baron Ashbourne. Many historians have wondered why he turned down the office of Home Secretary, with some speculation that he preferred the office of Lord Chancellor because it was significantly more lucrative. Jackson suggests the decision 'may be explained by Gibson's polite but cool relations with Salisbury, and by his desire to make financial provision for his large family' but it remains unclear.[31] Within days he began working on the 1885 Land Purchase Act and single-handedly drafted the legislation that is known as the Ashbourne Act. As Patrick Maume has written, 'Although the Ashbourne Act provided the relatively limited sum of £4 million, it laid down the method which was to be the basis for all future land purchase legislation.'[32] He was reappointed Lord Chancellor in 1886 (threatening to resign if not given a place in Cabinet again) and held the office again in the 'Conservative and Unionist governments of 1885–92 and 1895–1905', though Maume suggests 'he was never again a figure of more than departmental importance'.[33] As Lord Chancellor his 'judicial manner was marked by geniality and considerable "sound common sense", though limited legal knowledge'.[34] In 1898 he published a scholarly study of William Pitt entitled *Pitt: some Chapters of his Life and Times*. An adviser to successive Conservative leaders, Maume notes that in 'his last years Ashbourne won acceptance as a minor elder statesman'. He died in 1913.

Alvin Jackson suggests that Ashbourne 'lacked the ruthless political ambition of a Salisbury or a Randolph Churchill; and he lacked the remorseless physical and intellectual energy of a Gladstone or Lloyd George'.[35] It is possible that 'the effort of climbing the greasy pole of Conservative politics between 1875 and 1885 … exhausted his political energies. Or, perhaps, having made the ascent, he felt that the view was not worth the effort of sustaining.' Ashbourne's daughter, Violet, achieved international notoriety in

31 Alvin Jackson, 'Edward Gibson', *ODNB*.

32 Patrick Maume, 'Edward Gibson', *DIB*.

33 Ibid.

34 Ibid.

35 Alvin Jackson, 'Edward Gibson', *ODNB*.

1926 when she shot and wounded slightly Benito Mussolini in Italy. She was deported and spent the remainder of her life in an asylum in Northampton.

Despite achieving high office, David Plunket never quite achieved his potential. He became a barrister after graduation but his interests were always political. After running unsuccessfully for parliament in 1868, he was returned unopposed for Dublin University in 1870 and he held the seat for twenty-five years. One of his most successful interventions in the British House of Commons was to pass a resolution in 1873 requiring civil servants in Britain and Ireland to be paid the same and this was achieved despite considerable opposition from the Treasury. As the *Dictionary of Irish Biography* notes, 'In parliament Plunket was a skilful speaker and was soon recognized as one of the finest orators in the Commons.'[36] Considered a master of 'the grand style in parliamentary oratory', he was the proponent of a style that was all but dying away.[37] Indeed Plunket was later hailed as 'the last of the old-style parliamentary orators'.[38] *The Times* praised him as one of the most eloquent parliamentary speakers of the 1870s and 1880s.[39] A committed Unionist, he was regularly consulted for his views on Irish affairs.

Somewhat reluctantly, he accepted the post of Solicitor General for Ireland (1875–57), perhaps recognising that it would put a limit on his ambitions. Because of the quality of his oratory, Plunket was considered a power in the Commons. Gladstone was a political opponent but he respected Plunket because of his eloquence, most notably on the Irish land bill of 1881. In 1884 Plunket opposed the extension of the franchise to all male heads of households, regardless of property qualifications, arguing that it would help create a separate Irish nationality. Plunket served two terms as First Commissioner of Works (1885–86) and (1886–92). He retained his seat in the 1895 general election but resigned soon after to go to the House of Lords as Baron Rathmore of Shanganagh, Co. Dublin. He

36 P. M. Geoghegan, 'David Plunket', *DIB*.

37 T.H.S. Escott, *Social transformations in the Victorian Age* (London, 1897), p. 147

38 *The Contemporary Review* (1919), p. 668.

39 *The Times*, 28 August 1919.

was closely involved in the development of the Central London Railway, one of the earliest underground lines in London. He died in 1919.

W.E.H. Lecky became one of the most successful historians of the nineteenth century. As Donal McCartney writes in the *Dictionary of Irish Biography*, he 'was praised for his impartiality, judiciousness, moral tone, and liberal sympathies' and 'remained in the great tradition of the nineteenth-century English amateur historians.'[40] He wrote seven volumes on the history of England in the eighteenth century and five volumes of a history of Ireland in the eighteenth century.

As McCartney notes 'Irish nationalists, Gladstone, and other leading liberals all quoted from Lecky's historical work on Ireland in support of an independent Irish parliament'. But Lecky himself was a landowner, horrified by Parnellism, and he began writing pro-Unionist pamphlets. In 1892 Lord Salisbury offered him the Regius Professorship at Oxford but he turned it down, preferring to remain free of lecturing and other academic commitments. In 1895 Lecky succeeded Plunket as MP for Dublin University in the by-election and he took 'part in debates on the land bill of 1896, the local government bill of 1898, and the Department of Agriculture and Technical Instruction Bill of 1899. He spoke also in favour of university education for Catholics'.[41] A founding Fellow of the British Academy, he died in 1903.

In the *Oxford Dictionary of National Biography* Joseph Spence suggests that Lecky 'stood at the crossroads in the evolution of history writing between the age of the gentleman scholar in the library and that of the professional scholar in the archives'.[42] He hails him as 'a sharp critic of the careless or deliberately misleading application of arguments from Irish history to justify the patriotic cause' and believes that 'he was, therefore, both the first national historian of Ireland and the first "revisionist" of the nationalist idealization of Ireland.'

Considered 'the most brilliant of a brilliant generation produced

40 Donal McCartney, 'William Edward Hartpole Lecky', *DIB*.

41 Ibid.

42 Joseph Spence, 'W.E.H. Lecky, *ODNB*.

by the College', Gerald FitzGibbon became a Queen's Counsel in 1872 at the age of thirty-five.[43] As Patrick Maume writes in the *Dictionary of Irish Biography* he was 'the dominant figure in Irish legal circles for more than a generation. His powers of persuasion as a barrister were formidable and he was well known for his success in virtually every case he took in the Irish courts'. In 1873 he was the counsel for Fr Robert O'Keeffe in his libel action against Cardinal Paul Cullen. Despite all the odds, he won a verdict for O'Keeffe and this 'was regarded as one of his greatest forensic achievements'.[44] However, the verdict was later overturned by the Lord Chief Justice, James Whiteside, on the grounds of misdirection.

Ambitious for a political career, FitzGibbon made the mistake of standing aside in the 1875 by-election in the University of Dublin to allow Lord Cairns to run his protégé, a former Treasurer of the Society, Alexander Miller. This was a mistake as Edward Gibson stood against Miller and won and there was a noticeable cooling in FitzGibbon's friendship with Gibson after this. FitzGibbon became law adviser to Dublin Castle and was Solicitor General in Ireland (1877–78) and in 1878 he became a Lord Justice of Appeal. As a judge he was said to apply common sense, seeking 'to decide what the just outcome would be and then used his formidable dialectical skills to provide legal justification for it'.[45] FitzGibbon became a friend and mentor to Lord Randolph Churchill and was Churchill's candidate for Lord Chancellor of Ireland in 1886, but lost out to Gibson (now Lord Ashbourne). He died in 1909.

After his death both *The Times* and the Lord Chief Justice praised Fitzgibbon's judicial career 'and were unstinting in their praise of his devotion to the service of his country, his judicial integrity, and his social gifts'.[46] As his entry in the *Oxford Dictionary of National Biography* concludes, 'such a reference to an Irish judge from the English bench was unprecedented'.

43 Patrick Maume, 'Gerald FitzGibbon', *DIB*.

44 Ibid.

45 Ibid.

46 Sinead Agnew, 'Gerald FitzGibbon', *ODNB*.

'AN ECHO OF OLD TIMES': THE CONTROVERSY OF 1866

9

THE MOST CONTROVERSIAL inaugural paper – though not the most controversial inaugural meeting – in the history of the Society took place in the Dining Hall on 14 November 1866. The title of the paper was 'Science in Politics', but really it was about 'The Balance of Power in Europe', and it provoked immediate uproar, and generated waves of controversy that reverberated for weeks afterwards. One member, James Andrews, later described it as 'one of the greatest scenes of disorder at any of the meetings' he had ever attended.[1] At the centre of the controversy was the Auditor, Richard Ouseley Blake Lane, who felt obliged to tender his resignation afterwards as the address received massive coverage in local, national and British newspapers. Even Lane's attempt to resign was not without controversy and proved more difficult that he had imagined. It was traditional for opening addresses to be followed by two votes at the end of the meeting, one a vote of thanks to the Auditor, and the second a vote recommending the Society publish the address at its own expense. Neither vote was passed at the inaugural meeting. Instead it provoked a mixture of reactions amongst those present, ranging from profound anger and disgust to loud support. It was one of the most remarkable episodes in the entire history of the Society.

The Auditor at the centre of the storm, Richard Ouseley Blake Lane, was a large man, six foot four inches tall, and weighing fourteen stone, and had a reputation as 'a wag' and a troublemaker.[2] Despite his size, Lane was a successful athlete and was able to throw himself

1 Dagg, *CHS*, p. 227.

2 Ibid., p. 233.

over five feet in the university's high jump competition, and he was also a winner in weight-throwing. He had been a talented student, becoming a Scholar, and had recently graduated with his BA. Lane had been embroiled in controversy before. In his earlier years he had been a member of the Philosophical Society and he 'incurred the ire of the College authorities' when he read a satirical paper praising 'Fast' men at the expense of the 'Slow'. So there was some speculation afterwards that Lane was 'pulling the legs of his audience' with this inaugural address. From reading the paper it is clear that this was not intended as satire, although Lane clearly knew he was going to provoke a violent reaction. A profound meditation on European politics, and a devastating critique of British imperialism, it was no wonder that it provoked such a reaction.

Almost sixty years later, when Alfred Perceval Graves, a member of the Society, was asked for his recollections of the 'College Historical' he responded by recounting the story of that inaugural meeting, describing it as his 'most vivid recollection' and 'an eloquent and well-reasoned plea'.[3] Lane's speech was made possible by the College's relaxation of its own rules on the discussion of party politics. He mentioned this himself in his opening, when he praised the Society's 'marked inclination' in recent years 'to bring before your notice questions of present social and political importance'.

For the occasion the Dining Hall was packed with dignitaries as well as students. Napier, as President, was in the chair, and the guests included James Whiteside, the newly appointed Lord Chief Justice; the Lord Mayor; a number of judges and MPs; Sir William Wilde; Sir Robert Kane, the President of Queen's College, Cork; and many fellows and former members. Lane received much applause when he stood to speak, but very soon there were jeers as his attacks on British imperialism drew the ire of many of those present. Declaring that Britain would have to 'modify her maritime supremacy, her commercial rapacity, and her imperial arrogance', he insisted that Gibraltar must be handed over to Spain to 'evince the genuineness of her sympathy with European national rights'.[4] *The Irish Times* reported extensively on the speech the next day, and noted that while

3 Ibid.

4 Ibid., p. 224.

the criticisms of Britain received 'great applause', there were also repeated 'hisses'.[5]

Some of the language used was incendiary. Lane insisted that Britain had 'laughed to scorn every moral duty; she has forgotten every principle of justice'. British rule in Ireland was directly condemned, as Lane discussed 'six centuries of stupid oppression'. Lane admitted that it was not just foreign powers who had 'had their prosperity blighted by the commercial rapacity and domineering pride of imperial England. Nearer home a cry of misery has for centuries been ringing in her ears, exhorted from the bitter degradation of oppressed and suffering Ireland'. Lane believed it was no surprise that 'Ireland should prove a constant thorn in the side of the country which has so consistently wronged and misgoverned her'. And he suggested that Britain had 'been compelled from time to time to reap the whirlwind she has sown' (hisses and cheering).[6]

In later years the address received some praise for foreshadowing the League of Nations (before it was shown to be a failure), or the United Nations, as Lane called for the creation of a 'Confederacy of the West' to avoid future wars or anarchy.[7] Lane spoke of his dream of a time of 'universal peace, when war, with its long train of evils, shall be reduced to a minimum', and he quoted Tennyson in support:

> Till the war-drum throbb'd no longer, and the battle-flags were furl'd,
> In the Parliament of man, the Federation of the world.

The Irish Times reports that 'great confusion was here created which continued for some time, and during which there were frequent cries of "withdraw", "retract" etc.'

It took some time for Napier in the chair to 'quell the uproar and restore order', and the meeting was allowed continue. As the *Nation* reported, 'grave dons stirred uneasily on their chairs and looked about as if they expected to see apparitions of Robert Emmet and Wolfe Tone in some corner of the room'.[8] Lane explained that he

5 *The Irish Times*, 15 November 1866.

6 Ibid.

7 Dagg, *CHS*, p. 224.

8 *Nation*, 17 November 1862.

was trying to contrast the past with the present, but there was more uproar and shouts of 'Put him out.' Lane concluded his address despite the barrage of abuse that battled with the loud cheers. He sat down to huge applause.

Confusion and chaos reigned. The traditional vote of thanks was due to have been proposed by the Lord Chief Justice, Whiteside, and seconded by Mr Justice Keogh, but neither wanted to move it after hearing the address. There was huge embarrassment, prompting Professor Thomas Ebenezer Webb to intervene, and he stood-up and proposed the vote of thanks. There was applause and laughter when he declared that although he had heard many great addresses in the hall, he had 'listened to few with greater pleasure than that of Mr Lane'.[9] Webb admitted that he wouldn't commit to all of the sentiments (shouts of 'Hear! Hear!' and applause) and he praised the Auditor for achieving his object of stimulating thought.

The chairman then asked if anyone would second the motion, and for a time there was a horrible silence as no one was willing to support it. This was perhaps a little surprising, given that one report of the meeting claimed that 'there were many gentlemen on the platform who thoroughly approved of it, and it was most cordially received in the body of the hall', but it seems people were unwilling to be publicly associated with the sentiments. The motion was dropped.

Instead of the second motion, calling on the address to be published at the expense of the Society, an alternative was proposed by Whiteside. He suggested the wording: 'That this meeting regards with satisfaction the statements of the Auditor with regard to the progress of the Society during the past session', in other words, to compliment the opening section and ignore all the controversial later parts. This was seconded by Keogh, who delivered an attack on Lane's political analysis, especially the proposal to hand over Gibraltar. Keogh quoted Virgil to suggest that British imperialism had a noble purpose, 'to rule mankind and make the world obey'. At the end of this speech the medals for oratory for the previous session were awarded, Henry O'Hea receiving a gold medal and the Auditor a silver medal.

9 *Nation*, 24 November 1824.

The Irish Times devoted an editorial to the events in the Society the very next day. It suggested that while 'young and inexperienced speakers are allowed considerable latitude and indulgence' they should not be 'carried away by enthusiasm' and violate the rules 'of good taste' and of prudence. Declaring that the 'Common Hall of the University' was not 'the proper place for a vehement diatribe against England' or an attack on the political system, it accused Lane of poor taste, and in endangering the existence of the Society. However, it did acknowledge that the speech was 'eloquent, clever and independent'.

An extraordinary meeting of the committee of the Society was held on the evening of Friday 16 November and after a long discussion it agreed to give its own vote of thanks to the Auditor, 'without in any respect expressing its approval for the various opinions advanced'. The Society also agreed to publish the address at its own expense. However, when the officers approached the President of the Society over the weekend to report this decision and ask for his support, he advised them that the Committee should not attempt to reverse or modify the decisions taken at the opening meeting of the session.

The *Nation* newspaper published its own account of the meeting on Saturday 17 November. Calling it 'An echo of old times', it declared that 'a voice from the grave' or 'the stirring of dead bones' would not have generated more surprise than the inaugural address.[10] It praised Lane for breaking the 'cold chain of silence' which it believed had hung over the Society, the silence when it came to discussing patriotic issues. And it praised 'those few bold and truthful words' for breaking the spell that had been over the Society. It returned to the speech a week later, publishing a full account.[11] There were also stinging criticisms of the address in the *Daily Express* and in some British papers. *The Times* reported that the address 'was so anti-English in its tone that the audience refused to hear it to the end'.[12] The paper was astonished to learn that Lane was not a Catholic, but was in fact the son of a Munster clergyman.[13]

10 *Nation*, 17 November 1866.

11 *Nation*, 24 November 1866.

12 *The Times*, 16 November 1866.

That weekend Lane published a letter in the *Freeman's Journal* accusing Keogh of having misconstrued what he had said and attacking him for the 'positively ludicrous misrepresentation of the speech.[14] It seems Lane had only received a proof copy of his speech at 4 p.m. on the day of the address and while he had circulated it to Napier, Whiteside, Keogh, and Webb, it seems they had not had time to study it, and had certainly not read it through.

On Monday 19 November a conference was held to gather the opinion of a number of ex-Auditors and honorary members of the Society, including J.P. Mahaffy, David Plunket, and Gerald Fitzgibbon, with Napier presiding. The Revd G. A. Chadwick (later the bishop of Derry) attended this meeting, and in apocalyptic tones predicted that the Society would be ruined if it published the address.[15] However, he was ignored, and the meeting agreed to the resolution adopted by the Committee, recommending that it should be put to the Society at its next meeting in two days' time. Lane however, pre-empted this discussion, and the address appeared in print that very day. It seems following the address he had approached John Falconer, the publisher who usually printed the Society's addresses, and who had been present at the meeting, and arranged for the paper to be published without waiting for the Society to approve it. Extensive short-hand notes had been taken of all the contributions, and Falconer published the full text of Lane's address, as well as the contributions by Webb, Whiteside and Keogh. Falconer claimed that 'the address and the speeches which followed it were too valuable a contribution to be entrusted solely to the uncertain keeping of newspapers'. At the start of the pamphlet Lane contributed a note defending his address and standing over his comments. By pre-empting a formal decision of the Society, and arranging for the address to be published, Lane reignited the controversy.

A Committee meeting was held early on Wednesday 21 November to discuss this latest twist. The Secretary, Henry Edmund Hitchcock, announced that he was arranging another conference with the honorary members later that day to decide what to do next,

---

13 *The Times*, 19 November 1866.

14 Letter reprinted in *The Times*, 19 November 1866.

15 Dagg, *CHS*, p. 228.

following the decision of Lane to go ahead with publication. Upon hearing this, Lane tendered his resignation as Auditor, and the Committee accepted it. The conference took place in any case, and it agreed to submit a motion to the Society that evening noting that while it regretfully had to accept the resignation it wanted to assure the Auditor 'that its respect for him personally remains unabated'.

There were further twists in the story. At the public meeting of the Society that evening Lane announced that he was tendering his resignation. Standing orders were suspended and the motion agreed at the conference earlier that day was proposed by Richard O'Shaughnessy (Auditor in 1865–66), and seconded by Hitchcock. However, an honorary member, Gerald FitzGibbon, was present and he intervened to propose an amendment. He suggested that while the Society could not approve the course pursued by the Auditor in printing his address, it 'does not consider that the circumstances justify the acceptance of his resignation'. The motion was seconded by George Ferdinand Shaw, and there followed a long discussion of whether Lane should be allowed continue in his role. When the amendment was put to the house it was passed by thirty votes to ten. As the minutes record: 'Mr Richard O.B. Lane accordingly resumed his seat as Auditor.' The following week the Society voted a resolution praising the Auditor's address (again explicitly without expressing approval of the content) and agreed that its printing should be supported by the Society.

Nothing in the remainder of Lane's session as Auditor proved as controversial. Afterwards he was called to the bar, and he moved to Britain where he became a QC and pursued a successful career as a lawyer. He ended his career as a magistrate at Bow Street Police Court and it was noted that he confronted two generations of British criminals with his 'formidable though kindly personality'.[16] The controversy of 1866 was a reminder how quickly the Society could be plunged into crisis, and showed how the wider public and the wider media had an interest in what went on at meetings. These were lessons that the Society and the College were to not to forget in the years' ahead.

---

16 Dagg, *CHS,* p. 233.

10 'INJURIOUS TO PEACE': THE SOCIETY IN CONFLICT, 1867-1876

'The Society is popular with all classes on account of its national traditions, the distinguished names inscribed upon its roll, and the generous spirit which it infuses into the educated youth of the country.'

The Times, 4 December 1868.

WILLIAM CONNOR MAGEE, now Dean of Cork and of the Chapel Royal at Dublin Castle, returned to the Society in 1867. A young journalist, Thomas Power O'Connor, later to become a prominent figure in the Irish parliamentary party, was starting out in his career, and was assigned the task of recording the proceedings of the College Historical Society for *Saunders' News-Letter*. It was a measure of the reputation of the Society that two journalists were sent from the newspaper, and O'Connor later wrote a piece about his experience for *The Sunday Times* in 1923, noting that the Historical Society 'plays in the life of Trinity College the same part as the Union in Oxford'.[1] Unfortunately for O'Connor, his beginner shorthand was unable to keep up with the fast-paced eloquence of Magee – he compared it to trying to run a race with an express train – and he was soon left bewildered. However, it was a speech he never forgot, and he ranked Magee ahead of hundreds of other great orators he had heard.

Fearing 'great disorder', the opening meeting of the 1868–69

1 T.P. O'Connor, 'Men, women and memories', in *The Sunday Times*, 2 September 1923.

session was cancelled at the last minute by order of the Board, and notices were posted by the Junior Dean during the day.[2] Three of the opening meetings over the next eight years were to be similarly disrupted, and the final incident culminated in the resignation of the Auditor. This was a difficult period in the history of the Society, as it came into increasing conflict with College which feared disruption and the influence of national politics on the student body.

The opening meeting in October 1868 was set to take place the middle of a general election, with voting to take place seven days later for the city of Dublin constituency, and the Board objected because two of the candidates had been invited to speak to the Society. One, David Plunket, was well-known to the Society; the other, Sir Dominic Corrigan, was an eminent physician, and a leading Catholic in the city. A special meeting was called to discuss the ban, and the Society demanded to know how long the order applied for, and when it might be allowed hold the meeting. Corrigan had pulled out of the debate, in any case, so there seemed less risk of controversy being created. However, the Society was informed the debate would only be allowed take place once the election was over.

The inaugural meeting finally took place on 2 December 1868. The Auditor was Henry O'Hea, a brilliant young speaker and a Catholic, and he arranged a debate that generated huge publicity and interest. The meeting was attended by Plunket, who had been elected, and Corrigan, who had not, as well as leading figures from the world of law, politics and religion. As *The Irish Times* reported, the Dining Hall was packed 'to absolute inconvenience' and it was considered one of the largest crowds that had ever gathered.[3] O'Hea's own address was on the influence of university life on national life, and it was praised in *The Times* in London as being 'marked with great ability'.[4] It argued for a politics that went beyond the 'hostile camps' that were 'formed for us' and which could transcend 'old rancours, old grievances, and old crimes'. O'Hea traced the origins of the Society back to Burke's club in 1747, and the one of Yelverton

2 TCD HIST/MUN/SOC/31; Dagg, *CHS*, p. 230.

3 *The Irish Times*, 3 December 1868.

4 *The Times*, 4 December 1868.

in 1753, and took the story all the way through to the formation of the Society proper in 1770.

Plans began to be made for the centenary of the Society in 1870, and in a gesture of good faith there was a further relaxation from College in the subjects for debate that were allowed.[5] The central event was a major dinner held in the Dining Hall on 11 May 1870, and it was attended by many illustrious names from the Society's history. As could be expected there were many speeches. William Brooke, the Auditor in 1814, who was now Master in Chancery, spoke about the final days of the Society before dissolution. William Keogh, who had been Secretary in 1838–39 and was now a Justice of the Common Pleas, spoke about the Society in exile. Isaac Butt delivered a powerful concluding speech on the value of the Society, calling the centenary 'an historic event in the history of Ireland'.[6] Denying that he could speak 'words of immortality', he claimed that instead 'every word there spoken was in some sense a word of immortality', because it would be remembered in one hundred years' time and beyond that.

This was a period of change. For one thing, new rooms had to be found for the Society. On 12 April 1871 the Society discovered that House 27, which it had been using since its return to College, was to be demolished, so a request was made to the Board for new rooms. This was granted, and temporary accommodation was given in Number 17 and then Number 33, before a new home was found on the ground floor of Number 5. It was there the Society remained until the Graduates Memorial Building was constructed. At this time a proposal was made to merge the Society with the University Philosophical Society, but it was rejected.[7] In the election that year three candidates stood for Auditor: Albert William Quill, Gerald Fitzgerald, and Abraham Stoker, and Quill was elected. A former President of the University Philosophical Society, Stoker stood for election the following year, and defeated Cecil Robert Roche, who in turn was the successful candidate the following year.

Quill's opening address, on the value of a mixed university

5 Dagg, *CHS*, p. 234.

6 *The Irish Times*, 5 May 1870.

7 Dagg, *CHS*, p. 237.

education to combat sectarian animosities, received some criticism in the national media. The *Freeman's Journal* objected to some portions, and accused Quill of 'infidelity' to his religion because he was a Catholic. In a dignified response, Quill quoted Horace insisting he would not be shaken by the tyrant's threatening countenance, or the frenzy of his fellow citizens clamouring for what was wrong. Motions that session included one on the abolition of the viceroyalty and another on the removal of the social and political disabilities of women.

Nancy Whitelaw, one of Stoker's best biographers, has discussed how her subject 'learned to think and speak quickly' at the Historical Society.[8] Stoker believed that the Society was 'no ornamental appendage to the College' but played a key role as a 'supplementary school' and was necessary for the university 'to live and flourish'.[9] Serving as Librarian and Secretary before being elected Auditor, Stoker cut a remarkable figure. Unable to walk until the age of seven because of some undiagnosed illness, he grew into a large man and went on to become a prize-winning athlete, and was a leading figure in the Boat Club in Trinity. 'Bram' to his friends, he played competitive rugby and won silver cups in athletics and weight-throwing.[10] That session he opposed a motion attacking trade unionism, and supported the abolition of the viceroyalty, and intriguingly was in favour of a motion suggesting 'That the Novels of the Nineteenth Century are more Immoral in their Tendency than those of the Eighteenth'.

Stoker was elected Auditor for the 1872–73 session and delivered a stirring opening address on 13 November 1872 on 'The Necessity of Political Honesty'. The *Freeman's Journal* noted that the attendance in the Dining Hall was larger than usual, and it included Napier in the chair, the Lord Mayor, and various distinguished politicians (David Plunket among them) and lawyers. In his address,

---

8 Nancy Whitelaw, *Bram Stoker: author of Dracula* (Greensboro, 1998), p. 19.

9 Neil R. Story, *The Dracula Secrets: Jack the Ripper and the Darkest Sources of Bram Stoker* (Stroud, 2010).

10 William Hughes, *Beyond Dracula: Bram Stoker's Fiction and its Cultural Context* (New York, 2000), p. 5.

Stoker traced the history of the restrictions which had been placed on the motions the students could discuss, and how these had been eased by the College over the years. He recognized that the Society had evolved since 1770 in response to both a changing country and a changing College and that this was a good thing, 'that its prosperity has depended and still depends on this very change'.[11] Gerald FitzGibbon, proposing one of the votes of thanks, developed this theme, and suggested that there was no point just learning the dates and facts of the career of Oliver Cromwell; it was necessary to be able to go before a group of people and debate whether his career had been a success or not.

Perhaps the best speech, and certainly the best received on the night, was delivered by a Fellow of the University, Dr George Ferdinand Shaw. Shaw is fully deserving of a study in his own right, having been the founding editor of *The Irish Times* in 1859, a post he only held for fourteen weeks before resigning. The given reason was that he didn't have the time to combine editing the paper with his many academic responsibilities, and certainly he was remarkably busy. Among his many roles, he served as Registrar in Trinity, and in 1870 was a founding member, with Isaac Butt, of what became the Home Rule party. A famous theatre critic, he listed his hobbies in *Who's Who* as novels, plays and opera. Shaw had been Stoker's tutor in Trinity, and there was a close bond between the two men. In addition, Shaw had played a prominent role in the Society, even as a Fellow, and was the person who seconded the famous motion which allowed Lane to remain as Auditor, speaking regularly as well as chairing meetings.

Shaw was famous for his wit, and was greatly admired by another man who became a close friend and who bore the same surname (but was no relation), George Bernard Shaw. One of the official histories of Trinity describes George Ferdinand Shaw as a man who overflowed with 'tireless, if not clearly focussed energy' and someone who 'contributed little, perhaps, to the education of Dublin, but a great deal to its entertainment'. Certainly on the night of the inaugural address, Shaw contributed greatly to the entertainment of the audience. Shaw chose to oppose the central premise of the paper and

11 *The Irish Times*, 14 November 1872.

argued that what was needed instead was more dishonesty in politics. To great laughter, he insisted that 'he knew nothing more revolutionary or contrary to experience than that a politician should turn honest'.[12] Comparing national and international politics to a 'game of thimble-rig', where the public had to guess which cup the pea was under, he expressed a hope that when the Government began looking 'for the little pea of university education' they would not find that 'it had become thin air, and vanished up the operator's sleeve'.

A controversy erupted in 1873 that brought about the resignation of the Auditor. Cecil Robert Roche was elected Auditor for the 1873–74 session and he chose 'Federalism' as the subject for his opening address, and he prepared a text denouncing the principle of Home Rule. In 1886 Roche would be denounced in the British House of Commons as a 'fanatical firebrand', and his views had not changed much from when he was a student. The meeting was scheduled to take place on Wednesday 12 November 1873, but five days before a letter was received from the Board informing the Society the meeting had to be held 'with closed doors', in other words restricted to just members.[13] When the Society objected to this demand it received a second letter, on Saturday 8 November, informing it that because the public discussion of federalism, no matter how sensitively treated, 'would be prejudicial to the character of the College and injurious to its peace' it would not allow the Dining Hall to be used for the meeting.

Hearing this, the Society immediately convened an emergency meeting, attended by sixty-eight members later that same day. Motions suggesting holding the meeting outside the College, or inside closed to the public, were rejected. Instead the members supported the proposal of Henry O'Hea, seconded by Bram Stoker, to publish the Board's order in the newspapers, cancel the meeting, and submit a respectful remonstrance to College on the subject of the order. Two days later, at another special meeting of the Society, the Auditor announced that he was going to withdraw his address rather than enter into a contest with the Board which might 'end disastrously to either our liberty or our prosperity'. So instead he

12 *Nation*, 23 November 1872.

13 Dagg, *CHS*, p. 240.

proposed delivering his inaugural address, on a different subject, on Wednesday 14 January 1874.

What happened next was extraordinary. The motion approving the postponement was defeated by eighteen votes to thirteen, prompting Roche to submit his resignation. However, this was in turn rejected by the Society, which voted not to accept it. Roche could not be persuaded to remain in office and, after insisting that his position was untenable, he was allowed step down. Henry Tydd Lane, a former Record Secretary, was elected Auditor unopposed, and the session began with no inaugural address.

In the meantime Roche arranged for his inaugural address to be published as a pamphlet, and it was printed on 14 November.[14] Reading the text, it is perhaps easier to understand why the College felt obliged to restrict attendance. It was a strongly-worded discourse, full of noise and fury against the principle of an Irish parliament. *The Irish Times* praised it as 'an able exposition' and was critical of the College for engaging in 'paltry disputes with the Historical Society'.[15] In an editorial on 28 November it reminded readers that 'to be a student of the University of Dublin has been generally considered as a sort of stamp of respectability' and that 'the title of alumnus has authorised the bearer to regard himself as somewhat superior to those who could not affix to their names the magic letters of TCD'.

Roche continued to attend meetings of the Society and took part in debates that session, but the controversy cast a shadow over the year. After leaving Trinity Roche trained to be a barrister, but was unable to make much of an impression, and in 1886 he decided to campaign as a Unionist in the 1886 general election. Travelling around England, he denounced the Irish nationalists in extreme language, on one occasion claimed that 'when Hell was frozen over he would go down and fight the Parnellites on the ice'.[16] After the election he was rewarded for his activities by the new Conservative government, and was made an Irish Resident Magistrate, and his appointment was considered a scandal given his obvious political

14 Cecil Roche, *Federalism: the suppressed address to the College Historical Society* (Dublin, 1873).

15 *The Irish Times*, 15 and 28 November 1873.

16 *Hansard*, 17 July 1890, vol. 347, col. 116.

bias. Thomas Power O'Connor, in his history of the Home Rule movement, described Roche as 'the ruffian *par excellence* of the magisterial bench' and noted the 'harshness of his sentences, the brutality and insolence of his demeanour, his trickery'.[17] On one occasion, during a land protest in Ireland, Roche joined with the police in charging into the crowd, and assaulted a number with his heavy walking stick. In later years Edward Carson carried around a heavy Irish black-thorn walking stick, which he liked to boast had once belonged to 'a fearless Irish Resident Magistrate' named Cecil Roche who had used it on the heads of troublesome peasants.[18]

New members who joined the Society that year included Oscar Wilde, Edward Carson, William Ridgeway, and Arthur Warren Samuels. Debates were lively, and often controversial. A motion on 19 November 1873, discussing whether 'the Civil and Physical Disabilities of Women Ought to be Removed' was disrupted by a member of the public.

It what was now becoming an annual tradition, the opening meeting of the 1874–75 session was hugely controversial. The Society struggled to secure any external speakers to respond to the inaugural address, as twenty-one invitations were declined. In desperation, the Society accepted a recommendation from Lord Cairns, the Chancellor of the University (and the former British Lord Chancellor), and sent an invitation to Alexander Miller, Treasurer of the Society in 1852–53, who was now a candidate for the University of Dublin constituency in the upcoming by-election. This was a controversial move, because Miller was standing against Edward Gibson, the former Auditor of the Society. Gibson was a popular figure and was supported by many of the Fellows, whereas Miller was dismissed as 'Cairns' carrier pigeon', in the words of one Fellow, Dr Haughton.[19] It was soon joked in College that Miller had been 'let loose by Lord Cairns in London, with a label tied to its leg and on it the message "Elect me"'.[20]

17 T.P. O'Connor, *The Home Rule Movement* (New York, 1891), p. 652.

18 H.M. Hyde, *Carson: the life of Sir Edward Carson* (London, 1953), p. 122.

19 Dagg, *CHS*, p. 244.

20 Dagg, *CHS*, p. 247.

The by-election was all people wanted to talk about in College in the run-up to the event, and the Society was criticised for allowing itself to be manipulated by Cairns, and for appearing to show favouritism by inviting one candidate and not the other. In truth, the Committee had considered inviting Gibson as well, but because he had accepted an invitation to speak at the opening of the University Philosophical Society they decided against. By appearing to side with the unpopular candidate, the Society made things worse. Miller practised at the English bar and had just come over for the contest. His biggest liability was that he was seen as the puppet of Cairns, described in the *Freeman's Journal*'s report of the meeting as 'the most successful and the most unpopular Irishman of the time.'[21] It was believed that Miller's candidacy 'had not been managed with good taste or good sense', with Cairns criticised for trying to interfere in things, and among the student body Miller was 'eminently unpopular'. Afterwards the Dublin *Daily Express* accused the committee of having been manipulated by 'men who are older and deeper and more unscrupulous' than them, whom they blamed for the debacle. Another factor was that the Irish bar considered the Trinity seats as its by right, and resented an attempt by someone from the English bar to contest it. Thanks to all of these reasons, there was enormous interest in the opening meeting, with rumours prevalent that Trinity was at war. What followed was an 'unparalleled row'.

Reporting on what happened at the opening meeting on Wednesday 18 November 1874, the *Freeman's Journal* described it as 'the most extraordinary scene which was ever enacted within academic walls'.[22] First huge crowds gathered to try and get in, and the front of the Dining Hall was packed with 'a surging, swaying, densely-packed crowd of human beings trying to fight their way up [the steps] and in through the door'. Once inside, they had to fight their way through another crush, 'almost as bad as outside', to try and get in to the Dining Hall itself. This 'double scrimmage' resulted in broken hats, torn coats, and ripped shirts, until finally the Dining Hall was 'filled to overflowing with a vast throng'. The students present were described as 'collarless, stick-bearing, uproarious and "spilling for a fight"'.

21 *Freeman's Journal*, 19 November 1874.

22 Ibid.

The arrival of the President, Napier, with the Committee and guests (including the Chief Secretary and Lord Mayor), was the signal for 'the outbreak of the wild scene of tumult, uproar and riot, which raged for two long hours'. As a former Auditor, Gibson was part of the procession, alongside Miller, and there were loud cheers for him and groans for his rival. Ashantee bombs, a kind of fireworks, were exploded, and whistles and bugles added to the cacophony as they went by. Napier attempted to open the meeting, but he was unable to be heard as the students shouted 'Not for Joe.' and he was 'much distressed and annoyed by his reception'.[23] The Auditor, Charles Matheson, then rose to speak, and he raised up his hand calling out, 'Fair play, boys, fair play'. There were shouts of 'Shame' and 'Sit Down', but eventually the crowd calmed down so it could hear the majority of his address. Matheson's subject was the decline of the spirit of patriotism.

Towards the end of the paper, one student fainted because of the heat and this reignited the noise and disturbances, and there were shouts of 'Speak up', 'Sit down in front', and 'Open the windows'. Some potatoes were thrown from the crowd, and it was impossible to hear the concluding remarks.

Proposing the first vote of thanks was David Plunket and he joked that he was relieved not to be involved in the coming electoral context. At this, *The Irish Times* reports that there was much 'cheers, whistling and trumpet blowing'. Because of the enormous respect people had for him, Plunket was listened to for the majority of his speech. Somewhat mischievously, he chose to make a reference to what was happening, slightly misquoting lines from Thomas Campbell's poem, *Lochiel's Warning:*

> The sunset of life brings me mystical lore
> And coming events cast their shadows before.

Plunket ended his speech by quoting some lines from the *Nation* about unity between nationalists and unionists, calling for 'lasting peace from equal laws' and everyone joined 'in our common country's cause'.

The Lord Mayor was next, but he received no hearing at all and,

23 *The Irish Times*, 12 November 1874.

embarrassed, he sat down, after mumbling a few words. At this point some of the students released some carrier pigeons, which they had smuggled into the hall, and they flew around the room before eventually landing on some of the portraits. The reporters found it difficult to describe the scene: 'the appalling noise, the braying trumpets, the shrill shrieking whistles, the showers of exploding fireworks, the bewildered pigeons flying hither and thither, the missiles from outside, the free fights, the infernal tumult which reigned all round'.

When Miller was eventually invited to speak the noise reached a crescendo. *The Irish Times* described it as 'a perfect storm of cheers, hisses, cat calls, trumpeting etc.'. Ashantee bombs and other noisy explosives were thrown around the Dining Hall, and it was reported that the students 'yelled, screamed, roared, brayed' and began smashing up the wooden seats. It was turning into a riot. Miller's words were deliberately drowned out as the crowd ignored the attempts by Napier to calm things down. Defiant, Miller stood his ground for an hour, refusing to sit down, as the crowd began surging forward trying to reach the platform. The stewards pushed them back, and fighting broke out. 'This was the end' according to one reporter. Following this, the meeting had to be adjourned, and Anthony Traill, the Professor of Natural Philosophy, and some other Fellows formed a bodyguard for Miller as he was escorted from the hall. Because Traill was a popular figure with the students he was not harassed, but others were 'hustled rudely'. It brought to an end what the *Freeman's Journal* described as 'probably the stormiest meeting in the annals of the College Historical Society'.

The Board was quick to act, criticising the Committee for 'an injudicious selection of speakers'. In the correspondence which followed the Board made clear how it wanted debates to be conducted in future. The text of all opening addresses, and the lists of names of speakers, would have to be submitted to the Board in advance for approval.[24] All motions would have to be submitted to the Board at the start of a session for approval, and permission given for a subject in one year would not be considered perpetual. Later that year two motions, based on current events, were submitted, and

24 *The Irish Times*, 19 November 1874.

both were rejected. The first proposed 'That the Recent Action of the House of Commons towards John Mitchel was Constitutional', and given what had just happened (Mitchel had been elected MP for Tipperary but had been prevented from taking his seat because he was a convicted felon), it was bound to be controversial. The second proposed 'That Exceptional legislation for Ireland is Desirable' and also risked national politics inflaming tensions. Instead, over the year the Society debated whether political agitation had done more harm than good for Ireland (rejected), that the present social and political disabilities of women should be abolished (rejected), and 'that elements of weakness are discernible in the German empire' (passed). The by-election for the vacant seat took place in January 1875 and Gibson was elected, and it marked the beginning of a long and successful career in parliament.

The opening meeting of the 1875-76 session was also disrupted, though on a much smaller scale than in the previous year. The Auditor was the Revd Richard Campbell and at the start of his address on the Irish in the British Empire there was a disturbance in the crowd and a huge amount of noise was made. Standing firm, Campbell accused those involved of a 'most cowardly and ungentlemanly' act in disrupting the meeting, and noted, pointedly, that he had 'a good many friends in the hall' and hoped they would stand by him. This generated long applause and there was a stop to the disturbance. During the speech some firecrackers were let off, and towards the end of the speech the noise resumed again. Campbell accused the troublemakers of being strangers to Trinity, and called on the students to 'put it down and save the character of the College'.[25]

At this time the Board attempted to prevent the Society from using the Dining Hall for ordinary business meetings, claiming that the furniture was being damaged and that the introduction of gas lighting might add an unwelcome cost. The Society resisted these attempts, offering to pay for the cost of the gas, but the Board was adamant and claimed there was a risk that the roof of the building might go on fire if the lights were on for the duration of a full meeting of the Society.[26] Again, the Society objected, and proposed

25 *The Irish Times*, 11 November 1875.

26 Dagg, *CHS*, p. 253.

providing lamps at its own expense to light the building, and this was reluctantly approved, at least until 'a more suitable place could be found'. As a result, twelve lamps were purchased by the Society for use at meetings.

During that session the Society debated Pitt's Irish policy, which was extended to a second night because of the level of interest. A motion on whether the social and political disabilities of women ought to be removed was also extended to a second evening, and the motion passed by six votes at the end of a heated debate. Other motions included ones on the character and career of Cromwell, the character and conduct of Swift, secular education, and the emancipation of the colonies.

Edward Carson opened the debate proposing the abolition of capital punishment on 23 December 1875 in support of the motion 'That capital punishment ought to be abolished', but it was narrowly defeated.[27] On 7 June 1876 he opposed the motion that the system of land tenure in Ireland needs reformation, again on the losing side. At the review of attendance on 22 November 1876 it was revealed that Carson was one of the most frequent attenders at the meetings.[28] On 20 December 1876 he opposed the motion 'That the dramatic taste of the present day shows marked symptoms of degeneracy'.

James Campbell was elected Auditor for the 1876-77 session, defeating R.M. Hennessey, and Edward Carson defeated G.D. Burtchaell by two votes for the position of Librarian. The start of the session was marked by a clash between Campbell and Napier over the choice of subject for the inaugural address. Campbell wanted to speak on land tenure in Ireland, and prepared an address which he sent to Napier, but Napier objected to the subject matter and insisted that 'the general topic of land tenure in Ireland is too inflammatory and explosive for the occasion in College, however carefully considered and discussed, to be trusted for safe handling'. Claiming that the Board would veto the subject, Napier advised Campbell to find another subject.

Campbell was determined to proceed anyway, and in response he argued that his subject had been chosen with reference to

---

27 TCD MUN/SOC/HIST/33.

28 TCD MUN/SOC/HIST/34.

College's rules and regulations. He also pointed out that he had spent 'several months of study and reflection' preparing the address, and would be unable to continue with his coursework, and prepare for an important examination, and have time to write a new address in time for the opening meeting on 8 November. But Napier was not for budging, and he was adamant about 'the objectionable if not perilous character of the subject'. As a result, the inaugural address was postponed until after Christmas, while the ordinary meetings of the Society continued as normal. At this time Napier was in serious ill-health and was unable to attend meetings of the Society, and as he got worse (and his hearing failed) others were asked to chair the inaugural meetings in his absence.

On 12 January 1877 the Society submitted a list of motions to the Board for approval and nine were rejected. These included 'That the political career of Daniel O'Connell deserves our approval', and 'That the policy of the Home Rule Party merits our condemnation'.[29]

Campbell finally delivered his inaugural address on 7 February 1877. The subject of his new address was 'Social Tendencies' and he began by defending his previous choice of subject, arguing that 'as a general principle, I believe that your Auditor should be allowed a most extreme latitude in the difficult task of selecting a subject'. However, he conceded that Napier had acted as President with sincerity and discretion.

Carson was a regular speaker in this session. To give a selection of the debates he spoke on he argued in favour of approving Cromwell's political career (14 February 1877), and in support of Pitt's Irish policy (7 March 1877). On 8 June 1877 he spoke against Lecky's views on federalism (the former member's views now a subject for debate in the Society). A candidate for the auditorship on 13 June 1877, he was unsuccessful, and was defeated by Charles Andrew O'Connor. He continued to debate in the Society in the following session and was elected to the Committee in June 1878.

Called to the bar in 1877, Carson established himself as an effective and ferocious lawyer and impressed with his 'displays of moral courage and forensic ability'.[30] As his leading biographer, Alvin

29 TCD MUN/SOC/HIST/34.

30 Alvin Jackson, 'Edward Carson', *DIB*.

Jackson, notes in the *Dictionary of Irish Biography*, 'He was a crown prosecutor in some of the most celebrated trials of the period, and forged a reputation that he carried for the rest of his career.'[31]

Elected MP for Dublin University in 1892, his maiden speech made a considerable impression, in particular the assured way he handled interruptions. Jackson writes that 'The result was an instant metropolitan celebrity for a man who, though well known in Ireland, had as yet made no impression within the British political arena.'

At the same time he practised at the English bar and was involved in some of the most famous cases of the day, including the case which sent Oscar Wilde to Reading gaol, when he defended the Marquis of Queensbury. In 1910 he defended George Archer-Shee, a young naval cadet accused of stealing a five-shilling postal order. He won a famous victory and he was later portrayed as Sir Robert Morton KC in Terrence Rattigan's much filmed play *The Winslow Boy*.

In 1910 he became chairman of the Irish Unionist Parliamentary Party and led the campaign against the third Home Rule bill. A Southern Unionist from Dublin, he supported partition as a way of undermining the entire Home Rule project and adopted increasingly militant tactics to wreck it, including the creation of the Ulster Volunteer Force in 1913 and bringing the gun back into Irish politics with the Larne gun-running in 1914. With the outbreak of the first world war his career as a rebel was over and he was briefly Attorney General for England. Instrumental in the downfall of Asquith in 1916, he became First Lord of the Admiralty, but his time in office was a failure and he was made a minister without portfolio in July 1917. Bitterly opposed to the Anglo-Irish Treaty in 1921 he became a Lord of Appeal in Ordinary in May 1921 and took the title Lord Carson of Duncairn. Carson is recognized as 'one of the founding fathers of modern unionism', and he also left 'a stylistic legacy'.[32] Jackson notes that 'throughout his political and legal career' he was prone 'to brilliantly argued but often emotive or even belligerent speechifying' and 'bequeathed a model of tactical brinkmanship and histrionic style'.

James Campbell became a successful lawyer and was elected to

---

31 Ibid.

32 Ibid.

parliament as MP for St Stephen's Green division of Dublin (1898-1900) and as MP for Dublin University (1903-16). Solicitor General for Ireland (1901-05) and briefly Attorney General for Ireland (1905-06), in the years after he became 'a hate-figure for many nationalists because of his prominence as a Unionist spokesman'.[33]

Irish nationalists vetoed his becoming Lord Chancellor for Ireland in 1915, he instead became Attorney General for Ireland for the second time in 1916. Made a baronet in 1917, he became Lord Chancellor for Ireland a year later and served until 1921, becoming Lord Glenavy upon retirement. With the creation of the Irish Free State he accepted an invitation to become a Senator and he became the first chairman of the Senate. He retired from public life in 1928 and, according to his grandson, in his final years 'spent quite a lot of time and money on the tables at Monte Carlo, and on an attractive Spanish girl who numbered tennis among her accomplishments'. He died in 1931. Patrick Maume in the *Dictionary of Irish Biography* considers him 'certainly ambitious and financially rapacious even by the standards of early twentieth-century lawyer-politicians', but it also recognises 'that his arrogance manifested pride in his own genuine abilities and in what he conceived as the superior values associated with Britishness and Protestantism.'[34]

The member from this period who achieved the greatest international fame was Bram Stoker. After graduation he became a civil servant and began writing short stories and novels. In 1878 he left the civil service and moved to London where he joined Henry Irving at the Lyceum Theatre in London and there he came into contact with the leading literary figures of the time, including Arthur Conan Doyle, George Bernard Shaw, and Oscar Wilde.[35] The first of his eleven novels, *The Snake's Past,* was published in 1890 and came to the attention of William Gladstone. But his literary fame largely depends on his Gothic masterpiece *Dracula,* which was published in 1897 and interpreted and reinterpreted in every generation since. Writing in the *Dictionary of Irish Biography,* Paul Murray suggests that 'Uniquely among Irish writers, Stoker's reputation has been

33 Patrick Maume, 'James Campbell', *DIB.*

34 Ibid.

35 Paul Murray, 'Abraham Stoker', *DIB.*

maintained more by Dracula's continuing hold on the popular consciousness through adaptations in the mass media, primarily films, than to the quality of his writing. This has led to a certain ambiguity about his place in the Irish literary pantheon, his creation of the best known character in Irish fiction notwithstanding.'[36]

As Barbara Belford notes, 'Stoker, Maturin and Le Fanu constitute the Irish-Gothic triumvirate.'[37] In this way the Historical Society has a direct link to the Irish Gothic tradition through the works of three of its most prominent members in the nineteenth century: Charles Maturin, Sheridan Le Fanu and Bram Stoker. It is a remarkable literary legacy.

36 Ibid.

37 Barbara Belford, 'Abraham Stoker', *ODNB*.

'ALL THAT IS BEST AND MOST ILLUSTRIOUS IN IRISH LIFE', 1877-1900

II

'A FUNCTION of no little importance' was how Winston Churchill described the resolution which his father, Lord Randolph Churchill, was asked to make at the opening meeting of the College Historical Society on 14 November 1877.[1] Churchill's speech generated enormous publicity, and was reported internationally at the time as well as in the Irish and British newspapers.[2] Churchill had not been in Dublin very long, having arrived as the unofficial private secretary of his father, the Duke of Marlborough, the new Lord Lieutenant, and jumped at the opportunity to make an impression. An important influence here was Gerald FitzGibbon, the Irish administration's law adviser, who quickly became a lifelong friend and who introduced him to the Society.

Churchill agreed to reply to the inaugural address of the Auditor, Charles Andrew O'Connor, who had chosen as his subject 'Philosophy and Politics'. When Winston Churchill wrote a biography of his father, he included a detailed account of his visit to Trinity, and compared the Society to the Oxford Union.[3] Perhaps wisely he did not compare it to the Cambridge Union. Randolph Churchill had been a member there, but had been expelled for not paying his subscription.[4]

---

1 Winston Churchill, *Lord Randolph Churchill* (2 vols, London, 1906), i, 80; TCD HIST/MUN/SOC/77.

2 R.F. Foster, *Lord Randolph Churchill: A Political Life* (Oxford, 1981) p. 44, see for example New York Times, 10 December 1877.

3 Churchill, *Lord Randolph Churchill*, i, 80.

4 Joseph S. Meisel, *Public speech and the culture of public life in the age of Gladstone* (New York, 2001), p. 25.

In his address, on 'The Relation of Philosophy to Politics', O'Connor discussed the slenderness of the connection between philosophy and politics in the present day, and looked forward to a time when politics would be subservient to philosophy. He also argued that democracy tended to encourage mediocrity, with a suggestion that the United States was a good example, the home of 'speculative thinkers'.[5]

Rather than just praise the address uncritically, Churchill entertained the gathering by delivering a pointed and humorous response, in which he joked that he was connected by the closest ties to the United States – by his marriage. To much applause, he argued that a country that had produced the likes of Longfellow and Lincoln could not be said 'to be wanting in talent which is above mediocrity'. Claiming disingenuously that he had neither the time nor the courage to criticise the Auditor's comments, he suggested that instead he would point out 'in a perfectly friendly manner, that his [the Auditor's] promises were perhaps somewhat superficial and his conclusions a little hasty'. The students were loving this, and there was much laughter and applause throughout the speech. Years later, *The Irish Times* reflected that 'the speech was full of calculated indiscretion, and – to quote the Aristotelean definition of wit – refined insolence'.[6]

Addressing the relationship between philosophy and politics, Churchill reviewed the three principal schools of philosophy in the ancient world. The Stoics he dismissed as 'a most disagreeable school', the Platonists as 'a most unintelligible school', and settled on the Epicureans as 'a most attractive school'. Churchill suggested that there was a connection between the Epicurean school and Conservative politics, as it was a philosophy 'to let things alone as much as we can; to accustom ourselves to always look at the brightest side; to legislate for the moment rather than for the dim and distant future'.[7]

Churchill then developed his main argument, looking at the history of that year – 1877 – and the changes in the Irish

5 *New York Times*, 10 December 1877.

6 *The Irish Times*, 8 October 1923.

7 Churchill, *Lord Randolph Churchill*, p. 81; TCD HIST/MUN/SOC/77.

administration, the increased activity (which he described as 'volcanic uneasiness') of the Irish parliamentary party, the visit of one of Britain's greatest statesmen and orators to Ireland, and the publication of a superb new book, *New Ireland* by A. M. Sullivan. One newspaper at the time described the speech as 'gravely bantering, solemnly jocose'.[8]

During this session the Society appealed to have greater freedom in choosing subjects for debate, citing the example of the Oxford and the Cambridge Unions who by this point had secured uncontrolled freedom, but this was rejected by the Board.

Motions debated during this year included one warning about the undesirability of early marriages, a motion on the character and career of Daniel O'Connell, and one on Pitt's Irish policies. Seymour Bushe, a grandson of Charles Kendal Bushe, addressed the Society during the year and impressed with his oratory. The Society found itself prevented from using the Dining Hall for ordinary meetings, and the Museum Building was also closed off to it, so it was reluctantly forced to hold meetings from January 1878 in the new examination hall.

A talented Presbyterian student, John Ross, was elected Auditor for the 1878-79 session. A former President of the Philosophical Society, he was also captain of the hockey club and founder of the lawn tennis club in Trinity.[9] At his opening meeting he paid tribute to a distinguished former member and Vice-President of the Society, Judge William Keogh, who had recently died by his own hand. Ross called him 'a staunch friend' to the Society and noting that it was there as a member that 'his eloquence first attracted attention'.[10] Ross went on to become a successful barrister and defeated Justin McCarthy by twenty-six votes to become MP for Londonderry in 1892.[11] He became a judge in 1896 and helped draft the famous Wyndham Land Act in 1903. Appointed Lord Chancellor of Ireland in 1921, he was the final holder of the office before it was abolished in 1922.

8 *The Irish Times*, 8 October 1923.

9 William Murphy, 'Sir John Ross', *DIB*.

10 Dagg, *CHS*, p. 260.

11 William Murphy, 'Sir John Ross', *DIB*.

The death of Isaac Butt in May 1879 was mourned by the Society, and at the start of the new session on 12 November the Auditor, John W. Joynt, paid a powerful tribute to him. Joynt noted that the Society had long felt 'strong affection as well as ardent admiration' for him, and recognized that he provided the Society with a link to its own history as well as to the politics on the island. At that inaugural address, on 'Contemporary England', Randolph Churchill was again in attendance, and addressed the gathering.

International politics was sometimes a subject for debate in these years. In the 1880-81 session there was a motion on the Republican Party in the recent American presidential election, which had seen the election of James Garfield, and there were also debates on the abolition of trial by jury in Ireland, and the land question. Interestingly, a debate on whether 'the political sentiments of the Young Ireland Party deserve our approval' was tied, and required the casting vote of the chairman (former Auditor, John Joynt), to pass.

The meeting of Wednesday 10 May 1882 was dominated by the Phoenix Park murders which had taken place four days earlier. The new Chief Secretary for Ireland, Lord Frederick Cavendish and Walter Burke, the Castle Under-Secretary, had been knifed to death by the Invincibles while out for a walk, and the savagery of the attack horrified many in Ireland. Burke was a former member of the Society and the description of how he had been butchered shocked the members. At the start of the meeting standing orders were suspended and the Auditor proposed a motion, which was carried unanimously, which expressed its 'grief and horror' at the assassination. On 14 June another motion was passed expressing the Society's 'abhorrence at the foul murder of Mr Walter M. Burke, a former member of the Society'.[12]

There were many gifted speakers in the Society in this era. Richard Robert Cherry was elected Auditor unanimously, and went on to serve as Lord Chief Justice (1914–16). A student from Derry, Alfred Edward Crawford, won the gold medal for oratory and was considered by H. Cameron Lyster (Auditor for the 1884–85 session), as 'the most brilliant and promising member of the year'.[13] Crawford

12 TCD HIST/MUN/SOC/34; Dagg, *CHS*, p. 263.

13 View of the Auditor, H. Cameron Lyster (quoted in Dagg, *CHS*, p. 264).

was an ambitious young man, and spoke often of his desire to represent Derry in the imperial parliament. At a dinner to mark the end of the session, Crawford impressed the gathering with an extemporary speech on Peter Burrowes. It was so remarkable he was invited to give a second speech and he talked about the winning of legislative independence in 1782. He spoke of the events 'as if they were still in progress' and Lyster considered it to be 'the most brilliant extemporary speech I have ever heard'.[14] Crawford served as Librarian, but his health began to fail, and he was diagnosed with diabetes and he died in 1883.

During this period there were repeated clashes with the Board over the subjects for debate, and the College became increasingly strict about vetting the subjects for debate in advance. This reflected what was going on nationally, with a land war and increased Home Rule agitation as part of a new departure in Irish politics increasing fears about radical influences. In November 1882 the Board rejected nine of the forty-two proposed motions, which included ones on Pitt's Irish policy, federalism, Daniel O'Connell, and the Young Ireland Party. The Society objected on the grounds that many of the subjects had been debated before, with the full approval of the Board, and there followed a lengthy correspondence.

Tensions flared when the Society held a major debate on 7 February 1883 on the motion, 'That Grattan's denunciation of the Union has been justified by the results'. Patrick James Smyth, a controversial, rogue nationalist MP was in the chair, and he delivered a major speech at the end of the night which was covered in the newspapers. Smyth, described by Michael Davitt as 'our Irish national Don Quixote, eccentric, rhetorical and most thoroughly impractical' was a provocative figure to invite to the Society.[15] A school-friend of Thomas Francis Meagher, he had been involved in the 1848 rebellion and had been forced to flee Ireland afterwards, when he escaped to America with John Blake Dillon disguised as a peasant. Famously he facilitated the escape of John Mitchel from Van Diemen's Land in 1853, using the codename 'Nicaragua', and was preparing to assist the escape of William Smith O'Brien before

14 Dagg, *CHS*, p. 264.

15 David Murphy and Owen Magee, 'Patrick James Smyth', *DIB*.

he was pardoned.[16] Smyth was at one time considered a candidate for leadership of the party, but his views were too divergent from the other members. He wanted a full repeal of the Union, not just Home Rule, and he opposed the Land League, which he described as a 'League of Hell'. Clashing with Charles Stewart Parnell, he resented the autocratic leadership style, and formally seceded from the Irish parliamentary party in 1881.

The debate itself ran over two nights, and the motion was passed on the second by six votes. The Board was furious that the motion had been discussed, especially as it was one it had not approved, and it was even more angry that Smyth had been invited into Trinity. The Society claimed it had included the motion on the list it had submitted the previous autumn, but this was not the case, and the whether honest mistake or not, the Board was furious at this 'flagrant violation of the rules'.[17] As punishment, the Society was suspended from holding any debates in the month of March.

The death of Sir Joseph Napier, after a long illness, on 9 December 1882 necessitated the election of a new President. The meeting scheduled for 13 December was adjourned in his honour, and various tributes were paid to the incredible loyalty he had shown the Society over the years. The choice of new President was, in some respects, an easy one. Edward Gibson, now a King's Counsel and MP, was a Vice-President of the Society and a hugely respected figure. He was elected president on 7 February 1883. He chaired a meeting of the Society as President for the first time at the opening of the 114th session, in November 1883.

Douglas Hyde joined the Society in 1883 and in his journals he recounts going to meetings in May, including one where he listened to Lecky speak.[18] He was a steward at the inaugural meeting in November 1883 and received twenty-two votes for Auditor in June 1884, when H. Cameron Lyster was elected.

Thomas Davis's reputation remained extraordinarily high in the Society. In the 1884–45 session a motion 'That the career of Thomas Davis deserves our admiration' was passed unanimously. Other

---

16 D.J. O'Donoghue and Brigitte Anton, 'Patrick James Smyth', *ODNB*.

17 TCD HIST/MUN/SOC/34; Dagg, *CHS*, p. 266.

18 Dominic Daly, *The young Douglas Hyde* (Totowa, 1974), p. 55.

motions that session included one suggesting that emigration from Ireland should be encouraged by the state (defeated), and one supporting the revival of the Irish language (also defeated). The debate on 11 March 1885 was on the motion 'That a system of proportional representation is desirable' and the opening speaker was Dr Anthony Traill, a fellow of the College (and future Provost). The motion was passed by a substantial majority. Throughout the year there were attempts to open the membership of the Society to Freshman students, but the Board was unwilling to relax its restriction and the policy went nowhere.

During this session Douglas Hyde spoke in favour of the motions 'That the Church of England ought to be disestablished' and 'That the political institutions of 1782 deserve approval'. On 3 March 1885 he spoke on 'Celts and Teutons' and boasted afterwards that he 'did wonderfully well. Everyone said I was the best speaker.'[19] On 13 May he argued that England was going downhill, and on 3 June 'gave a very good talk' on 'Irish Rule in Ireland'. At the end of the 1885–86 session he was awarded the gold medal for history because of 'the superior style' of his answering.[20] However, he spoke 'very badly' on Female Emancipation at another debate, and he was disappointed because it was a subject he felt very strongly about.[21] On 11 November 1885 he spoke at the opening meeting in favour of disestablishment of the Church of England and his biographers write that 'although his arguments were unpopular, his eloquence was unchallenged'.[22] Hyde won the silver medal for oratory in 1887 and the gold medal for composition in 1888.

Hyde's later career is so well known as to almost need no summary. A lifelong enthusiast for the Irish language and culture, a few years after leaving Trinity he delivered one of the most influential lectures in Irish history on 'The necessity for de-anglicising Ireland'. A year later, in 1893, he became the first President of the Gaelic League and in 1909 he became the first Professor of Irish at UCD, a

19 Ibid., p. 56.

20 Dagg, *CHS*, p. 271.

21 J.E. Dunleavy and G.W. Dunleavy, *Douglas Hyde: a maker of modern Ireland* (Los Angeles, 1981), p. 119.

22 Ibid.

post he held until 1932. A powerful symbol of the Irish Gaelic Revival, on 26 June 1938 he was inaugurated the first President of Ireland, and Taoiseach Éamon de Valera spoke of how the Irish people saluted him as the rightful successor of their native princes after centuries of foreign usurpation. As Patrick Maume writes in the *Dictionary of Irish Biography*, 'Hyde ignited cultural debates which have raged ever since...This outwardly simple man was a complex blend of Ireland's traditions; those who chose him to symbolise the new state wrought better than they knew.'[23]

One of the most remarkable figures in the Society in the 1880s was Henry Simpson Lunn, a student from England. At Trinity he studied for degrees in medicine and theology at the same time, while preaching in local Methodist chapels two Sundays out of three.[24] Born in England, he was a devout Wesleyan Methodist and had two conversion experiences in his early life that convinced him to become a minister and do missionary work in India, and his studies had brought him to Ireland.[25] Elected treasurer of the Theological Society in his second year, he become Secretary of the College Historical Society (defeating Thomas Bethune Moffat by a large majority) and President of the University Temperance Society. Among his closest friends in Trinity was Douglas Hyde (who was also close to Moffat).

After learning of the persecution of the Irish Catholics through his study of history in the Society, Lunn became a passionate Home Ruler and was a founding member of the Irish Protestant Home Rule Association. During the general election campaign in 1886 there was a great demand for speakers from Ireland to come to Britain, especially those who were Protestant and supported Home Rule, and Lunn travelled over with J.G. Swift MacNeill. In London he met with Michael Davitt, who arranged a meeting for him with Charles Stewart Parnell. It seems Parnell wanted Lunn to stand for parliament himself, but he declined because of his mission to go to India, which he said 'stood before any political ambition'.[26]

Lunn viewed the auditorship of the Historical Society as 'the blue

23 Patrick Maume, 'Douglas Hyde', *DIB*.

24 H.S. Lunn, *Chapters from my life* (London, 1918), p. 36.

25 Stella Wood, 'Henry Simpson Lunn', *ODNB*.

26 Lunn, *Chapters*, p. 43.

ribbon of university life', and people knew for months in advance that he was going to be a candidate in the summer of 1886. Unfortunately for his chances, he gave the inaugural address at the Purity Society, a new group formed in College to promote wholesomeness and social purity, and this was used against him. Stories were told, 'in graphic terms', that he had gone out in the streets of Dublin with a lantern to harass men who were visiting prostitutes, and had succeeded in getting two men fired from the Bank of Ireland because of their nocturnal activities. Despite Lunn receiving a letter from the secretary of the bank confirming that no one had been fired, the rumour would not die. His popularity in College went into sharp decline, and Lunn was sometimes pelted with eggs by other students. One night, when he was away in England campaigning, his rooms were broken into by a group of loyalist students who called themselves 'moonlighters' and they wrecked everything. As Lunn later recounted in his memoir, they 'passed a unanimous resolution consigning me and Parnell to the abyss, destroyed my furniture, broke my pictures up, cut my bedding to pieces, and poured oil from my lamp upon it'. It seems they only stopped from setting fire to the whole thing because of the fear that it would 'burn half Trinity down'.

George Ferdinand Shaw had been Lunn's tutor before being replaced by John P. Mahaffy, and he supported Lunn's attempts to get compensation for Trinity for all the damage even though he didn't support Lunn's views on Home Rule. As Shaw remarked to Mahaffy on Front Square, 'It is men who take their own line who are the salt of the earth. Would you have us all crushed beneath the juggernaut of identity?' However, the Board viewed it differently, and no compensation was paid.

Auditorial elections tended not to be controversial, but the election in 1886 was different and it proved to be one of nastiest in the Society's history. Three candidates put themselves forward: Henry Simpson Lunn, Thomas Bethune Moffat and Percival Gaussen, but only the first two were serious contenders. Lunn's candidacy that year seemed doomed from the start and there were too many people against him.[27] For one thing his fervent support for Home Rule meant that he was away in England for much of the

27 Lunn, *Chapters*, p. 366.

year. Another impediment was that he was viewed as 'a rather aggressive Englishman'.[28] As Stella Wood in the *Oxford Dictionary of National Biography* describes him, he was 'determined and forceful. His optimism and desire for progress were infectious but were accompanied by an impatience and oversensitivity which sometimes made him difficult to work with.' These traits were there as a student as well. In short, Lunn was heavily disliked, and long before the election a vicious smear campaign was waged against him and it proved devastating to his candidacy.

The auditorial campaign took place in the context of these tensions. In addition, rules were broken to facilitate his defeat. Moffat's brother, Charles, was an honorary member of the Society, and attempted to influence the election by canvassing other voters in writing. Canvassing was forbidden under the rules of the Society and Charles had compounded the matter by including some hostile comments about Lunn in his letters. Lunn was furious and complained to Charles Moffat, and received a formal apology. But he was still not satisfied and brought the matter before the Society. Motions were discussed, including one proposing that Charles Moffat should be suspended for a year, leading to a counter-motion suggesting that the Auditor should be impeached if anyone was suspended. In the end, Moffat was allowed continue as a member and the motion to impeach the Auditor was dropped.

H. Cameron Lyster, the former Auditor, later admitted that the 'very bitter contest' had 'aroused more heated feelings' than he had ever known. In the end, Moffat won by a considerable margin, with Lunn a distant second, and Gaussen only receiving a handful of votes.

Lunn was ordained a Methodist minister in 1886, and did some missionary work in India, but was forced to resign after falling out with the ministry. In later years he was obsessed with the idea of church reunion, and campaigned across the world promoting closer co-operation between churches. He also became a travel agent, setting up his own company, which later became the hugely successful Lunn Poly, at one time the largest chain of travel agents in the United Kingdom. A friend of Asquith, Lunn ran for

28 Dagg, *CHS*, p. 272.

parliament twice unsuccessfully, and was knighted in 1910. But he never forgot his defeat in the auditorial election, and spent much time on the subject in his first memoir, *Chapters from my Life.* He returned to the subject in his chapter on the first world war, when discussing a successful libel action Asquith's wife had brought against a newspaper. It reminded Lunn of his 'own case when I was in Dublin and of the barrister who defeated my candidature for the chair of the Historical Society by spreading lies about me'.[29]

The Board continued to veto motions of which it disapproved. In the 1887–87 session some suggested topics were rejected, but there were good debates on trial by jury, the American Civil War ('the revolt of the Southern states'), and whether 'the principles of the Chartists were radically vicious' (which was defeated). In the 1888–89 session one of the best debates was on the motion 'That the encouragement of the higher education of women is desirable', and this was passed by the House.

As President, Gibson (now Lord Ashbourne), had one issue that was a source of regular annoyance. He objected to the rule which stated that only the Auditor (or pro-Auditor) could answer points of order, and believed that, in his own case, 'the rule is simply absurd'.[30] Given that he was the President of the Society, the Lord Chancellor of Ireland, and a former Auditor, he believed that he should be authorised to decide on all points, instead of having someone else go 'over my head (and it might be against my clear opinion)'. But the Society refused to address the point, regretting the anomaly in a letter to him, but avoiding making any change.

Edward Carson chaired the debate on 20 January 1890 on Pitt's Irish policy and addressed the meeting at the end. One of the most important changes to the regulations of the Society occurred at this time. On 19 March 1890 the Auditor, Gerald F. Brunskill, brought forward a motion to allow Freshman students join the Society. This was carried without a division. Brunskill had been doing much work behind the scenes, and had secured Board approval for the change, and the reform changed both the membership and the very character of the Society. It was now a Society for all the university. A second

29 Lunn, *Chapters,* p. 232.

30 Dagg, *CHS*, p. 277.

motion, also passed unanimously, removed the entrance fee of five shillings. Until this point the Society had sometimes been criticised for being too exclusive, now it had a real opportunity to transform its image and its role in College.

These changes were discussed by William J. Hardy, the new Auditor, at the opening of the 1890–91 session on 12 November. Speaking on the subject of 'New Journalism', Hardy began by recognising that 'the charge of exclusiveness sometimes brought against the Historical can no longer be maintained', and he welcomed the addition of new members from across the different years.[31] The Board was relaxing its restrictions and only blocked one motion that year.

William Macneile Dixon was the Auditor for the 1891-92 session, and in his inaugural address he discussed the subject of 'University Education in Ireland'. At this time he was working on his history of Trinity College Dublin. The construction of the Graduates' Memorial Building, occupied the Society during the 1890s, especially as it was proposed to give it rooms within it. Much of the concern centred on the proposal to create some kind of Union in the building, and it was feared that this would attempt to replace the Society. An extraordinary general meeting was called for the afternoon of 4 April 1894 and at it Lord Justice FitzGibbon proposed a motion, seconded by Professor Cherry, asserting the independence and separate existence of the College Historical Society. The students' strategy was at times disorganized and haphazard. In December 1895 it dissolved the sub-committee it had established to watch over the society's interests in the building, only to reconstitute the sub-committee two months later. The GMB was eventually opened on Friday 30 May 1902.

Beauclerk Upington was elected Auditor of the Society for 1896–97 and delivered his inaugural address on the future of South Africa on 11 November 1896. Upington was the son of Sir Thomas Upington, the Cork-born Prime Minister of the Cape Colony in South Africa between 1884 and 1886.[32] Upington would go on to become a 'legendary King's Counsel' in the Cape Colony, described

31 *The Irish Times*, 13 November 1890; Dagg, *CHS*, p. 280.

32 Oliver Rafferty (ed.), *Irish Catholic identities* (Manchester, 2013), p. 266.

in one account as 'the most famous criminal lawyer that the Cape has ever seen'.[33] One writer called him, 'a man you could not forget: tall and spare, dark-eyed, with almost hawk-like features'.[34] Upington appears in many South African legal memoirs, and was said to be 'a real character, who might have stepped out of the pages of Dickens'. A brilliant speaker, he was celebrated in South Africa for his 'legal oratory and honeyed words'.[35] Upington could be aggressive when he wanted to be, and was withering to those who crossed him. His insults to the bench become legendary. When one judge remonstrated, 'Mr Upington, you do nothing to conceal your total contempt for me', Upington replied, 'With respect, my lord, I do my best to conceal it'[36]

Upington's inaugural meeting attracted a huge attendance, so much so that the Dining Hall was overcrowded, and this created its own problems.[37] The crowd was in an exuberant spirit, and spent much of the first part of proceedings making noise – throwing crackers, blowing horns, and making cat calls. Few onlookers were able to hear anything. But Upington gradually took control of the crowd, and he ended the speech with a powerful message of how one day South Africa would achieve 'the great goal of national freedom and prosperity', which was its 'ultimate and manifest destiny'.

Lecky was one of the guest speakers at Upington's inaugural and he gave his personal impressions of President Paul Kruger: 'He has been more than once in my house ... a strong stubborn man, with indomitable courage and resolution, with very little tinge of cultivation, but, with a natural shrewdness in judging men and events'. Upington returned to Cape Town in 1898 and became, in the words of the *Dictionary of South African Biography,* 'a brilliant advocate', and his success was described as 'phenomenal.'[38] He served one term in parliament (1915–19) where he was considered one of

---

33 Leslie Blackwell, *Of judges and justice* (Cape Town, 1965), p. 18.

34 Marius Diemont, *Brushes with the law* (Cape Town, 1995), p. 39.

35 Jean St Leger Lawrence, *Coming home to roost* (Cape Town, 1986), p. 118.

36 *Frontline* (1980), vol, 1, issue 1, p. 32.

37 *Irish times,* 12 November 1896.

38 V.G. Hiemstra, 'Beauclerk Upington', *Dictionary of South African Biography* (1977), vol. 3 p. 7.

the 'most compelling' speakers in the House of Assembly and 'where he constantly pleaded for the poor and oppressed'. Terrible with his own money, he suffered severe financial difficulties in his final years. Many friends wrote him cheques to help him out, but he was too disorganized to cash them, and left 'cheques for hundreds of pounds in his drawers and in books'. He died in 1938.

That session the Society debated among other subjects, press censorship, socialism, Pitt's Irish policy, and British rule in India. Standish James O'Grady, the writer and journalist, was the guest chair for the debate on whether Dickens was the greatest novelist of the nineteenth century (it was defeated), while Timothy Harrington, MP, chaired the debate on whether the career and conduct of Daniel O'Connell was worthy of admiration (it was carried).

Ashbourne could be a demanding president. The inaugural meeting of the 1897–98 session was scheduled for 10 November 1897, and the day before he sent the Auditor a letter stating that as that year was the centenary of the death of Edmund Burke, the address should be on his life. The Auditor, George Freeman Irwin, had no choice but to comply, and he borrowed from the Library every book he could find on Burke. Then, with the help of the Record Secretary, Robert Romilly Smylie, he stayed up all night, preparing his address, which was delivered with some success.

To celebrate the life of Burke, the Society organized a Burke Memorial Dinner, which was held in the Dining Hall, on 7 December 1897. The dinner was presided over by the Provost, and was attended by the Lord Lieutenant, and a range of dignitaries. It was noted that almost every one of the hundred people present had been a member of the Society, and the gathering included seventeen ex-Auditors.

One of the best toasts of the night was delivered by Lecky to the memory of Edmund Burke. Lecky noted that while they owed much to Burke – 'we claim him as the founder of the Historical Society' - it was also true that 'Burke certainly owed much to us'. He explained that it was at the Society that 'he first practised the art of debating, of which he became so great a master'.[39] Another toast was to The College Historical Society. In response to this, Irwin delivered a

39 Dagg, *CHS*, p. 292.

speech that was described by the new student journal *TCD* as 'brilliant, perfect in matter and delivery and apt in illustration'.[40] It is possible the praise was justified, although it probably did not hurt that Irwin was the first editor of the publication.[41] Mahaffy also spoke, and he noted that the Society was necessary to 'keep alive the sacred flame', by holding 'aloft the beacon of eloquence amid the surge of over-instructed and stammering mediocrity'.

W.B. Yeats chaired a meeting of the Society at the end of the 1898–99 session, a debate on 20 May 1899 on whether any attempt to further an Irish Literary Movement would lead to provincialism.[42] After the motion was defeated, Yeats stood to address the gathering to much applause. Expressing a hope that the university would 'be one of the instruments that would express that which was distinctive' in the country, he rejected the idea that a literature based on national characteristics was provincial. For Yeats, 'a peasant dressed in his national costume was not provincial', but a small shopkeeper who copied the costumes of London or Paris was, because cosmopolitanism was never a creative force. Recognising that Ireland had a destiny shaped by its history, he argued that Ireland 'with its legends, its profound faith, with its simplicity, its sincerity would lift up its voices in an empire of spirit greater than any material empire'.

The opening meeting of the 1900–01 session was an opportunity to reflect on the previous century. The Auditor, John Edward Walsh, delivered a major address on 'Trinity College in the nineteenth century'. The Historical Society had endured considerable trauma in the nineteenth century – including death and resurrection – before re-establishing itself as the place for aspiring public speakers to develop their skills and test their ideas. It was where writers and poets, clergyman and lawyers, politicians and academics developed the friendships, skills and resilience that were to serve them well in the years ahead. Young Ireland could trace its lineage to the Society but so too could Irish Unionism. The Irish Gothic tradition owed a debt to the Society. Perhaps it was no wonder that in response to the

40 Ibid.

41 Kenneth Claude Bailey, *A history of Trinity College Dublin, 1892-1945* (Dublin, 1947), p. 176.

42 *Freeman's Journal*, 1 June 1901.

inaugural paper Lecky decided to assert that 'there was no other institution which was so closely connected with all that was best and most illustrious in Irish life'. [43]

43 Dagg, *CHS*, p. 298.

12

'THE FINEST DISPLAY OF ORATORY I EVER HEARD': THE COLLEGE HISTORICAL SOCIETY AND THE RIDDLE OF *ULYSSES*

IN JAMES JOYCE'S MASTERPIECE, *Ulysses,* published in complete form in 1920, there is a notable reference to the College Historical Society bestowing a kind of literary immortality upon it. In the 'Aeolus' chapter, Professor McHugh begins reminiscing about 'the finest display of oratory I ever heard' and gives the honour to 'a speech made by John F. Taylor at the college historical society'. Taylor's speech was one that inspired Joyce and resonated with him. In 1924, when he was asked to record some of *Ulysses* for Sylvia Beach, his first choice was McHugh's account of the oration.[1] Joyce claimed he chose the piece because it was 'declamatory' and therefore would work well for reading out-loud. But Beach rightly suspected that it was really because 'it expressed something he wanted said and preserved in his own voice'.[2] Taylor's speech was one that impressed many Irish nationalist and literary figures in Joyce's lifetime, including Roger Casement who made it the centre-piece of his short pamphlet, *The Language of the Outlaw.* W. B. Yeats was also hugely influenced by it, although he could only remember it taking place at 'some College society perhaps'.[3]

---

1 Neil R. Davison, *James Joyce, Ulysses and the construction of Jewish identity* (Cambridge, 1998), p.80.

2 So Onose 'A great future behind him: John F. Taylor's speech in "Aeolus" revisited', in *A long the Kommerun: selected papers from the Utrecht James Joyce symposium* (London, 2016).

3 W.H. O'Donnell and D.N. Archibald (eds), *The collected works of W.B. Yeats. Vol. 3. Autobiographies* (New York 1999), p.101.

Thanks to its mention in *Ulysses*, the College Historical Society is referenced in many Joycean studies, including the detailed annotated studies of *Ulysses*, and its name continues to reach an international literary audience. For example, Don Gifford and Robert J. Seidman's masterly *Ulysses Annotated: Notes for James Joyce's Ulysses* contains a lengthy note on the College Historical Society, including its claim to be 'the oldest university debating society in Ireland or Great Britain', and discusses how many of the historical figures mentioned in the text were members at one point or another.[4] Specialist studies also pay tribute to the society. The distinguished German academic, Wolfgang Wicht, in his study of *Utopianism in James Joyce's Ulysses,* discusses how one of the most 'positive and sympathetic' references to the Moses story was contained in Taylor's speech extemporised 'before the Trinity College Historical Society'.[5] There are numerous other examples, from studies of *Ulysses* as a comic novel, to general studies.[6]

This chapter is in some ways a digression, analysing as it does a literary reference to the Society, even if it is in one of the most significant literary texts of all time. But it is also the exploration of a puzzle. Because the speech which impressed Joyce so much did not occur in the College Historical Society, or indeed anywhere in Trinity. Instead Joyce incorrectly attributed the debate to the Society, and it is worth exploring why he did that, whether it was intentional, and the proper context of the speech. It is also worth discussing because through *Ulysses* the name of the Society reached an international audience of readers, literary scholars, and literary theorists. Finally it is noteworthy that the person who Taylor was debating against in *Ulysses* – the villain of the piece – was a major

4 Don Gifford and R.J. Seidman, *Ulysses Annotated* (London, 1974), p. 147.

5 Wolfgang Wicht, *Utopianism in James Joyce's Ulysses* (Heidelberg, 2000), p. 173.

6 Zach Bowen, *Ulysses as a comic novel* (Syracuse, 1989), p. 50; Willi Erzgraber, *James Joyce: oral and written discourse as mirrored in experimental narrative art* (London, 2002), p. 231; Harry Blamires, *The new Bloomsday book: a guide through Ulysses* (London, 1996), p. 54.

figure in the history of the Society, Gerald FitzGibbon, and through *Ulysses* an unfair and distorted version of FitzGibbon's views was presented to the world.

The debate that impressed Joyce so much took place on 24 October 1901. It was not a meeting of the College Historical Society (its inaugural meeting did not take place until November) but rather the inaugural meeting of the Law Students' Debating Society in King's Inns. There is no evidence that Joyce attended the debate. He did, however, purchase a copy of Casement's short pamphlet in 1904 which quoted extensively from the speech and this formed the basis of his own retelling of the debate. There are at least four versions of Taylor's speech. First is the account of the debate in the *Freeman's Journal* published the day after, on 25 October 1901. Second was a version that appeared in the *Manchester Guardian* on 14 November 1902, in a letter signed X, which was published as a tribute to Taylor who had just died. It was this version, word-for-word, which Casement used in his short pamphlet, first published privately in 1904 and reprinted in the *United Irishman* in 1906.[7] The third version of the speech is Joyce's version that appears in *Ulysses.* And the fourth is one that W.B. Yeats reworked and presented in two different places in his autobiography. There are significant differences between all versions.

In *Ulysses* the speech is presented as part of a debate on the revival of the Irish language, which followed the reading of 'an essay (new for those days), advocating the revival of the Irish tongue'. In this version, Gerald FitzGibbon, then Lord Justice of Appeal, rose to deliver a scathing attack on the proposal. McHugh believed Fitzgibbon's style of oratory needed no real introduction. Turning to a friend he said, 'You know Gerald FitzGibbon. Then you can imagine the style of his discourse.' It was a speech, 'mark you', said McHugh, 'of a finished orator, full of courteous haughtiness and pouring in chastened diction'. According to McHugh, he treated the new movement with contempt, 'We were weak, therefore worthless.' The speech that impressed Joyce so much was delivered in response by John F. Taylor, an Irish barrister and journalist who was Dublin correspondent for the *Manchester Guardian.* Many people believed

7 *United Irishmen*, 17 February 1906.

that Taylor was 'the finest orator of his time' and that 'his gifts as an orator were of a remarkable order'.[8] Roger Casement described him as 'one of the most eloquent of modern Irishmen'.[9] Yeats called him 'an obscure great orator' and considered him to be perhaps the finest orator he had ever heard.[10] Patrick Maume in the *Dictionary of Irish Biography* reflects on Taylor's oratorical prowess and notes that Maud Gonne believed that only Patrick Pearse came close to matching his prowess.[11]

According to McHugh in *Ulysses*, Taylor 'had come there, you must know, from a sick bed'. The speech had not been prepared in advance, and he arrived wearing 'a loose neck-cloth', his 'dark lean face had a growth of shaggy beard', and 'he looked (though he was not) a dying man'. Taylor compared FitzGibbon's arguments to some Egyptian high-priest addressing Moses: 'Why will you Jews not accept our culture, our religion and our language?' Taylor insisted that had Moses listened to these warnings, 'had he bowed his head and bowed his will and bowed his spirit before that arrogant admonition' then 'he would never have brought the chosen people out of their house of bondage ... nor ever have come down with the light of inspiration shining in his countenance and bearing in his arms the tables of the law'. As Joyce has MacHugh say, without any contradiction: 'That is oratory.'

The version of Taylor's speech that appears in *Ulysses* was largely Joyce's own creation. In effect, he took a published account of the debate and rewrote in his own style. The imagery was the same, but the language very different. In the *Manchester Guardian* account, used word-for-word by Casement, it is not some 'high-priest of the land' addressing Moses but rather 'a fashionable professor with an attachment to the Egyptian court'. After outlining at length the reasons why the Israelites should submit, Taylor's response is to ask, 'if Moses had listened to those arguments what would have been the

8 Herbert Mackey (ed.), *The Crime Against Europe: The Writings and Poetry of Roger Casement* (Dublin, 1958), p. 114; Gifford and Seidman, *Ulysses Annotated,* p. 147.

9 Text in Herbert Mackey (ed.), *Crime against Europe*, p. 113.

10 O'Donnell and Archibold (eds), *Autobiographies*, p. 101.

11 Patrick Maume, 'John Francis Taylor', *DIB.*

end? Would he ever have come down from the Mount, with the light of God shining on his face, and carrying in his hands the Tablets of the Law written in the language of the outlaw?'[12] Joyce took Casement's pamphlet as his starting point – including its mention of Taylor having come from his sick-bed – and made the speech his own. The Tablets of the Law become the Tables of the Law, and the changes to the text of the argument are also substantial.

FitzGibbon is cast as the villain in the version of the speech published in the *Manchester Guardian* and used by Casement. We are told that FitzGibbon 'made a dialectical discourse of a kind with which we are all familiar on platforms' except that he had 'surpassed the ordinary advocate in the skilful irrelevance of his argument and in the covering (no less skilful) of his manner of delivery'.[13] It was, the article concluded, 'conventional fireworks'. It is in response to this attack that Taylor makes his strong defence of the Irish language.

Joyce was not the only one to present a reimagined version of the debate. In Yeat's *Autobiographies,* first published in 1955, there are numerous references to Taylor, and in two places Yeats gives his own version of the speech, which owes much to his imagination and invention. According to Yeats the speech was so famous he once overheard in Dublin 'a man murmuring [it] to another'. Getting some details wrong in his first and more detailed account of the speech, Yeats names Taylor's opponent as the Lord Chancellor and has him speaking first (FitzGibbon was Lord Justice of Appeal), in 'balanced unemotional sentences, now self-complacent, now derisive'. In response, Taylor begins hesitantly, 'stopping for words, but after speaking very badly for a little, straightened his figure and spoke as out of a dream'. In this vision, Yeats has Taylor say that he is 'carried to another age, a nobler society, and another Lord Chancellor is speaking. I am at the court of the first Pharaoh.' The language is very different in this version. Taylor has the Egyptian Lord Chancellor ask the children of Israel: 'If you have any spirituality as you boast, why not use our great empire to spread it through the world, why still cling to that beggarly nationality of yours?' Then Taylor's 'voice changed and sank' and he cried, 'had he

12 Mackey (ed.), *Crime against Europe,* p. 115.

13 Ibid., p. 114.

obeyed he would never have come down the mountains carrying in his arms the Tables of the Law in the language of the outlaw'. Yeats version is his own take on the Casement version of the speech, refracted through the prism of *Ulysses.*

Yeats himself was inconsistent about whether he had actually been at the original debate. In the 1932–36 page proofs Yeats references the debate he was describing and admitted that 'Taylor made an even more imaginative use of Egypt, but I did not hear the speech'.[14] Later in the autobiography he seemed to recall having been at the debate, this time correctly placing Taylor against FitzGibbon. In this version he has Taylor present his opponents as saying: 'Join with our greatness! What in comparison to that is your little, beggarly nationality?'[15] Yeats claimed to 'recall the excitement, the shiver of the nerves' as Taylor's voice 'rose to an ecstatic cry' as he declaimed, 'Out of that nation came the salvation of the world.'[16] It becomes impossible to reconcile Yeats' different accounts.

There is no doubt that Yeats was entranced by Taylor's oratory, even though they had a difficult relationship and there was much tension between them. 'He hated me', says Yeats simply at one point.[17] Taylor was critical of Yeats for publishing Irish folklore in English rather than Irish, and for finding fault with the Young Ireland poetry and prose. Nevertheless, in another section of the *Autobiographies,* Yeats describes Taylor's oratory as 'noble, strange, even beautiful, at moments the greatest I have ever listened to'.[18] He compared him to 'a man under a curse, compelled to hide his genius, and compelled to show in conspicuous places his ill-judgement and his temper'.[19] Later again he described him as 'a great orator, the greatest I have heard' but 'doomed by the violence of his temper to speak before Law Students' Debating Societies, obscure Young Ireland societies'.[20] Yeats described him as having an angular body,

14 O'Donnell and Archibold (eds), *Autobiographies*, p. 192.
15 Ibid.
16 Ibid., p. 193.
17 Ibid., p. 313.
18 Ibid., p. 179.
19 Ibid., p. 180.
20 Ibid., p. 313.

'often rigid with suppressed rage, his gaze fixed upon some object, his clothes badly made, his erect attitude suggesting a firm base'. He believed that unlike many other speakers Taylor had style, evident in his 'flights of oratorical frenzy' and concluded that 'drunk or sober, idle or toiling, this man had it'.[21]

So in terms of reworkings of the speech we have the Casement version of the speech, the Joyce version of the speech, and the Yeats version. None of them reflects the reality of what really took place at the debate on 24 October 1901, and all present distorted versions of the order of events and the format. The reality of the debate was very different from the version Joyce re-imagined over a decade later, based on the account used by Casement, or the versions Yeats imagined. In fact the debate that occurred on 24 October 1901 bore very little resemblance to any of the later descriptions. Apart from the incorrect attribution of where the debate took place, the order of the speeches was different and this changes completely the nature of the retellings. The real event was a packed meeting of the Law Students Debating Society in the King's Inns, attended by the Lord Mayor and the Archbishop of Dublin and a host of dignitaries. FitzGibbon was the President of the Law Students Debating Society and he chaired the meeting, and it began with an address on the Irish revival by the Auditor, St Lawrence Devitt. Taylor spoke after him, moving the resolution that the best thanks of the Society were given to the Auditor. So the crucial point is that Taylor spoke before FitzGibbon, who only addressed the gathering from the chair at the end of the meeting. Taylor was not responding to some attacks by FitzGibbon, rather he was replying to the Auditor's address in favour of the revival of the Irish language. It was not a response to some unprovoked denunciation of the Irish language.

In his speech, Taylor began his speech praising Thomas Davis's by now famous address to the College Historical Society in 1840, reminding people that it had been criticised by many at the time who did not see its value.[22] Taylor argued that all political statesmanship in Ireland could be considered a failure as long as forty thousand young people were emigrating every year. In his peroration

21 Ibid., p. 315.

22 *Freeman's Journal*, 25 October 1901.

he compared the dismissive views on the Irish language to the 'intellectual Egyptian' who had told Moses not to bother doing anything for his people. Instead Moses had 'come down from the mountain, his face glowing as a star, and bearing the Tablets of the Law'. The greatest strength of the Irish language, he argued, was that it was not a 'language encrusted with commercialism and materialism' but a 'pure language that was kept aloof and unsullied with contamination with the world'. This resolution was passed without controversy. It was only then, to conclude the meeting, that FitzGibbon addressed the gathering from the chair.

Far from denouncing the Irish language, FitzGibbon delivered a thoughtful closing speech in which he admitted that 'the old language of Ireland was an object of intense interest and affection from his earliest days'. He challenged the Auditor's claim that the Irish people had only spoken Irish one hundred years earlier, citing as evidence Daniel O'Connell, 'the greatest master of invective and the greatest advocate', who had grown up speaking English as well as Irish. FitzGibbon argued that it was all well and good to speak of reviving the Irish language, but he wanted to know what language was going to be revived, whether it would be classical Irish, or some newer invention. Looking across the world to the Irish diaspora in the United States, Australia and New Zealand, FitzGibbon argued that there was a 'greater Ireland' there of emigrants who spoke English as their first language but who were no less Irish. On behalf of these people, and for himself, he repudiated the theory that the proof of an Irishman was their ability to say 'conas tá tú'. This was greeted with loud applause and the meeting terminated.

So the mystery is why did Joyce attribute the debate to the College Historical Society? Of course, if he had known the confusion it would have caused he might have done it deliberately, a puzzle for later scholars, something for them to analyse and trip themselves up over. It could also be argued that there was a strong internal logic in the context of the novel. Earlier in the chapter there is a wider discussion of oratory, and many of the great speakers are referenced – 'Henry Grattan and Flood and Demosthenes and Edmund Burke'. Given the profile of the College Historical Society, and its rich history involving some of these names, it perhaps made sense to name-check the recognisable student society instead of a more obscure one. But there is a simpler and more obvious explanation: Joyce made a mistake. He had not attended the debate, and based his version of the event on the Casement pamphlet. From that he drew all the details about the order of speeches, the behaviour of FitzGibbon denouncing the Irish language, and the brilliant performance by Taylor, who overcame his illness to provide a stirring vindication. But he did not know from the pamphlet where the debate had taken place. Or rather, he knew where it could not have taken place. And this is the key to the entire puzzle.

Apart from rewriting the speech, there was one other major change Joyce made to the version in the Casement pamphlet. There the debate is said to have taken place at the 'University College Debating Society', in other words the Literary and Historical Society in University College Dublin. Joyce was a leading member of this Society, indeed he was one of its most impressive orators at this time. It made no sense for Joyce to attribute the event to the debating society in Trinity, if it had in fact occurred in his own debating society in his own university. It is not likely to have been something he misremembered, or changed deliberately. The only explanation is that when Joyce read Casement's pamphlet he realized that the author had got the venue wrong. It had not taken place in the L&H, because if it had he would have known about it and would have attended it. But because Joyce had not seen the account in the *Freeman's Journal* (if he had he would have known the correct order of speeches), he did not know where it had actually taken place and had no way of finding out. Making a guess, he incorrectly assumed it must have taken place in Trinity. And so he refers to the debate having taken place in the 'college historical society', with the name in lower case for personal or stylistic reasons.

Most Joycean scholars have attributed the debate to the College Historical Society, while only a handful have correctly identified that it took place at King's Inns, most notably the greatest of them all, Richard Ellmann.[23] One UCD researcher, So Onose, has proposed that in fact two debates took place on the same subject with the same protagonists within weeks of each other. The first was the one

23 See also John Garvin, *James Joyce's disunited kingdom and the Irish dimension* (Dublin, 1976), p. 67.

recorded in the *Freeman's Journal,* which took place in King's Inns. The second was a debate in University College Dublin in November, when FitzGibbon and Taylor effectively had a 'rematch'. Onose bases this on the fact that the *Freeman's Journal* account clearly shows that FitzGibbon spoke after Taylor and in 'moderate terms', and argues that the only explanation for this contradiction is if two debates took place. He believes that this explains FitzGibbon's vehemence at the second encounter, 'as well as the finesse with which Taylor counters it', as they were 'reprising their previous arguments'. However, there are major problems with this ingenious theory and it does not stand up to scrutiny.

First, Onose deploys as evidence the fact that Ellmann described the Taylor speech at King's Inns as 'pallid' and, agreeing with this, suggests that it could never therefore have been considered great oratory.[24] However, Ellmann does not dismiss the speech itself as pallid, only the limited coverage in the newspaper. Second, while Taylor did address the L&H inaugural meeting on 20 November 1901, FitzGibbon was not present. The debate was on socialism, not the Irish revival movement, and followed the Auditor's paper on the 'Social Problem'.[25] The supposed rematch never took place.

As it happens, the L&H did debate the Irish language later in the month, on 30 November ('That the Promotion of the Irish Language Movement is Essential to the Preservation of Irish Nationality'), but neither FitzGibbon nor Taylor were present. Indeed we learn from *St Stephen's* that the committee meeting which decided the topic was a fractious one, with two ex-Auditors involved, and 'that the Senior Secretary had to resign no less than three times'.[26] But, unfortunately, that is all that is said, and we are told 'a veil of impenetrable secrecy' hung over the affair.

Joycean scholars have long debated whether Joyce actually heard Taylor's speech on 24 October 1901. The evidence appears conclusive that he did not. If he had attended the debate in the King's Inns he would have known the real order or events and would not have got key details wrong, including the venue. He would also have been able

24 Onose, A great future behind him', p. 48.

25 *St Stephen's* (December 1901), p. 45.

26 Ibid.

to add his own details to the descriptions. Instead he based the structure of his debate entirely on the Casement pamphlet. But the reason he chose to write about Taylor, and rewrite his speech for *Ulysses* was because he had heard him speak on a different subject at a different student event, and that was the debate on socialism on the 20 November 1901 in the L&H. It was this speech that made Joyce consider Taylor the finest orator he ever heard. According to the student journal, *St Stephen's,* we know that Taylor delivered a powerful address that was the 'speech of the evening', and that 'with his cause undoubtedly the victory rested'. As the student reporter explains, 'in Mr Taylor we found a prophet', and there is considerable praise for how he addressed 'the miseries of the poor and the cruelties of the compulsory individualism of the Saxon'. Present at the debate was Joyce, who was described as 'Dreamy Jimmy ... standing on a window-sill' looking as if he could 'say things unutterable.'[27]

In *St Stephen's* a considerable compliment is paid to Joyce: his oratory is compared to Taylor's. We are told that Taylor spoke 'with a style that reminds one of our own Joyce at his best'. However a qualification is added that Taylor 'has a broadness of sympathy that the latter has yet to acquire'. It must have been flattering for Joyce to read in the student magazine that Taylor was 'the only true descendent of Grattan and Flood at the Irish bar' and that he himself had a similar speaking style.[28] It is surely no coincidence that in *Ulysses* the discussion of Taylor's oratory comes directly after a reference to Grattan and Flood; Joyce was drawing from the account in *St Stephen's* as well as the Casement pamphlet. Sometime in 1904 Joyce purchased a copy of *The Language of the Outlaw* and read an account of a Taylor speech at a different debate, and later decided to incorporate this into *Ulysses,* inspired by the speech he had actually seen him deliver.

So James Joyce's discussion of 'the finest oratory' he ever heard was a speech he wrote himself, inspired by a debate he did not attend, based on a pamphlet which got key details wrong. The Joycean scholar, Mark Osteen, has commented on 'the intertextual layers of appropriations' in Joyce's borrowing from the account of a

27 Ibid., p. 46.

28 Ibid., p. 45.

real event and 'placing his version of the real man's words in the mouth of a fictional character, who quotes the fictional version of the real orator, who himself cites the words of an imaginary priest'.[29] The reality was even more complicated than that. Nevertheless, by mentioning the College Historical Society Joyce ensured that the name of the Society reached an international literary audience, and it continues to be named and praised in studies of the novel.[30] It turns out that the most famous and widely discussed debate in the history of the College Historical Society was one that never took place there. Joyce might well have appreciated the irony.

---

29 Mark Osteen, *The economy of Ulysses: making both ends meet* (Syracuse, 1995), p. 208.

30 See for example, Bowen, *Ulysses as a comic novel*, p. 50; Erzgraber, *James Joyce;* Blamires, *The new Bloomsday book*, p. 54.

IN THE SHADOW OF WAR, 1901-1914

13

WINSTON CHURCHILL visited the College Historical Society in November 1902 to speak at the inaugural meeting of the Society. Even in 1902 Churchill was considered 'distinguished alike in war, in literature and in parliament'.[1] The Auditor was James Andrews, future Lord Chief Justice of Northern Ireland, and the subject 'Imperial Federation'. Writing about the visit in 1923, *The Irish Times* noted that 'Apart from his well-known connection with various legislative attempts to settle the Irish problem, culminating in his signature of the Anglo-Irish Treaty, Mr Churchill is associated with Ireland through the medium of the College Historical Society.'[2] And it praised the Society as one 'which has always attempted to demonstrate to English public men that there is one place in Ireland from which the spirit of religious and political bigotry has been successfully exorcised'.

In his address, Andrews called for the creation of 'a Federated Empire', with countries having a similar role to states in the United States of America.[3] He suggested that 'the scattered members of the Empire' would 'find one real national life in Imperial unity' through such a construct. Greeted with 'loud cheers', Churchill delivered a stirring response, and challenged elements of the proposal. He joked that the Auditor had provided a garment to cover the issues of tariffs, federation and defence but if it was 'not actually dangerous to public health, [it] might be somewhat subversive to public decency'. Churchill believed it was better to keep the countries separate,

1 *The Irish Times,* 8 October 1923.

2 Ibid.

3 *The Irish Times,* 6 November 1902; TCD/MUN/SOC/HIST/39.

suggesting that in a federation they would be dragged into 'the sport of party politics' and become 'pawns or the counters in a game they could never play'.

In another brilliant sound-bite, Churchill summed-up the difference between the Liberals and the Conservatives: 'The Tories, in trying to keep the Empire, nearly lost it, and the Liberals have kept it while trying to throw it away.' Churchill joked that he was speaking 'in the temple of truth', in a country 'where no whisper of dissension ever disturbed the serenity of the air'. Other speakers included the former Auditor, James Campbell, and the Duke of Connaught, Prince Arthur, who was the third son of Queen Victoria.

Significant debates during the year included one on a motion that Greek should not form a compulsory subject in the university curriculum. Nine members spoke on the evening, and the debate was adjourned so it could continue on the following night. Six speakers spoke on the next day, at which point an amendment was introduced 'That Greek and Latin should not form compulsory subjects in a university curriculum'.[4] A further eight speakers debated this amendment. Following which, votes were taken and the motion and the amendment were both defeated. The writer, George Russell (AE), chaired a debate on the motion 'That the Irish literary movement is deserving of the support of every Irishman' and the motion was passed.[5]

A prominent member at this time was Oliver St John Gogarty, a young medical student, and occasionally he could be too boisterous. Twice in February 1903 the Auditor fined him one shilling for obstruction.[6] Gogarty would return to speak the Society in later years and won fame as a surgeon and man of letters, writing many poems and books. A supporter of Sinn Féin during the War of Independence, he provided a safe house to Michael Collins, and attended to his friend, Arthur Griffith, in his final days.[7] A senator between 1922 and 1936, Gogarty was kidnapped by anti-Treaty republicans in 1923, but he escaped by jumping into the Liffey. As

4 TCD/MUN/SOC/HIST/39.

5 Dagg, *CHS*, p. 303; TCD/MUN/SOC/HIST/39.

6 TCD/MUN/SOC/HIST/39.

7 Patrick Maume, 'Oliver St John Gogarty', *DIB*.

Patrick Maume notes in the *Dictionary of Irish Biography*, 'in gratitude he ceremonially introduced two swans to the Liffey'. 'Best remembered as the model for the irrepressible Buck Mulligan in Joyce's *Ulysses.*' Maume notes that 'he retains admirers who believe his art was undervalued'.

On 6 March 1903 Trinity hosted a major debate where speakers from the society competed against debaters from the Oxford and Cambridge Unions. The motion was 'That this House Disapproves of the Principle of Party Government'.[8]

At the inaugural meeting in November 1903 the Auditor, John Mary FitzGerald, delivered a paper on 'the Industrial Future of Ireland' and Sir Horace Plunkett was one of the speakers in response. From Cork, Jack FitzGerald was one of the leading debaters of his generation and graduated with a gold medal in English literature. He went on to become a skilful barrister, and when he died unexpectedly in May 1946 he was eulogised by T.C. Kingsmill Moore who called him 'one of the most quick-witted of a quick-witted profession ... entirely original in his methods and unpredictable in his sallies'.[9]

Other motions debated that year included a controversial one on whether the American government should take measures by which the lives and liberties of the black population would be secured, which was defeated.[10] Opposing the motion were two South African students, Johann Hahn and Willhelm Van Zijl. Van Zijl won the gold medal for oratory that year and later became a member of the legislature of Cape Colony.

In 1904 the decision was taken enabling women to attend Trinity and take degrees, though not debates of the Society, and a motion was passed welcoming the admission of women to the university.[11] That summer the Society moved from House 5, where it had been since 1872, to the newly opened Graduates Memorial Building. The Society developed one room as its Library and created a billiards room in the attic. H. Lloyd Cowdy was elected Auditor for the 1904–

8 Dagg, *CHS*, p. 304; TCD/MUN/SOC/HIST/39.

9 *The Irish Law Times and Solicitors' Journal* (1946), p. 140.

10 TCD/MUN/SOC/HIST/39.

11 Dagg, *CHS*, p. 309; TCD/MUN/SOC/HIST/39.

05 session and chose the subject of 'The British Policy of Free Imports' for his inaugural, despite a warning from Ashbourne, the President of the Society, about the political nature of the subject.

One of the most controversial debates of the session was one on 23 November 1904 on the motion 'That the Socialistic Ideal is Economically Unsound'. Four members of the Socialist Party of Ireland were invited to speak opposing the motion, with standing orders suspended to allow this to happen, but they were unable to convince the students of their cause and the motion was carried by 19 votes to 13.[12] Following the failure of revolt in Russia in 1905 a motion was passed 'That this House views with regret the failure of the recent revolutionary movement in Russia'.[13]

In February 1905 the College Historical Society took part in a debate at the Oxford Union for the first time in its history. Initially the Oxford Union had wanted a debate on the Act of Union of 1800, but eventually it was agreed to have a debate on a matter relating to present-day politics: 'That the conduct of the Irish Parliamentary Party is not conducive to the best interest of Ireland'. There were three speakers on each side, with Trinity sending the Auditor, Henry Lloyd Cowdy, the Treasurer, Harold Murphy, and Cecil Darley, to oppose the motion. The debate on Thursday 16 February was widely reported in both the *Oxford Review* and the *Oxford Magazine,* where it was noted that 'the debate was by far the most interesting of the term'.[14] Described as 'an admirable debate', it was noted that 'the delegates displayed that eloquence which we associate with Irish speakers'. Harold Murphy, in particular, was praised for achieving 'real eloquence'.

In his twenty-minute oration, speaking from first opposition, Murphy acknowledged how much the speakers from Trinity were looking forward to discussing a political question, given that 'political speeches had been completely debarred' back home. Murphy quoted an Irish MP in Isaac Butt's time who had claimed it was the duty of Irishmen to be gentlemen first and patriots second. A grandson of Judge William Keogh, and a son of the prosecutor in

12 Ibid., p. 318.

13 TCD/MUN/SOC/HIST/39.

14 *Oxford Magazine,* 22 February 1905.

the Phoenix Park murder trials, Murphy was a remarkable orator, almost certainly the finest speaker of his generation at Trinity. He was later described as having 'a clear head, an admirable command of language, and a wonderful gift of witty and apposite illustration'.[15]

To much applause, Murphy suggested that 'his firm conviction was that in the case of Ireland it was the duty of a man to think first of his own country and afterwards of his own self-respect and dignity'.[16] And he concluded by suggesting that Home Rule for Ireland would result 'in Ireland taking her place amongst the great nations of the world'. Despite his oratorical flourishes, Murphy was unable to convince the House, although he came close, and the motion was only passed by 100 votes to 78.

By this time, Murphy had already marked himself out as a leader, both inside and outside of the classroom. He won the Littledale Prize in English Literature in 1901 and the Cluff Memorial Prize in 1902 and graduated with a first class degree and gold medal in Modern History and Political Science in 1903. During this time he was described as 'perhaps the best cox ever possessed by the Boat Club' and 'his cool and balanced judgement and his extensive vocabulary, helped the senior eight to victory on many occasions'.[17] He was also a talented hockey player, and played four times for Ireland. In 1905 he was made assistant to the Professor of History, John Wardell, and attracted large numbers to his lectures, and he became Barrington Lecturer in Political Economy in 1910. More interested in a career in the law than in academia, he was called to the Irish bar in 1906 and the English bar in 1910 and soon built up a large practice. Deciding to enter politics, he stood as a Liberal candidate in a by-election in Crewe in July 1912, but was narrowly defeated. Sir John Simon, the Solicitor General and a leading Liberal politician, described him at the time as the finest orator in England, and claimed that when sharing a platform he always insisted on speaking first so he would not have to follow him.

There was controversy in April 1905 when the Auditor, Henry Lloyd Cowdy, missed three meetings of the Society in a row and was

---

15 *The Irish Times*, 8 January 1942.

16 *Oxford Review*, 18 February 1905.

17 Dagg, *CHS*, p. 419; TCD/MUN/SOC/HIST/39.

deemed to have vacated the office under chapter five of law seventeen. A new election was called, and a member of Committee, Edward Sullivan Murphy, the brother of Harold Murphy, put his name forward and it looked like he would be elected unopposed. However, at the last minute Cowdy insisted on putting his name forward, and Sullivan Murphy withdrew his name to avoid a split. Cowdy was re-elected unopposed and Sullivan Murphy thereupon resigned from the Committee. He later served as Attorney General for Northern Ireland between 1937 and 1939 and was a Lord Justice of Appeal in Northern Ireland from 1939 until his death in 1945. Cowdy enlisted in the British army during the First World War and was killed in action.

The outstanding speaker of his generation, Harold Murphy was elected Auditor for the 1905–06 session. At the beginning of the session a motion was passed by eighteen votes to eleven to allow smoking during private business. However, the Auditor realized that this went against a custom of the Society, so it was debated again the following week and rejected by sixteen votes to eight.

During the year a motion 'That the political methods of Parnell contained the elements of failure' was defeated, as was a motion 'That some measure of female suffrage is desirable'. A debate on whether the supremacy of the British in South Africa was essential to the welfare of the country was opposed by William Francis Casey, a student from Cape Town, and it was rejected by the House. Casey later became a very successful editor of *The Times* newspaper in London. The Librarian that session was Maurice Cherry Greene, known as 'Mottie'. Greene was a nephew of a former Auditor, Richard Robert Cherry, who at this time was Lord Chief Justice. During the year, if it ever looked like the Committee was going to be outvoted on an issue, 'Mottie' would 'disappear quietly' only to return shortly with a number of Society members drawn from the rugby club 'sufficient to ensure a majority', and these became known as 'Mottie's tail'.[18] After leaving College he joined the British Colonial Service and served in Nigeria, Cyprus, Palestine and Gibraltar.

At the inaugural meeting of the new session, on 7 November 1906, the Auditor, Thomas Dagg, announced that the Society had

18 Dagg, *CHS*, p. 420.

made a deal with College about which rooms it would have in the Graduates Memorial Building. The ground-floor room became the reading room for the University Philosophical Society, with the first floor for the College Historical Society. Dagg's address was on 'The University and the State'. During the year W.B. Yeats chaired a debate on the motion 'That Decadence is the Prevailing Characteristic of the Modern Stage', which passed, while a motion 'That the principle of hereditary legislative chambers is unsound', chaired by J.G. Swift MacNeill MP, was defeated.[19]

Notable motions during the 1908-09 session included one on extending the franchise to women, which was defeated, as one on appointing Indians to the governing body of India which was likewise rejected. William Hugh Art O'Grady was Auditor for the 1909-10 session. O'Grady was a son of Standish James O'Grady, a major figure in the Irish Literary Revival, and motions include one on whether the result of the battle of the Boyne was beneficial to Ireland (defeated) and whether England's attitude towards the South African Republics in 1899 is justified (also defeated).[20]

Arthur Purefoy Irwin Samuels was elected Auditor unanimously for the 1910-11 session. Samuels had a remarkable passion for the history of the Society and came up with the idea of producing an edition of the minutes of the 1747 Society that were in Edmund Burke's handwriting. This inspired him to begin work on a book on Burke's career in Trinity, which he had almost completed before the outbreak of the First World War.[21] 'Irish Possibilities' was the title of Samuels' inaugural address, which took place on 2 November 1910. Lord MacDonnell, known as 'The Sphinx of the Empire' delivered the first response, and spoke for almost an hour outlining some of his suggestions for the future of Ireland, including a scheme for devolution. MacDonnell noted his happiness that his first public pronouncement on Irish affairs was given at a neutral venue. During the session the members debated and supported the motion 'That this Society Deplores the Growth of Republicanism in Europe', as well as 'That this Society Approves of the Action of the United Irishmen in

19 TCD MUN/SOC/HIST Uncatalogued Papers, 1907-19.

20 Ibid.

21 *The Irish Times*, 20 September 1916.

1798'. The Auditor, Samuels, spoke against the motion 'That this Society Deplores the Growth of the Military Spirit in Universities'.

Samuels was a member of the Officers Training Corps and subsequently lost his life in the First World War. His book, *The Early Life Correspondence and Writings of The Rt. Hon. Edmund Burke,* was completed by his father, Arthur Warren Samuels, a former MP for the University of Dublin, and published in 1923. It remains a standard text and has been described as 'remarkable' by the distinguished historian, Professor Louis Cullen.[22]

Speaking on the life of Edmund Burke, Cullen has noted that in this period Burke was neglected by Trinity, who seemed uncomfortable with him 'inside its walls'.[23] The centenary of his death in 1897 seems to have gone unnoticed, except by the Society, and he barely featured in histories of the College. It was the Society which commemorated him and Cullen suggests, admittedly 'with some exaggeration', that it was the College Historical Society which rescued him for Trinity. Cullen dates the change to 1923 and the publication of Samuel's work posthumously and he says that 'in this way, father and son brought the Hist[orical Society] and College together.'

Valentine Holmes was the Auditor for the 1911–12 session and he delivered his inaugural address on 8 November 1911 on 'The Doctrine of Nationality'. Speakers included John Pentland Mahaffy, Douglas Hyde, and A.M. Sullivan. Once again women's suffrage was debated that session, and was rejected, as was a motion supporting compulsory military training. James Maxwell Henry was elected Auditor for the 1912–13 session, but ill-health prevented him attending the inaugural meeting in November. In his absence, J.G. Acheson, a member of Committee, read his paper entitled 'Economic Independence for Ireland'. Arthur Davies was named as Pro-Auditor in his absence.

College politics and national politics combined to shape the most contentious debate of this period. The Board of the University suggested in 1912 that the University of Dublin should be excluded from the Home Rule Bill if it passed, thus cutting Trinity off from

---

22 L.M. Cullen, 'Edmund Burke', Trinity Monday Discourse 1997 (www.tcd.ie).

23 Ibid.

the rest of the island. On the 13 November 1912 a motion was proposed by E.M. Stephens and seconded by C.S. Power for debate in private business the following week: 'That this Society Disapproves of any Legislation which would Tend to Separate Trinity College from the Rest of Ireland, believing such legislation opposed to the best interests of the University and of this Society'. However, on 20 November the Pro-Auditor, Davies, ruled that the motion was out of order, and this caused uproar and Dermot Coffey suggested adjourning the meeting to discuss the conduct of the Pro-Auditor. Stephens was a nephew of John Millington Synge and became a barrister after graduation. He served as Joint Secretary to the Constitutional Committee in 1922 and ended his career as Assistant Registrar of the Supreme Court.[24]

The heated debate in the Society over the future of Ireland was reported in the *Irish Independent* on Friday 22 November. The following week Thomas Dagg proposed a motion, condemning the publication of the proceedings of private business, calling it 'unprecedented', and threatening to expel any member who breached the confidence of the Society and was guilty of dishonourable conduct. During this discussion it was revealed that a reporter from the newspaper was outside and wanted a report of proceedings. This promoted one member to propose a motion to adjourn the meeting so that the journalist could be put 'under the pump', in other words drenched with water, but as Dagg notes, wiser heads prevailed and the motion was rejected, 'and the newspaper representative departed in blissful ignorance of the fate which had threatened him'.[25]

While all of this was going on the Auditor decided to resign because of ill-health. James Maxwell Henry realized that continuance in office was impossible and he resigned on 27 November. Arthur Davies was unanimously elected Auditor in his place. Motions that session included some of the most imaginative of the period, including 'That a Democratic Nation has no Conception of Honour' (defeated), 'That the Fatalist Makes the Best Soldier' (defeated), 'That the English Nation is Degenerate' (passed) and

24 F.X. Martin, *The scholar revolutionary: Eoin MacNeill, 1867-1945, and the making of the new Ireland* (Dublin, 1973), p. 212.

25 Dagg, *CHS*, p. 348.

'That Medical Science is Tainted with Quackery' (defeated).[26]

In May 1913 the President of the Society, Lord Ashbourne, died and on 28 May the meeting was adjourned as a mark of respect to a man who had served the Society for thirty years. Sir John Ross was proposed as President, and was elected on 26 November 1913. Ross chaired the inaugural meeting of the 1913-14 session.

In the middle of the great Dublin Lockout of 1913 the Society decided to tackle the issue with one of its first debates. The motion, 'That this Society Considers the Present Methods of Trade Unionism Unjustifiable' was selected for 26 November and a King's Counsel, Henry Hanna, was asked to chair it. However when he was unable to do it, the Committee decided upon a controversial choice. Captain Jack White, a soldier who had fought in the Second Boer War, and served at Gibraltar and in India, had returned to Ireland, after various detours (including a time as lumberjack in Canada and a member of a nudist free-love colony at the Cotswolds), where he became a co-founder of the Irish Citizen Army and a leading trade unionist.[27] White was controversial because of a speech he had made to the Gaelic Society in Trinity on 18 November in which he had called on the students to go on strike in protest at what was happening, and invited the students to a meeting the following night. The Provost, Dr Traill, quickly intervened banning students from attending. Realising that they were on a collision course with the College, the Committee decided to withdraw the invitation to White and change the wording of the motion for debate on 26 November, and they informed the Provost of their plans.

There was uproar at the meeting on 26 November when the revised motion was read out. C.S. Power proposed a motion, seconded by E.M. Stephens, calling on the house to adjourn so that the conduct of the officers and Committee in changing the chairman could be discussed. After a long debate this was narrowly defeated by 14 votes to 13. In the end, there was no time left for debating the new motion, and it was put to the house and carried without any speeches. Captain White was furious and sent a letter demanding an apology at the next meeting. When this was declined, he sent his

26 TCD MUN/SOC/HIST Uncatalogued Papers, 1907-19.

27 Fearghal McGarry, James Robert ('Jack') White, DIB.

correspondence with the Society to the newspapers for publication.

Other debates that session included many that touched on the increasing international tensions. A motion 'That this Society would Welcome a Holiday in Armaments' was rejected, as was one 'That this Society Considers the Attitude of President Wilson with Regard to Mexico Unjustifiable'. A motion suggesting 'That this House Approves of Compulsory Military Service' was approved. Other notable debates were on educational matters, for example 'That this Society is of the Opinion that the Maintenance of the University System is Undesirable in the Present Age of Specialisation', or national ones, 'That this House Deplores the Establishment in Ireland of a New "Pale"'. [28]

On 25 February 1914 Trinity hosted a major competitive debate between the College Historical Society and Edinburgh University Union on the motion 'That this House Views with Concern the Interference on the Part of the South African Government with the Liberty of the Subject'.[29] The debate was a topical one, involving a recent case where some men in South Africa were seized and brought back to England for trial. Two speakers from each university proposed and opposed the motion, which was solidly defeated at the end of the night by 58 votes to 19. Speaking from the chair at the end of the debate, Sir John Ross, the President of the Society, disagreed with the vote of the House, and noted that this was the kind of subject that meant more to people as they grew older. In the course of making his case, he referenced the arrest of Wolfe Tone and illegal trial in 1798, and argued that 'liberty depended on the maintenance of the law' and 'if the law was lightly broken or set aside, no man could see the end of it'. At the end of the session, Douglas Hyde was elected a Vice-President of the Society.[30]

With the prospect of the third Home Rule bill being enacted in 1914, the Society debated whether it should seek any special privileges in the new dispensation. Barry St John Galvin proposed a motion in private business calling on the Correspondence Secretary to write to the various party leaders requesting that the College Historical

28 Dagg, *CHS*, p. 350.

29 *The Irish Times*, 26 February 1914.

30 *The Irish Times*, 13 June 1914.

Society be granted the privilege of having its own gallery in the new Irish House of Commons. However, after a lengthy debate, his motion was rejected by 29 votes to 13. Galvin was a remarkable student. He became a Scholar in 1913 and was heavy-weight champion in Trinity as well as a talented rugby player. He was later described in *The Irish Times* as 'one of the outstanding personalities in College just before the war' and shared the distinction with 'Mottie' Green of having 'the greatest number of stories told about him'.[31] With the outbreak of the First World War in the summer of 1914 Galvin, like many of his fellow students, decided to enlist. For the next five years the war was to overshadow everything else in the Society.

31 *The Irish Times*, 3 October 1941.

'THE GREAT STRUGGLE FOR EMPIRE': THE SOCIETY AND THE FIRST WORLD WAR AND ITS AFTERMATH, 1914-1920

14

THE OUTBREAK of the First World War created massive upheaval across Europe and the Society was similarly disrupted. At a committee meeting on 10 September 1914 it was agreed to postpone the inaugural meeting indefinitely, and there were no large meetings, with distinguished invited guests, for the duration of the conflict. Many of those involved with the Society enlisted and went off to fight; some never came back. After the war it was calculated that 251 members of the Society, almost 75% of the total membership, fought in the British army during the war.[1] When former members were included in the list, the figure rose to approximately 700. Of these, 137 died. A number of those who served won distinction in combat. Sixteen became Companions of the Distinguished Service Order, fifty-five won Military Crosses, four won the Crois de Guerre, and ten won other awards. The rush to serve in the war left the Society without many people to serve on the Committee, or attend debates, and the Society was reduced to one-fifth of its usual number. This placed a burden on the Society's finances, though two grants from the Board of the College of £30 and £25 enabled it to keep functioning. Nevertheless, cuts were made, and it was decided to only hold a limited number of debates each year. War regulations were introduced by the Society in December 1915 and revised throughout the conflict, and initially it was agreed to only hold two debates each term and thus place 'the

1 Dagg, *CHS*, p. 364; *The Irish Times,* 30 January 1919.

Society on a war footing while the great struggle for Empire continues'.[2]

In February 1915 the Society praised 'the magnificent spirit of patriotism evinced by its officers and members in the present crisis'.[3] The Auditor, T.D.M. Bartley, had enlisted as soon as war was declared and missed the entire session, having been given a leave of absence by the Society, and a pro-Auditor, A.O. Hardy, was appointed in his place. Bartley was commissioned a Captain in the British army and later went on to become a Judge of the Supreme Court in Kenya. Because the Auditor, a number of officers, and members were on active service it was decided to postpone the inaugural meeting indefinitely, and this announcement was published in *The Irish Times* on 2 November 1914.[4] The first meeting of the Society took place on 4 November 1914, but following the reading of the minutes the meeting adjourned as a mark of respect to the Provost, Dr Traill, who was also a Vice-President of the Society, who had died.[5]

Barry St John Galvin, the Correspondence Secretary, and Kevin O'Duffy, the Librarian, were two Committee members who enlisted, and a Pro-Correspondence Secretary and a Pro-Librarian were appointed in their place. In January 1915 letters were received from both Galvin and O'Duffy from their training camps tendering their resignations. Galvin was commissioned a Captain in the Royal Dublin Fusiliers. O'Duffy joined the 7th Royal Munster Fusiliers and was promoted to lieutenant in January 1915. He was killed at the Dardennelles in August.[6] Menzies Murray, the Treasurer, attended meetings of the Society until Christmas, but he received a commission in the army and so he tendered his resignation.

It is worth looking in detail at Galvin's wartime service, in part because of his distinguished career in the Society, in part because it exemplifies the experience of members during the war. In the first part of the war, Galvin served in the 8th (Service) Battalion of the

2 *The Irish Times*, 11 December 1915.

3 Dagg, *CHS*, p. 352.

4 *The Irish Times*, 2 November 1914.

5 *The Irish Times,* 6 November 1914.

6 *The Irish Times*, 24 August 1915.

Royal Irish Fusiliers of the 16th (Irish) Division and won the military cross for 'gallantry and devotion' in 1916. Despite his Falstaffian appearance, he was an effective soldier. The official report revealed that during a raid south-east of Loos on 11 July 1916 he continued to lead his party despite being wounded in action. Knocked unconscious by an exploding bomb, he resumed fighting as soon as he recovered and crossed into the German front line, where he was again wounded. Afterwards he required hospitalisation, and was evacuated to the base hospital at St Omer and from there to the Kitchener Hospital in Brighton, with a gun-shot wound to the right chest and another in his left shoulder. Following his recovery he went on to serve with the 1st battalion Royal Irish Fusiliers of the 36th (Ulster) Division. Captured at Andechy on 27 March 1918, he was held at a prisoner of war camp in Germany until the end of the war. There he learned how to play chess and in later years he was a skilful player, becoming a member of the Munster Interprovincial Chess team.[7] Instead of returning home immediately, he joined the North Russian Relief Force, the British Expeditionary Force which fought in Russia against the Bolshevik revolutionaries in 1919.[8] In the words of the new British Secretary of State for War, Winston Churchill, they wanted 'to strangle at birth the Bolshevist state' and Galvin was part of the attempt to relieve the White Russian forces at Archangel. As *The Irish Times* reported, he was 'at Murmansk with the famous Churchill Expeditionary Force'.[9] Galvin returned to Trinity after this, completing his studies and rejoining the Society, and as we shall later see became Auditor in the summer of 1920.

At the meeting on 10 February 1915 the resignations of the Treasurer, Correspondence Secretary and Librarian were announced, and details were given for the nomination of new officers, and also to fill the five seats on the regular Committee. The following week, 17 February, Theodore Conyngham (T.C.) Kingsmill Moore was elected Librarian, marking the beginning of a period of distinguished service to the Society.

Debates that session reflected the mood and politics of the time.

7 *The Irish Times*, 3 October 1941.

8 National Archives, War Office 339/13046.

9 *The Irish Times*, 3 October 1941.

A motion 'That this House Approves of Conscription' was rejected, as was a motion 'That this House is of the Opinion that a Lasting International Peace can only be Secured by the Growth of Democracy'. Likewise a discussion about whether the end justified the means when it came to the development of nations was also rejected. A motion suggesting that the growth of nationality necessitated the growth of armaments was passed, as was one declaring that oratory no longer moulded public opinion. However, a proposal that international law could have no binding force in time of war was rejected. Attendances were small, however, averaging fourteen members.[10] At the end of the session, the pro-Auditor, Hardy, received the equivalent of 'marked thanks' for having 'piloted the Society most successfully through a period of stress'.[11]

Isaac Roundtree was elected Auditor for the 1915–16 session and on 21 October it was agreed by the committee not to hold any inaugural meetings for the duration of the conflict. Only one debate was held that year, on a topical motion attacking American neutrality, 'That this House Condemns the Attitudes of the USA in the Present War'. Six members spoke, and the final vote was five in favour and four against. There were four other meetings of the Society, but each time standing orders were suspended and resolutions were passed allowing the House to move straight to private business without a debate. The average attendance during the session was eight.

Kingsmill Moore, who was Record Secretary, took a leave of absence in Hilary Term, partly so he could concentrate on the Officers Training Corps, based in Trinity. It was in that role that he was involved in the defence of Trinity during the Easter Rising in 1916, waiting for an attack that never came. Writing about this afterwards, in the editorial of *TCD,* he said that 'Trinity has never passed a more anxious time than on the fateful first night of the rebellion, when the houses held by the enemy loomed ominously over the low building, where a handful of students watched and waited for an attack.' Kingsmill Moore attributed the fact that the rebels had not attacked Trinity to its status in Irish society, 'that the

10 Dagg, *CHS*, p. 354.

11 Ibid.

honoured fame of our university made the rebels loath to attack it'. He believed that 'The love of Trinity and pride in it are the heritage of all Irishmen, and whatever be the form of our government, whatever the party in power, we believe that they will regard our College as one of Ireland's greatest possessions.'

In the 1916–17 session only five meetings of the Society were held, and at two of these there was no debate. Attendances continued to be small, usually on average fifteen people. The first debate was on 5 December 1916, again on the subject of American neutrality, 'That this House Condemns the Attitude of the USA in this War'. For the second time, the motion passed. It was at this meeting that a resolution was passed paying tribute to the former Auditor, Arthur Purefoy Irwin Samuels, who had been commissioned a captain in the army and who had been killed in the fighting. He joined the Royal Irish Rifles at the start of the war, was promoted to Captain in February 1915 and was wounded by a shell fragment at the beginning of the great offensive at the Somme in July 1916.[12] However, an operation was deemed inadvisable, so he was patched up and returned to his battalion where he served continuously in the fighting line until he was fatally wounded in action on Saturday 23 September 1916, and he died the following day.[13]

On 14 February 1917 the motion was 'That this House is of the Opinion that a Universal Peace can be Secured by a League of Nations to Enforce it'. Eight speakers took part in the debate, two proposing the motion, and six opposing, and the motion was defeated. The third and final debate took place on 13 June 1917 in favour of admitting women to the franchise. Five speakers spoke in favour, and six against, and when the motion was put to the House it passed by ten votes to nine. Given the reduced numbers involved in the Society, and the desire for some consistency, Roundtree was asked to continue as Auditor for the following year.

There were seven meetings of the College Historical Society in the 1917-18 session and seven debates. The members rejected a motion suggesting that the Central Powers should suffer a commercial boycott after the war. However, there was support for the motion

12 *The Irish Times,* 8 July 1916.

13 *The Irish Times,* 30 September 1914.

'That this House Considers that in Time of War the Civil Authorities are Subordinate to the Military'. Other motions had wider influences. A motion on whether the British Medical Council was unduly conservative in its attitude to bone-setters was rejected, while one arguing the merits for the place of History in higher education was passed. The shadow of the 1916 Rising influenced one debate, a motion 'That this House Disapproves of the Doctrine that Nationality is a Basis of Political Independence', which included guests from Oxford University, and which was defeated.

In Hilary Term problems arose over the absence of the Auditor, Isaac Roundtree, and a motion was passed by the Committee on 5 February 1918 suggesting that it was desirable for the Auditor and officers to be in Dublin to promote the interests of the Society. At the same time, Roundtree resigned as Auditor, and it appears he was pushed into stepping down because of general dissatisfaction. New elections for the committee were held on 11 February and Kingsmill Moore was elected Auditor. Captain Bartley, the former Auditor, agreed to serve on Committee. The first motion under the new Auditor was on 13 February on the motion 'That this House is of Opinion that a Benevolent Despotism is Preferable to a Democratic Government'.[14] New temporary laws of the Society were drafted and adopted, and these confirmed that there would be no opening meeting of the Society until the declaration of peace. On 29 May the outgoing Auditor and his Committee were proposed for re-election for the following session and this was approved.

A week before the Armistice brought an end to the First World War, a motion was passed on 4 November 1918 allowing British officers quartered in College to make use of the Society's rooms and to take part in Wednesday debates. This motion was proposed by Captain Bartley and passed unanimously. Two days after the Armistice was announced, on 13 November Kingsmill Moore brought forward a proposal to hold his inaugural meeting in the first week of Hilary term, and that women should be allowed attend. At this meeting it was also agreed to hold a debate on the proposed League of Nations the following week, on 20 November. A sub-committee was also established to report on the services of the past

14 *The Irish Times*, 13 Feb 1918.

and present members of the Society in the war. However, when the Society met on 20 November the proposal to admit women to the inaugural meeting was dropped because of considerable opposition.

The motion 'That the League of Nations is a Practical Policy' passed, despite opposition from the new Lecky Professor of History, W. Allison Philips. The members also rejected a motion suggesting that the attempt to revive the Gaelic language was in the best interests of Ireland. Recent events in Russia were debated, and the motion 'That the Bolshevist Regime in Russia should be Suppressed by External Force' was supported. There was also support for the minimum wage.[15]

The Peace Inaugural Meeting was the name given to the first inaugural meeting held in almost six years, which took place on Wednesday 29 January 1919 in the Dining Hall. Kingsmill Moore discussed the developments in the Society since November 1913 and suggested that although 'the Great War had caused such a break in the usual functions of the Society', it had 'added a new and glorious chapter to its history'.[16] Kingsmill Moore's address was on 'Socialism and the War' and the guest speakers included the Lord Primate, Professor W. Allison Philips, W. B. Yeats, and Thomas Johnson, the leader of the Labour Party.

The meeting was chaired by the President of the Society, Sir John Ross, and began with the presentation of the medals, which included two for Kingsmill Moore – the gold medal for oratory as well as the President's gold medal.[17] In his speech, Kingsmill Moore noted that in 1914 few people feared a workers' rebellion, but that things had changed during the war. Looking at the socialist movement in Germany, France, Britain and Austria, he discussed how the socialist parties had viewed the war, and why so many had supported it. A major theme of the speech was Russia, and he called the revolution an event 'which may prove the most important event in European history since 1789'. Attacking the Russian autocracy, he argued that revolution had been inevitable 'and its course certain to be violent', given that 'the mass of Russians were crushed' by a system 'utterly

15 TCD MUN/SOC/HIST Uncatalogued Papers, 1907-19.

16 Dagg, *CHS*, p. 364.

17 *The Irish Times*, 30 January 1919.

unscrupulous, whose methods were espionage and the agent provocateur, and whose arguments were the knot and the cell'.[18] It was in this context, he said, that Lenin and Trotsky had succeeded.

Kingsmill Moore ended his stirring address by claiming that 'our generation will be one of change, of social renaissance, of a fresh combat between altruism and self-interest', and he declared that 'the task for men of goodwill is to act as midwives who can ease the throes of the new birth'. The Lord Primate proposed the vote of thanks to the Auditor and denounced the Bolshevik Revolution as 'a saturnalia of cruelty and crime and lust'. Professor W. Alison Philips was less inclined to praise the Auditor's address and argued that it was 'by no means true that the condition of the Russian people before the revolution was worse than it had been in the past'. He suggested that Kingsmill Moore had drawn 'a somewhat lurid picture of these conditions' and credited the capitalist system with all the beneficial changes that had taken place.

In his speech, W. B. Yeats declared that 'Russia, had, in the name of progress and in the name of human freedom, revived tyranny and torture of the worst description'. And he expressed his hope that the Irish revolutionary government would not seek an alliance with revolutionaries elsewhere or risk splitting the nation in two. Thomas Johnson admitted that the socialists had failed to prevent the war, but argued that the war had taught people that those who did the work should control the work. Concluding the debate, Sir John Ross claimed that Johnson was under the delusion that capital was 'the diabolical influence that kept the whole world in unhappiness'. And he joked that 'a little association with their university would shake that idea out of Mr Johnson's head'.

A number of American soldiers were residing in College in 1919, awaiting demobilisation and a return home, and Provost Mahaffy arranged for them to attend classes. On 23 April he wrote to the Society inviting them to meet with him and asking that the Americans might also be allowed use the reading rooms and take part in debates as 'they are strange here and wandering about'. Mahaffy's letter to the Society was one of the final ones he wrote, and he died on 30 April.

---

18 *The Irish Times,* 30 January 1919.

The Society was happy to assist and invited the officers and soldiers to use the Society's rooms, informing them of the fact that the Society 'was founded by Edmund Burke, the great champion of the rights of the American colonies during their struggle with the Mother Country'. A debate between the Society and the Americans was arranged for 28 May, but it never went ahead as the soldiers were demobilised in the meantime.

C.J.L. Brock, who as Record Secretary had done impressive work preparing the list of names of members who had fought and died in the First World War, was elected Auditor for the 1919–20 session. At the inaugural meeting, on 5 November 1919, he received the gold medal for oratory and delivered an inaugural address on 'History in politics'. Reviewing the history of the Society since 1770, Brock claimed that 'one of the greatest functions of the College Historical Society was that, by encouraging its members to study history and to apply it to modern problems, it discovered for them the great underlying principles which should be within the grasp of every citizen who wished to serve the state'.[19] In addition, by cultivating the gift of oratory, the Society prepared people to follow in the footsteps of those who had gone before. As *The Irish Times* noted in one of two leading articles about the debate, 'Mr Brock applied his own – or rather, his Society's – principles to the many aspects of the vexed and tormented world of 1919'.[20] And it congratulated 'the Historical Society on its return, sane and vigorous as of old, to the paths of peace'. It believed that during the war the members had adorned its name with a new honour: 'they have been more than students of history; they have helped to make it'.

Brock also noted that Society was 'to be congratulated in having so successfully survived a period of such great difficulty in carrying out its functions, and of such great financial strain'. He proudly asserted that 'every fit member of the Society served in the war', and while this left it 'temporarily in a most depleted condition' it also 'added one of the most glorious passages to its glorious history'. A further cause for celebration was that the Society's debts had been paid, and the attendance at debates was once again at a high,

19 *The Irish Times*, 6 November 1919.
20 Ibid.

matching pre-war figures. Brock became a leading figure in British liberal intellectual circles in the 1920s, a member of the Cobden Club (of which he later co-authored a history), and wrote pamphlets on *Peace and disarmament* (1928) and *The moral case for free trade* (1943). The first vote of thanks was moved by the Provost, and he praised Brock's speech and joked that it was 'a chastening discipline to be assured on such high authority that in the conflict between the College and the Board one hundred years ago the Society was nearly always right and the Provost and Senior Fellows were always wrong'.

Barry St John Galvin, who had returned to complete his studies after fighting in the war, was elected Treasurer of the Society on 11 March 1920 following the resignation of Walter Starkie. On 9 June 1920 he delivered a major speech supporting the motion 'That Dominion Home Rule for Ireland is Desirable'.[21] He suggested that people had got used to bloodshed because of the war, 'and they had at the back of their minds the conviction that, if beaten on the use of constitutional methods, they could still make an appeal to force'. He believed that this was what was happening with Irish nationalists fighting the War of Independence. Opposing the motion, J.R. Halpin suggested that dominion home rule was code for a republic and that 'the remedy for the present condition of affairs was firm, consistent government'. The motion passed by a single vote.

In terms of later career, perhaps the most significant member from this period was T.C. Kingsmill Moore who was called to the bar in 1918, served in the Seanad in the 1940s, and became a High Court Judge in 1948 and a Supreme Court Judge in 1951. Another eminent Judge, Gerard Hogan, in the *Dictionary of Irish Biography*, argues that 'Kingsmill Moore must therefore rank as one of the greatest judges that the State has produced'.[22] He notes that 'the quality of Kingsmill Moore's legal writing and analysis remains undimmed. His skill in judgment writing has been matched by only a select few of great judges such as Hugh Kennedy… and Adrian Hardiman'. A man of many talents, Kingsmill Moore also published a book of poetry entitled *Misconceptions* (1921) and his book on angling, *A Man May Fish* (1960) 'is regarded as a classic'.

21 *The Irish Times*, 10 June 1920.

22 Gerard Hogan, 'Theodore Conyngham Kingsmill Moore', *DIB*.

The Society emerged from First World War enhanced. It had survived a difficult and painful period where it lost members and former members, and where it was forced to reduce its operations to a minimum. As Sir John Ross noted at the Peace Inaugural Meeting the sacrifice of the members of the Society during the war had 'conferred on that university and on that ancient Society such a glory as never was before, and they had handed down a tradition for the benefit of those present and of those who would succeed them'.[23] This view was a popular one; it gave members a new self-confidence and a renewed sense of destiny about the Society's ability to contribute to national and international debates that would drive it forward in the 1920s.

23 *The Irish Times*, 30 January 1919.

15 'THE HIST' IN THE AGE OF PUBLIC DISCOURSE, 1920-1929

IN THE 1920S the College Historical Society assumed a new position in Irish life. In addition to being a place where aspiring speakers found their voice, it also became somewhere the great topics of the day could be discussed and the proceedings reported to the public. People were interested in what happened in the Society and the content of speeches and results of debates became widely known. The records for the Society in the 1920s are poor and not all have survived, but it is possible to reconstruct the great debates from the way they were reported in the newspapers of the day. We also see it being referred to as 'The Hist' for the first time in national media, a shorthand that had been popularised by members.[1] The Society became a forum for public discourse, sometimes taking on the issues that could not be safely discussed elsewhere. No longer just open to Sophisters, 'the Hist'was now a place where all students could apply for membership and observe, listen, and take part.

At the end of June 1920, Barry St John Galvin was elected Auditor of the Society. For his inaugural address he chose the subject of Bolshevism and invited the controversial British MP, Cecil L'Estrange Malone, to speak at the meeting on 9 November 1920. A war hero, Malone had been awarded the OBE, and had recently become the first ever Member of Parliament for the Communist Party of Great Britain after defecting from the Liberals. He had also published a glowing account of his visit to the Soviet Union. Two days before heading to Ireland, on 7 November he delivered a provocative speech at the Albert Hall in London, where he asked

1 See for example *The Sunday Independent,* 24 November 1929.

rhetorically what were 'a few Churchills or a few Curzons on lamp-posts compared to the massacre of thousands of human beings?' As a result, New Scotland Yard decided to charge him with sedition under the Defence of the Realm Act and his arrest took place in the Common Room, over the Dining Hall, at Trinity College Dublin. The timing could not have been better in terms of publicity for the Society and it received international attention because of the arrest.

On the day of the inaugural Dublin was swirling with the story that Malone was going to be arrested. In the afternoon the Committee telephoned Dublin Castle to ask if there were any plans to arrest Malone, but were told there were none. Malone arrived early for the debate, and was having tea in the Common Room in Trinity, where the guests were being entertained, when an officer and some men arrived shortly before 7.30 p.m. After a brief conversation with the Auditor, the officer went across the room and took Malone into military custody. He was helped into his overcoat by one of the men, and taken out a side door and removed to the police station in College, before being driven to the Bridewell prison.

A large crowd had gathered to hear Malone speak, but they were unaware of his arrest and when the doors were opened 'there was an immediate rush for good seats'. The meeting proceeding as normal, and the only time Malone's absence was mentioned was when it came for him to speak, when the chairman, Mr Justice Samuels, a Vice-President of the Society, said that Malone was 'quite unexpectedly not present'. News of his arrest had by now travelled around the hall and there was laughter and applause. Towards the end of the evening someone in the audience asked 'Where is Colonel Malone?' The chairman refused to answer. The same person asked about another speaker who had been advertised, but was also unable to attend, Oliver St John Gogarty. Here the chairman had a reply. 'Dr Gogarty' he said, 'telegraphed that he could not come'. 'For the same reason?' asked someone mischievously.

Galvin's speech had to compete with such distractions. It was a powerful address, blaming the present distress on not so much the 'inherent contradiction in the theory of Bolshevism', or on 'any conscious rascality in its prophets', but on 'its complete impracticability'. In his peroration he claimed that if other European countries embraced 'the gospel of Bolshevism' and pulled down the 'mighty structure of ordered society' then 'assuredly we shall perish under its ruins'. Two days later, on 11 November, Malone was sent back to Britain on the mail steamer to Holyhead and was meant to have been arrested on his arrival, but the police missed him.[2] He was eventually intercepted at Euston Station in London, where he was arrested. Put on trial, he was convicted and sentenced to six months in prison. There he rethought his revolutionary politics and decided to leave the Communist Party, and upon his release he joined the Independent Labour Party. Malone was stripped of his OBE in 1921 and lost his seat in 1924, but returned to parliament four years later.

Debates in the session reflected the ongoing War of Independence, included one on 2 December 1920 on the motion 'That no Solution of the Irish Problem should at Present be Attempted'. One speaker on the proposition denied that the Irish were a single nation and suggested that 'Ireland had been spilt into a number of small states, one waging war against another'.[3] Opposing the motion, another speaker argued that 'the Union had brought nothing but disunion'. After speeches on both sides, the House divided evenly 13 votes to 13, at which the chairman cast his deciding vote to defeat the motion.

A motion suggesting that Pitt's Irish policy was worthy of approval was likewise rejected. However, a debate on whether dominion home rule for Ireland was desirable, chaired by Jean Allery, ended in the motion being passed. International politics also featured. A debate on the Versailles Treaty took place on the motion, 'That the Provisions of the Peace Treaties are Unwisely Severe on the Central Powers'. It was defeated. A motion that war criminals should be brought to trial was also defeated. After leaving Trinity, Galvin became a solicitor in 1923 and built up a large practice in Co. Cork, serving as law agent to Cork Corporation before his death in 1941.

At the end of the term, William Patton proposed a motion that in future the private business of the Society should be conducted in Irish, and it was seconded by F.M. O'Connor. However, when it came up for debate at the next meeting, the Auditor ruled it out of order.

To celebrate the 150th anniversary of the Society speakers were

2 *The Times*, 12 November 1920.

3 *The Irish Times*, 3 December 1919.

invited from the Speculative Society in Edinburgh, and from the Oxford, Cambridge and Durham Unions for a major debate. The actual anniversary of 21 March fell during the legal circuit, so instead it was decided to hold the debate during Trinity Week. The debate took place on 2 June 1920 in the Public Theatre on the motion 'That Attempts to Create or Foster Small Nations are Harmful to the Progress of Civilisation'. Trinity speakers were on both sides of the debate, with J.C. Donaldson, the Librarian, opening the debate by suggesting that small nations were a menace to the world, and claiming that Irish independence would bring the country 'into the wilderness of ancient feuds and bitterness, unproductive, barren, hopeless'. (Ralph) Brereton Barry was the final speaker of the night, opposing the motion, and he denounced 'the hideous doctrine of the super-state' that was born in Germany, and believed that small states, including Ireland, should not be denied their rights.[4] The motion was defeated without a division.

A commemorative dinner followed in the Dining Hall the following night. In his toast, the Provost, John Henry Bernard, acknowledged that for some years relations between the College and the Society had been strained. But he conceded that Trinity owed a real debt to the Historical Society 'for the part that it has taken in preserving the continuity of academic tradition'. While other groups forget their history, and lost their identity, the Society had always been unafraid 'to rest itself upon the proud traditions of the past, while it looks forward with eager hope to the days that are coming'.[5]

Brereton Barry was elected Auditor for the 1921–22 session. Praised byThomas Dagg for his 'courtesy, wit and charm of manner', Barry 'was an excellent amateur actor', with a great love of the art and the theatre.[6] His inaugural meeting was on Saturday 19 November 1921 on 'Labour in Parliament' and looked at the problem of the Labour Party in Ireland not having contested the 1918 general election and thus not having any parliamentary representation.[7] He suggested that the future of the Labour Party rested on whether it

4 Dagg, *CHS*, p. 370-371.

5 Ibid., p. 372.

6 Ibid., p. 425.

7 *The Irish Times*, 21 November 1921.

wanted to be a party of class or a party of ideas. To much applause he suggested that Labour, because of its international contacts, had a great opportunity to work for disarmament and for the establishment of world peace. The leading Liberal politician, the Rt Hon. Sir John Simon (who would go on to hold three of the four great offices of state in Britain: Home Secretary, Foreign Secretary and Chancellor of the Exchequer) proposed the vote of thanks and argued that until the Labour Party got rid of class consciousness in its movement it would never succeed in being a real Labour Party.

The most notable debate of the session took place on 15 March 1922 when the Society debated whether two legislative chambers are essential to successful parliamentary government. It was at the very time that Arthur Griffith and others were working on the constitution of the new Irish Free State, so it was a topical motion, and the meeting was chaired by Darryl Figgis who was a key member of the Constitution Committee responsible for it. Brereton Barry joked that 'they all knew that a Constitution was being evolved and they did not wish to know any more'.[8] The motion was passed by 18 votes to 6. Speaking from the chair, Figgis said that 'Ireland, as a nation, should refuse to be threatened by the past and the experience of other nations'. And he suggested that there might be a role in a second chamber for people who had served Ireland well in various capacities in the past.

After leaving Trinity, Brereton Barry was called to the bar and in 1922 and, as his *Irish Times* obituary notes, made 'remarkable progress in his profession' becoming a senior counsel and appearing in some high profile cases, including the Ring College case, where his cross-examination skills were widely praised.[9] He stood for election, unsuccessfully, for Fine Gael in 1938, but was narrowly defeated, before his death in 1941.

The inaugural meeting of the 1922-23 session took place on 8 November 1922 and was on 'International Peace and the League of Nations'.[10] The Auditor, Mark Wilson, spoke of his hope that because Ireland now had her own parliament it might be able to

8 *The Irish Times*, 16 March 1922.

9 *The Irish Times*, 3 December 1941.

10 *The Irish Times*, 9 November 1922.

'stimulate and revive general interest in the social and political problems of the country'. Wilson was optimistic that the League of Nations had succeeded in creating a permanent organisation for promoting international co-operation and securing the peace of the world, through the Permanent Court of International Justice. Proposing the vote of thanks, Lord Parmoor, the Labour peer, argued that 'some body of international supervision, by whatever name it may be called, had become a necessity'. The motion was seconded by Professor W. Allison Philips, who took a typically unconventional line and suggested that the root objection to the new body was that it had replaced specific obligations with 'a whole series of vague and general observances', and this was more likely to undermine the sure foundations of international peace. Hugh Kennedy, the Attorney General and soon to become the state's first Chief Justice, joked that the problem with the League of Nations was that it was the product of chancery lawyers. To great laughter and applause, he suggested that if it had been developed by the great criminal lawyers it would be far more effective. More seriously, he argued that Ireland would think carefully about whether to join the League and would do so after studying whether it could 'maintain and establish peace and prevent and stamp out national crimes'. Later in the year the sweepstakes were the subject of a lively debate on 14 March 1923, with the house divided equally on whether they were a good thing for charitable purposes.[11] In the end, the casting vote of the chairman was needed to defeat the motion.

The remarkable Patrick Bourke was elected Auditor for the 1923-24 session. Born into poverty, Bourke had worked from an early age and had a full-time job with the Inland Revenue when he started in Trinity in 1918. His first preference had been to go to University College Dublin, but they had rejected his application on the grounds that he could not attend all of the lectures because of the requirements of his job. For Bourke, this marked the institution out as 'neither national nor a university'.[12] Trinity was the beneficiary, and over the course of a stellar undergraduate career he was a Scholar, the Auditor of the Gaelic Society (1922-23) as well as the College

11 *The Irish Times,* 15 March 1923.

12 Pauric Dempsey and Shaun Boylan, 'Patrick Bourke', *DIB.*

Historical Society, and won four gold medals and three silver medals. After leaving College he had a distinguished career as a civil servant and in banking, and played a major role in the creation of Allied Irish Bank.

For his inaugural address Bourke chose the subject of 'Democracy'. The meeting was chaired by a former Auditor, Charles Andrew O'Connor, now Master of the Rolls and a Vice-President of the Society, who reflected on how he had been the one delivering the inaugural address almost fifty years earlier. Bourke received the gold medal for oratory before his speech, which was a thoughtful reflection on how men's minds and habits had been disturbed by years of war and now found it difficult to return to a quiet and steady groove.[13] Looking at the development of democracies around the world, across history, he ended by discussing the new Irish state which had been born out of revolution. For Bourke, Irish people were 'witnessing one more experiment in democracy' and he expressed his hope that it would give people rights and liberties to help them realize a higher and fuller life.

Proposing the vote of the thanks was James Ramsay Montagu Butler, MP for Cambridge University, and later Regius Professor of Modern History at Cambridge. Butler joked that he was there under false pretences because he was a Butler and not an Irishman, and a Trinity man but not from Dublin. Butler spoke about the corrosive effects of cynicism in politics. To much applause, Butler looked around the world at those who wore redshirts and blackshirts and suggested that this was 'a reckless gamble in rouge et noir'. For Butler, education was the key to protecting democracy from the threats it faced. He believed that universities had a role to play here, because although not everyone in society might be able to go to one, the universities could carry 'knowledge and education to the people who have not the time or the means'. In this way, he believed that 'this extra mural work is one of the great new tasks that the modern university' must undertake.

Kevin O'Higgins, the Minister for Home Affairs, was the other high-profile guest and he delivered a major speech. Discussing the recent civil war, which had only just come to an end, O'Higgins

13 *The Irish Times,* 8 November 1923.

suggested that the State 'had been challenged in its infancy, and democracy had been, actually and metaphorically, a burning question here in our recent past'. For Higgins the civil war had been fought over the principle 'that the people must be the arbiters of their own destiny', which he believed had been 'contested bitterly by the faction which rallied to the cry that the people have no right to do wrong'. Arguing that 'democracy is the balance between varied and sometimes conflicting political ideas', he suggested that this was 'a delicate balance, which it is ill work to upset'. O'Higgins quoted Edmund Burke to show that in a real democracy a majority could not oppress a minority, and showed how the new Constitution provided for minority views to be represented. He concluded his speech to much applause by saying that he 'believed that this Society would play an important part in the solution of the problems that lay ahead for Ireland'.

Other successful debates in the session included one on 5 December 1923 which approved a motion deploring the neglect of classical education and one on 6 February 1924 supporting the admission of women to universities.[14] On 13 February 1924 the Society debated whether 'the Revival of Despotism is Necessary for the Future of Europe' and the best speech of the evening was delivered by an ancient classics and legal and political science student, Frederick Boland, the future Irish diplomat and Chancellor of the university.[15]

On 12 March 1924 the motion was 'That Principles Ought to be Sacrificed for Expediency' and the debate is famous for the fact that Samuel Beckett was one of the members who spoke at it[16] Unfortunately the records of the Society are poor for this period and we do not know what Beckett said, or on what side, but we do know that the motion was carried by a single vote.[17] Beckett was involved in a number of clubs and societies and his exploits with the Chess and Cricket Clubs were documented in the national media at the time.[18]

14 *The Irish Times,* 6 December 1923;6 February 1924.

15 *The Irish Times,* 13 February 1924.

16 *The Irish Times,* 12 March 1924.

17 *The Irish Times,* 13 March 1924.

18 See for example, *Freeman's Journal*, 31 May 1924 and 15 December 1924.

Although a shy student, Beckett had debated at Portora Royal School before coming to Trinity, and had made a 'violent and eloquent speech' in favour of women's rights.[19] Beckett's later career almost needs no mention. The winner of the Nobel Prize for Literature in 1969, he worked with the French Resistance during the Second World War and was one of the greatest writers and playwrights of the twentieth century.

In June 1924 a major competitive debate was hosted where Trinity took on teams from the Cambridge Union, the Edinburgh Speculative Society, and the Edinburgh Union, on the motion 'That Nationalism rather than Internationalism is the Hope of the Future'. The debate was, in part, a thank you for the hospitality Trinity teams had received at the different societies over the past year. The Auditor, Patrick Bourke, proposed the motion and he attacked the League of Nations as 'a pale ghost of a covenant' calling it 'the finest piece of fiction that he knew'.[20] Following strong speeches on both sides, the motion was defeated.

'Free Trade' was the subject of T.J. Johnston's inaugural address for the 155th session on 29 October 1924. Guests included Ernest Blythe, the Minister for Finance, and Francis Hirst, the former editor of the *Economist* and the current editor of *Common Sense.* Johnson argued persuasively against protectionism, suggesting that it did not increase employment, and that the 'panacea for unemployment lies in the expansion of foreign markets'.[21] Johnson was a theology student, and his choice of subject was commented upon by Hirst, who joked that he was surprised the Auditor had chosen 'a subject so mundane, so clogged with earth, so far below the pure upper air of his daily aetherial speculations'. To much laughter and applause, he suggested that free will might have been chosen as the subject instead of free trade, before delivering a powerful reflection on the dangers of protectionism and the value of free trade. In his speech, Blythe accepted that 'there was a lamentable lack of enterprise in this country, and a lamentable lack of confidence in Irish enterprises'. While he accepted this was irrational,

19 James Knowlson, *Damned to Fame: the life of Samuel Beckett* (London, 2014), Chapter 2

20 *The Irish Times*, 19 June 1924.

21 *The Irish Times*, 30 October 1924.

he believed it could not be ignored. He rejected suggestions made by other speakers that the British Empire might consolidate into a superstate such as the United States, insisting that 'he did not wish this nation to be a province in a backwash'. And to cheers of 'Hear, hear', he warned that 'there was a national feeling in this country which would stand against that, and any party in this country that went for it would go down'.

Other notable debates included one on the motion 'That American Culture is Superior to European' on 12 November 1924, where Frederick Boland, now a Scholar and the Correspondence Secretary, spoke for the proposition.[22] The debate on 26 November 1924 was on whether military training should form a part of all education, and speaking against the motion F.G. Budd argued that 'military training led to militarism and gave the idea that war was a perfectly natural thing, whereas, in reality, it was nothing but carnage'. The debate on 25 February debated and approved a motion in favour of plural voting, in other words giving extra votes to those who were best qualified to cast them. On the losing side was Frederick Boland, who argued for the principle that all people were equal.[23]

The future of Germany was debated on 13 May 1925 and was to feature regularly in the years ahead. A motion passed approving the result of the recent presidential election in Germany, with the debate chaired by the historian, Professor Edmund Curtis.[24] On 27 May 1925 the students debated whether India should be gradually evacuated by the British, with the Record Secretary, W.L. Greer, arguing that since Ireland had gained her own freedom they should not deny another nation what 'they had so ardently desired'.[25] However, the motion was defeated by a large majority. At the end of the session, Eric Porter Goff, the Treasurer of the Society and later to become a distinguished clergyman, went on a three-month debating tour of the United States with a colleague from the Oxford Union, and they visited seventy centres discussing most notably

22 *The Irish Times*, 12 November 1924.

23 *The Irish Times*, 26 February 1925.

24 *The Irish Times*, 14 May 1925.

25 *The Irish Times*, 29 May 1925.

America's relations with the League of Nations.[26]

The opening of the 1925-26 session was dominated by the controversy over the non-appearance of Lord Birkenhead. Birkenhead, who as F. E. Smith had been one of the greatest lawyers of the day, was a former British Lord Chancellor and had helped negotiate the Anglo-Irish Treaty. Now Secretary of State for India in the British Government, Birkenhead had accepted an invitation to speak at the inaugural meeting on Wednesday 28 October 1925 on the subject of 'Unemployment'. The meeting was to be chaired by Lord Glenavy (the former Auditor, James Campbell), who had recently succeeded Sir John Ross as President of the Society. However, on the day before the meeting, Birkenhead sent a telegram sending his apologies, saying that because a Cabinet meeting had been summoned for the next day he was unable to attend. The Governor-General of the Irish Free State, Tim Healy, agreed to take his place.[27]

The purported real explanation for the last-minute cancellation emerged in the following days. It was reported in the British media that Birkenhead had received a number of death threats, and that security concerns had prompted him to cancel, with claims that these 'threats of violence' were 'so seriously regarded by the authorities' in both countries that neither would accept responsibility for his safety.[28] Kevin O'Higgins, now Minister for Justice, released a statement denying this story, and claimed that the Irish police were not aware of any threats or planned disturbances. He insisted that 'Lord Birkenhead will always be as safe as he would have been had circumstances permitted him to keep his engagement at Trinity College.'

At the inaugural meeting, the Auditor William Greer delivered a thoughtful paper on unemployment, and there was much praise in the newspapers for 'a striking speech' made by Tim Healy.[29] Greer later became a clergyman and educationalist and was bishop of Manchester. Debates that session included one on whether the dole should be abolished (4 November 1925) and whether civilisation had progressed since the Society had first met (11 November 1925), a

26 *The Irish Times*, 13 June 1925.

27 *The Irish Times*, 27 October 1925.

28 *The Irish Times*, 2 November 1925.

29 *The Irish Times*, 29 October 1925.

debate which was chaired by W.B. Yeats. A controversial motion was debated on 25 November, 'That Germany's Precipitation of War was Justified'.

J.G. Swift MacNeill wrote a letter to *The Irish Times*, published on 2 November 1925, complaining about the exclusion of women from the Society.[30] MacNeill noted that during the period outside of College between 1815 and 1843 women had attended some meetings, and that in 1857 the Society had attempted to extend membership to women but had been blocked. Believing that there was no solid reason for continuing the exclusion, he praised the Society for being so far seeing in 1857, eight years before the suggestion in the British House of Commons that women should be admitted, but was greeted with laughter.

William Hopkins was the Auditor for the 157th session and he chose the subject of 'Imperialism' for his inaugural address. Speakers included Viscount Charlemont, the Minister for Education in Northern Ireland, and Professor Eoin MacNeill TD, with Lord Glenavy, the President of the Society, in the chair. The Governor General was in attendance, and at the meeting Glenavy presented the gold medal for oratory to Frederick Boland with the silver medal to the Auditor.

In his address, Hopkins argued that 'the value of liberty depended not on liberty itself, but on the use that is made of it'.[31] He suggested that throughout history imperialism was 'a guilty thing', as it was 'a lust for domination' that 'had left its mark down along history in blood and ruin'. He was grateful that Ireland was unlikely to ever conquer any other land, or master the seas, but would instead spread themselves across the world through 'the fields of art, science, and literature' to the advantage of the world. In this way, he believed, Ireland could 'be in the forefront for the benefit of humanity'.

Responding to the address was Sir Thomas Myles who had been a brilliant student in Trinity in the 1870s, a member of the Society, and a notable athlete. Myles graduated BA in 1880 and took his medical degrees in 1881 before becoming resident surgeon at Dr Steevens'

30 *The Irish Times*, 2 November 1925.

31 *The Irish Times*, 28 October 1926.

Hospital at the age of twenty-four.[32] He was called to the Phoenix Park in 1881, the scene of the crime, to tend to Lord Frederick Cavendish and T.H. Burke after the attack by the Invincibles. Burke was already dead and Cavendish died soon after, and he gave evidence at the subsequent trial of those involved. A supporter of Home Rule, he became more radical in the 1910s and helped Erskine Childers and the Irish Volunteers with the gun-running in 1914. Myles began by saying that 'Trinity students were just as enthusiastic and as eager to listen to a brilliant address as they were fifty years ago'. Suggesting that people were misled about the dangers of imperialism, he said that he had no illusions about what the British Empire had done around the world, and pointed out the contradiction that one of the seemingly happiest and most prosperous countries in Europe was Italy, ruled by a despot, Mussolini.

Eoin MacNeill discussed the idea of state worship and suggested that it was particularly prevalent in Ireland, and he was critical of politicians like Éamon de Valera who believed that he only needed to look into his own heart to find out the wishes of the Irish people. Quoting Plato, Aristotle and Socrates, he argued for a government 'based upon a universally recognized standard of right' based upon 'a principle of self-determination'.

Prominent debates that session included one on 1 December 1926 that Trinity College Dublin should become 'a centre of culture'. There was also a three-way debate with the Cambridge Union and the Speculative Society in Edinburgh on 16 March 1927 on restricting the sale of intoxicating liquor. Held the day before St Patrick's Day, the motion was defeated by 109 votes to 65.[33]

In the years after Irish independence, the Society self-consciously acted as a bridge between north and south. Attempts were always made to have speakers from both parts of the island for major debates, especially for the inaugural meeting. The 1927–28 session was a case in point. The Auditor, B.W. (Brendan William) Lloyd chose as his subject 'The World in Revolt' and among the speakers was W.T. Cosgrave, President of the Executive Council, and Mr Justice Daniel Wilson of Northern Ireland. Lloyd's thesis was that

---

32 David Murphy, 'Thomas Myles', *DIB*.

33 *The Irish Times*, 17 March 1927.

the problems of the world stemmed from having false perspectives of the past. In the lead-up to the First World War the great powers had 'gloried in its stupendous material progress' and believed that prosperity and peace were bound to continue. It was a false hope, and this overconfidence had given way to war and then a general confusion afterwards.

Cosgrave was late arriving, coming from a debate in the Dáil, and he missed the first part of the address. He was greeted with warm applause, and there was similar support when he rose to propose the vote of thanks. Cosgrave expressed his delight at speaking to a Society, which he suggested had 'an honoured place in the history of Trinity' and 'I may say, of Ireland'.[34] Listing some of the great names who had been involved with the Society, from the time 'of the silver-tongued Edmund Burke' who founded the original 'Club', he listed Grattan, Tone, the Emmets, Davis, Dillon, Butt and Lecky as among those who had achieved distinction in every sphere.

Cosgrave argued that the real value of History was not 'the sentimental reverence' for 'our childhood fairy tales' but in 'the stern lessons to be learned from the successes and failures of past generations'. He believed that the 'knowledge accumulated throughout the ages' was of the utmost benefit to society. Suggesting that when a community set out to oppress a weaker people it sowed the seeds of war, he argued that 'history shows that abuse of power begets misery, misery begets resentment, resentment begets revolt, revolt begets war, war begets domination' and the vicious circle goes on. Cosgrave's speech was a plea for the League of Nations, as a way of avoiding the abuse of nationalism, and preventing the clash of nations in arms.

The educationist, positivist, and historian, Professor F.S. Marvin, also spoke and suggested there was cause for optimism. Instead of 'the world in revolt' he believed it was 'the world in renaissance', and he predicted a new struggle for freedom, freedom of thought and of knowledge as well as freedom from tyranny.

Owen Sheehy Skeffington, the son of Francis Sheehy Skeffington, the pacifist murdered by a British soldier during the 1916 Rising, and of Hannah Sheehy Skeffington, a leading women's rights campaigner,

---

34 *The Irish Times*, 27 October 1926.

entered Trinity in 1927 and soon after joined the Historical Society. For the bicentenary in 1970 he published a vivid account of his time in the Society in *The Irish Times,* calling it 'a wonderful stamping ground and workshop for those who value wit coupled with rational debate, who favour persuasion rather than the bludgeon, who are prepared to give a fair hearing as well as demand one'.[35] As important, he said, it 'has been – is – good fun'.

When he first put his name down to join the Society some students joked that if the Society was to admit such 'Sinn Féiners' it might as well admit de Valera. There were usually five debates in Michaelmas Term, seven in Hilary Term and seven in Trinity Term, and usually ran until 10.30 p.m. There followed private business and there the midnight closure rule was always strictly observed. Private business was conducted very strictly, with fines awarded which sometimes grew to large amounts. One way around this was to talk the clock down until the clock struck midnight, forcing the meeting to an end. Towards the end of the 1929–30 session a special 12 hour private business meeting was arranged to go through all the fines and other business, and various ways were found to kill the meeting. 'The occasion', in the words of Owen Sheehy Skeffington, 'was an epic one', with the opposition effectively led by Gerard Sweetman, later Fine Gael TD and Minister for Finance in the first Inter-Party Government.[36] The discussions could be humourous and frustrating, echoing the role playing that had begun with Edmund Burke's Club in 1747. For example, a privileged motion was put down to give leave of absence to the Librarian, R.P.P. Wallace, even though he made clear that he did not want to and would not take a leave of absence. None the less, the motion was debated for three hours, and it was suggested that 'he *looked* as if he wanted it, that he worked too hard for the Society, that a rest would do him good' and so on.

There was much interest in the debate on 23 November 1927 on the motion 'That this House Considers that Modern Civilisation should Slow Down'.[37] The debate was chaired by Sir Robert Tate KBE, who had been commanding officer of the Officer Training

35 *The Irish Times*, 5 March 1970.

36 Ibid.

37 *The Irish Times*, 24 November 1927.

Corps in Trinity in the 1910s. Oliver McCutcheon proposed the motion and argued that people were acting recklessly at the present time, with questionable progress in the area of medical science. W. J. Mandy opposed the motion and argued that progress should be judged not in material terms 'but in the realm of ideas'. He criticised the lack of progress in morality, religion, or education, and suggested that it was therefore impertinent to propose the motion. The Auditor, Brendan Lloyd, and Eoin O'Mahony also spoke, and the motion was carried by 41 votes to 35.

The Auditor for the 159th session, (John) Donough Bryan, chose 'The Significance of Race' as the subject for his inaugural. Chaired by Glenavy, the meeting heard Bryan suggest that racial thinking was responsible for 'a whole brood of errors, of which the most prevalent was to confuse race with nation'.[38] Attacking the idea that it was possible to tell anything about people by examining the shape of their skulls, or the proportion of their noses, he argued that poor anthropology was 'an international peril'. The work of anthropologists such as Houston Chamberlain was particularly popular in Germany, and Bryan argued that these 'racial fictions' were of obvious political use.

Tim Healy, the noted politician and lawyer, spoke at the meeting and joked that the Auditor's speech was 'a destructive attack on the heresy of predestination'. He remembered a speech he had heard at the Society fifty years previously, when Lord Killanin had said that 'no man ever mistook me for anything but an Irishman, drunk or sober'. Speaking from the chair, Glenavy gave a warm welcome to Healy, despite being political opponents, and called him 'one of our most distinguished honorary graduates and absolutely indispensable'. Glenavy dismissed craniology as little more than 'crazeology' and spoke in favour of the Jewish race.

Bryan, a scholar in 1926, was described in *Studies* as 'a talented and promising young author', and was a promising historian of early modern Ireland. He took a gold medal in history and won the Blake scholarship and briefly lectured in history at Trinity, before he died tragically in October 1932. His first (and only) book, *The Great Earl of Kildare,* was published posthumously.[39]

38 *The Irish Times*, 1 November 1928.

39 *Studies*, vol. 23, (1934) p. 339.

On 21 November 1928 the Society debated the motion 'That the Worst Form of Snobbery is that of Wealth'. Eoin O'Mahony proposed the motion, and the Auditor, Donough Bryan, opposed.

On 16 November 1928 there was an attempt to steal the minute-book and letters for Burke's Club. A thief broke into the GMB through a basement window and attempted to open the showcase, but failed to prise open the door.[40] Wallace, the Record Secretary, discovered the attempt the following morning and raised the alarm, and the documents, medals and certificates were brought to the Library for safe keeping.

To mark the bicentenary of the birth of Edmund Burke, and to raise some much needed funds because the Society was £2000 in debt, a number of events were organized, including a surprise visit by Lord Birkenhead, who spoke at the GMB on 12 December 1928. The invitation cards did not indicate the name of the speaker, but a large crowd had gathered none the less, which included the Provost, and various professors, judges and bishops and students, and the room was overflowing. Birkenhead, however, was two hours late arriving, after spending the morning playing golf at Portmarnock. Glenavy presided, and joked that 'the distinguished visitor is conspicuous by his absence, and I have some slight misgivings that he may have taken the wrong train'.[41] Entertaining the waiting crowd with a short history of the Society, and his own time as Auditor, Glenavy suggested that from the year 1770 to the present day most of 'the prominent leaders of public or patriotic life in this country' were directly associated with the Society.

As Glenavy was concluding, Bryan announced that the special guest had arrived, and there were loud cheers. Birkenhead joked that the reason why he was late was because he knew Glenavy was speaking before him, and he had 'never known him to make a speech that lasted less than an hour, and I thought I had calculated most closely the correct time to arrive'. Discussing the debates in Britain over women attending university, Birkenhead suggested the creation of an all-woman university, where men were excluded.

That evening, a major intervarsity debate was held in the Public

40 *The Irish Times*, 24 November 1928.

41 *The Irish Times*, 13 December 1928.

Theatre with speakers from Trinity taking on the Oxford Union, the Cambridge Union, the Durham Union, the Edinburgh Speculative Society, the École Normale Supérieure in Paris and the Literary and Historical Society in UCD.[42] The motion was 'That a censorship of literature is desirable' and speakers spoke as individuals rather than in teams.

Cecil Harsmsworth, the former British Under-Secretary for State, chaired the debate, and Donough Bryan spoke on the Trinity side, arguing against the fundamental principle of censorship. Admitting that 'certain literature had an evil effect on unbalanced and ignorant minds', he suggested that 'a censorship could have no useful result and would do a vast deal of harm'.[43] To cheers of 'Hear, hear' he argued that 'he did not think that government or any body of men in the world had the right to say to an individual "this subject you shall not read"'.

As far as Bryan was concerned innocence was not the same as virtue. Virtue, he believed, was 'a thing that came from strife and victory rather than a thing that was obtained by shutting people off in a corner where they have no temptation'. In a brilliant and stirring peroration, he asked the house to oppose the motion because 'it would be a pitiable thing if the first thing which this country did when it got its freedom was to fetter public opinion, and if the fight for freedom would end in intellectual servitude'.

Perhaps the best speech of the night was delivered by André Parreaux, a student from Paris, who went on to have a distinguished career as an academic and historian. Parreaux proposed the motion, but in a mock-serious way that punctured its pretensions. Wondering where censorship should stop, he argued for a censorship of the Bible as 'the innocent reader' might be influenced by David's adultery. To much laughter and applause, he suggested that 'the merciless application of censorship was really the only logical attitude to adopt'. As *The Irish Times* reported, 'while ostensibly speaking in the affirmative', Parreaux 'dealt a number of shrewd blows at the censorship theory'.[44] The motion was defeated by 241 votes to 91.

---

42 *The Irish Times*, 12 December 1928.

43 *The Irish Times*, 13 December 1928.

44 *The Irish Times*, 22 December 1928.

Other influential debates that session included a motion 'That this House would Welcome an Open Discussion on the Problem of Sex' on 6 February 1929.[45] On 6 March 1929 the motion was 'That Record-Breaking Competitions are Absurd', where Terence de Vere White opposed the motion.[46] Debates could be historical or topical. On 13 March it was 'That the Execution of Charles I was Justifiable'.[47] On 8 May 1929 the students debated modern technology, in a debate chaired by the sculptor, Jerome Connor, with a motion 'That the "Talkie" is an Undesirable Innovation'.[48] The debate on 29 May 1929 was on the motion 'That Nationalism is an Obstacle to World Peace'.[49]

White would later recount his memories of the Society in his book, *A Frefiful Midge,* described by Owen Dudley Edwards as 'an autobiography of masterful diplomacy and atmospheric realism pretending to be the work of a (fictitious) Bernard Vandeleur.'[50] In it he admitted that his maiden speech had been a disaster: 'I heard it quite distinctly because my voice seemed to leave me and speak from a distant point in the ceiling.'[51] He stopped speaking suddenly and he had 'two impulses equally strong – to burst into tears and to run away', but he resumed his speech and finally concluded. Leaving the hall as soon 'as decency allowed', he claimed that he stayed out of Trinity until he felt the report of his shame had died, before realising that 'No one, of course, gave a damn.' Eventually he found the courage to return to speak at the chamber, and over time developed 'an epigrammatic and would-be sophisticated style that was not common in Trinity' and which won much praise. However, he admitted that as the audience became accustomed to it, 'they ceased to be impressed by it'.

A major debate on Irish education was held on 27 February 1929. The motion was 'That Irish Boys should be Educated at Irish

45 *The Irish Times*, 6 February 1929.
46 *The Irish Times*, 7 March 1929.
47 *The Irish Times*, 13 March 1929.
48 *The Irish Times*, 8 May 1929.
49 *The Irish Times*, 29 May 1929.
50 Owen Dudley Edwards, '(Herbert) Terence De Vere White', *DIB.*
51 Terence De Vere White, *A Fretful Midge* (London, 1957), p. 63.

Schools' and it attracted wide interest because of some claims that English schools were better. W.J. Mandy proposed the motion, suggesting that 'definite racial characteristics' were better than 'a cosmopolitan outlook'.[52] Terence de Vere White opposed the motion and argued that 'every boy was entitled to the best education that his parents could afford'. He did not believe a child had to be educated in Ireland 'for sentimental reasons', and suggested that 'the training of a boy to be a good citizen was of more importance than party politics'. And he denounced the motion as one of the most narrow-minded ever discussed by the Society, similar to Government proposals to censor literature.

Eoin O'Mahony proposed the motion and argued that 'Irish boys, educated in an Irish school, were the best men to run the country, because they knew the country and the people'. G.R. Quirke, opposing the motion, argued that 'all the English schools were loyal to the Constitution', meaning presumably the British Constitution, and 'unfortunately that was not the case in Ireland'. The motion was carried by 34 votes to 10.

The value of science was debated on the evening of 22 May 1929, with a motion 'That Scientists Should take a Ten Years' Holiday'. The debate was open to the public, and attracted a large crowd, and three of the speakers were guests from Sydney University. The motion was proposed by N.G. Godsall who argued that 'humanity was a finer thing than science'.[53] He suggested that 'the effect of science was to rob the world of its beauty and man of his humanity'. Scientists were blamed for reducing the world to a factory, and man to a machine.

Opposing the motion was the Auditor, Donough Bryan, who defended scientists from the accusation that they had attacked the religious faith. Instead, he argued, it was 'certain ecclesiastics who had most unjustifiably attacked the scientists'. Bryan believed that 'science had been of assistance to mankind'. The arguments were convincing, and the motion was defeated by a large majority.

One of the speakers opposing the motion was (Charles) Bueno McKenna, a Scholar (1925) with a degree in experimental science,

52 *The Irish Times*, 28 February 1929.

53 *The Irish Times*, 27 May 1929.

and he was elected the new Auditor of the Society a couple of days later, unopposed.[54] McKenna had started a second degree in Law, and was also an Associate of the Institute of Chemists. Described in a profile in *The Irish Times* as 'a person of many parts', and later in the year as 'one of the most brilliant of the younger Trinity men', he played a role in the founding of the TCD Students Association, the forerunner of the Students Union, and was an able orator.[55] A keen golfer, it was noted in the paper that 'he has also been known to enjoy occasional dances very thoroughly', and his proudest possession was said to be his collection of college ties in all patterns.

Eoin O'Mahony was elected Record Secretary unopposed. Given his subsequent status in Society folklore, it is worth spending some time on O'Mahony. Known as 'Pope' O'Mahony since his days in Clongowes, apparently because, with characteristic innocence, he said that his ambition in life was to be pope.[56] In another account it was because he was believed to be infallible, knowing all the answers in class.[57] Born in 1904, O'Mahony was older than many of his contemporaries when he arrived in Trinity, having already gone to UCC where he failed to complete his medical degree, but where he became gold medallist and Auditor of the university's debating society. Studying for the bar at King's Inns, he became a prominent debater in Trinity, and impressed with his oratorical powers. In his obituary in *The Times* of London, Charles Lysaght wrote that 'he was without doubt the outstanding Irish talker of his time', a 'memorable personality, kindly, lovable, eccentric and improvident'.[58] De Vere White described his 'rich Cork brogue' as 'one of the most mellifluous in Ireland', and claimed that 'only James Dillon could compare with him in organ power, in copiousness and volume'.[59]

After leaving Trinity O'Mahony became state counsel in Cork for a time, before breaking with Fianna Fáil on the treatment of

54 *The Irish Times*, 24 May 1929.

55 *The Irish Times*, 24 May 1929, 31 October 1929.

56 Charles Lysaght, 'Eoin O'Mahony', *DIB*.

57 J. Anthony Gaughan, *Alfred O'Rahilly* (Dublin, 1992), p. 54.

58 *The Times*, 19 February 1970.

59 White, *Fretful Midge*, p. 66.

republican prisoners. He achieved some success as a genealogist, and has been described as 'an authority on aristocratic families, especially those who had nationalist connections'.[60] He also worked as a broadcaster, and was a visiting lecturer in the United States, but his attempts to win a seat in either the Dáil or Seanad ended in failure, and he was unable to secure a nomination to run in the 1966 presidential election, the first person to ever attempt to secure a nomination through four local authorities. In one profile it was noted that 'the best of his talk was good, but his compulsive loquacity and way of life led some not to take him seriously'.[61] Charles Lysaght writes that he poured 'forth torrents of information in a mellifluous Cork accent, entertaining and sometimes insightful, but at other times long-winded, wanting in accuracy and slightly absurd'.[62] Although a staunch republican, he campaigned for Daniel O'Connell's home at Derrynane to be saved, and he was the only Irish person to go to Messines in 1967 to commemorate the fiftieth anniversary of the death of Willie Redmond.

For his inaugural address, on 30 October 1929, McKenna chose as his subject the theme of the depopulation of Ireland. The meeting was chaired by the Provost, Dr Gwynn, and gathered a large attendance. McKenna looked at the decline of the Irish population since the Famine, and how many had gone to live and work in American cities. He suggested that 'the Irish race has abandoned the ancestral soil, not for El Dorado, but for Hoboken and the Bowery'. Instead of finding a land of milk and honey, 'they have become the hewers of wood and the drawers of water for the modern Pharaoh'. Speaking passionately about the towns and villages in Ireland where there was 'an absence of hope', he questioned whether anyone could blame them when those who remained at home faced 'cramped opportunity and illiberal life'. Some of his proposed solutions, however, were impractical. For example, he wondered whether farmers should be forbidden to sell land. But his faith in the country's future resonated and was seen as a strong appeal for greater investment in education.

---

60 *History Ireland,* (2004), vol. 12, number 2.

61 Ibid.

62 Charles Lysaght, 'Eoin O'Mahony', *DIB*.

V.I. Dobrznski, the Consul General for Poland, spoke later in the meeting and discussed the growth of the Polish economy since 1921. Linking the stories of Ireland and Poland, he suggested that as their destinies were now in their own hands they could be hopeful of a future of prosperity and progress.

The chairman of the Free State Senate, T.W. Westropp Bennett, proposed that the address was printed and called for the government to intervene to ameliorate conditions. Concluding the debate, the Provost noted that the address had been received 'with an enthusiasm he had rarely seen in the College'. But he admitted that he disagreed with the central thesis that emigration was an evil as he believed 'it had largely contributed to make the name of Ireland known and honoured the world over'.

Motions under McKenna's auditorship were a little more spiky and far-seeing. On 13 November 1929 the students debated 'That Politicians should Not be Tolerated in a Civilised Community', a debate reported in *The Irish Times* with the headline 'Hard words for politicians'. White proposed the motion and argued that politicians had no qualification 'except the ability to blather' and were not even half-honest.[63] Reviewing the record of politicians, from Cassius to Lloyd George, he claimed that English and Irish politicians had ruined Ireland in the past and were ruining it at present. D.P. Owens opposed the motion and suggested that there could be no civilisation without government. Government's aim was to raise the standard of civilisation. The motion, however, was carried by a majority. Sir Philip Hanson, the chair of the Commission of Public Works, chaired the debate and he suggested that politicians were people who were paid for guessing what the public wanted. The difference, he said, between politicians and autocrats, was that autocrats often guessed wrong about what people wanted and could not be put out of office so easily.

A debate about bicameralism was one of the highlights of the session. On 20 November 1929 the motion 'That this House Regrets Upper Chambers' was debated, with Hugh Law TD in the chair. Eoin O'Mahony proposed the motion and said he had developed his aversion to second chambers from reading St Thomas Aquinas.

---

63 *The Irish Times*, 14 November 1929.

Arguing that there was no room for two chambers in the Irish Free State, he called for the abolition of the Free State Senate.[64] Opposing the motion was Gerard Sweetman, who noted that the Senate had allowed Thomas Johnson, the Labour leader, to continue in parliament after losing his seat. J.J. Auchmuty also spoke in favour of the motion, with Owen Sheehy Skeffington, in his maiden speech, opposing. After a vote, the motion was defeated.

Senator James Douglas was in the chair a week later for a debate on the motion 'That this House would welcome a United States of Europe'. D.P. Owens proposed the motion and suggested that European solidarity could be a bulwark against Americanism and the evils it brought with it 'jazz, the talkies and broadcasting'.[65] Opposing the motion, White argued that European nations differed widely in creed, race, traditions and general outlook and could never be unified. The motion was lost by 13 votes to 21.

The debate on 4 December 1929 was on 'tabloid knowledge', the term for having potted histories of events rather than detailed examinations. Tim Healy chaired the debate, 'That this House Deplores Tabloid Knowledge', and it was opened by the Auditor, McKenna, who regretted that there was an increasing tendency to shirking the road to true knowledge by taking shortcuts.[66] Blaming America for this trend, because there 'hustle was the thing', he suggested that 'tabloid knowledge was fatal to scholarship'. Eoin O'Mahony opposed the motion and argued that Macaulay had driven home his knowledge through so-called tabloid histories. He suggested that an attack on tabloid knowledge was ultimately an attack on the whole basis of the present civilisation. The motion was defeated by 32 votes to 24. Speaking from the chair, Healy praised the quality of the 'scholarly, effective and eloquent' debate. He quoted King George III who said lawyers were people who did not necessarily know more law than anyone else, they just knew where best to find it. This, he believed, was the best example he could find of tabloid knowledge. As the year came to a close, the Society was in a strong position, its debates regularly featuring in the national

64 *The Irish Times*, 21 November 1929.

65 *The Irish Times*, 28 November 1929.

66 *The Irish Times*, 5 December 1929.

newspapers, and a stream of talented debaters coming through its ranks. It was proud of its position in society, informing, influencing, and shaping national debates, as it entered a decade where these things were needed more than ever.

ILLUSTRATIONS

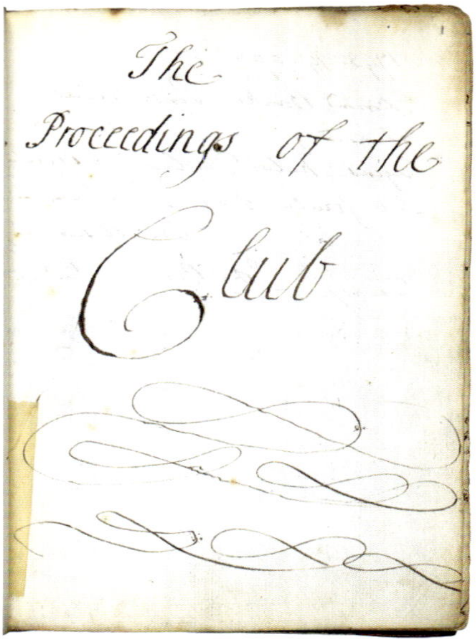
The
Proceedings of the
Club

Burke Minute Book: Title-page
TCD MUN SOC HIST 81 p .5

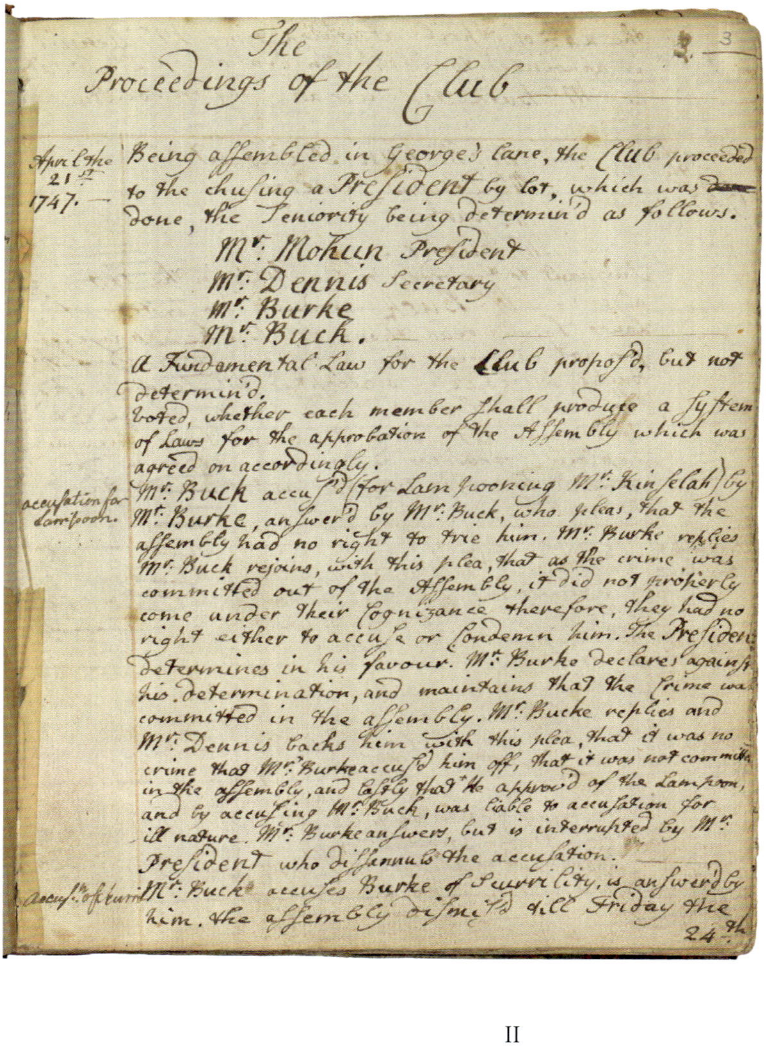
3

The
Proceedings of the Club

April the 21st 1747. — Being assembled in George's lane, the Club proceeded to the chusing a President by lot, which was done, the Seniority being determin'd as follows.

Mr. Mohun President
Mr. Dennis Secretary
Mr. Burke
Mr. Buck.

A Fundemental Law for the Club propos'd, but not determin'd.
Voted, whether each member shall produce a system of Laws for the approbation of the Assembly which was agreed on accordingly.

accusation for lampoon. Mr. Buck accus'd (for Lampooning Mr. Kinselah) by Mr. Burke, answer'd by Mr. Buck, who pleas, that the assembly had no right to trie him. Mr. Burke replies Mr. Buck rejoins, with this plea, that as the crime was committed out of the Assembly, it did not properly come under their Cognizance therefore, they had no right either to accuse or condemn him. The President determines in his favour. Mr. Burke declares against his determination, and maintains that the Crime was committed in the assembly. Mr. Bucke replies and Mr. Dennis backs him with this plea, that it was no crime that Mr. Burke accus'd him off, that it was not committed in the assembly, and lastly that he approv'd of the Lampoon, and by accusing Mr. Buck, was liable to accusation for ill nature. Mr. Burke answers, but is interrupted by Mr. President who dissannuls the accusation.

accus. of scurril. Mr. Buck accuses Burke of Scurrility, is answerd by him. the assembly dismiss'd till Friday the 24th

Burke Minute Book:
First Meeting 21st April 1747
TCD MUN SOC HIST 81 p. 7

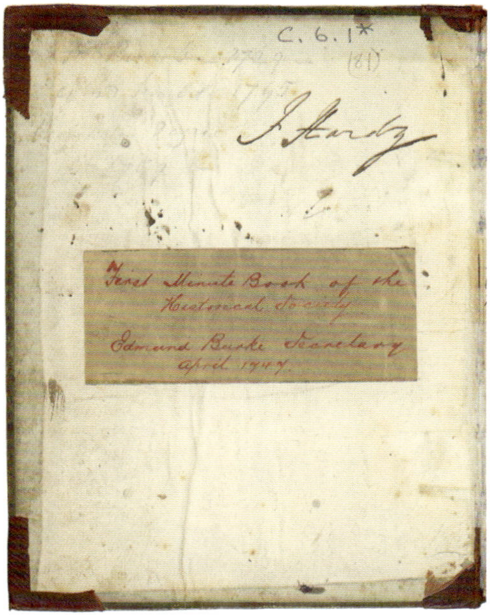

ABOVE LEFT

Burke Minute Book: Front cover

TCD MUN SOC HIST 81 p. 1

ABOVE RIGHT

Burke Minute Book: Note on inside cover 'First Minute Book of the Historical Society, Edmund Burke Secretary April 1747'

TCD MUN SOC HIST 81 p. 2

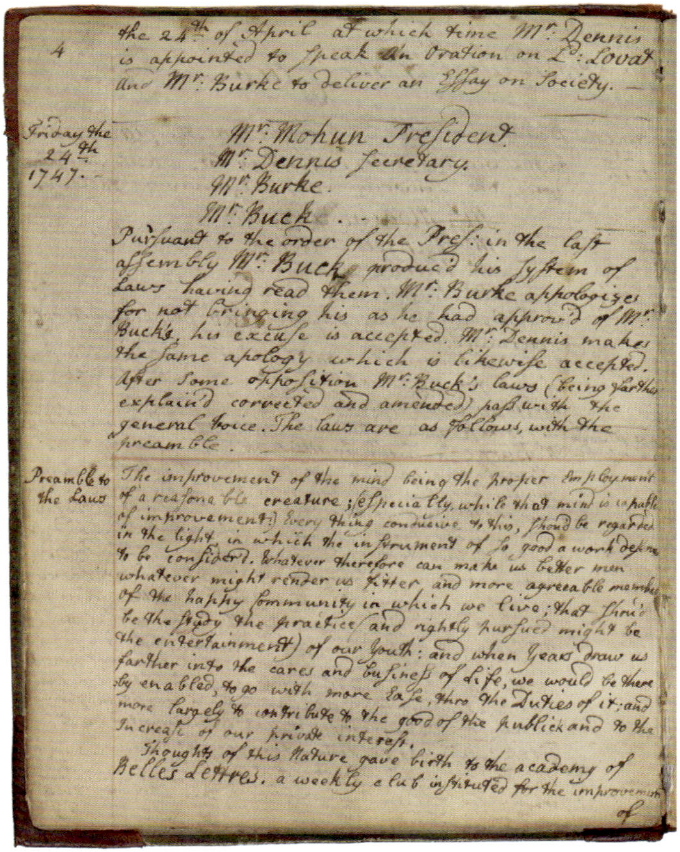

4 the 24th of April at which time Mr: Dennis is appointed to speak an Oration on Ld: Lovat And Mr: Burke to deliver an Essay on Society. —

Friday the 24th 1747. — Mr: Mohun President.
Mr: Dennis secretary.
Mr: Burke.
Mr: Buck. . .

Pursuant to the order of the Pres: in the last assembly Mr: Buck produc'd his system of Laws having read them. Mr: Burke appologizes for not bringing his as he had approv'd of Mr: Buck's, his excuse is accepted. Mr: Dennis makes the same apology which is likewise accepted. After some opposition Mr: Buck's laws (being farther explain'd corrected and amended) pass with the general voice. The laws are as follows, with the preamble.

Preamble to the Laws — The improvement of the mind being the proper Employment of a reasonable creature; (especially, while that mind is capable of improvement:) Every thing conducive to this, shoud be regarded in the light in which the instrument of so good a work deserves to be consider'd. Whatever therefore can make us better men whatever might render us fitter and more agreeable members of the happy community in which we live; that shou'd be the study the practice (and rightly pursued might be the entertainment) of our youth: and when Years draw us farther into the cares and business of Life, we would be thereby enabled, to go with more Ease, thro the Duties of it; and more largely to contribute to the good of the publick and to the Increase of our private interest.

Thoughts of this Nature gave birth to the academy of Belles Lettres. a weekly club instituted for the improvement of

RIGHT

Burke Minute Book: Second Meeting 24th April 1747

TCD MUN SOC HIST 81 p. 8

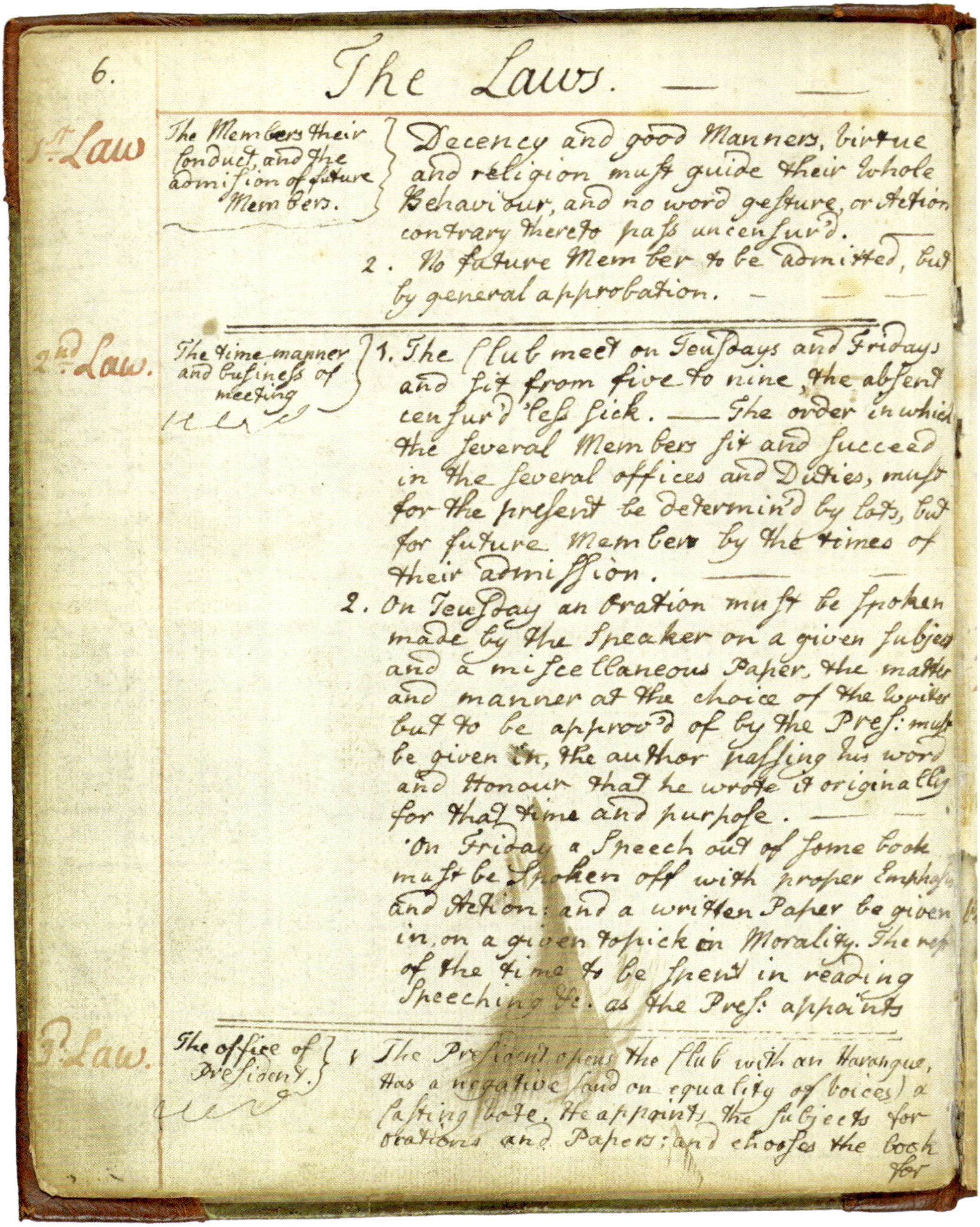

6. The Laws. —— ——

1st Law | The Members their Conduct, and the admision of future Members.

Decency and good Manners, virtue and religion must guide their whole Behaviour, and no word gesture, or Action contrary thereto pass uncensur'd.

2. No future Member to be admitted, but by general approbation. — — —

2nd Law. | The time manner and business of meeting

1. The Club meet on Teusdays and Fridays and sit from five to nine, the absent censur'd less sick. —— The order in which the several Members sit and succeed in the several offices and Duties, must for the present be determin'd by lots, but for future Members by the times of their admission. —— ——

2. On Teusday an Oration must be spoken made by the Speaker on a given subject and a miscellaneous Paper, the matter and manner at the choice of the Writer but to be approv'd of by the Pres: must be given in, the author passing his word and Honour that he wrote it originally for that time and purpose. ——

On Friday a Speech out of some book must be spoken off with proper Emphasis and Action: and a written Paper be given in, on a given topick in Morality. The rest of the time to be spent in reading Speeching &c. as the Pres: appoints

3rd Law. | The office of President.

1 The President opens the Club with an Harangue, Has a negative (and on equality of voices) a casting vote. He appoints the subjects for Orations and Papers; and chooses the book for

Burke Minute Book: The first page of The Laws
TCD MUN SOC HIST 81 p. 10

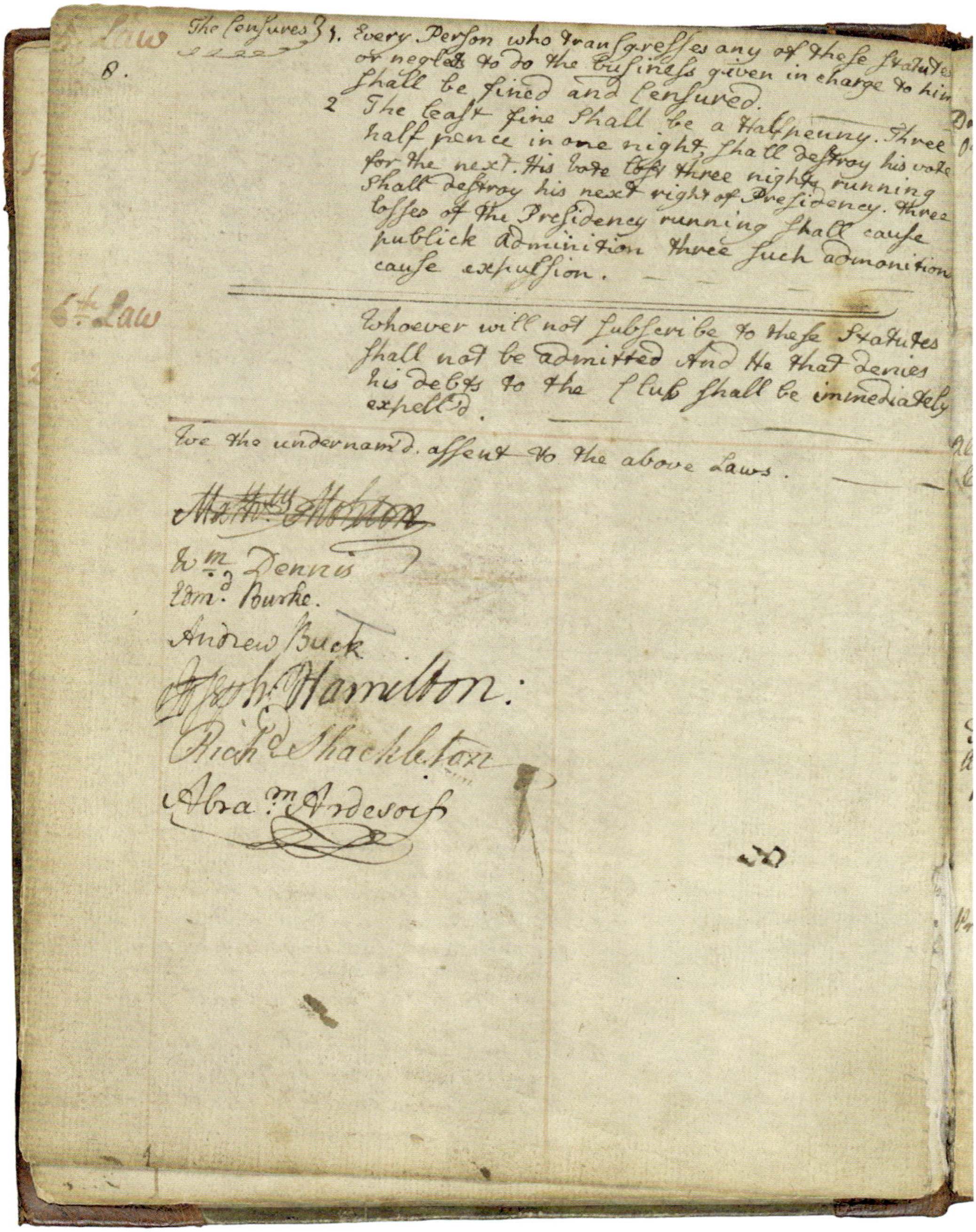

Law The Censures 1. Every Person who transgresses any of these Statutes or neglects to do the business given in charge to him shall be fined and censured.

8\. 2 The least fine shall be a Halfpenny. Three half pence in one night, shall destroy his vote for the next. His vote lost three nights running shall destroy his next right of Presidency. three losses of the Presidency running shall cause publick admonition three such admonition cause expulsion.

6th Law Whoever will not subscribe to these Statutes shall not be admitted And He that denies his debts to the Club shall be immediately expelled.

We the undernam'd. assent to the above Laws.

~~Matthw Mohun~~

Wm. Dennis

Edmd. Burke.

Andrew Buck

Josh. Hamilton:

Richd. Shackleton

Abram. Ardesoif

Burke Minute Book: Signatures of those assenting to The Laws: Mohun, Dennis, Burke, Buck, Hamilton, Shackleton and Ardesoif

TCD MUN SOC HIST 81 p. 12

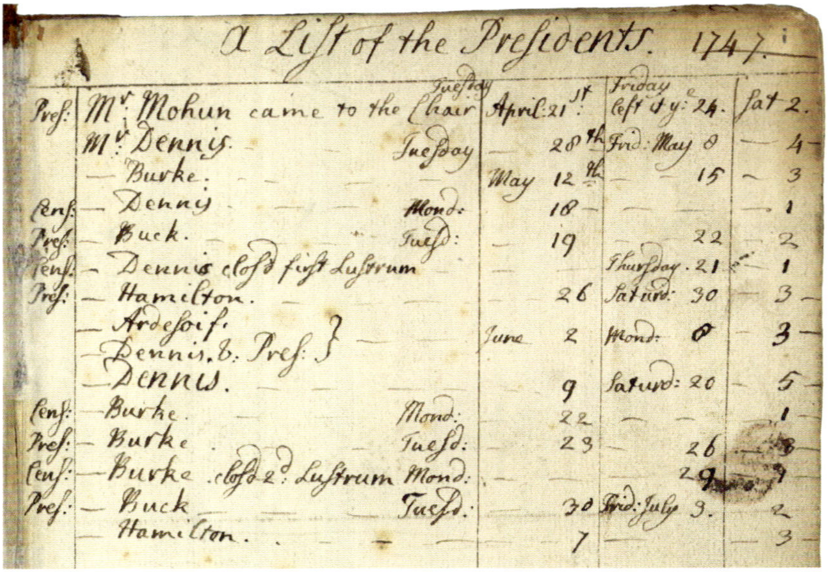

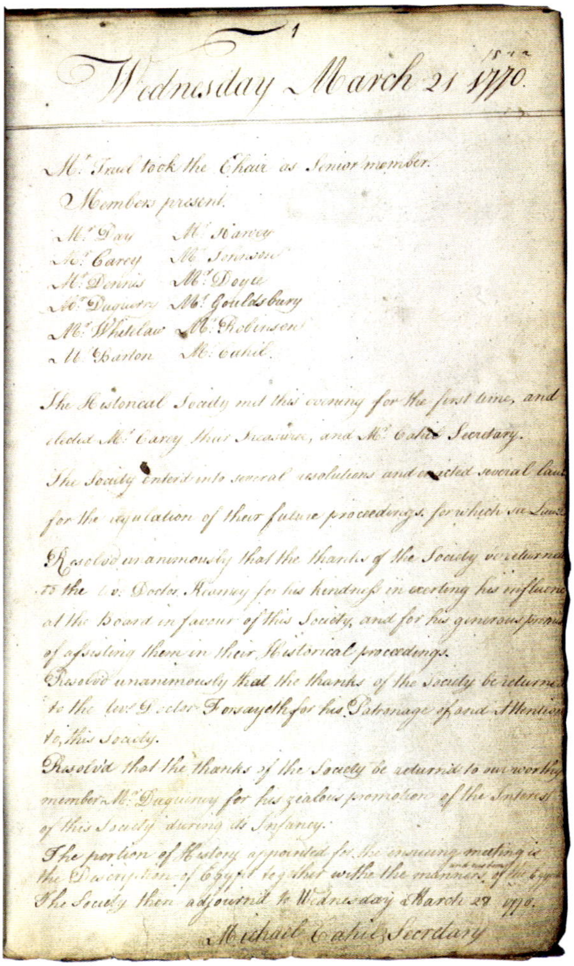

ABOVE

Burke Minute Book: A list of the Presidents who presided over the meetings
TCD MUN SOC HIST 81 p. 3

LEFT

The minutes of the first meeting of the Historical Society on Wednesday 21st March 1770
TCD MUN SOC HIST 1 p. 1

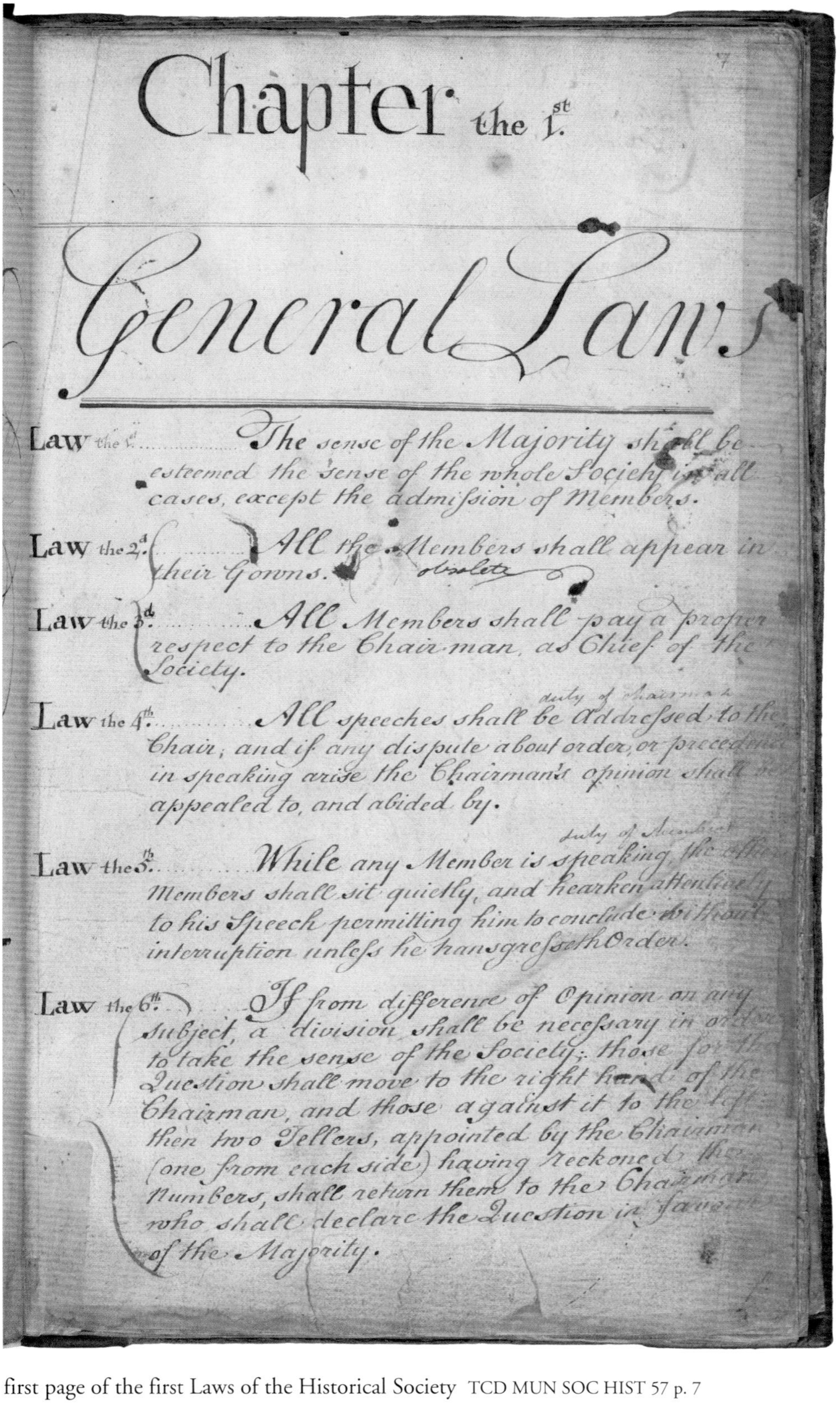

Chapter the 1st

General Laws

Law the 1st .... The sense of the Majority shall be esteemed the sense of the whole Society in all cases, except the admission of Members.

Law the 2d .... All the Members shall appear in their Gowns. obsolete

Law the 3d .... All Members shall pay a proper respect to the Chair-man, as Chief of the Society.

Law the 4th .... duty of Chairman All speeches shall be addressed to the Chair; and if any dispute about order, or precedence in speaking arise the Chairman's opinion shall be appealed to, and abided by.

Law the 5th .... duty of Members While any Member is speaking, the other Members shall sit quietly, and hearken attentively to his Speech permitting him to conclude without interruption unless he transgresseth Order.

Law the 6th .... If from difference of Opinion on any subject, a division shall be necessary in order to take the sense of the Society; those for the Question shall move to the right hand of the Chairman, and those against it to the left then two Tellers, appointed by the Chairman (one from each side) having reckoned the Numbers, shall return them to the Chairman who shall declare the Question in favour of the Majority.

The first page of the first Laws of the Historical Society TCD MUN SOC HIST 57 p. 7

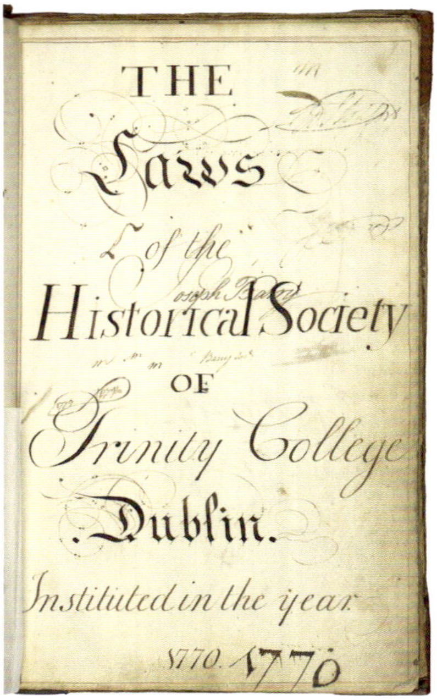

The title-page of The Laws of the Historical Society
TCD MUN SOC HIST 57, title page

Signatures opposite the first page of The Laws of the Historical Society, with an elaborate large one of Theobald Wolfe Tone
TCD MUN SOC HIST 57 p. 6

RIGHT

10th September 1914: A minute of the meeting which decided that the Inaugural meeting be postponed indefinitely due to the start of the First World War
From TCD MUN SOC HIST series

BELOW LEFT

Cover of the volume containing the Laws and Declarations of the members of the Historical Society containing 997 autographs 1770 to 1794
TCD MUN SOC HIST 57 COVER

BELOW RIGHT

Title-page of the Essays of the members of the Historical Society
TCD MUN SOC HIST 49 p. 61

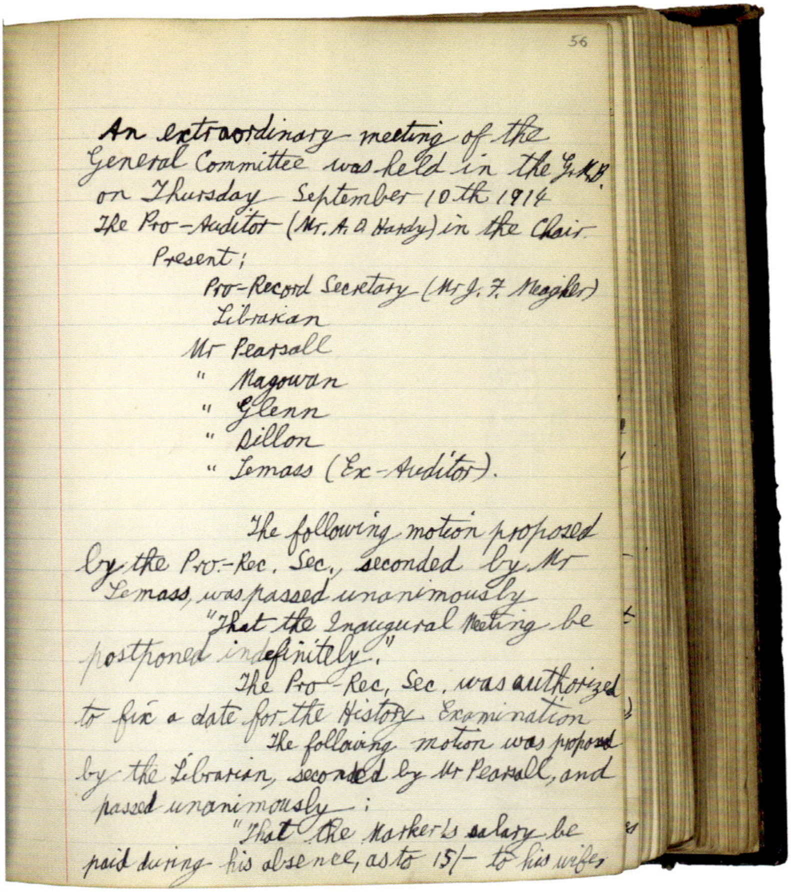
56

An extraordinary meeting of the General Committee was held in the G.K.R. on Thursday September 10th 1914
The Pro-Auditor (Mr. A. D. Hardy) in the Chair.
Present;
Pro-Record Secretary (Mr J. F. Meagher)
Librarian
Mr Pearsall
" Magowan
" Glenn
" Dillon
" Lemass (Ex-Auditor).

The following motion proposed by the Pro.-Rec. Sec., seconded by Mr Lemass, was passed unanimously
"That the Inaugural Meeting be postponed indefinitely."
The Pro-Rec. Sec. was authorized to fix a date for the History Examination
The following motion was proposed by the Librarian, seconded by Mr Pearsall, and passed unanimously;
"That the Marker's salary be paid during his absence, as to 15/- to his wife

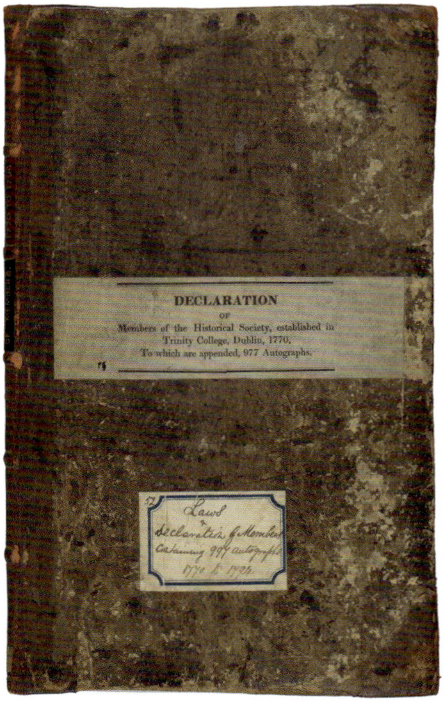

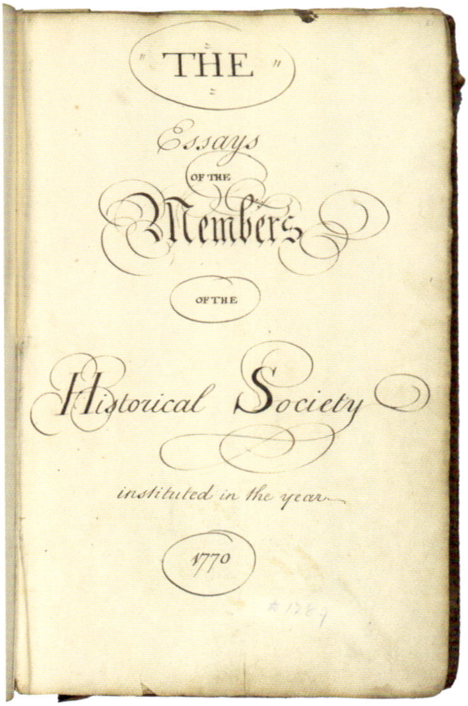

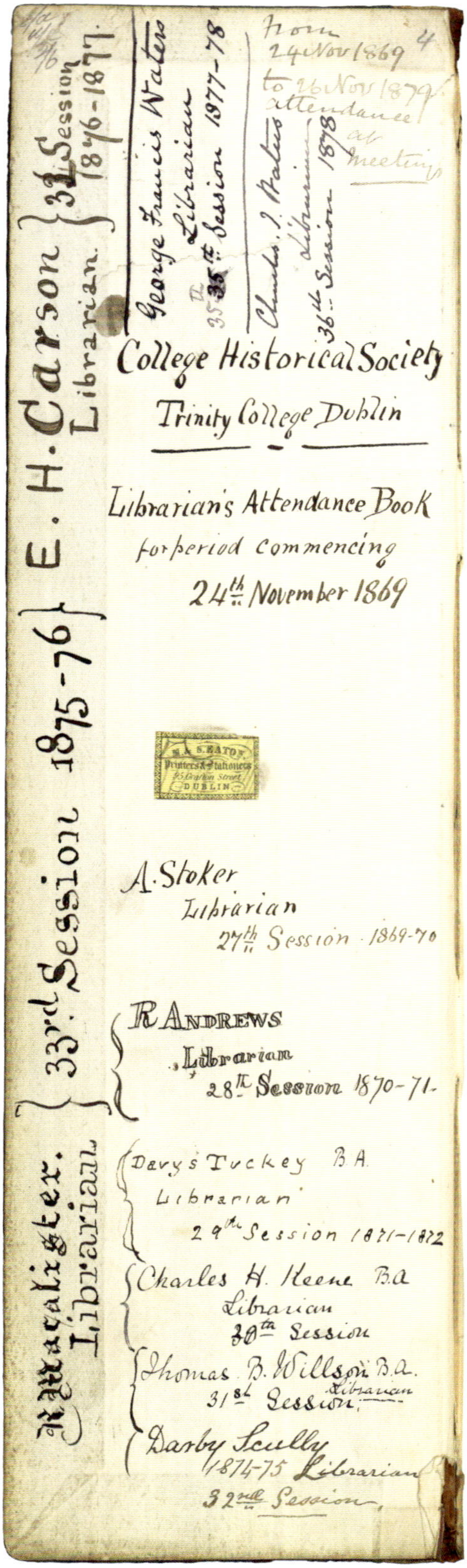

LEFT

A page from the Librarian's Attendance Book commencing on 24th November 1869 to 26th November 1879, including the names of the Librarians Bram Stoker and Edward Carson

From TCD MUN SOC HIST series

BELOW

A list of new members in 1873-74 including Oscar Wilde and Edward Carson

From TCD MUN SOC HIST series

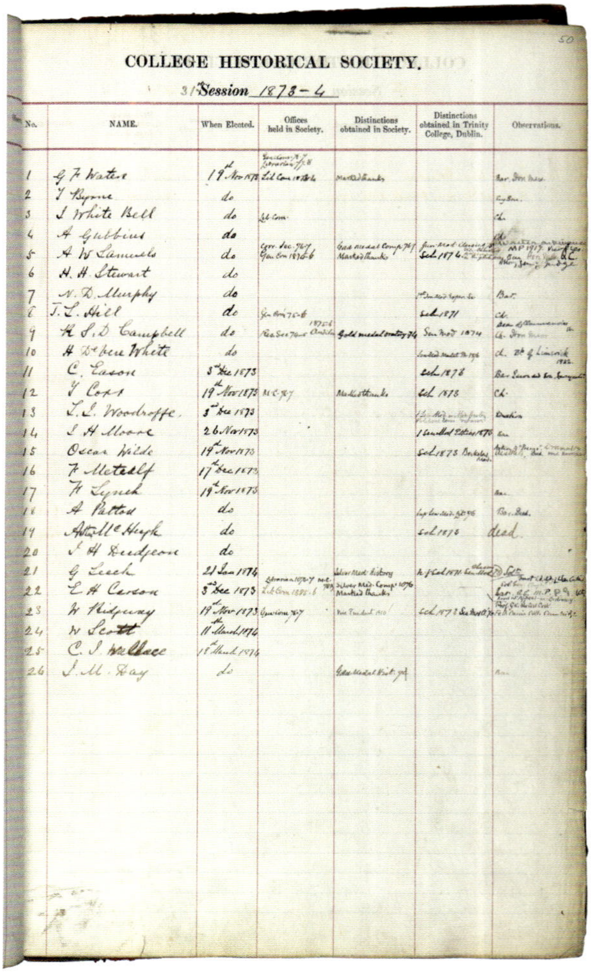

LEFT

Cover of the 1874 Historical Society petition to the Board for the continued use of the Dining Hall, the petition bound in leather and the title gold blocked
TCD MUN SOC HIST 42, COVER

BELOW

Text page of the Historical Society petition to the Board 1874 for the continued use of the Dining Hall
TCD MUN SOC HIST 42, folio 10r

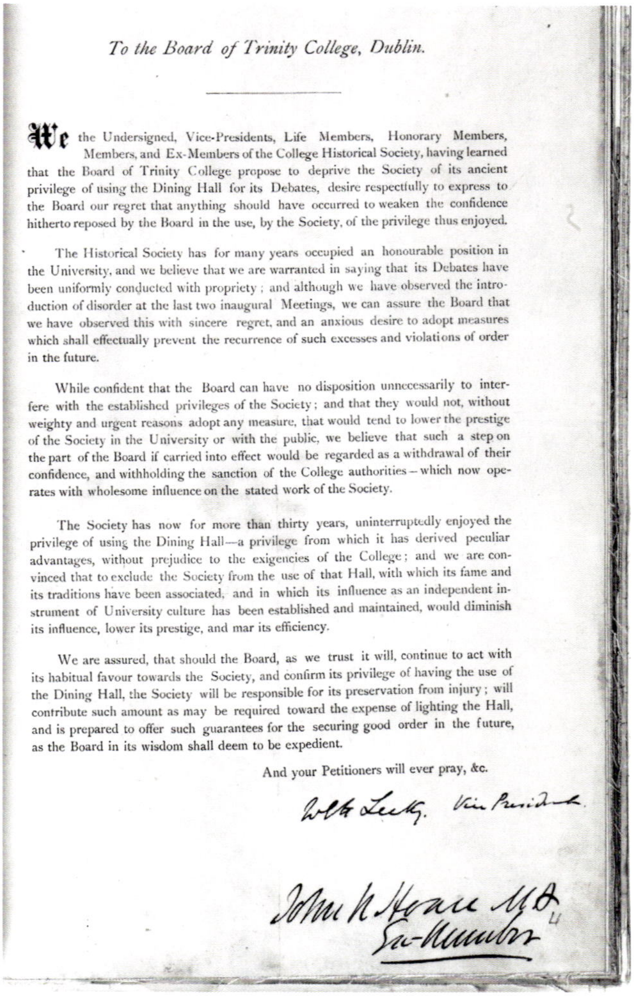

To the Board of Trinity College, Dublin.

We the Undersigned, Vice-Presidents, Life Members, Honorary Members, Members, and Ex-Members of the College Historical Society, having learned that the Board of Trinity College propose to deprive the Society of its ancient privilege of using the Dining Hall for its Debates, desire respectfully to express to the Board our regret that anything should have occurred to weaken the confidence hitherto reposed by the Board in the use, by the Society, of the privilege thus enjoyed.

The Historical Society has for many years occupied an honourable position in the University, and we believe that we are warranted in saying that its Debates have been uniformly conducted with propriety; and although we have observed the introduction of disorder at the last two inaugural Meetings, we can assure the Board that we have observed this with sincere regret, and an anxious desire to adopt measures which shall effectually prevent the recurrence of such excesses and violations of order in the future.

While confident that the Board can have no disposition unnecessarily to interfere with the established privileges of the Society; and that they would not, without weighty and urgent reasons adopt any measure, that would tend to lower the prestige of the Society in the University or with the public, we believe that such a step on the part of the Board if carried into effect would be regarded as a withdrawal of their confidence, and withholding the sanction of the College authorities – which now operates with wholesome influence on the stated work of the Society.

The Society has now for more than thirty years, uninterruptedly enjoyed the privilege of using the Dining Hall—a privilege from which it has derived peculiar advantages, without prejudice to the exigencies of the College; and we are convinced that to exclude the Society from the use of that Hall, with which its fame and its traditions have been associated, and in which its influence as an independent instrument of University culture has been established and maintained, would diminish its influence, lower its prestige, and mar its efficiency.

We are assured, that should the Board, as we trust it will, continue to act with its habitual favour towards the Society, and confirm its privilege of having the use of the Dining Hall, the Society will be responsible for its preservation from injury; will contribute such amount as may be required toward the expense of lighting the Hall, and is prepared to offer such guarantees for the securing good order in the future, as the Board in its wisdom shall deem to be expedient.

And your Petitioners will ever pray, &c.

W E H Lecky. Vice President.

John K Hoare M.D.
Ex-Member

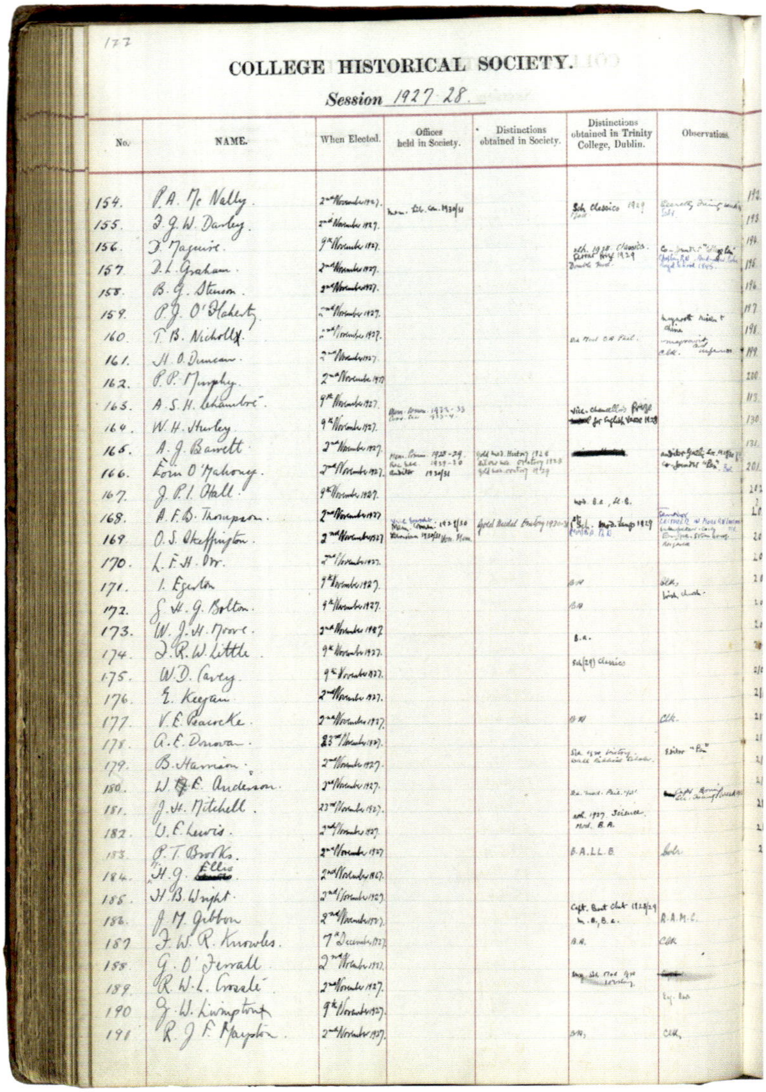

177

COLLEGE HISTORICAL SOCIETY.

Session 1927-28.

No.	NAME.	When Elected.	Offices held in Society.	Distinctions obtained in Society.	Distinctions obtained in Trinity College, Dublin.	Observations.
154.	P. A. McNally.	2nd November 1927.			Sch. Classics 1929	
155.	J. G. W. Darley.	2nd November 1927.				
156.	J. Maguire.	9th November 1927.				
157.	J. L. Graham.	2nd November 1927.				
158.	B. G. Stinson.	2nd November 1927.				
159.	P. J. O'Flaherty.	2nd November 1927.				
160.	T. B. Nicholls.	2nd November 1927.				
161.	H. O. Duncan.	2nd November 1927.				
162.	P. P. Murphy.	2nd November 1927.				
163.	A. S. H. Chambré.	9th November 1927.				
164.	W. H. Hurley.	9th November 1927.				
165.	A. J. Barrett.	2nd November 1927.			[redacted]	
166.	Eoin O'Mahony.	2nd November 1927.				
167.	J. P. I. Hall.	9th November 1927.				
168.	A. F. B. Thompson.	2nd November 1927.				
169.	O. S. Skeffington.	2nd November 1927.				
170.	L. F. H. Orr.	2nd November 1927.				
171.	I. Egerton	9th November 1927.				
172.	J. H. G. Bolton.	9th November 1927.				
173.	W. J. H. Moore.	2nd November 1927.				
174.	J. R. W. Little.	9th November 1927.			B.A.	
175.	W. D. Carey.	9th November 1927.				
176.	E. Keegan.	2nd November 1927.				
177.	V. E. Peacocke.	2nd November 1927.				Clk.
178.	A. E. Donovan.	23rd November 1927.				
179.	B. Harrison.	2nd November 1927.				
180.	W. F. E. Anderson.	2nd November 1927.				
181.	J. H. Mitchell.	23rd November 1927.				
182.	V. E. Lewis.	2nd November 1927.				
183.	P. T. Brooks.	2nd November 1927.			B.A. LL.B.	
184.	H. G. Ellis	2nd November 1927.				
185.	H. B. Wright.	2nd November 1927.				
186.	J. M. Gibbon	2nd November 1927.				R.A.M.C.
187.	J. W. R. Knowles.	7th December 1927.			B.A.	Clk.
188.	G. O'Ferrall.	2nd November 1927.				
189.	R. W. L. Croxale.	2nd November 1927.				
190.	G. W. Livingstone.	9th November 1927.				
191.	R. J. F. Mayston.	2nd November 1927.				Clk.

A list of new members in 1927-28 including Eoin O'Mahony and Owen Sheehy Skeffington

From TCD MUN SOC HIST series

Medal presented to William Ball for his poem read on 'Wednesday the 26th of April MDCC75'. The medal is clearly one of a batch with the name cut in script and the year in a curious mixture of cast Roman (MDCC) and cut Arabic numbers (75)

TCD MUN SOC HIST 89/20

OFFICERS & MEDALLISTS 1858-61

Standing: David R. Plunket, Henry Stewart, Freeman Wills
Seated: Edward Gibson, Conway Cartwright, W.E.H. Lecky

COMMITTEE 1872-73

Standing: not named, not named, not named, Cecil Roche,W.F. O'Shaughnessy, Henry W. Adair
Seated: R.D. Murray, Henry Lane, Abraham Stoker, Charles Matheson, Charles H. Keane

COMMITTEE 1905-06

Back: M.H. Meeredy, M.C. Green, J.H.G. Brookes, R.J.C. Maunsell, H.S.B. Taylor, H.L. Cowdy
Middle: T.S.C. Dagg, H.L. Murphy, J.G. Dougherty
Front: D.L.C. Dunlop, R.J.H. Shaw

COMMITTEE 1914-15

Officers (order uncertain): T.D.M. Bartley Auditor, M. Murray Treasurer, I. Roundtree & B.St.J. Galvin Secretaries, K.E. O'Duffy & T.C.K. Moore Librarians

COMMITTEE 1923-24

Standing: W.D.L. Greer, D.R. Dutt, F.G.O. Budd, C.ff Young, E.H. Hall, J.K. MacCarthy Morrogh
Seated: J.B. Gregg, F.D. MacCarthy Morrogh, P. Bourke, T.J. Johnston, E.N.P Goff

COMMITTEE 1929-30

Standing: K.F. Purcell, T.E. Lloyd, R.W. Jackson, J.A. Wallace, T. de Vere White
Seated: A.M. Gwynn, T.D. Gwynn, C.B. McKenna, E. O'Mahony, R.P.P. Wallace

COMMITTEE 1934-35

Inset:
J.C. Cole,
G.T. Farley,
R.B. McDowell
Standing:
N.W. Kennedy,
J.A. Walmsley,
J.R.C. Green,
H.L.S. Jefferson
Seated:
C.A. Preston,
D.G. Neill,
J.W. Wellwood,
J.H. Douglas

COMMITTEE 1956-57

Seated: C.St G. Sides, R.St G. Sides, B.C.J. Udenze, E.C. Emekekwue, A.S. Talalla
Standing (names uncertain): from J. Miller, P.C. Bourke, R.D. Jackson, R.H. Bolster, V.S. Young

COMMITTEE 1959-60

Standing: W.N. Keery, D.A.S. Butler, P.P. Mannion, J.P. Gilmartin, W.P. Morris, N.N. Wachuku
Seated: J.S. Wilkins, J.A. Francis, I.H. Simons, P.R.M. Hinchcliffe, B.Hagard

COMMITTEE 1963-64

Standing: C.S. Ó hÉigeartaigh, W.D. Cinnamon, J.B.L. Rose, J.S. Keery, H.J. O'Neill, J.E. Liddle
Seated: M.J. Morgan, P.R. Evershed, J.M. Craig, E.H. Lowry, R.M. Ervine-Andrews, D.J. McConnell

COMMITTEE 1969-70

Standing: Donnell Deeny, Ted Smyth, Derek Moran, M. Woodhouse, P. O'Sullivan, Frank Bannister
Seated: Fergus O'Ferrall, Jonathan Peel, Nicholas FitzGerald Browne, Ian Ashe, Richard Clarke, William Hamill

COMMITTEE 1975-76

Standing (order uncertain): Maurice O'Connell, Ruth Sheil, Caroline Ward, Keith McBean, John Thompson, Andrew Galligan
Seated (order unceratain): G.J. Murray, George Birmingham, Michael Hanna, Mary Harney, W.D. Alexander, C.G.M. O'Floinn

COMMITTEE 1986-87

Standing (names uncertain): Anthony Whelan, Kim Humphreys, Frank Smyth, Joe McAdams, Michael Clarke, Orla McCabe
Seated (names uncertain): Jill Godsil, John Francis, Doreen Shivnen, Barbara Boyle, David Langwallner, Marc Caron

COMMITTEE 1990-91

Standing (names uncertain): Fiona McLoughlin, John Smith, Kitty Moloney, Brendan Fitzpatrick, Leo T. O'Shaughnessy
Seated: Andrea Carter, Paul Kelly, Kerida Naidoo, Una Ní Dhubhghaill, Bernard Dunleavy

COMMITTEE 2004-05

Standing (order uncertain): David Boughton, Mary O'Brien. David Walker, Claire Kennedy, Andrew Byrne, Cormac Quigley
Seated (order uncertain): David Bowles, Claire Hartnett, Cormac O'Dea, Ann O'Brien, Cathal McCann, Hannah Murphy, Niall McCarthy

Bicentenary Address 3rd March 1970
William Hamill, Fergus O'Ferrall, Ted Smyth, Derek Moran, Edward Kennedy, Frederick Boland, Ian Ashe

International Debate 4 March 1970: Andreas Papanderou, Conor Cruise O'Brien(partially hidden), Michael Foot, James Dillon, Eugene McCarthy, Frederick Boland, Jack Lynch, Ian Ashe

Charles Haughey, Minister for Finance, opening the Art & Oratory Exhibition 1970 in the National Gallery, Ian Ashe Auditor, James White Gallery Director, Frederick Boland President of the Society

Irish Times 2010 winners Hist team Niall Sherry and Niamh Ní Mhaoileoin, with Sean O'Quigley, individual winner from Griffith College

Irish Times 2013 individual winner, Kate Brady, with Sir Donnell Deeny and Justice Frank Clarke

Irish Mace 2013 team winner Sally Rooney speaking at the final. The other member of the winning team was Ian Curran

Irish Times 2019 Hist team winners, Ronan Daly and Daniel Gilligan with Chair Jack Chambers TD

CHALLENGES TO FREEDOM: THE 'HIST' IN THE 1930S

16

THE POLITICAL TURBULENCE of the 1930s was reflected in the debates of the Society and we find the rise of fascism and the fear of communism at the centre of many of the biggest debates each year. It is notable that the allure of Hitler was rejected, and there was a regular majority against totalitarianism in all its shapes. The role of women internationally, nationally, and in Society was also the subject of a number of significant debates, sometimes with unexpected results. In 1931 the Society made history by voting in a debate to admit women as members, but the motion was not considered to have any binding power and afterwards was completely ignored. As international tensions mounted the Society increasingly debated the darkening future and the debates were widely reported and discussed in national media.[1]

The role of women in higher education was debated on 29 January 1930 with a motion 'That in the Opinion of this House, the Time has now come for the Establishment of a Women's University'. Eoin O'Mahony proposed the motion, suggesting that as women couldn't live on campus they were missing the 'whole object and end of a true university education'.[2] Opposing the motion, Terence de Vere White suggested that while 'women were a necessary evil, educated women were an unnecessary evil'. Owen Sheehy Skeffington accused White of having 'an inferiority complex' and pointed out that the most intelligent and aesthetic elements in any university were not the rugby players or those who secured high places in

1 TCD MUN/SOC/HIST Uncatalogued Papers, 1930-39.

2 *The Irish Times*, 30 January 1930.

examinations. As far as Skeffington was concerned 'the best types never passed an examination'. For him, 'co-education led to a franker attitude of mind'. J. Wallace supported the motion and 'sighed for the type of woman idealised in Elizabethan sonnets' as *The Irish Times* memorably described it.

Partition was debated on 19 February 1930. The motion was 'That this House Abhors Partition' and opening the debate for the proposition was the Auditor, Bueno McKenna, who attacked the absurdity of a very small country having two separate governments and civil services. Trinity, he believed, was the only place in Ireland where Irish people from north and south could meet on neutral ground. So he suggested that 'Trinity College could do much to reconcile the present absurd differences; for any Irishman with any sentiment must abhor partition as a thing unnatural'.[3] James Auchmuty opposed the motion and suggested that as the people of both parts of the island were very different 'in numerous respects' they should not have the same political institutions. Owen Sheehy Skeffington argued that Irish unity was of the utmost importance, for Ulster and for the rest of Ireland, for economic reasons while W. Bedell Stanford opposed the motion. The motion was passed by 22 votes to 12. The debate was chaired by Lynn Doyle, the novelist and short-story writer, and speaking from the chair he argued that there could be no permanent unity between the two parts of the country if it was accomplished by force.

The Irish sweepstakes had become a popular way of raising money for charity, although there were criticisms of the gambling culture which accompanied it. This was the focus of the debate on 5 March 1930, 'That Sweepstakes for Charitable Purposes are Undesirable'. The debate was opened by the Librarian, R.P.P. Wallace, who suggested that the Sweepstakes bill was 'a striking example of Machiavellianism'. He argued that if the people wanted to gamble they should do so honestly, and not under the pretence of charity.[4] Supporting him was D.P. Owens, who argued that sweepstakes catered for the gambling instinct, and to say that the end justified the means 'was an immoral and demoralising doctrine'.

---

3 *The Irish Times*, 20 February 1930.

4 *The Irish Times*, 6 March 1930.

The Auditor, Bueno McKenna, supported the motion, and argued that the small element of chance involved was as nothing compared to the good it did for charity. He was supported by A.M. Gwynn, the Correspondence Secretary, who suggested that people no longer gave money to support charitable hospitals and so something else was needed. The motion was carried by 14 votes to 11.

The chair for the sweepstakes debate was Sir William Taylor, of Sir Patrick Dunn's Hospital, and he admitted that he had previously been against the idea of sweepstakes. However, he revealed that extraordinary circumstances had changed his mind, and he now believed they were necessary. Addressing the criticism that gambling was immoral, he listed the countries where sweepstakes were legal, including Canada, Australia, and South Africa, and suggested the Free State was no more immoral than them.

The final meeting of the session was a major debate on the motion 'That this House approves of Henry Ford' on 24 June 1930. McKenna and White proposed the motion, with O'Mahony opposing. The motion was defeated by 35 votes to 22. Glenavy chaired the debate and suggested that there was a great deal to admire about Henry Ford, and that his great genius and enterprise had brought many benefits to Ireland.[5] This was a time when Ford's democratisation of the means of travel were widely celebrated, though his darker anti-Semitic campaigning was less well known in Ireland.[6] At the end of the year Eoin O'Mahony was elected Auditor and Owen Sheehy Skeffington, described at the time in *The Irish Times* as 'cricketer and linguist' was elected Librarian.[7]

O'Mahony's inaugural meeting on 5 November 1930 was talked about for years later because of what happened at the dinner afterwards. The meeting itself was a flop. O'Mahony had not written a paper, and spoke for an entire hour on the subject of 'Canada: a Travail' off the back of a few envelopes. In a cruel but entertaining description, White described it as 'quite incomprehensible' and suggested that 'whatever the pains of Canada may have been, the

5 *The Irish Times*, 25 June 1930.

6 Neil Baldwin, *Henry Ford and the Jews: The Mass Production of Hate* (New York, 2001).

7 *The Irish Times*, 7 June 1930.

audience, upon whom a twilight sleep had mercifully descended, were oblivious to them'.[8]

O'Mahony suggested that the British Commonwealth could not hold together as it was presently constituted. Instead he argued that the British Empire should concentrate on the parts that would last for a hundred years.[9] The Canadian Separatist Party leader, John Ewan, responded, and made the case for independence. As White noted acerbically afterwards, 'the party consisted of himself; and his surprise at being invited to express his views in public must have put his health in considerable peril. For he was very old.'[10] He claimed that Ewan seemed to 'address his boots in a mumbled monotone' for what seemed like hours, as for him 'it was the opportunity of a lifetime'.

Afterwards there was the usual supper in the Dining Hall, and by tradition there a toast was made to the King. A strong republican, O'Mahony had agonised about this for days, seeking advice from his Committee about what he should do. The decisive moment seems to have been when he overheard some students talking about him on the way in and say, 'Thank God we have taught him to behave like a Trinity man and a gentleman.'[11] When the time came for the toast, O'Mahony jumped to his feet and shouted 'Gentlemen, I give you the toast of Ireland!' White claimed that 'his officers, of whom I was one, were as panic-stricken as if he had elected to sup in the nude'.[12]

As Sheehy Skeffington remembered afterwards 'farce followed'. All rose for the toast, and some could be heard saying 'Ireland – and the King. I mean, the King and Ireland'. The chairman, Professor W. Allison Philips, jumped up and proposed the royal toast, which was drunk by some and not by others. There was a huge uproar, 'the echoes of which reverberated for years'.[13] Those disgusted by O'Mahony's action stormed out of the supper, and Professor Phillips

8 White, *Fretful Midge*, pp. 66-67.

9 *The Irish Times*. 6 November 1930.

10 White, *Fretful Midge*, p. 67.

11 *The Irish Times*, 5 March 1970.

12 White, *Fretful midge*, p. 67.

13 Terence de Vere White, 'Social life in Ireland, 1927-1937' in *Studies* (1965), vol. 54, p. 77.

left soon after, although he later claimed that this was because he had some trouble with his bladder and not because he was offended. Despite the uproar, there was one important result: 'that toast was never given again'.

The events of that night dominated the Society for the whole session. Attempts were made to impeach O'Mahony, who himself had to be persuaded by his friends not to resign. Terence de Vere White remembered that 'Owen Sheehy Skeffington was one of Mr O'Mahony's most vigorous supporters in the ensuing rumpus.' New members flooded into the Society, some determined to impeach the Auditor, others to support him. Every week a motion for impeachment was put down in private business, and each week Sheehy Skeffington and others intervened to prevent it being heard by adopting various procedural and delaying tactics.

Michael Farrell joined the Society that year, at the age of thirty-one, after an eventful life which had seen him imprisoned for six months during the War of Independence for carrying incriminating documents, a period working in the Belgian Congo as a marine superintendent, and some time as a journalist and sailor, in a career that was described by *The Irish Times* as 'infinite in its variety'.[14] Having dropped out of medicine in UCD years some time earlier, he came to Trinity to resume his medical training, and made his maiden speech in the Society on 12 November 1930. Unusually for the time, it was reported in *The Irish Times,* mainly because, as the paper noted, Farrell was 'well known in Dublin's intellectual and Bohemian circles'. In its report it said that he 'showed no trace of the usual nervousness of the oratorical novice, but, on the contrary, spoke with remarkable fluency'. The debate was on whether doles and outdoor reliefs created 'a paradise for parasites', which required the casting vote of the chairman to be defeated.[15] Farrell's career in the Society came to a premature end although he returned in later years to chair debates. He dropped out of College towards the end of 1930 to pursue a career in journalism. As Diarmaid Ferriter notes in the *Dictionary of Irish Biography,* Farrell was remembered by his neighbour Sean O'Faolain 'as humorous, talkative

14 Diarmaid Ferriter, 'Michael Farrell', *DIB*; *The Irish Times*, 15 November 1930.

15 *The Irish Times*, 13 November 1930.

and argumentative'.[16] A successful journalist, writer and broadcaster, Farrell's novel *The Tears Might Cease*, published posthumously, became a huge bestseller in Ireland, Britain and the United States.

A hugely provocative motion 'That Women Take Too Great a Part in Public Life' was debated on 26 November 1930. The headline in *The Irish Times* the next day was 'Women in Public Life' and it carried the devastating subheading: 'Sixty men decide their usefulness'.[17] The paper noted that the Society 'has already been described as anti-feminist' and that no women were present to 'defend their rights'. Instead they had to depend on 'a great number' of men to 'to take up the cudgels of the helpless women'.

D.P. Owens and Bedell Stanford and three other speakers proposed the motion, but it was ably opposed by Owen Sheehy Skeffington, Michael Farrell, Terence de Vere White and four others. One speaker opposing the motion (the paper did not specify who), argued that the alleged inferiority of women was a myth. Another 'caused considerable laughter' by suggesting that in many cases men were imitating women, pointing out that Lord Mayors, men in courts, and even members of the Historical Society 'not only wore gowns, but sometimes grew long hair when they wanted to look important'. Sheehy Skeffington suggested that the Society would benefit considerably if women were admitted to membership, but this provoked cries of 'Shame'. The motion was lost by a single vote, 32 to 31.

The most notable guest to the Society that session was George William Forbes, the Prime Minister of New Zealand, who spoke to the Society on 29 November 1930, debating the motion 'That Monarchy is the Ideal Form of Government'.[18]

Former Auditor, R. Brereton Barry, returned to the Society to chair the debate on 4 February 1931 on the motion 'That this House approves of Dean Inge's views'. This referenced William Inge a controversial figure. A former Professor of Divinity at Cambridge, and now the Dean of St Paul's Cathedral in London, Inge supported eugenics, birth control and nudism, and dismissed democracy as an

16 Diarmaid Ferriter, 'Michael Farrell', *DIB*.

17 *The Irish Times*, 27 November 1930.

18 *The Irish Times*, 20, 26, 29 November 1930.

'absurdity'. In the debate, Inge was criticised for his views on eugenics and especially birth control, and for dismissing Irish emigrants to the North of England as 'low-grade Irish'.[19] Proposing the motion, James Auchmuty called Inge 'the greatest exponent of scientific broad-mindedness and Christian tolerance of the present day'. D.P. Owens, however, attacked Inge for going beyond his expertise to make unprovoked attacks. The motion passed narrowly by two votes.

Speaking from the chair, Brereton Barry said that he disagreed with Inge's attitude to democracy, believing it was founded on prejudice, not on a rational objection to a working system. Accusing him of 'misusing his intellectual powers', Barry said that Inge rationalised the prejudices of the ordinary, conservative Englishman, especially his opposition to the 'dole'.

American influence on European culture was debated on 12 February 1931 with the motion 'That the Cultural Influence of America on Europe is to be Commended'. Stanford opened the debate and appealed to his listeners to put aside their prejudice when considering the motion. He praised the mixing of the races in America and believed that it was producing 'a great culture – a mixture of influence'.[20] Claiming not be worried about the introduction of American slang into the English language, Stanford reminded people that the Romance languages were all developed from Roman slang.

D.P. Owens opposed the motion and said that it was still to be proved that America had a cultural influence. In a great turn of phrase, he suggested American culture was 'only to be tolerated, sometimes to be deplored, but never to be commended'. Attacking 'the talkies' as the antithesis of culture, he contrasted the queues for the cinema in Ireland with the queues for the National Gallery. A.J. Quirke also opposed the motion and suggested that wealth in America had begotten vulgarity. He claimed that 'all vulgarisms in the English language today were mainly American'.

Owen Sheehy Skeffington supported the motion and deplored the references of previous speakers to American vulgarity. He said the word was too easy to use, and should be backed up by examples.

19 *The Irish Times*, 5 February 1931.

20 *The Irish Times*, 13 February 1931.

He also suggested that American crudities could be matched by English ones at any time.

History was made in the Society on 18 February 1931 the Society voted by 19 votes to 13 to admit women as members.[21] The driving force was the Librarian, Owen Sheehy Skeffington, who opened the debate, suggesting that the standard of oratory at the debates would be raised if women were admitted. In a dig at the sartorial habits of the men, he wondered whether it would also lead to an improvement in the dress of the members. As far as he was concerned, the old idea of the segregation of the sexes was completely out of date.[22]

D. P. Owens opposed the motion, suggesting that the admission of women would be contrary to the traditions of the Society. He believed they would introduce 'an element of pettiness into the Society's discussion' and would take offence too easily. Putting himself in the mind of Edmund Burke, he argued that their founder 'would never have approved of the Society becoming a playground for feminine sulks'. Instead of being a great forum for debate, he said the Society would become a social rendezvous, similar to Switzer's.

The Auditor, Eoin O'Mahony, answered these charges in support of the motion, and he argued persuasively that there was nothing to prevent the admission of women. He noted that 'some of the best intellects in the university' were women, and they ought not be excluded.

Despite passing the motion, the Society did not make any real attempts to admit women. It was regarded as an interesting result, nothing more, something to be debated at regular intervals in the years ahead as an intellectual exercise rather than as a driving force for change. *The Irish Times* noted in 1938 that the motion had 'long since become a hardy annual', often discussed, concluding that 'it is safe to prophesy that, whatever the result of the debate, it is unlikely that the motion will ever be carried into practical effect'.[23]

The debate on 18 March 1931 was 'That Russian Communism is the Only Cure for our Economic Ills', and it was chaired by Jim Larkin, the legendary labour leader of 1913 Lockout fame. His speech

21 *The Irish Times*, 19 February 1931.

22 TCD MUN/SOC/HIST Uncatalogued Papers, 1930-39.

23 *The Irish Times*, 5 March 1938.

from the chair was so brilliant that Sheehy Skeffington claimed afterwards that 'if he had asked us there and then to storm the Dáil we would at once have done so'.[24] It had quite the impression on a number of students. Years later, W.B. Stanford reminisced about hearing Jim Larkin speak at this meeting 'and mesmerising the members with his description of the poverty in homes on the quays not more than a quarter mile' from the university.[25] Afterwards the students crowded around Larkin and asked him what they could do, but he 'just disentangled' himself and walked away. Larkin attended debates regularly in this period, and returned a couple of months later on 20 May 1931 to chair a debate on whether the individual should conform to the wishes of the majority in a state.[26]

In March 1931 the attempts to impeach O'Mahony culminated in a special twelve-hour public business meeting being called. Sheehy Skeffington knew it would be passed, so he introduced an amendment, also passed, which included the officers and Committee in the impeachment. The next week the entire Committee, starting with the Auditor, had to tender their resignations, all of which were refused. As Sheehy Skeffington remembered afterwards, it was 'good fun while it lasted and not bad parliamentary training. Hist issues are not always important, but learning to wield the instrument of speech and use fairly the structures of democratic procedure *can* be of vital importance.'[27]

Reflecting on the controversy years later, White was still critical of the way O'Mahony handled the issue, going about in the wrong way, and making his stand 'in an undignified manner'. But he accepted that the action had the effect 'of shaking us into politics: some found themselves more on the right than they had expected; some more on the left'.[28] He suggested that 'all were forced to discover that man is by nature a political animal' and O'Mahony had succeeded in teaching 'this ancient lesson'.

Lord Glenavy died in March 1931 and his death was mourned by the Society. *The Irish Times* noted his contribution as President of

---

24 *The Irish Times*, 5 March 1970.

25 *The Irish Times*, 5 January 1956.

26 TCD MUN/SOC/HIST Uncatalogued Papers, 1930-39.

27 *The Irish Times*, 5 March 1970.

28 White, *Fretful Midge*, pp 67-68.

the Society, and how his advice and assistance were always helpful.[29] A new President was needed and Douglas Hyde was invited to succeed him. His response was typical of his humour and style. Admitting that he would 'esteem the honour highly', he said he would only accept it 'if you cannot get anyone better'.[30]

The educational offering at Trinity was debated on 17 May 1931 with the motion 'That Education in this University is Not Up to Date'. Terence de Vere White spoke in favour of the motion, which was opposed by D. P. Owens and others.[31] The final debate of the session was on 23 June 1931 on the motion that 'This House Deplores the Defeat of the Spanish Armada', which was defeated by 27 votes to 3.[32]

James Auchmuty was elected Auditor for the 162nd session and he chose as his subject the theme of 'Ireland Abroad'. The meeting was chaired by Professor Douglas Hyde, and included the Governor General, James McNeill, among the speakers, in one of his final events before he stepped down. McNeill made an impression when he praised the great role the Society had played in the history of the College. In his paper, Auchmuty spoke of how the Irish had travelled across the world and had 'always been impelled by some great idea'.[33] Suggesting that India, Australia and Canada owed much to the Irish, he said it would be one 'of the calamities of their country's history if they should cut the cord which bound them ever so slightly to their blood brothers across the sea'. These were lifelong beliefs of Auchmuty, who came from Portadown, and had been elected a Scholar at Trinity in 1929. He went on to become a schoolmaster at Sandford Park School, before returning to Trinity to lecture on education, where he was recruited by MI6 during the Second World War. Becoming a Professor of History in Australia, he became the first Vice-Chancellor of the University of Newcastle in Australia in 1965.[34]

29 *The Irish Times*, 28 March 1931.
30 Dunleavy and Dunleavy, *Douglas Hyde*, p. 359.
31 *The Irish Times*, 18 May 1931.
32 *The Irish Times*, 24 June 1931.
33 *The Irish Times*, 5 November 1931.
34 Kenneth R. Dutton, *Auchmuty: The Life of James Johnston Auchmuty* (Brisbane, 2000).

At this meeting the gold medal for oratory was awarded to Owen Sheehy Skeffington. Sheehy Skeffington graduated with a first-class degree in 1931 and moved to Paris, where he knew Beckett and Joyce, and began work on his Ph.D. Returning to Trinity as a lecturer in 1939, the *Dictionary of Irish Biography* notes that 'he was a brilliant orator, a fearless champion of civil and human rights, and an inspiring teacher, known simply and affectionately to generations of Trinity students as "Skeff"'.[35] Elected to the Seanad for Dublin University in 1954 on his third attempt he served 1954 to 1961 and 1965 to 1970. *The Irish Times* hailed him as 'the Man of the Senate' and he 'spoke, often at length, to some 300 motions, persistently assailed complacency and apathy in high places'. The story is told of how, 'on one occasion he proposed, without a seconder, a motion regretting that the Government had failed to act on its statements against unlawful paramilitary activity; when asked in mid-flow if he was continuing to speak simply in the hope of finding a seconder, he replied 'Yes', and continued.' He died of a heart attack on 10 June 1970 and was praised by the Cathaoirleach of the Seanad for his 'honesty, integrity and moral courage'. His letters to *The Irish Times* between 1940 and 1970 have been described as 'a lesson in style' as well as 'a commentary on the social history of the Republic in those years' and covered issues such as the mother-and-child scheme, apartheid, and the proposed merger of Trinity and UCD. Indeed the paper published tributes and commentaries after his death which were usually only accorded to 'a major figure of State.'

A debate on Irish unity on 25 November 1932 was one of the highlights of the 1932-33 session. Speaking on the motion that 'The Unity of Ireland is an Impossible Ideal', the Auditor, James Auchmuty, argued that the main differences between the people in Northern Ireland and the south were cultural and not racial or lingual. He suggested that the centre of imperialism in the north of Ireland was in London, while in the south of Ireland it was Rome. Regretting that this dependency had been growing since independence, he argued that this would have to be resolved first and that the minority would have to be granted legal safeguards before unification could be considered.[36]

35 C.E.J. Caldicott, 'Owen Lancelot Sheehy Skeffington', *DIB*.

36 *The Irish Times*, 26 November 1932.

D.P. Owens rejected the motion and argued that the differences between the people were 'largely artificial and insignificant', the result of history rather than any real difference. Regretting the 'weakness of both extremes in fanning the dying flames of Unionism and Republicanism', he pointed to India as an example of far greater differences and difficulties being resolved. Stanford also spoke in favour of the motion, arguing that disagreement was an essential part of the Irish character. 'Unity in diversity', he believed, 'was the spirit of Ireland.' J.P. Wallace pointed to the Irish rugby team as an example of how both parts of the country could keep their individual characteristics with a common aim. The motion was defeated by 21 votes to 9.

The debate on 18 May 1932 was on contemporary politics, 'That this House has Confidence in the Present Government of the Irish Free State'. The debate was chaired by Senator Joseph Connolly, the Minster for Posts and Telegraphs, and the motion was proposed by the Librarian, C.L. Flynn, who argued that the new economic policy of the Government 'would benefit the plain people of Ireland'. It was opposed by Terence de Vere White who hoped that de Valera would succeed, though he feared the contrary.[37] D.P. Owens asked the House to deliver a vote of no confidence in the Government, on the grounds that they were driving the country out of the Commonwealth without giving the people a chance to decide, and because they were perpetuating partition. The motion was defeated by 56 votes to 9, a decisive rejection of the incoming Government. Speaking from the chair, Senator Connolly said he was disappointed that only nine members had voted for the motion, 'having regard to the republican traditions of the College'. He believed the only way to persuade people in Northern Ireland to join the Irish State was to establish a prosperous economic State in the south.

A debate on freedom of speech took place on 25 May 1932. The motion was 'That the State should allow Complete Freedom of Speech', and it was chaired by the Irish dramatist, Lennox Robinson.[38] E.H. Gwynn spoke in favour of the motion and said that freedom of speech encouraged people to be public spirited and that

37 *The Irish Times*, 19 May 1932.

38 *The Irish Times*, 26 May 1932.

was a great asset to the state. Opposing the motion, J.S. Alcorn asked why people should have absolute freedom of speech but not absolute freedom of action. He suggested that people should not be allowed put forward propaganda that would have a harmful effect. The motion was passed by 15 votes to 7. Speaking from the chair, Robinson said that he was very glad the motion had been carried. However, he then added a warning, saying that what was happening in Russia and in Italy gave him reason to wonder if the opponents of the motion were not right. They were 'two great experiments so similar in many ways and so ruthless in their attempt against freedom of ideas and action', that one needed to be concerned. Referring to freedom of speech on the stage, he said that the American stage had broken down every verbal barrier. There were only about six words that could not be said, and he believed that the restriction on them would be lifted over the next ten years.

The inaugural meeting of the 1933-34 session dealt with the challenge of communism and was described by *The Irish Times* as 'one of the most stimulating' in recent years.[39] G.K. Chesterton had agreed to speak, but withdrew after a piece ran in the *Irish Press* suggesting 'that he had been tricked into appearing in a College obnoxious to Irish national and Catholic beliefs.'[40] Terence de Vere White was the Auditor and the formal title of the paper was 'Leninism and Laissez faire'. The meeting was chaired by Douglas Hyde, the new President of the Society. Guest speakers included H. N. Brailsford, the leader of the Socialist League, who has been described by Paul Foot as 'perhaps the best socialist writer in Britain at the time'; Compton MacKenzie, the Scottish writer and nationalist who had co-founded the Scottish National Party in 1928 and was currently Lord Rector of Glasgow University; and Desmond FitzGerald, the Cumann na nGaedheal TD.

White argued that it was important to separate the aims of the Bolsheviks from their achievements. Comparing Russia and Italy, he argued that 'although Lenin has been the first to lead the world one way, and Mussolini leads another, I should not be surprised if they both arrive at the same destination'. White dismissed the fear of Bolshevism

39 *The Irish Times*, 3 November 1932.

40 Owen Dudley Edwards, 'Terence de Vere White', *DIB*.

as a foolish one. He suggested that communism could not be transplanted to France or England without being changed in innumerable ways. So he advocated for a third way, with limited nationalisation of industry over time. After leaving Trinity White became a solicitor and writer, and his first book, *The Road of Excess* (1945) was a sympathetic study of Isaac Butt. A named partner in McCann, White and FizGerald, he retired from the firm in 1961 to become literary editor of *The Irish Times,* and he continued to write works of fiction and non-fiction until his death in 1994.[41] In the *Dictionary of Irish Biography* Owen Dudley Edwards notes that he was 'a generous and shrewd patron of younger critics and historians, and several major writers of late twentieth-century Ireland owed their initial success to his sponsorship' and praises his inspiration, 'capacity for atmosphere, nuance, charm, social analysis, and historical symbolism'.

Moving the vote of thanks, Brailsford spoke in favour of taking over the key parts of the country in the interests of the community, starting with banking and moving on to the railways, electricity and finally to the land. Desmond FitzGerald launched an attack on the Bolshevik revolution, suggesting that 'fifteen years' experience had proved only one thing – that the reign of Bolshevism was co-terminous with the reign of dictatorship and the suppression of human liberty'. Dismissing Marxism as 'essentially Victorian', he said that Marx's reasoning was sound, but his premises were false.

One of the most impressive speeches was delivered by Compton MacKenzie who launched an attack on communism, calling it 'anti-democratic'. Howeve, he also criticised capitalism, joking that he would not recognise a stock or share if he saw one. He said he was 'quite convinced that capitalism was a very bad system, for he never practised it'. Becoming more serious, he predicted that a great struggle between communism and the present social system was coming and that 'the individual needed to be prepared to examine the merits on each side and to decide on his position'. He said the 'next battle would be to decide which way humanity would go, and that would be a holy war'. It would, he said, be 'a great war to decide whether people should live as ants or live to support their individuality'. At this meeting the leading speaker of the previous

41 Ibid.

session, D.P. Owens, was awarded the gold medal for oratory.

The debate on 9 November 1932 was on the motion 'That Irish Boys should go to Irish Schools', and was chaired by Stephen Gwynn. R.P. McDermott, who would win the gold medal for oratory at the end of that session, proposed the motion and praised Trinity for being 'a guardian of the Anglo-Irish tradition' and for building up a heritage for the people.[42] Opposing the motion, A.R. Booth said that public schools in England trained men for independence of thought and action, and he attacked the 'nationalisation of culture'. Contemporary politics was also debated that session. The motion on 16 November 1932 was 'That this House would not deplore the dissolution of the League of Nations'. Other notable debates included one on the motion 'That Trinity College Needs a Root and Branch Reformation', on 22 November 1932, which was defeated.[43]

One of the largest debates of the year took place on 7 December 1932, a major inter-varsity competition involving all the College debating societies on the island. The motion was 'That Sentiment Plays Too Large a Part in Irish Life', and it was proposed by the Auditor, who delivered the best speech of the night. Suggesting that sentiment played a dangerous part in Irish life, White defined sentiment as using your heart when your head was needed. The election victory of Fianna Fáil earlier that year was attributed to 'an orgy of sentiment', and he claimed that 'De Valera had captured the public imagination' more that W.T. Cosgrave 'because it was quite easy to get sentimental about him'.[44] He saw the government's policies on censorship and compulsory Irish as sops 'to those who are morally superior'. He also objected to the phrase 'the plain people of Ireland', which was then commonplace, calling it 'an insult to Irish intelligence'. Tim Walsh from UCD opposed the motion, and there were also speakers from Queen's University Belfast and Cork. The motion was carried.

Other debates that session included on 1 February 1933 'That the Athletic Side of Life in this College is Over-emphasised and Over-

---

42 *The Irish Times*, 10 November 1932.

43 *The Irish Times*, 23 November 1932.

44 *The Irish Times*, 8 December 1932.

subsidised', and one on whether 'the Victorian Age is Under-Rated' on 22 February, chaired by the playwright, Denis Johnston.

Lennox Robinson returned to the Society to chair the debate on 15 February 1933, 'That this House Deplores the Decay of Puritanism', which was defeated by a single vote. Speaking from the chair, Robinson defined puritanism as an attitude of mind, and said that it had led 'to cruelty and destruction of beautiful things'. He revealed he was against it because he would not shut himself off from 'music and colour and exquisite things which did not hurt anybody'.

The debate on 8 March 1933 was whether 'This House Approves of George Bernard Shaw', and it was chaired by George Russell (AE). The distinguished Trinity academic, Dr Walter Starkie, proposed the motion and said that Shaw needed to be appreciated from a world view as well as an Irish one. He said Shaw had killed the stage Irishman, and had also killed 'the absurd plays and art of the nineteenth century'.[45] 'The modern girl', said Starkie, 'is partly the creation of Shaw, and a very good creation too, if we compare her with the simpering heroines of the previous century.' Starkie claimed that he disagreed with much of Shaw's philosophy completely, 'and that is one of the reasons why I approve of him. He had an ability to irritate you, and that irritation forced you to think.

R.P. McDermott opposed the motion and denounced Shaw as an irresponsible propagandist, who used the theatre as his medium, and who deceived nations in a way he would never have deceived Ireland. White suggested that if Shaw was sincere he would practice socialism as well as preach it, and would not admire people like Mussolini. The motion was passed by 28 votes to 20. Speaking after the vote from the chair, Russell spoke of what Shaw was like as a person, 'the kindest, most sensitive, and most generous of men'. He praised Shaw for having 'a completely detached and disinterested mind' and said this quality had made him a world figure.

A controversial motion was chosen for debate on 10 May 1933, 'That in the Opinion of this House, Women Should Have No Place in Trinity College'. White proposed the motion and said that the three plagues of the generation were Lord Northcliffe, the media baron; Marie Stopes, the woman who had founded the first birth

45 *The Irish Times*, 9 March 1933.

control clinic in Britain; and 'the serious woman'.[46] Claiming that women were not improved by College life, he suggested that Kilmainham Jail might make a suitable women's college if it was available and if funds were forthcoming. Other speakers opposed the motion, but the Auditor's speech was decisive, if misguided, and the motion was passed.

American civilisation was debated on 17 May 1933 and whether the House approved of it, in a debate chaired by Senator Oliver St John Gogarty. St John Gogarty's style in the chair was to comment aloud on the speakers as the debate went on, which many found disconcerting, although some members appreciated him as 'the last of the wits'.[47] The motion was rejected by 16 votes to 10, with the House rejecting American civilisation. When he spoke from the chair St John Gogarty was in agreement, saying that America mass-produced the inventions of other countries but did not invent anything itself. He claimed that in America 'men of university education were looked down upon' because they produced nothing, and he said 'art for art's sake was difficult'.

A year after debating confidence in the new Fianna Fáil Government, on 26 May 1933 the Society met to debate confidence in it once again. Noel Hartnett supported the motion of confidence, claiming that it was a Government with 'a truly democratic outlook' and that 'class interests and bitterness had ceased to exist'.[48] D.P. Owens, the Treasurer, attacked the Government claiming they had failed to keep all their election promises and that he objected to being governed by idealists. The motion was defeated by 43 votes to 10 as the students once again voiced their displeasure with the Government, regardless of the change of party.

The most controversial motion of the year, and a hugely topical one given events in Germany at the time, was a debate on Hitler on 31 May 1933. The motion was 'That this House Approves of Herr Hitler' and it was chaired by Professor Daniel Binchy, who had been Ireland's ambassador to Germany between 1929 and 1932. R.P. McDermott proposed the motion and suggested that Hitler was

46 *The Irish Times*, 11 May 1933.

47 White, *Fretful Midge*, p. 72.

48 *The Irish Times*, 27 May 1933.

necessary to fight the menace of communism, claiming that many of the reports of Jewish persecution could be discounted. In a speech which reflected the anti-Semitism of the time, he argued that 'the existence of a foreign organism in a national state was a very serious problem, which could only properly be solved by Hitler's methods'.[49] Terence de Vere White opposed the motion and said the appeal of Hitler was purely emotional, and attracted people who were 'void of intellectual interests'.

Dr Helmut Bauersfeld, a brilliant young German scholar who was teaching in Trinity as an exchange lecturer in 1933 delivered a passionate apology for Hitler. An archaeologist, Bauersfeld was also a Nazi and was well-known for defending Hitler having written many pieces for the national media giving his perspective on events at home. In his speech he denied that Hitler was a dictator because he had the support of the Reichstag. Blaming the hostility of newspapers in England on 'some malign influence', he wondered why the English people were so interested in the Jews. He claimed the Jews in Germany had flooded into the country after the war to take advantage of the weak currency and were hated, not because they had jobs, but because they had got the jobs by unfair means. Bauersfeld insisted that Hitler was the friend of the worker and 'stood for peace'. This was one of Bauersfeld's last acts in Trinity, and he left that summer to take up a post at Hamburg and he became a prominent and active SS officer.[50]

The motion was defeated by 17 votes to 12 as the members rejected Hitler. After this, Binchy spoke from the chair and said that he disapproved of Hitler, having first met him in Munich at the start of his career, and again in Berlin. He encouraged the students to read *Mein Kampf*, calling it 'the bible of the Nazi movement'. While Binchy blamed the Allies for the harsh treatment of Germany after the war, he said 'the past sufferings of Germany should not be used as a cloak for the doings of Hitler'. He dismissed National Socialism as 'sham socialism' and called Hitler 'the supreme demagogue of our time'.

---

49 *The Irish Times*, 1 June 1933.

50 Michael Fahlbusch and Ingo Haar (eds), *German Scholars and Ethnic Cleansing, 1919-1945* (New York, 2005), p. 220.

The final meeting of the session took place on 20 June 1933 and was an honorary members' debate on the motion 'That modern Ireland should not look to the ancient Gael for inspiration'. White opened the debate and suggested the Ireland should look to the future rather than the past, and the country had started a new life.[51] Opposing the motion, Dr Walter Starkie said that the ancient Gael had inspired the great quartet of Swift, Goldsmith, Burke and Berkeley and that Ireland risked losing the greatness of the Gael in 'this narrow policy of cooping us up in this narrow island'. James Auchmuty also proposed the motion, and said the tendency in Ireland was to revert to the years of oppression. To advance as a country they had to dispose of that, he suggested. R. Brereton Barry also spoke in favour of the motion and said that the danger of the current Gaelic revival was that it might make people anti-English. He suggested that there was nothing more foolish than 'a mere blind, negative attitude'. Jack B. Yeats also took part in the debate, although unfortunately the content of his speech was not recorded.

Arthur Quirke was the Auditor for the new session and he chose 'Modern Education' as the subject of his inaugural address, which was held in the Dining Hall on 1 November 1933, with Douglas Hyde in the chair. Quirke suggested that there needed to be a balance between the cultural and the utilitarian, and that a love for literature should be inculcated in a child from his earliest years. Sir Thomas Molony, Vice-Chancellor of the University, proposed the vote of thanks, and argued that home education was of the first importance. In a noted rebuke of the Society, he criticised it for not admitting women, even to its opening meeting, and he called this 'an old prejudice'.[52] He hoped the day would soon come when women would be admitted and would grace the Society's meetings with 'their eloquence and common sense'. Oliver St John Gogarty also spoke, and in a humorous address said what the country needed was an education to make it fool-proof from politicians. In a more serious and profound conclusion, he suggested that the universities should have as their ideal the individuality of the human soul. This, he believed, was the way of inspiring the people.

51 *The Irish Times*, 21 June 1933.

52 *The Irish Times*, 2 November 1933.

German politics was again debated on 8 November 1933, on a motion 'That this House Approves Germany's Withdrawal from the Disarmament Conference'. R.M. Smyllie of *The Irish Times* proposed the motion and suggested that if Germany had been treated fairly after the First World War then there would be no Hitlerism today. He argued that Hitler, for all his faults, had forced people to face reality and exposed what he called 'the humbug of Geneva', the home of the League of Nations. R. S. Nesbitt disagreed and argued that the League was the best institution for securing world peace, and that Germany's actions were a serious blow to its ideas. Helmut Clissmann, a German who was visiting Dublin as part of the 'Young Prussian League' spoke next.[53] As W.J. McCormack has written, Clissmann's group 'stunned Dublin with their lavish accoutrements', with their grey military uniforms. A Nazi and almost certainly a spy, Clissmann had a number of targets and one of them was spreading propaganda at Trinity College Dublin. At the debate Clissmann claimed the League of Nations had an imperialist spirit and was only intended as an instrument for the great powers to keep the weaker ones in subjugation. Early the next year, Clissmann put on a play at the Gate Theatre with the Modern Languages Society in Trinity, and remained active in student activities. During the Second World War, Clissmann served as a German intelligence officer, and in Irish intelligence files he was described as a former 'German Gauleiter in Dublin'.[54]

Denouncing the motion, Owen Sheehy Skeffington claimed that if Germany was sincere in its desire for peace it would have stayed in the league and taken every opportunity to criticise it. The motion was defeated by 21 votes to 17. Speaking from the chair, Bolton C. Waller, who had published notable books on the League of Nations and the politics of the period, suggested that the Versailles Treaty had been too harshly interpreted against Germany, but that Germany should not have abandoned the League. He said it would not be an easy task to satisfy Germany's self-respect, but that it would have to be achieved in some way.

53 See W.J McCormack, *Blood Kindred: W. B. Yeats, the Life, the Death, the Politics* (London, 2005).

54 Ibid.

A quirky debate took place on 15 November 1933, chaired by Dr Thomas Bodkin, the director of the National Gallery of Ireland. The motion was 'That this House Prefers the Gentlemen of the Eighteenth Century to that of the Twentieth Century', and R.P. MacDermott proposed the motion claiming that the tradition of the eighteenth-century gentleman prevailed longer in Ireland than anywhere else, and perhaps longer still in Trinity.[55] W.H. Hurley opposed the motion and said that in the eighteenth century they had bear-baiting, in the twentieth prize-fighting. The eighteenth-century man, he suggested, was 'a three bottle man', while the twentieth-century gentleman drank cocktails.

Other notable debates that session included the debate on 31 January 1934 on the motion 'That Pacificism is the Truest Form of Patriotism', chaired by the businessman, Albert Le Brocquy. Another was the one on 14 February 1934, 'That this House Prefers the Eccentric to the Orthodox'. On 21 February 1934 R.M. Smyllie returned to chair a debate on the motion 'That this House is Disgusted with Modern Journalism'.

Hitler was again debated on 17 May 1934, this time a motion 'That this House Approves of Herr Hitler's Attitude to Women', was defeated by a single vote. The debate extended far beyond Hitler's views of women into his general attitude to foreign policy. H.T. Rooke proposed the motion and said that all lovers of peace and security must support Nazi policies.[56] Opposing, Noel Hartnett, who would win the gold medal for oratory at the end of the session, said that he only agreed with Hitler when his policies were directed against 'the bitter insolence of the French and the stupidity of the English' in an attempt to revive the honour and greatness of Germany.

The opening of the 1934-35 session was one of the most significant in many years. The President of the Executive Council, Éamon de Valera, agreed to speak, and the event was broadcast on Irish radio.[57] Taking place on Wednesday 7 November in the Dining Hall, the debate was also broadcast in the GMB for those who were

---

55 *The Irish Times*, 16 November 1933.

56 *The Irish Times*, 17 May 1934.

57 *The Irish Times*, 7 November 1934, 10 November 1934.

unable to secure tickets. The Auditor, James W. Wellwood, spoke on 'The University and the Nation' and the main guest speaker was Professor Harold Laski of the LSE. The meeting created a record for attendance, although we do not have an exact figure.[58] A student from England, Wellwood later became a successful barrister, and in 1954 stood as a Labour candidate in the by-election in East Croydon, but was defeated.[59]

De Valera used his speech to discuss the desire of the Irish people to live at peace with Britain. Declaring 'we are prepared to co-operate with them in the things that we both agree to be of common interest', he insisted 'we are not prepared to have them dictate to us, and tell us that a thing is to our advantage, when we are convinced otherwise ourselves'.[60]

Responding to the subject of the paper, de Valera said there was a huge mistake made in confounding the work of the universities with what was really the aims and functions of primary and secondary schools. Discussing whether it was better for students to specialise in university, or receive a broad education, de Valera highlighted the tension between preparing students for employment and preparing them for life. He also took the opportunity to criticise experts whose caution created inertia. Looking at his own experience of politics, he said that whenever he wanted to do anything he was usually told a thousand reasons why it could not be done. So there needed to be 'a good deal of trial and error and experiment' and courage, because 'if you listened to every warning that is given you as to the dangers of any line of action, you will never move at all'. de Valera believed that Trinity had a role to play in the life of the nation, 'uniting the two parts of the country that are divided'. He denied that Irish people hated English people, instead they hated injustice, and 'what they hated in the past was the injustice done to them'.

A major political theorist, Harold Laski has been called 'the best-known socialist intellectual of his era'.[61] He was a brilliant teacher and writer who devoted his energies in an attempt 'to combine

58 *The Irish Times*, 20 November 1937.

59 *The Times*, 21 September 1954.

60 *The Irish Times*, 17 November 1934.

61 Michael Newman, 'Harold Laski', *ODNB*.

liberty, equality and international in theoretical terms and to promote these ideals through teaching and participation in public life'.[62] Owen Sheehy Skeffington considered Laski to be the best speaker he ever heard, and his performance that night was 'brilliant'.[63] He began his speech with the words: 'There is one thing at least that Mr de Valera will have to admit, and that is that we English are always ready to forgive…' On hearing this, about half of the crowd, those opposed to de Valera, began cheering. However, Laski had not completed his sentence, and added '…those whom we have most grievously wronged'. At this there was 'a moment of stunned silence, and then a wild cheer from the other half of the audience'. It was described as 'a splendid stirring up of listeners'.

On 21 November 1934 the students debated the motion 'That this House Considers the Results of the Battle of the Boyne were Beneficial', which was defeated by two votes and a rising star in the Society, R.B. McDowell, was among those who proposed the motion.[64]

International politics loomed over a debate on whether Trinity should abolish its Officer Training Corps in the interests of peace, held on 29 November 1934. The debate was chaired by Sir Robert Tate, and it was his casting vote which defeated the motion after the House split evenly on the motion. The Record Secretary, J.H. Douglas proposed the motion, and suggested that young people should be taught to avoid fighting other nations, and what was needed was a labour organisation such as existed in Germany which had the spade as its symbol instead of the rifle. Opposing the motion, W.B. Armstrong jumped on the mention of Germany and attacked it as 'the most war-like country in a war-like Europe' and declared that 'so long as fascism exists there is no hope of peace'.[65] R.B. McDowell also opposed the motion, though his speech is not reported. Despite not having detailed records of McDowell's speeches we know that they were among the finest of the year, as at the end of the session he was awarded the gold medal for oratory.[66]

62 Ibid.

63 *The Irish Times*, 5 March 1970.

64 *The Irish Times*, 22 November 1934.

65 *The Irish Times*, 30 November 1934.

66 TCD MUN/SOC/HIST Uncatalogued Papers, 1930-39.

American politics was debated on 6 February 1935 with a motion 'That this House Considers President Roosevelt's New Deal is a Misdeal'. A deliberately provocative motion was chosen for the major intervarsity debate with Cambridge, Edinburgh and Durham held on 13 February 1935. The motion was 'That this House Approves of the Totalitarian State' and the meeting was chaired by the Provost. In a decisive rejection of totalitarianism the motion was defeated by 39 votes to 13.

James Wellwood, the Auditor, proposed the motion, and suggested that democracy had failed throughout the world in the post-war era because it had never been properly tried.[67] Recognising the faults of the totalitarian states in Germany and Italy, he called for an economic and social order that gave every man and woman the fullest opportunities in life. Desmond Neill, the Treasurer of the Society, opposed the motion, and argued that the application of religious ideals to politics could only lead to disaster. Visiting speakers included Cuthbert Alport, proposing the motion for the Cambridge Union, who was later a Conservative MP and peer. Charles Fletcher-Cooke also spoke for Cambridge, and opposed the motion, suggesting that if the philosophy of the state was so important 'then they could not have any regard for men like O'Connell and Parnell, who were not afraid of strife'. At the time a communist, after the war Fletcher-Cooke became a Conservative MP from 1951 to 1983 and brought through the legislation to decriminalise suicide in 1961.

The motion on 6 March 1935 was 'That this House would Welcome a Thirty-Two County Irish Republic' and Frank MacDermott TD chaired the debate. Proposing the motion, David Greene suggested that a republic along the ideals of Pearse would have 'fewer political parasites' than at present.[68] Greene was a brilliant student of Celtic and Modern Languages (and was to graduate in 1937 with a gold medal in each) and he later won the gold medal for oratory in the Society as well as Colours for his ability at water polo.[69]

Opposing the motion in a humorous speech, N.L. Jefferson

67 *The Irish Times*, 14 February 1935.

68 *The Irish Times*, 7 March 1935.

69 *The Irish Times*, 20 November 1937.

compared a thirty-two county republic to a mixed marriage and joked that it would produce the most unfortunate offspring. The motion was defeated by 24 votes to 12 and speaking from the chair, MacDermott suggested that the only things that were standing in the way of Irish unity were in the hearts of Irish citizens. He suggested if they wanted to get rid of partition they would have to govern Southern Ireland soundly, and to do that they had to get rid of class warfare.

Russian politics was the subject of the debate on 22 May 1935 with a motion 'That this House Wishes it Were in Moscow'. Proposing the motion was R.B. McDowell, and it was opposed by the Auditor, Wellwood. The motion a week later was 'That this House Approves of Blood Sports'.[70]

An individual signing himself 'CRP' and giving the 'College Historical Society, Dublin' as his address, wrote a letter to *The Irish Times* that was published on 22 August 1935 denouncing attempts to rally support to fight Italy for invading Abyssinia. CRP claimed to be speaking for 'a considerable body of present-day undergraduates – the choicest food of canons' and argued that he would 'refuse to poison my personality in a hellish, soul-destroying conflict to preserve a nation of semi-savages'. He insisted he was 'sorry for the Abyssinians, but they must look after themselves'. And he concluded by saying that 'in the twentieth century it is a full-time job for a man to save his soul'. CRP insisted he was writing 'not as an individual' but as a 'representative of a body of opinion', which was why he said he was using the Society as his address. The letter drew a response from someone styling themselves 'ERG' who suggested the letter should form a good subject for debate in the Society when it was next in session.[71] Recognising that war was terrible, but sometimes moral issues required it, he quoted from William Meynell the lines that 'He who made the earthquake and the storm, Perchance made battles too'.

Desmond Neill was elected Auditor for the 1935-36 session and he chose 'The Use of Force as a Political Weapon' as the subject of his inaugural address on 6 November 1935. He suggested that in a

---

70 TCD MUN/SOC/HIST Uncatalogued Papers, 1930-39.

71 *The Irish Times*, 24 August 1935.

normal democracy a citizen had waived 'his sacred right of rebellion', but if he was deprived of a legal way of securing his rights then rebellion was justified. Arguing that the declaration of unionists to oppose Home Rule by force should have been considered 'an illegitimate threat' by the British Government, he suggested that the Republicans were justified in using force in those circumstances.[72] He attacked the use of armed force for leading to the destruction of lives, and argued for increased powers for the League of Nations.

John Strachey, a left-wing Marxist described in *The Irish Times* as 'the most powerful English exponent of communist principles', also spoke.[73] Strachey was the author of a number of influential books, including *The Nature of Capitalist Crises,* and had been prevented from travelling across the United States on a lecture tour because of his views. However, he had been rejected from membership of the Communist Party, ostensibly because he was considered a hopeless intellectual, and suffered a nervous breakdown.[74] Strachey said that from the communist point of view the Irish struggle was both justified and inevitable. He argued that the capitalist class would not hesitate to use force and violence to crush the working classes if it could, and he claimed that the working classes were committing suicide if they did not prepare for it. A grandson of John Blake Dillon, James Dillon TD, rejected the appeal of communism and criticised it for wanting to convince the world that the only object in life was the achievement of material prosperity. At the end of the meeting, the President, Douglas Hyde, presented the gold medal for oratory to the Auditor.

Controversial debates that session included the one on 13 November 1935 on the motion 'That this House Believes in Racial Superiority' or, closer to home, 'That this House Considers that the Book of Kells should be Sold' on 27 November 1935. Women in the Society was again debated on 4 March 1936, when the motion 'That this House would Approve of the Admission of Women to the Floor of the House' was discussed.

Harold Laski returned to the Society in 1936 to chair a debate on

---

72 *The Irish Times*, 7 November 1935.

73 *The Irish Times*, 24 October 1935.

74 Michael Newman, 'John St Loe Strachey', *ODNB.*

12 February on the motion 'That this House Agrees with the Auditor of the Session 1785–86 that Ireland must Break the Connection with England'. D.W. Greene proposed the motion and described Tone's theory as 'the finest conception of Irish nationalism that had ever evolved'.[75] The motion was opposed by R.B. McDowell who said he objected to the introduction of religion into politics. The Auditor, Neill, also spoke and said that every Irishman should first be a European, and secondly an Irishman. With the aim of peace in mind, he said they needed to break the connection with the British Empire, which he considered the greatest obstacle to world peace. The motion was defeated by 31 votes to 19. Speaking from the chair, Laski delivered a powerful speech on Anglo-Irish relations, and discussed how Ulster could achieve a more peaceful and prosperous future.

An intervarsity debate on whether the state intervenes excessively in the life of the individual took place on 20 February 1936, when the motion was defeated by a single vote. There were speakers from Glasgow and Manchester, as well as a representative from UCD's L&H.[76] A week later the motion was 'That this House Approves of Euthanasia', which was chaired by Dr Bethel Solomons, the former Master of the Rotunda, who was a former rugby international and a world famous obstetrician and gynecologist.

General Eoin O'Duffy, the founder of the Blueshirts, chaired the debate on 6 May 1936, 'That this House Approves of Organised Displays of Public Emotion', a proxy motion for debating fascist rallies. The motion was defeated by 24 votes to 6, a resounding rejection of fascist principles. Speaking from the chair, O'Duffy denied that the debate was really about fascism, or that the vote was a rejection of it, insisting that there was now no fascist movement in Ireland. He accepted that 'the display of spiritual emotion' had been made use of by both Mussolini and Hitler and suggested that Hitler held the key to the peace of Europe.[77]

Peadar O'Donnell, the socialist agitator and influential IRA figure, chaired the debate on 20 May 1936 on whether socialism

75 *The Irish Times*, 13 February 1936.

76 *The Irish Times*, 21 February 1936.

77 *The Irish Times*, 7 May 1936.

would be the salvation of Ireland, a motion that was defeated by 22 votes to 10. The debate the following week was 'That this House Sympathises with Minorities'.[78]

W.A. Beers was the Auditor for the 167th session and he chose as the subject of his inaugural 'This Freedom' at the meeting on 4 November 1936. Addressing the right to freedom of association, he argued that dictatorships grew more extreme as they grew older and more sensitive to criticism.[79] He insisted that people were capable of wise political action, it was the very principle of democracy itself, and the right of freedom of association represented 'the very end of liberty in society'. However, he warned that such a right could not be absolute as you could not provide an unlimited right to those who wished to overthrow the state by violence.

Sir Arnold Wilson, the British MP who would later enlist and be killed in the Second World War, proposed the vote of thanks and attacked the League of Nations as 'an immoral institution' because it tolerated the bad actions of its members. He argued that intolerance based on conviction was better than tolerance based on indifference. Peader O'Donnell also spoke and he claimed that the people who controlled the wealth of nations controlled capitalist democracy. Sean O'Faolain also spoke and joked that Ireland was one of the freest countries in the world, because everyone was free to do what they did not want to do. Attacking the government for inducing a 'mental inertia' in the people, he said that the greatest of all natural forces was the heart of the common people.

The Spanish Civil War was debated a week later, on 10 November 1936, with a motion 'That this House would Welcome a Victory for the Madrid Government'. The Auditor, Beers, proposed the motion, and D.W. Greene argued that although the Spanish government was accused of being communist or socialist, this was preferable to General Franco coming to power.[80]

Opposing the motion, C.A. Preston argued that the insurgents were trying to free Spain from the menace of an extreme anarchist or Bolshevik regime. Standing orders were suspended during the

78 TCD MUN/SOC/HIST Uncatalogued Papers, 1930-39.

79 *The Irish Times*, 5 November 1936.

80 *The Irish Times*, 12 November 1936.

debate to permit Francis Noone, a member of the Irish Christian Front (ICF), to speak to the gathering. The ICF was a strongly pro-Franco organisation, and Noone claimed that if the communists won the civil war the capital of Spain would be Moscow not Madrid.

Eoin MacNeill chaired the debate on 18 November 1936 on whether the House would welcome an Irish-speaking state (it was defeated by 26 votes to 16). R.B. McDowell, now Correspondence Secretary, opposed the motion, arguing that if the state was to tell people what language they were to speak they might soon begin to tell people what they were to say, and 'gradually would do all the talking itself'.[81] After the motion was defeated MacNeill spoke form the chair and he declared that 'the chief enemy of the Irish language was sheer, stark snobbery'.

Motions that session included 'That the Family is a Necessary Institution' (25 November 1936) and 'That Britain's Contribution to World Peace is Negated by the Existence of her Empire' (2 December 1936). Dr Nicholas Mansergh chaired the debate on 17 February 1937 on a motion 'That this House has Full Confidence in the Present Government'. D.W. Greene proposed the motion and called Fianna Fáil the less bad of two parties, and de Valera 'the greatest leader of the Irish party since Parnell'.[82] R.B. McDowell opposed the motion and attacked de Valera's policy towards Ulster Unionists, comparing him to John Knox, someone who had 'the same straightforward honesty and the absolute incapacity to see the other person's point of view'. The Auditor, W.A. Beers, supported the motion and praised de Valera for trying to govern along democratic lines. Attacking the opposition for flirting with fascism, he said, to much applause and laughter, that it was 'evident that it was not a policy for this country, and the Blueshirts were getting paler and paler and fading into the Celtic twilight'. The motion was passed by 25 votes to 17, as the House divided in favour of the Government and it was reported the next day in *The Irish Times* under the headline: 'Confidence in Mr de Valera' with the sub-heading 'Compared to Parnell'.

The idea of a classless society was debated in an inter-university debate on 24 February 1937, with student speakers from Cambridge,

81 *The Irish Times*, 19 November 1936.

82 *The Irish Times*, 19 February 1937.

Durham and Edinburgh. The Auditor, Beers, said that he was the last person to pretend that capitalism was a perfect system, but warned people should be sure of what they were getting in exchange before they replaced it.[83] Jack B. Yeats chaired the debate on 3 March 1937 on the motion 'That the House Deplores the Tendencies of Modern Literature', which was defeated by 12 votes to 6. Speaking from the chair, Yeats said that writers were fighting a losing battle in their search for new slants on life. He regretted that speech was decaying into slang, as writing followed speech, and he credited Joyce's genius to being from Dublin 'where vigorous speech still survived'.[84]

De Valera proposed a new constitution in 1937, to be voted on by the people in a national plebiscite on 1 July. The proposal was debated in the Society on 19 May with a motion 'That this House Welcomes the New Constitution', in a debate chaired by the former Auditor, T.C. Kingsmill Moore, now a distinguished lawyer. D.A. Murphy praised the proposed new constitution as a blunt instrument with which to strike the final and greatest blow for Irish freedom.[85] Opposing it, D.W. Greene warned that the new constitution could give way to dictatorship and attacked the preamble for containing 'a theological statement of a very doubtful validity'. Arguing that the Christian view of life did not appeal to a large number of people in the country, he believed it imposed a sectarian view of life on the country. The motion was rejected, by 28 votes to 15, and *The Irish Times* reported that debate under the headline 'Against the New Constitution: College Historical Society Debate'.

'The Search for Peace' was the subject of the inaugural address of the new Auditor, W. Ivan McCutheon, on 10 November 1937. Speakers included Jim Larkin, now a TD, and Frank MacDermott. McCutheon attacked war as beastly and blamed the Treaty of Versailles for many of the problems of the present day. Proposing pacifism as a solution to the challenges of their generation, he suggested it was the only way of avoiding international catastrophe. MacDermott suggested that pacifism in all circumstances was not possible or desirable, because sometimes injustice needed to be

83 *The Irish Times*, 25 February 1937.

84 *The Irish Times*, 4 March 1937.

85 *The Irish Times*, 20 May 1937.

prevented. He used the example of a hypothetical attempt to restore the Protestant Ascendancy in Ireland and suggested that sometimes force was necessary to resist. Former Auditor, R. Brereton Barry, also spoke and he warned that there were now people in Europe who did not want peace and who 'deified the qualities of the fighting men'. He called for international arbitration, backed up by force, as the only way of maintaining order.

To give a flavour of debates that session, the war between China and Japan was the subject of a racially charged and clumsily worded motion which was debated on 2 March 1938, 'That the Fate of the Far East Should be Left in the Hands of the Yellow Races'.[86] The issue of women becoming members of the Society was debated again at the Society on 9 March 1938, with the motion for debate 'That this House Approves of the Admission of Women to its Membership', with Peter Allt proposing the motion. The decline of the observance of the Sabbath was debated on 11 May 1938. An inter-university debate with Glasgow and UCD took place on 1 June 1938, with the motion 'That this House prefers evolution to revolution' and R.B. McDowell seconded the motion. One of the most entertaining debates of the session took place on 15 June 1938, when McDowell proposed the motion 'That this House Prefers Liars to Bores'.

The election of Douglas Hyde, unopposed, as President of Ireland in June 1938 meant that the Society had the President of Ireland as its President. For the inaugural meeting of the new session, Hyde chaired the debate, and speakers included the poet, Cecil Day Lewis, and the artist, Seán Keating. The new Auditor, (George Daniel) Peter Allt, was a scholar in modern languages and a winner of the gold medal for oratory in the Society. After graduation he showed some promise as a literary scholar, but his drug abuse and erratic temperament derailed his ambitions. Conor Cruise O'Brien was an early rival of Allt's but they soon became friends, and Allt gave him advice on how to win the gold medal for oratory at the Society. His 'Machiavellian suggestion' was 'to follow a pro-fascist line' to attract attention.[87] O'Brien decided against this advice, mainly because it would mean a break with his cousin, Owen Sheehy

86 *The Irish Times*. 2 March 1938.

87 Conor Cruise O'Brien, *Memoir: my life and themes* (Dublin, 1999), p. 77.

Skeffington, otherwise he admitted he might have been tempted. In the event he won the gold medal for oratory without compromising his political beliefs and integrity.

O'Brien will feature prominently in later chapters, playing an important role in the campaign for women becoming members of the Society in the 1960s, and later being elected President of the Society. A diplomat, historian, university vice-chancellor, politician and journalist, he has been described by Frank Callanan in the *Dictionary of Irish Biography* as 'a familiar, formidable and distinctive figure in the dramatis personae of contemporary Irish life.'[88] Roy Foster has acclaimed O'Brien as 'the pre-eminent Irish intellectual of his generation (and a few others). In his numerous books and essays, profound reflections and an astonishing range of cultural references were expressed in a lapidary style, replete with implications and often horribly funny.'[89] He notes that 'he was a great faller-out with political colleagues ... he also aroused controversy'. Assessing his principal contribution to Irish political life, Callanan suggests it 'lies in his sustained attack in the 1970s on the terrorism of the IRA, and on the moonlit penumbra of condonation and evasiveness that surrounded it in southern politics. He understood that this had to be an assault of great intellectual clarity and measured passion.'[90]

Allt's drinking and drug abuse was a problem during his time in Trinity. On one occasion, after a heavy session, he persuaded O'Brien to accompany him as he broke into the rooms of the Vice Provost, W.A. Goligher, carrying a hammer and nail, determined 'to put an end to Goligher's wicked existence'.[91] Fortunately the Vice Provost was away that evening. On another occasion, he threw an ash-tray out a window, injuring an elderly woman. After leaving College he

---

88 Frank Callanan, 'Conor Cruise O'Brien', *DIB.*

80 Roy Foster, 'The Cruiser: Conor Cruise O'Brien (1917-2008): A tribute to Ireland's greatest modern public intellectual', *Standpoint* (February 2009), https://standpointmag.co.uk/issues/february-2009/the-cruiser-february-09-text-conor-cruise-obrien-roy-foster/.

90 Frank Callanan, 'Conor Cruise O'Brien', *DIB.*

91 Ibid., p. 77.

edited a collection of W.B. Yeats poems, and other works, but his promising literary career was cut short when he fell in front of an Underground train in London in 1954. O'Brien did not believe it was suicide, writing in his memoir that he believed 'his fall must have been a drug-induced accident'.

Future Irish president, Erskine Childers, TD, chaired the debate on 9 November 1938, which came in the wake of the Munich Agreement, 'That this House has Confidence in Mr Chamberlain's Foreign Policy', although unfortunately we do not have a record of how the motion was decided.[92]

One of the most interesting debates of the decade took place not at a meeting of the College Historical Society, but at the DU Modern Language Society on Tuesday 22 November 1938. Christine Foster chose a deliberately controversial title to provoke debate: 'Is the Jew Guilty?'[93] The title was taken from a book published by the Nazis in Germany, and Foster used it as an opportunity to attack the racial policies of the Nazis. She pointed out the contradictions in Hitler's anti-Semitism and blamed Germany and ultimately Christianity for anti-Semitism. Other speakers included students Prince Alexander Lieven and C.B. McMullan. A member of the College Historical Society, Lieven was a student of modern languages and history, and was a fluent in German, English, Russian and French. Lieven's family had been forced to flee Russia after the revolution and Lieven wrote plays as well as debated.

Not a single person answered the question being posed in the affirmative. The debate was a perfect example of what the Society was missing by its exclusion of women, with some of the most interesting and thought-provoking debates happening elsewhere because of the restriction. Instead the Society debated Censorship the following night, in an Irish inter-university debate. Foster was a brilliant campaigner on the rights of women, forcing her way into the Dining Hall to help herself at the buffet lunch during Trinity Term 1938, in contravention of the custom that it was only for men, to protest against the inadequate facilities provided for women in

---

92 TCD MUN/SOC/HIST Uncatalogued Papers, 1930-39.

93 *The Irish Times*, 26 November 1938.

College.[94] As a result, College conceded more space to women students for lunch. Foster also campaigned against the rule that women students had to leave the grounds at 6 p.m., and against their exclusion from the major societies, including the College Historical Society. In September 1939 Christine Foster married a fellow student, Conor Cruise O'Brien and their daughter, Kate Cruise O'Brien, was to play her own part in challenging the exclusion of women from the Society in the 1960s.

Russian politics was debated on 23 November 1938, on the motion 'That this House Considers that the Russian Experiment has Failed'. S.S. Ó hÉigeartaigh, the Librarian, argued that the Russian revolution had been wrong in its ideals, wrong in the way it had come about, and wrong in its subsequent policies.[95] Opposing the motion, Vivian Mercier said that more time was needed before the Russian experiment could be judged, and he insisted that if the decision was that it had failed, then it must be concluded that the English, American, French and other revolutions had failed as well.

War was on the minds of the students at the start of 1939. The motion for debate on 25 January was 'That this House Will Take Part in No War', which was defeated by 21 votes to 9. Speaking from the chair afterwards, Professor J.T. Wigham, said that fear was one of the most important causes of war. He said he was glad the motion was defeated because even if people tried to keep out of war, they could not prevent war being brought to them.[96] It also loomed large over the intervarsity debate on 15 February with Edinburgh, Cambridge and Durham. The motion was on whether 'the Rational Man Today Must be a Pessimist' and students discussed what was going on in Germany and Japan with the production of armaments and war in Spain. Pieter Keuneman, the Secretary of the Cambridge Union, delivered one of the best speeches of the evening, attacking Japan for indulging in its national pastime of 'picking up bits of China', and England for 'seeking a peace that passed all understanding'.[97] Keuneman was from Sri Lanka and interrupted his

94 *The Irish Times*, 21 January 1939.

95 *The Irish Times*, 24 November 1938.

96 *The Irish Times*, 26 January 1939.

97 *The Irish Times*, 16 February 1939.

studies to go to Spain to fight Franco, before later serving as a member of parliament in Sri Lanka, a leading figure in the Communist party, and a cabinet minister.

Opposing the motion, Patrick Butler, the President of the Cambridge Union (and later eighteenth Baron Dunboyne), rejected pessimism as contributing to the confusion of the present world. He believed that 'man had become deluded and had surrendered himself to the wills of dictators and the call of a political phrase'.

Conor Cruise O'Brien spoke at the debate on 22 February 1939, seconding the motion 'That the Present System of Education in Ireland is Confused, Misdirected and Harmful'. On 1 June he proposed the motion 'That this House Disapproves of the Leisured Classes', but the motion was defeated. Returning to the Society, Michael Farrell, now a successful broadcaster, chaired the debate and he criticised 'the growing harshness and utilitarian outlook' of people in the Society and in the country as a whole, arguing that leisure conferred many benefits on the individual and upon society.[98]

The debate on 17 May 1939 was on whether 'Conscription on this Island is at the Present Moment Undesirable', and it was carried by 25 votes to 10. The chair of the debate was Charles Felce, an exchange lecturer from the University of Paris, who attacked the 'chicken-hearted' attitude of some of the speakers who did not want to fight. He declared that there were 'few joys comparable to that of transpiercing an opponent with a bayonet'.[99] The outbreak of war in September 1939 was to provide far too many opportunities for this kind of rhetoric to be tested.

---

98 *The Irish Times*, 3 June 1939.

99 *The Irish Times*, 20 May 1939.

17 'THE CAUSE OF TRUTH': THE SOCIETY AND THE SECOND WORLD WAR, 1939-1945

THE OUTBREAK of the Second World War on 3 September 1939 created a new dynamic in debates. On top of the official Government censorship, the College decided to impose a second layer of censorship. All College societies were forbidden from holding any political debate that was open to members of the public, and even the tamest of political motions had to be discussed in private with a chair chosen from the College staff.[1] College, it seemed, was determined to be neutral in word and in action, and avoid anything that might cause offence to anyone, or compromise the independence of the university. Nevertheless, the Society struck a courageous and independent line in continuing to debate what was happening across the world, despite the College's restrictions, as it engaged with the global crisis.

John Derrick Hughes was the Auditor for the 1939-40 session, and he invited Sir John Maffey, the British ambassador to Ireland, to speak at his inaugural meeting on 1 November 1939 on the subject 'History and the War'. The sympathies of the members was in no doubt and when Maffey rose to propose the vote of thanks 'the audience broke into enthusiastic applause, which was maintained for several minutes'.[2] In a humorous speech, Maffey compared the path of democracy to a group of drunken men staggering home. It may not look very

---

1 Michael B. Yeats, *Cast a cold eye: Memories of a poet's son and politician* (Dublin, 1998), p.41.

2 *The Irish Times*, 2 November 1939.

organized when viewed from afar, but there was a general sense of direction and a line of objective. In contrast, if the path of a dictator was viewed from the same distance it would appear 'sharp and straight' as if there were no precipices or turns, 'but history showed that the precipices were there'. D.L. Keir, the Vice-Chancellor of Queen's University Belfast, also spoke and attacked the absurdities of Aryan racial doctrine and the moral debasement of Nazism. Other speakers included Senator Desmond FitzGerald who warned that the Europe they knew was in danger. Dr W.B. Stanford blamed historians for contributing to the war by giving the impression in their text books that the chief subject of history was war.

Hughes's own paper had a strong historical dimension, as befitted someone who had just been awarded a gold medal along with his degree. He argued that although Ireland was neutral it had a duty to keep 'clear thinking and free speech alive'. Denying that history repeated itself identically, he said the same problems presented themselves, and the same solutions were used. At the end of the meeting, Conor Cruise O'Brien, and the former Auditor, Peter Allt, were awarded gold medals for oratory.

Irish neutrality was debated a week later, with the motion 'That this House Approves of the Splendid Isolation of Eire'. Other motions that month included 'That this House Believes that the Soldier is the Maker of History' (22 November 1939), and 'That this House Believes All is Fair in Love and War (29 November 1939). One of the most interesting debates was around a proposal to create a united states of Europe on 31 January 1940, which was supported by 22 votes to 13.[3] Senator Sir John Keane, who chaired the debate, said he saw little hope of such a federation developing, but he hoped experience of war would give nations a greater sense of the real issues.

The continuing exclusion of women from the Society was debated on 14 February 1940. Judge Kenneth Sheils Reddin chaired the debate on the motion 'That this House Regrets the Exclusion of Women from Membership', which was defeated by 30 votes to 11. After the vote, Reddin, who was also a noted playwright and novelist, said that it seemed strange women should still be excluded from the Society in 1940. He said that women played such an important part

3 *The Irish Times*, 1 February 1940.

in modern life that the Society could not 'remain Victorian' by continuing to exclude them.[4] *The Irish Times* reported the debate with the headline: 'Women still outside College Historical'.

The 6th Earl of Longford chaired the debate on 21 February 1940 on the motion 'That this House Deplores the Tendencies of the Modern Theatre'. Proposed by R.B. McDowell, and opposed by Alexander Lieven, the motion was passed by a majority. Longford was a former chair of the Gate Theatre and a playwright and poet. Speaking from the chair, he expressed a view that a national drama in a foreign language was impossible, and he wondered how war in Europe would affect Irish theatre.[5]

On 8 May the members of the Society rejected a motion 'That Expediency is the Only International Law', while a more relaxed, humorous debate took place at a following meeting on the motion 'That Beer is Best'. Sean O'Faolain chaired the debate on 22 May 1940 on the motion 'That this House is Ashamed of the History of Ireland'. A controversial motion was proposed on 5 June 1940, 'That this House Regrets the Abolition of Slavery', but unfortunately the records do not show whether it was successful or not.[6]

At the end of the year, William Rooke was elected Auditor. Rooke was a popular figure in College, a keen cricketer, and regarded as 'a fluent and humorous speaker'.[7] Rooke spoke at the final debate of the year, for honorary members, on the motion 'That this House Believes in Orthodoxy' with the debate chaired by R. Brereton Barry.

Rooke chose the subject of 'Some Obstacles to Clear Thinking' as the subject of his inaugural. Exploiting the difficulties of ascertaining truth in an era of propaganda, he said that propaganda was used 'as a means of persuading people to a point of view through the press, the wireless and the cinema' by people who 'whitewashed their own cause and blackened that of the enemy'.[8] David Gray, the United States Ambassador to Ireland, was the guest of honour, and he suggested that the 'Institute of 1770', also known as 'The Hasty

4 *The Irish Times*, 15 February 1940.

5 *The Irish Times*, 22 February 1940.

6 TCD MUN/SOC/HIST Uncatalogued Papers, 1940-49.

7 *The Irish Times*, 8 June 1940.

8 *The Irish Times*, 7 November 1940.

Pudding Club', the Harvard social club he was a member of, owed its existence to the refounding in that year of Edmund Burke's debating society, and called it another debt America owed to Ireland. Leslie A. Montgomery, who wrote under the name Lynn C. Doyle, also spoke and attacked those 'dangerous liars' who believe that they alone possess the truth. In a stirring oration, he said that 'at this moment, the world was lying like blazes in the cause of truth'.

A student Scholar, J.V. Luce, proposed the motion 'That All Poets are Fools' on 20 November 1940, and claimed that poets were insincere and appealed only to the emotions.[9] The poet, Austin Clarke, opposed the motion and said he would only be able to support it if the medieval interpretation of 'fool' was applied, someone who clad wisdom in imaginative speech. In a humorous and effective speech, Clarke claimed that the eccentricities of poets had disappeared in 1910 and had been taken on 'by bikers and fresh air friends'. A student, T.A. Bradshaw, developed a similar line of argument, suggesting that only pseudo poets, who suffered from an inferiority complex, wore long hair and corduroy trousers. The motion was rejected by 27 votes to 15.

Sometimes because of the College restrictions there is no record of what was said at a debate. This was the case for two interesting debates that session. On 27 November 1940 the motion for debate was 'That this House Would Welcome the Union of Ireland for the Purpose of Defence', chaired by James Dillon. Censorship was the subject for the debate on 29 January 1941, chaired by R.M. Smyllie, by this time the editor of *The Irish Times*.

The poet, Patrick Kavanagh, chaired the debate on 5 February on the motion 'That the Cinema is a Better Form of Entertainment than the Theatre', which was defeated. Kavanagh used the debate as an opportunity to attack the directors of the Abbey Theatre, claiming they had 'lost the confidence of the poets and writers of Ireland' and calling on them to resign. If they did not, he threatened that a new group of writers would meet in some back street in Dublin and establish a new literary theatre. Attacking the Abbey Theatre for never being an actors' theatre, or a Gaelic theatre, or an orthodox theatre, he insisted that 'The Abbey Theatre looks like becoming,

9 *The Irish Times*, 21 November 1940.

in the words of a popular simile, as low-class as a certain radio programme'.[10]

On 12 March 1941 the Society debated the motion 'That this House Disapproves of the Anglo-Irishman' and John Betjeman, who was press attaché to the British Ambassador and not yet an established poet, defined the Anglo-Irishman as someone with a small drop of Irish blood and a great deal of devotion to Ireland. He suggested that the interchange of culture had helped both Ireland and England. To the English the Irish had given culture and politeness, and to the Irish the English gave energy and creative ability. Henry Francis Reade Morris suggested that no race on earth of its size had done as much for 'the culture, literature and art of their country as had the Anglo-Irish'. Dr W.B. Stanford proposed an amendment 'disapproving of the perpetration of the term Anglo-Irishman' but it was defeated. The motion itself was also defeated by 23 votes to 17.[11]

The election for Auditor in May 1941 was somewhat unusual. Three candidates were nominated for the position, the Record Secretary, Mark Mortimer, the Correspondence Secretary, Alexander Lieven, and Horace Porter. The contest was believed to be fairly close, so before the ballot, it was decided that two prominent honorary members would take an unofficial straw poll to ascertain the strength of the candidates. There was some debate in the Society as to whether such polling was allowed, as it was feared it might influence the eventual outcome.[12] In the event, Lieven was elected Auditor, with Porter having the consolation of winning the gold medal for oratory. The gold medal for oratory the following year was won by Lieven.

For his inaugural address, on 5 November 1941, Lieven chose the subject of 'Intellectuals at Bay' and he attracted a star-studded line-up of speakers. Lieven argued that the term 'intellectual' had become a term of abuse and contempt and regretted that the 'thinking community' had lost interest in anything except the purely immediate. The English literary critic, Cyril Connolly, author of *Enemies of*

10 *The Irish Times*, 6 February 1941.

11 *The Irish Times*, 13 March 1941.

12 *The Irish Times*, 24 May 1941.

Promise, proposed the vote of thanks and confirmed that there was a strong prejudice against intellectuals in England. Comparing Ireland to one of the ancient Greek city-states, he said that Ireland was one of the last European countries where the lights had not gone out. He said that 'Irish people must use the lights; they must burn the midnight oil and give an example of a united democratic country.'[13]

The scientist Erwin Schrodinger, who had fled to Ireland because of his opposition to Nazism, was another high profile respondent. Schrodinger expressed his doubts that the world's intellectuals would work together to improve the world, claiming that 'intellectuals were not likely to strain themselves very much, simply because they had not power to impose their will on the world's course'.[14] He argued that there seemed to be 'a sort of absolute incompatibility between the sphere of action and the contemplative sphere'. Looking at the instances when single people exerted an overwhelming influence on historical events, he suggested that these people were 'rather products of history than producers of it'.

The poet and writer, Stephen Spender, was another guest speaker, and he talked about how intellectuals across Europe who had attempted to act had been threatened by tyranny. In response, Jim Prendergast of the Communist Party of Ireland expressed his adherence to Marxism and Russian Soviet principles, and celebrating the 'wonderful resistance' that Russia was putting up against Germany.

The revival of the Irish language was debated on 12 November 1941, with the House decided by 27 votes to 20 against supporting it. Alexander Lieven, the Auditor, spoke in favour of Irish, saying that the language as the last remaining barrier preventing the country from being swamped by the influx of English influence.[15] Benjamin Maguire, the Treasurer of the Society, claimed that Irish was already dead and could not be revived. Suggesting that whether people said 'and' or 'agus' would not fill an empty stomach, he said the language was being forced on people who did not want it.

Other motions that session included 'That Our Schooldays are the Happiest' (18 November 1941) and 'Socialism is the Only Basis

13 *The Irish Times*, 6 November 1941.

14 *The Irish Times*, 6 November 1941.

15 *The Irish Times*, 13 November 1941.

for a United Ireland' (3 December 1941). General Eoin O'Duffy chaired the debate on 11 February 1942 on the motion that 'This House Would Welcome Conscription'.

John Ross was the Auditor for the 173nd session and he chose as the subject of his inaugural address the forward-looking, 'Post-war Ireland' on 4 November 1942. Former Attorney General and future Taoiseach, John A. Costello, was one of respondents to the paper. The former head of Government, and leader of Fine Gael, W.T. Cosgrave spoke at the Society a week later, on 11 November, rejecting the motion 'That the Irish Nation is Living in the Past', a debate which was really about Irish neutrality. Suggesting that people in Ireland had long memories, and disliked anyone interfering in their national life, he said this was perfectly understandable. Cosgrave dismissed 'sentimental Englishmen' who were critical of Irish people for talking about their past, saying that their own feelings for their past had given them strength in their darkest hour in 1940. He believed that partition had poisoned the relationship between the two countries and kept efforts at reconciliation to a minimum. However, he suggested that reunion would come about 'as sure as night follows day'.[16] The motion was supported by 31 votes to 14.

The war continued to affect the Society in different ways. Fearing that the records of the Society would be destroyed in an air raid, the Committee decided to put the historic books in a bank for safekeeping, including the proceedings of Burke's Club and the Librarian's attendance book which had belonged to Edward Carson.[17] Then, in November the Auditor, John Ross, resigned his office to fight in the Second World War. This caused something of a sensation at the time.[18] Replacing him was a member of the Committee, J. Louis Lord, who was a graduate in History. Ross saw active service in France and Belgium, ending the war with the rank of Captain. He returned to Trinity to complete his degree, went on to become a successful solicitor and represented the University of Dublin in the Seanad between 1961 and 1965.[19]

---

16 *The Irish Times*, 12 November 1941.

17 *The Irish Times*, 16 November 1943.

18 *Sunday Independent*, 1 January 2012.

19 Ibid.

Motions in the 173nd session included 'That this House Distrusts the Scientist' (18 November 1942), which was defeated by 24 votes to 12, and 'That the World will be a Better Place after the War' (12 May 1943). The admission of women was once more debated on 26 May, while the different traditions in the Society's history was debated on 2 June, 'That this House Prefers Edmund Burke to Wolfe Tone'. To mark the 100th anniversary of the Society returning to College in 1843, a special debate was held on 16 June 1943 on the motion 'That Revolution is Preferable to Evolution'. T.C. Kingsmill Moore was among the speakers who opposed the motion, which was proposed by (Alexander) Norman Jeffares, the Auditor-elect.[20] Jeffares later became a noted literary scholar and was Jury Chair of English at the University of Adelaide, and afterwards Chair of English at the University of Leeds and then at the University of Stirling.

'Whither Education' was the subject of Jeffares' inaugural meeting on 3 November 1943, and it proved controversial when six women were refused admission. Invitation cards had been sent to the officers of the other student clubs and societies, and some were sent to women officers by mistake, even though they were not allowed attend. Six women who were officers of other College societies received their invitation cards and decided to make a point by seeking admission. The group attempted to gain entrance to College at Front Gate but were refused entry, and the Auditor was asked to make a formal decision. Eventually Jeffares sent word down that they would not be admitted, but added that if they sent their names up they would receive a formal apology.[21] *The Irish Times* covered the story on the front page and quoted one of the women, unnamed, as saying: 'It is ridiculous that anybody can walk in off the street and attend this meeting, provided he is a man, and we, who have received formal invitations are debarred from attending just because we are women.' It was noted that there were as many women officers and committee members as men in the other College societies and given the educational subject matter of the inaugural women should be allowed to attend.[22]

20 *The Irish Times*, 17 June 1943.

21 *The Irish Times*, 4 November 1943.

22 *The Irish Times*, 4 November 1943.

The inaugural itself, and the controversy, made front page news in *The Irish Times* the next day, and it reported Jeffares calling for more funding for primary education and demanding major reform for secondary education, claiming it had become an extended and uncoordinated mass of subjects. Sir Richard Livingstone, the President of Corpus Christi College in Oxford, gave the speech proposing the vote of thanks to the Auditor, and said that 'the outstanding absurdity of our education in the past has been that 80 per cent of our population have been given no education at all after they reach 14 years of age'.

Unfortunately for the Society, the controversy over the refusal to admit women to the meeting overshadowed the event itself. It continued to rumble in the days ahead as the women waited for the formal apology. *The Irish Times* reported that they felt that something should be done about the Society's constitution and that they were the people to do it.[23] In an editorial on 8 November 1943, headed 'Women's Rights', it was noted that the incident recalled 'the days of the suffragettes'. Accepting that 'naturally, the women concerned are annoyed', it observed that with a little forethought the officers of the Society could have avoided 'marring their otherwise excellent meeting with such discourtesy'.[24] There was some sympathy for the Auditor, despite the clumsy way the matter had been handled. Because the College forbade women to be on the grounds after 6 p.m. he would have been in trouble if he had broken the restriction. It is also likely he would have faced impeachment if he had contravened the Society's own laws.

The Irish Times took a strong line on the controversy. Advocating 'a *blitzkrieg*' on the College Historical Society, it described it as 'the oldest, and probably the most conservative society in the College'. Praising the six women as 'pioneers', it supported their attempt to change 'a mighty tradition'.[25] It noted that other societies had lost nothing 'by surrendering their masculine exclusiveness' and recognized that women members would bring their 'obviously abundant energy' to the benefit of the Society.

Debates during the year included one on whether Radio Éireann

23 *The Irish Times*, 5 November 1943.

24 *The Irish Times*, 8 November 1943.

25 Ibid.

was doing a good job (16 February 1944), and an inter-university debate on 1 March 1944 on the motion 'That this House would Welcome a Gaelic Nation State' chaired by T.C. Kingsmill Moore. Speakers from UCD, Oxford and Edinburgh took part, and the motion was opposed by the Auditor, Jeffares, who suggested that those who write in Irish had contributed only a small amount to Irish literature. Criticising what Ireland had achieved since independence, he insisted the country was 'drifting in a backwater', and the only problem was that people could not see the truth.[26] He called compulsory teaching of Irish the direct antithesis of everything Ireland should claim to stand for, as he delivered the best speech of the night, and the one that was most reported afterwards. The motion was defeated by 51 votes to 29.

Jeffares delivered a paper on 'Women in Greek Literature' at a special meeting of the Society on 3 March 1944, which was chaired by Provost Alton. Speakers included Dr W.B. Stanford, and the meeting was open to women to attend, in what was a deliberate attempt to make amends for the debacle over the inaugural. He also threw a lavish party in the rooms of the Society later in the year to which women were invited, and it was reported that 'all important College personalities and many well-known figures of Dublin life, as well as many graduates and undergraduates were present'.[27]

American President Franklin Delano Roosevelt's 'Four Freedoms' was the subject of the debate on 8 March 1944 as the students discussed the four fundamental freedoms he believed all people in the world should be able to enjoy: freedom of speech, freedom of worship, freedom from want, and freedom from fear. The motion was 'That this House believes the four freedoms are unattainable', and the star speaker was T.F. O'Higgins Snr, the leader of Fine Gael in the Dáil, and brother of the assassinated minister, Kevin O'Higgins. Attacking de Valera for driving a wedge between north and south, he accused the government of having failed on many levels. Going through each of the four freedoms, he argued that freedom of speech had been threatened in 1932 when W.T. Cosgrave and other politicians were shouted down at meetings in a concerted

26 *The Irish Times*, 2 March 1944.

27 *The Irish Times*, 12 June 1944.

campaign against them. As a result, the Army Comrades Association had been founded (with O'Higgins instrumental in its creation) which he insisted had been 'a non-political body' there 'to protect any meeting challenges, no matter what party held the meeting'.[28] O'Higgins claimed that over a twelve month period 'of strenuous and heroic work in defence of free speech', where 'heads were split and blood was spilt', the Government had finally intervened to protect free speech. Arguing against isolationism after the war, O'Higgins suggested that doing so would only ensure that Irish people lived 'in fear and want, watching hungrily as the world's trade flows by us'. The motion was defeated by 26 votes to 17.

During the 1940s and early 1950s the membership of the Society changed significantly to reflect the large numbers of international students ('most from Africa but from Asia as well') studying in the university.[29] Their contribution, according to one prominent member, 'was profound'. Years later it was recognized that 'a high proportion of them, on returning to their own countries' were 'prominent in the emergence of those nations and the political and cultural development of their peoples'. They also had an enormous impact on the Society.

The best example was Jaja Anucha Wachuku, the finest speaker in the Society in 1944–45. A brilliant law student from Africa, Wachuku later became the first Speaker of the Nigerian House of Representatives, the first Nigerian Ambassador to the United Nations, and the first Nigerian Minister for Foreign Affairs, and was widely respected as a 'lawyer, statesman, politician, diplomat and humanitarian'[30]. At Trinity he began acquiring books at an incredible rate, and when he returned to Nigeria he brought with him one of the biggest private collections in the country.[31] Wachuku represented the Society at an inter-university debate at the University of Durham during the year, and excelled in competitive debate as well as in the weekly format. Wachuku graduated with a first-class degree in legal science and studied at King's Inns, before returning to Nigeria in

28 *The Irish Times*, 9 March 1944.

29 *The Irish Times*, 10 March 1970.

30 Lanre Alayande, *Our Rainmaker* (New York, 2010), p. 155.

31 *The Times*, 11 January 1961.

1947. No gold medal for oratory was awarded at the end of the 1943-44 session, with no-one having met the requirements, but Wachuku was the sole recipient of the silver medal for oratory that year, narrowly missing out on the higher prize.

Described in one study as 'a peerless jurist, humanist and orator of our time', it was at Trinity that Wachuku honed his oratorical skills, and they were skills which served him well over a long and distinguished career.[32] His time in the Trinity was often referenced in international profiles, for example *Time* magazine in 1960 noted that 'a law degree came easily, along with a medal for oratory'.[33] As a minister he often wore his Trinity tie (just like many colleagues on the front bench) and himself always spoke warmly about his time in Trinity and in the Society, and it was said that he 'never missed an opportunity of speaking about the intellectual environment and charm of TCD'.[34] Wachuku's exploits at the Society were long remembered. In one profile in 1960 it was recalled that 'he galvanised more than one debate [in the Hist] by turning up in full Nigerian dress' and he was hailed as 'a fiery orator'.[35]

In later years Wachuku was praised for having 'the energy, versatility shrewdness and gift of oratory' wrapped up in his sturdy frame, and it played a key role in his diplomatic and political life.[36] Wachuku was one of the central figures in Nigeria declaring independence in 1960, and in 2014 he was honoured posthumously by the Nigerian President as a 'hero of the struggle for Nigeria's independence' and a 'pioneer political leader'. Oratory played its part in the story.[37] During the campaign Wachuku often ridiculed British officials who claimed that Nigeria was not capable of nationhood, and articulated a vision for when the country should be independent. In 1957 the Nigerian Federal Legislature wanted to give a mandate to its

32 N. Enuma el Mahmud-Okereke, *OUA, time to admit South Africa* (Abuja, 1983), p. 2.

33 *Time* (1960), vol. 78, p. 30.

34 Emeka Anyoku, *The Missing Headlines: Selected Speeches* (Liverpool, 1997) p.441; *New Commonwealth*, vol. 40 (1962), p. 411; *The Irish Times*, 25 January 1966.

35 *The Irish Times*, 16 February 1960.

36 *New Commonwealth*, p. 411.

37 *The Niger Times*, 10 March 2014.

delegates to demand independence from Britain at a constitutional convention held in London, but there were splits between the various politicians from the regions. *The Times* reported that 'It was Mr Wachuku's oratory which brought a compromise' as he explained the need for unanimous consent if they were to have any authority.[38] In his speech to the delegates which won them over he said, 'We cannot expect to become self-governing and independent today and become a laughing-stock tomorrow. It will be better when the whole nation is geared to this one objective, and when the whole country is charged with the spirit of independence... For a long time we have felt that our right to independence, to control our own destiny, has been unduly restricted. We feel now that we have come to the stage where a definite and positive demand must be made, demanding it as of right, not begging.'

Time magazine carried a profile of Wachuku in 1961 under the headline 'Pride of Africa', and it praised a speech he made in front of the UN General Assembly where he revealed that he was 'losing confidence in the great powers' and calling on them to end their quarrels.[39] In a fiery piece of oratory he declared that they were 'climbing from the pedestal of greatness to the pedestal of insanity'. The final words were widely quoted afterwards: 'we expect leadership from them; they give us destruction. We expect wisdom from them; they give us lack of knowledge. We expect objectivity, they present us with blurred visit.'

Wachuku's oratorical and diplomatic skills helped save the life of Nelson Mandela in 1963-64. When Mandela and other leaders of the ANC were arrested and put on trial for sabotage and other crimes, in what became known as the Rivonia Trial, the South African Government pressed for the death sentence. By this time, Wachuku was the Foreign Minister for Nigeria, and he persuaded both the British and American governments to intervene. As Kenneth Broun notes in his book, *Saving Mandela,* 'contact by both Governments was initiated based upon a request from the widely respected and moderate Nigerian Foreign Minister Jaja Wachuku'.[40] Wachuku was convinced that the execution of the leaders, and

---

38 *The Times,* 11 January 1961.

39 *Time,* 20 October 1961.

40 Kenneth S. Broun, *Saving Nelson Mandela* (Oxford, 2012), p. 111.

Mandela especially, would 'greatly weaken the position of those such as the Nigerian Government who were trying to counsel moderation' and destabilise African politics. The intervention proved decisive and when Mandela was convicted he was sentenced to life imprisonment.[41] In the years ahead Wachuku had a distinguished political career, showing courage in the face of civil war and much criticism, for example when he worked behind the scenes to dismantle the apartheid system in South Africa. Wachuku continued to campaign on behalf of Mandela until he was finally released from Robben Island in 1990; Wachuku died six years later.[42] In the entire history of the Society there are many remarkable individuals who stand out for their oratorical powers and contribution to national and international affairs. There are a handful whose contribution was exceptional. Jaja Anucha Wachuku is one of them.

Other motions in the 174th session included one on 'That this House Approves of the Student Representative Council' (8 May 1944), the forerunner of the Students' Union. The chair of the SRC that year was Michael Butler Yeats, a son of W. B. Yeats, and nephew of Jack B. Yeats. Michael was an enthusiastic chess player, and had graduated with a first in History and Political Science in October 1943. A talented debater, who claimed he only joined the Society to counteract his shyness, he was also a member of the General Committee of the Society.[43] In May, the Correspondence Secretary, F.G.C. Cornwall resigned, and Yeats was elected to replace him. Yeats was one of three candidates for the Auditorship a month later, and was elected.

For his inaugural meeting, Yeats secured a number of big name speakers, including the Taoiseach, Eamon de Valera, and Dr Jan Masaryk, the Foreign Minister of the Czechoslovak Government-in-Exile. In his autobiography, Yeats recounted being brought into Government Buildings to meet the Taoiseach who asked him who else he had invited to speak. When Masaryk's name was mentioned he replied, 'Right, I will speak if he comes'.[44] Behind the scenes, the Government negotiated with Masaryk over the terms of the visit, and

---

41 Ibid.

42 See Jaja Wachuku et al, *Africa: the political pattern* (Toronto, 1961).

43 Yeats, *Cast a Cold Eye*, p. 43.

44 Ibid.

refused him permission to speak at any other event while he was in Ireland. A few days before the meeting, Provost Alton called in Yeats and asked him to invite de Valera to dine on Commons before the meeting. Afterwards Yeats reflected on how peculiar it was that the Provost would be forced to send a student to invite the Taoiseach of the day, and concluded 'that his strange behaviour reflected the nervousness felt by the College authorities at that period in their dealings with the "new" Ireland outside the College walls'. Yeats went to Government Buildings to meet de Valera for the second time, and de Valera asked him to pass on his apologies to the Provost, saying, 'you might think it strange after all the years I have been in public life, but I still like to have some time to myself before making a speech'. However, he did agree to dine with the students after the event.

The inaugural meeting took place on 1 November 1944 on the subject of 'The Small Nations', and was the main news story on the front page of *The Irish Times* the next day, with a photo of the Auditor and Masaryk accompanying the piece. In his address, Yeats suggested that small nations did not share any of the blame for the failure of the League of Nations. Instead 'the law of the jungle' had been allowed govern international affairs, and he suggested which the way to stop this in the future was to ensure that small nations exercised 'the greatest possible influence, both material and moral, on the post-war world'.[45]

Proposing the vote of thanks, de Valera admitted that he did not see a solution to wars in their time, because he believed 'that the only solution which would guarantee peace is a universal world state'.[46] He suggested that 'until such a coercive power was at the disposal of a central world authority, with world police to prevent aggression of all kinds' then 'there could not be an effective instrument to maintain peace'. Discussing the failures of the League of Nation, he speculated about a successor organisation which could succeed, 'an organisation for the maintenance of a lasting peace'.

Masaryk was the son of the first President of Czechoslovakia and served as Ambassador to Britain until the German occupation of the Sudetenland in 1938 when he resigned and went into exile. During

45 *The Irish Times*, 2 November 1944.
46 *The Irish Times*, 2 November 1944.

the war he served as Foreign Minister in the Government-in-Exile and made regular radio broadcasts for the people in occupied Czechoslovakia. In his speech Masaryk suggested that they were now on the threshold of a new chapter in the history of the planet. He therefore called on the citizens of small nations to once again think about how best they could serve their own and the greater interest. Declaring that it had 'never been possible to destroy small nations, or to incorporate them into larger units by mere force', because although they were small in terms of numbers of people, they were 'distinguished by a marked power of resistance'. Masaryk called for a system of collective security in the future to protect small nations from the aggressive policy of neighbours. Referencing the great contribution of Irish people to literature and culture, he cited W.B. Yeats, Synge, Hyde, AE, and George Bernard Shaw, and suggested that spiritual values emanated from small nations, and this was one of their greatest contributions to the world. 'It is in the depths of the inner life', he commented, 'that the real losses and gains take place. It is there that are situated the real battlefields, not marked on any maps, but which nevertheless decide the destinies of myriads.'

After the war, Masaryk continued as Foreign Minister following the liberation of Czechoslovakia, but after the Communist takeover he died in suspicious circumstances on 10 March 1948 after falling from his window. The death was claimed to be a suicide, but he was almost certainly murdered by Soviet agents. It was joked, with much black humour, that he was such a tidy man, he even closed the window after himself. As *Life* magazine noted in 1968 he was 'freedom's only spokesman' in the country, and how, even 'today his name is still spoken reverently and, every Sunday, thousands stream to the cemetery in a small village outside Prague where he and his father lie buried'.[47] The defenestration of Masaryk was a portent of the defenestration of democracy in Czechoslovakia.

Dr Owen Sheehy Skeffington, now a lecturer at Trinity, also spoke at the inaugural meeting and he thanked de Valera for not being 'afraid to enter Trinity College'. He suggested that some people viewed Trinity 'as a sort of leper colony', and that you would be

47 *Life,* 23 May 1968. See also Claire Sterling, *The Masaryk Case* (New York, 1969).

contaminated as soon as you entered the Front Gate. However, he said he was glad that de Valera and others recognized 'the immense contribution' of the College to the country. In a 'brilliantly challenging speech', he denied that the Wilsonian principle of self-determination had been applied in Ireland after the 1918 general election, which had essentially been a vote for self-determination, and instead there followed 'a regime of military repression and coercion unparallelled in history'.[48] During the speech it looked like the British High Commissioner was about to rise in protest, but he remained seated. Masaryk turned to Sheehy Skeffington after he sat down and told him, 'I was delighted with what you had to say. I couldn't speak my mind tonight, but invite me back after the war.'

After leaving Trinity, Michael B. Yeats ran unsuccessfully for the Dáil for Fianna Fáil in 1948 and 1951, but was appointed to the Seanad (1951–54). A delegate to the Council of Europe in 1953 he took a huge interest in European affairs.[49] Returning to the Seanad in 1961, he served as a Senator until 1980, and was elected Cathaoirleach in 1969 (both Mary Robinson and Owen Sheehy-Skeffington voted against him). Yeats became one of Ireland's first MEPs in 1973 and made the opening speech on behalf of the Irish delegation on 16 January. He missed out on becoming President of the Parliament in 1975 by one vote, and became a Vice-President. After losing his seat in 1979 he served as a Director in the Secretariat of the EEC Council of Ministers until his retirement in 1986.

Debates that session included 'That Irish Culture is Dying' (31 January 1945), presided over by Terence de Vere White, and 'That This House Regrets the Decline of Monarchy' (14 March 1945). The monarchy debate attracted some attention as among the speakers were Sean MacEoin, the War of Independence hero and Fine Gael TD, who said that all governments that had a ceremonial head of State were monarchistic in their mentality. The motion was passed by 2 votes.[50]

On Monday 7 May 1945 Germany surrendered unconditionally,

---

48 Quoted in Andrée Sheehy Skeffington, *Skeff: A Life of Owen Sheehy Skeffington 1909-1970* (Dublin, 1991), p. 122.

49 Helena King, 'Michael B. Yeats', *DIB.*

50 *The Irish Times*, 15 March 1945.

a week after Hitler had committed suicide in the bunker. It was announced that the next day, 8 May, would be Victory in Europe Day, and this prompted some disturbances in Dublin, including in Trinity. At 3 p.m. on the Monday a group of students, including members of the Society, decided to raise the flags of the victorious powers, and the Red Flag, the Union Flag, the Stars and Stripes, and the French Tricolour were flown from the roof.[51] This was initially a good-natured event, but as time passed some people grew unhappy that the Irish Tricolour was at the bottom of the mast, underneath the other flags. There were some protests, and eventually the flags were taken down, but the controversy intensified when two Northern Irish students decided to set fire to the Irish flag. Soon there were large crowds gathering to protest in the city centre and 'Trinity burns the Tricolour' was the placard carried by one man. The gates of Trinity were locked and Gardaí were forced to form a protective cordon, and there were baton charges to force the crowd back. UCD student Charles J. Haughey is credited with climbing up a lamppost outside Trinity and burning a British flag, starting a minor riot.

These events became the subject of the debate in the Society on Wednesday 9 May, when the motion 'That this House is Ashamed of the History of Ireland' was interpreted by speakers to discuss recent happenings. P.S. O'Hegarty, the writer, editor and former IRB man (and future father-in-law of Michael B. Yeats), chaired the debate and wore Gaelic evening dress for the occasion. Frank Hill suggested that the people of Ireland were probably ashamed of Trinity today, while another said that the 'Orangemen who had disgraced themselves on the roof of the college were representatives of the students' at large.[52] G.D. Sullivan opposed the motion and said that 'We feel ashamed of the minority of students who misrepresented it, and ashamed that the authorities, who bungled it, could not have handled the situation better.'

Yeats, as Auditor of the Historical Society, joined with Ann Stephens, the President of the Elizabethan Society, Raymond Oliver,

---

51 See Patrick Geoghegan, 'Calling time on the war', *Irish Independent,* 18 February 2017.

52 *The Irish Times*, 10 May 1945.

the President of the Philosophical Society, and D.P. Leighton, the Chair of the Students' Representative Council, to write a letter to *The Irish Times* pointing out that 'the insult offered to the national flag' on Monday 8 May was 'not the act of the student body as a whole'. They insisted that it was 'carried out and supported only by a small and irresponsible minority'.[53]

The controversy rumbled on. A member of the Committee, signing himself '*Another of the Many*, College Historical Society' wrote a letter to *The Irish Times* which was published on 11 May where he suggested that 95 per cent of the people in Trinity were ashamed of the attempted burning of the Irish flag. He insisted that the majority of students in Trinity had supported the Allied powers (who he refers to throughout as the 'United Nations') and condemning the two men ('neither of them citizens of Eire') who attempted to burn the flag ('the reaction throughout College to this incident is a unanimous feeling of disgust'). He apologised for having the Irish flag underneath the other flags, and also criticised those outside of College who exploited it as an opportunity to attack 'the outlook of this university', because 'it fitted in with their ideas, founded on ignorance'.

This controversy marked the final engagement of the students with the Second World War, bringing to an end a period in which the Society had managed to navigate various restrictions to provide a forum for independent thinking and debate. The Society had articulated its own vision in the cause of truth, at a time when discussion of the war in Ireland was limited and prescribed. At a time of censorship and propaganda it had lived up to its mission as a school for oratory, debate, and democratic principles.

---

53 *The Irish Times*, 10 May 1945.

'A SPHERE OF IDEAS': THE SOCIETY IN THE POST-WAR YEARS, 1945-1959

18

THE INFLUENCE of Thomas Davis on the history of Ireland and beyond was the subject of a paper by Dr T.W. Moody at an event in the Society on 12 June 1945 to mark the centenary of his death. Moody praised Davis for having worked to create mutual understanding between Catholics and Protestants and said that 'the nation of his dreams was a tolerant and all-comprehending nation, conscious of its deep roots in the past'.[1] Therefore, he said, Davis recommended the study of Irish history, literature and the language as the best way of promoting national feeling.

The winner of the gold medal for oratory for the session, Robert Francis Vere Heuston, was elected Auditor for the new session and he chose the subject of 'Public Opinion and Politics' for his inaugural meeting on 7 November 1945. In the course of his paper he blamed the decline of the influence of public opinion on politics, suggesting that expert opinion had now replaced it.[2]

Professor D.W. Brogan, Professor of Political Science at Cambridge, proposed the vote of thanks and reminded people that a dictatorship which controlled all the mechanisms for gauging public opinion never really knew what the people were thinking. Sir Shane Leslie, the writer and diplomat (and a first cousin of Winston Churchill), also spoke and said that he had always failed to grasp what public opinion meant because he had always come bottom of the polls. Public opinion, he suggested, was a luxury of democracy. R.B. McCallum, the Oxford academic who coined the word

1 *The Irish Times*, 13 June 1945.

2 *The Irish Times*, 8 November 1945.

psephology to describe the academic study of elections, proposed the motion that the Society was worthy of support. It was seconded by P.S. O'Hegarty who praised the Irish Government of 1922 to 1932 as 'the best', regretting that it had lost power because they had 'got slightly out of touch with public opinion'. However, he also praised de Valera's actions during the war, calling him 'a man who had moral fervour' who was 'in touch with the intimate feelings of the country'.

A remarkable student, Heuston was a direct descendant of a first cousin of Robert Emmet, and was immensely proud of the connection.[3] After graduating in law with first-class honours, he went to the King's Inns and was called to the bar in 1947. Deciding upon an academic career, he became a fellow at Pembroke College, Oxford, and was so popular that according to Ronan Keane, one-time Chief Justice, 'there were often queues to gain admission to his lectures'. After a time as Professor of Law in Southampton, he returned to Trinity as Regius Professor of Laws in 1970, and served on the Law Reform Commission from 1975 to 1981. His two-volume *Lives of the Lord Chancellors,* is considered a classic.

The nascent Irish tourism industry was debated on 27 Febraury 1946, with a motion 'That this House Approves of Tourist Development in Ireland'. It was chaired by Senator Gerard Sweetman, the President of the Irish Tourist Association, who argued that Ireland needed to invest in an efficient transport system or it would not have any attraction for tourists.[4] The motion was carried.

Heuston was involved in choosing a faux controversial motion for 6 March, 'That the Law is an Immoral Profession'. A Trinity correspondent in *The Irish Times* joked that given the Society's role in producing so many 'of Ireland's greatest men of law' it was a motion that 'may well shake this venerable institution to its foundation'.[5] The motion was defeated.

The death of an IRA hunger-striker, Sean McCaughey, on 11 May 1946, after a twenty-three day protest in Portlaoise prison, created a genuine controversy in the Society at the first meeting after it happened. On Wednesday 15 May, before the debate proper began, a

3 Ronan Keane, 'R.F.V. Heuston', *DIB*.

4 *The Irish Times*, 28 February 1946.

5 *The Irish Times*, 6 March 1946.

privileged motion was proposed by James John Skinner calling on the House to adjourn as a mark of respect to the relatives of McCaughey. This was ruled out of order by Heuston, who argued that it was 'a highly controversial matter of a political nature' and could not be discussed without the prior sanction of the Board.[6] The debate proceeded, but after the first speaker had concluded, Skinner asked the House to adjourn to 'to consider the conduct of the Auditor in ruling the original motion out of order'. This was, as Skinner himself admitted, 'a grave step', but he was determined to punish Heuston and praise McCaughey, who he called 'a great Irishman'.

Refusing to accept the objections of the House, Skinner delivered a tribute to McCaughey, before he was forced to stop after various interruptions from members. Dr R.B. McDowell was in the chair and he criticised the motion for violating a gentleman's agreement that political matters were not raised in the House without prior sanction.

A law student, Skinner was a prominent debater with the Society, and had received the thanks of the Society for the previous session. His subsequent career is worthy of mention. After graduation he emigrated to Northern Rhodesia in 1951 and represented African nationalist defendants, later saying that it was in part because he was 'a natural radical anyway', and in part because he rejected the 'social and racial atmosphere of the time'.[7]

A founding member, and legal adviser to the United National Independence Party, Skinner played a leading role in the foundation of the Republic of Zambia in 1964 and helped draft the new country's Constitution.[8] He served as Minister for Justice in President Kaunda's Government, and was the only white member of the first Cabinet. He followed this with a period as Attorney General where he was praised in *The Lusaka Times* for 'working miracles in maintaining the standards of Zambian justice in recent years' and for 'never letting his political sympathies guide his legal opinions'.

Skinner became Chief Justice of Zambia in 1969, but resigned soon after clashing with Kaunda over his decision to support the quashing of a conviction of two Portuguese soldiers for a minor

6 *The Irish Times*, 16 May 1946.

7 *The Irish Times*, 13 January 1969.

8 Turlough O'Riordan, 'James John Skinner', *DIB*.

infringement. Kaunda encouraged protests, and a juvenile paramilitary organisation stormed the court building in Lusaka and Skinner was forced to barricade himself in a strong room in fear of his life. On the verge of a breakdown, Skinner fled the country and resigned his post. Later in the year he was appointed Chief Justice of Malawi, and he served there until 1985. Unfortunately his tenure was tainted by his swearing-in of Hastings Kamuzu Banda as President for Life in 1971, and the judiciary's support for a dictator damaged his reputation, although some argued he maintained 'a credible independence for Malawi's judiciary'.

Heuston's successor as Auditor of the College Historical Society was Vincent Delany. In terms of their later careers it is interesting that both were Regius Professor of Laws in Trinity – with Delany holding the chair before Heuston. Delany chose 'The Challenge of Socialism' as the subject of his inaugural address, which took place on 6 November 1946. Bad fog affected numbers, which were smaller than usual, but the debate was praised in *The Irish Times* for providing 'plenty of meat for the hardy people who ventured' to the Dining Hall.[9]

Harry Diamond, Socialist Republican MP in the Northern Ireland parliament, was one of the speakers, and he suggested that people in Ireland should 'look with the greatest sympathy on the socialist experiment now taking place in Great Britain and to a lesser extent in New Zealand'.[10] It was, he declared, an evolutionary experiment that has the force of the people behind it and would be successful.

Liam Cosgrave, Fine Gael TD, also spoke and he noted how all countries with a socialist form of government elevated the rulers to positions far above the ordinary people. Arguing that Hitler's Germany and Mussolini's Italy had been a different kind of socialist system, he attacked the kinds of society that attempted to impose an unrealistic economic model. According to a newspaper report the debate never rose 'to the great heights of left or right fire', but provided plenty of substance.[11] Other notable debates that session

9 *The Irish Times*, 13 November 1946.
10 *The Irish Times*, 7 November 1946.
11 *The Irish Times*, 13 November 1946.

included 'That this House Regrets the Decline of Sunday Observance' (13 November 1946).[12]

After leaving Trinity, Vincent Delany lectured in law at Queen's University Belfast before returning to become Professor of Laws and then Regius Professor of Laws in 1963. The author of some major pieces of scholarship, including *The Administration of Justice in Ireland* and a study of *The Canals of the South of Ireland,* when he died suddenly in 1964 he was hailed as a law teacher, as a scholar, and as someone who 'left behind a substantial quantity of legal writing'.[13]

Censorship in Ireland was debated on 12 February 1947, with the motion 'That this House Considers the Irish Censorship an Undesirable Institution'. The motion was carried by 12 votes to 6. The entrepreneur, E. Keith Eason, owner of Eason and Son Ltd. on O'Connell Street chaired the meeting. He suggested that the publisher should be the main censor, and he criticised the Board of Censors for publishing lists of undesirable books, claiming that nine-tenths of them would never be heard of if it wasn't for this publicity.[14] 'Censorship Board "Useless"' was the headline the next day in *The Irish Times* in its report of the debate.

To celebrate the bicentenary of the founding of Burke's Club, Professor Harold Laski returned to the Society to deliver a paper on Burke on 14 March 1947. Desmond FitzGerald, the former Minister of Defence, also spoke, as did Professor Robin Dudley Edwards of UCD. Beforehand some 'unpleasantness' was predicted, mainly because College was uncomfortable with having a left-wing intellectual speak and had refused the Society permission to use the Dining Hall.[15] In the end it passed off without major incident, although there was a degree of tension at the meeting. Laski argued that Burke was not a liberal who had betrayed his principles in 1789 but a consistent conservative who advocated change only when injustice and cruelty had made it necessary.

FitzGerald proposed the vote of thanks in somewhat unfriendly terms, suggesting that Laski was a Moscovite (which he was not),

12 TCD MUN/SOC/HIST Uncatalogued Papers, 1940-49.

13 *Northern Irish Legal Quarterly* (1964), vol. 15, n. 4, p. 470.

14 *The Irish Times*, 13 February 1947.

15 *The Irish Times*, 26 March 1947.

adding sarcastically that the Moscovites had done a service to the world 'by making murder respectable' by calling it 'liquidation'.[16] Dudley Edwards, a former Auditor of the L&H in UCD, and a legendary charismatic if difficult figure, also attempted to take on Laski, making a weak joke about his name, and suggesting that while he, himself, was only an academic, and a bit out of touch with the big world, he understood that Laski had 'something to do with politics'. It was an ungenerous and somewhat bitter speech to second the traditional vote of thanks.

Laski made a short reply that was both brilliant and devastating. He said that he was 'particularly impressed' with FitzGerald's comments about murder and liquidation, because he was only a university teacher, while FitzGerald was 'a former member of the Cosgrave Government' which had 'practical experience' of such things. Turning to Dudley Edwards, he observed that 'the ivory tower' inhabited by Professor Edwards' was one where 'apparently no light penetrated'. However, he urged him to enjoy his time in the open, 'before lapsing back into that state of resentful coma, which the universities call research'. It was, as Sheehy Skeffington recalled afterwards, 'a double oratorical knock-out'.

The Society published Laski's paper the following year and it was noted in *The Irish Times* that while 'it might seem incongruous that the great prophet of socialism should be asked to eulogise the high priest of conservatism, but there is such broadness of humanity and spaciousness of mind that they have much in common'.[17] The paper praised the Society for continuing 'the enlightened practice of hearing, and publishing, papers on the numerous famous men who have been among the Society's members'.

A Classics Scholar, Robert Hugh Steele Boyd was the Auditor for the 19478 session and he chose 'Beyond Pessimism' as the theme of his inaugural on 5 November 1947. Victor Gollancz, the prominent English publisher, spoke at the meeting and he suggested that Britain should 'throw in her lot with a larger European unit, and as a member of that unit, share and share alike'.[18] He suggested that there

16 *The Irish Times*, 5 March 1970.

17 *The Irish Times*, 10 April 1948.

18 *The Irish Times*, 6 November 1947.

should be less nationalism and more internationalism, and defended the Labour Party in Britain for its work. Christopher Hollis, the Conservative British MP and writer, also spoke and challenged the idea that communism had anything to do with economics. He claimed that communism 'was nothing more than a gang getting into power and staying in power'.

Following the defeat of Fianna Fáil in the 1948 general election, John A. Costello became Taoiseach as head of an Inter-Party Government. He attended the inaugural meeting of the 1948-49 session, his presence described by *The Irish Times* as 'a tribute to the special position that these meetings still occupy in Irish public life'.[19] The Auditor, a Legal Science Scholar, John Leonard Barry Deane, chose as his subject 'Citizens – Masters or Servants?' and the President of the High Court, Mr Justice Gavan Duffy also attended. The meeting took place on 3 November 1948 and Deane argued that the right to intern a citizen without trial, which had been done in Britain and Ireland during the war, was something that could only be justified in the gravest of emergencies.

In a major speech, Costello claimed that it was important to persuade the public to take a greater interest in politics, or risk falling prey to 'impractical dreamers' or 'the insane imaginings of barbarous minds'.[20] Attacking the growth of totalitarianism and the spread of communism, he said that 'many who cavil at state interference without having taken the trouble to examine the reasons for it frequently have no one but themselves to blame for their grievances'. Supporting the idea of social security protections, he said that these were only possible if the economy was strong. 'If our national income becomes stagnant', he warned, 'if we refuse to work hard and produce more, social security becomes merely a delusion and a deception.' Costello suggested that people in Ireland could be proud of their institution for having maintained a strong democracy, 'while safeguarding their moral and spiritual values'. Lord Killanin also spoke and he warned that civil servants too often believed that they were the masters, and that was bureaucracy at its worst.

Deane graduated with a first in law, but he had the distinction

19 *The Irish Times*, 13 October 1947.

20 *The Irish Times*, 4 November 1948.

of living well without ever working in paid employment. He played the stock market with some success, and this gave him an income to devote his life to voluntary work.[21] He was chairman of the Church of Ireland Pensions Board for fifteen years and was credited with 'putting the scheme on a sound footing to the benefit of clergy, widows and orphans'. A layman, he was made an Honorary Canon because of his lifetime of service to the Church of Ireland, and became known as 'the Canon from Bandon'. What he finally retired, it was hailed as 'the end of an era' by Archbishop Eames.

On 1 February 1950 the House rejected the motion 'That the Irish Lack the Qualities which Go to Make a Great Nation' by two votes.[22] James Kilfedder, the Record Secretary, proposed the motion and suggested that the Irish had the same hatred and bigotry as in 1921. Opposing the motion, R.B. Henderson claimed that Ireland would be one day called a great nation, meaning 'a prosperous, independent, thriving community'.

The Chief Justice, Conor Maguire, chaired an Irish intervarsity debate in the Society on 9 Match 1949 on the motion 'That Ireland is Out of Touch with the Rest of the World', a motion which was carried by 48 votes to 17. A debate with Edinburgh, Durham, Oxford and Cambridge took place on 8 March 1950 on the motion 'That the Past is No Passport to the Present', which was defeated by 54 votes to 43. Lord Killanin chaired the debate, and Norman St John-Stevas of Cambridge was the star speaker on the night, arguing that most countries had little historical sense, but Ireland had an excess of it.[23] William Rees-Mogg was one of the speakers for Oxford.

James Kilfedder was elected Auditor for the 1950-51 session and he delivered his inaugural address on 'War in Our Time' on 1 November 1950, suggesting that Ireland had an outmoded conception of nationalism and by her neutrality had deprived herself of her only hope of making a useful contribution to European defence. He called on Ireland to join the Atlantic Pact or return to the British Commonwealth. Sir John Esmonde, the Fine Gael TD for Wexford who had the distinction of also having sat in the House

21 *The Irish Times*, 5 May 2001.

22 *The Irish Times*, 2 Feb. 1950.

23 *The Irish Times*, 9 March 1950.

of Commons before independence, delivered a stinging attack on the British Government in his speech, who he accused of having made 'a wild attack upon the Republic'. He declared he was tired of 'having people who never got the smell of gunpowder, or saw rotting corpses, trying to make this country a playground for other people to fight their battles in'.[24]

Kilfedder later became an Ulster Unionst MP in the British House of Commons (1964-66, 1970-95), and formed his own party, the Ulster Popular Unionist Party, in 1980. In the *Dictionary of Irish Biography,* Patrick Maume notes that he 'generally avoided sectarian rhetoric', although he 'publicly welcomed the death of hunger strikers in 1981' and called for Northern Ireland 'to be placed under martial law after the Enniskillen bombing in 1987'.[25] Knighted in 1992, he died of a heart attack in 1995, and it was afterwards claimed that the gay rights group Outrage had threatened to 'out' him as a homosexual after he voted to maintain a restricted age of consent. As Maume notes, 'it was widely believed in Northern Ireland political and journalistic circles that Kilfedder was indeed homosexual' and 'Outrage was accused of blackmail and blamed for Kilfedder's death'.

A controversial debate on Northern Ireland was held in camera, at the request of the Board, on 29 November 1950. The motion was 'That this House Would Arm Now to Take the North' and eighteen members spoke, the majority against the motion. It was defeated by 57 votes to 12.[26]

Noel Browne, the controversial Minister for Health, spoke before the Society on 31 January 1951 on the motion 'That this House Deplores Party Politics'. He criticised those who opposed party politics, claiming that 'to do so is to deplore intelligent collective action towards the effective solution of these problems which face any community'.[27] The Record Secretary, Maurice Abrahamson, proposed the motion and suggested that party politics sacrificed the interests of the nation for the interests of the party. He suggested

---

24 *The Irish Times*, 2 November 1950.

25 Patrick Maume, 'James Kilfedder', *DIB*.

26 TCD MUN/SOC/HIST Uncatalogued Papers, 1950-59.

27 *The Irish Times*, 1 February 1951.

that the individual was subsumed by the party system. The motion was defeated by 29 votes to 19.

There was an attempt to amend the motion at the debate on 30 May 1951, when it was proposed to change 'That Patriotism is the Last Refuge of the Scoundrel' to 'That Fine Gael is the Party of Scoundrels Whose Last Refuge is Patriotism'.[28] The amendment was debated at length before being defeated by 29 votes to 17. Ben Udenze spoke on the amendment and then opposed the motion in the debate proper, delivering one of the best speeches of the night. The motion was defeated by a single vote.

Following the death of Douglas Hyde in 1949 a new President of the Society was needed and in March 1951 Sir Robert Tate, a Senior Fellow at Trinity, known as 'Major' to his friends, was elected. Upon accepting the office he declared that it was 'one of the greatest honours he had ever received'.[29] A leading Classicist, he had been the head of the Officer Training Corps in Trinity during the First World War.

Maurice Abrahamson was elected Auditor for the 1951–2 session, becoming the first Jewish Auditor of the Society. Abramson later became a successful stockbroker and was President of the Irish Stock Exchange (1961–63) and chair of the Jewish Representative Council of Ireland. The Treasurer of the Society was Mahomed J. Jaffer, who was born in Karachi in what became Pakistan and went on to become a successful international lawyer in the United States. Abrahamson's inaugural address on 7 November was on the subject of 'Left or Right? and speakers included Seán MacBride; Osbert Lancaster, the political cartoonist of the *Daily Express;* and Sir Andrew McFadyean, the Liberal politician and philosopher. The debate was chaired by Sir Robert Tate, the President of the Society, and Abrahamson argued for a new approach to ensure a political system was in place to safeguard the interests of all sections in society, both nationally and internationally. MacBride, now out of office, used his speech to attack a recent Central Bank report for advocating economic policies he believed had caused the rise of communism in Europe in the 1920s and this was reported in the papers the next day.[30]

---

28 TCD MUN/SOC/HIST Uncatalogued Papers, 1950-59.

29 *The Irish Times*, 12 March 1951.

30 *The Irish Times*, 8 November 1951.

Other debates that session included one on 28 November 1951 on the motion, 'That this House Deplores the Rearmament of Western Germany', with the motion proposed by Henry Barron, future Supreme Court judge.[31] 'That European Civilisation is in a State of Decay' was the motion for the intervarsity debate on 5 March 1952, which was defeated by 86 votes to 65. Professor W.B. Stanford chaired the debate, and argued that European civilisation was in less danger in the 1950s than in the 1930s. One of the speakers from Cambridge was Douglas Hurd, the Vice-President of the Cambridge Union and future British Foreign Secretary (among other offices), who gave a humorous speech and said the fact the *News of the World* was banned in Ireland was a sign of the country's superior civilisation.[32]

For John Wood's inaugural meeting on 5 November 1952 he posed the question of 'Overlord Cabinet?' and his guest speakers included Patrick Gordon Walker, the Labour MP, and Professor Nicholas Mansergh. Gordon Walker, who would later serve briefly as Foreign Secretary despite having lost his seat in Parliament in controversial circumstances, described the British Cabinet as an 'elusive institution', in remarks that were widely reported.[33] In his speech, Mansergh suggested that no other form of government could have carried out 'the present social revolution' in such a quiet way.

Major debates that session included the one on 4 March 1953 on the motion 'That Democracy is Not Worth the Effort'. This was an intervarsity debate, with speakers from UCC, Glasgow, Bangor, Edinburgh, Queen's and UCD, with Wood, the Auditor, proposing the motion. The motion was defeated by 46 votes to 23, and speaking from the chair, Senator Noel Hartnett, of Clann na Poblachta, described the speeches as 'anaemic'.[34] Claiming that this was a symptom of attitudes at the time, he argued that democratic power was moving from parliament to 'specialised, and even secret society groups' such as the Knights of Columbanus and the Freemasons. He also condemned those who criticised Hitler but gave a free pass to

31 *The Irish Times*, 28 November 1951.

32 *The Irish Times*, 6 March 1952.

33 *The Irish Times*, 6 November 1952.

34 *The Irish Times*, 5 March 1953.

Franco, in a speech that drifted into conspiracy theory and wild accusation.

In the same month, Hartnett put himself forward as a candidate for the Presidency of the College Historical Society, Sir Robert Tate having died in January 1952. The other candidates were A. A. Luce, the distinguished Berkeley authority and former Vice-Provost, and Frederick Boland, the Irish Ambassador to London. Boland was successful and it was noted in *The Irish Times* that 'no more suitable candidate could have been found'.[35]

Now out of office following the Mother and Child scheme debacle, the former Minister for Health, Noel Browne, returned to chair a meeting of the Society on 11 March 1953. The motion was 'That Socialism is No Longer Fashionable', and it was carried by a small majority. Browne delivered a stinging attack on the health service in Ireland, which he called a two-tiered system, one for the wealthy who could afford to pay for treatment, and the other a pauper-type of service for the poor.[36]

Edward Carson was honoured with a debate on 3 June 1953, on the motion that 'This House Reveres the Memory of Lord Carson' and speakers paid tribute to someone who was described as 'personally a most charming man' even if you disagreed with his political ideals and opinions.[37]

'Empire and Liberty' was the subject of Eric Gorton's inaugural address on 4 November 1953, and his speakers included James Dillon TD, and Forbes Burnham, the chairman of the People's Progressive Party in British Guiana, who became the first Prime Minister of Guyana in 1964 and the country's second President in 1980. Burnham defined liberty as the right of his people to run their own country, and suggested that the 'thirst for liberty, for freedom, that desire of people regardless of race to run their own country', was something that would always disappoint the imperialist powers, especially those who believed 'in a wonderful empire where the sun never sets'.

These views were challenged by Dillon who argued that the

35 *The Irish Times*, 7 March 1953.

36 *The Irish Times*, 12 March 1953.

37 *The Irish Times*, 4 June 1953.

definition of liberty was larger than Burnham's conception. Dillon insisted it meant 'that the smallest minority and the humblest man or women in a community shall have the right to say or do, within the law, whatever his conscience directs him to do'.[38] Accusing Burnham of being a Soviet supporter, wrapped in the flag with the 'hammer, sickle, all', Dillon warned him not to 'take the hammer out of his waistcoat or the sickle out of his pocket'. He joked that 'When I meet an animal that has feathers like a duck, that quacks like a duck, that walks like a duck and lays eggs like a duck, I will believe it is a duck, even though it says it is a Picasso peace dove'. He went on to attack Fianna Fáil's policy of external relations in the 1930s as 'a disgusting fraud' and 'detestable experience', and suggested that the world needed a new commonwealth of nations.

One of the funniest and most entertaining debates in the Society's history took place on 18 November 1953. Myles na gCopaleen (Brian O'Nolan, aka Flann O'Brien) was in the chair and he ran proceedings in his own unorthodox and inimitable way. The motion was that 'This House has no Faith in Tradition' and he persistently interrupted speakers and ordered them to sit down before they had time to develop their argument.[39] One student proposed the idea that tradition kills initiative. The chair immediately interrupted and ordered the student to talk about something else. Handling this challenge well, the student developed another line of argument, but was then told to sit down. The motion was defeated by 45 votes to 13. Speaking from the chair, na gCopaleen denounced all the speeches as rubbish, before delivering his own speech on Egyptology and arbitration before concluding a memorable evening.

On Monday 4 May 1954 the Society joined forces with the Philosophical Society as part of Trinity Tóstal Week, a celebration of Irish culture, to debate the motion 'That this House Approves of the Union'. The novelty was that all the speakers wore period costume and represented some of the great college personalities of the past. Gorton proposed the motion as Edmund Burke and was 'suitably bewigged and wearing a yellow frockcoat and white

38 *The Irish Times*, 5 November 1953.

39 *Trinity News*, 25 November 1953.

breeches'.[40] Desmond Kimmitt (soon to be elected Auditor) spoke as Robert Emmet, while other speakers played the parts of Mahaffy and Oscar Wilde.

On Wednesday 5 May the Society debated whether it would 'Welcome a New Approach in Irish Politics', which was passed by 25 votes to 2. Peadar Doyle, a Fine Gael TD and former Lord Mayor of Dublin, delivered 'a moving speech' admitting that he had never set foot in Trinity before, where Wolfe Tone, his political hero had been educated.[41] The debate was chaired by Stanford, who complained of the 'petty party feeling' in the debate and claimed that a fault of the Irish was their love of words rather than deeds. Other motions included 'That this House Reveres the Memory of F.D. Roosevelt' (2 June), which was passed by 21 votes to 16.[42]

R.D.F. (Desmond) Kimmitt's inaugural address was on the subject of 'Certain Inalienable Rights' on 3 November 1954. The main attraction was Lord Halisham, the Conservative peer who (as Quintin Hogg) had won a reputation for 'hard-hitting intelligent debate' in parliament and in his regular appearances on television and radio.[43] Halisham later served as British Secretary of State for Education in the 1960s and as Lord Chancellor in the 1970s. T.F. O'Higgins, the Minister for Health, also spoke at the debate.

An arch-Unionist and conservative, Kimmitt had strong prejudices which he made no attempt to conceal and this caused many problems in the Society. A hostile environment was created for anyone with even the mildest liberal or nationalist feelings, or who was Catholic. After his election Kimmitt had many arguments with his Librarian, Connolly Cole, and over the summer announced that he would not tolerate Cole continuing in the role. Cole resigned in November 1954 claiming that 'one could forgive the political atmosphere in the Hist, but it is the very definite religious bias which makes it intolerable'.[44]

The debate on 10 November 1954 was on the motion 'That this

40 *The Irish Times*, 5 May 1954.

41 *Trinity News*, 14 May 1954,

42 TCD MUN/SOC/HIST Uncatalogued Papers, 1950-59.

43 *The Irish Times*, 1 November 1954.

44 *Trinity News*, 2 December 1954.

House would prefer a Communist Regime to a Third World War'.[45] Ben Udenze was the opening speaker of the night and the motion was passed by 17 votes to 11. Kimmitt spoke in favour of censorship in the debate on 2 February 1955 that 'This House Approves of Moral Censorship in Literature and in Films'. He argued that Ireland was in a better position that Britain or the United States to fight filth, and suggested that 'spiritual integrity' was vital in the present fight against communism. A law student, Ben Udenze, distinguished himself in opposition to the motion.[46] Kimmitt was a gold medallist for oratory in the Society, and later became a prominent Anglican archdeacon in Canada.

Graduates of Trinity were urged to take a more active part in public life at the debate at the honorary members' debate on 15 June 1955. The motion was 'That this House Wishes Itself Back in the Eighteenth Century', and a number of former Auditors spoke. John Ross warned that they were in 'great danger of becoming a petty people' if they did not engage in national affairs.[47] The Auditor-elect, Colin Nicholls, claimed people needed 'to go back to a great classical age, an age which had confidence in itself instead of disillusion and fear'. Terence de Vere White also spoke and claimed that it required more imagination, more courage, and more judgement to live in their own time than in any previous age. Bueno McKenna suggested that the eighteenth century was a time of considerable violence and that ordinary people were much better off now. The House divided evenly on the motion, and the chair, Kingsmill Moore, cast the decisive vote to pass it.

Clement Atlee, the former British Prime Minister and Leader of the Labour Party, was the star attraction at the inaugural meeting on 2 November 1955 on the subject of 'Peace in Our Time'. The Auditor, Colin Nicholls, argued that principle should not be sacrificed for practice, claiming that the principle of self-determination was the most important one of all. In a brilliant response, Atlee asked 'Can we live together and disagree?' suggesting that it would 'be a dull world in which we all agreed'.[48] Believing

45 TCD MUN/SOC/HIST Uncatalogued Papers, 1950-59.

46 *The Irish Times*, 3 February 1955.

47 *The Irish Times*, 16 June 1955.

48 *The Irish Times*, 3 November 1955.

that this was where democracies set a good example, he expressed his hope that for real peace to be preserved you needed a world 'of the utmost diversity and cheerful controversy, in which all our battles may be fought in a sphere of ideas and not on the battlefields'.

Atlee argued that the people of Africa and Asia had as equal a right as the people of Europe to influence in the world, he delivered a plea for toleration, an optimistic vision for the future, grounded in his experience of the past. Atlee had flown over especially for the meeting, and at the airport had been met by journalists who asked him about Partition. In his response he said it was a matter entirely for the Irish, adding with a smile, 'It's your show'.

There was no debate on 22 February 1956 as a motion was proposed by the Auditor and seconded by the Treasurer suggesting that the meeting adjourn 'in order that it may observe from the television of a suitable hostelry the progress of its representatives in the finals of the *Observer* debating tournament in London'. This was carried without a division.[49] The Society, however, lost the final with Glasgow Union winning the competition, then in its third year. Significant debates that session included the one on 28 February 1956 against UCD on the motion 'That this House would favour the amalgamation of TCD and UCD', which was defeated by 19 votes to 14. On 14 March 1956 the motion was one that was dated even for the time: 'That the Happiest Nations, Like the Happiest Women, Have No History'.[50] The motion was defeated. There was an attempt to change the motion on 13 June from 'That this House Reveres the Memory of Marshall Jan Christian Smuts' to 'That this House Reveres the Memory of Joseph Vissarionovich Stalin', and it failed thanks to the casting vote of the chairman.[51] The original motion passed by a narrow majority.

The Treasurer of the Society, Benedict Chukwuemake Udenze, won the silver medal for oratory at the end of Trinity Term in 1957, and was elected Auditor for the 187th session, becoming the first black student, and the first native African to hold the office. Richard St G. Sides became Record Secretary, with (Emmanuel) Chuku

49 TCD MUN/SOC/HIST Uncatalogued Papers, 1950-59.
50 TCD MUN/SOC/HIST Uncatalogued Papers, 1950-59.
51 TCD MUN/SOC/HIST Uncatalogued Papers, 1950-59.

Emekekwue as Correspondence Secretary. Born in Awaka in Nigeria, Udenze went to school at King's College in Onitsha, which was run by Irish priests. There he played football for the school, and excelled in tennis, a sport he continued to play at Trinity.[52] Upon leaving school he worked as a teacher, going against his father's wishes, and almost made it his career. However, he decided to wanted to pursue a career in public life and came to Trinity to train to be lawyer, as the first step to a political career.

Known as Ben Udenze during his time in Trinity, he was described in a profile in *Trinity News* as 'an unassuming kind of man, quick in making friends and good in keeping them'. His ambition was to return to Nigeria and establish a legal practice there, before getting involved in national politics. It was even predicted that 'the experience he has acquired here should ensure that Nigeria gains a wise and good servant when he returns'.[53]

Udenze chose to take on the legacy of colonialism in Africa in his inaugural address, to which he gave the title of 'Created Unarmed'. It was delivered on 7 November 1956 and was a passionate indictment of the many failures of the colonial powers on the continent. Udenze argued that 'The African people have had to follow flags which do not represent their aspirations'.[54] He then suggested that the good things done by colonial powers were mitigated by their reluctance to grant the countries some measure of freedom, insisting that 'Only when colonial powers live up to their standards, and realize that democracy must not be vague, will peace, progress and prosperity result.'

Responding to the paper, Senator Roger McHugh, the academic and playwright, argued that Ireland should join in a UN police force if it was created. He suggested that it was not a simple issue of democracy against communism, because colonial imperialism was also a threat to the international community. Brigadier General Eric Dorman-O'Gowan also spoke and suggested that the worst examples of imperialism could be found in Europe.

Dorman O'Gowan was an extraordinary figure, having fought

52 *Trinity News*, 8 November 1953.

53 Ibid.

54 *Trinity News*, 15 November 1956.

in the British army in the First and Second World Wars, before becoming an adviser to the IRA in the 1950s and allowing them to train on his estate. A friend of Ernest Hemingway, he became embittered after being dismissed from the British army in irregular circumstances in 1943, and moved to Ireland.[55] In his speech he attacked having Russia on the UN Security Council, suggesting that it was like having a poacher on a bench of magistrates, able to use his veto in any case of poaching he supported, and able to charge the other magistrates with poaching in their own lands.[56] A Dr John O'Donovan also spoke and began by promising a poor speech. According to the student report, 'he kept his word'.[57]

In November 1956 the Society debated the recent re-election of the President of the United States with the motion 'That this House Welcomes the Election of Mr Eisenhower'. M.H. Proctor proposed the motion, and showed the audience the cover of *Time* magazine which had Eisenhower and Nixon together, arguing that Eisenhower was a man of strong personality and good experience who could settle international misunderstandings.[58] Albert Talalla opposed the motion, and warned about the dangers of Nixon becoming president. Chuku Emekekwue said that he wished Eisenhower could have a third term. *Trinity News* reported that 'in general the Society was very critical of Eisenhower's administration and of Mr Dulles' foreign policy' and the motion was defeated. The chair of the debate was R. B. McDowell, and he said that while Adlai Stevenson may have been the choice of the intellectuals, Eisenhower had the popularity of a great soldier. Emekekwue graduated in medicine before returning to Nigeria where he had a distinguished career as a physician.[59]

Dorman O'Gowan returned to the Society to chair the debate on 30 January 1957 on whether the House should join the volunteer force that had been established in Britain by some students to aid those in Hungary fighting against communism. The motion was defeated, and Dorman O'Gowan argued that the principles

55 Patrick Maume, 'Eric Dorman-O'Gowan', *DIB*.

56 *The Irish Times*, 8 November 1956.

57 Ibid.

58 *Trinity News*, 29 November 1956.

59 *Africa's Who's who* (1991), p. 604.

presented and emotions on display should not 'only operate where anti-communism is concerned'.[60]

Éamon de Valera chaired the intervarsity debate on 13 February 1957 on the motion that patriotism was the last refuge of the scoundrel, and was pictured alongside the Auditor in *The Irish Times* the next day. Udenze supported the motion and claimed that many crimes had been committed in the name of patriotism. There were also speakers from Durham, Glasgow, Bangor, Cork, Galway, and UCD. The motion was defeated by 42 votes to 15 and, speaking from the chair, de Valera said that love of one's country was a natural virtue, criticising those who said it was unnatural.[61] He suggested that 'the youth of today' was too cynical, adopting a pretence that created unhappiness. 'If I had my way', said de Valera, 'I would try and foster it [a love of country] in little children', believing that 'through that love of country they would make greater sacrifices for the common good'. During the debate the Civil War had been referenced, and de Valera defended those who had opposed the Treaty claiming that those who were dubbed Irregulars were in fact defending the State.

The Archbishop of Dublin, George Otto Simms, a former Vice-President and member of the Society, was welcomed back to the Society on 13 March 1957 for a debate on whether 'the Happiness of Society Depends on Material Wealth Rather than Culture'.[62] Simms said that it was a pleasure for him 'to come from time to time and renew his associations with the Society and its cut and thrust in debate'.

Other significant debates that session included one 'That Ireland Should Rejoin the British Commonwealth' on 8 May 1957. Sir Ivone Kirkpatrick, the former Permanent Head of the British Foreign Office, arguing that 'in the modern world, no single country, large or small, can afford to be completely isolated'.[63] The motion was carried by 16 votes to 8. Another was the debate, 'That the Emancipation of Women is Detrimental to Society', which was defeated by 13 votes to 8 at a debate on 15 May 1957.[64]

---

60 *The Irish Times*, 31 January 1957.

61 *The Irish Times*, 14 February 1957.

62 *The Irish Times*, 14 March 1957.

63 *The Irish Times*, 9 May 1957.

The playwright and future director of the Abbey Theatre, Gabriel Fallon, chaired the debate on 5 June 1957 as the Society debated a motion on its former member, with the motion that 'This House Reveres the Memory of Oscar Wilde'. Fallon described *The Importance of being Earnest* as 'a miracle of indestructability', and claimed that even if Wilde had written nothing else he would be entitled to be called a man of genius.[65] And he wondered what might have been his 'even greater contributions to English literature' if only for 'his downfall.'

Many Nigerian students came to Dublin in the 1950s to pursue a third-level education, and Trinity had a thriving Nigerian student population. Udenze was elected President of the Dublin branch of the Nigerian Students Union, and welcomed the Nigerian Commissioner to the UK, Matthew Taiwo Mbu, who came to Ireland in April 1957 to meet with the students and visit the universities where they studied. Udenze praised the generosity of the Irish people, and thanked them for the welcome the Nigerian students had received in the country.[66]

After graduating with his LLB degree in 1959, Udenze returned to Nigeria and set-up practice in Onitsha, where he went by his middle name, and was known as Chukwuemaka Udenze. Elected Mayor of Onitsha, he moved his practice to Enugu after the Nigerian Civil War. During the Nigerian Second Republic he was elected to the Senate and he served as a Senator until the military coup in 1983 brought it to an end. In a study of this period Senator Udenze has been described as 'an astute politician', and he was an eloquent speaker in parliament.[67] After the fall of the Republic, he remained in practice as Head of Chambers until his death in April 1990. The law firm he founded in 1959, Chukwuemeka Udenze & Co., continues to this day and honours the memory of 'Senator Udenze' and is proud, in its own words, 'to maintain his legacy.'[68]

64 TCD MUN/SOC/HIST Uncatalogued Papers, 1950-59.

65 *The Irish Times*, 6 June 1957.

66 *The Irish Times*, 11 April 1957.

67 Patrick J. O. Nwadinigwe, *Umu-Nshi Royal Stool from 558 BC to Date* (Awka, 2000), p. 94.

68 http://www.cudenzeandco.com/.

There was a massive controversy at the start of the 188th session, over an invitation to the Soviet ambassador to the UK, Jacob Malik, to speak. First, the Department of External Affairs, was upset that an invitation had been sent to someone representing a country that Ireland had no diplomatic relations with, and Frank Aiken, the Minister, rejected the invitation that was sent to him.[69] Second, the Auditor, Christopher St George Sides, and his Committee, made a dreadful error in misinterpreting the response from the Soviet embassy. The letter they received gave no indication that Malik would accept, being a polite refusal noting that the Ambassador was busy with events planned to mark the 40th anniversary of the Russian Revolution, but might be able to send one of his officials if not free. In their naiveté, or desire for publicity, the Committee took this as a confirmation, and announced that Malik was coming and made their plans accordingly.

In the run-up to the event there was massive confusion, as no one at the Russian embassy in London had applied for a visa to visit Ireland, and speculation mounted that he would not show. When the Correspondence Secretary, Haley-Dunne, was asked to produce the letter of acceptance he claimed, weakly, that they had sent it back to the embassy to remind the Ambassador of what he had agreed. The front page story in *Trinity News* was 'Who knows the truth?' with the subheading 'Did Malik accept?' An unnamed Irish journalist and commentator was quoted as saying that 'This sort of letter is a polite refusal in diplomatic usage. The Auditor shouldn't have jumped to false conclusions.' He also revealed that an official in the Department of External Affairs had let the Russian Embassy know that any request for a visa would likely be refused.

As a result, the Auditor's paper on 6 November 1957 on the 'Destiny of Europe' was completely overshadowed by the controversy. Despite the absence of the Ambassador, there was a distinguished line-up of speakers. Herbert Morrison, the Labour MP, attended and suggested that if every country honoured the commitments they had made upon joining the United Nations there would be no more war in the world. However, he warned that some governments did not 'play the game' and it only needed one great

69 *Trinity News*, 7 November 1957.

power to 'upset the apple cart'.[70] Without naming names, he pointed the finger at the Soviet Union, who he accused implicitly of not playing the game, and using its satellite countries to make the UN ineffective. This, he said, was the tragedy of the United Nations.

Seán MacBride also spoke and said that if Western Europe was to survive economically, politically and culturally it needed to unite and co-operate to a much greater extent than it had in the past. In a powerful defence of human rights, he said that 'every denial of human liberty and justice constituted a blow to the foundation of the free world'. MacBride pointed to the elephant in the room, and joked that he was curious why Ambassador Malik had been unable to attend, wondering 'was it a guilt complex in regard to human rights? Or, to be charitable, perhaps it was a "previous engagement", or Asian flu, or lumbago, or, simply, cold feet'. Thomas Dagg, the senior Vice-President of the Society, chaired the meeting, and regretted that Malik had been unable to come, suggesting that 'he may have found some little trouble at home'.

Myles na Gopaleen wrote an article about the controversy in *The Irish Times* on 9 November, joking that 'the notion of Jacob Malik landing in the Phoenix Park in a low-flying Sputnik is an engaging concept',[71] He also took a few swipes at Herbert Morrison, suggesting that he spoke in platitudes and mocking his metaphor of the apple-cart. Reviewing the theory that Malik did not come because he believed he would not get a visa, he described this as 'the Gaelic Leprechaun openly taunting the Russian Bear'.

On the general Committee that year was Count Nikolai Tolstoy-Miloslavski, a Russian émigré and distant cousin of Leo Tolstoy, who later became a successful writer under the name Nikolai Tolstoy. Tolstoy stood for UKIP in four British general elections between 1997 and 2010, losing each time. Motions that session included 'That the Individual is of No Consequence in Modern Society' (2 December 1957, chaired by Noel Browne), and 'That Castles in the Air are Not Worth Defending' (an inter-university debate on 6 March 1958).[72]

---

70 *The Irish Times*, 7 November 1957.

71 *The Irish Times*, 9 November 1957.

72 TCD MUN/SOC/HIST Uncatalogued Papers, 1950-59.

We get a good impression of what the debates were like in the articles of *Trinity News.* The report of the debate in June 1958, 'That this House Reveres the Memory of James Dean', shows how a straightforward motion could go off in unexpected directions. There was 'a fireworks display' when one of the speakers suggested amending the motion to something about de Gaulle, prompting a furious debate and 'several chaps had a bash in the free-for-all'.[73] It was reported that 'Mr Knight insulted Mr Dillon, Mr Burke insulted Mr Dillon, and Mr Doral was illogical enough not to insult Mr Dillon'. 'Two unknown men then spoke' with the paper helpfully pointing out that one wore a red and white tie, and the other apologised for being unshaven, 'so that they may recognise themselves. The motion was defeated. The honorary members' debate that session was on the motion 'That the English are a Nuisance' and it was defeated by 31 to 29 on 18 June 1958.[74]

One of the most charismatic figures in the Society at this time, and a frequent debater, was Jan Kaminski. Born in 1932, Kaminski was a Polish Jew who had spent time in a concentration camp during the Second World War. As a profile in *Trinity News* recounted, he had 'seen more of life than most of his fellow students ever will and looks on the present as both a challenge and a joke'.[75]

Lord Altrincham accepted an invitation to speak at the inaugural meeting of the 189th session, as the Society once more brooked controversy with its proposed guests. 'A genuine Tory radical', and editor of the *National and English Review*', Altrincham had become embroiled in controversy in August 1957 when he had written an article criticising Queen Elizabeth II, an incident later dramatized in the television series *The Crown*. Altrincham 'deplored the narrowness of her entourage, 'almost without exception people of the "tweedy" sort', cut off from the larger nation, and also criticized her public manner, with its appearance of 'a priggish schoolgirl', and her speaking style, 'a pain in the neck'. [76] His intention was to make the point that to be relevant in the second half of the twentieth

73 *Trinity News,* 12 June 1958.

74 *The Irish Times,* 19 June 1958.

75 *Trinity News,* 30 October 1958.

76 Geoffrey Wheatcroft, 'John Grigg' [Lord Altrincham], *ODNB.*

century the monarchy needed to modernise, and many of the suggestions he made were gradually adopted. Indeed, the Queen's Private Secretary later thanked Altrincham for 'the terrific service he had done', calling it 'a watershed moment for the monarchy'. Not everyone, however, saw it like that, and Altrincham was verbally and physically attacked.

The Society's guest speakers were usually given rooms in the University Club on St Stephen's Green, but Altrincham was refused because of his comments about the Queen (although no reason was officially given) and he was obliged to take rooms in College.[77] The Auditor, Michael Knight, gave his inaugural address on 5 November 1958 on 'Sons of Gloriana' and suggested that university graduates should look forward to entering the public service, because it needed 'original thought, ideas and expression'.[78] It was a provocative paper and in it he dismissed British students studying at Trinity as 'rejects of English universities'.

In his response, Altrincham proposed that the voting age should be lowered from twenty-one to eighteen, or perhaps even to 16. 'I know how strong an allergy there is to any innovation', he said, arguing that 'if you can swing for your country, fight, breed and work for your country, why should you not be allowed to vote for your country'. He also made what he called a 'slight protest' against the title of the Auditor's paper, disputing both the 'Gloriana' part and the 'sons' part. After renouncing his title in 1963, Altrincham (now John Grigg) wrote a number of important works, including an acclaimed three-volume study of Lloyd George.

H. Montgomery Hyde, the brilliant historian and MP, also spoke at the inaugural, and advised the audience 'do not be a "yes" man', and not to be afraid 'of taking an independent line'. He suggested that too many people in public life were 'yes' men and it led to unpopularity, suggesting that he had lost votes by taking his own position on Suez and other crises. The debate was chaired by Mr Justice Kingsmill Moore, now a Supreme Court Judge and Vice-President of the Society, who defended those students who had been dismissed by the Auditor as 'rejects of English universities', claiming

77 *The Irish Times*, 6 November 1958.

78 *The Irish Times*, 6 November 1958.

that they were independent people who were 'a very valuable element in our university'.

'Students vote for divorce' was the headline in *The Irish Times* after the motion, 'This House Favours Divorce' was carried on 19 November 1958 by 41 votes to 29. The Revd Gerald Myles, headmaster of Wesley College, chaired the debate and said that, while people who accepted the Christian teaching could not accept divorce, they had no right to force their views on others.[79]

The legalisation of homosexuality was debated on 6 May 1959 in a debate on the Wolfendon report, which had been published in the UK two years earlier. Dr Bethel Solomons, the former Master of the Rotunda and former President of the Royal College of Physicians, chaired the debate, which decided by 19 votes to 17 in favour of decriminalising homosexual activity between two consenting adults.[80]

Ian Simons was elected Auditor for the 1959–60 session and he chose 'Ten years of NATO' as the subject of his inaugural on 4 November 1959, with Paul-Henri Spaak, the Secretary General of NATO, as the star speaker. 600 people gathered to hear Spaak, including most of the diplomatic corps in Dublin, and the number included a large number of students in the GMB who watched the proceedings in the Dining Hall on closed-circuit television. Introduced by Mr Justice Kingsmill Moore, who chaired the meeting, as 'the presiding genius of NATO', Spaak (who spoke in French throughout, with a script provided for the audience) suggested that the failure of communism to make any further inroads in Europe was due to NATO.[81] But he warned that 'we are now entering a new phase', and urged that there could be no 'exaggerated optimism' or they would be deluding themselves.

Manny Shinwell, a British Labour MP, who as Minister for Fuel and Power had nationalised the coal mines in 1946, and who had also served as Minister for Defence, used his speech to attack Spaak and the previous speakers. In *Trinity News* it was reported that 'all on the platform moved uncomfortably and forced smiles ... and

79 *The Irish Times*, 20 November 1958.

80 TCD MUN/SOC/HIST Uncatalogued Papers, 1950-59.

81 *The Irish Times*, 5 November 1959.

Spaak beamed (in blissful ignorance) whenever his name was mentioned.'[82] Shinwell attacked Ireland's international policy and condemned NATO, suggesting that the money might be better spent raising living standards in underdeveloped countries. 'Only rarely does a Hist audience take a speaker to heart as dearly as it took Mr Shinwell' was the view afterwards.

Spaak was furious when he discovered from his translator what was being said. He demanded a right of reply, which wasn't possible, and afterwards he threw a tantrum. Skipping the dinner, he went straight to his room. There was a strained atmosphere afterwards among the guests, but for the students 'the cat amongst the pigeons was a joy to watch and a pleasure to listen to'.

During this period the Society was prepared to debate subjects that challenged people's views of what was happening at home and abroad. Other debates that session included 'That the USA is Bunkered' (11 November 1959), which was carried by 52 votes to 46. The motion on 18 November 1959 was 'That White Africa is Doomed' and it passed by 57 votes to 46.[83]

On 2 December 1959 the motion was 'That Ireland should Forget the Past', which was defeated. Ernest Blythe, the Director of the Abbey Theatre, was one of the speakers proposing the motion, and he suggested that, while he wanted people to remember the past, there were some aspects that were better forgotten. It was a powerful plea for the connection between religion and politics to be broken, with Blythe arguing that there could be no Irish nation if the Irish language was lost.[84] Senator Owen Sheehy Skeffington also spoke and said that 'The Irish language is dying and it is dying chiefly because of the strange methods employed to keep it alive.'

'TCD Society debates actions of Government' was the headline in *The Irish Times* following the debate on the motion 'That this House has No Confidence in the Government of the Republic of Ireland' on 27 January 1960.[85] Neville Keery suggested that there was no notable difference between the two main parties in the Dail,

82 *Trinity News*, 12 November 1959.

83 *The Irish Times*, 19 November 1959.

84 *The Irish Times*, 3 December 1959.

85 *The Irish Times*, 28 January 1960.

except that they fought on different sides in the civil war. Supporting the government on its UN policy, and on nothing else, Keery (who was a talented debater and would go on to win the gold medal) suggested that the main opposition party (Fine Gael) had all the faults of the Government party (Fianna Fáil). Laurence Roche opposed the motion and blamed the physical-force element in modern Ireland on the success of Fianna Fail's indoctrination of physical force nationalism. Noel Browne TD argued that the Government had not honoured its republican ideas, and called on people to be inspired by a similar spirit of sacrifice as the leaders of 1916. Senator W. B. Stanford also spoke and suggested that while the current government was not ideal, it was the best they could have. He said he hoped more people from the Historical Society would enter politics and become parliamentarians and ministers, and serve the country in that way. The motion was defeated by 84 votes to 67.

Students from universities in the United States came to the Society on 3 February 1960 to debate the threat of nuclear annihilation, in a motion about whether diplomacy (Hyde Park) was better than Hiroshima. R.L. Nichols, of the University of Kansas, told the gathering the story of how the people manning the radar look-outs along the coast in 1954 detected unidentified objects on the screen. General Curtis B. LeMay, the officer in command of the Strategic Air Command, was called, and emergency monitoring was ordered. In the event, it turned out to be geese flying, but Nichols reminded listeners of how World War Three could have started if LeMay had decided to lift the red telephone.[86] H.A. Hovey, of Wabash College, Indiana, and Harvard, opposed the motion, and predicted that there would be no surprise attacks by the United States or the USSR on the other, as the results would be too horrifying for both nations. The motion was carried by 43 votes to 26. With the 1950s over, the Society was entering a period when there was much public interest in its debates and it was determined to confront the biggest issues of the day.

86 *The Irish Times*, 4 February 1960.

19 'SOMETHING FUNDAMENTALLY CONSTITUTIONAL AND DEMOCRATIC': THE SOCIETY IN THE 1960S

THE 1960s were dominated by debates over the admission of women to the Society, a long-running controversy that was only resolved at the end of the decade. The decade began with a female student, Felicity Miller, being elected a member of the Society, after taking advantage of a loophole in the rules. For a number of days she visited the Conversation Room of the Society to peruse the day's papers, 'surrounded by shocked and speechless officers, gentlemen etc.'[1] However, she decided against attempting to attend a meeting of the Society, despite having developed a deep affection for it, and enjoyed her unique position until an auditorial ruling removed her. This was also a period of remarkable intellectual activity in the Society, as motions were discussed which reflected the turmoil of the 1960s, with debates on the civil rights struggle in the United States and Northern Ireland, apartheid in South Africa, the proposed merger with UCD, and the other dominant issues of the time. These debates were reported extensively in the national media and there was a remarkable public interest in what was said and how the students voted on the issue.

The motion on 16 November 1960 was that 'This House has Confidence in the Government of Ireland'. Senator Brian Lenihan of Fianna Fáil, who proposed the motion, argued that the Government had made real progress, with incomes up and unemployment down. Opposing the motion, Alexis FitzGerald Snr, of Fine Gael, suggested that there were real grounds for optimism

1 *Trinity News*, 24 November 1960.

in the future of the country because there was evidence of a lively mind at work.[2]

The motion on 23 November 1960 was on arts funding, 'That the State should not Legislate for Culture' and Mervyn Wall, secretary of the Arts Council, argued that while the State should support art financially it should not 'call the tune'.[3]

'Students debate value of democracy' was the headline in *The Irish Times*, reporting on the debate of 8 December 1960. The motion was 'That this House has No Faith in Democracy', which was defeated, and James Murnaghan, the retired Supreme Court judge who chaired the debate, criticised politicians who jumped to their feet and talked without any thought about what they were going to say.[4]

On 1 March 1961 the Society debated the apartheid regime in South Africa and rejected it decisively, by 35 votes to 8. The headline on page 3 of *The Irish Times* the next day was: 'Apartheid condemned in TCD debate'.[5] The best speech of the evening was delivered by Oladele Olusiji Kale, a Nigerian student who was studying medicine in Trinity. Kale argued that 'this evil called apartheid is the greatest evil since Nazism', pointing out that it 'was welcomed by the man who rules South Africa today, [Hendrik] Verwoerd. He welcomed the idea of rule by a "superior race" in Europe'. Comparing how Verwoerd condoned the atrocities of Hitler with how he condoned the atrocity at Sharpeville the previous year, when seventy-five Africans were shot in the back, he suggested that one of the most objectionable features of apartheid was the way it devalued Africans and equated them with pigs. Kale also discussed events in the Congo. 'Once upon a time there was a man named Patrice Lumumba', he said, 'he lived the life of a fool and he died a fool'. But he suggested that Lumumba's death had ensured that there were fewer fools in Africa today, because it 'changed the minds of Africans about the intentions of the western powers', and 'it was now extremely difficult for them to assume that they could trust the West'. During this

2 *The Irish Times*, 17 November 1960.

3 *The Irish Times*, 24 November 1960.

4 *The Irish Times*, 9 December 1060.

5 *The Irish Times*, 2 March 1961.

speech a black student entered the chamber carrying a large placard with the words 'I'm all white, Jack', written in 'red, lurid letters'.

In a stirring peroration, Kale, called the House to action: 'stop telling us you hate apartheid if you are not going to do something about it'. He insisted that 'we have heard enough about it. Now we want something to be done'. Kale later became a successful medical academic, Professor of Preventative and Social Medicine at the University of Ibadan, and served on various scientific and medical steering committees including the World Health Organisation's working group on tropical disease. A keen chess and darts player, he was also national games co-ordinator for the All Nigeria Darts Federation.[6]

Europe featured largely in the 192nd session, with Patrick Branigan choosing 'The European Community' as the subject of his inaugural address on 1 November 1961. Jack Lynch, the Minister for Industry and Commerce, was one of the main speakers, and he expressed his belief that the EEC would consider Ireland's recent application to join 'with sympathy and goodwill'. [7] Lynch believed that 'Ireland has a higher aim and ambition', one that could only be achieved through membership of the EEC, and he declared that the country was attracted 'by the wider objectives of the community' which they would work to achieve.

A major Eurosceptic speech was delivered by Viscount Hitchingbrooke, a Conservative MP and eldest son of the Earl of Sandwich. He dismissed the EEC as 'a patch-work' of ancient rivalries and feuds held together by the obsessive fear of communism. Suggesting that it was likely to end in failure, he called on Ireland to put its faith in the British Commonwealth. Roy Jenkins, the Labour MP, asked whether Britain could afford to stay out of the Common Market, and suggested that the answer was 'No'. He believed that pooling sovereignty was the only practical step for Britain and for Ireland.

The debate on 8 November 1961 was 'That Ireland's Patriots Died in Vain', and the motion was proposed by Senator Owen Sheehy Skeffington, who argued that the limited achievements since

---

6 Biographical Legacy and Research Foundation, *Who's Who in Nigeria* (https://blerf.org).

7 *The Irish Times*, 2 November 1961.

independence suggested that they had. Claiming that Ireland's dead, and Ireland herself, had been betrayed by the living, he said that the only ideal worth achieving was the 'effective betterment of the living conditions of the people'.[8] Noting that Ireland exported her best young people, he pointed out that at the same time there were 320,000 houses in the country (out of a total of 662,000) which did not have internal toilet facilities, and only 250,000 had piped water.

Seán MacBride opposed the motion and said he agreed with 90 per cent of what Sheehy Skeffington had said. He blamed a failure of successive governments in education for holding back the country's political evolution, and called it 'one of the most urgent needs of the nation'. Pointing to other failures, he suggested that possibly only a thousand people in the country backed the Rising in 1916, and only a handful of the leaders believed in social reform and they were all dead by the time independence was achieved. The motion was carried by 62 votes to 53.

A Dominican priest, Fr Joseph Collins, chaired the debate on 22 November 1961, 'That Marching to Disarm is Marching to Disaster'. The motion was passed by 50 votes to 27.[9] A week later, on 29 November, the debate was held in camera by order of the Board because of the controversial subject matter, 'That this House Condemns the Practice of Birth-Control'. It was the most attended debate of the year and after a long debate the motion was defeated by 82 votes to 35.[10]

Europe again featured in the debate on 31 January 1962, on the motion 'That this House had No Confidence in the British Government'. The motion was defeated by 25 votes to 22, and speaking afterwards from the chair, Dr David Thornley suggested that the Common Market was aimed at creating an enclave of prosperity in a world of poverty.[11] He suggested that Ireland was 'being carried into the Common Market on the Johnsonian principle of fleas upon fleas'.

Four women students attempted to attend the meeting of the

---

8 *The Irish Times*, 9 November 1961.

9 TCD MUN/SOC/HIST Uncatalogued Papers, 1960-69.

10 Ibid.

11 *The Irish Times*, 1 February 1962.

Society on 23 May 1962, but they were removed. The incident was reported to the Junior Dean, R.B. McDowell, who fined the students £2 each for breaking the rule on attendance. Ann Carr, a student from New York, was one of the organisers, and she was adamant afterwards that banning women from the Society was an anachronism. She said the old rule was not good for Trinity, and was part of the 'old regime' which needed to change.[12] Carr noted that debating was an important part of women's education and no other society in Trinity offered the same opportunity for debate.

The Correspondence Secretary, J. Michael Newcombe, from Stockport in England, was elected Auditor for the new session (winning by just two votes), and upon taking office he issued a firm policy statement on the admission of women to the Society, upholding the existing restrictions. As *Trinity News* noted, Newcombe was 'no woman hater ... He is simply convinced that the essentially masculine character of the Hist must be maintained'.[13] A talented speaker, unafraid to speak his mind, he found in the Society a way of nurturing 'his gift for outspoken expression of strong conviction'. Newcombe was a devout Catholic, and believed strongly that some reforms were necessary, and he was vocal in his campaign to persuade the Catholic hierarchy to appoint a Catholic chaplain in Trinity.

Newcombe chose the subject of 'Christ, Class and Communism' for his inaugural address on 31 October 1962, and delivered it 'with customary panache' according to the report in *Trinity News*.[14] Despite his religious views, Newcombe delivered a speech that was hugely critical of the Catholic Church as an institution, and blamed it for not doing enough to help the poor in the nineteenth century. This, he claimed, was the starting point of communism. He also suggested that children were more brutally treated in schools run by religious orders.

Bill Carritt, a member of the British Communist Party, proposed the vote of thanks, and suggested that the ideals of communism were built on a principle of communal morality, similar to Christ's

12 *The Irish Times*, 26 May 1962.

13 *Trinity News*, 8 November 1962.

14 *Trinity News*, 8 November 1962.

teachings.[15] According to the student reporter, he was 'the epitome of the leftist intellectual, with lean and hungry look, a high forehead and impressive spectacles', quoting everyone from Berthold Brecht to C.P. Snow.

Owen Sheehy Skeffington also spoke and called Ireland a 'deeply and sincerely materialistic country', before going on to attack both the Catholic Church and Communist states for being totalitarian. The barrister Donal Barrington spent much of his speech criticising the Auditor's paper, praising the Church for what it had done, and insisting that although there was no doubt that children had been treated brutally in schools, he did not believe the religious orders were any worse. The most entertaining speech was delivered by Professor A.A. Luce, who 'rolled his R's and was plaintive about new-fangled things like communism'.[16] One solution, he suggested, was for Mr Kruschchev to read the works of Mr Berkeley.

The chamber was packed on 28 November 1962 as a large crowd gathered to debate the continuing restriction of women. The motion was that 'This House Would not Admit Women', as the Society discussed, in the words of *The Irish Times,* 'a 215 year tradition' (going back to 1747).[17] Newcombe proposed the motion and claimed that he had not been impressed by the contribution of women to other debating societies in Ireland or Britain, suggesting that allowances had to be made for women speakers and the standard of debate was lowered as a result.

A number of Vice-Presidents of the Society spoke on the night. Owen Sheehy Skeffington opposed the motion with skill and passion, arguing that mixed membership would result in 'a more adult, more balanced, and more adjusted Society'. Reviewing other traditions that had been abandoned, such as fining members half a crown for sitting behind the chair which had been ignored that evening, he suggested the Society should adopt to a changing world, in the same way as Catholics had been admitted after 1793.

R.B. McDowell, another Vice-President of the Society, supported the ban, and claimed that to disregard the considerable differences

---

15 *The Irish Times*, 1 November 1962.

16 *Trinity News*, 8 November 1962.

17 *The Irish Times*, 29 November 1962.

between men and women in terms of tempo, manner and outlook was silly. Women, he believed, would be a distraction, and he suggested that there were other opportunities outside of the Society for men and women to mix. The motion, upholding the ban, was passed by a decisive majority, 173 votes to 39. In its review of the 'three hours of lively debate', *The Irish Times* noted that the arguments had ranged from 'the best interests of the Society to the love-making of pigs', but in the end the Society 'decided to remain an all-male entity'.

Newcombe was afterwards forced to defend the Society's stance in the pages of *Trinity News,* after criticisms about the continuing exclusion of women. In an article on 29 November 1962 he claimed that admitting women would 'involve the abolition of the present Society and the founding of a new debating society which might, perhaps, bear the name of College Historical Society but whose resemblance would go no further'.[18] However, in May 1963 the Society agreed to hold debates with the women-only society, 'the Eliz' on the condition that the women attended only as 'guests'.[19]

One of the best debates of the session took place on 13 February 1963 on the motion, 'That this House has No Confidence in the United Nations'. The Auditor proposed the motion, and those in favour included David McConnell, with another future Auditor, Eric Lowry, against. The debate was chaired by the Chief Justice (and future President) Cearbhall Ó Dálaigh, and was defeated by 27 votes to 20.

The Auditor for the 194th session, Eric Lowry, chose the United Nations as the subject of his inaugural address on 30 October 1963. He delivered what was described in *Trinity News* as a 'provocative assessment', accepting the idea of the UN as excellent, but also suggesting what needed to be done to make it more effective.[20] Ranbir Singh, the Charge d'Affaires for India also spoke and provided an historical perspective, arguing that the UN reflected the desire of people over centuries for unity and peace. Patrick O'Donovan of the *Observer* gave 'a sparkling speech' and paid tribute to the Irish delegation, which he felt had made a very real contribution to the

18 *Trinity News*, 29 November 1962.

19 *Trinity News*, 16 May 1963.

20 *Trinity News*, 7 November 1963.

United Nations. Charles Haughey, the Minister for Justice, was meant to speak, but was delayed in the Dáil, so Senator John Ross spoke in his place. According to *Trinity News* the meeting provided 'food for thought and considerable entertainment' and the general impression was one of optimism rather than idealism.

A Churchill family tradition continued to the next generation when Winston's son, Randolph, writer and former MP, addressed the Society on 6 November 1963. The motion was 'That Young Men Should be Angry', and Brendan Behan was also due to speak, but he didn't show. At the start of the meeting, the Auditor, Eric Lowry, read a statement that 'Mr Behan had a bad attack of diabetes in the morning. He went to see his doctor and we haven't been able to find him since.'[21]

Churchill began his speech by referencing the exclusion of women: 'Gentlemen, I'm sorry I can't say "Ladies and Gentlemen"', before pausing to add, 'Well, I'm not really.' In Society legend it is understood he was very drunk at the despatch box. One would certainly hope so. In a bellicose, rambling, over-the-top speech he banged the table a number of times, and instructed the gathering on how to do it properly. He claimed it was a well-established custom in debating circles and needed to be done at exactly the right time, such as by saying 'I will NOT' - and here he banged the table – 'put up with that.'

Criticising the 'modern silly prissy world', Churchill wondered if the absence of women allowed them to speak more freely, and he suggested that men 'ought to be castrated for safety's sake before you embark on a political career'. Regretting the absence of Behan, he suggested that it 'was only a knockabout bizarre masquerade' without him, and the excuse of being in hospital was only a euphemism.

Terence de Vere White reviewed the debate for *The Irish Times* and noted 'the orator was taking time to come to grips with his subject'. Churchill at one point took out some pages of notes, and admitted that he had spent the afternoon reading the Book of Job. 'It is full of very good stuff', he insisted, revealing that he had almost brought some copies with him, but 'you can probably get copies in the library'. Eventually Churchill returned to the motion, criticising

21 *The Irish Times*, 7 November 1963.

the Auditor, who had spoken earlier, for discussing South Africa. 'He knows nothing about it', Churchill claimed, 'and it was none of his bloody business.' It was one of the most bizarre and entertaining speeches ever delivered to the Society, enjoyable precisely because it was all over the place. As White concluded, 'It was very like a dream. Perhaps it WAS a dream. But it was noisy enough while it lasted.'

Motions that session included 'That God will Not Save the Queen' (an intervarsity debate on 20 November 1963), which was defeated by 41 votes to 31, and 'That this House Reveres the Memory of the British Empire' (15 April 1964). To commemorate the bicentenary of the birth of Wolfe Tone, R.B. McDowell delivered an entertaining lecture on his life on 26 November 1963 where he described him as a man of action rather than a scholar or profound thinker.

Brendan Corish, the leader of the Labour Party, spoke at the debate on 22 January 1964, 'That Ireland Needs a de Gaulle'. He reminded the House that democracy was only as strong or as weak as the people who made it, and appealed to Irish citizens to take a more active part in politics. Noting the tendency to refer to anyone in power as 'they', he pointed out that 'they' were really 'ourselves'.[22] Corish challenged the idea that a de Gaulle type was the answer to the problems of Ireland, dismissing his leadership as a 'type of mitigated dictatorship'. The motion was defeated. At the meeting the Society sent a message of congratulations to Frederick Boland, the President of the Society, on being elected the new Chancellor of the University of Dublin.

The Society found itself embroiled in controversy in February 1964 when it passed a motion expressing regret at the Board of the University banning an issue of *TCD* and forcing the editor to resign. A correspondent to *The Irish Times* criticised the students for standing up 'for students rights and freedom of speech' without knowing all of the facts.[23] This prompted Eric Lowry, the Auditor, to write a letter to the paper, published on 11 February, defending the action, saying that nineteen speakers spoke on the subject, they were well informed and the debate was serious.[24] As Lowry argued,

22 *The Irish Times*, 23 January 1964.

23 *The Irish Times*, 8 February 1964.

24 *The Irish Times*, 11 February 1964.

the motion showed that the students had demonstrated 'that we do care when the principle of freedom of speech is unjustifiably thrown to the winds' and he insisted that they had performed their duty and their right. By defending the right to freedom of speech Lowry had defended a tradition going back to the foundation of the Society.

On 29 April 1964 the motion was 'That Blood Sports be Banned', and it was presided over by Herbert Jackson, the chairman of the newly founded Irish Society for the Abolition of Cruel Sports. The motion was defeated by two votes, and Jackson accused some unscrupulous greyhound trainers of giving their dogs live hares and rabbits to give them a taste of blood. He also criticised fox hunting, and the practice of throwing a captured fox to the hounds, as comparable to throwing the Christians to the lions.[25]

'That Trinity's First Duty was to Ireland' was the motion on 6 May 1964, in a debate chaired by the University Chancellor, Frederick Boland. Proposing the motion, Sheehy Skeffington suggested that Trinity had something to give that was found nowhere else in Ireland, 'the principle and practice of using our minds freely on any topic'. Arguing that when students entered Trinity they learned how to defend their ideas, 'convincingly and intelligently', and that these ideas were either strengthened or abandoned as a result. Kingsmill Moore opposed the motion and suggested that a university's first duty was to itself, 'to be a leader of all thought, and a disseminator for all thought'. The motion was defeated by 57 votes to 36. Speaking from the chair, Boland admitted that he did not agree with the result and would have voted in favour of the motion. Praising the Hist, he said that debating societies were one of the most valuable things in a democracy, because they enabled people to express ideas and convictions freely.[26]

The Auditor for the 195th session, David McConnell, chose 'A Terrible Beauty' as the title of his inaugural address on 6 November 1964, and delivered what Owen Sheehy Skeffington described as 'a balanced, thoughtful, charitable and forward-looking paper' on the progress and problems of the Irish state since independence.[27] Calling for greater access to foreign markets as a way of supporting

25 TCD MUN/SOC/HIST Uncatalogued Papers, 1960-69.

26 *The Irish Times*, 7 May 1964.

27 *Trinity News*, 12 November 1964.

Irish agriculture, McConnell praised the two programmes for economic expansion in 1958 and 1963 as national attempts to solve the problems in the economy.[28]

The new Minister for Justice, Brian Lenihan, replied to the address, and called on political parties, trade unions, employment and farmer organisations, as well as the people of Ireland, to join together in 'an act of faith in the future of our country.[29] He suggested that partisanship and sectional differences were luxuries which could not be afforded at that time, when Britain had imposed a 15 per cent levy on Irish goods.

In advance of the meeting McConnell had invited Fr James McDyer to speak, a pioneering priest who had established the Glencolumcille Folk Village in Co. Donegal, praised in *The Irish Times* as 'The miracle of Glencolumcille'.[30] Unfortunately McDyer was refused permission to attend, admitting to McConnell that he had tried twice to approach 'the proper quarters; but 'the fuse burned out before it reached target'.[31] However, he recommended Peadar O'Donnell in his place, providing a contact number, admitting 'how earnestly I would wish to be with you on that night!'

O'Donnell, now considered 'one of the most influential socialist republican theorists and an important voice of dissent in twentieth-century Ireland', accepted the invitation to speak, returning to the Society he had first addressed in 1936.[32] As Fearghal McGarry writes in the *Dictionary of Irish Biography*, O'Donnell 'was prominent in the Irish Campaign for Nuclear Disarmament and served as its president in the early 1960s. He was a supporter of African anti-colonial movements such as that against apartheid. In later years he was involved in the 'Save the West' campaign.' In his speech to the Society O'Donnell regretted that the people of the west of Ireland had suffered the most economically and in terms of emigration. Closing the night, Owen Sheehy Skeffington argued that the

28 TCD MUN/SOC/HIST Uncatalogued Papers, 1960-69.

29 *The Irish Times*, 7 November 1964.

30 *The Irish Times*, 24 January 1963.

31 Fr James McDyer to David McConnell, 13 August 1964 (Private collection, David McConnell papers).

32 Fearghal McGarry, 'Peadar O'Donnell', *DIB*.

measure of freedom won after 1916 had not been enough and that social freedom was needed to achieve the 'terrible beauty' mentioned in the Auditor's paper.

Apartheid was debated once again that session, with the motion 'That this House would Boycott South Africa' on 25 November 1964. The best speech of the evening, one that was cheered for several minutes and reported in detail afterwards, was by Joe Slovo, a white South African barrister with the Anti-Apartheid Association, who was also a leading figure in the military wing of the ANC. In later years, Slovo helped negotiate the end of apartheid, and became Minister for Housing in Nelson Mandela's first Government. Slovo claimed that no other country in the world imposed such a cruel and barbaric system on black people as South Africa, and he suggested that this was why its government cheered acts of cruelty against black people elsewhere in the world, for example, at Little Rock or the Congo. It was, he said, 'because it seemed to justify their way of life'.[33] Suggesting that Verwoerd had not 'a monopoly of racial evil', he noted that 'he has cornered the market in pernicious practices against the black man'. 'Conditions in South Africa', he said, 'form a daily insult to all civilized people, white or black' and he listed all of the things that could get a black person in trouble, including being sent to jail for being friendly with a white woman, not holding the proper pass, or being out past a certain time. It was an extraordinary speech, laying bare the reality of racial oppression in South Africa, and *The Irish Times* reported it in detail with the headline 'Trinity students cheer anti-apartheid speech'.

The poet, Micheal O'Siadhail, entered Trinity in 1964 and won the maiden's speaker prize in the Society in his first term as well as the Scottish-Irish debating competition. He served on Committee and was elected Correspondence Secretary unopposed for the 1966-67 session, but he resigned because he felt 'that debating and arguing only one side of a case you might not fully support separated heart and mind in a way that was unhealthy for a poet'.[34] His friendships,

33 *The Irish Times*, 26 November 1964.

34 Micheal O'Siadhail, 'Facing each other', in Tom Greggs, Rachel Muers and Simeon Zahl (eds), *The Vocation of Theology Today: A Festschrift for David Ford* (Eugene, OR, 2013), p. 361.

however, with members of the Society continued, in particular with David Ford, who went on to serve as Auditor. Combining innovation and tradition, O'Siadhail's collections *The Chosen Garden, Our Double Time, The Gossamer Wall: Poems in Witness to the Holocaust, Love Life,* and *Globe* confirmed his reputation as one of the leading Irish poets, with their profound meditations on life, love, despair, and competing histories.[35]

The exclusion of women from the Society continued to be a source of contention. Upon taking office, McConnell established a subcommittee, chaired by Michael Cameron, the Treasurer, to look into the question, and gather opinions from the members on the subject. Independent of this, Aideen McCloskey and eleven other female students circulated a petition to show support for admitting women, and this was accepted by the sub-committee as evidence of wider views. Reporting on these developments, *The Irish Times* assessed the likelihood of change in what it called 'this traditionally "misogynist" society'.

Conor Cruise O'Brien, now Vice-Chancellor of the University of Ghana, was one of the people who responded to the survey, writing a letter on headed notepaper on 11 January 1965, and he declared that he strongly opposed 'the present system of complete exclusion of women'.[36] He suggested that 'the effect on the Society and the College if women were admitted could not fail to be one of enrichment'. And he noted, from his experience of other mixed debating societies, that women were good debaters 'with little of the exhibitionist element which used in my days to be often characteristic of the young male orator'.

To mark the 150th anniversary of the birth of Thomas Davis, the Society organized a major lecture on 1 December 1964 on his life and legacy by the great historian, Professor J.C. Beckett. Arguing that Davis was by no means a great literary figure, and was a flawed historian, Beckett explored the secret of his fame. It was, he suggested, because Davis expressed in practical form the ideals for which he stood, 'an all-embracing concept of Irish nationalism'.[37]

35 Marc Caball and David F. Ford (eds), *Musics of Belonging: The Poetry of Michael O'Siadhail* (Dublin, 2007).

36 TCD MUN/SOC/HIST Uncatalogued papers [1960-69].

37 *The Irish Times*, 2 December 1964.

Accusing Davis of showing 'an optimistic misunderstanding' in using history as political propaganda, he suggested that Davis had influenced a form of nationalism which perpetuated divisions which he himself 'had given his young life's work to break down'. R.B. McDowell also spoke and said that the Young Ireland period interested him immensely because it was a time when intellectuals dominated the political scene.

One of the biggest debates of the session was on 3 February 1965, an intervarsity debate on the motion 'That the Easter Rising Stands Betrayed'. The debate was chaired by Hugh McAteer, a former chief of staff of the IRA and the brother of Eddie McAteer, the leader of the Nationalist Party in Northern Ireland. David McConnell, the Auditor, introduced him at the start as someone who had been jailed in 1936 for seven years, in 1942 for fifteen years, and had spent various other spells in prison.[38] Proposing the motion, McConnell described the Easter Rising as one of the strangest events in the history of Ireland, one that was not supported at the time, and which brought together poets, socialists, and many others, to try and create a new Ireland. In a characteristically nuanced and eloquently delivered speech, McConnell regretted that the founding fathers' guarantee of equality of opportunity was not being fulfilled. Suggesting that people succeeded in Ireland, not because of their abilities, but on the wealth of their parents, he said that until there was equality of opportunity for all the principles of the Easter Rising were betrayed. There were also speakers from UCD and Columbia University in New York, before the motion was defeated by 31 votes to 21.

Speaking from the chair, McAteer attacked the recent visit of Taoiseach Seán Lemass to Northern Ireland, describing the crossing of the border as 'the greatest betrayal since 1916'. Recognising that those who wished to continue the fight of 1916 were dismissed as 'a lunatic fringe', McAteer noted that Pearse and his fellow rebels had been called the same, as he asked for a new spirit of sacrifice to continue their work.

In March 1965, McConnell and his debating partner, Cian Ó hÉigeartaigh, won *The Irish Times* debating competition, proposing

38 *The Irish Times*, 4 February 1965.

the motion 'That Ireland's Need is Socialism'.[39] At the end of the session, McConnell was awarded the gold medal for oratory.

Martyn Lewis, (later a successful broadcaster) proposed a motion in the Society to admit women in 1965 and he argued that 'it is intolerable that women who enjoy full membership of this university should not be allowed to debate in the premier debating Society in College'.[40] He suggested that the wearisome clinging to tradition was not in the best interests of Society, and was 'hopelessly incompatible with the social sphere to which we all belong'. He concluded that 'Society in general has emancipated women, but the College Historical Society has not'.

Reviewing the session in *The Irish Times,* a student noted that 'Quite consciously the Hist this year has been more Irish, more left-wing, and more interested in science than at any time in the recent past'. This was directly down to the range of interests of McConnell (who went on to become Professor of Genetics in Trinity and President of the Society) and his Committee.

Michael Cameron, a student from England, was elected Auditor for the 196th session, defeating Ó hÉigeartaigh. The session began well, with a successful inaugural meeting on 5 November 1965. The subject was 'Ireland's influence on British politics', and Cameron used his paper to announce his support for women becoming members of the Society, to some cheers. He then went on to praise the British Labour Party and attack the Liberals. In his response, James Dillon, the former Fine Gael Leader, attacked the main political parties for being 'flocks of sheep led by hard-faced men'. In what was described by *The Irish Times* as 'a masterly performance', he took up a position a few paces to the right of the lectern and, 'with his voice booming out down the hall, he chided' the audience with being afraid of freedom, 'afraid of sneezing except according to a plan'. 'My hackles rise at the mention of a plan', he roared, 'I don't want to be planned'.

There was some surprise later in November when Cameron read a paper to the Philosophical Society, the first time that an Auditor of the Society had done so. His paper was on 'The life and

---

39 *The Irish Times*, 8 March 1965.

40 *Trinity News*, 29 April 1965.

Achievements of Pandit Nehru' and he described Nehru and Churchill as 'the two greatest Harroverians who died within a few months of each other'.[41]

In November 1965 the minute book of Burke's Club was stolen, for the third time in its history. It was later returned in an unmarked package in 1967, and the story made the front page of *The Irish Times*.[42]

The Society was engulfed in a College controversy in February 1966 after it sent a team to the UK to compete in *University Challenge.* Granada television approached June Rodgers, a student from Co. Antrim studying English, who had taken part in the competition for the Phil in 1963, enquiring about the possibility of Trinity sending a team. Rodgers immediately approached the Hist, thinking it was only fair that the honour should be rotated. Unfortunately, Cameron appears to have left selecting a team until the last minute, and chose a team with the help of Rodgers. A notice asking for participants was posted, although Rodgers said afterwards that 'some people who replied to our advertisement were not contacted, because we believed they were not suitable at all'.[43] Two Scholars, Mary Bourke (later Robinson) and David Norris were approached and agreed to take part, and the rest of the team was made up of David Wagstaff (former Correspondence Secretary) and Michael Shiels, the Records Secretary. It was, Norris admitted later, 'put together in a not entirely democratic fashion'.[44]

The competition did not go well. In his autobiography, David Norris (by now a Senator representing the University of Dublin), described how they defeated their opponents, Somerville College, Oxford, in the dress rehearsal and this led to 'a surfeit of confidence'. They relaxed during the break and Norris remembered a few of them 'downing a celebratory gin in the hospitality room'. The real contest went very differently, with the Trinity team having lost its edge, 'and our expected victory march began to unravel'. At one point, the team got so many questions wrong that their score threatened to go into

41 *The Irish Times*, 19 November 1965.

42 *The Irish Times*, 24 April 1967.

43 *Trinity News*, 10 February 1966.

44 David Norris, *A Kick Against the Pricks: The Autobiography* (Dublin, 2013), p. 62.

minus figures. In the event, the final score was 150 to 50. As Norris recounted, 'there was an awful stick when we came home, and *Trinity News* lambasted us for bringing "shame" on the university'. But it proved a ratings success, as 'the audience loved it as it was like a public execution' and 'it became so famous that it was repeated on ITV on several occasions'.

Notable debates that session included one chaired by Charles Haughey, the Minister for Agriculture, on 9 February, on the motion 'That this House Would Turn Swords into Ploughshares'. The motion was carried. 'That the Press is Too Powerful' was the motion debated on 23 February 1966. The Librarian, Francis Sheehy Skeffington, the son of Owen and Andrée, opposed the motion and argued that a press which was free, diverse and independent could never be too powerful. He suggested that it was a weak press that was a sign of a totalitarian press. The motion was defeated, and Brian Inglis, the journalist and broadcaster, who chaired the meeting, suggested that Irish newspapers were more responsible and better balanced than British newspapers.

Representing the Society, David McConnell and Cian Ó hÉigeartaigh won *The Irish Times* debating competition for the second time in a row on 9 February 1966, speaking on the motion 'That this House Would Rather Live in any Age than its Own'.[45] The team went on to win the Observer Mace competition against teams from the UK and Ireland, the first victory in the competition for the Society. In recognition of this achievement, the Society awarded special medals to both speakers to mark the occasion.[46]

1966 was the 50th anniversary of the Easter Rising, and on 14 April 1966 the Society passed a resolution congratulating the members of Misneach, an Irish-language activist group, 'on their courageous stand'. These were thirteen people, mainly students from Trinity and UCD, went on hunger strike to protest against the way the Irish language was being treated by the State. The protest lasted from Easter Monday to the following Saturday and the motion praised them for protesting against 'the non-achievement of the aims of the signatories of 1916'.[47]

---

45 *The Irish Times*, 10 February 1966.

46 TCD MUN/SOC/HIST Uncatalogued papers [1960-69].

47 *The Irish Times*, 15 April 1966.

The Second Vatican Council, which had concluded in December 1965, was the subject of the debate on 27 April 1966, with the motion 'That the Vatican Council was a Flash in the Pan'. Norman St John-Stevas, the Conservative MP and writer, told the meeting that he believed in their lifetime they would see 'every religious service celebrated in common, with the exception of the Eucharist'.[48] Cian Ó hÉigeartaigh supported the motion and looked at the trends which existed before the Council and those which emerged afterwards, before concluding that the real reforms had started before. He criticised the Catholic church for its position on papal infallibility, divorce, mixed marriages and 'various other theological points', as working against Christian unity. Religious segregation in schools, he said, went against the principles of Wolfe Tone, and meant that real unity was as far away as ever. The motion was defeated.

The former British Prime Minister, Sir Alec Douglas-Home, was the star attraction for the debate on 4 May 1966 on the motion 'That in Politics Principles Should Give Way to Pragmatism'. There were queues of people waiting to get into the GMB, for a debate that was also attended by the British Ambassador, the Provost, and the President of the Society. As one student commented at the time, 'It's good for the Hist to get big names, but why do they always have to be Tories?'[49] Douglas-Home's luggage had been misdirected on the way over, so he was forced to borrow evening dress from the Provost. As chair, Douglas-Home spoke at the end of the debate, after the motion had been narrowly defeated. He began by joking about the number of speakers who had used dictionaries to define 'principle' and 'pragmatism', saying he was surprised to find that there were so many dictionaries at Trinity; at his university they had only written the one.[50]

Addressing the confrontation between the Communist and free worlds, Douglas-Home suggested that it had its roots in the early days of the Russian revolution, when the principle that the ends justified the means meant that force was believed to be justified. He claimed that it was only when this force had been met with greater

48 *The Irish Times*, 29 April 1966.

49 *Trinity News*, 9 December 1965.

50 *The Irish Times*, 5 May 1966.

force that some sort of pragmatic formula for co-existence had been found. Criticising the principle of egalitarianism for compelling people to be equal, restricting liberty, he argued instead for individual liberty. He concluded by discussing one of the great paradoxes of modern life, the fact that technological advances were bringing people closer together but nationalism was driving people apart. The United Nations, he believed, was the best combination of idealistic principle and pragmatism that existed in the world.

During the summer there was some public criticism of the Society for being allegedly anti-Irish, but the charges were answered ably by Cian Ó hÉigeartaigh in the letters page of *The Irish Times*, who revealed that some of the Society's official minutes were recorded in Irish (a practice he himself had started) and that the majority of the officers and competitive speakers were also Irish.[51]

(Robert) Brian Williamson was elected Auditor for the 197th session and delivered his inaugural paper on 'Television – Its Impact on Politics' on Friday 4 November 1966. Speakers included the 7th Earl of Longford, who at this time was Leader of the House of Lords and Lord Keeper of the Privy Seal.

The debate on the motion 'That this House Looks Forward to a United Europe' on 9 November 1966 was interrupted by eight women, led by June Rodgers, now a final year student. The idea had come to Rodgers earlier in the day and she arranged the plan with the help of a member of the Society. On the way in they were spotted by one man, but he was so surprised he didn't say a word.

A diversion was arranged to allow them to get through the entrance, and they burst through, taking seats around the chamber. As *Trinity News* reported afterwards, 'Like so many Mafia gunmen, the eight moved in for the kill.' Or, as Rodgers said afterwards, 'like a knife through hot butter' they were in.[52] Wearing her academic gown, Rodgers presented herself before the Auditor, Brian Williamson, who was described as 'astonished' in *The Irish Times*, and asked for permission to address the Society. 'There was absolute panic on the part of the officers of the Society', Rodgers told an *Irish Times* journalist afterwards, and a sub-committee was immediately

51 *The Irish Times*, 9 August 1966.

52 *Trinity News*, 17 November 1966.

established to discuss the matter. The request was rejected and the students were forcibly removed from the chamber, having been on the floor of the House for about seven minutes in total. The British Labour MP, Patrick Gordon Walker, was proposing the motion, and he clapped loudly in support of the students. Walker had an interesting history. He was appointed Foreign Secretary by Harold Wilson in 1964, despite having lost his seat in the general election, and it was arranged that he would stand for a safe seat so he could return to parliament. However, he lost this election as well, and was forced to resign as Foreign Secretary. He returned to parliament in the general election earlier in March 1966. He later became a member of the European Parliament.

A group of students in gowns gathered at the steps of the GMB on 16 November but were refused entry to the debate. The motion was 'That this House Regrets the Offences against the State Act' and it was chaired by Alfred George Hinds, who could best be described as a celebrity criminal. Jailed for a jewellery robbery in 1953, Hinds organized three separate escapes from high security prisons, developing a reputation as 'Houdini' Hinds. Earlier that year he published an account of his escapes, and the successful libel action he had taken against his arresting officer, and became a much sought after speaker on the circuit. The motion was amended on the night, changing the word 'Regrets' to 'abhors' and it passed by 74 votes to 9. Speaking from the chair, Hinds said that 'any government should give a citizen the right to speak against it, but not the right to use or advocate violence'.[53]

Other debates that session included one supporting euthanasia (18 January 1967), which was defeated, and the traditional vote of no confidence in the Government (1 March 1967), which was carried. Sanctions against Rhodesia were debated on 12 April 1967, while on 19 April 1967 the motion was 'That the Americans Should Get Out of Vietnam'. The Australian Ambassador to Ireland, Hugh Robertson, spoke at the debate about Vietnam and supported the United States in its war which he said had won the admiration of the Australian people.[54] The motion was carried.

---

53 *The Irish Times*, 18 November 1966.

54 *The Irish Times*, 20 April 1967.

There 'were howls of indignation from the members', according to *The Irish Times,* when five female students found a way into the debate on 25 January 1967 after arranging another diversion.[55] The meeting broke up in disorder, as fighting broke out between those who supported the women and those who wanted them ejected. Professor David Greene, of the Department of Celtic Studies in Trinity, who was chairing the meeting, exited the chamber, followed by the officers and the guest speakers. The motion was 'That a Nation Without a Language is a Nation Without Spirit' and one of the women students said afterwards that she had organized the protest because it was an issue that affected both men and women, and therefore the opinion of women should be heard. After a short adjournment, the meeting resumed in another part of the building. In the official record of the Society it is noted that 'this debate was disrupted somewhat by the invasion of women'.[56]

Michael Foot, the Labour MP and 'rebel with so many causes', was the guest speaker for the debate on 26 April 1967 on the motion 'That the System of Government by Party has not been Beneficial to Public Welfare'.[57] Foot admitted that he had been unsure whether to propose or oppose the motion, but eventually decided against it. There was some confusion when Foot also claimed to have come to Dublin primarily to take part in the tercentenary celebrations of the birth of Jonathan Swift, claiming that Swift was 'one of the most effective and vituperative enemies of the party system'.[58] At the time there was much debate about a possible merger between Trinity and UCD, and a student heckled, 'He would not approve of us joining up with UCD'. According to the report in *The Irish Times*, Foot 'blandly agreed that the Dean probably would not, and then proceeded to the serious business of defending the party system'.

Attacking political parties for demanding rigid obedience of its members, Foot insisted that the idea of a consensus on political opinions was a dangerous one. Later in the debate a student asked him 'Do you not think that Harold Wilson is a twister?' Foot replied that

55 *The Irish Times*, 26 January 1967.

56 TCD MUN/SOC/HIST Uncatalogued papers, 1960-69.

57 *The Irish Times*, 27 April 1967.

58 *The Irish Times*, 27 April 1967.

he did not approve of such language, and if he was going to call Wilson anything 'I'll choose my own language. And if that was a subject for debate we could go on for a long time.' Frank Sherwin, the colourful independent TD, also spoke at the debate and claimed that 'Democracy is a great moral conception, but in practice it has failed'.

'TCD to "Open gates wide to the world"' was the headline in *The Irish Times*, following the honorary members debate on 3 May 1967.[59] George Dawson, the respected Professor of Genetics, said 'to hell with tradition', as he argued that 'what we are is more important that what we have been'. He stressed that as Trinity became more international in its outlook 'we must see the value of things that are new as well as old'. John Ross also spoke at this debate, and suggested that the quota of English students coming to Trinity should be reduced from 30 to 10 per cent because they were dominating the clubs and societies. The Auditor, Williamson, argued that Trinity could not play a part in Ireland until it played a part in Europe.

During the year Williamson invited Maurice Macmillan, the son of the British prime minister, over to Trinity to debate a motion about the sons of great men. A friendship was struck up, and after graduating in economics, Williamson went to work for him as a private secretary, later serving as a kind of special adviser in Government in the 1970s. Becoming part of the City of London establishment, he was appointed chair of the company Liffe, and was later knighted.[60]

William (Gully) Stanford was the Auditor for the 198th session and he chose 'Church and State in Ireland since 1922' as the subject of his inaugural address on 25 October 1967. From the Auditor's correspondence we get an insight into what it was like securing guests at this time. A letter was sent on 1 July to the Roman Catholic Archbishop of Dublin, John Charles McQuaid, inviting him to speak, but McQuaid declined on 4 July saying that he feared he was 'not competent to speak on the relations between the Anglican Church and the Irish State since 1922'.[61] Having deliberately misrepresented the invitation, McQuaid wished him well and

59 *The Irish Times*, 4 May 1967.

60 *Irish Independent*, 24 June 2001.

61 Private correspondence courtesy of Gully Stanford.

expressed his hope that he would 'speak with justice' during his term in office. Undaunted, Stanford wrote to McQuaid a second time on 17 July clarifying that he would be speaking about the relations between the Catholic Church and the State as 'it would be illogical in an ambitious paper to concentrate on a minority church whose dealings as such with the State have been, naturally, minor.' He concluded by suggesting that 'Your Grace's presence appears essential – whatever comment you may choose to make'. This line seems to have irritated McQuaid, who responded on 28 July, suggesting that he could not see 'how my presence at your treatment of the Catholic Church's relations with the Irish State could be at all regarded as essential'. Agreeing with the Auditor that his paper was 'ambitious', he suggested that he did not believe Stanford had 'the evidence that would allow a full and just estimate of a thesis so vast and so complex'. Stanford made one last attempt to change McQuaid's mind on 10 August but it was not a case of third time lucky. A formal typed letter on behalf of the Archbishop was sent on 7 October declining the invitation.

Stanford also invited the Minister for Education, Donogh O'Malley, to speak at the inaugural. O'Malley declined, suggesting that 'the present moment is perhaps not the best for my direct participation', and addressing his response to 'Professor Stanford'. It seems he had mistakenly believed that the invitation had come from Stanford's father, W.B. Stanford, the Professor of Greek, and said he looked forward to hearing 'from you the conclusions you have drawn from your wide experience and wisdom in the matter'.

On the night of the inaugural Stanford accused the first Inter-Party Government of 'an unscrupulous act of cowardice' for deserting Noel Browne during the Mother and Child crisis and there was 'prolonged and long applause'.[62] Other speakers included the Archbishop of Dublin, George Otto Simms, and Professor Patrick Corish, of St Patrick's College Maynooth.

Erskine Childers, the Minister for Posts and Telegraphs, chaired the debate on 1 November 1967 on the motion 'That this House has Confidence in Radio Telefis Éireann'. He used it as an opportunity to condemn as 'completely wrong' the 'hustling, rude and impatient

62 *The Irish Times*, 26 October 1967.

interviewing in RTE'. During the debate itself, Stanford opposed the motion and claimed that RTE spent too much money importing externally made trash and should concentrate on a small amount of well-made home programmes. David Ford, the Librarian, proposed the motion and argued that a television service should not be expected to be a schoolteacher to the nation. He suggested that much of the criticism of RTE sprang from 'the rage of Irish society at seeing its own face on the screen'. The motion was defeated.

The former Taoiseach, Seán Lemass, chaired the debate on 17 January 1968 on the motion 'That Trade Unions have forgotten the working man'. Controversy erupted half way through the debate when a speaker opposing the motion, Eoin Ó Murchú, the former Censor in the Society, attempted to introduce a privileged motion to replace 'trade unions' in the motion with 'Fianna Fáil'. Stanford refused to take the motion, at which Ó Murchú attempted to adjourn the debate so they could consider the 'improper conduct' of the Auditor. For twenty-minutes the debate was at a standstill, as Stanford and Ó Murchú argued the point back and forth, and their exchanges 'were the subject of cheers and counter-cheers and, indeed, boos and counter-boos'.[63] During it all, Lemass 'sat unmoved, except for the occasional flicker of amusement'. In the end, Ó Murchú withdrew his motion, saying he did not want to deprive the House of an opportunity to hear from Lemass. Ó Murchú was a founding member of the Republican Club in Trinity and went on to have a successful career as a writer and journalist.

The original motion was carried by 48 votes to 23 and Lemass began his speech by suggesting that many proposition and opposition speakers had been unfair in blaming Fianna Fáil for all that was wrong. He reminisced about a time he had asked to meet a delegation from the different unions representing the Great Southern Railway and discovered that there were 33 different unions involved and they each sent four or five delegates to the meeting. Fragmentation, he believed, was the great weakness of the trade union movement, and he suggested that free organized trade unions were vital to the progress of a free democratic society.

The Society provided a public forum for politicians to get a

63 *The Irish Times*, 18 January 1968.

message across, sometimes directed against opponents, sometimes directed against those on their own side. Senator Garret FitzGerald spoke to the Society on 7 February 1967 and used it as an opportunity to criticise his Fine Gael party colleague, Oliver J. Flanagan, over comments he had made on television defending jobbery. In a speech that was widely reported, FitzGerald insisted that if Flanagan did not accept party 'policy against corruption he is in conflict with his party and has an honourable course open to him – resignation'.[64] Politicians knew that the Hist was an effective medium for sending a political message, because the debates were reported in the national newspapers, and it ensured publicity for what they wanted to say.

Oxford, Cambridge, Edinburgh and Durham came to Trinity to debate the motion 'That Honour Sinks where Commerce Long Prevails' on 14 February 1968. However, the speakers from the Oxford Union decided to boycott the event on the night because of the continuing exclusion of women. They said they could not associate with a society which barred women students, especially as their own President, Geraldine Jones, was a woman (and indeed the first woman President of the Union).[65] During the debate, Stanford argued that honour did not live with commerce, citing the continuation of the war in Vietnam as proof of that. Afterwards the Oxford Union announced that its boycott of the Hist was likely to continue, and in an interview Jones said that 'We wouldn't like it if someone said "Well, you can send your people provided they're not Jews or Negroes or Roman Catholics"'.

The proposed merger with UCD was debated on 28 February 1968, with the controversial and attention-grabbing motion, 'That Merger Means Murder'. The Minister for Education who had suggested the idea, Donogh O'Malley, made an unexpected appearance at the debate, though he chose not to speak. However, the fact that the Minister considered it worth hearing the arguments on both sides, and gauging reactions, is revealing. Proposing the motion, R.B.D. French, a lecturer in English in Trinity, in the best speech of the night, attacked those running Trinity for being

64 *The Irish Times*, 8 February 1968.
65 *The Irish Times*, 15 February 1968.

dominated by what he called 'a desire to please.'[66] He called the proposed merger a forced marriage, likely to end in divorce, and was nothing less than an extremely dangerous experiment in which the dice were heavily loaded against success. Opposing the motion, Professor J.J. O'Meara of UCD called on the staffs of the two institutions to prepare a common policy document as the best way forward. The motion was carried by 108 votes to 32.

Donogh O'Malley died a month later, and in the reports of his death it was mentioned that his decision to attend the debate was an example of his willingness to hear arguments on both sides of an issue, and to be influenced by other thinking.[67] At the meeting on 10 April 1968 the Auditor paid tribute to O'Malley saying that, after forty years of educational stagnation, he was the first Minister for Education worthy of the name.[68]

The debate on 10 April was on the motion 'That Racial Integration is a Dangerous Delusion', and it was defeated by 45 votes to 25. A motion 'That this House would Support a National Lottery' was carried by 26 votes to 19 a fortnight later, on 24 April. Lord Chalfont, the Labour Peer and Minister for State with Responsibility for Common Market Affairs, chaired the debate on 1 May 1968 on the motion 'That Peking is the Rome of Tomorrow'. Declan Budd, the Record Secretary, proposed the motion and predicted that 'just as the past of Rome is a glorious past, so the future of China is a glorious future'.[69] Mao Tse Tung, he argued, was 'the great statesman and political theorist of this century'. Frank Bannister opposed the motion and predicted that China would never become a world power or a world threat. The motion was defeated by 40 votes to 18. Speaking from the chair, Chalfont called for a united and integrated Europe as the only way of dealing with the challenges of the future. Discussing China's potential to become a great power, he said there was an immediate and urgent need 'to bring the China of today into the community of nations'.

The motion for the honorary members debate that session was

---

66 *The Irish Times*, 29 January 1968.

67 *The Irish Times*, 11 March 1968.

68 *The Irish Times*, 11 April 1968.

69 *The Irish Times*, 2 May 1968.

'That the West Can Never be Saved', and an otherwise dull debate was enlivened by a spiky, if controversial speech by R. B. McDowell. Suggesting that if the West of Ireland was dying it should be let die, McDowell attacked the campaigners on the issue for representing 'a form of selfish, bogus nationalism which made him want to reach for his gun'.[70]

Five women were made Fellows on 10 June 1968, making it possible for a woman to become Provost, and from January 1969 female students were allowed rooms on campus. This all increased the pressure on the Society to admit women. Conor Cruise O'Brien, a Vice-President of the Society since 1964, spoke at the inaugural meeting of the Philosophical Society and he expressed concern at the state of the Historical Society which excluded 'half the human race' from membership.

The new Auditor of the Society, David Ford, revealed at his inaugural meeting on 'Student Power' on 23 October 1968 that he was in favour of admitting women. One of his guest speakers, David Adelstein, one of the leaders of the Radical School Alliance in Britain, said at the same meeting that he would never have come over to speak if he had known women were excluded. A white South African, Adelstein was a former Students Union president at the LSE, where he was still a student. In an excoriating speech, he attacked the Society's 'arrogant ceremonial and stultifying procedures of debate' and it was noted in *The Irish Times* that he was fortunate not to have been fined sixpence.[71] In a wide-ranging attack on teaching methods and values in modern universities, Adelstein argued that not only was the curriculum highly biased, but the teaching structures themselves were also. These comments were widely reported the next day. Also on the platform was Michael Foot MP, who said there was only a limited number of points on which he agreed with the advocates of student power. Criticising the occasional advocacy of violence by the supporters of student power, he argued that this was a betrayal of reason and argument and a betrayal of the greatest cause the Left possessed.

'TCD debate abandoned in uproar' was the headline on the front

70 *The Irish Times*, 9 May 1968.

71 *The Irish Times*, 30 October 1968.

page of *The Irish Times on* Thursday 14 November 1968 the day after a major intervarsity debate was meant to have taken place in Trinity. The motion was 'That this House would Uphold the Concept of a Just War', with teams from Aberystwyth, Belfast, Edinburgh, Durham and UCD, and Conor Cruise O'Brien in the chair. Before the competitive debate began a member of the Society, Bill McCormack, rose to move a suspension of standing orders so the admission of women could be considered, and began a lengthy filibuster. As *The Irish Times* reports, 'he continued to speak for 20 minutes in spite of constant appeals from the Auditor to desist, and an increasing barrage of comments and points of order from all sides'. 'As the noise increased', O'Brien decided to intervene from the chair. He said: 'there are certain principles on which I cannot pretend to remain impartial. The disorderly scene which is taking place tonight is the normal and expected result of a situation which has its root cause in social exclusiveness, whether racial, religious or sexual.'[72] He then asked for permission to leave the chair as he would not consent to remain until the question of admitting women was resolved. As he said afterwards, 'I did not think that I could simply sit there like a stuffed owl, which was what I apparently was expected to do.'[73]

At this, a member of the Society accused O'Brien of 'cheek and rudeness' in having accepted an invitation to chair despite knowing of the restriction. In reply, O'Brien said that he had not intended any discourtesy, but could no longer act as chairman, and with that he left the room. There was 'a great deal of scuffling and shouting, and even the exchange of a few blows' before McCormack's motion was voted on and declared lost. According to the report in the *Trinity News,* under the headline 'Suffragette Histeria', O'Brien knew what was coming, having arranged things with his daughter, Kate Cruise O'Brien, who was campaigning for women to be admitted.[74]

The Irish Times reported that the students from the other universities at first sat quietly and non-committedly while these extraordinary scenes went on around them. In one of the 'infrequent lulls' one was heard 'mildly inquiring' if there was any chance of

---

72 *The Irish Times*, 14 November 1968.

73 Ibid.

74 *Trinity News*, 21 November 1968.

getting on with the debate as originally arranged. But as the meeting descended into chaos they got up and left as a body, with one of them saying that they 'would not tolerate any more of this nonsense'. The meeting thus came to a halt abruptly, with *The Irish Times* wondering if some damage had been done 'to the prestige of the College Historical Society'.

At the meeting, the Censor, Joe Revington, spoke loudly in favour of women being admitted and it created a major fissure in the Society, with the Committee meeting the following week to debate whether to expel him and revoke his membership. After a heated discussion, the Committee voted by six votes to five to expel him, accusing him of flouting the rules of the Society in the way he pursued the issue of admitting women. This prompted the five members who had voted for him to remain to resign in protest. In later years, Revington boasted of the fact that he was the only student since Robert Emmet to have been expelled from the Society.[75]

The controversy reignited in the debate that evening. The motion was 'That this House Welcomes the Outcome of the US Presidential Election', but the real debate was over the civil war that was tearing the Society apart. At the start of the meeting, one of the remaining members of the Committee, the Treasurer, Victor Allen, declared his intention to resign, but denied it had anything to do with the recent controversy. As the debate began there were shouts of 'resign' directed at the remaining Committtee members, with one member of the Society appealing from the floor for calm. 'We don't want this put in the papers tomorrow', he said, in words that were quoted verbatim on the front page of *The Irish Times* the next day, as he expressed his hope that the College's name wouldn't be 'dragged through the mud'. At this point Allen asked for permission to state his reasons for resigning, but this was ruled out of order and he was told the matter would be discussed afterwards in private business. This prompted shouts of 'We want Hitler' from the angry crowd.

When the debate finally started, Dermot Ryan, the successful Dublin businessman, proposed the motion and expressed his great pleasure that he was there. This led to immediate shouts of 'Out'

75 Joe Revington, 'Irish Life and Lore Oral History' (www.irishlifeandlore.com).

and the Auditor asked him to confine himself to discussing the motion. Shane Ross also spoke, in favour of Richard Nixon, and he suggested that Nixon was best person to deal with Vietnam and the problem of race relations in America.

Afterwards Allen released a statement, which was reported in *The Irish Times*, saying that he had resigned because he was 'not prepared to accept revolutionary action'. Claiming that the events of the past few weeks had put a great nervous strain on the Committee members, he said that the laws of the Society were no longer being followed or respected. He also praised the Auditor for doing his best in 'a thankless task' and apologised for 'deserting him'.

In the days ahead there was talk of a special meeting of the Society to strip Conor Cruise O'Brien of his Vice-Presidency. However this would have required a five-sixths majority, and Ford did not believe this was likely. Ford, a supporter of women being admitted, said he believed O'Brien had harmed the cause and that he had met 'many people who've said they will not vote for women if individuals are going to try and bully the Society into a certain position.'[76]

With the Society in turmoil, and the civil war being played out in public, the continuing exclusion of women was no longer tenable. It all came to a head on the night of 4 December 1968 as the Society debated once again to end the ban. At the start of the evening two women attempted to crash the meeting, or so it was reported the next day, accompanied by twenty men who defended them from being ejected. As *The Irish Times* described it, 'blows were struck, eggs were thrown, and a Law student was pulled by the hair as he tried to push the women out'.[77] One over-enthusiastic member of the Boat Club rushed to the Chamber purely for the purposes of opposing the women. He told the journalists afterwards that he was proud to be a 'right wing reactionary', and that he would prefer if women were not allowed into Trinity at all. He declared proudly that 'If the 1,000 women were removed, 1,000 Irishmen could take their place, and men, after all, are the breadwinners'.

The architect of the campaign was Kate Cruise O'Brien and years

76 *The Irish Times*, 20 November 1968.

77 *The Irish Times*, 5 December 1968.

later she reflected on the night and what had really happened. She said that panic had ensued when she had announced that she planned on attending the debate, though she admitted she was bluffing, and 'had no real intention of invading such a fiercely defended male domain'.[78] However, the members were not to know this. O'Brien put on her academic gown and went with her best friend and sat outside the theatre. It was intended to persuade the Society that a 'female invasion' was imminent and it had the desired effect. Four men were sent to guard the doors and others watched the windows and balcony. As O'Brien recounted, 'male hysteria invaded the debate more than I could have done'. Indeed she later remembered how the member from the Boat Club (she misremembered him as a Committee member) told the media that 'Troublemakers and Amazons' had interrupted an historic debate. According to O'Brien there had been no interruption, but the men's own fear had made them think that one was coming. Answering the charge that women could not debate effectively because they lacked the necessary emotional detachment, O'Brien revealed that she had 'never witnessed collective female hysteria which came near the collective and virulent male hysteria that I witnessed on that night in Trinity'.

According to *The Irish Times* the next day there had been an interruption and it lasted fifteen minutes until the women were finally forced out, and they continued their protest outside, 'repeatedly tampered with the fuse box, causing the lights to go on and off'. As the debate went on four men, one armed with a three-foot baton, guarded the entrance so there would be no further interruptions. After three hours of heated debate, the Society voted by 82 votes to 67 to admit women. History was finally made. Speaking as Auditor, David Ford said, 'I am delighted to have women as members. I think they will revitalise this Society and we shall enter a new era.'

The new era began on 15 January 1969 when women spoke officially in the Society for the first time. The headline in *The Irish Times* the next day was: 'Feminine voices heard at the "Hist":

78 *Irish Independent*, 12 March 1987.

emancipation conceded after 199 years'.[79] The motion was 'That this House Reveres the Memory of Emily Pankhurst' and Sheelagh Murnaghan, the British Liberal MP, chaired the debate, an event she celebrated as 'this occasion of reform'. The meeting was described as 'a rumbustious first meeting' of the term, with almost twenty speakers, including five female students who were 'uproariously introduced as making their maiden speeches'. The meeting was packed, with many women standing. Some appealed to the Auditor to ask the men to give up their seats, but Ford, 'who was occasionally audible, said he couldn't'. As a result 'the men remained seated and the women remained on their feet'.

The first speaker of the night, and the first woman to speak officially at the Society, was Rosaleen Mills, the Vice Principal of Sutton Park School and a lifelong champion of women's rights. Mills defended Pankhurst robustly, and criticised Churchill who she claimed had said that in certain circumstances votes for women would mean Britain would be ruled by prostitutes. In a rousing peroration she expressed her hope that one day there might be a society where justice could be obtained without recourse to violence.

The first female member of the Society to speak was Barbara Hoare, who opposed the motion, and agreed with Pankurst's own ironical description of herself as a hooligan. According to Hoare, Pankhurst was a tyrant who neglected her family and encouraged violence. As for her campaigns, she dismissed them saying that 'any chimpanzee can be trained to throw stones'. A Miss Murnaghan spoke about the Civil Rights protests in Northern Ireland and warned of the danger of the movement being driven into a corner by the actions of some people with different motivations from those campaigners.

It was a three-hour debate and much of the meeting was taken up with an intermittent discussion about whether Joe Revington should be allowed speak. The Auditor insisted that Revington wasn't a member of the Society, having been expelled, but others argued that he had earned the distinction to speak as a distinguished guest. Ford refused to suspend standing orders to allow Revington to speak, ruling the matter out of order, but Revington was not to be silenced.

79 *The Irish Times*, 16 January 1969.

He 'interrupted with alacrity during the evening and announced that he found the Society's liberalism "skin deep"'.[80] The motion was defeated by 51 votes to 45.

Other debates that session included one on the motion 'That Parliament is the Graveyard of Socialism' (6 November 1968) and 'That this House would March on Stormont' (22 January 1969). The Catholic Church's position on birth control was the subject of the debate on 12 February 1969, with the motion 'That the Pill is Mightier than the Pope'. Joseph Foyle, the chair of the Lausanne Group, a Catholic group founded in 1968 to combat those promoting a liberal agenda, chaired the debate and argued that there were emotional and psychological effects of the pill which had been glibly overlooked.[81] In time, he believed, the Pope would be shown to have been right. This was an attempt to do God's will, he argued. Dr Raymond Cross, a consultant obstetrician and gynaecologist at the Rotunda Hospital in Dublin hailed the pill as the most important discovery in modern gynaecology. However, he warned that while it was a good therapeutic weapon, it was a 'lousy contraceptive', and he believed there still needed to be work done to find a way of controlling family planning without interfering with the natural physiology of women.

'That this House Supports the State of Israel' was the motion on 19 February 1969, with a large attendance supporting the motion by a large majority. At the start of the debate there was a minute's silence 'in memory of all the victims and in recognition of their sacrifices and everybody's loss'. Rabbi Isaac Bernstein proposed the motion and argued that if Israel was granted its rights it would benefit Jews and Arabs alike.[82] Prince Michael Grousinki, the self-styled head of the Georgian people in exile and a Georgian nationalist, led the opposition to the motion and questioned the right of Jews to settle in Israel. He argued that the Jewish people in Israel were invaders and should be expelled.

Having been refused permission a few years earlier, Fr James McDyer chaired the debate on Wednesday 29 January 1969, on the

80 *The Irish Times*, 16 January 1969.

81 *The Irish Times*, 13 February 1968.

82 *The Irish Times*, 20 February 1969.

motion 'That this House would Emigrate'. The debate was remembered for what happened afterwards. As the Committee was having supper someone broke into the Conversation Room of the GMB and stole the framed petition of the Society in the 1840s requesting permission to return to College, signed by several hundred eminent people in the city.[83] It was later recovered in May with *The Irish Times* covering the story with the headline '"Hist" recovers lost scroll.'[84]

On Tuesday 25 February the Minister for Education, Brian Lenihan, was due to speak at the auditorial meeting of the Business and Economic Society, but it was disrupted by protestors and he was unable to do so. He was forced to take refuge in the bathroom where, as *The Irish Times* later reported, 'he eventually made a flying getaway, climbing through a window and jumping six feet into a hedge'.[85] Lenihan himself admitted 'That's what one can expect from political life. I'm not worried about it'. At the Society the next night, David Ford proposed a motion regretting the disruption as a 'grave threat to the right of free speech and association in this university'.[86] The motion was passed unanimously. The motion that evening was 'That this House would join the Labour Party', and the main speaker proposing it was Barry Desmond, then a member of the Labour Party Administrative Council. He argued that 'Labour must get on the march again, state its policies, and carry them to the electorate with fire in its belly'. And he predicted that the policies of James Connolly would 'one day be vindicated by the new and younger generation of Irish men and women who, after 50 years of this sterile Irish political controversy, seek a fresh alternative'. The motion resulted in a tie when it was put to a vote, and Dr John O'Connell (then a Labour TD, and later a Fianna Fáil Minister for Health) who was chairing the debate used his casting vote to carry it.

The Society continued to excel in competitive debating. In 1967 Cian Ó hÉigeartaigh won the McCausland Trophy in the 8th national inter-varsity debating competition, while David Ford won

---

83 *The Irish Times*, 31 January 1969.

84 *The Irish Times*, 8 May 1969.

85 *The Irish Times*, 11 Febraury 1977.

86 *The Irish Times*, 27 February 1969.

it in 1969, debating the motion 'That Dogmatism is the Brandy of the Damned'.[87] Ford later became a distinguished academic as well as Regius Professor of Divinity at the University of Cambridge. Bill McCormack, who had played a leading role on the radical side, also became an academic and Professor of Literary History at Goldsmith's College, and a respected author. Joe Revington, who had been expelled from the Society, went on to become a barrister and served as an adviser to Dick Spring when he was leader of the Labour Party.

The 1960s was a remarkable decade in the history of the Society, at the forefront of major national debates, while also riven by its own internal conflict about the admission of women. Years later a notable tribute was paid to David Ford for the leadership he had shown in this period and for steering a middle path between hardliners on both sides. As Micheál O'Siadhail recalled, Ford 'eschewed the extremes of the conservative males who wanted no truck with women and those who wanted to bring women in by protest and disruption'.[88] Instead he wanted women as members and to achieve this through changing the laws of the Society 'and he succeeded after much struggle and some knife edge votes'. For him, 'Burke's Club represented something fundamentally constitutional and democratic'. It is a description that could equally apply to the Society over a tumultuous decade.

87 *The Irish Times*, 6 March 1969.

88 Micheal O'Siadhail, 'Facing each other', p. 361.

20 'THE GREATEST OF ALL THE SCHOOLS OF THE ORATORS': THE HIST IN ITS BICENTENARY YEAR

IAN ASHE was the Auditor for the 200th session of the Society and he presided over one of the most exciting years in the Society's history as the bicentenary of its founding was marked with the kind of rigorous, outward-looking debates which had been a hallmark of its history. The Record Secretary for the session was the talented Richard Clarke, who went on to become a Church of Ireland clergyman and achieved distinction as Archbishop of Armagh and Primate of All Ireland. The Librarian was Fergus O'Ferrall, later Adelaide Professor in Health Policy at Trinity College Dublin and a distinguished historian. The Treasurer was Nicholas FitzGerald Browne, who later became a successful novelist and writer under the name Nicholas Best. The session began with Ashe's inaugural, on 'Freedom of Speech in Politics', and ironically, it became embroiled in controversy over that very issue. One of the guest speakers was John Taylor, the parliamentary secretary to the Stormont Minister for Home Affairs, who went out of his way to antagonise the gathering of almost 500 people.

In his address, Ashe claimed that protest marches were not community challenges to the government, but 'a community concession'.[1] And he criticised the political parties in the Republic for being 'too sensitive', criticising in particular Fine Gael and the Labour Party. In response, Richie Ryan, the Fine Gael TD and future Minister for Finance, said he regretted that Ashe had 'succumbed to the fashionable denigration of political parties'.

---

1 *The Irish Times*, 25 October 1969.

The real controversy was still to come. Taylor had not prepared anything, as he revealed to the audience at the start of his speech, before going on to say 'nothing at great length'.[2] Afterwards Taylor boasted that 'some people wanted a riot, and I decided to give them what they wanted'. The speech lasted an estimated fifty minutes and was overlong, gratuitously offensive, and deliberately rude. Looking to the future, Taylor claimed that only when the Irish government considered the rights of the individual in divorce and birth control, as well as tackling other issues 'honestly' such as lowering the voting age to eighteen, would the Stormont Government be willing to talk to them. He also threw in comments belittling Gaelic games, and attacking the Irish language. 'Most people told me not to come', he said at one point, at which a heckler responded, 'Quite right'.

During Taylor's speech he was frequently shouted down by the audience. At one stage there was a series of slow handclaps, and a verse of the Irish national anthem was sung as well as snatches of 'I'll take you home again, Cathleen' and other songs.[3] Joe Revington, by now the President of the SRC, attempted to interrupt Taylor and speak in his place, shouting 'I refuse to sit here and listen to this man.' The Chancellor of the University (and President of the Society), F. H. Boland, who was chairing the meeting, was horrified and called the interruptions a 'disgrace'. According to *The Irish Times*, the meeting was 'close to anarchy' by the end of his speech, and Boland 'seized the microphone and demanded that interruptions cease. But they continued.'

Despite Taylor's provocations, Boland believed the episode did 'no credit to the College Historical Society.... I am sorry that the right of free speech was not respected tonight'. Jim Hamilton was one of the members of the Society who interrupted Taylor and later defended his actions in the letters page of *The Irish Times*. 'Far from being denied freedom of speech', he argued, 'Mr Taylor got far more than he had hoped for – so much, in fact, that it rapidly became clear he had very little to say.'[4] He concluded by saying he was angry at Taylor's 'abuse of the hospitality of the College Historical Society',

---

2 *The Irish Times*, 25 October 1969.

3 *The Irish Times*, 23 October 1969.

4 *The Irish Times*, 25 October 1969.

claiming he had 'never met a more cynical politician or one whose actions disgusted me more.' Taylor was a politician, he believed, where manners have very little place. Taylor went on to have a significant career in Ulster Unionism, and continued to court controversy by making deliberately provocative comments, most notably in 2017 when (as Lord Kilclooney) he dismissed former Hist man, Taoiseach Leo Varadkar, in a tweet as a 'typical Indian'.[5] When asked about the comment in the Dáil Varadkar replied with devastating simplicity: 'I had thought it was a parody account, but seemingly it is not. It is for real...that is all I will say about it.'[6]

The motion on 29 October 1969 was that 'Ireland has a Worthy Parliamentary Opposition' and Maurice O'Connell, a former member of Dublin City Council, made headlines when he accused a small group in Fine Gael for keeping it a minority party. An honorary member, Senator Neville Keery of Fianna Fáil, claimed the opposition parties (Fine Gael and Labour) played a vital role in creating the national image of the politician, possibly even more than the Government party. The debate was chaired by the journalist and broadcaster Prionsias Mac Aonghusa and the motion was defeated.[7]

Religion was debated on 5 November 1969, with the motion 'That Religious Denominations will Kill Christianity'.[8] The Jesuit priest, Fr Michael Sweetman, suggested that the Catholic Church was not a denomination, 'but the authoritative true Church of Christ'. The motion was defeated.[9]

Dr Hilda O'Malley, the widow of Donogh O'Malley, chaired the debate on 12 November 1969 on the motion 'That Female Governments would Hasten World Peace'. The motion was defeated by 38 votes to 16, and speaking from the chair O'Malley suggested that it was as difficult for a women to get elected to Dáil Éireann on her own achievements as it was to break down the walls of Jericho.[10]

A former president of the GAA, Alf Murray, spoke to the Society

5 *The Irish Times,* 1 May 2018.
6 Ibid.
7 *The Irish Times,* 30 October 1969.
8 *The Irish Times,* 6 November 1969.
9 TCD MUN/SOC/HIST Uncatalogued papers, 1960-69.
10 *The Irish Times,* 13 November 1969.

on 19 November 1969, debating the motion 'That Politics Ruins Sports'. He argued that the GAA 'is not anti-anything, but it is definitely pro-Ireland' and suggested that it was 'in favour of what Ireland should mean to the other nations of the world'.[11] Kadar Asmal, a Law lecturer in Trinity, also spoke and recognized that the GAA had played a large part in the regeneration of Ireland at the start of the twentieth century. He admitted that 'politics plays a part in sport', but said that he wanted to remove 'the obnoxious role which sectarianism and party politics also play'. This brought him on to a discussion of Apartheid in South Africa and its pernicious influence on sport, comparing it to a hypothetical situation in Ireland where only members of Fianna Fáil were allowed play competitive sport. The motion was carried by 16 votes to 11.

Other motions that session included 'That this House would Shun the Common Market' (3 December 1969) which was chaired by newly elected Senator for the University of Dublin, Mary Bourke, and defeated by 30 votes to 16, and 'That this House has no Faith in the American People' (4 February 1970) where the American Ambassador to Ireland, John D. Moore, suggested that protests, dissent and internal violence had been a part of American life for 200 years.[12]

The highpoint of the session, however, was the week of events in March 1970 organized around the bicentenary. 'An Art and Oratory' exhibition was launched in the National Gallery of Ireland by the Minister for Finance, Charles J. Haughey, as part of the commemorative programme, where he paid tribute to Edmund Burke as 'one of the greatest political thinkers of all time'. He was courageous and controversial. He was a formidable orator. And he was a man whose words, no matter what the words, had a kind of richness to them.'[13] Haughey ended his speech with a quote from Burke which he said for him 'had its own special appeal'. It was an attack on 'the presumptuous judgement of the ignorant' who criticised those involved in 'great public schemes'.

11 *The Irish Times*, 20 November 1969.

12 TCD MUN/SOC/HIST Uncatalogued Papers, 1960-1969 and 1970-79.

13 *The Irish Times*, 3 March 1970.

Senator Edward Kennedy, whose two brothers had been assassinated, one in office, one running for office, delivered a bicentenary address on Edmund Burke on 3 March 1970. The event in the Public Theatre was packed and was chaired by the Chancellor, F.H. Boland. There was one banner in the theatre, carried by members of the Trinity United Nations Association, which was in Greek and called for 'Free Greece'.

Kennedy began by saying how delighted he was to have been invited calling it 'one of the greatest honours of my public life, as well as an opportunity to express myself on matters that I feel are vital to our time'. He called the College Historical Society 'the greatest of all the schools of the orators' and said that it was fitting that Edmund Burke had been instrumental in its founding. Praising its tradition for 'open debate', he said it had served as 'a centre of controversy and discussion', hearing the voices of Irish nationalists such as Wolfe Tone, Robert Emmet, John Blake Dillon, and Thomas Davis, 'as well as those who opposed their thoughts and actions'.

Kennedy's speech was interrupted six times, five for applause. The most unexpected interruption, according to *The Irish Times*, was when one young man in the Gallery stood on his seat and shouted 'Down with US imperialism, the greatest enemy the Western world has ever known.'[14] Four students carried him out, as he shouted 'Long live Mao Tse-Tung'. Kennedy responded with a quick quip: 'There goes one of the great debaters', inviting him back the following night, which line prompted loud applause.

The speech contained 'salvoes of impeccable Kennedy rhetoric', for example as he argued that 'every society is a mixture of stability and change, an irrevocable history and an uncertain future. We are both what we have been and what we desire to be. We are creatures of memory and hope, struggling with uncertainty as we try to fulfil the promises that we know we must keep.' The theme of the speech was the rejection of violence as a way of bringing about social change. Recognising that the young had their own harsh rhetoric, Kennedy added that 'As one who shares many of their hopes and aspirations for the future I feel constrained to warn that history is a harsh judge of those so caught up with revolution that they forget reformation.'

14 *The Irish Times*, 4 March 1970.

Warning the audience about 'the two greatest dangers to peace and the future existence of mankind', Kennedy said that 'the continuation of human oppression, whether conscious or unconscious' and 'the toleration of weapons that can destroy our planet' had to be put under the control of humane and reasonable people 'if we are to be optimistic about the future of the world'. It was, he said, 'a profound struggle for the future of our common civilisation', and he quoted his brother, President John F. Kennedy, during his visit to Dublin in 1963 when he said that 'the supreme reality of our time is our indivisibility as children of God, and our common vulnerability on this planet'.

The full text of the speech was printed the next day in *The Irish Times*, and the event was praised for being 'a curious mixture of the formal and the informal, the undergraduate cheerfulness and the pomp and circumstance of academicism'. Afterwards, Senator Kennedy was met by a crowd of 50 protestors, positioned outside of the gate of the Provost's House, who obstructed his car as it left and pounded on the roof for two minutes, while a 200-strong crowd of protestors looked on from Grafton Street. There was a large Garda presence, who were accused of being 'fascist pigs', and one arrest was made.

The Taoiseach, Jack Lynch, was in the chair the following night, 4 March 1970, with a debate on the motion 'That the Only Liberty is a Liberty connected with Order', and there was an impressive line-up of speakers. Senator Eugene McCarthy, who had challenged sitting president, Lyndon B. Johnson, for the Democratic nomination in 1968, discussed how liberty is related to environment, and he suggested that the real challenge was not so much what one sought by way of liberty, but about the order in which one would seek it.[15] Professor Andreas Georgios Papandreou, the son of the former Greek Prime Minister (and a future Prime Minister himself, as well as the father of a future Prime Minister), suggested that 'the democratic vision is getting dimmer day by day'. He argued that popular sovereignty was becoming 'a mere slogan' and 'liberty is on the retreat'.

James Dillon, the former Fine Gael leader, began his speech in

15 *The Irish Times*, 5 March 1970.

Irish and he was subjected to some heckling by Maoists, prompting him to note, 'There is no need to get so excited about Irish'. He reminded the gathering that his grandfather, John Blake Dillon, had been President of the Society in the nineteenth century, and suggested that those interested in freedom should read *Animal Farm* by George Orwell. There was some jeering when he mentioned protestors waving their little red books and he told the jeering students, 'Thank God for America. You would not dare boo in China or you would be hung up in the morning.' Dillon made a persuasive case that the only effective safeguard against that kind of slavery was parliamentary democracy. Michael Foot, the Labour MP, also spoke and offered his hope that 'the smaller nations would combine to give the world a different offering'.

In his speech from the chair, Lynch spoke out against abuses of liberty which created 'chaotic and anarchic' situations. He suggested that 'a democratic Government must respond to majority opinion with action, to minority opinion with consideration'. However, when the announcement of grievances is accompanied by force then a Government has 'to act as the custodian of order so that the liberty of all its country's citizens' are assured.

The public debates marking the bicentenary celebrations came to end with a debate on 6 March 1970 in a packed Public Theatre on the motion 'That Emmet's Epitaph be now Written'. As *The Irish Times* reported afterwards, it was a debate 'in which various speakers cheerfully declined to speak on the side on which they had originally been chosen'.[16] John Hume argued for the removal of injustice as the prerequisite for 'the necessary and inevitable remarriage of the two parts of Ireland'.[17] In a powerful speech against violence, he said that the border would only be removed by the spilling of common sweat, not the spilling of blood. 'It may not be popular', he admitted, 'but it is the only way.' Vincent Browne referenced the Arms Crisis in his speech and attacked Neil Blaney and Kevin Boland for making reunification impossible by their actions and attitudes. He also called for Articles 2 and 3 of the Constitution to be abandoned at the earliest opportunity. A talented young Law student, and member of

16 *The Irish Times*, 7 March 1970.

17 *The Irish Times*, 7 March 1970.

the Committee, Donnell Deeny, was the only student to speak at the debate, and delivered what *The Irish Times* called 'one of the best speeches of the evening, pouring scorn equally on the domestic factions north and south'. If Emmet's epitaph could now be written, he implied, it was because we were now as bad as the rest of them.

Erskine Childers, the Tánaiste and Minister for Health, also spoke, and was the subject of some protests outside, with chants of 'Down with Childer's Health Bill' and 'Down with Childers, imperialist lackey'. Childers argued for the economic advantages that would come to a united Ireland in the EEC and expressed his hope the full civil rights for all in Northern Ireland would soon become a reality. Other speakers included Michael O'Kennedy TD, Michael O'Leary, the Labour TD, and Gerry Fitt MP.

The 200th session came to a close with an honorary members' debate on Wednesday 13 May 1970 on the motion 'That Fashion kills Fashion'.[18] It marked the end of a year that would be long remembered by members, and form the template for future commemorative events. Perhaps the final word can be left with R. B. McDowell, who delivered a spellbinding lecture, almost entirely without notes, on 'Personalities in the Hist' on Thursday 5 March during the commemorative week. McDowell ended his speech with a tribute to Lecky, who he suggested epitomised the virtues which were most needed today 'in particular those of moderation, of attempting to listen to another person's point of view, and of attempting really to be objective'. These characteristics, he argued, were the 'cement of our civilisation'.[19]

18 TCD MUN/SOC/HIST Uncatalogued Papers, 1970-79.

19 *The Irish Times,* 6 March 1970.

DEBATING BELIEF, DEBATING FACTS, 1970-1979

21

THE WINNER OF THE GOLD MEDAL for oratory for the 200th session, Donnell Deeny was elected Auditor for the 201st session, and his Committee included the first woman on the General Committee, Linda Best, who was elected with 123 votes, a record number.[1] Bernadette Devlin, the MP for Mid-Ulster, spoke at Deeny's inaugural on Friday 30 October 1970 and called for an advanced form of socialism as the solution to Ireland's problems.[2] She suggested that 'we are the people, we do the work, and we have the power if we stop crawling about the feet of our leaders'. Noel Browne, now a Labour TD, also took part in the debate, and criticised the 'Republican' leaders of the past – Cosgrave, Lynch, de Valera, MacBride, Costello and Lemass – for being unable to subordinate their loyalty to the Catholic Church to the objective of achieving a united Ireland. In a prescient speech, Lord Longford argued that the only solution to the problems in Northern Ireland was some sort of coalition in which the minority was represented. In Deeny's own paper he suggested that two things were necessary to end sectarianism in Northern Ireland. The first was the integration of the educational system, with integrated housing, and the second was that 'Ulster itself must cease to exist... [it] must be absorbed into a greater unit before religion can decline into irrelevance'.[3]

A debate on the abolition of the Seanad saw the motion carried by 56 votes to 27 on 4 November 1970. Five of the six candidates for the

---

1 *The Irish Times*, 9 May 1970.

2 *The Irish Times*, 31 October 1970.

3 TCD MUN/SOC/HIST Uncatalogued Papers, 1970-79.

Trinity seats in the upcoming election spoke at the debate, and the headline the next day in *The Irish Times* was 'Candidates lose in debate on Seanad'.[4] One of the candidates, Catherine McGuinness, future Supreme Court judge, argued that to abolish the Seanad was to throw away a great opportunity of improving its membership.[5] Proposing the motion, Jim Hamilton attacked the principle of the universities having the exclusive right to directly elect representatives to the Seanad, and attacked the body for being impotent and ineffective. He suggested that a better way for the Government to bring issues before the public's eye was to take out a one-page ad in *The Irish Times* every day, as it would save time, money and space. Donnell Deeny also supported the motion and argued that the Seanad was a waste of money, an undemocratic body, unrepresentative of the people, which slowed down change and where the debates were of a poor quality.

There were other notable debates that session. Liam Cosgrave, the Fine Gael TD, and future Taoiseach chaired the debate on 3 March 1971 on the motion 'That Politics is an Honourable Profession'. The motion was defeated. 'That Violence is Necessary for an Irish Solution' was debated on 27 January 1971 with Tomás Mac Giolla, the President of Official Sinn Féin in the chair. The motion was defeated. '"That this House would Liberate its Women' was debated on 3 February 1971, and speakers included Mary Kenny, the women's editor of the *Irish Press*, and Alan Amsby, who was better known as the cabaret entertainer, 'Mr Pussy'. The motion was carried. 'That Stormont is Dead' was debated on 14 April 1971 with Robert Babington, the Ulster Unionist MP, in the chair. The motion was carried. The debate on 28 April 1971 was 'That these Islands should Remain outside the EEC'.[6]

The My Lai massacre during the Vietnam War was the subject of the annual impromptu debating competition on 21 April 1971 when the motion was 'That Lieutenant Calley should Go Free'. The prize was shared by Jim Hamilton and Declan Kiberd and the motion was defeated. Hamilton won the gold medal for oratory that session and later served as Director of Public Prosecutions in Ireland (1999-2011).

Deeny was part of the winning College Historical Society team in

4 *The Irish Times*, 5 November 1970.
5 *The Irish Times*, 5 November 1970.
6 TCD MUN/SOC/HIST Uncatalogued Papers, 1970-79.

The Irish Times debating competition that year, and went on to win the competition a record three times (in 1971, and again in 1972 when he had the unique achievement of being part of the winning team and also named best individual speaker). The other member of the Hist team in 1971 was Greg Murphy, a red-headed socialist in a three-piece pin-striped suit, who went on to win the *Observer* Mace individual prize. Marian Finucane, representing Bolton Street, was the winner of the best individual speaker in 1971, with Frank Bannister partnering Deeny in 1972 to win the team prize..[7]

'That Abortion should be Legalised' was the motion on 24 February 1971, in one of the most contentious debates of the year. Diana Mundy, of the British Abortion Law Reform Association, proposed the motion and suggested that 'abortion law reformers did not invent abortion and neither is it the product of the permissive, or what I prefer to call the civilized, society'.[8] She pointed out the fact that the birth-rate in Ireland was not noticeably higher than in other countries, even though contraception and abortion were illegal, showing that Irish women went to Britain to have abortions or deliver their babies. She argued that 'we are dealing in the region of belief not in fact', and she insisted that 'I have thought about abortion a great deal and I sincerely believe that it is not murder'. Martin Mears, of the Child Preservation Society, opposed the motion, and argued that society was never justified in taking away the life of another human being. He denied that it was better to legalise abortion because it was happening anyway, saying that it was never moral to legalise infanticide just because it was prevalent. Expediency, he insisted, was no justification. The motion was carried by 53 votes to 31 and *The Irish Times* reported the debate extensively with the headline 'Reform of Law on Abortion Urged'.

There was further controversy with the motion on 5 May 1971 that the Catholic church 'is an Enemy of the Irish People', was organized as the honorary members debate. Many honorary members as *The Irish Times* reported, 'declined to attend the meeting, in protest against the indelicacy of the motion'.[9] Unbowed, Deeny proposed the motion

7 *The Irish Times*, 12 February 1971.

8 *The Irish Times*, 25 February 1971.

9 *The Irish Times*, 6 May 1971.

and said that one area where the Catholic church was an enemy of the people was in opposing integrated education in Northern Ireland. James D'Arcy SC, opposed the motion and reminded people that the Catholic Church had educated Irish people when no one else would. Stephen Harris, a Vice President of the Society, attacked the motion as a joke in very bad taste and claimed that it could only be supported from an extreme socialist point of view.[10] The motion was carried by 39 votes to 35.

'Speakers demolish EEC at TCD Society debate' was the headline in *The Irish Times* on 28 October 1971, the day after Ted Smyth's inaugural meeting. 'The debate began with a thorough roasting of the EEC and all its works from the Auditor of the Society, Mr Edward Smyth', according to the report, before Garret FitzGerald, the Fine Gael TD, presented the case for Europe. FitzGerald challenged one of the guests, Professor Nicholas Kaldor, a Cambridge economist who had been an adviser to Harold Wilson, to clarify whether he agreed with all the conclusions in an anti-EEC pamphlet by Raymond Crotty given that he had written its foreword. Kaldor declared that 'he could not follow Dr FitzGerald's specific questions, and none of them seemed to matter anyway'. The British trade union leader, Clive Jenkins, also spoke and declared his conviction that Britain would never join the EEC as support, he believed, 'was wafer thin' and would evaporate before the necessary legislation was passed.

Michel Rocard, the French radical socialist leader (and future Prime Minister), provided what *The Irish Times* called 'the meat of the evening'. He claimed that the EEC had failed to produce common policies, except on agriculture and 'if you are going to join, don't do it because of an agricultural policy which has no future'. Justin Keating, Labour TD, concluded the evening predicting that Irish industry would be sucked out of Ireland if it joined the EEC.

'That Coalition is Dishonest' was the motion on 3 November 1971, with Declan Costello, the former Fine Gael TD and author of 'The Just Society' document, arguing that political parties could not be defined in clichés. He suggested that it was possible to see 'a reforming government formed by a coalition of the Labour Party and Fine Gael', as no party 'has a monopoly of talents'.

10 *The Irish Times*, 6 May 1971.

On 26 January 1972 the motion for debate was 'That Western Democracy has Failed' and Dr Kadar Asmal suggested that 'the greatest threat to democracy is the role of the large corporation, which shows a total disregard for sovereignty'.[11] Opposing Irish entry to the EEC, he argued that membership would destroy Irish people's right to make its own meaningful decisions. 'It is up to the people to take part in the national argument against joining the EEC if we are to retain our limited form of democracy', he said. Dr Ronald Segal, the South African author and historian, and, like Asmal, a leading figure in the Anti-Apartheid movement, proposed the motion and suggested that democracy had failed by its own standards because it had become 'about the power of money, not the power of people'. The motion was carried.

Writing about his time in Trinity some years later, the Auditor, Ted Smyth, recalled that while 'Trinity was an incubator of change, the Hist was a petri dish where the the issues of the day were fiercely debated'.[12] He recalled that he learned as much about politics from the Society as in class. On Wednesday 2 February 1972 he adjourned the meeting of the Society 'as a mark of respect to the thirteen people killed in Derry on Bloody Sunday', a few days earlier.[13] That evening Smyth joined a protest march to the British embassy in Merrion Square on the night the embassy was burnt down by protestors. He later recalled that it 'seemed to me at the time like a natural symbolic reaction', though he regretted that 'such acts also contributed to the murderous cycle of retaliation that followed'. Smyth later became a distinguished Irish diplomat and played a significant role in the Irish peace process and as a supporter of European integration. A successful businessman, he also became a trustee of the Ireland Funds and Glucksman Ireland House.

Perhaps the most controversial debate of the year was the one on 9 February 1972 on the Barry Goldwater-inspired motion 'That Extremism in the Defence of Liberty is no Vice', chaired by Tim Pat Coogan, the editor of the *Irish Press.* Coming weeks after Bloody

---

11 *The Irish Times*, 27 January 1972.

12 Kathy Gilfillan (ed.), *Trinity Tales: Trinity College Dublin in the Seventies* (Dublin, 2011), p. 89.

13 Ibid., p. 90.

Sunday, there was much interest in what one of the guests, Neil Blaney, the former Minister for Agriculture who had been dismissed from office for his role in the Arms Crisis, would say and the debate was packed. Blaney accused the Government of collaborating with Britain, suggesting that 'Pontius Pilate did no worse.'[14] Defending the actions which had seen him dismissed, Blaney insisted that 'force is morally justified in certain circumstances ... A people is justified in using force to destroy an oppressive and unjust regime when all other recourse has failed'. Blaney believed that such a situation existed in Northern Ireland, and he accused southern political leaders of 'paying lip service to the dead', even after 'the recent massacre in Derry'. He was answered by Senator John Kelly, of Fine Gael, who attacked 'the sheer, bitter stupidity of the British government in the Derry shootings'. Denouncing violence on all sides, Kelly insisted that he would not 'go an inch of the road with people who take it upon themselves to shoot anyone else'.

A controversial new building in Trinity was debated on 5 April 1972, with the motion 'This House Supports the Board's Proposal for the New Arts Block'. Condemning the plans, Senator Mary Robinson argued that they must look at the new building from the point of view of Dublin as a whole, criticising it as 'an awful, imposing façade facing on to Nassau Street'.[15] Paul Koralek, the architect, defended the project, wondering if it was a monster that was being talked about. Blaming nostalgia for the criticisms, he suggested that the new block would open great opportunities and make new things possible. The motion was defeated by 36 votes to 24.

Northern Ireland was debated again on 26 April 1972, with the motion 'That this House supports the Two Nation Theory', as speakers criticised the failure of successive governments in the Republic to make the state more favourable to Northern Irish Protestants. Dr David Thornley, Labour TD, criticised a 'pretty sectarian state', and Dr John O'Connell, his Labour colleague, argued that work was needed to create an unsectarian constitution acceptable to all.[16] Rosemary Mitchell of the Two Nations Study Group questioned

14 *The Irish Times*, 10 February 1972.

15 *The Irish Times*, 6 April 1972.

16 *The Irish Times*, 27 April 1972.

whether the South had anything to offer Protestant workers.

During this year the team of Donnell Deeny and Frank Bannister won *The Irish Times* debating competition, while the Correspondence Secretary, Declan Kiberd, won *The Irish Press* trophy and the Censor, James Connolly, won the *Irish Independent* debate.[17]

Winner of the gold medal for oratory for the 202nd session, Declan Kiberd was elected Auditor for the 203rd session and his committee included future President of the Irish Legal History Society, Robert Marshall, as Correspondence Secretary (following the resignation of John Stephenson at the end of the summer) and James Connolly as Record Secretary. Kiberd chose as his subject for his inaugural the subject of universities in crisis. It took place on 24 October 1972 and in his paper he argued that universities needed to be saved from technicians and return to being a truly humanist institution. Kiberd wondered 'if arts and ethics had still been compulsory this century' whether the napalm bomb would have been invented, 'and perhaps Trinity might have produced fewer money-grabbing doctors and less careerist academics.'[18] Arguing that the student revolts of recent years were not a subversive communist plot, he suggested that rather it was 'an attempt to recapture the university from technicians and give it back to free-thinking humanists, an attempt to hold the university true to its own deepest traditions'. One of the best speeches of the night was delivered by a young Michael D. Higgins, then a lecturer at University College Galway. However, *The Irish Times* criticised the debate for going on too long and being 'at times uninteresting to the point of boring'.

Notable debates that session included 'That this House would Re-elect Richard M. Nixon' (1 November 1972) which was defeated, and 'That Irish Men make Lousy Lovers' (8 November 1972), with David Norris and Nell McCafferty speaking, which was carried. The motion 'That Dáil Éireann is Dead' was debated on 18 January 1973, and speakers included Dr Garret FitzGerald, Dr David Thornley and Captain James Kelly. FitzGerald, the Fine Gael spokesperson on finance, criticised those who used the cloak of civil rights to associate with 'the very elements in our society which threaten our lives and

---

17 TCD MUN/SOC/HIST Uncatalogued Papers, 1970-79.

18 *The Irish Times*, 25 October 1972.

freedom'.[19] The motion was carried. Charity was debated on 24 January 1973, with the motion 'That Social Work hinders Social Progress', with Declan Costello in the chair. Máirín de Burca, the joint secretary of Official Sinn Féin argued that people who engage in charitable activities should also fight for justice and inequality, otherwise they were shoring up the system. The motion was defeated.

'Pornography is the Opium of the Impotent' was the motion debated on 31 January 1973. John Calder, the British publisher, argued that people would be better off discussing the real obscenities in life, such as violence in both parts of Ireland, instead of flogging the dead horse of pornography.[20] The writer Monk Gibbon proposed the motion, and suggested that pornography was the exploitation of sex by the unsexed. The motion passed by 21 votes to 13.

David O'Sullivan won the gold medal for oratory that session, while the winner of the Maiden Speaker's prize that year was Arthur Deeny, the younger brother of Donnell Deeny. A man of many talents, Deeny went on to become a successful copywriter and creative director for a number of advertising companies and penned the instantly recognisable jingle that became famous in the 1990s: 'Fleetwood would, would Fleetwood'.[21] When he died in March 2018 he was remembered in *The Irish Times* as 'a much-loved and colourful figure in the worlds of Irish advertising, cricket and humanism.'[22]

The most controversial debate of the session took place on 4 April 1973 on Northern Ireland as members and guest speakers engaged with the motion, 'That this House Welcomes and Supports the White Paper' of the British Government, published on 20 March, which proposed devolution and power-sharing.[23] In the early stages of the debate it almost had to be abandoned, with protests from Republican, Internationalist, and Maoist agitators. The former Stormont Minister, Roy Bradford MP, was in the chair, and he was

19 *The Irish Times*, 19 January 1973.

20 *The Irish Times*, 1 February 1973.

21 *The Irish Times*, 9 April 2018.

22 Ibid.

23 *The Irish Times*, 5 April 1973.

denounced as a 'bloody Protestant murderer', to which he replied that he had been insulted many times by much more intelligent people. Three times the Auditor, Declan Kiberd, was forced to threaten abandoning the meeting to try and restore order. Speakers included Gerry Fitt MP, leader of the SDLP, Bob Cooper of the Alliance party, and Stanley Orme MP, of the British Labour Party. Fitt was loudly heckled when he suggested that if the British army was withdrawn from Northern Ireland then there would be a massacre and many thousands of his constituents would be killed. He criticised the British White Paper for spending so little time on the Irish dimension, and suggested that a united Ireland would be a long drawn out process and would only come about by necessity. The debate was covered in the media, and the result of the vote, approval of the White paper by 40 votes, was the headline in *The Irish Times* the next day.

The inaugural meeting of the 204th session was even more chaotic, turning into a 'mini riot' and made the front page of *The Irish Times*.[24] Jonathan Guinness, the chairman of the Conservative Monday Club, a controversial pressure group which opposed decolonisation and immigration and supported apartheid, was invited to speak, and stories of his attendance promoted various left-wing groups, some within College, some outside, to gather and protest. In the event, Guinness had to postpone his visit, but the protestors were unaware of this, and were also determined to prevent the Minister for Justice, Paddy Cooney, from speaking. A group of about thirty demonstrators padlocked the door of the Public Theatre before the meeting, demanding 'free speech for Republican socialists'. [25] The Senior Dean, Professor George Dawson, ordered the protestors to leave, 'in the interests of free speech', but they refused. As a result, the officers of the Society decided to move the meeting to the Dining Hall. The demonstrators attempted to rush the door of the Dining Hall, but were kept out by the students.

The Gardaí were called to the scene and some scuffles broke out. The demonstrators abused the Gardaí for being 'Free State

24 *The Irish Times*, 26 October 1973 and *The Irish Times*, 15 November 1973.

25 *The Irish Times*, 26 October 1973.

collaborators' and shouted 'Cooney out' and 'Up the Provos'. The demonstrators, about 30 in total, not all students of Trinity, also claimed that debating societies like the Historical Society were 'an outmoded feature of our class structured society'.

The meeting began an hour behind schedule with the Society issuing a statement that to postpone the meeting would be a victory for the protestors. James Connolly, the Auditor, read a paper on 'Crime – Punishment or Treatment' in which he criticised the prison system for not having changed very much in one hundred years. Speaking in support was the Earl of Longford, and Seamus Sorohan SC. In Cooney's speech he spoke of the need for prison reform, and listed some of the areas the Government was working on.

Having been unable to attend the inaugural, Jonathan Guinness accepted an invitation to speak to the University Philosophical Society, but it retracted the invitation after all of the protests. The Historical Society invited him to be at its meeting on 14 November 1973 on the motion 'Profits before Prophets', but did not advertise his attendance in advance, and the meeting passed without incident. Nigel Cox, a former President of the Philosophical Society criticised the Historical Society publicly for having Guinness speak 'under a cloak of secrecy', claiming this was making a mockery of free speech.[26] But he was answered by the Auditor, Connolly, who said it was regrettable that controversial speakers could only be heard when their visits were unannounced.

The Middle East was debated on 28 November 1973, with a motion 'That this House desires Yaweh to lead Israel out of Egypt'.[27] Atif Matouk, the President of the Irish-Arab Society, argued that the problem in the Middle East was not the conflict between Arabs and Israelis but the need to redress an injustice and give the Palestinian people their land. Maurice Abrahamson, the former Auditor of the Society, opposed the motion, and suggested that the root cause of Israel's uncertainty was the constant state of insecurity in which her population lived. Calling on Arab states to recognise the state of Israel, he defended Israel occupation of certain territories because of Arab aggression. The motion was defeated by 77 votes to 12.

26 *The Irish Times*, 15 November 1973.

27 *The Irish Times*, 29 November 1973.

'That this House finds the Sunningdale Agreement Unacceptable' was the motion for debate on 16 January 1974.[28] Chaired by Tomás Mac Giolla, the President of Official Sinn Féin, the best speech of the evening was delivered by Hugh Logue, the SDLP member of the Northern Ireland Assembly for Derry, who suggested that they had created an institution 'which will bring together Catholic, Protestant, and Dissenter'. The motion was defeated.

Dick Burke, the Minister for Education, chaired the debate for the Edmund Burke Memorial Trophy on 30 January 1974, and there was controversy when the students proposed and passed unanimously a motion condemning his inaction on the question of student grants.[29] Burke was cutting in his response from the chair. He suggested that there were loans for students available in Russia, and that was where the proposer of the motion could go 'if he wants loans for students'. Other notable debates that session included 'That 1984 is but a Decade Away' (13 February 1974), 'That Women's Lib Degrades Women' (20 February 1974) chaired by Professor Otway-Ruthven, and 'That this House would Restrict the Right to Strike' (10 February 1974). All three motions were defeated.

David O'Sullivan was elected Auditor for the 205th session, with Mícheál O hUigín as Treasurer and Louise Leonard (who had won the silver medal for oratory at the end of the previous session) as Record Secretary. Mary Harney was elected to the general Committee. The 2nd Lord Brookeborough, the son of the former Northern Ireland Prime Minister, was the star attraction at the debate on 23 October 1974 on the motion that 'This House should get Tough with Terrorists'. Defending internment, he suggested that the death penalty may need to be introduced to deal with terrorism, although he warned it was a two-edged weapon and may only make things worse. Eamonn McCann opposed the motion and condemned the British army for only protecting certain parts of Belfast, while ignoring some Catholic areas, where 'sectarian assassins cruised about hunting their prey'.[30] Máiriín de Burca of Official Sinn Féin claimed that five years ago she would have made a better speech than

28 *The Irish Times*, 17 January 1974.

29 *The Irish Times*, 31 January 1974.

30 *The Irish Times*. 24 October 1974.

McCann's, but not now, with more than 1,000 dead. Arguing that 'the principal terrorists in a portion of our country are in uniform', she also attacked the Provisional IRA as terrorists whose activities bore no relation to the IRA in the period from the 1920s to the 1950s. The motion was defeated.

David O'Sullivan's inaugural paper was read on 1 November 1974, on 'The Need for a Students' Union'. It was particularly hard-hitting, suggesting that 'at present, the universities are stagnant. Instead of being organic, growing, self-critical, flexible and inspirational, they have become staid, dull, institutionalised and depersonalised'.[31] O'Sullivan called for a new university structure to deal with the day to day problems of dissatisfied students, arguing that the aim of a students' union should be to effect a real change within the educational system as a whole. And he argued that 'we need to restore vitality to the educational process. We need to restore its humanity.' The Censor, George Birmingham, later recalled that O'Sullivan 'was always forceful and often inspirational'.[32]

Michael O'Leary, the Minister for Labour, spoke at the meeting, and had to face interruptions from one student who, as *The Irish Times* reported, 'had overestimated his alcoholic capacity'. This student was removed, but a second person 'indulged in not only ill-mannered but also ill-informed heckling'. Describing a university as a 'community of learners', O'Leary suggested that 'it should connect its work with the range of problems faced by the community which succours it'.

The Middle East was debated on 27 November 1974, with the motion 'That an Independent Secular Palestinian State is the Solution to the Middle Eastern Problem'.[33] Dr M. R. Mehdi of the Palestinian Liberation Organisation proposed the motion and called for co-existence between Israel and Palestinian statelets, with the aim of ultimately uniting them in a new state. Dr Marcus Einfeld of the World Jewish Congress opposed the motion, questioning aloud why this was the first time such a proposal had been made by the PLO, and warning that the 'speech was a mask for worse things yet to

31 *The Irish Times*, 4 November 1974.

32 Declan Budd and Ross Hinds, *The Hist and Edmund Burke's Club* (Dublin, 1997), p. 379.

33 *The Irish Times*, 28 November 1974.

come'. George Birmingham later recalled O'Sullivan speaking at this debate and receiving a standing ovation.[34]

The debate on 4 December 1974 was unusual because of the format of the motion. It was a debate on Northern Ireland and it consisted of a proposition with four sub-parts to be voted on. The motion was 'Recognising that the Unity of Ireland is a Desirable if Distant Prospect' (this part was carried) this House would: 1. Remove the territorial claim to Northern Ireland suggested in Articles Two and Three of the Constitution (this part was defeated); 2. Desire the British Government to suspend elections in Northern Ireland until such time as a power-sharing administration may receive support (also defeated); 3. Replace juries by commissions of magistrates (defeated); and 4. Continue to intern extremists who may not legally be convicted' (defeated). The motion was amended on the night to include a fifth clause: 'Replace Merlyn Rees as Secretary of State for Northern Ireland', which was carried. Liam Hourican, the respected and talented RTÉ news reporter, who had been Northern Ireland correspondent, was in the chair and he displayed great skill in explaining the concept of the multi-part motion and keeping the debate on track.

Other notable debates that session included an intervarsity debate on the motion 'That the Royal Family has been Too Long in the Saddle (19 February 1975), which had writer, Ulick O'Connor, in the chair, which was carried, and 'That Trade Unions Pose a Threat to Democracy' (9 April 1975) which was defeated. Although it was not called this, Brexit was debated on 16 April 1975 with the motion 'That this House would Encourage Britain to Leave the EEC'. The motion was defeated.[35]

Michael Hanna was elected Auditor for the 206th session, with Mary Harney as Treasurer. Harney later recalled coming to Trinity from a conservative catholic family background and finding in the Hist a place where liberal social issues were debated and discussed. 'There was no divorce, homosexuals were regarded as criminals and contraception was illegal', and she believed that 'being sometimes obliged to debate on the opposite side to one's own views honed

34 Declan Budd and Ross Hinds, *The Hist and Edmund Burke's Club*, p. 379.

35 TCD MUN/SOC/HIST Uncatalogued Papers, 1970-79.

our capacity to see the world as others do'.[36]

The inaugural meeting of the session took place on 24 October 1975 on the motion 'To Practice or to Preach – the Political Dilemma'. Speakers included John Hume, the deputy leader of the SDLP, Jack Lynch, the leader of Fianna Fáil, Michael Foot, the British Labour MP and Employment Secretary, and Maurice Manning, a Politics lecturer in UCD. In his speech Hume suggested that the Irish question had been simplified by too many people into meaning the British presence in Northern Ireland. 'If this alone was the problem we had to face', he explained, 'it would be very easy to solve.' Calling for moral courage instead of the more praised political courage, he argued that people needed to look at the traditions of both sides, 'irrespective of the way in which we held the Gods from which these traditions descended'.[37] Hume set out his critique of Irish nationalism. It was based on too romantic a notion of Ireland that bore little reality to life on the island and, from it, people claimed a right to die and to kill.

Jack Lynch used his speech to set out the long-term objective of his party on Northern Ireland. It was 'to bring about the re-unification of Ireland by peaceful means, because we believe that this is the way in which a true peace, and enduring friendship and a mutual understanding can be forged among all the people of this island.'

'That only Israeli Intransigence in the Middle East is a Stepping Stone to a Third World War' was the motion on 5 November 1975, chaired by Liam Hourican, with Michael Adams and Ben Briscoe, the Fianna Fáil TD, speaking. The motion was defeated. The debate 'That Contraception would Ruin Irish Society' on 12 November 1975 heard Fr Denis Faul from Northern Ireland argue that if Senator Mary Robinson's family planning bill became law then fornication, adultery and abortion would be 'on the rates'. Not only that, love and loyalty would be undermined and venereal disease and sexual perversion would spread across the country.[38] Opposing the motion,

36 Kathy Gilfillan (ed.), *Trinity tales: Trinity College Dublin in the Seventies*, p. 207.

37 *The Irish Times*, 25 October 1975.

38 *The Irish Times*, 13 November 1975.

Frank Crummey, the founding member and director of Family Planning Services, suggested that Robinson's bill was too conservative, and wondered 'how Catholics can achieve salvation if they never have the opportunity to avoid temptation'.

'That this House would Embrace a Gayer Culture' was the motion on 27 November 1975. Dr Noel Browne proposed the motion and suggested that too many Irish homosexuals had been forced to emigrate because of blackmail or the threat of exposure. In his critique of Irish society he suggested it was destructive that Irish homosexuals had to either suppress their natural sexuality or face imprisonment. Also proposing the motion was Dr David Norris, then a lecturer in English at Trinity and representing the Irish Gay Rights Movement. The motion was carried.

The value of coalitions was debated on 14 January 1976 with a motion 'That Two Parties Make Twice the Mess'. Opposing the motion, Dr Garret FitzGerald, Minister for Foreign Affairs, argued that the present Fine Gael-Labour Government had shown a unity when it came to Northern Ireland and the world economic crisis that few one-party governments had been able to maintain. And he suggested that the great ideological debates now took place within parties rather than between them. The motion was narrowly defeated.[39]

Other motions that session included 'Equality Leads to Mediocrity' (4 February 1976) where Máirín de Burca, joint secretary of Official Sinn Féin, attacked the Labour Party for its 'acrobatics' on equal pay for women.[40] On 11 February 1976 the motion was 'That Ireland Unfree shall Never be at Peace', and Paddy Harte, Fine Gael TD, blamed Irish society north and south for creating a situation where teenagers could be persuaded into 'camps of hate' believing that the best way of serving their cause was through 'vicious murder'.[41]

Senator Mary Robinson delivered one of the standout speeches of the session at a debate on 14 April 1976, opposing the motion 'That this House has faith in Western Democracy.'[42] Robinson revealed that she had little faith that western democracies had the

39 TCD MUN/SOC/HIST Uncatalogued Papers, 1970-79.

40 *The Irish Times*, 5 February 1976.

41 *The Irish Times*, 12 Febuary 1976.

42 *The Irish Times*, 15 April 1976.

capacity to respond adequately to the internal and external challenges facing them. These challenges included economic recession and uneven rates of inflation across countries, as well as a shift of values, and Robinson suggested that 'The Irish Republic had been given the opportunity to become a deeply democratic State but the opportunity had not been taken up.'

The election of Mary Harney as the first woman Auditor of the Society in May 1976 made history. It came seven years after the ban on membership had been lifted and *The Irish Times* reported the news on page 4 of the paper, giving her details as 'Miss Mary Harney, an economics student and a member of Fianna Fáil'.[43] As Harney later recalled, 'I like to think of this as my first exercise in mould-breaking'.[44] It was the start of a distinguished career, and a year later she became the youngest Senator in Irish history when appointed to the chamber by Taoiseach Jack Lynch, following the general election that year. It was customary for the Auditor of the Society to be elected to membership of one of the clubs on St Stephen's Green, but this was not awarded to Harney. As she later remembered, 'it was explained that the failure to elect me was not because I was a woman, but because I was not a man'.[45]

Harney delivered her inaugural paper on 22 October 1976 entitled 'Who Governs our Society?' Guest speakers included the former leader of the British Liberal Party, Jo Grimond MP, the leader of the SDLP, Gerry Fitt MP, and the Bishop of Ardagh and Clonmacnoise, Dr Cathal Daly.

Jack Lynch returned to the Society to debate the motion that 'Today's Politicians have Betrayed the Men of 1916' on 10 November 1976.[46] Lynch admitted that the 1916 leaders would probably now admit that there was more to 'the Northern problem' than their analysis suggested. He argued that the men of 1916 would be horrified to see 'the acts of barbarism perpetrated in the name of the Republic they held dear' in Northern Ireland. On a more optimistic

43 *The Irish Times*, 6 May 1976.

44 Kathy Gilfillan (ed.), *Trinity Tales: Trinity College Dublin in the Seventies*, p. 208.

45 Declan Budd and Ross Hinds, *The Hist and Edmund Burke's Club*, p. 382.

46 *The Irish Times*, 11 November 1976.

note, he suggested that the European Movement, and Ireland's entry to the EEC, represented 'the adoption on a vast European scale of those concepts of equal citizenship which have always been an intrinsic part of the Irish Republican movement'.[47]

Opposing the motion, Eamonn McCann argued that the Provisional IRA was the only sizeable movement in Ireland which was striving to advance the central idea of the leaders of 1916. Rejecting the idea that their methods would have been abhorrent to the revolutionary generation, he gave the example of 'the revered leaders of the War of Independence' who had sanctioned the execution of alleged informers on flimsy evidence and 'as casually as another man might order a pint'.

Mary Whitehouse, the British campaigner against pornography, spoke at the debate on 24 November 1976, proposing the motion 'That the People need the Protection of Censorship'.[48] Arguing that society's moral and cultural strength was being undermined by the permissive blight, she linked this with the failure to deal with economic problems. Opposing the motion, John Mulcahy, editor of *Hibernia,* argued that it was disrespectful to suggest the public was 'incapable of discerning the truth or is unfit to be confronted with reality'. The motion was defeated.

Other motions that session included 'That this House would Nationalise the Banks' (1 December 1976), which was defeated, and 'That Parliament is the Graveyard of Socialism' (20 April 1977), which was carried, with the journalist, Auberon Waugh, as the guest speaker.

One of the most interesting took place on 26 January 1977 on the motion, 'That this House Mourns the Death of Irish Culture'. Particularly notable was the way Dr Micheál MacLiammóir and Dr Hilton Edwards, iconic figures in the history of the Gate Theatre, as well as life partners, took opposing points of view. Hugh Leonard, the writer and playwright, also opposed the motion and suggested that 'in living and working in this country, Dr MacLiammóir is a refutation that culture is dead in Ireland'.[49] Joan O'Brien of the Language Freedom Movement delivered a lengthy speech in which

47 *The Irish Times*, 11 November 1976.

48 *The Irish Times*, 25 November 1976.

49 *The Irish Times*, 27 January 1977.

she denounced 'Gaelic extremists' for holding 'extreme left-wing totalitarian views.'

When MacLiammóir rose to speak he received a standing ovation and he spoke in favour of the motion, suggesting that Irish, 'that tragic language', was 'dead as a living language and nothing can restore it'. Defining culture as 'a strange dream of a certain type of achievement, not capable of being adequately explained in words', he suggested that only a half-witted nation would have shed so much blood to prove it was not British and then not speak its own language.

Opposing the motion, Hilton Edwards began by claiming that he 'knew less about Irish culture than anybody else in the world'. Attributing his longevity in Irish theatre, fifty years, to the fact that he had kept clear of Irish politics, he suggested that culture in Ireland was not dead, it was only beginning. Edwards reminded the audience that when he had first arrived in Ireland it would have been impossible to put on certain plays, but that had now changed, and he claimed that 'the voices of censorship are now crying in the wilderness.' The motion was defeated.

On 9 February 1977 the Society held an intervarsity debate on the motion 'That Men should be Reared to be Husbands and Fathers'. Anatoly Kaplin, the Soviet ambassador to Ireland, was invited to chair the debate, but the meeting was interrupted by five Maoists who began denouncing 'Soviet Social Imperialism' and tried to prevent him from speaking at the end of the debate. The Auditor, Mary Harney, offered the protestors the opportunity to address the meeting, but they refused to do so. Instead they created a disturbance and threw eggs at the ambassador, apparently hitting his suit.[50] As Harney and Ruth Sheil, the Record Secretary, explained in a letter to *The Irish Times* a few days later, 'Freedom of expression is the essence of this Society's activities'.[51] And they reiterated the mission of the Society to 'continue to offer a peaceful forum to speakers representing every shade of opinion'.

The Northern Ireland debate that session was on the motion, 'That Principle must be Compromised if Peace is to be Attained in Northern Ireland' and took place on 16 February 1977. Speakers included Austin

50 *The Irish Times*, 11 February 1977.

51 *The Irish Times*, 14 February 1977.

Currie of the SDLP, Michael O'Kennedy, the Fianna Fáil spokesperson on foreign affairs, Kevin Boland, Máirín de Burca of Sinn Féin, the Workers Party, and Tim Pat Coogan, the editor of *The Irish Press*. O'Kennedy accused the Government in general, and Conor Cruise O'Brien in particular, of wanting to replace Articles 2 and 3 of the Constitution and perhaps bring in a new Constitution entirely. He suggested that they 'should refrain from chipping away at the Constitution which is the guarantee not only of our national integrity but also of our commitment to peace and harmonious relations with other states'.[52] In an eloquent speech, Currie argued that there was only one principle in relation to the north that was worth working towards and that was 'reconciliation of Irishmen of the different political traditions'. The motion was defeated.

Years later, during the debate in the Seanad, Senator David Norris referred to Harney as someone he remembered 'as a brilliant debater in Trinity'.[53] Mary Harney subsequently wrote that her 'years at the Hist had equipped me well for a career in political life, upon which I had already embarked as I left Trinity'.[54] She remembers how Trinity was exciting in the 1970s because 'it was in the process of evolving as an institution to become a broad-based Irish university, growing rapidly in both stature and number of students'.[55] Harney went on to become the first woman leader of a political party in the Dáil when she became the leader of the Progressive Democrats in 1993, and she became the first female Tánaiste, serving in office between 1997 and 2006. Despite much opposition, including from colleagues in Government, she succeeded in bringing in a ban on the sale, distribution and marketing of coal in Dublin in 1990, thus ending the problem of smog in the city and saving many lives.[56] Harney served as Minister for Health between 2004 and 2011 and after leaving politics became Chancellor of the University of Limerick.

Peter Charleton was elected Auditor for the 208th session and for

52 *The Irish Times*, 17 February 1977.

53 Seanad debate, 15 November 2001 (www.oireachtas.ie).

54 Kathy Gilfillan (ed.), *Trinity Tales: Trinity College Dublin in the Seventies*, p. 208.

55 Ibid., p. 210.

56 *The Irish Times*, 26 September 2015.

his inaugural meeting on 21 October 1977 delivered a paper on 'The Irish Question – Republicanism Renewed'. The line-up of guest speakers was impressive, and included Mairead Corrigan, recent winner of the Nobel Peace Prize, Professor John A. Murphy of UCC, Dr Noel Browne, Senator Conor Cruise O'Brien, Bernadette McAliskey (formerly Bernadette Devlin), and Lord Brookeborough.[57] Corrigan spoke of how there were two tribes in Northern Ireland who had not yet learned to live together. She suggested that she had more in common with a Protestant in the Shankill Road area than with a Catholic in Dublin. In his speech, O'Brien called for a return to the co-existence and fraternity exemplified by the Lemass-O'Neill meetings of 1965, arguing that the marking of the 1916 Rising in 1966 had undermined this. Browne claimed that republicanism had disappeared in Ireland in the twentieth century because 'an arrogant triumphalist authoritarian Catholic church became our Government'. McAliskey used her speech to attack Sinn Féin, the Workers' Party, for posthumously converting Wolfe Tone to socialism.

Motions that session included 'That this House Reveres the Memory of Karl Marx' (26 October 1977) where Richie Ryan, the former Minister for Finance, suggested that if the teachings of Marx had been adopted in Ireland, the country would have failed and would have become 'the back garden of England'.[58] The motion was defeated. 'That Gay Rights are Human Rights' was the motion on 16 November 1977 with Professor Mary McAleese in the chair and Senator Mary Robinson and David Norris both speaking in favour of the motion. 'That de Valera was a Dodo' was the motion for a competitive debate on 30 November 1977.[59]

On 12 January 1978 the motion was 'That Fianna Fáil are more Promise than Practice' and Michael Keating, the Fine Gael spokesperson on urban affairs, accused Fianna Fáil of being 'guilty of fraud and deceit on a massive and organized scale' because of the election promises it had made to win the 1977 general election. Senator Seamus Brennan, the General Secretary of Fianna Fáil, rebutted these claims, suggesting that 'political promises' were 'a

57 *The Irish Times*, 22 October 1977.

58 *The Irish Times*, 27 October 1977.

59 TCD MUN/SOC/HIST Uncatalogued Papers, 1970-79.

legitimate and indeed necessary part of the democratic process'. Also opposing the motion was Fianna Fáil TD, Liam Lawlor.

'That Only Violence will Free South Africa' was the motion on 25 January 1978, and Seán MacBride used the event to accuse NATO of collaborating in secret with South Africa, creating the possibility of an East-West clash in Africa. Stating that he was 'technically opposing' the motion, MacBride explained that he did not believe violence was the only solution in South Africa.[60] MacBride discussed the high mortality rate among blacks in South Africa and suggested that the people were quite entitled to rise up in arms to prevent this 'genocide'. Kadar Asmal, now a senior lecturer in Law at Trinity and a major figure in the Irish Anti-Apartheid Movement, spoke in favour of the motion. Insisting he was not a pacifist, he said that the panoply of legislation in South Africa made any form of non-violent opposition impossible. Both MacBride and Asmal warned that it was wrong to make comparisons between Ireland and South Africa. Asmal suggested that international pressure was important and would continue to be important, but that only the people of South Africa could liberate themselves.

Peter Charleton went on to become a successful barrister (described as 'stellar' by *The Sunday Business Post*), criminal law author, and Supreme Court judge.[61] As a barrister it was noted that he was 'diligent, organized and quick on his feet with keen analytical skills. He could cut through a brief with knife-like precision. Even when defending in a criminal case, his approach was direct, never flowery.'[62] A lawyer noted that 'he'd focus on the points which could be won, rather than wasting the time of the court'. Charleton chaired the Disclosures Tribunal and in October 2018 published a hard-hitting report which exonerated the whistleblower, Maurice McCabe, and vindicated Frances Fitzgerald, the former Minister for Justice. An editorial in *The Irish Times* praised Charleton's 'lucid, clear-eyed prose' and said he had succeeded in painting 'a picture of almost total dysfunction' in the Gardaí.[63] In its review of the year,

60 *The Irish Times*, 26 January 1978.

61 *The Sunday Business Post*, 4 March 2017.

62 Ibid.

63 *The Irish Times*, 12 October 2018.

The Times noted that the report 'excoriated Martin Callinan, the former Garda Commissioner, and David Taylor, the former press officer, for carrying out "a campaign of calumny" against Mr Mc Cabe'.[64]

'Do you enjoy bad taste, vulgarity and the occasional obscenity?' asked a poster around Trinity during Fresher's Week in October 1978, 'Then join the Hist'.[65] The poster belied the seriousness of what was happening in the Society in this period. Joseph Jackson was elected Auditor for the 209th session, and his Committee included Roy Dooney (who later became a Government adviser) as Treasurer, Rory Montgomery as Librarian and Brian Lenihan as Censor. During this period Rory Montgomery shared rooms with his close friend, Brian Lenihan. Described as 'clever and clubbable', he helped negotiate the Good Friday Agreement and was described in *The Irish Times* as 'the intellectual powerhouse on all things European' and he went on to play a leading role during the Brexit negotiations.[66] Brian Lenihan's subsequent career is well known. He became a Fianna Fáil TD and Minister, and was Minister for Finance during the crisis years of 2008 to 2011, where he worked to stabilise the Irish economy despite being diagnosed in December 2009 with pancreatic cancer. The leader of Fine Gael, Enda Kenny, praised his 'wonderful courage' while 'carrying out his public duties in the most challenging economic circumstances'.[67] He died in June 2011, a few months after leaving office.

Jackson delivered his inaugural paper entitled 'A New Direction for Ireland' on 25 October 1978 and speakers included Dr Garret FitzGerald and John Ross. 'That the Men of 1916 Should have Saved their Ink' was debated on 8 November 1978 with Conor Cruise O'Brien in the chair. At this time O'Brien was back in the Seanad, having lost his seat in the 1977 general election following his time as Minister for Posts and Telegraphs in the coalition government. O'Brien suggested that Pearse's words at the grave of O'Donovan Rossa had provided republicans with 'a licence to kill'.[68] He claimed

64 *The Times (Ireland),* 26 December 2018.

65 *The Irish Times,* 12 October 1978.

66 *The Irish Times,* 30 March 2018.

67 *The Guardian,* 13 June 2011.

68 *The Irish Times,* 9 November 1978.

that the insistence that 'Ireland unfree shall never be at peace' were 'powerful words... They are the bidding to the killers'. In his conclusion he accused Pearse of blasphemy in his approach to the blood sacrifice, describing the 1916 Rising as 'the terrorist acting out the sacrifice of Christ'. The motion was defeated.

Notable debates that session included 'That Wedlock is Padlock' (18 October 1978) with Nuala Fennell speaking, and 'That Fianna Fáil has given you Your Kind of Country' (10 January 1979). The meeting on 24 January 1979 was adjourned to mark the death of T. C. Kingsmill Moore. Professor Mary McAleese chaired the debate on 18 April 1979 'That this House Calls for a British Withdrawal from Northern Ireland', which was carried.

The 1970s was the last great decade of the Society in terms of the debates being covered in national media. Politicians began to use radio and television to get their message across and, as the power of the speech was eroded, coverage of the Society began to dwindle. In the years ahead the Society was obliged to reinvent itself and take on a new identity. What remained consistent was its determination to provide a forum where new ideas could be tested and challenged, and where its members could be shaped by a mixture of ideas, some prolix, some provocative, and some profound.

22 A NEW ERA, 1979-1989

THE SOCIETY HAD A CHANGING PLACE in Irish society in the 1980s. There was no longer the same level of media interest in the big debates taking place on campus, or what the major guest speakers said and, as a result, we no longer have the same level of detailed accounts of debates in national newspapers as we had before. Sometimes a major debate was covered, sometimes the records of the Society or the student newspapers provide details, but more often we have a list of speakers and the result of a debate (and not always even that), and often no details about what was said. Television and radio were proving more effective for people wishing to make a public statement on something, taking the place of making a speech in a debating society that would be reported the next day. In this decade we see the Society finding a new role for itself, both within College and outside of it, less visible in terms of media coverage, but more determined than ever to provide a forum for old orthodoxies to be challenged and new ideas to be tested and developed.

Alexander Owens was Auditor for the 210th session and his inaugural meeting took place on 26 October 1979. His paper was entitled 'Abuse of Power' and guest speakers included Professor John Kelly TD, Austin Currie, Senator Noel Mulcahy, and the former deputy leader of the British Labour Party, George Brown. Debates that session include one on the motion 'That this House deplores the Pernicious Influence of the Media on Public Taste and Opinion' on 31 October 1979, chaired by broadcaster Pat Kenny, which was carried.[1]

The first joint meeting of the College Historical Society and the University Philosophical Society (or 'with the Other Society' as the records note) took place the following night, on 1 November 1979,

1 TCD MUN/SOC/HIST Uncatalogued Papers, 1970-79.

chaired by Professor Mary McAleese, with a debate between the candidates for the University of Dublin Seanad seat recently vacated by Conor Cruise O'Brien. The motion was suitably provocative: 'That this House Believes that Dr O'Brien's Seat is not Worth Filling'. One of the candidates, David Norris, thanked the societies for 'reconciling their historical and philosophical differences' to enable the meeting to take place, a meeting which was described as somewhat surreal given that none of the undergraduates present had a vote in the upcoming election.[2]

The star speech was by Norris, 'impeccably turned out in a well-worn academic gown', who opposed the motion. Catherine McGuinness, who went on to win the seat, criticised the other candidates for outlining policies on a whole range of national issues, 'as if, once elected, they would be forming a one-man government'. And she criticised O'Brien for his record of non-attendance and non-participation in the life of the Senate. Shane Ross called for Trinity to have greater self-confidence, suggesting that 'the College seems to be ashamed of its past, frightened of its own shadow, and it has no reason to be'. Summing up at the end of the debate, Mary McAleese wished the candidates the best and said that whoever was elected would be lost in the Seanad because the chamber had no real power, but that any of them would be a great asset in the Dáil, where there was such a lack of real talent.[3]

Mary McAleese later recounted that one of the best speakers she remembered from this period was Brian Lenihan, the son of the Fianna Fáil politician, who was elected Treasurer for the 211st session, and who went on to serve as Minister for Finance, showing courage and ability at one the most difficult periods in modern Irish history. She recalled that he was, 'even then, a very passionate debater' and 'on the floor of the debating chamber ... he showed an ability to both analyse very quickly and to respond very quickly'.[4]

Conor Cruise O'Brien, now editor-in-chief of the *Observer* newspaper, chaired the debate on 14 November 1979 on the motion

2 *The Irish Times*, 2 November 1979.

3 Ibid.

4 Brian Murphy, Mary O'Rourke and Noel Whelan (eds), *Brian Lenihan: In Calm and Crisis* (Dublin, 2014).

'That this House reveres the memory of Patrick Pearse', which was defeated.[5] Mary McAleese returned to chair the debate 'That this House would Decriminalise Abortion' on 6 February 1980, and proposing the motion was Anne Connolly, Director of the Well Woman Centres in Dublin. The motion was carried. Other motions included 'That this House has Confidence in the Government' on 13 February 1980 which was defeated.[6]

For his inaugural meeting on Friday 17 October 1980, the Auditor for the 211st session, Sean Moran, delivered a paper on 'Ireland, Independence, and our World'.[7] In it he argued that other countries were not interested in the problem of Northern Ireland, and that the United States in particular would be reluctant to do anything to upset the UK, 'its head boy at the NATO school'. The Minister for Foreign Affairs, Brian Lenihan, also spoke, and he suggested that it was for Ireland and Britain to work together, in co-operation with the communities in the North, to resolve the conflict of rights which was at the heart of the violence. In his speech, Conor Cruise O'Brien argued that Irish people needed to accept without reservation the right of other Irish people to remain in the United Kingdom. He said he hoped Garret FitzGerald would be the next Taoiseach, admitting that 'he talks a certain amount of nonsense about Northern Ireland, but at least it is generous nonsense with no threats about it'.[8]

Other motions that session included 'That this House would be Pleased to see the Election of Ronald Reagan' (29 October 1980) which was defeated, and 'That this House supports Capital Punishment' (5 November 1980), also defeated.[9] The hunger strikes were debated on 19 November 1980 with the motion 'That this House would Yield to the Hunger Strikers', which was rejected.[10]

On 11 February 1981 the proposed IRFU tour to South Africa was debated with the motion 'That the Tour should Go Ahead'. The meeting was chaired by the rugby broadcaster, Tom McGurk, and

---

5 TCD MUN/SOC/HIST Uncatalogued Papers, 1980-89.

6 Ibid.

7 *Irish Independent*, 18 October 1980.

8 *Evening Herald*, 18 October 1980.

9 TCD MUN/SOC/HIST Uncatalogued Papers, 1980-89.

10 Ibid.

Kadar Asmal, the chair of the Anti-Apartheid Movement, denounced the tour as a 'ghastly mistake'.[11] The motion was defeated. The Provost, F.S.L. Lyons, a Vice-President of the Society, chaired the intervarsity debate on 8 April 1981 on the motion 'That History Televised is History Trivialised'. At this point, Lyons had already tendered his resignation as Provost, but carried on in the role until September, and unfortunately the records do not reveal his thoughts from the chair.[12] The motion was defeated.

The inaugural meeting on 6 November 1981 was controversial, with the new Provost, William Watts, refusing to chair the event because one of the invited speakers was Owen Carron, the MP for Fermanagh and South Tyrone. Carron had been the election agent for Bobby Sands, and following his death in 1981 had stood at the by-election in his place as an Anti H-Block candidate and had won the seat, becoming the youngest MP at the time. Watts was influenced by an incident which had taken place in March 1981 in College, at the height of the hunger-strikers campaign in Northern Ireland, when Geoffrey Armstrong, the chairman of British Leyland and director of the Confederation of British Industry, was giving an invited lecture in the Arts Building. Three masked gunmen burst into the theatre and shot Armstrong three times in the leg, shouting 'This action is in support of the H-Blocks'.[13]

Watts explained that Carron's 'association with groups supporting violence and responsible for violent act's made it impossible for him to attend.[14] In the event, David McConnell, former Auditor and at this time a lecturer in the College and a Vice-President of the Society, stepped into his place. William R. Maguire delivered his inaugural address on 'Authority and Freedom' and other speakers included Senator John A. Murphy, Albert Reynolds, the former Minister for Posts and Telegraphs (and future Taoiseach), and Ivan Yates, the Fine Gael TD.

During the meeting, Carron said that nationalists in Northern Ireland could not be criticised for defending themselves against a

11 *Irish Independent*, 12 February 1981.

12 TCD MUN/SOC/HIST Uncatalogued Papers, 1980-89.

13 *The Irish Times*, 6 November 1981.

14 Ibid.

regime which had consistently denied them a share in government. Arguing that the so-called political criminals of today were the martyrs and saints of the next age, he asked 'Do we not admire freedom fighters in other parts of the world?'[15]

Albert Reynolds used his speech to defend his decision as minister to continue the ban on RTE for members of illegal organisations, saying that 'Freedom can be hampered in many ways, and not least by the projection of attitudes onto society'. He argued that society needed to be able to protect itself, especially when individuals harbour hatreds for others in the community. In his speech, Ivan Yates said the voice of authority and freedom in the country should condemn all violence, terrorism and intimidation, so that the most important principle of all was retained, that of 'respect others as yourself'.

'That Abortion is a Necessary Evil' was the motion on 25 November 1981, and speakers included Anne Connolly of the Well Woman Centres in Dublin. The motion was defeated.[16] The maiden speaker's final took place on 2 November 1981 with the motion 'That Solidarity puts both Communism and Trade Unionism to Shame'. The winner was Iseult O'Malley and later that year she won the National Maiden Speaker's Competition. 'That violence is the only answer to Apartheid' was debated on 20 January 1982, with Kadar Asmal one of the speakers. The motion was carried.[17]

Northern Ireland was again debated on 7 April 1982, with the motion 'That the Solution for the Northern Ireland Problem lies in a United Ireland', chaired by Conor Cruise O'Brien. The debate was notable for the fact that two British politicians spoke in favour of a united Ireland, Kevin McNamara, the Labour MP, and Paul Rose, the branch secretary of the SDP. McNamara argued that the validity of a united Ireland was something that was 'stark and glaring', suggesting that it was the solution 'we have run away from'.[18]

The first meeting of the 213rd session was on the motion 'That Gay Rights are Human Rights'. Speakers included Áine Lawlor, the

---

15 *The Irish Times*, 7 November 1981.

16 TCD MUN/SOC/HIST Uncatalogued Papers, 1980-89.

17 TCD MUN/SOC/HIST Uncatalogued Papers, 1980-89.

18 *The Irish Times*, 8 April 1982.

President of Trinity Students Union and future RTÉ broadcaster, and Mary Kennedy of the Irish Family League, with the debate chaired by David Norris. Lawlor returned to the Society to chair the final meeting of the session on 30 March 1983 'That this House supports a General Student Strike', which was defeated.[19]

The second meeting of the 213rd session debated the legacy of perhaps the most dominant Irish political figure of the twentieth century, with the motion 'That this House Reveres the Memory of Éamon de Valera'.[20] Jack Lynch rose to propose the motion and the Auditor, Eoin McCullough, later recounted how he was greeted by a standing ovation before he said a word, 'the affection that those present felt for him was a reflection of his decency, but also of what had happened in his party since he resigned as Taoiseach in 1979'.[21] Lynch suggested that no leader had more totally dedicated himself to the service of his country, calling de Valera a visionary and also a practical man, and insisted that 'to an extent Dev's strength was the nation's weakness'. Also supporting the motion was Seán Haughey, the son of Charles J. Haughey. Opposing the motion, Professor Robin Dudley Edwards of UCD said that if the Society passed the motion it would be going against its tradition by saying that it revered a man whose doctrine was that he was a Catholic and that this was the normal religion of Irish people. The motion was narrowly passed, by 122 votes to 120.

'That the Abortion Referendum is a Cosmetic Exercise' was the motion on 17 November 1982.[22] Trinity lecturer (and future President of DCU) Ferdinand von Prondzynski chaired the debate, and speakers included Senator (and future Supreme Court judge) Catherine McGuinness, Patsy Buckley and Dr Máire Woods.[23]

A motion of no confidence in the Fine Gael-Labour Government, which had only come into office on 12 December 1982, was debated on 12 January 1983 with the meeting chaired by the

19 TCD MUN/SOC/HIST Uncatalogued Papers, 1980-89.

20 *The Irish Times*, 21 October 1982.

21 Kate McGuinness (ed.), *Trinity Tales: Trinity College Dublin in the Eighties* (Dublin, 2014), p. 43.

22 TCD MUN/SOC/HIST Uncatalogued Papers, 1980-89.

23 TCD MUN/SOC/HIST Uncatalogued Papers, 1980-89.

political scientist, Dr Tom Garvin. Opposing the motion, Michael Keating, the Fine Gael TD, argued that now was the time to put national interest before self-interest, calling for 'a rebirth of patriotism, in the best sense of that word'.[24] Michael O'Kennedy, the Fianna Fáil TD, supported the motion and noted that it was unprecedented for the Society to propose a motion of no confidence in a Government in its first month in office. Other speakers include Bertie Ahern, the Fianna Fáil TD, and Richard Bruton, the Fine Gael TD. The motion was carried.

The Society hosted the Irish *Observer* Mace final on 26 January 1983 and the competition was won by their own team, with Declan McCavana and Iseult O'Malley speaking on the motion 'That University Education should be a Right, not a Privilege'.[25] McCavana later became a Senior Lecturer at the Ecole Polytechnique in Paris, and President of the French Debating Association and was awarded an OBE for services to the promotion of the English language in France, while O'Malley later became a successful barrister and Supreme Court judge.

McCullough delivered his inaugural paper entitled 'Towards a Just Society' on 25 February 1983 in the Mansion House. The security staff in Trinity were on strike and two of the speakers, the Tánaiste and leader of the Labour Party, Dick Spring, and the trade unionist, Donal Nevin, refused to cross the picket line, so an alternative venue outside of College was found. Other speakers included Mr Justice Declan Costello (author of the original *Just Society* document) and Conor Cruise O'Brien. Writing about the evening years later, McCullough noted that he remembered little of the occasion, except that he was 'interrupted consistently by a drunk' from the back of the room.[26]

Declan Sheehan was the Auditor for the 214th session and his first meeting was the Freshers' debate on 12 October 1983 with the motion 'That Venereal Diseases are the Wages of Sin', which was defeated, with David Norris one of the guest speakers. Michael Foot, who had stepped down as leader of the British Labour Party a few

24 *The Irish Times*, 13 January 1983.

25 TCD MUN/SOC/HIST Uncatalogued Papers, 1980-89.

26 McGuinness (ed.), *Trinity Tales*, p. 44.

weeks earlier after a disastrous electoral defeat in June, chaired the debate on 19 October 1983, with the motion 'That Socialism is an Outmoded Philosophy'. Foot was a major draw and, according to *The Irish Times*, over 500 people attended the meeting.[27] Proposing the motion was John Kelly, the Fine Gael TD, and opposing the motion was Senator Michael D. Higgins. When the motion was defeated, 'gloriously defeated' according to the chair, Foot delivered his own speech, attacking Kelly for wanting to introduce Thatcherite economic policies into Ireland. The main focus of his speech, however, was a plea for disarmament.[28]

Senator Mary Robinson chaired the debate on 30 November 1983 on the motion 'That Prostitution must be Legalised' which was carried. This meeting was notable for the election of Conor Cruise O'Brien, unopposed, as President of the Society, following the resignation of F. H. Boland.[29] Having resigned as editor-in-chief of the *Observer*, O'Brien was now a journalist with *The Irish Times*, later moving to the *Irish Independent*, and eventually to the *Sunday Independent*.[30]

'That this House would Proscribe Sinn Féin' was the motion on 15 February 1984. Danny Morrison, of Sinn Féin, opposed the motion, and urged the members to dismiss the 'creeping fascism' of the motion.[31] Morrison defended the military actions of the IRA and suggested that 'the limited freedoms' enjoyed in the south today were as a result of violence in the past. Supporting the motion was Jeffrey Dudgeon, who in 1982 had won a case in the European Court of Human Rights that British homosexual legislation should be extended to Northern Ireland, who argued that the IRA was winning a war that was unwinnable because it could only be won by destroying a tribe of people. Professor John A. Murphy suggested that refusing to deal with Sinn Féin delegations was a 'gesture of perverse stupidity'.

Sheehan presented his inaugural paper on 6 April 1984, on the theme 'Limits to Social Justice'. Arguing that most public

---

27 *The Irish Times*, 21 October 1983.

28 *The Irish Times*, 21 October 1983.

29 TCD MUN/SOC/HIST Uncatalogued Papers, 1980-89.

30 Frank Callanan, 'Conor Cruise O'Brien', *DIB.*

31 *The Irish Times*, 16 February 1984.

expenditure benefitted the better off than the less well off.', he made an eloquent plea for a better way of doing things[32] Senator Brendan Ryan (Independent, NUI) spoke at the meeting and suggested that conflict was inevitable in society as 'the oppressed of this world, already restless, will rise up in outrage and change will be achieved'. However, he added the caveat, 'unless, that is, the greedy and powerful obliterate us all first'.

A team representing the Society won *The Irish Times* debating competition in 1984, with former Auditor, Eoin McCullough, and future Auditor, Brian Murray, achieving a sixth overall team victory for the Hist. Murray, the outgoing Treasurer, was elected Auditor for the 215th session unopposed. The first meeting of the session took place on 10 October 1984 with Lord Longford in the chair for a debate on the motion 'That Pornography is the Opium of the Impotent'. Speakers included the talented actor and comedian, Dermot Morgan, and David Norris.[33]

The distinguished Supreme Court Judge, the Hon. Mr Justice Niall McCarthy, chaired the debate on 24 October 1984 on the motion 'That our Written Constitution has Served Us Well'. Speakers included Senior Counsel (and future Supreme Court Judge) Niall Fennelly, and Senator Mary Robinson. The motion was tied and, remaining impartial, the chair does not appear to have used his casting vote to have settled it. The debate the following week was also tied, on the motion 'That this House would Legalise Divorce'. Speakers included Desmond Fennell, Proinsias de Rossa TD, and Fr Brendan Purcell, with Mr Justice Rory O'Hanlon of the High Court in the chair. Again the chair, a member of the judiciary, seems to have decided against settling the debate one way or another.[34]

Murray's inaugural paper was on the subject 'Liberty and Equality' on 9 November 1984 and guest speakers included Dr John Bowman; the former Auditor, Dr Declan Kiberd; Mr Justice Niall McCarthy; and Clive Soley, the British Labour MP. Other notable debates that session included 'That Nationalism is a Bar to Progress' on 16 January 1985, chaired by Kader Asmal, which was defeated.[35]

32 *The Irish Times*, 7 April 1984.

33 TCD MUN/SOC/HIST Uncatalogued Papers, 1980-89.

34 TCD MUN/SOC/HIST Uncatalogued Papers, 1980-89.

35 TCD MUN/SOC/HIST Uncatalogued Papers, 1980-89.

The Auditor was part of the winning team in the Irish *Observer* Mace final on 6 February 1985 hosted by the Society, speaking alongside Declan McCavana, on the motion 'That this House would declare Western Europe a Nuclear Free Zone'. One of the final debates of the session was on 3 April 1985 on the motion 'That every Embryo is Sacred'. The distinguished geneticist, Professor George Dawson, was in the chair and speakers included Senator Catherine McGuinness and Dr Mary Henry. The motion was defeated.[36]

Sallyanne Godson was elected Auditor for the 216th session and her opening meeting was on the motion 'That Morality is the Last Refuge of the Hypocrite', with the journalist Mary Kenny one of the guest speakers. There was some controversy afterwards when Kenny criticised the students in an article in the *Sunday Independent* for being 'scruffy' and lamented the fact that the students seemed to have lost their manners.[37] In a response in the same paper, Godson dismissed these comments as 'exaggerated, unfair and unjustified'.[38] She noted pointedly that 'the purpose of the College Historical Society is not to appeal to the snobbish prejudices of the reformed, London-based journalists, but to provide an open forum for serious debate'.

Notable debates that session included 'That a Right to Strike is a Danger to the Community' (30 October 1985) which was defeated and which included two future leaders of the Labour Party among the guest speakers, Pat Rabbitte and Ruairi Quinn.[39] Godson's inaugural paper was delivered on 15 November 1985 and was entitled 'Pluralism and Ireland' and speakers included the Hon. Mr Justice Declan Costello, Desmond Fennell, Professor John Kelly, and Dr Aidan Doyle. The Taoiseach, Dr Garret FitzGerald, had agreed to speak, but had to cancel at the last minute so he could travel to Hillsborough Castle to sign the Anglo-Irish Agreement. Others included 'That the Students' Union needs a Shake-up' (5 March 1986), which was carried, and 'That this House rejects the Principle of Coalition' (12 March 1986) which had the brilliant Trinity historian, Dr David Fitzpatrick, in the chair.[40]

---

36 TCD MUN/SOC/HIST Uncatalogued Papers, 1980-89.

37 *Sunday Independent*, 13 October 1985.

38 *Sunday Independent*, 27 October 1985.

39 TCD MUN/SOC/HIST Uncatalogued Papers, 1980-89.

Senator Mary Robinson chaired the debate on Wednesday 20 November 1985 on the motion 'That Dublin has no Role in the Government of Northern Ireland'. This was a dramatic appearance, given that she had resigned from the Labour Party two days earlier over her opposition to the Anglo-Irish Agreement. Robinson believed that the Agreement was 'unworkable' because of Unionist opposition and would not achieve its objective of securing peace and stability in Northern Ireland.[41] Guest speakers at the debate included Professor John A. Murphy and Paddy Devlin, the founding member of the SDLP who was now a member of the United Labour Party.

After leaving Trinity Godson joined the BBC as a researcher on a politics programme called 'On the Record', presented by Jonathan Dimbleby. She credits her 'Hist training' with getting through the selection process, and it meant she could 'hold my own at On the Record team meetings which were modelled on Oxbridge seminars: my contemporaries there included Nick Robinson, Martha Kearney, John Rentoul, Sean O'Grady, all prominent political journalists in the UK to this day'.[42] Godson later became a producer on *Newsnight* and other programmes, before returning to Ireland and becoming a producer on RTE's *Prime Time.*

Committee member Doreen Shivnen stood for election to succeed Godson as Auditor, raising the prospect of two successive women Auditors for the first time in the Society's history, and this seems to have made some people uneasy. Comments were made that 'it would be inappropriate or unseemly or unbecoming or, failing all else, unlikely that another woman would be elected in direct succession to the second female Auditor.'[43] It was hinted that if Shivnen wished to run for Auditor it might be better 'to try her hand some other year?' However, Shivnen ignored these 'hints' and stood for election, winning a decisive victory. After graduation, Shivnen studied at the King's Inns and became a successful barrister, specialising in Probate and Chancery matters.

The officers for the 217th session included David Langwallner as

---

40 TCD MUN/SOC/HIST Uncatalogued Papers, 1980-89.

41 *The Irish Times*, 19 November 1985, 21 November 1985.

42 Correspondence with the Author.

43 Ibid.

Record Secretary, with Anthony Whelan on the Committee. The first meeting took place on 11 October 1986 with the motion 'That the Medium is the Message'. The main guest speaker was Oliver J. Flanagan, the Fine Gael TD and former Minister for Defence, and he accused the media of being one-sided during the recent abortion and divorce referendums. Flanagan noted that he was still in public life after thirty years, despite 'a badly-created public image by the media'.[44]

Ernest Walton, the Nobel Prize winning physicist and retired Trinity professor, chaired the debate on 18 October 1986 on the motion 'That Scientific Advance is Logical Regression', but unfortunately we do not have a record of what he said. Other notable debates that session included 'That this House would Embrace a Gayer Culture' (19 November 1986), which was defeated, with speakers including Nell McCafferty, and 'That this House would Decriminalise Prostitution' (28 January 1987), which was carried.[45]

The Anglo-Irish Agreement was debated a second time on 14 November 1986 on the occasion of the Auditor's inaugural paper, entitled 'Politics and Government'. Senator Mary Robinson was in the chair and speakers included Baroness Ewart-Biggs, Professor Brian Farrell, John Hume, the leader of the SDLP, and Mr Justice Niall McCarthy.[46] In his speech, John Hume said that the British Government was doing a service to all communities in Northern Ireland by standing firm against Unionist blackmail. And he posed the question whether Irish nationalism and republicanism was up for the challenge of persuading the Protestant minority in Ireland that Irish unity and freedom were a matter for Irish people to decide.[47]

Lady Jane Ewart-Biggs, the widow of Christopher Ewart-Biggs, the British ambassador to Ireland who had been blown up shortly after his arrival in Ireland in 1976, delivered a powerful speech, drawing on extracts from her late husband's diary. She admitted that she found it surprising that in Ireland, both north and south, where there were 'so many problems of poverty and deprivation', there was not a proper socialist party. Praising the Anglo-Irish Agreement as

44 *The Irish Times*, 2 October 1986.

45 TCD MUN/SOC/HIST Uncatalogued Papers, 1980-89.

46 Ibid.

47 *The Irish Times*, 15 November 1986.

'tangible evidence of reconciliation', she suggested that it offered a framework within which the people of Northern Ireland could learn to live together. Speaking from the chair, Robinson argued that an opportunity had been lost when a proposal to modify Articles 2 and 3 of the Irish Constitution had been dropped. She argued that this was 'a tragic omission of a vital piece of the jigsaw of putting together the framework for lasting peace in Ireland'.

Former Taoiseach, Jack Lynch, chaired the final of *The Irish Times* debating competition on 3 February 1987, which was hosted by the Society and televised on RTE. The motion was 'That the GAA has been a Positive Influence on the Development of Irish Society' and the mood became 'raucous and celebratory' as the Hist team of Paul Gavin and Aidan Kane won the competition, a seventh team win overall.[48]

One of the Vice-Presidents of the Society, John Ross, returned to chair the Honorary Members' debate on 1 May 1987 on the motion 'That this House would Praise Famous Men', and speakers included former Auditor, Maurice Abrahamson, and former Record Secretary, the chair's son, Shane Ross.[49]

The former Censor, Kane, won the gold medal for oratory at the end of the session, but is reported to have declined the award for reasons that are not explained in the records.[50] None the less, he is listed as a gold medallist in the records at subsequent appearances in the Society. Kane was elected Auditor of the 218th session unopposed and his first meeting took place on 7 October 1987 on the motion 'That this House Respects the Private Lives of Public Figures'. The debate was chaired by Senator David Norris and guests included Angela Phelan and Jonathan Philbin Bowman, with the motion defeated.

Founding member of the Progressive Democrats, Michael McDowell, spoke to the Society on 14 October 1987 opposing the motion 'that this House Reveres the Men of October 1917' and made headlines for his attack on the Workers' Party, calling them 'dangerously subversive'.[51] In a dramatic denunciation, he accused

---

48 TCD MUN/SOC/HIST Uncatalogued Papers, 1980-89; Correspondence between Doreen Shivnen and Author.

49 TCD MUN/SOC/HIST Uncatalogued Papers, 1980-89.

50 Ibid.

51 *The Irish Times*, 15 October 1987.

them of having 'a wing which clearly extends into violent subversion, racketeering and, on occasion, murder'. He suggested that 'they have no commitment to liberal politics, liberal values or civil liberties'. Afterwards, the leader of the Workers' party, Tomás Mac Giolla, dismissed the attack as 'a whole baggage-pack of lies and innuendo straight out of his own twisted mind' and called it an 'unbelievable attack'. Other speakers included the Trinity historian, Dr John Horne, and the UCD historian, Dr Hugh Gough, as well as the broadcaster Marty Whelan. Despite McDowell's denunciation the motion was carried.

The debate on 21 October 1987 was on the reform of the Constitution, and the leader of Fine Gael, Alan Dukes, argued that the Constitution was 'not written in tablets of stone, nor does it have the status of Holy Writ'.[52] He suggested that it was a mistake to think that what was needed was a new Constitution, or no change at all, because in reality the Constitution was 'not a single seamless garment' but 'a series of prescriptions relating to discrete areas of activities' where changes could be made to some areas without affecting others. Speaking against him was Dr Mary Lucey of the Society for the Protection of the Unborn Child (SPUC), who asked 'How can we trust our politicians? How can we rely on them? Their promises, like the Treaty of Limerick, are broken before the ink is dry.' Lucey suggested that it was 'nonsense' to praise the former Taoiseach, Garret FitzGerald for showing courage with his constitutional crusade, as apparently 'all that is required today to qualify as a folk hero is to take on the bad old Catholic church'.

Other debates that session included 'That our Children will Revere the Name of Margaret Thatcher', chaired by the Trinity economist Dr Seán Barrett (and later Senator and Pro Chancellor of the University). Speakers included Lady Olga Maitland, the British journalist who had failed to win a seat for the Conservatives in that summer's general election, the journalist James Downey and Captain James Kelly, and the motion was carried.[53]

The leader of Sinn Féin, Gerry Adams, proposed the motion on 17 February 1988 'That this House would Repeal Section 31 of the

52 *The Irish Times*, 22 October 1987.

53 TCD MUN/SOC/HIST Uncatalogued Papers, 1980-89.

Broadcasting Act'. This was a time when most members of the Society would not have heard the voice of Adams because of the ban on broadcasting the voices of those suspected of being involved in terrorist activities. The chamber filled early and the door outside was blocked as 'a huge crowd tried to get in'.[54] One student at the time, Ivana Bacik, recalls being smuggled into the meeting with a few others by a friend on the Committee. She notes that 'this was a highly charged event' and 'the campus was crawling with both uniformed and undercover Gardaí, all on the alert for trouble'. Despite all of this drama, she remembers that 'the speech itself was somewhat underwhelming.' Opposing the motion that evening was Senator John A. Murphy and the barrister Frank Callanan. The motion was carried.

A memorial debate was held on 2 March 1988 to honour the former President of the Society, F. H. Boland, who had died in 1985. The motion was 'That Diplomacy is an Honourable Profession' and speakers included the Irish diplomat Philip McDonagh, and the Australian and British ambassadors. The motion was carried.[55]

The Correspondence Secretary, Anthony Whelan, a Scholar and silver medallist of the Society, was elected Auditor unopposed for the 219th session and his first debate was on the motion 'That this House would Limit the Power of the Press', with guests including George Birmingham, Mary Kenny and Conor Brady. Michael McDowell and Proinsias de Rossa squared off on 11 October 1988 debating the motion 'That the Future of the Left is On the Right', with the debate chaired by Shane Ross. Mark Little, the President of Trinity's Students' Union, spoke at the debate on 19 October 1988, 'That the Catholic Church has been Good for Ireland', and a week later the Chief Justice of Ireland, Thomas Finlay, chaired the debate, 'That the Death Penalty is a Necessity'. Speakers included Michael Noonan, the Fine Gael TD, and Roger Gale, the British Conservative MP.[56]

Northern Ireland was debated on 9 November 1988 with the motion, 'That this House believes the Time has come to Talk to

54 Account of Ivana Bacik, correspondence with Author.

55 TCD MUN/SOC/HIST Uncatalogued Papers, 1980-89.

56 Ibid.

Terrorists', in a debate chaired by Baroness Ewart-Biggs.[57] Opposing the motion, Ken Maginnis, Official Unionist MP, said that allowing Sinn Féin members to speak on the air waves about community issues was like allowing paedophiles to speak about society's problems. Both posed a threat to society, and both were rejected by an overwhelming majority. He argued that 'we cannot afford these people the same rights' and concluded from this that 'if we cannot afford them the same rights and freedom of the air waves how can we talk to them and sit down with them around the table'? Supporting the motion was Alban Maginness, the chair of the SDLP, who discussed his party's new strategy of engaging in talks with Sinn Féin. Even though they had ended in failure, he prophesised that in historical terms the SDLP's initiation of talks would be seen as successful. The motion was carried.

Anthony Whelan delivered his inaugural paper on 17 November 1988 on the subject of 'Party Politics', and the meeting was notable for the clash between the leader of the Progressive Democrats, Des O'Malley, and the Minister for the Environment, Pádraig Flynn. Flynn spent most of his speech attacking the Progressive Democrats, claiming they had broken no moulds, and had lost their initial optimism, having reached 'organisational middle age'.[58] In response, O'Malley dismissed Flynn's speech as 'almost theatrical'. Professor John Kelly of Fine Gael suggested that Ireland was bound to coalition governments because of the narrow majorities and the PR voting system. He described the current Fianna Fáil minority government as 'an effective coalition' because there was broad agreement between Fianna Fáil and Fine Gael on economic policy.

Arthur Scargill was the main attraction for the debate on 31 November 1988 on the motion that 'That the Share-Owning Democracy is a License for Greed'. In a passionate oration he denounced the British Prime Minister, Margaret Thatcher, at every turn. He asked rhetorically whether there was a future for coal, and then suggested that 'Of course there is. That is why Mrs Thatcher is trying to privatise it.'[59] Warning that nuclear-powered electricity was

57 TCD MUN/SOC/HIST Uncatalogued Papers, 1980-89; *The Irish Times*, 10 November 1988.

58 *The Irish Times*, 18 November 1988.

59 *Sunday Independent*, 4 December 1988.

dangerous, he claimed that the Irish Sea had 'radioactive levels 26 times higher than those recorded in the American nuclear testing grounds in the South Pacific'. Arguing against Scargill was John Bruton, Fine Gael TD, and future Taoiseach. During the debate, a student speaker, described in the *Sunday Independent* as 'the intense young man with the jutting chin', proclaimed that 'Apathy is the enemy of Democracy'. At this, someone heckled 'Who cares'? prompting much laughter and 'even Arthur Scargill giggled'. The motion was carried by a significant majority.

The Maiden Speakers' Final on 7 December 1988 was hugely controversial. The motion was 'That this House supports gradual reform in South Africa'. The Society had invited Justus de Goede, the South African Minister Plenipotentiary at its Embassy in London, to chair the event, but had not publicised this fact, or told the sponsor of the competition, Bank of Ireland. [60] However, news leaked out, and shortly before the debate was to begin, with de Goede in the GMB, College received news that a protest was being organized, and it instructed the Society to remove de Goede from the campus. The Society had only told College of 'the secret invitation' the day before, and had agreed 'in the event of a mass demonstration, not to proceed'.[61] As the Correspondence Secretary, Chris Hayden, later explained, the Senior Dean, Peter Boyle, when he heard what was being planned, 'told me to get him the hell out of there'. The student officer with Bank of Ireland, Brendan King, later revealed that had he known there was going to be a South African diplomat in the chair he would also have objected to him.

The debate proceeded without de Groede and at one stage was interrupted by a middle-aged woman 'who said she wished to protest at the invitation issued to the South African diplomat'. *The Irish Times* reported, 'the woman was surrounded by a group of students and was manhandled as she continued to protest', but this was later corrected by the Auditor, Anthony Whelan. Whelan explained that 'the woman was repeatedly called to order, and eventually was asked to leave because she would not allow a student speaker to continue

60 *The Irish Times*, 8 December 1988.

61 *The Irish Times*, 8 December 1988.

uninterrupted'.[62] The Censor, Orla Corrigan, was asked to escort the woman from the chamber, but when the woman refused, security was called to 'ensure her quiet eviction'. As Whelan correctly noted, 'the only violence was when she assaulted a student who challenged her views'.

The private business meeting that followed the public meeting was 'stormy'. One speaker threatened that if the Society ever invited a similar guest 'you will be in deep trouble'. Defending the Society's position in *The Irish Times* on 13 December 1988, Whelan argued 'That anyone should take it upon themselves to dictate the course of debate on any issue is offensive. To accompany that with threats is considerably worse.' He urged the public, and especially students in Trinity, 'to condemn and oppose the violence and threats of those who gag those with whom they do not agree'. The alternative, he suggested, was 'the sort of mob rule which has raised its ugly head in this College'.

Afterwards, de Goede attacked the College for preventing him speaking, calling their attitude 'quite amazing'. He said 'You have free speech or you do not. I am sure the reception would have been a lively one. I am disappointed in the sense that I had something important to say and I was prohibited.' The Auditor, Anthony Whelan, won much praise for his defence of the Society in the pages of *The Irish Times*, and went on to have a distinguished career in the European Commission, serving as *chef de cabinet* for EU Commissioner Neelie Kroes between 2006 and 2013, and becoming digital policy counsellor in the cabinet of European Commission President Ursula von der Leyen in 2019.

Other notable debates that session included one chaired by the Provost, William Watts, on 22 February 1989 on the motion, 'That Education is a Right, not a Privilege'. Speakers included Ivana Bacik, of Trinity's Students' Union; the education correspondent of *The Irish Times,* Christina Murphy; and the Workers' Party politician, Pat Rabbitte. The motion was carried. The businessman Tony O'Reilly chaired the debate on 5 April 1989 on the motion 'That this House would have Sunk the *Mayflower*', and the guest speaker was the writer and journalist, Dr Charles Lysaght (who had won the inaugural *Irish*

62 *The Irish Times*, 13 December 1988.

Times debating competition in 1960 for the King's Inns).

The first meeting of the 220th session on 5 October 1989 was notable for having the Tánaiste and Minister for Defence, Brian Lenihan, in the chair for a Freshers' debate on the motion 'That our Children will Revere the Memory of Charles J. Haughey'. The motion was deliberately provocative and took place only weeks before Haughey dismissed Lenihan from office during the Irish presidential election. Opposing the motion was the President of the Society and long-time antagonist of Haughey, Conor Cruise O'Brien, who delivered a trenchant denunciation. The debate itself was won by a young student who would go on to have a distinguished career in the Society, John Smith.

Orla Corrigan was the Auditor for this session and notable debates included 'That this House would Muzzle the Media (11 October 1989) with Hugh Leonard and Vincent Browne speaking, and 'That the Right to Life is Preferable to the Right to Choose' (18 October 1989), with Máire Kirrane and Maria Baghramian speaking. Both motions were defeated. 'That this House would Extradite Terrorist Suspects to Britain' was the motion on 8 November 1989, with Mr Justice Niall McCarthy in the chair, and former Auditor (and future Supreme Court Judge) Peter Charleton speaking. The motion was defeated.[63] Green issues were debated on 10 January 1990 with the motion 'That this House would put the Environment First'. Roger Garland, Green Party TD, proposed the motion, with Dr George Dawson in the chair. The motion was carried.

The winner of the Maiden Speaker's competition, Bernard Dunleavy, together with Fiona McLoughlin, won the Friends of the Irish Debate Series Intervarsities on 31 January 1990 speaking on the motion 'That this House has Nothing to Fear from German Unity'. On 7 February 1990 the Society won the Thomas Davis Intervarsity Competition, with the Censor, Kerida Naidoo, and John Smith speaking on the motion 'That this House would Unite Ireland'. Provost Watts chaired the debate on 28 February 1990 on the motion 'That Student Radicalism has Seen its Day'. Ivana Bacik, the President of Trinity's Students Union, opposed the motion, which was defeated.[64]

---

63 TCD MUN/SOC/HIST Uncatalogued Papers, 1980-89.

64 Ibid.

In terms of the life of the College, the 1980s was a decade when the great issues of the day were debated, no matter how controversial, from Northern Ireland, to women's rights, to the state of the country. The Society was no longer covered as extensively in the national media, but debates still had the potential to resonate, especially when controversy flared. To paraphrase Edmund Burke, a Society without the means of change, was without the means of its own conservation. By demonstrating its capacity to evolve in the 1980s, the Hist continued to be relevant, and it continued to inspire, entertain, infuriate and inform.

23 MAKING A DIFFERENCE, 1990-1999

THE MAKE-UP AND MEMBERSHIP of the Society in the 1990s was reflective of Trinity's changing role within Ireland. The large influx of undergraduate students from all over Ireland meant that Trinity was now competing with UCD in the education of the future leaders of Irish society. This was a period when future Taoiseach, Leo Varadkar, future Minister for Finance, Paschal Donohoe (who was an officer in the Phil) and the future Deputy Leader of Fianna Fáil, Dara Calleary, (who was an officer in the Hist), were active in the GMB over the course of the decade, and the same impact is seen in the worlds of law, media, business, and across Irish life.

Kerida Naidoo was elected Auditor for the 221st session and his committee included Una Ní Dhubhgaill as Record Secretary, Mark Tottenham as Correspondence Secretary, and Bernard Dunleavy as Librarian. There were a number of notable debates that session, including one chaired by Shane Ross, now a Senator for the University of Dublin, on 17 October 1990 on the motion 'That Sanctions will Not End Apartheid'.[1] Justus de Goede was one of the guest speakers, and was allowed attend the meeting this time, and other speakers included Roger Garland, the Green Party TD. The motion was defeated.

The Kingsmill Moore Intervarsities debate was held in the Society on 24 October 1990, with the Chancellor of the University (and a Vice-President of the Society), Dr Frank O'Reilly in the chair. The motion was 'That this House Condemns the National Lottery' and the winning team was from the King's Inns, composed of the former Auditor of the Hist, Anthony Whelan, and the former

1 TCD MUN/SOC/HIST Uncatalogued Papers, 1990-99.

Record Secretary, David Langwallner. The motion was defeated.[2]

On the day Margaret Thatcher left Downing Street for the final time as Prime Minister, 28 November 1990, the Society debated her legacy with the motion 'That Margaret Thatcher is the Antichrist'. The motion was defeated. 'That Evil is the Way to Heaven' was debated on 30 January 1991, with Sr Rita Lane in the chair. The motion was defeated.[3]

Naidoo delivered his inaugural paper on 8 March 1991 on the subject of 'The Use of Force as a Political Weapon'. Senator Shane Ross chaired the meeting, and guest speakers included Ken Maginnis, the Ulster Unionist MP; Proinsias de Rossa, the Workers' Party TD and MEP; Nell McCafferty and Vincent Fagan. The singer, Chris de Burgh, chaired the National Maiden Speakers' Final held as a meeting of the Society on 3 April 1991, on the motion 'That Musicians should Entertain and not Preach'. The motion was defeated, with UCD winning the competition.

Bernard Dunleavy was elected Auditor for the 222nd session, and his Committee included John Smith as Correspondence Secretary and Fiona McLoughlin as Record Secretary. For the Freshers' Debate on 2 October 1991 the motion was 'That the State has no Place in the Bedroom'. Senator David Norris was in the chair, and the guest speaker was the rebel priest, Fr Pat Buckley. The motion was carried, with Mervyn McCullough winning the prize for best speaker.[4]

'That this House would Retain Articles Two and Three of the Constitution' was the motion on 9 October 1991, with Paddy Harte, the Fine Gael TD in the chair. Speakers included Michael McDowell and Bernadette McAliskey, and the motion was carried. The Kingsmill Moore Intervarsities debate took place on 30 October 1991, on the motion 'That this House acknowledges its Debt to the Empire'. The motion was defeated, and the winning team, from the King's Inns, was composed of former Auditor, Kerida Naidoo, and former Librarian, Marguerite Bolger.

The inaugural meeting took place on 15 November 1991, as Dunleavy read a paper entitled 'The Destiny of Europe'. Senator

---

2 Ibid.

3 Ibid.

4 TCD MUN/SOC/HIST Uncatalogued Papers, 1990-99.

David Norris chaired the meeting and guest speakers were all familiar faces in the Society, with Michael Foot MP, Senator Maurice Manning, Dr Garret FitzGerald TD, and the former Auditor, Aidan Kane. This was a busy month for the Auditor, as he won the semi-final of *The Irish Times* debating competition a few days later on 21 November, speaking at a meeting of the Society with his debating partner, John Smith, on the motion 'That Mother Ireland has Failed her Children'. A few days later, on the 25 November 1991, the Society held a special event in the old House of Lords chamber, now the Bank of Ireland, with the distinguished UCD historian, Dr Art Cosgrove, in the chair. At this meeting Dunleavy, read a paper entitled 'Wolfe Tone: the Revolutionary'.

In 1992 Trinity celebrated its quatercentenary and the World Student Debating Championships was held in Dublin and organized by the Society. The final took place on 7 January 1992 in the National Concert Hall, with Dr Garret FitzGerald in the chair, as competitive speakers from around the world debated the motion 'That Nationalism is a Hangover from History'. Guest adjudicators for the evening included Lord Jenkins of Hillhead (formerly Roy Jenkins, the Chancellor of the University of Oxford and a former President of the European Commission), Dr Anthony Clare (the distinguished psychiatrist and broadcaster), David Lange (the former New Zealand Prime Minister), Mary Holland (the distinguished Irish journalist) and Kenneth Harris (the distinguished British journalist and broadcaster). The motion was defeated and the winning team was Robin Marshall and Gordon Peterson from Glasgow University Union.[5]

Motions that session included 'That this House would Relock its Chastity Belt' (22 January 1992), which was defeated, and 'That this House would Keep Ireland White' (4 March 1992), which was carried. Dessie Ellis, who had become the first person to be extradited from Ireland to Britain under the 1987 Extradition Act, despite going on hunger strike, was a guest speaker opposing the motion, 'That this House would Extradite' (5 February 1992), and the motion was defeated.

The Supreme Court Judge, Hugh O'Flaherty, chaired the

5 TCD MUN/SOC/HIST Uncatalogued Papers, 1990-99.

Frederick H. Boland Gold Medal debate on 8 April 1992, with the motion 'That this House would give Land for Peace'. The adjudication panel was composed of three eminent figures from the Society's recent past, Donnell Deeny QC, Mr Justice Declan Budd and Jim Hamilton. The motion was carried when put to the House and the winner of the medal was Marguerite Bolger.[6] On 9 May 1992 there was an open day in Trinity for the general public to celebrate the 400th anniversary and the Society held a special debate at 3 p.m. in the GMB on the motion 'That Politics has No Place in the Bedroom'.[7]

The Correspondence Secretary (and silver medallist for the 222nd session), John Smith, was elected Auditor for the 223rd session. The first meeting of the session was the annual Freshers' debate, with Senator David Norris in the chair, as the students debated the motion 'That this House would Legalise Prostitution'. The motion was defeated and the winner of the competition was Paschal Donohoe, future Fine Gael TD and Minister for Finance and Public Expenditure and Reform. Runners up were Eleanor Edmond, future advocacy and human rights lawyer, and Léan Ní Chuilleanáin, poet and writer.[8] Despite this promising start to his career in the Society, Donohoe found a home in the 'Other Society' and became a prominent member of the Philosophical Society.

The by now annual Northern Ireland debate was 'That this House would Retain Articles Two and Three of the Constitution' (14 October 1992), with speakers including the writer, Ulick O'Connor, Senator Éamon Ó Cuív of Fianna Fáil, and the journalist and historian, Tim Pat Coogan. The motion was defeated. Professor David McConnell chaired the annual Colours debate on 28 October 1992, with the motion 'That God is a Trinity Graduate'. The Society won best team, but the best individual speaker was future comedian and broadcaster, the talented Dara Ó Briain, who was representing the L&H team from UCD.[9]

The Maiden Speaker's Final was chaired by Michael McDowell

6 TCD MUN/SOC/HIST Uncatalogued Papers, 1990-99.

7 *The Irish Times*, 9 May 1992.

8 TCD MUN/SOC/HIST Uncatalogued Papers, 1990-99.

9 TCD MUN/SOC/HIST Uncatalogued Papers, 1990-99.

SC on 2 December 1992, with the motion 'That Marx is the Opium of the People'. One of the speakers was Paschal Donohoe, who argued that opium provoked a denial of reality.[10] Other debates that session (and unfortunately we do not have records of whether they were carried or defeated or what was said) included 'That the Legal Profession is More Interested in Fees than Justice' (13 January 1993), chaired by the Chief Justice, Thomas A. Finlay, with Iseult O'Malley the guest speaker, and 'That a Share-Owning Democracy is a License for Greed' (4 February 1993) with businessman Dermot Desmond in the chair and Damien Kiberd the guest speaker.

The final of *The Irish Times* debating competition was held in Limerick that year, with the motion 'That Coalition is the Natural Form of Government of Ireland' and Des O'Malley, the leader of the Progressive Democrats, in the chair. Eight of the twelve speakers were from Trinity, an unprecedented number, and the Demosthenes trophy was won by the Hist team of Brendan Foley and Gavan Titley who were proposing the motion.[11]

Smith delivered his inaugural paper on 5 March 1993, entitled 'Created Unarmed – 70 Years of the Irish State'. Brian Lenihan, the Fianna Fáil TD, chaired the meeting, and guest speakers included Robert Ballagh, the artist and commentator, David Trimble, the Ulster Unionist MP, Austin Currie, the Fine Gael TD, and Eoghan Harris, the journalist, director, and writer.

A Classics Scholar, Eugene Downes, was elected Auditor unopposed for the 224th session. His Committee included Gavan Titley as Correspondence Secretary and Dara Calleary as Librarian. Downes went on to have a distinguished career in the world of the arts and culture, serving as a successful director of the Kilkenny Arts Festival, before becoming Cultural Director at the Department of Foreign Affairs and Trade. Gavan Titley became an expert in multiculturalism and the challenge of racism, lecturing in media studies at Maynooth University. Dara Calleary was elected a Fianna Fáil TD for Mayo in 2007 and became Deputy Leader of the party and Director of Policy in March 2018.

The first debate of the session was the Fresher's Debate, chaired by

---

10 TCD MUN/SOC/HIST Uncatalogued Papers, 1990-99.

11 *Trinity News*, 2 March 1993.

Kerida Naidoo, on the motion 'That the Twenty-first Century Would Not be Socialist'. Guest speakers included Eoghan Harris and Arthur Scargill, and the student winner was Natalie McDonnell.[12] The annual debate on abortion took place a week later, on 20 October 1993, with the motion 'That Abortion is Sometimes the Lesser of Two Evils'. Speakers included Professor William Binchy, Senator Mary Henry, and Professor David McConnell. Other notable debates that session included 'That Articles 2 and 3 Stand in the Way of Peace' (10 November 1993) with the journalist, Richard Ingrams, in the chair, and Robert Kee, the historian, and Ken Maginnis MP, among the speakers. On 19 January 1994 Sir Bob Geldof chaired the debate 'That Human Rights Should be the Price for Development Aid', but unfortunately we do not have a record of his speech from the chair.

John Connolly (a journalist with *The Irish Times* before becoming a globally successful novelist) provides an eye-catching account of the final of the *Irish Times* debating competition held in University College Galway on Friday 25 February 1994. The debate was chaired by twice former winner, Adrian Hardiman SC, and a number of Society members (and former members) took part, debating the motion 'That the Private Lives of Public Figures are of No Concern to the Body Politic'. Representing the Hist, Douglas Clarke began with what Connolly described as 'a criminally bad pun', as he deployed the 'Tonya Harding' argument, suggesting it was one which 'leaves the opposition weak at the knees'.[13] Nevertheless Clarke was successful at setting out clearly 'what would become the twin towers of all the proposing speakers' arguments that evening', namely that knowing about the private lives of public figures 'was irrelevant and an unreliable basis for assessing their suitability, and detrimental to the interests of the body politic itself.' Clarke's team-mate, Brian Kennedy, argued that 'there was no sustainable link between a politician's suitability for office and his private life, and that an informed choice could be made simply on the basis of public performance'.

Eugene Downes, representing the Society as an individual, opposed the motion, and Connolly described him as having 'presented a beautifully paced and delivered argument'. The Record

12 TCD MUN/SOC/HIST Uncatalogued Papers, 1990-99.

13 John Connolly, 'It's how you say it', *The Irish Times*, 1 March 1994.

Secretary, Sinéad McBrearty, also represented the Society as an individual, and Connolly suggests that her speech was 'perhaps over-colloquial', which attracted 'a certain amount of good-natured heckling with which she dealt well'.

Also opposing the motion was Bernard Dunleavy and John Smith, both now at the King's Inns. Before the debate, Dunleavy was observed pacing the hall outside the lecture theatre 'like an expectant father.' This prompted Smith to joke to Connolly that, 'In his position I usually say "Bernard, there's only one parachute on this plane, and you're the one wearing the lead boots"'. Dunleavy's speech, however, was nerveless and Connolly praised it for being 'both witty and substantial'. Dunleavy 'argued that people cannot compartmentalise their lives, and that the private and business allegiences of politicians had a great effect on their public lives'. In a stirring piece of oratory, which won him the prize for best individual speaker, Dunleavy accused the proposition of being 'fundamentally undemocratic' in denying the public the information they needed to make a balanced judgment. His team-mate and best friend, John Smith, 'produced one of the best lines of the night' when he claimed that 'Bertie Ahern's knowledge of finance was such that when he visited New York he was furious that Dow Jones did not meet him personally'.

The winning team on the night was Marcus Dowling and Dara Ó Briain, representing UCD's L&H. Dowling's 'confident, assured delivery was reinforced by the witty speech' of Ó Briain, who suggested that 'the representatives of the nation should not be expected to be superhuman and pointed out that even those whose private lives might be suspect do not legislate with their libido'. In his entertaining report, Connolly praised Hardiman for chairing the debate in 'a witty, understated way which did not draw attention away from the speakers themselves'. Hardiman's own reflections on debating are worth noting here. Speaking from the chair, he suggested that it helped to build confidence and lose self-consciousness, saying 'You only have to look at somebody who hasn't done it to see the difference'.[14]

Eugene Downes presented his inaugural paper on 4 March 1994

---

14 *The Irish Times*, 22 February 1994.

entitled 'Squaring the Circle? National Identity in Northern Ireland'. The meeting was chaired by the Provost, Dr Thomas Mitchell, and speakers included the Secretary of State for Northern Ireland, Sir Patrick Mayhew MP; Dr Jim McDaid, the Fianna Fáil TD; Seamus Mallon, the SDLP MP; and Michael McDowell SC. Mayhew used his speech to advance the ongoing peace process, by sending a carefully worded message to Sinn Féin about the so-called Unionist veto. This had been identified by Martin McGuinness of Sinn Féin as the central stumbling block to a cessation of violence, and Mayhew was able to use his speech to allay those concerns. Arguing that 'self-determination, in other words, democracy' would prevail in the days ahead, Mayhew suggested that 'it is in democracy that we find the supreme concept in which the ideas of national identity can be accommodated. No one should claim a veto to override that.'[15] *The Irish Times* reported extensively on his 'carefully worded address to students', and quoted his message that 'all who are serious about consent – and we are – have to recognise that consent must be freely given'.

The Correspondence Secretary, Gavan Titley, was elected Auditor for the 225th session, with Dara Calleary elected Treasurer, and Douglas Clarke and Treasa Ní Mhiochain were both unopposed in becoming Correspondence Secretary and Record Secretary respectively. The Freshers' debate saw Alan Amsby return to the Society and chair the debate as his alter ego, 'Mr Pussy', with the motion, 'That this House Wants a Permissive Society'. The debate was won by Ruth McAvinia, who went on to have a distinguished career in the Philosophical Society and later became News Editor for the European Space Agency and a member of faculty of the International Space University.

Notable debates that session included 'That Divorce Weakens the Structure of Society' (12 October 1994), with Professor Anthony Clare in the chair, and speakers including Joe McCarroll (the vice-chair of the Anti-Divorce Campaign), Mags O'Brien (who chaired the Divorce Action Group during the referendum the following year), and Dr Gerard Casey (head of the Christian Solidarity Party). The motion was defeated.

---

15 *The Irish Times,* 5 March 1994.

'That the Arts should be Political' was debated on 26 October 1994, in a debate chaired by broadcaster Mike Murphy, and speakers included the artistic director of the Abbey Theatre, Patrick Mason, the writer, Anne Enright (soon to publish her first novel), and the poet, Theo Dorgan. Northern Ireland was debated on 16 November 1994, with a motion 'That this House has Nothing to Fear from a United Ireland'. Gerry Danaher SC chaired the debate, and speakers included Mitchell McLaughlin of Sinn Fein, Peter Temple-Morris, the Conservative MP, and Joe Hendron, the SDLP MP. The motion was carried.

Titley delivered his inaugural paper on 25 November 1994, entitled 'Debating Society: the Role of an Intellectual Forum', with the Chancellor of the University, F. J. O'Reilly in the chair. The guest speakers were Fintan O'Toole, Professor Terry Eagleton, Dr Stuart Murray, and Dr Declan Kiberd. Other notable meetings that session included, 'That the Pill is Mightier than the Pope', motion for the Maiden Speakers' Final (30 November 1994), chaired by the presenter of the *The Den*, Ray D'Arcy. The motion was carried and the winner of the competition was Edain Lysaght. Abortion was debated on 18 January 1995, with the motion 'That this House would Legalise Abortion'. The debate was chaired by Senator Mary Henry, and speakers included law lecturer and barrister, Diarmuid Rossa Phelan, and Dr Noreen O'Carroll. The motion was defeated.[16]

Chief Justice Liam Hamilton chaired the debate on 25 January 1995, as the Society debated the motion 'This House would Rewrite the Constitution'. The debate was notable for including a future Chief Justice among the guest speakers, Frank Clarke SC, alongside distinguished barristers, James Nugent SC, Michael McDowell TD, and honorary member (and future Judge of the Court of Appeal), George Birmingham. The motion was carried.[17]

To commemorate the 25th anniversary of the admission of women to the Society a debate was held on 1 February 1995 on the motion 'This House Believes that Feminism has Run its Course', chaired by the first woman to serve as a High Court judge, Mella Carroll. Speakers included former Auditor, Sallyanne Godson, and the motion was defeated.

16 TCD MUN/SOC/HIST Uncatalogued Papers, 1990-99.
17 Ibid.

Bernard Dunleavy returned to the Society to chair the final of the Thomas Davis Intervarsity on 15 February 1995. The motion was 'That this House would Silence Tarantino', which was defeated when put to the floor, with the team from Glasgow of Lynne Roach and Nick McGrath winning the competition, and John Smith named best individual speaker.

The annual Colours debate took place a week later, on 22 February, with the motion 'That this House would Bury Eric Cantona under the Patio'. The L&H team from UCD proved victorious, with Dara Ó Briain, and future leading barristers, Marcus Dowling and John Berry, defeating the Hist team, although Nick Royle was named best individual speaker. Jenifer Ní Ghrádaigh, representing the L&H for UCD, was victorious in the National Maiden Speakers' Competition at the meeting of the Society on 5 April, speaking on the motion 'That this House believes in the Necessity of the US as a World Police Force'. The final debate of the session was the honorary members debate on 19 April 1995, with Eric Lowry in the chair, and the motion the amusing, 'That this House would Debate another Motion'.

Douglas Clarke was elected Auditor for the 226th session, with Rachael Murphy as Treasurer, Alex Massie as Correspondence Secretary (later replaced by Catherine Donnelly), Nathy Dunleavy as Record Secretary, and Nick Royle as Censor. The General Committee included Adrian Langan, who would go on to have a significant career in the Society.

The session began with the Fresher's debate, chaired by the talented comedian and actor, Dermot Morgan, and his presence was a huge draw for students following the screening of the first season of *Father Ted* earlier in the year. Popular culture was debated on 11 October 1995, with the motion 'That this House would Pulp Hollywood's Fiction', with film critic, Michael Dwyer, in the chair, and film producer, Ron Stoneman, the guest speaker. Dara Calleary returned to chair the debate on abortion on 18 October 1995. The motion was 'That this House would Legalise Abortion' with Neville Cox (future Dean of Graduate Studies in Trinity) proposing the motion, and Éamon Ó Cuív, the Fianna Fáil TD, opposing. Trinity won the annual Colours' debate that year, with Colm Ó Mongáin (future RTE broadcaster and deputy foreign editor) and Joe Guerin, successfully proposing the motion 'That God is a Trinity Graduate' on 25 October 1995.[18]

In a significant recognition of the role of the Society in providing a forum for debate on sensitive issues, the Northern Ireland debate on 1 November 1995 was recorded for use on RTE's *Prime Time* television programme. The debate was chaired by Colin Parry, whose son, Tim, twelve-years-old, had been killed in the Warrington bomb attack in 1993. The motion was 'That Decommissioning is Necessary before All-Party Talks' and *Trinity News* reported that 'Members of the College Historical Society heard an emotional call for dialogue between the parties involved in the Northern Ireland conflict.'[19] Parry told the packed house that it was only through a frank exchange of views that a stable peace could be secured. 'There has to be passion, and heat, and anger generated', he pleaded, 'that is the heart of the debate'. There was a prolonged ovation following his speech. Douglas Clarke, the Auditor, described Parry as a 'source of inspiration and encouragement for us all'. Other speakers included Kevin McNamara, the British Labour Party MP; David Ervine, the Progressive Unionist Party figure who had helped deliver the loyalist ceasefire in 1994; and the motion was defeated. The debate was long remembered for Parry's moving tribute to his son, and his considered views on the impact of conflict and the need for reconciliation, left a lasting impression.

Clarke delivered his inaugural paper on 16 February 1996, entitled, 'The Twilight Zone: Law and the Media'. The meeting was chaired by the Chief Justice, Liam Hamilton, and guest speakers included Brian Sedgemore, the British Labour Party MP, Robert Marshall-Andrews QC (later a British Labour Party MP), Michael McDowell, the Progressive Democrats TD, and Alun Jones QC. A skilled orator, Clarke, won the prize for best speaker in the *Irish Times* debating competition that year.

Many of the major debates of that session involved questions of social change in Ireland. The most memorable of these was held on Wednesday 22 November, two days before the referendum to decide whether to change the constitutional ban on divorce. The GMB was

---

18 Ibid.

19 *Trinity News*, 16 November 1995.

more packed than members could ever recall, as people gathered to consider the motion 'That this House would Vote in Favour of Divorce' and the subject was thrashed out with passion and conviction. The recently retired High Court judge, Rory O'Hanlon, in the chair, a surprising choice some felt, given that he was also chairman of the No Divorce Campaign. The motion was proposed by Adrian Hardiman SC and the journalist Vincent Browne, and was opposed by Dr Gerard Casey, the vice chairman of the No Divorce Campaign, and Professor William Binchy, of the Anti-Divorce Campaign.

In a powerful speech, which was reported extensively in *The Irish Times* the next day, Hardiman argued that the case for a ban on divorce 'is purely sectarian and exists for no other reason'. Suggesting there was a 'moral policeman' view among some of those who opposed divorce, one that believed that people 'are not to be trusted – neither people who want it nor the judiciary who will implement it'. *Trinity News* also reported the debate and quoted Hardiman as suggesting that the same people who were opposing divorce were the same 'Hardy Boys' who had fought against the decriminalisation of homosexuality and contraception.[20]

Opposing these arguments, Binchy argued that 'individualism is at the heart of the divorce debate – the right to pursue happiness without regard to its effect on others'.[21] And he suggested that the introduction of divorce would have the effect of facilitating individualism. Speaking from the chair, O'Hanlon quoted some past popes, expressed his admiration for some of the work of Opus Dei, before revealing he was against the motion. The motion was carried narrowly, which surprised many people, but it reflected the national mood. Two days later the referendum also passed by the narrowest of margins, by 50.28 per cent to 49.72 per cent.

Ray D'Arcy returned to chair the Maiden Speakers' Final on 29 November 1995, with the motion, 'That this House would Bomb the Vatican'. The motion was defeated, with Nicola Doherty winning the competition.

The Government's proposed changes to university governance

20 *Trinity News,* 7 December 1995.

21 *The Irish Times,* 23 November 1995.

were contentious at this time and on 24 January 1996 the Society debated 'That this House would Defend Trinity's Autonomy', chaired by the Chancellor, F.J. O'Reilly. The Minister for Education, Niamh Breathnach, defended the Government's position, but a significant speech against was made by Dr Sean Barrett, the Junior Dean. Micheál Martin, the Fianna Fáil TD (and future Minister for Education), delivered a nuanced speech, with new ideas for the future of higher education.

In a significant coup, Sir John Hall, the chairman of Newcastle United Football Club, then leading the Premier League, chaired the debate on 21 February 1996 on the impact of Sky Sports, 'That Sport does not Need Murdoch'. The guest speaker was the acclaimed football journalist and writer, Simon Kuper.[22]

Northern Ireland was debated again on 3 April 1996, with the Provost, Dr Tom Mitchell, in the chair. The motion was 'That this House Believes in All-Party Talks without Preconditions', and speakers included the Secretary of State for Northern Ireland, Sir Patrick Mayhew, Dr Joe Hendron, the SDLP MP, Dr John Alderdice, the leader of the Alliance Party, Councillor Gary McMichael, and the Minister for Social Welfare, Prionsias de Rossa TD, the leader of Democratic Left. Mayhew argued that 'his Government wanted to see Sinn Féin at the table but the party's presence would be determined by an unequivocal restoration of the IRA ceasefire'.[23] In his speech, de Rossa claimed that peace could not be achieved by threats or ultimatums, before adding, 'Nor will it be met be the kind of ill-judged, bad-tempered display we saw from David Trimble at the Ulster Unionist Council'. The motion was carried.

Nathy Dunleavy was elected Auditor for the 227th session, and his officers included Catherine Donnelly as Treasurer, Adrian Langan as Correspondence Secretary, and Frank Mitchell as Record Secretary, with Roddy Maguire elected to the Committee. The first debate of the session was the Fresher's debate, on the motion 'That This House does not Value Virginity'. The debate was chaired by Peter Temple-Morris MP, and the winner was first year student, Paul Gleeson.

Colin Parry returned to chair the Northern Ireland debate that

---

22 TCD MUN/SOC/HIST Uncatalogued Papers, 1990-99.

23 *The Irish Times,* 4 April 1996.

year on 9 October 1996. The motion was 'That Decommissioning must Precede All-Party Talks', and speakers included the Revd Martin Smyth, the Ulster Unionist MP; the Minister of State in the Department of Finance, Hugh Coveney, Fine Gael TD; the journalist and writer, Ruth Dudley Edwards, and former Taoiseach, Dr Garret FitzGerald. The motion was defeated.

The broadcaster Charlie Bird was the guest speaker a week later, debating the motion 'That the Private Lives of Public Figures are of No Concern to the Body Politic'. Other notable debates that session included 'That this House wants a Federal Europe' (6 November 1996), chaired by Dara Calleary, with Anthony Coughlan and Bernie Malone, the Labour MEP, the guest speakers. The motion was defeated. 'That Film Diminishes the Actor' was the motion on 20 November 1996, with Mike Murphy in the chair, and the guest speaker was the playwright and journalist, Hugh Leonard.

Dunleavy delivered his inaugural paper on 7 February 1997 entitled 'Liberty in Chains'. The meeting was chaired by the Chancellor, and was notable for the presence of Lt Colonel Oliver North, whose role in the Iran-Contra scandal in the 1980s made him a high profile and somewhat controversial speaker. The other guest speakers included the successful barrister, Shane Murphy; the former leader of the British Labour Party, Michael Foot, and Dr Germaine Greer.

Before the debate, North stopped off in the Stag's Head for a pint, where he told a journalist for the *Irish Independent* that his message was 'Get Government off my back, out of my face, get its fingers out of my wallet'.[24] Attending the debate wearing the medals he had received in the marines, North called on the audience to 'Stand up and call evil what it is, and fight for what is right.'[25] 'Never one to mince his words' according to *The Irish Times,* 'the man at the centre of the Iran-Contra affair launched one offensive after another at familiar targets: abortion, homosexuality, and euthanasia. Peppering his speech with biblical references, he warned that failing to protect certain liberties could lead to social unrest and violence 'Such as that witnessed at abortion clinics in the United States'. Under the headline, 'Hist backs North in his war against evil', the

24 *Irish Independent,* 8 February 1997.

25 *The Irish Times,* 8 February 1997.

paper reported that although North 'enjoys the role of the lone protagonist, he must have been disappointed as the assembled audience gave him more applause than heckles'.

Bertie Ahern, the leader of Fianna Fáil (and a few months away from becoming Taoiseach) chaired the final of *The Irish Times* debating competition, held as a meeting of the Society, on 11 February 1997, with the motion 'That this House would support Public Funding of Political Parties'. The Leinster Schools Final was also held at the Society, on 7 March 1997, as the students debated the motion 'That Feminism has Run its Course'. The winning team was Aoife Titley and Catherine Bannon, representing Loreto College, St Stephen's Green, with Mary Fay of Santa Sabina College in Sutton named best individual speaker. The Society's role in the organisation of the Leinster Schools' Debating Competition, in conjunction with the L&H in UCD, was a notable public engagement of the Society, deserving of a study of its own. This was a major part of the work of the Librarian, and involved finding chairs and adjudicators to travel across the province, and the success of the competition owed much to the willingness of officers and members to give up their time, many having taken part in the competition themselves.

The Correspondence Secretary, Adrian Langan, was elected Auditor for the 228th session. A History and Political Science student from Co. Mayo, Langan had the rare distinction of also being elected President of the Students' Union during his time in Trinity. The officers that session included Donal Kane as Treasurer, Aoife Scannell as Correspondence Secretary succeeded by Padraic Lyons, Roddy Maguire as Record Secretary, Aisling Kelly as Censor, and Eilís Murphy as Librarian, with Sarah Fennell and Paul Gleeson elected to the Committee. Debates looked different that year, thanks to the introduction of a ban on smoking in the chamber, something that pre-dated the national ban on smoking in workplaces by seven years. The first meeting of the session took place on 1 October 1997, with the annual Freshers' debate on the motion 'That this House Wants a Permissive Society'. Ray D'Arcy chaired the debate, and the competition was won by Ciaran Walsh.

During this period, the annual debate on Northern Ireland, always held in the Michaelmas Term, was the most well-attended and anticipated event in the calendar. Full houses and lively views would be expressed as Ireland, north and south, inched itself towards compromise, settlement and peace. Many of the issues which enveloped that process – decommissioning, the rights and wrongs of the conflicts, the shape of the ultimate settlement, and police reform – were discussed and debated annually. They were enlivened by a large cohort of students from Northern Ireland who were members, Committee members and officers at the time, as well as by the willingness of many politicians from the Unionist tradition to come to Trinity, and to the Hist, to outline their views. Notable guest speakers from that tradition during this time included David Trimble MP, John Taylor MP, David Ervine, the Revd Martin Smyth MP, and Jeffrey Donaldson MP. The Secretary of State for Northern Ireland, Sir Patrick Mayhew, was a regular guest as was General John de Chastelain, the co-chairman of the Northern Ireland peace process and the Chairman of the Independent International Commission on Decommissioning,

It is notable that General John de Chastelain accepted an invitation to chair the Northern Ireland debate on 15 October 1997, on the motion 'That Paramilitaries cannot Negotiate Peace'. Also speaking at the meeting was Ulster Unionist MP, Jeffrey Donaldson, and Dr Martin Mansergh, a special adviser to the Taoiseach, Bertie Ahern, who was closely involved in the peace process. De Chastelain used the visit to Dublin to send a clear message to paramilitaries 'that mechanisms were being put in place to facilitate the decommissioning of paramilitary weapons, after which decommissioning would be a matter for the paramilitaries "just like the ceasefires."'[26]

The high focus on Northern Ireland in the 1990s was reflected in that session's inagural meeting. It took place on 6 February 1998, with the President of the Society, Dr Conor Cruise O'Brien, in the chair. This was the bicentenary year of the 1798 rebellion, with negotiations ongoing which would lead to the Good Friday Agreement in April 1998, and Langan's paper was an eloquent and timely reflection on Northern Ireland, entitled '1798 and all that: solving the Irish Question'. It was responded to by the leader of the United Kingdom Unionist Party, Robert (Bob) McCartney MP; Professor John A. Murphy; the leader of the Labour Party, Ruairi Quinn TD; and Lord Alderdice (the recently elevated John Alderdice).

26 *The Irish Times*, 16 October 1997.

To commemorate the 250th anniversary of the foundation of Burke's Club in 1747, a series of celebrations were organized by the former Auditor, Bernard Dunleavy. This included a major international student debate held that year as the Kingsmill Moore Intervarsity on 12 November 1997. The Chancellor chaired the meeting, with the motion 'Conservatism is a Doomed Philosophy'. The motion was carried and the winning team was the Society team of Adrian Langan and Gavan Titley.

The highlight of the celebrations was the special meeting held the next day on 13 November 1997 where the former French President, Valéry Giscard d'Estaing, delivered a major speech on Burke. The meeting was chaired by the Chairman of Goldman Sachs, and former EU Commissioner, Peter Sutherland, and also speaking was the President of the Society (and Burke biographer), Conor Cruise O'Brien. In his speech Giscard d'Estaing confessed to being a closet Burkian, and said that his motto in the 1974 Presidential election was 'change within continuity'.[27] Three years later, he discussed his visit to Trinity in his book on the future of nations, *The French: Reflections on the Destiny of a People,* a book inspired by having read Burke's *Reflections on the Revolution in France* to prepare for this visit.[28]

Other notable meetings that session included 'That this House wants a Federalist Europe' (29 October 1997), where speakers included Alan Dukes, Peter Lilley, the British Conservative MP, and Brian Crowley, the Fianna Fáil MEP. Dara Ó Briain returned to the Society at the meeting on 16 January 1998 which took a different format. Instead of a formal debate there was an interview with the award-winning actor, Jeremy Irons, and this was an approach that was to become a successful occasional format in the years' ahead.

The annual abortion debate took place on 21 January 1998 on the motion 'That this House Supports a Woman's Right to Choose', and speakers included the head of Women's Studies at UCD, Ailbhe Smyth; as well as Nora Bennis, the head of the strongly anti-abortion National Party; and Professor William Binchy. One of the student speakers, proposing the motion, was a first-year medicine student,

---

27 TCD MUN/SOC/HIST Uncatalogued Papers, 1990-99.

28 *The Irish Times*, 4 November 2000.

Leo Varadkar, who twenty years later as Taoiseach would successfully bring forward a referendum to repeal the 8th amendment.

In terms of competitive debating that session, Paul Gleeson won best individual speaker in the *Irish Times* debating competition, with Adrian Langan and Gavan Titley winning the Irish Mace competition. Langan was later *chef de cabinet* to the Labour leader, Pat Rabbitte, before going on to work in communications, public affairs and education.

Roddy Maguire was elected Auditor for the 229th session and his officers included Ciara Bradshaw as Treasurer (later succeeded by Emmet Coldrick), Ciarán Toland as Correspondence Secretary, Paul Gleeson as Record Secretary, Sarah Fennell as Censor, and Emmet Coldrick as Librarian (later succeeded by Paul Geaney). The Committee included Yvonne Campbell, Paul Geaney, and Aoife Titley, with Leo Varadkar missing out narrowly on election to the Committee by a fraction of a vote. Varadkar later recalled being devastated by the result and it is possible it changed the trajectory of his career. The very next week he successfully ran for election as a Chairman of the YFG (Young Fine Gael) branch in Trinity, and from there was elected to the National Executive in Fine Gael, where he took his first steps in national politics. He admits that it is 'impossible to know if history would have been different if I spent my spare time in second year dedicated to the Hist rather than politics and FG'.[29]

The first meeting of the 229th session took place on 7 October 1998, the annual Freshers' debate, with the motion 'That this House would Sleep with the Boss'. The guest speaker was the actor and comedian Brendan O'Carroll, and the competition was won by Jim McElroy (who also won the Maiden Speaker's competition later that year).

The challenges of migration, and how Ireland should treat refugees, were debated on 14 October 1998. Iseult O'Malley returned to the Society to chair the debate, 'That Ireland Should Embrace Refugees', and speakers included the spokesperson for the Bosnian Community Development Project, Haris Bijedic; Joe Higgins, the Socialist Party TD; and Khalid Ibrahim, of the Organisation for Human Rights in Iraq. The motion was carried.

29 Correspondence with Author.

Northern Ireland was debated on 21 October 1998 with the motion 'That Immediate Decommissioning is Necessary for Northern Ireland'. The motion was defeated and speakers included Caoimhín Ó Caoláin, the Sinn Fein TD, Willie Thompson, the Ulster Unionist MP, Dr Arthur Aughey, Ruth Dudley Edwards, and Kevin McNamara, the British Labour MP.

Notable meetings that session include the Colours' debate, held in Trinity that year on 28 October 1998, on the motion 'That this House would Burn Belfield'. The motion was carried and the winning team included Paul Geaney, Eoghan Cole and Ciaran Walsh. On 2 November 1998 the meeting was a special interview with the film critic, Barry Norman, with the Auditor in the chair. Dara Ó Briain returned to the Society to interview another award-winning actor, this time Ben Kingsley, on 1 March 1999.

The Society won the final of the Kingsmill Moore Intervarsity on 11 November 1998, on the motion 'That this House Believes that Nationalism is a Wicked Force'. The winning team was Padraic Lyons and Paul Gleeson. They also won the AIB Wolfe Tone's Final on 17 February 1999, speaking on the motion 'That this House Believes there's Something About Mary'. The broadcaster Jimmy Magee chaired the debate on 20 January 1999, on the motion 'That the Irish Media Doesn't Play Fair', with Eamon Dunphy the star attraction on the night. The motion was defeated.[30]

Maguire delivered his inaugural paper on 12 February 1999, entitled 'As Good as it Gets: Irish Society on the Brink of the Millennium'. The meeting was chaired by Mr Justice Declan Budd, and the guest speakers included Joe Higgins, the Socialist Party TD, Michael McDowell SC, and Professor William Binchy.

At the end of the session Paul Gleeson was awarded the silver medal for oratory and he was elected Auditor unopposed for the 230th session. His officers included Sarah Fennell as Treasurer, Mary Lynch as Correspondence Secretary, Paul Geaney as Record Secretary, Aoife Titley as Censor, and Yvonne Campbell as Librarian. Jim McElroy, Eoghan Cole, Louis Mooney and Catherine Bannon were among those elected to serve on the Committee.

The 230th session brought the Society out of one century (indeed

---

30 TCD MUN/SOC/HIST Uncatalogued Papers, 1990-99.

out of one millennium) and into the next, debating many of the contentious social issues that would divide and dominate Irish society over the years to come, such as marriage equality and access to abortion. The annual Northern Ireland debate took place in the juncture between the signing of the Good Friday Agreement and the successful operation of the institutions it created, with the issue of how to decommission paramilitary weapons the thorn in the side of Northern politics (and as Gleeson notes, this 'was rarely short of thorns').[31]

The opening debate of the session was the Fresher's Debate on 6 October 1999, with a subject that was now becoming tiresome to anyone who had attended in previous years: 'That this House Believes Virginity is a Virtue'. Joe Duffy, the RTE broadcaster as former SU President, was in the chair, and the competition was won by Susan O'Malley and John Lynham. Michael D. Higgins, the Labour TD, spoke at the debate on 13 October 1999, on the motion 'That this House Believes the Media is More Powerful than the Government'.

A year after the Good Friday Agreement, Colin Parry returned to the Society for the third time to chair the Northern Ireland debate on the motion 'That this House Believes No Guns Must Mean No Government'. Speakers included Ken Maginnis MP, Dr Garret FitzGerald, Gerry McGeough, Dr Martin Mansergh, and Dr Joe Hendron.

In a notable tribute, the President of Ireland, Dr Mary McAleese, accepted an invitation to deliver an address to the Society in November 1999 entitled 'Irish Society on the Brink of the Twenty-first Century'. The speech began with an acknowledgment that it was 'a great pleasure to return to my old, familiar haunt here in Trinity'.[32]

In a brilliant oration which covered the course of Irish history, McAleese considered how Irish identity had been shaped by these experiences, and how 'centuries of conquest, famine, war, emigration, poverty, unemployment, still-born hope – drained many of our people of confidence and energy, filtered into a self-perception of victimhood, coloured our self-belief in what we were capable of, set self-imposed limits on our ambitions, our preoccupations.'

31 Correspondence with Author.

32 https://www.president.ie/en/media-library/speeches/address-by-president-mcaleese-at-the-college-historical-society-of-trinity.

Looking ahead to the role Ireland would place in the new millennium, McAleese suggested that the 'so-called land of saints and scholars has been recaptured in our engagement with the European Union, our new position as one of the world's largest per capita exporting nations, our expertise in the new technologies, our service with the United Nations, our powerful and loyal global Irish family.' It was a speech which captured the Irish experience over a millennium, and prophesied a new direction for the country in the Twenty-first century, a new direction which she herself was helping Ireland take. Quoting the words inscribed on the Statue of Liberty, McAleese wondered how the new Ireland would treat 'a few of the world's tired and poor [who] make their weary way to our door'. And she lay down a challenge for those listening and the country as a whole, 'What invitation are we willing to offer?' There are choices and it is you, the inheritors of our future, who will make them.'

The speech ended on a profoundly uplifting note: 'Do we dare to dream of the death of hate, the death of poverty? What birth are we standing on the brink of? Stillborn hopes or a new reality to be profoundly proud of? No other brink on this island has ever offered so much to so many.' It was one of the great orations in the history of the Society.

Tommy Tiernan returned to the Society to chair the Maiden Speakers' Final on 1 December 1999, on the motion 'That this House Regrets the Role of the Catholic Church in Twentieth-Century Ireland'. The competition was won by John Lynham. Dr Germaine Greer visited a week later and was interviewed by Dr Neville Cox.[33]

Gleeson delivered his inaugural paper on 3 March 2000 on political reform, entitled, 'Ireland Beyond 2000: Challenging the Comfort Zone'. Lord Henry Mountcharles chaired the meeting and speakers included the political scientist, Professor Michael Laver, Senator Shane Ross, Pat Rabbitte, the Labour TD, and Des O'Malley, the Progressive Democrats TD.

'That this House Believes Ireland has Outgrown Religion' was debated on 13 April 2000, with the meeting chaired by Fr Aidan Larkin, the SDLP politician and lawyer, who became a Columban missionary and was at the time a University Chaplain in Trinity. Taking strongly

33 TCD MUN/SOC/HIST Uncatalogued Papers, 1990-99.

opposing views, and with strongly contrasting styles, were Tommy Tiernan proposing the motion, and Rónán Mullen opposing.

Debates in 2000 included 'That this House would Disband the RUC' (2 February 2000), a competitive debate won by Yvonne Campbell and Bríd McGrath, 'That this House would Legalise Abortion in Ireland (23 February 2000), with Senator Mary Henry, Professor Ivana Bacik and Professor William Binchy, and 'That this House would Celebrate Clinton's Presidency' (8 March 2000). The final debate of the session was the hosting of the All-Ireland Schools Final, with former Taoiseach, John Bruton, in the chair. The motion was 'That this House Believes Ireland's Future Lies in a Federal Europe', and the winning team was Mánus de Barra and Abie Philbin Bowman of Sandford Park, with David Whelan of Gonzaga College the best individual speaker.

Attendances at debates was strong during the sesssion and it was an indication of the strength of the Society at the start of the twenty-first century. While there was a growing tendency in Trinity, and in debating societies in other universities, to focus on inviting celebrity guests for interview, sometimes with a dubious 'award' or 'recognition' created for the event to lure them along, the Hist tried, as far as possible, to keep the focus on issues. As Gleeson recalls these were 'political or social issues of contention or importance' and much time was spent 'crafting motions which best facilitated passionate argumentation and good rhetoric.'[34]

By this time the reading of the records at the start of a meeting had become an opportunity to deliver humorous accounts of the week before and the Record Secretary that session, Paul Geaney, delivered some of the most memorable. After leaving Trinity, Geaney went on to become a successful entrepreneur and businessman. He was a founder of Avolon, one of world's largest aircraft leasing companies, becoming part of the senior leadership team. Included in *Irish America's* Wall Street fifty, in 2016 he was listed by *Airline Economics* as one of the top forty executives under forty in the global aviation industry.[35] Based in New York, he has discussed how the

34 Correspondence with Author.

35 See https://irishamerica.com/2011/12/paul-geaney/ and *Airline Economics,* June-July 2016.

Society helped shape his career, noting that it is usually associated with figures in politics, law, media, academia and so on, and that business is often forgotten. As an officer in the Hist, Geaney believed he developed communication skills which were invaluable in business, and he also learned about organising major events, for example through the running of the Leinster Schools' Debating Competition with UCD. More importantly, the debates encouraged members to think internationally, and this engagement with global ideas, more than anything else, helped define a career which has been global in its focus.

Reflecting on his time in the Society, the Auditor for that session, Paul Gleeson, notes that his years in the Hist provided him with friendships which endure twenty years later and which he calls 'the greatest legacy you could wish for.'[36] He adds that the skills developed in competitive debating and as Auditor served him well too in a career with the Department of Foreign Affairs (DFA), 'where being able to talk on your feet – and not getting stuck for a response – is a vital skill.' Gleeson joined the Department in 2001 after having his interest piqued by a DFA stand in a careers fair in the GMB, and went on to serve abroad in Brussels, South Africa and Atlanta in the United States, as well as in Dublin working on issues around overseas aid, Northern Ireland and Brexit. In 2018 he was appointed the Irish Ambassador to Chile, Peru and Ecuador, based in Santiago.

Gleeson also recalls that 'our regular attendees that year also included a future Taoiseach, Leo Varadkar, who was an active participant in many Hist debates throughout his time in College. He also represented the Hist at the Cambridge Intervarsity, where he was partnered with Mark Byrne, and they performed creditably although they did not win. Unfortunately for those curious about what the future Taoiseach said at this time, or the positions he adopted, the records of the Society are little help. As has been stated, by the 1990s the records had become humorous accounts, rather than detailed accounts of who spoke and what was said. There are no official records (or at least none that have been catalogued) of Varadkar's speeches to the Society, so we are unable to analyse what positions he took or what he said. The interest in his youthful

36 Correspondence with Author.

positions is something he himself has referenced. In a speech on the future of relationships North and South, delivered in Queen's University Belfast, on Friday 4 August 2017, Varadkar referenced Edward Carson's time in the College Historical Society, and the different issues he had spoken on, and joked that he feared 'the day when some future historian looks at the positions I adopted as a student'.[37]

In an interview with *Trinity Today* in 2017, shortly after becoming Taoiseach, Varadkar discussed his time in the Society. He noted that:

> I joined the College Historical Society when I started in Trinity and really enjoyed my time in the Hist. There were some very good people involved in the Society and it was a great place for making friends and learning about yourself. Adrian Langan was the Auditor when I started College and it was a very memorable year in terms of speakers and debates. Adrian later went on to set-up the 'Ireland in Europe' campaign and was campaign director for the 'Irish Alliance for Europe' during the second Nice referendum campaign and I really admired the role he played during that important debate.[38]

When asked what, in particular, he learned from his time in the Society Varadkar answered:

> I suppose the first thing I learned was how to think on your feet. As Taoiseach I face Leaders' Questions twice a week, on Tuesdays and Wednesdays, and over half an hour you can be asked about anything at all, with no advance notice or warning. Of course you prepare as much as you can, but sometimes you have to rely on your memory and wider reading and ability to formulate a response on the spot.

In a notable tribute to the value of student debating he added that:

> The great thing about student debating is that you get used to points of information and having your train of thought

37 https://merrionstreet.ie/en/News-Room/Speeches/Speech_by_the_Taoiseach_Mr_Leo_Varadkar_TD_Queen_s_University_Friday_4_August_2017.html.

38 *Trinity Today*, Autumn 2017.

> interrupted. You learn the importance of thinking quickly and being able to develop arguments and responses under pressure. It's very useful training for a politician, or indeed for life!

Varadkar ran for Fine Gael in the local elections in June 1999 for Mulhuddart while a second year student. He secured 380 votes and was eliminated on the 9th count, but he later commented that 'sometimes you learn more from your defeats than your victories'. As he told *Trinity Today*, 'I learned how to hone a message, to run a professional campaign, and I learned never to give up.' He said he 'would tell any young, idealistic student reading this to just go for it. It's not about winning, it's about standing for what you believe in and making a stand.' Varadkar ran again in the local elections in 2004, this time for Castleknock, and topped the poll with 4,894, virtually a Dáil quota. Elected to the Dáil in the 2007 general election for Dublin West, he became a cabinet minister following the 2011 election.

Varadkar has referenced his involvement in the Society on a number of public occasions. As Minister for Transport, Tourism and Sport he delivered a speech to the Hibernian Society in Savannah, Georgia on St Patrick's Day in 2014, where Paul Gleeson was then Consul General. Varadkar reminisced that they had been students at Trinity College Dublin, and 'were both debaters in the College Historical Society.'[39]

The event in Savannah was a politically tricky one, because the gathering was exclusively male, and the year before the Tánaiste, Eamon Gilmore, had boycotted the event. Varadkar ended his speech with an eloquent plea for toleration, suggesting that 'real change requires that we find the courage within ourselves to make our future as it ought to be – free and independent, equal and just. Catholic, Protestant, believer and non-believer, gay, straight, male, female.' The speech received a standing ovation and was reported in the *Irish Independent* under the headline, 'Varadkar calls for equality at men-only dinner in US'.[40]

---

39 https://merrionstreet.ie/en/News-Room/Speeches/speech-by-minister-for-transport-tourism-sport-leo-varadkar-to-the-hibernian-society-in-savannah-georgia-on-st-patricks-day-2014.58761.shortcut.html.

40 *Irish Independent,* 19 March 2014.

A couple of days after returning home, Varadkar spoke to the Road Safety Authority International Conference on Driver Distraction in Dublin Castle on Thursday 20 March 2014 and delivered an even more significant speech. It is remembered for a single word, but a word which had enormous implications for Irish politics. Raising the issue of Garda whistle-blowers (whose conduct had been described as 'disgusting'), he praised them for shining 'a light into a dark place' and for forcing 'those who would rather turn a blind-eye to face up to the truth'.[41] The speech concluded the simple but emphatic: 'There have been many words used to describe their actions. But if I was to use one word, the word I would use is "distinguished."' Few political interventions have been as consequential.

Varadkar was elected Taoiseach on 14 June 2017, becoming the youngest Taoiseach in Irish history and the first to have been educated at Trinity. Even many who opposed Fine Gael in office welcomed his election as Taoiseach, symbolising as it did a more modern and inclusive Ireland, indeed the kind of Ireland that had been the focus of many of the debates in the Society throughout this period. As Varadkar announced upon his election as leader of Fine Gael, in words that were reported around the world, 'prejudice has no hold in this Republic'.[42] His election meant, he said, that 'every proud parent in Ireland today can dream big dreams for their children'.[43]

Varadkar spends much time thinking about what he wants to say, and will spend hours rewriting and revising his speeches, believing that what a Taoiseach says is as important as what he does. Two notable speeches from his time in office are worthy of examination, because the value of what he learned in the Society are evident from the way they were constructed and delivered.

When Pope Francis visited Ireland in August 2018 there was a televised reception in St Patrick's Hall in Dublin Castle. In his speech, Varadkar praised the Catholic Church for all it had contributed to Ireland throughout history before discussing the dark history of abuse, which had 'created a bitter and broken heritage for

41 *Irish Independent,* 21 March 2014.

42 *Wall Street Journal,* 2 June 2017, online; *Daily Telegraph,* 3 June 2017.

43 *Irish Examiner,* 3 June 2017.

so many people, leaving a legacy of pain and suffering.'[44] Noting that Ireland was a very different country than it was in 1979 when Pope John Paul II visited, Varadkar emphasised that 'modern Ireland is still very much a country of faith and spirit and values. Family, community, enterprise, social justice, diversity, openness to the world, equality before the law, and individual liberty – these values describe the Republic which we aspire to build.'

As the *Sunday Independent* reported, 'in a speech broadcast around the globe, the Taoiseach said it is time for Church and State "to build a new relationship" fit for the twenty-first century.'[45] Noting that the Taoiseach had spent the summer working on the speech, *The Irish Times* praised it for being 'what many judged to be one of the finest speeches of his career and one of the best of our recent political history.'[46] In the paper, Simon Carswell suggested that 'the mastery of Varadkar's address, delivered before the 266th Pontiff in St Patrick's Hall, was the balance he struck: being both gracious and grave; praiseworthy and condemnatory; honest but never confrontational. He showed it was possible to be charitable and critical.'

A second speech received international media attention was made during his St Patrick's Day visit to the United States in 2018. Speaking at a breakfast hosted by the Vice President Mike Pence, Varadkar noted that he stood there 'this morning as leader of my country, flawed and human, but judged on my political actions and mistakes and not on my sexual orientation or my skin tone or my gender or my religious beliefs.'[47] In words that went viral on social media, he added, 'I do not believe my country is the only one in the world where my story is possible. It is found in every country where freedom and liberty are cherished. We are, after all, all God's children.'[48]

---

44 https://www.gov.ie/en/speech/d9f784-speech-of-an-taoiseach-leo-varadkar-on-the-occasion-of-the-visit-of-/?referrer=/eng/news/taoiseach%27s_speeches/speech_of_an_taoiseach_leo_varadkar_on_the_occasion_of_the_visit_of_pope_francis.html/.

45 *Sunday Independent,* 26 August 2018.

46 *The Irish Times,* 27 August 2018.

47 https://www.gov.ie/en/speech/6a1b9d-speech-of-an-taoiseach-vice-president-pences-st-patricks-day-breakfa/.

48 *The Irish Times,* 16 March 2019; https://www.thejournal.ie/leo-varadkar-donald-trump-capitol-hill-lunch-4542885-Mar2019/.

The College Historical Society has a remarkable record of attracting Taoisigh to speak to its members. Some spoke before they became Taoiseach, others while they were Taoiseach, and a few after they left office. Varadkar is unique in being the only one who spoke before the Society as a member, while as a student in Trinity in the late 1990s and early 2000s.

The rise to prominence of former Trinity students such as Varadkar is something the Provost, Patrick Prendergast, hailed in 2017 as representing the university's new position 'at the heart of Irish public and political life' after what he termed the 'wilderness years' of much of the twentieth century, 'when Trinity was isolated for various reasons not of the College's making, including Archbishop McQuaid's infamous ban on Catholics attending'.[49] The Hist played its part in helping Trinity find that new position in Irish society. But it also served a wider function in the service of democracy and debate. By offering a safe space to send public messages and advance ideas, it helped advance debate on the major issues of the day, most significantly on Northern Ireland, and also on the social and political issues that would come to dominate in the first two decades of the new century.

49 https://www.tcd.ie/provost/addresses/2017-2018/2017-09-05-economy-of-ireland.php.

24 THE SCHOOL FOR ORATORY IN THE TWENTY-FIRST CENTURY

It is impossible to tell the story of the Society in the first part of the twenty-first century in the same way as for previous eras. For one thing, it is too soon to identify the figures who will go on to achieve prominence in later life, although some, as we will see, have already begun to make their mark. Debates and speakers may also assume a greater significance with the passage of time, and similarly some events which seemed important at the time may later fade into obscurity. Rather than provide a detailed narrative, this chapter will provide a snapshot of the Society in the first two decades of the new century, the major debates, the guest speakers, and some of the controversies, as the Society entered a new era of debate and intellectual inquiry.

One challenge with contemporary history is writing about people known to the author and recounting events witnessed first-hand. The ancient Greek chronicler of Rome's imperial triumphs, Polybius, provided one model of how to approach this challenge, by deliberately writing himself into the history for the events he had witnessed or been involved in.[1] Thomas Dagg, in his brilliant archival study of the Society, published posthumously in a limited edition of twenty-five copies in 1969, showed much ability and dexterity when writing about his own time as Auditor (1906-07), and his involvement in the Society, and avoided making subjective assessments.[2] Avoiding another challenge with contemporary history completely, he chose to end the story in 1920, to ensure there was a

1 Brian McGing, *Polybius' Histories* (Oxford, 2010), p. 15.

2 Dagg, *CHS.*

suitable distance between the reader and the events being discussed. In the book on the Society by Declan Budd and Ross Hinds, published in 1997, they avoided this problem, while skilfully ensuring the study was up-to-date, by bringing together an anthology of first-hand accounts of recent events to provide a multiplicity of voices for the modern era.[3]

In a profile of university debating, published in *The Irish Times* in 2015 ('This house believes debating societies are here to stay: they are where witty, argumentative students go to earn their stripes'), Nora Ida McAuliffe assessed the reasons why students were drawn to societies such as the Hist. For some, it was to provide 'a platform for their opinion', for others it was to overcome 'a fear of public speaking', and more 'were into debating at school and just never left'.[4] For some students in Trinity a major attraction is the very history of the Society, the opportunity to follow in the footsteps of the politicians, revolutionaries, and orators of past generations, to develop one's skills as a speaker, and to be challenged against the very best of the current generation. The laws of the Society, archaic as they are, fulfil a useful function, training members in how to navigate a world of complex rules and procedures, invaluable for anyone interested in a career in politics or the law, or indeed the church, academia and many other professions.

Niamh Ní Mhaoileoin, one of the most talented orators in the history of the Society, has provided a brilliant insight into how the Society changed during her time as a member (2007–11) and it has a wider application. The Hist did not merely reflect the changes that were going on in Irish society. Often it prefigured what was to come, with the thinking that was driving debates in the Society anticipating new thinking on old issues more widely. In her first two years Ní Mhaoileoin recalls the members regularly debated whether same-sex marriage should be legalised, both in the Chamber and in competitive debates. In 2009, when she was an officer, the Society ran the debate 'This House Believes Gay Marriage is Unfair on Children'. She notes that it 'was difficult to find speakers on the anti-

3 Declan Budd and Ross Hinds, *The Hist, and Edmund Burke's Club* (Dublin 1997).

4 *The Irish Times*, 6 October 2015.

LGBT+ side', but 'we considered them reasonable two-sided arguments'. By the time she graduated in 2011, however, this had changed. Most had 'already concluded that those topics – and the rights of LGBT+ people – were beyond the scope of reasonable debate.' The debating society itself reflected how attitudes had changed among the younger generation, a change that was to drive the victory in the referendum on marriage equality in 2015.

The Irish Times profile on student debating in 2015 concluded that although it 'may not play the same role on campus as in the mid to late twentieth century', the 'Irish debating scene is still strong and vibrant', with the standard 'regarded as among the best in the world'.[5] Within the world of Irish debating the *Irish Times* debating competition has a special significance, in part because of the distinguished careers of many of its winners, in part because it has the most participants and is believed to 'reward oratory'.[6] In the modern era the Hist has had considerable success in the competition, becoming the debating society with the greatest number of team wins, and winning a remarkable four-in-a-row between 2007 and 2010. It is therefore worth spending some time on the Society's record in the competition in the first two decades of the twenty-first century.

In terms of competitive debate, 2001 was an historic year for the Society. That year the Society won all the prizes in the final of the *Irish Times* debating competition, with Yvonne Campbell and Bríd McGrath winning the Demosthenes trophy for best team and the Auditor, Aoife Titley, named best individual speaker. The final was held in UCD on 23 February 20001, with the motion 'That this House Agrees Sinn Fein has a Place in this Republic's Government', and the debate chaired by Martin McGuinness, the Northern Ireland Education Minister.[7] Speaking afterwards, McGuinness described the debate as 'exciting, stimulating and interesting'.[8] In *The Irish Times* report of the debate, it was noted that Campbell and McGrath 'displayed their skill in their speaking and as they interrupted other speakers with points of information', while Titley 'delivered a superb

5 *The Irish Times,* 6 October 2015.

6 Former winner, Frank Kennedy, quoted in Ibid.

7 *The Irish Times,* 24 February 2001

8 *The Irish Times,* 6 March 2001.

performance to win the individual speaker's prize'. All three were proposing the motion. As part of the prize, the three winners travelled to the United States to take part in a three-week debating tour (perhaps the biggest prize in Irish debating), visiting Chicago, Denver, San Diego, San Antonio, Virginia and New York.[9] In Virginia they found themselves 'called upon to defend George W. Bush's foreign policy', something McGrath admitted afterwards 'presented us with a real challenge'. All three were distinguished orators in the Society, and at the end of that session Bríd McGrath won the silver medal for oratory.

The Society's good run in the competition continued the next year. The 2002 final was held in Maynooth on 22 February, and the convenor of the competition, Paul Gleeson, joked on the night that there was an incongruity in debating the motion 'That this House Regrets the American Response to September 11th' in order to win a prestigious trip to the United States.[10] The debate was chaired by the Minister for Foreign Affairs, Brian Cowen. The Auditor, Louis Mooney, was part of the winning team speaking alongside Brendan Kelly. Proposing the motion, Mooney argued that the bombing campaign had succeeded in 'sparking a wave of anti-Americanism throughout the Islamic world' and he suggested that the correct course of action for President Bush was peaceful conflict resolution.[11] The Society also excelled in the other major national debating competition that year. In the Irish final of the John Smith Memorial Mace competition the Society team of Jim McElroy and Mánus de Barra, runners up in the *Irish Times* final, proved victorious.

The 2003 final of the *Irish Times* debating competition was unique in having an all Trinity-UCD line-up, with six UCD speakers proposing the motion, and six Trinity speakers opposing it. *The Irish Times* afterwards described this as 'an unprecedented coincidence' and also noted that Alison McIntyre, the Censor of the Society, was 'the only female among the twelve speakers'.[12] The motion for the debate was 'That this House Believes History will Judge [Bertie]

9 *The Irish Times*, 24 April 2001.

10 *The Irish Times*, 26 February 2002.

11 *The Irish Times*, 23 February 2002.

12 *The Irish Times*, 22 February 2003.

Ahern's Ireland Harshly', with the leader of the Labour Party, Pat Rabbitte, in the chair. McIntyre won the Christina Murphy Memorial Trophy for best individual speaker, with Colm Coyne and Leo Mulrooney of the L&H winning the Demosthenes trophy, but unfortunately we do not have a report of McIntyre's winnning speech.

In each year between 2007 and 2010 the Society won the Demosthenes trophy in the final of the *Irish Times* debating competition, an unprecedented achievement, and one that has never been matched since. It also confirmed the Society as the most successful in the competition's history. The run began in 2007 when the team of David Boughton and Ciaran Denny won the final of the competition, debating the motion 'That this House Believes that a Neutral Ireland cannot fulfil its Global Responsibilities in the Twenty-first Century'. The Hist team argued that it can take a day to start a war, but a decade to recover from one, with Boughton praising Ireland for successfully treading the line between 'passion and pragmatism'.[13] Opposing the motion, both speakers successfully argued that in an increasingly 'black and white' world, where supporters are 'allies' and opponents are labelled 'terrorists', Ireland's position as a neutral country provided some much needed colour. The debate was held in Trinity and chaired by Mary Robinson, who used her speech after the formal debate to criticise rendition flights and make the case that Ireland had a role to play internationally when it came to climate change.[14]

The following year, the team of Christopher Kissane and David Kenny won the final on 29 February 2008, opposing the motion 'That this House Believes that Ireland Owes a Debt of Gratitude to the Catholic Church'. Arguing that the Church's moral authority had gone, 'because we know the truth', the team suggested that the 'compassion agenda' was used to increase its own authority and control.[15] Kenny claimed that a community which relied on 'shaming' and on 'guilting people' was not a community, and he described Catholicism as the 'stickiest religion there is', whose genius was to 'get you while you are young' and convince people they were 'bad Catholics'.

---

13 *The Irish Times*, 19 February 2007.

14 Ibid.

15 *The Irish Times*, 3 March 2008.

In 2009 the Hist team of John Gallagher and Andrea Mulligan won the final of the competition, held in the University of Limerick, opposing the motion 'That this House Believes the Partition of Ireland should Remain Permanent'.[16] Unfortunately we do not have an account of the speech of Mulligan, a superb debater and a leading figure in the Society, but *The Irish Times* reports Gallagher as saying that Britain had kept Northern Ireland on 'life support' in order to 'keep it quiet' and he suggested that this 'stifles innovation and it stifles creativity'. An all-Ireland economy was recommended as making better economic sense, especially for those living in border counties.

The remarkable four-in-a-row was achieved by the team of Niamh Ní Mhaoileoin and Niall Sherry on the fiftieth anniversary of the competition, debating the motion 'That this House Believes that Ireland Owes a Debt of Gratitude to Fianna Fáil, 1926-2010'. The debate was held in DCU on 21 February 2010 and was chaired by the former First Minister of Northern Ireland, David Trimble, and the *University Times* reported that 'the winning team achieved a confident victory to take the prestigious prize'.[17]

Opposing the motion, Ní Mhaoileoin suggested that it was Fianna Fáil which owed a debt of gratitude to the Irish people for entrusting them with their governance. Pointing out the damage done by corrupt politics to the trust of the electorate, she said, 'In 1926, Ireland gained a new political movement ... and we gave them the opportunity to build a nation. Eighty-four years later, we are left with one of the most difficult questions ever posed to an Irish nation: was it for this?'[18] Sherry developed this argument, suggesting that much of Ireland's progress had come about despite, and not because, of Fianna Fáil. 'They owe us for the decades of power that they have squandered' he declared to applause.

The Society had other successes in the competition in the years afterwards, though not on the same scale. In 2013 Kate Brady won best individual speaker representing the Society at the final in Belfast, debating the motion 'This House would Emigrate'. The only

16 *The Irish Times*, 21 February 2009.

17 *University Times*, 10 March 2010.

18 *The Irish Times*, 22 February 2010.

woman speaker among the twelve in the final, and opposing the motion, Brady contrasted the emigrant, who left home in the belief they would never return, with the explorer, who travelled in the hope of return. The explorer, Brady suggested, 'can see new worlds on their own terms'.[19] The Demosthenes trophy for best team was won by the Bram Stoker Club, another Trinity team, composed of former Auditor, John Engle, and Liam Brophy.

'Irish neutrality has always been a grand act of self-exception' argued Daniel Gilligan on Friday 22 February 2019 as the Society won the Demosthenes trophy for a record fifteenth time (as of 2019). The Hist team of Ronan Daly and Gilligan proposed the motion that 'This House would Rescind Ireland's Position of Neutrality in Favour of a European Standing Army', in a debate held in UCD and chaired by the Fianna Fáil TD, Jack Chambers. Daly was reported as arguing that that 'this debate is about the profound distance between who we are, and we believe ourselves to be'.[20]

The Society in the modern era had its share of turmoil, with some auditorial resignations, various controversies, and occasional in-fighting, sometimes blighting its ability to be a leader in challenging old orthodoxies, developing new ideas and providing a space for the clash of ideas. One Auditor, in correspondence with the author, considered it one of the achievements of his year that there were no resignations from the Committee. None the less, there were significant triumphs as well during this period as the Society worked to be 'a school of oratory', a forum for the testing and development of new ideas. This book is a study of oratory, debate and argument, as well as of the individuals who made their mark in the Society and afterwards, not of the controversies and in-fighting except where they impact on the themes of the book. The remainder of this chapter will therefore provide a snapshot of some of the debates and speakers who contributed to the success of the Society in the twenty-first century. Unfortunately we do not always have records of what was said, or how motions were decided, but occasionally we have reports in the Trinity or national newspapers and, from 2009 (but more regularly from 2013), video recordings of the majority of meetings.

19 *The Irish Times*, 1 March 2013.

20 *The Irish Times*, 25 February 2019.

Aoife Titley was Auditor for the 231st session and presented her inaugural paper on 21 February 2001 on 'People v. Peoples: Distinguishing the Difference between Human Rights and Culture', with guest speakers Michael D. Higgins, Dr Ronit Lentin, and Senator David Norris. Notable debates included 'That this House would Name Paedophile Offenders' (11 October 2000), with speakers including Senator Mary Henry and Ivana Bacik (by now Reid Professor of Law at Trinity).[21]

Adrian Hardiman returned to the Society on 25 October 2000, this time as a Supreme Court judge, to chair the Kingsmill Moore Intervarsity, with the motion debated 'That this House Believes Europe Will Never be United'. Mr Justice Hugh O'Flaherty of the Supreme Court chaired the debate on 1 November 2000 ('That this House would Elect the Judiciary') and speakers included the talented lawyer, Paul Anthony McDermott, and James Nugent SC. 'That this House Believes that the Celtic Tiger has Proved to be a Burden rather than a Boom' was debated on 22 November 2000 and speakers included businessman Denis O'Brien, Senator Fergal Quinn, and honorary member, Adrian Langan. That session the maiden speaker's competition was won by Alison McIntyre, debating the motion 'That this House believes that Socialism is the Whine of the Weak' (29 November 2000). [22]

Louis Mooney was elected Auditor for the 232nd session, with Jim McElroy as Treasurer, and Brendan Kelly replacing Aoife Carroll as Correspondence Secretary during the year. Mooney presented his inaugural paper on 8 February 2002 entitled 'Freedom of Speech v. the Right to Good Names: Do our Libel Laws Strike the Right Balance?' and guest speakers included Dr Gerard Hogan SC, Fintan O'Toole, and Charlie Bird.

Notable debates included the Northern Ireland debate on 17 October 2001 on the motion 'That this House would Keep the Belfast Agreement Alive'. Chaired by Dr Garret FitzGerald, the meeting had one of the most impressive array of stakeholders and experts ever assembled at a single meeting, including Sir Ivor Roberts (the British ambassador to Ireland), Jeffrey Donaldson (the Ulster

21 TCD MUN/SOC/HIST Uncatalogued Papers, 2000-2019.

22 Ibid.

Unionist MP who had walked out of the Good Friday negotiations), Jane Morris (of the Northern Ireland Women's Coalition), Albert Reynolds (former Taoiseach), Gerry McGeough (former IRA activist), Duncan Shipley-Dalton (Ulster Unionist MLA), Edwin Poots (DUP MLA), Austin Currie TD, Sean Farren (SDLP MLA), and the Revd Martin Smyth (Ulster Unionist MP).[23]

Senator David Norris chaired the debate 'That this House Supports Gay Adoption' (7 November 2001) with speakers including Peter Tatchell (the co-founder of the British LGBT campaign group, OutRage!) and Máire Kirrane, of the National Party. The meeting on 9 January 2002 was an interview with disgraced former Conservative MP, Neil Hamilton and his wife, Christine. Former Ireland football manager, Jack Charleton, chaired the debate on 12 February 2002, with the motion 'That this House would Keep Politics Off the Pitch'. The comedian Ardal O'Hanlon chaired the meeting on 6 March 2002, which was a 'Student Stand-Up Comedy Night'.

Brendan Kelly was elected Auditor for the 233rd session, and his officers included Claire Gleeson as Record Secretary and Alison McIntyre as Censor, with Anne O'Brien on the Committee. Kelly's inaugural paper was presented on 19 February 2003 entitled 'International Law since September 11th, 2001'. Speakers included High Court judge, Roderick Murphy, former Auditor, Paul Gleeson, and the journalist, Deaglán de Bréadún.

Four days before the second Nice Referendum, the subject was debated on 15 October 2002, with the motion 'That This House would Give Nice a Chance'. The impressive line-up of speakers included Adrian Langan (Campaign Director of the Irish Alliance for Europe), Roger Cole (chair of the Peace and Neutrality Alliance), Prionsias de Rossa (Labour MEP), Patricia McKenna (Green MEP), Dana Rosemary Scallon (Independent MEP), Brian Lenihan (Fianna Fáil TD), Caoimhghín Ó Caoláin (Sinn Féin TD), Paul Gogarty (Green TD) and Caroline Lucas (British Green MEP).[24]

General John de Chastelain returned to the Society to chair the Northern Ireland debate on 30 October 2002, with the motion 'That this House Believes the War is Over'. George Galloway, the Labour

---

23 Ibid.

24 Ibid.

MP, spoke at the debate on 6 November 2002 on the motion 'That this House would Bomb Iraq'. John McGuirk was the winner of the Maiden Speaker's competition on 27 November 2002, speaking on the motion 'That this House Regrets the Role of the Catholic Church in Twentieth Century Ireland'. McGuirk would later become a prominent writer, media commentator and activist and involved in opposing the Lisbon referendums in 2008 and 2009, and the abortion referendum in 2018.

The victory of Fianna Fáil in the 2002 general election was debated on 26 February 2003, with the motion 'That this House Believes the Government was Re-Elected on False Promises'. Speakers include a veritable line-up of current politicians (including some future ministers and even a future Taoiseach) with Enda Kenny proposing the motion, and Finian McGrath, Barry Andrews, Joe Higgins, Séamus Brennan, Averil Power, Trevor Sargent, and Killian Forde all taking part.

To mark the bicentenary of the death of Robert Emmet, a special honorary members debate was held as part of the Robert Emmet commemoration on 5 March 2003. The debate was chaired by the new President of the Society, David McConnell, who had succeeded Conor Cruise O'Brien, and who would go on to be a remarkable influence on the Society in the years' ahead as a supporter, adviser, and champion. The motion was 'That this House Believes the Time has Come to Write Emmet's Epitaph' and speakers included Philip Emmet (a direct descendent of Thomas Addis Emmet), Dr Patrick Geoghegan (from the Department of History in Trinity and the author of a biography of Emmet), Dr Ruán O'Donnell (whose two volumes on Emmet and the 1798 and 1803 rebellions would be published later that year), Adrian Langan (making his second appearance before the Society that year), and Brian Cleary (the chair of the Robert Emmet Association).

Alison McIntyre was elected Auditor for the 234th session, and the officers included Niall McCarthy as Record Secretary, Anne O'Brien as Librarian, and with Hannah Murphy, Claire Hartnett and Cathal McCann on the Committee. McIntyre delivered her inaugural paper on 20 February 2004, entitled 'An Ghaeilge: the Changing Status of National Identity in a New Europe'. Notable debates that session included 'That this House Supports Gay

Marriage' on 8 October 2003, chaired by Ailbhe Smyth. Hannah Murphy was one of the students proposing the motion, with John McGuirk the first opposition speaker. The motion was carried.[25]

On 22 October 2003 Dr Mary Kelly, the Director General of the Environmental Protection Agency, chaired the debate 'That this House Believes Green isn't Always Best'. Cathal McCann proposed the motion, which was opposed by Trevor Sargent of the Green Party, Fergus O'Dowd, the Fine Gael TD, and Paddy Cosgrave (then a student and later co-founder of Web Summit). The motion was defeated.

Increasingly in this period we see interviews or set-piece lectures taking the place of regular debates once or twice a session. On 18 November 2003 the broadcaster Philip Boucher-Hayes chaired the meeting of the Society, which was an interview with Charles and Diana Ingram, the couple at the centre of a notorious cheating scandal on the British version of *Who Wants to Be a Millionaire* two years earlier. On 3 December 2004 Martin McGuinness, the deputy leader of Sinn Féin, spoke to the Society on 'Reflections on the Northern Assembly Elections'. On 28 January 2004 the Taoiseach, Bertie Ahern, delivered a lecture (what was billed as 'the Inaugural Robert Emmet memorial lecture' but which does not appear to have been repeated) to the Society.

On 29 January 2004 there was another debate on Europe, 'That This House Believes the EU Constitution is the Final Nail in the Coffin of National Sovereignty'. Proposing the motion was Joe Higgins TD, Mary Lou McDonald (soon to become a Sinn Féin MEP), Patricia McKenna (Green Party MEP) and John McGuirk, with Ruairí Quinn and John Bruton opposing. The motion was defeated.

During the session the Society ran an online poll to find out who was the Greatest Irish Person, and the highest ranking ten people were brought forward to be proposed and debated at a meeting on 21 April 2004, chaired by the President, David McConnell. Síle de Valera, the Fianna Fáil TD, proposed her grandfather, Éamon de Valera, Robert Emmet was proposed by Patrick Geoghegan, Daniel O'Connell by Adrian Langan, Patrick Pearse by Jim McElroy, Gerry Adams by Alison McIntyre, James Connolly by Colm Ó Mongáin, Michael

25 Ibid.

Collins by Yvonne Campbell, Bono by Brendan Bruen, and Roy Keane by Cathal McCann. It is revealing that Bobby Sands, who had also made the shortlist, was unable to find a proposer. At the end of the debate the House voted by secret ballot to decide the winner, with Robert Emmet coming first on 18 votes, and Daniel O'Connell and Michael Collins tied in second place on 17 votes.

Anne O'Brien was elected Auditor for the 235th session, with Hannah Murphy as Correspondence Secretary and Cathal McCann as Record Secretary. Notable debates that session included one on President George W. Bush on 13 October 2004 in the run-up to the American presidential election ('That this House would Remove George from Washington') which was carried, and a debate on the administrative changes in Trinity which were underway 'That this House would Restructure Trinity' (27 October 2004), which was defeated.

Cathal McCann was elected Auditor for the 236th session, with James O'Brien as Record Secretary, This was the first year that the Auditor was enabled to take a sabbatical (similar to Students' Union Officers). McCann was a Human Genetics student and wouldn't have been able to balance running the Society with his heavy class-load, and he used a year of his Scholarship to live on campus, and this added to the professionalism and prestige of the office.

'That this House would legalise abortion' was debated on 12 October 2005, and was the first time the issue had been debated in the Society in a number of years, and speakers included Professor William Binchy; Frances Kissling, the President of Catholics for a Free Choice in the United States; Dr Rebecca Gomperts of the Women on Waves Foundation from the Netherlands; Catherine Forde, the chairwoman of the Irish Family Planning Association; and Anne Scanlon of 'LIFE', a British pro-life charity.

The annual Northern Ireland debate a week later was historic, featuring two former Taoisigh: Garret Fitzgerald who chaired, and Albert Reynolds who spoke, along with Jeffrey Donaldson, Mark Durkan, and the Secretary of State for Northern Ireland, Peter Hain. Other notable debates that session included 'That religion has no place in Bunracht na hÉireann', where the Church of Ireland Archbishop of Dublin, John Neill, spoke, and 'That this House believes the Legal Profession Should Be Deregulated' in Hilary Term, with Minister for Justice, Michael McDowell. 'That This House Would Legalise Euthanasia' proved controversial, and there was a huge attendance, with people from Youth Defence protesting outside. The debate was recorded for a documentary on the pro-euthanasia group Dignitas for the Canadian Discovery Channel. Speakers included Ludwig A. Minelli from Dignitas; Margaret Braithwaite, former chair of the Voluntary Euthanasia Society; Fr Kevin Bacon, the Secretary of the Irish Bishops Conference on Bioethics; Professor Nigel Biggar of Trinity; and Rita L. Marker, Director of the International Taskforce on Euthanasia and Assisted Suicide.

McCann presented his inaugural paper on 8 February 2006, a passionate rallying call for a new generation, entitled 'Student Apathy and Social Disengagement' and the Chancellor of the University, Mary Robinson, was one of the respondents, alongside Adrian Langan, the Labour Party *chef de cabinet*. Other guests that year included the celebrated actors Ralph Fiennes and David Kelly.

James O'Brien was elected Auditor for the 237th session, and (following some resignations) his officers included Timothy Smyth as Treasurer and William Quill as Correspondence Secretary. Quill would be one of the most influential figures in the Society in this period, his advice and guidance often sought and highly respected. The Librarian was Andrea Mulligan and Debates Convenor was Christopher Kissane, two of the standout debaters from this period.

O'Brien's inaugural paper was entitled, 'The Happiness and Glory of a Representative: Burke and the Potential for Real Leadership in Politics', and speakers included the Secretary General to the Government, Dermot McCarthy, as well as the Czech Republic Ambassador to Ireland Josef Havlas, and broadcaster and comedian, Abie Philbin Bowman. Notable debates that session included 'That this House would Re-elect the Government' and speakers included Brian Lenihan of Fianna Fáil and Mary Lou McDonald of Sinn Féin with Brian Dobson in the Chair. The annual Northern Ireland debate had Jeffrey Donaldson, by now with the DUP, and Ken Maginnis, of the Ulster Unionist Party, as guest speakers, with Nobel Peace Prize winner, John Hume, in the Chair. In terms of student speakers, O'Brien remembers Christopher Kissane being 'phenomenal all year', and Josephine Curry as 'excellent'.

The Treasurer, Timothy Smyth, was elected Auditor for the 238th session, and his officers included Andrea Mulligan as Treasurer, William Quill as Correspondence Secretary, John Gallagher as Record Secretary, and Thomas Kinsella as Librarian, with Jamie Walsh a member of the Committee. History was made on 19 October 2007 when the First Minister of Northern Ireland, the Revd Ian Paisley, attended the Society for the first time to deliver a lecture on Edward Carson. This was reported widely across Ireland and the UK, with the *Observer* noting that it was the first time Carson was to be honoured in Dublin since the foundation of the Irish State.[26] Smyth commented at the time that it was 'long overdue' for a man of Carson's reputation and magnitude to be commemorated in Trinity, saying that 'we are absolutely delighted that the current leader of unionism' should be giving the lecture.

Wearing a 'Jesus is God' badge, a Dublin Fusiliers tie, and a heart-shaped Union Jack tie-pin, Paisley arrived to a standing ovation and it was noted in *The Irish Times* that 'the often rancourous debates held by the Hist during the Troubles seemed to belong to another era'.[27] Paisley spoke for thirty minutes on Carson, before taking fifty minutes of questions, including whether he had any regrets. His response was that he wished he had come to Dublin more often, 'to evangelise the heathens'. In a moment of honesty and reflection, Paisley noted that 'we are a strange race... we love and we hate... when we love, we love hard and when we hate, we hate hard'.[28] The meeting ended with Paisley inviting the audience to come up to the Giant's Causeway, telling them 'I'm the MP for the area, that's why I'm a giant'.

Smyth brought a new vision to the Society, determined to innovate in terms of speakers and events. The session included an interview with the acclaimed writer and barrister, John Mortimer, by his biographer, Valerie Grove, on Tuesday 30 October 2007 where he discussed how he came to write his *Rumpole of the Bailey* series of novels. The next night, on Wednesday 31 October, there was a regular debate, with the motion, 'That Israeli Intransigence is the Root of the Crisis in the Middle East', and guests included, the Palestinian Ambassador to Ireland, Hikmat Ajjuri; David Landy,

26 *Observer,* 7 October 2007.

27 *The Irish Times,* 20 October 2007.

28 *Irish Independent,* 20 October 2007.

of the Irish Palestine Solidarity Campaign; Dr Rory Miller of Kings' College London; and Susan Philips, the political analyst.

The inaugural meeting took place on 21 November 2007 in a packed Dining Hall, as Smyth delivered a brilliant paper on 'Overcoming Conflict and the Legacy of History'. Acclaiming the Downing Street Declaration as a turning point in the conflict in Northern Ireland, he recognized the role of the British Prime Minister of the time, John Major, in achieving it. Major himself was the star attraction at the meeting, and he spoke of the painstaking work that had gone into achieving the Declaration and what needed to be done afterwards. Also speaking were Noel Dorr and Sir Roderic Lyne, two diplomats who gave revealing insights into the backstage diplomacy behind the Declaration. Dr Martin Mansergh, the Fianna Fáil TD who had played an influential role in the peace process, then provided detailed and humorous portraits of Albert Reynolds and John Major when discussing how the Declaration was negotiated.

'That This House Believes that Scotland Should Declare its Independence' was debated at the honorary members' debate on 23 April 2008. Other notable events included an interview with *Divine Comedy* frontman Neil Hannon, and the debate 'That Russia is Again a Threat to the West'.

Thomas Kinsella was elected Auditor for the 239th session, and his officers included Niamh Ní Mhaoileon, as Librarian. Former Taoiseach Bertie Ahern received the Society's gold medal for outstanding contribution to public discourse at the debate on Wednesday 22 October 2008 and then spoke on the motion 'That this House would Reunite Ireland'. Ahern attended the meeting on crutches, having fractured his leg while falling down the stairs in his house the day before. Ireland had been drawn in the football World Cup qualifying group with Italy and a student joked that the medal should be presented to the Italian national football team, and 'may they all break their legs'.[29]

For his inaugural meeting in February 2009 (described in one account as 'captivating') Kinsella spoke about the role of religion in the public sphere and Archbishop Desmond Tutu was the star attraction,

29 *The Irish Times,* 23 October 2008.

but unfortunately we do not have a record of what was said.[30]

A different kind of event took place on the night of the American Presidential Election, on Tuesday 4 November 2008. The Society decided to hold an all-night event in the GMB to watch the results come in, and permission was granted by the Junior Dean, Dr Emma Stokes, on the condition that a member of staff supervised it and that there was no alcohol consumed on the premises. Dr Patrick Geoghegan of the Department of History agreed to take responsibility, and arrived at midnight after having delivered a speech on the history of American presidential elections at the Kildare Street and University Club. Despite the Society having promised to be on its best behaviour, he expected to find a party in full swing, with the election being used as a pretext, and was pleasantly surprised (and indeed a little disappointed) to find the students earnestly following the results on laptops and on a large screen in the Conversation Room of the GMB. Most of the students were supporting Barack Obama, but he never forgot how the students gathered in respectful silence to listen to the concession speech of his opponent, John McCain, in the early hours of the morning, applauding at the end.

Jamie Walsh was elected Auditor for the 240th session and his officers included Mark Kearney as Treasurer, Kate Brady as Correspondence Secretary, and Colm Denny as Librarian. The Fresher's debate was on whether marriage is an outdated institution ('If you like it then you should put a ring on it!') and Niamh Ní Mhaoileoin remembers it as her favourite debate during her time in the Hist. Ardal O'Hanlon chaired the debate ('very funny and charming') and guest speakers included Katherine Zappone and Dr Ann-Louise Gilligan, who had married in Canada in 2003 and whose legal case in Ireland set off a decade of debate on marriage equality and helped pave the way for its achievement in 2015. Both 'gave extraordinarily powerful speeches in defence of marriage'. The debate was opened by Catherine Murphy, a talented speaker who went on to achieve success as a comedian under the name Catherine Bohart. Ní Mhaoileoin spoke in favour of the motion, with Huw Duffy in opposition, and she remembers it as 'the best clash' the two friends ever had in the Society.[31]

30 TCD MUN/SOC/HIST Uncatalogued Papers, 2000-2019.

31 Correspondence with Author.

Professor Joseph Stiglitz, the winner of the Nobel Prize for Economics, and the former chief economist of the World Bank, spoke to the Society about the impact of globalisation on the poor on Wednesday 7 October 2009. Discussing the bank bailout in Ireland, he compared it to the 'type of thing happening in banana republics all over the world'.[32] Other notable guests that session included the author of *Wild Swans*, Jung Chang, and Bill Bryson, author of *A Short History of Nearly Everything*.

The liguist, philosopher and political activist, Professor Noam Chomsky, was interviewed by the journalist Robert Fisk at the Society on 3 November 2009, and he warned that Israel's greatest enemies were those supporting 'its moral degeneration and ultimate destruction'.[33] Chomsky suggested that disillusionment with the policies of John F. Kennedy in the 1960s had prompted people to become involved in the civil rights campaigns and the feminist movement.

Walsh's inaugural paper was delivered on 27 January 2010 in a packed Public Theatre. Entitled 'Economics in the Global Sphere' it advocated a renewed approach to global governance in fighting extreme poverty and global warming, and was responded to by Joan Burton TD, Professor Patrick Cunningham and Senator Shane Ross.[34] The keynote response was delivered by Professor Jeffrey Sachs, the Special Advisor to the United Nations Secretary-General, and in his speech he suggested that for the first time in history the world was 'intensely and completely' interconnected'.[35] Sachs claimed that globalisation and the challenge of environmental sustainability were the defining issues of the current generation, warning that 'the impact of society on our physical earth and the physical environment is an unprecedented challenge'.

Huw Duffy was elected Auditor for the 241st session, and his officers included Anthony McDonnell as Correspondence Secretary, Kate Oliver as Record Secretary, and Liam O'Neill as Librarian, with Eamonn Bell, Ruth Hoey, Hannah McCarthy, and Joanne Pedrina

32 *Sunday Business Post*, 11 October 2009.

33 *The Irish Times*, 4 November 2009.

34 TCD MUN/SOC/HIST Uncatalogued Papers, 2000-2019.

35 *The Irish Times*, 28 January 2010.

four notable members of the Committee. Major debates that session included 'This House Believes That the Catholic Church is a Force For Good' (29 September 2010), with Colm O'Gorman as one of the guest speakers, and he delivered a powerful speech drawing on his own experience of clerical abuse. An outstanding speech was delivered by Niamh Ní Mhaoileoin, who used it to announce publicly that she had lost her faith in the Catholic Church. In previous years she had spoken in defence of Catholicism, but in 2010 she changed her views. It was, she believes, her 'best ever speech in the Chamber', which in itself gives an indication of the quality.

The debate on the motion 'That this House believes that Development Aid has Done more Harm than Good' on Wednesday 6 October 2010 featured 'a darkly charismatic Bob Geldof' on the side of the opposition.[36] Justin Kilcullen of Trócaire also opposed the motion, with Professor Yash Tandon, a Ugandan activist, policymaker and professor of political economy, arguing for the proposition.[37] According to the report in *Trinity News*, 'the knighted former rocker Sir Bob stole the show'. Reminding the audience that human life was at stake, he posed the following challenge: 'I don't care who they are, but if they are made mute by poverty you will hear my voice on their behalf. Whose voice will be raised with mine?' Arguing that 'charity is what most human beings can do in order to stop another hurting', he warned that if that was lost 'then something that is purely human withers and dies'.[38] Geldof insisted that 'poverty is soluble' and his speech was credited with the defeat of the motion. At this meeting Geldof also received the gold medal for outstanding contribution to public discourse (but was said to be distinctly unimpressed by the quality of the medal being awarded to him).

Former British Prime Minister Gordon Brown received the gold medal for outstanding contribution to public discourse on 10 December 2010. The meeting was reported in the *Irish Independent* which revealed that 'there was standing room only at the venue'.[39]

36 Correspondence with Huw Duffy.

37 *Trinity News* (http://trinitynews.ie/2010/10/geldof-addresses-attentive-listeners-at-the-hist-debate-on-development-aid/).

38 *Irish Independent*, 7 October 2010.

39 *Irish Independent*, 11 December 2010.

Brown had recently authored a book, *Beyond the Crash,* and it was noted that 'he wooed his audience well, weaving amusing anecdotes into his persistent efforts to plug his book – which insists that only a global response will be successful in tackling the current crisis.'

Alastair Campbell, the former Downing Street Press Secretary (1997-2000) and Director of Communications and Strategy (2000-2003), was the guest speaker at the Society in February 2011 at a specially arranged Tuesday morning event. In a thirty-minute speech he discussed 'the media age' and was critical of the decline in journalistic standards, complaining that 'the line of who is and isn't a journalist is being constantly blurred.'[40] Warning that people may not want to enter into politics because of the public scrutiny, he defended politics as 'a noble calling'. During questions from the floor, Campbell was asked about David Cameron, who had succeeded Gordon Brown as British Prime Minister after the 2010 general election. In a scathing answer, Campbell was quoted as suggesting that Cameron had 'little empathy, he doesn't understand people, he doesn't have a sense of what he wants to do in power, his background is disproportionate to the population.'

The novelist Roddy Doyle received the Edmund Burke medal for his contribution to the arts on Tuesday 15 February 2011. According to the report in the *University Times,* Doyle delivered a message of hope 'to the room of eager onlookers' and suggested that 'the notion that Ireland has nothing to offer the world anymore is warped. Fight it. Fight it by laughing. Sure the country doesn't like you anyway. You've no manners, no attention span, no time for anything but Facebook, and as for your morals…!'[41]

Huw Duffy's inaugural paper was a brilliant reflection on 'The Piety of Atheism' and speakers at the meeting included American naturalist philosopher Daniel Dennett, Senator Ivana Bacik, Professor of Philosophy in Trinity, Peter Simons, and the biochemist, *Irish Times* columnist and, in his own words, 'token theist', William Reville.

Antonin Scalia, the United States Supreme Court Judge, visited Trinity on Thursday 10 March 2011 and spoke to the Society in a packed Edmund Burke Theatre. The subject of his paper was 'Mullahs

40 *University Times,* 11 February 2011.

41 *University Times,* 19 February 2011.

of the West' and he argued that the courts must have the courage to interpret the Constitution truthfully to 'stop the majority doing whatever it wants – that's why the Constitution's there'.[42] Recognising that this might be unpopular, he cited as evidence his ruling against a law prohibiting flag burning. Although he didn't agree with the practice, dismissing the people who wanted to do it as 'probably a bunch of bearded, sandal-wearing, hippie-types that were doing it anyway', he argued that the Constitution granted people the right to freedom of speech, and that this had to be upheld.

The American civil rights leader, the Revd Jesse Jackson, received the gold medal for outstanding contribution to public discourse on Tuesday 22 March 2011, and received a standing ovation from the students.[43] In a stirring call to arms, Jackson told the packed gathering of students that their generation was responsible for building on the advances that had been made over the previous sixty years and had to fight to protect democracy which was threatened by rich and powerful elites.

'College debaters are just students wearing ill-fitting formal clothes, and most of them aren't even very good. But, crucially, some of them kind of are.'[44] So wrote Sally Rooney of her debating career. In this period of the Society's history one of the best debaters was Rooney herself, the Censor of the Society for the 242nd sessions (2011-12).

Rooney excelled in competitive debate, winning a number of competitions, and she also took part in the World and European Universities Debating Championships. In 2013 she was ranked the best speaker at the European Universities Debating Championships held at Manchester. In the final she opposed the motion 'That this House give more votes to citizens according to their performance on a current affairs test' and her speech was a devastating critique of the proposal, demonstrating how the poorer members of the society would be marginalised and excluded. In a brilliant rebuttal of the

---

42 *University Times*, 14 March 2011.

43 *Irish Independent*, 23 March 2011.

44 Sally Rooney, 'Even if you beat me', *Dublin Review* (September 2015), https://thedublinreview.com/article/even-if-you-beat-me/.

suggestion that geographical knowledge would form part of the test, she noted archly: 'Iraq isn't a current affair. Its location isn't a current affair. Iraq's been there for quite a while.'[45]

'Eerily clever and stunningly eloquent in equal measure' was how one of Rooney's debating partners described her and it is an accurate description.[46] Others remember Rooney as a 'brilliant' debater, who 'gave many rousing and moving speeches, both in the chamber and competitively'.[47] The Society was gifted with talented orators in this period with Niamh Ní Mhaoileoin, Huw Duffy, Kate Brady, and Sally Rooney among the stand-out speakers of the twenty-first century.

In 2015 Rooney wrote an account of her career as a competitive debater for the *Dublin Review*.[48] Sharp, insightful and at times scathing, it was written in the assured style she would soon become known for, and it helped launch her career as a writer. Rooney noted how when she first started attending College debates, 'I was a nearly friendless teenager living away from home for the first time; for me, the most talented speakers seemed to possess a subtle power and command that was almost glamorous. I started watching debates every week, just sitting in the audience, mostly on my own.' *The New Yorker* later discussed this in its profile of Rooney and it noted that 'What Rooney loved about debating was entering a state of "flow," that magical mental hum when disparate facts and ideas effortlessly assembled themselves in her mind and poured from her mouth as argument.' It also highlighted how she was uncomfortable in competitive debates 'advocating morally dubious positions, like capitalism's benefits for the poor, or "things oppressed people should do about their oppression."' Later she wondered that, 'maybe I stopped debating to see if I could still think of things to say when there weren't any prizes'.[49]

---

45 https://www.youtube.com/watch?v=vzj_su8st8I.

46 *Belfast Telegraph*, 3 June 2017.

47 Correspondnece between Ursula Quill and Author.

48 Sally Rooney 'Even if you beat me,' *Dublin Review* (September 2015), https://thedublinreview.com/article/even-if-you-beat-me/.

49 *The New Yorker*, 31 July 2017.

What happened next, as *The Daily Telegraph* later reported, was that in 2016, 'shortly after embarking on a master's in American literature at Trinity College Dublin, where she had read English as an undergraduate, Rooney, then twenty-four years old, sat down at her laptop'.[50] Within 'three breakneck months, writing for ten hours a day until her eyesight went fuzzy and her head began to spin', Rooney completed 'a really rough, unreadable first draft', of what would eventually become *Conversations with Friends*, 'the story of Frances, a Trinity College student, her intense relationship with a former girlfriend and her affair with an older married man.'

A literary agent, Tracy Bohan, at the Wylie agency in London, read Rooney's essay on competitive debating and made contact, asking her what else she had written. This promoted Rooney to finish *Conversations with Friends* which according to *The Daily Telegraph* was 'sold in a seven-way auction to Faber and Faber as part of a two-book deal lucrative enough to enable Rooney to write full-time.'[51] The novel was published in May 2017, 'it was greeted with critical approval and commercial success; Rooney was hailed as the voice of her generation'. As *The New York Times* noted, Rooney was praised as 'Salinger for the Snapchat generation'.[52] The actor, Lena Denham, even tweeted, 'Sally Rooney is my fave writer working in modern fiction.'[53]

When discussing 'all the praise lavished' on the novel, *The Guardian* noted 'that it was glittering, witty, addictive, elegant, heartbreaking'[54] and hailed the follow-up *Normal People* as 'A superb evocation of a couple at Trinity College Dublin who show what it is to be young and in love', calling it 'a future classic'. In January 2019 Rooney, then twenty-seven, became the youngest novelist ever to land the Costa awards' best novel category. *The Guardian* reported that 'in one south London bookshop, the owner has put a sign in the window advising that yes, they do have copies of Sally Rooney's *Normal People,* the literary phenomenon of the year.'[55] It was

---

50 *Daily Telegraph,* 1 September 2018.

51 Ibid.

52 *New YorkTimes*, 26 April 2019.

53 Ibid.

54 *The Guardian,* 1 September 2018.

reported that 'booksellers have said they are keeping a stash behind the counter, putting them in the hands of customers before they can even blurt: "Do you"'. Sian Cain in *The Guardian* claimed that it was the first novel she had 'read that has convincingly captured what it is to be young today: often overeducated, neurotic, slightly too self-aware.' The book was nominated for the 2018 Man Booker Prize, and according to *The Bookseller*, it was the year's most critically praised book in the United Kingdom.[56] At the end of 2019 former American President, Barack Obama, listed it as one of his favourite books of the year.[57]

Today many people ask Rooney whether debating helped her as a writer and she has replied, 'I honestly don't know'.[58] She recalls that debating was 'a way for her eighteen-year-old self (the only girl from her school to go to Trinity) to achieve popularity in a new environment'. In an interview with the *Observer* in December 2018 Rooney described her debating career as 'definitely interesting', but dismissed competitive debating for being 'like a game. I was going to say like football but I think it's less intellectually involved than football. Really it's more like Scrabble.'[59] Rooney's debating skills are often in evidence in her writing, and they are often praised in the media. For example, the *Observer* interview commended 'a powerful essay' in the *London Review of Books* earlier in 2018 where 'she deployed the full might of her debating skills in articulating her rage, concluding a thorough demolition of the case against abortion'. In particular, it highlighted Rooney's powerful conclusion that 'in the relationship between foetus and woman, the woman is granted fewer rights than a corpse'.

Debating – and some of the people who are active in debating societies – is briefly mentioned in *Normal People,* published in August 2018. As *The Daily Telegraph* noted, 'Gareth, Marianne's

55 *The Guardian,* 9 January 2019.

56 *The New Yorker,* 7 January 2019.

57 https://www.irishtimes.com/culture/books/sally-rooney-s-novel-among-barack-obama-s-favourite-reads-of-2019-1.4126771.

58 *Belfast Telegraph*, 3 June 2017.

59 *Observer*, 2 December 2018.

privileged sometime boyfriend, is identified pointedly as a member of a debating society that invites a neo-Nazi to give a speech.'[60] Gareth, we learn, is in favour of 'free speech', and another character, Connell, jokes to Marianne, 'Yeah, that's good. Thank god for white moderates. As I believe Dr King once wrote.'[61] Hearing this Marianne laughs. This was directly based on Rooney's experience in Trinity. When *The Times* interviewed Rooney the journalist noted that 'talking to Sally Rooney makes you feel clever', and reported that in 'her third year she was involved in a successful campaign to stop the BNP leader at the time, Nick Griffin appearing at the debating society'.[62]

The 'debating society' in question was the Philosophical Society, which had invited Nick Griffin to take part in its debate on the motion 'This House Believes that Immigration has Gone too Far' on 20 October 2011. This prompted a backlash against The Phil and a meeting of Students Against Facism took place in Trinity on 11 October 2011. One of the speakers was Gavan Titley, who denied that the idea of stopping Griffin was a denial of freedom of speech, calling that 'a very thin understanding of freedom of expression'.[63] According to the report published online by the *University Times*, he accused The Phil of being 'a small, self-selecting members' club which had decided it's going to have its brush with controversy with no consequences for them, other than perhaps a sherry hangover'. Challenging the vagueness of the motion, Titley even questioned whether the debate was valid. In its defence, The Phil released a statement clarifying that Griffin would be speaking for ten minutes in a sixty-eight minute debate, and there would be speakers on both sides of the motion, as it called for 'a healthier discourse on campus, and one founded on truth'. The incident clearly had an impact on Rooney and in years to come literary critics will study the influence of debating on her writing career, as well as how an essay on debating helped bring her to prominence in the first place.

The Auditor for the start of the 242nd session was Liam O'Neill,

60 *Daily Telegraph*, 1 September 2018.

61 Sally Rooney, *Normal People*, (London, 2018).

62 *The Times*, 19 January 2019.

63 *University Times*, 12 October 2011.

but he resigned because of ill-health and was succeeded by the Correspondence Secretary, Ursula Ní Choill in October (and who as Ursula Quill later became Programme Director of Hist250, the plans for the 250th anniversary of the Society in 2020). The officers included John Engle as Treasurer, Ben Blunnie as Correspondence Secretary, Hannah McCarthy as Record Secretary and Sally Rooney as Censor, with Cormac McGuinness serving on the Committee. Debates that session were on topics as diverse as the Arab Spring, Abortion, the Philosopher King, Human Genetic Engineering, Julian Assange, the Irish Language, and the Travelling Community.

The Rubberbandits visited the Society on 13 December 2011, wearing plastic bags over their heads, and the *Irish Independent* reported that 'the Limerick-based hip-hop pranksters said they are no strangers to the posh halls of higher learning.'[64] The two men were reported as 'swigging from a couple of bottles of Bavaria beer and cheap white wine', and they were joined at the podium by *Hot Press* journalist Olaf Tyaransen 'who quizzed them on their success after their hit song 'Horse Outside' propelled them to fame last year'.

Dr Lobsang Sangay, the leader of the Tibetan Government-in-Exile, visited Ireland for the first time in March 2012 and was presented with the gold medal for outstanding contribution to public discourse by the Society. Accepting the award on behalf of the people of Tibet, Sangay discussed his rise from poverty and compared his story with the Tibetan struggle.[65] Entertaining the audience with stories of his election campaign in 2011 to become president, when he had travelled across five continents, he became serious when discussing the Chinese occupation of Tibet. There had been twenty-four self-immolations in Tibet since 2009 and Sangay said that while he denounced the act he believed 'Tibetans are doing so because they have no other means of calling for freedom and for the return of the Dalai Lama. When you cannot have a peaceful demonstration, or paste up posters, or have a rally – when there is no possibility for protest without the likelihood of being arrested or shot, then their only way is self-immolation.' Following the speech Sangay presented the members of the Committee with a traditional

64 *Irish Independent,* 14 December 2011.

65 *University Times*, 6 March 2012.

Tibetan scarf, before mingling with the audience and then 'leaving the building to a final rapturous applause'.

Ní Choill presented her inaugural paper on 22 February 2012 on 'A Global Approach to Feminism' and it was a brilliant synthesis of what was happening around the world with some suggestions for future progress. Discussing the impact same-sex marriage (not yet legalised in Ireland) was having on feminist discussions around marriage, and about sexual violence and consent, she noted that: 'feminism is based on empathy and solidarity and ultimately on recognising the humanity in both women and men.' Speakers on the night included Kashmiri intellectual, Dr Nitasha Kaul; historian Dr Mary McAuliffe; the director of AkidWa, Salome Mbugua; and Dr Olive Braiden. Ní Choill recalls that at the end of the evening, the chair, President David McConnell, spoke 'movingly' about what he had learned and it was a thought-provoking discussion on different and complex approaches to feminism and gender equality. Two gold medals for oratory were presented that evening. The first was to Niamh Ní Mhaoileoin, the second to Huw Duffy.

An American student, John Engle, was elected Auditor for the 243rd session and presented his inaugural paper on 'Pax Americana', a sophisticated analysis of United States foreign policy in the twenty-first century, in October 2012. Former US Secretary of Defence William Perry spoke at the meeting, and delivered a brilliant first-hand account of the times when the world had come close to nuclear annihilation, often because of accident or error.

Engle resigned as Auditor on 31 October, following a controversy over a loan to cover immigration requirements and the subsequent passing of a vote of no confidence by the Committee.[66] Hannah McCarthy was elected to succeed him and her officers included Ruth Hoey as Treasurer, John Doody as Correspondence Secretary, Cormac McGuinness as Record Secretary, and Briony Somers as Librarian, with Isobel D'Arcy the senior member of the General Commitee. International affairs featured prominently during the session with speeches by General Romeo Dallaire, the Force Commander of the UN Peacekeeping Mission to Rwanda (who criticised William Perry over the US's refusal to send troops to

66 *University Times*, 18 October 2012.

Rwanda); the Dean of Harvard Law School, Martha Minow; and Nobel Laureate and former Finnish Prime Minister, Martti Ahtisaari.

During Michaelmas term, a Hist debate on legalising abortion for any reason coincided with the publication of details of the death of Savita Halpanaver, who had died after her requests for an abortion were denied by hospital staff due to Ireland's constitutional restriction on abortion. A large crowd of pro-abortion protesters gathered outside Government Buildings on Merrion Street and around Trinity College the night of the highly charged debate at the GMB, which featured contributions from Dr William Binchy and Sally Rooney.

The second Inaugural of the 243rd session took place in Hillary Term when Hannah McCarthy delivered a highly praised paper on 'The Role of the Arts in the Twenty-first Century' in the Public Theatre. There were impressive responses from Professor Germaine Greer, Festival Director Willie White, and artist Dorothy Cross RHA. Under McCarthy's leadership the session was notable for involving more figures from the arts than in previous sessions and for recognising the role that creative figures play in public discourse. During the year the 'Burke Medal for Outstanding Contribution to Public Discourse through the Arts' was awarded to the artist Tracy Emin, the actor and comedian Eddie Izzard and the author, Sir Alexander McCall Smith. It was during this session Kate Brady won best individual speaker of the *Irish Times* Debating Competition (as we have seen) and Sally Rooney and Ian Curran won the Irish Mace.

José Manuel Barroso, the President of the European Commission, visited the Society on 28 February 2013 and two hundred students gathered to see him be awarded the medal for outstanding contribution to public discourse. Speaking first about the low turnout for European elections, Barroso expressed his belief that Britain would not leave the EU in a future referendum. There was praise for Ireland's 'long tradition of public debate' and Barroso suggested that 'the subject of Europe is not immune from that debate, nor should it be. Constructive criticism does not pose a threat ... passivism and indifference does'. Barroso noted that 'since the Hist was founded by Edmund Burke, it is perhaps only natural that any discussion on the future of the EU turns to the issue of democratic participation', before quoting Burke's line that 'in all forms of government the people is the true legislator'. Suggesting that although the European Union was complicated, Barroso said there was also a responsibility on citizens to make themselves informed about it.[67]

Michael D. Higgins returned to the Society as President of Ireland on 19 November 2013 and received the gold medal for his contribution to public discourse. This was during Cormac McGuinness's year as Auditor and Fionn McGorry in the *University Times* reported that 'the entire room was brought to its feet several times, not merely out of a sense of civic obligation, but out of real affection for the poet, sociologist, and politician that stood before us.'[68] As the *University Times* reported, the event was attended by the Provost, Patrick Prendergast, and the Senior Lecturer (Dean of Undergraduate Studies), Patrick Geoghegan, and was chaired by the President of the Society, David McConnell. At the start of his speech President Higgins referenced the many times he had visited and spoken at the Society. And he noted the significance that 'the years when this venerable Society held its first sessions, in the second half of the eighteenth century, coincided with a key moment in the development of Western aesthetic philosophy.'[69]

In a brilliant speech, President Higgins argued that 'The challenge in this beginning of the twenty-first century, is to reaffirm forcefully that the value of the arts lies primarily in the quality of depth, the intensity of vision, and the loyalty to the infinite possibilities of human imagination, that their practice can yield.' Suggesting that 'the real value of creativity lies in the exploration of how we are to live ethically together with joy and fulfilment', he ended by calling for an 'Ireland of tomorrow where economic discourse will be relocated within the wider frame of our culture, a place where among the ethical issues posed will be the important one of defending the integrity and freedom of that which can be imagined but which has not yet managed to be.'

McGorry wrote in the *University Times* that 'in the Q&A which

67 *Irish Independent*, 1 March 2013.

68 *University Times*, 21 November 2013.

69 https://president.ie/en/media-library/speeches/the-worthiness-of-the-arts-in-the-21st-century-address-to-trinity-college-h.

followed, he [the President] clearly showed that his verbosity and eloquence are not restricted to the printed page, managing to refer to theorists, books, articles and anecdotes, in answering each of the questions'. Many of the answers were self-deprecating. In answering a question on his days as a lecturer, President Higgins said his taxing lectures attracted voyeurs, as he lectured on 'Sociology of Deviant Behaviour.' When discussing how he would swap with colleagues to give lectures to students outside of his faculty, he ridiculed himself, stating "We eccentrics looked after each other'.

The Questions and Answers session ended with some uplifting words for the students. President Higgins advised them, 'Don't waste your life by entering in to something that's tired and jaded, when the whole world is out there for the taking.' As McGorry concluded in the *University Times* 'his comment was one of hope, and, of exasperation, and it is rare that students would be given the opportunity to interact with the president in such an intimate setting, one that both Higgins and the students present seemed to relish.'

There was controversy in the Society at the meeting of 5 February 2014 when members of the Committee raised the issue of sexism within the world of debating. A series of proposals were made to the Committee and were then published on Facebook. At the meeting the Auditor agreed to create a new position of Equity Officer and introduce a gender quota for a minimum of 30% female speakers at events, to be increased to 50 per cent if this was found feasible.[70]

The award-winning singer, Sinéad O'Connor, spoke to the Society in February 2014, debating the motion 'This House Believes the Catholic Church can be Salvaged'. O'Connor wrote about her appearance in the *Sunday Independent* a few days later and suggested that 'we need to rescue God from religion. We have the ability to make God's best intentions for us manifest with our own voices.'[71]

'This House Believes in a Right to Die' was debated on Wednesday 26 September 2014 in one of the first debates of the 245th session, with Michael Coleman the Auditor. Proposing the motion was Tom Curran, the partner of Marie Fleming, who had

70 *University Times*, 6 February 2014.

71 *Sunday Independent*, 23 February 2014.

died the previous year and who had campaigned to make assisted dying legal in Ireland and had taken cases to the High Court and the Supreme Court seeking recognition of a right to assisted suicide in Ireland. Curran was the Irish co-ordinator of Exit International, an organisation campaigning to make legal wider options in end-of-life care, and he argued that 'We have an obligation to die. The question is of when and how.'[72] Visibly shaking during his speech, Curran suggested that people had the right to die on their own terms, in the absence of pain and suffering.

Opposing the motion was Senator Rónán Mullen who argued for the value of palliative care and suggested that thanks to medical advances 'so much can be done to alleviate suffering'. According to the report of the debate, Mullen claimed that some people felt coerced into taking their own lives for the benefit of their families. The journalist, Ollie Donnelly, suggested that 'the night's most striking quote' belonged to a student speaker, Clare Ní Cheallaigh, who said that 'it's important for people to be able to say "I've lived my life, and I'm ready to leave'. When the motion was put to the house it was almost unanimously passed, 'with only one dissenting "Nay", coming from one of the opposition bench's speakers'.

The debate was chaired by Senator Ivana Bacik and she referenced the event in the Seanad the next day. She discussed how 'last night's student debate was instructive to me' and showed how legislators needed to 'ensure that we act with compassion to meet the needs of people with terminal illness and others whose needs are currently not being met in this country'.[73]

The award-winning film director, Ken Loach, spoke to the Society on Wednesday 12 November 2014 and he discussed his struggle to present different points of view at a time when those in power were 'ruthless in their suppression of the weak'.[74] Moving on to tell the story of why he made *The Wind That Shakes the Barley*, he dismissed Gordon Brown's claim that Britain needed to stop apologizing for the empire, saying, 'I've never heard anyone apologise for the British Empire, and it was a reign of terror.' As *Trinity News*

72 *University Times*, 1 November 2014.

73 https://www.oireachtas.ie/en/debates/debate/seanad/2018-09-27/8.

74 *Trinity News*, 14 November 2014.

reported, Loach ended his speech urging the crowd to take action: 'Our politicians will do nothing. So what do we do? The answer is we have to boycott. It's the only way.'

Membership of the Society reached 3000 in 2012 but hit 10,000 when a new four-year membership was introduced in 2015, ensuring that once students joined as freshers they were registered for the duration of their undergraduate degree. The number of active members, however, was much less. As Julia McCarthy, the Auditor for the 246th session told *The Irish Times* around fifty to one hundred attended an average debate, with up to two hundred people for the big ones.[75]

That session there were some changes, with the Committee expanded to include a new Events Convenor and other members with the rationale to provide more time for debating. That session Daire Courtney and Michael Coleman reached the World University Debating Championship quarter final in Thessaloniki and the final of the European university debating championship in Warsaw. Guests included the economist and Nobel Prize laureate Angus Deaton, author Dan Brown and actor Robert Sheehan. The students debated global capitalism, Syriza, and Brexit, the latter against Cambridge University for the Student Economic Review. The honorary members debate was 'That this House believes the Rising Deserves to be Commemorated' and brought back speakers from recent decades to debate against each other.

In advance of the 2016 general election a debate was held as a political party debate on 22 January 2016, chaired by broadcaster Gavin Jennings. Not all parties were represented, with the smaller parties excluded, and Sinn Féin and Fianna Fáil both apologising for declining the offer to attend. Speakers included Minister for Communications, Energy and Natural Resources, Alex White (Labour), the leader of Renua, Lucinda Creighton, Alan Farrell (Fine Gael), Glenna Lynch (Social Democrats), and Annette Mooney (People before Profit).[76]

The Auditor for the 247th session was Ronan Mac Giolla Rua and he presented his inaugural paper in October 2016 on 'The Future of

75 *The Irish Times*, 6 October 2015.

76 *Trinity News*, 22 Jaunary 2016.

Europe' and speakers included Ambassador of the European Union to the United States (and former Auditor), David O'Sullivan; the Executive Director of European Movement Ireland, Noelle O'Connell; Ireland's 'principal-level Brexit-negotiator' (and former officer) Rory Montgomery; as well as the Chief Economist of Friends First, Jim Power.[77] As *Trinity News* reported, O'Sullivan discussed all the benefits that Ireland had received from EU membership, and then 'went on to criticise the ineffectiveness of the EU's response to the current refugee crisis, stressing that Europe must become more tolerant towards inward migration and that the numbers seeking refuge from conflicts such as Syria's civil war are equivalent to a tiny percentage of the EU's current population'.[78] In his closing remarks, the Chairman, David McConnell, noted the Auditor's background in mathematics and said it provided a clear example that everyone, 'whatever our discipline', should interact with the pressing questions of the day through forums such as student societies.

The American singer, songwriter, photographer and poet, Patti Smith, received the gold medal for outstanding contribution to the arts on 4 November 2016, in an event that was attended by students, journalists and Bono.[79] The Auditor, Ronan Mac Giolla Rua, praised Smith for broadening 'our understanding of the world'. Smith spoke about how suffering helped us understand ourselves better as humans and 'a parallel between the lessons she learned from life and her recent visit to Reading Gaol where Oscar Wilde was imprisoned'.[80] Describing poets as 'saints', she suggested they inspired people and articulated what we cannot express. At the end, Smith decided to grant the students 'a little benediction' and performed a song that was her own tribute to Wilde.

A debate on the tactics which should be used for repeal of the 8th amendment took place on Wednesday 22 March 2017, with the motion 'That this House Supports all Forms of Civil Disobedience to Repeal the 8th Amendment'.[81] This was the final of an internal

---

77 *University Times*, 10 October 2016.

78 *Trinity News*, 11 October 2016.

79 *University Times*, 4 November 2016.

80 *University Times*, 4 November 2016.

81 *Trinity News*, 23 March 2017.

debating competition open exclusively to female and non-binary genders and was chaired by Anna Cosgrave, the founder of the Repeal Project. As *Trinity News* reported, 'because this was a competitive debate participants were unable to choose their sides in the motion and so what they said may not be representative of their views,' and the same caveat applies here (and indeed when considering anything said in a competitive debate). Catherine Kelly proposed the motion and suggested that that civil disobedience was an effective way to bring attention to the injustice of the 8th amendment. Catherine Prasifka also spoke in support of the motion and delivered what was reported as 'a passionate speech that mentioned how the state "does not have a meaningful say on the laws" when it denies women abortion.' Ríona Morris warned that civil disobedience could damage public opinion and set back the cause for a decade. The competition was won by Catherine Prasifka, with Ríona Morris the runner up.

The former British Deputy Prime Minister (and former leader of the Liberal Democrats) Nick Clegg spoke to the Society on 5 April 2017. In his speech he attacked the first past the post electoral system ('outrageous') and suggested that the British Prime Minister, Theresa May, was 'an unelected Remainer pursuing a hard Brexit strategy'.[82] Dominic McGrath, who covered the event for the *University Times,* discussed 'the sheer variety of insults he hurled at Theresa May, Michael Gove, Boris Johnson *et al*'. Denouncing those who led the UK out of the EU as 'opportunists and charlatans', Clegg discussed the 'astonishing interdependence' between Ireland and the UK.

A huge crowd gathered to try and gain entry to hear the American civil rights leader, the Reverend Al Sharpton, speak to the Society on 25 September 2017 as part of Empowerment Week in Trinity. As the *University Times* reported, 'By a quarter to seven a queue had formed as far as Front Square, as people eagerly waited in line to gain entry to the GMB.'[83] Sharpton was awarded the gold medal for outstanding contribution to public discourse, and then delivered a powerful speech in which he discussed the 'politics of regression' across the world. By this, he meant the forces who were trying to undo decades of work on

82 *University Times*, 5 April 2017.

83 *University Times*, 25 September 2017.

civil rights, and he cited as an example the way President Donald Trump had described professional athletes fighting racial injustice as 'sons of bitches'. This, argued Sharpton, was Trump attempting to 'escape his responsibilities as president'. Concluding his speech, Sharpton asked the students 'whether your generation will continue to fight or join the regressive forces?'

In the Questions and Answers session, Sharpton suggested that no matter what the odds, one should always be 'faithful and loyal to a cause'. When the discussion moved to President Trump, Sharpton advised those who disagreed with Trump's politics to 'use his unpredictability against him. Trump will beat himself if you keep him in the spotlight'. Advising the students to get involved in activism, he warned them not to confuse this with posting messages on social media. As he noted, 'you need to get people in politics who mightn't subscribe to your Instagram'. Sharpton received a standing ovation.

One of the biggest controversies in the Society's history occured that session when the Society announced in September 2017 that it was planning to award the former UK Independence Party (UKIP) leader, Nigel Farage, the Society's gold medal for outstanding contribution to public discourse in early 2018. A number of former Auditors and members of the Society objected, with some claiming that that it was one thing to invite Farage to a debate where his views on Brexit could be challenged and engaged with, it was another to present him with a gold medal for public discourse when there was such controversy over the way he had acted during the Brexit referendum in the UK in 2016. Others rejected the idea of Farage speaking at the Society as a matter of principle.

The Auditor, Paul Molloy, issued a statement on 6 October 2017 apologising for the decision to offer him the gold medal, suggesting that it was never the intention of the Society to 'endorse any particular viewpoint individuals may hold, but rather to recognise the impact which they have made which has them stand out'.[84] Denying that the invitation was an endorsement of Farage's beliefs, he insisted that 'it should not be taken as a reflection of the views of the General Committee or as an endorsement of them by the College Historical Society'.

84 *University Times*, 6 October 2017.

The controversy did not end there. On Monday 29 January 2018 the Auditor announced that Farage would be a guest at a debate at the Society that Friday. This unleashed another storm, with 23 members of the Society (including three former Auditors) issuing an open letter on Wednesday 31 January which they hoped would be read out during private business that evening. The letter denounced Farage in the strongest terms and suggested that the invitation to invite him did not represent them 'as members, or the values the Society should be promoting by giving them a platform within College, in 2018.'[85] Molloy defended the invitation in a statement, saying that the inviting of people of divergent views 'is the nature of free enquiry in a democratic society' Upholding a value of the Society going back to its foundation, Molloy suggested that 'it is by that enquiry the strength of ideas and the validity of beliefs are challenged and upheld'.

After all the controversy Farage came to the Society on Friday 2 February 2018, not to take part in a debate, but to deliver a speech and be interveiwed by *Irish Times* political editor, Pat Leahy. As Dominic McGrath reported in the *University Times*, for all the controversy about the visit the speech itself was 'remarkably dull'.[86] Dimissing the Taoiseach, Leo Varadkar, as the 'Irish Blair', and questioning where his interests really lay, Farage made the 'somewhat predicable' call for Ireland to consider its own place in the EU. Leahy was praised as 'an apt choice' of moderator, and it was noted that 'he took Farage to task point by point'. Two male audience members wore 'Make America Great Again' hats, and Farage received 'plenty of appluase throughout his speech', with critics of the visit choosing to avoid it completely. When one audience member rebuked Farage for all the lies told during the Brexit referendum, Farage shot back, 'You're quite right to talk about lies. Fifty years of them.' Towards the end of the meeting Farage claimed that he had done more 'than any politician since 1945 to destroy the far-right in Britain', something McGrath recognized was 'a lie, of course', before concluding that 'Farage's brand of nationalism has become all too predicable'.

85 *University Times*, 31 January 2018.

86 http://www.universitytimes.ie/2018/02/farage-asks-ireland-to-consider-its-eu-future/.

A week later, on 9 February 2018, former British Chancellor of the Exchequer, and noted pro-European, Kenneth Clarke, received the gold medal for outstanding contribution to political discourse, in an event that was much less controversial. Clarke directly addressed the visit of Farage in his speech from the chair and, as Simon Foy, noted in *The University Times,* the event was 'as surely as close to the antithesis of that speech given by Nigel Farage as one could find.'[87] He described Brexit as the event which had 'shattered the political situation in Britain' and described the political malaise which had followed the referendum as having 'caused quite the biggest shambles I have seen in my political life'. Stating that he believed in 'parliamentary democracy', he said he hoped he would never 'see another referendum again in my lifetime'.

Two weeks before the Society' AGM, on 20 March 2018 Molloy announced that he was stepping down as Audior citing personal reasons. Thanking his Committee for their efforts, he said the Society 'had performed well, even under difficult circumstances'.[88] The next night, Wednesday 21 March 2018, was the honorary members debate on the motion, 'This House would Pull the Lever,' a debate on Philippa Foot's trolley problem, which asks the question is it ethical to kill one person in order to save five.[89] Former Librarian of the Society, Ross Hinds, proposed the motion, and *Trinity News* reported that his reference to the 'Emperor's New Clothes to reflect the falsity of certainty in situations of human experience was thought-provoking'. Also speaking was former Auditor, John Smith (whose 'toy train related stories truly tickled the audience'), and Senator David Norris and Catherine Prasifka. The report concluded by noting that 'if the passion amongst those present tonight is anything to go by, The Hist shall remain omnipresent within college life long after these celebrations' [the 250th] conclusion'.

Catherine Kelly was elected Auditor for the 249th session. Highlights of the year included the talented actor, Natalie Dormer,

87 http://www.universitytimes.ie/2018/02/ken-clarke-is-sick-of-brexit/.

88 http://www.universitytimes.ie/2018/03/molloy-steps-down-as-hist-auditor/.

89 *Trinity News,* 22 March 2018.

receiving the Burke Medal for outstanding contribution to the arts on 6 December 2018. Renowned for her work as Anne Boleyn in *The Tudors* and as Margaery Tyrell in *Game of Thrones,* as well as for her stage and screen work, Dormer delivered a speech, described in *Trinity News* as 'an effective ode to the arts and their importance and significance in technological modern times'. Reminiscing about her childhood, Dormer recalled 'submerging herself with stories ... I often found myself moved to tears, and adults telling me to stop being silly because the actors were only pretending.' However, she believed that behind the pretence was a deeper truth: 'they were authentic, and therefore cathartic.' When introducing the speaker, the Auditor, Catherine Kelly, 'talked about the society's history and notable alumni, emphasizing its never-ending dedication and interest in contributing to political discourse'.

#MeToo was debated on Wednesday 13 February 2019 with a debate chaired by former Labour Minister, Joan Burton TD. The motion was 'That this House Believes that the #MeToo Movement is Succeeding'. The debate was opened by Senator Ivana Bacik who argued that 'although "there's still a huge amount left to do", #MeToo has effectively "highlighted the hugely pervasive nature of sexual harassment" and drawn attention to a "power imbalance in society"'.[90] As Gráinne Sexton reported in *Trinity News,* Bacik 'concluded by reminding the audience that there has been "very visible change due to the #MeToo movement in Ireland", affirming this with reference to a 10 per cent rise in the reportage of sexual offence allegations to the Gardaí from 2017 to 2018.'

Taryn de Vere, a journalist for Her.ie and advocate for victims of sexual and domestic abuse, 'highlighted the power of #MeToo to unify the voices of millions of victims due to its accessibility for "anyone who has an internet connection"'. The Auditor, Catherine Kelly, closed the case for the proposition and emphasised 'the importance of the #MeToo movement in creating space for empathetic dialogue around issues of sexual violence'. The motion passed with a strong majority in favour. Speaking from the chair, Joan Burton said that 'Ireland is a better place for debates like this tonight'. Senator Bacik discussed the debate in the Seanad the next

90 *Trinity News,* 15 February 2019.

day, and noted that it 'was quite chilling to hear about the levels of sexual harassment the young women speakers had experienced. They are continuing to experience harassment, even with the #MeToo movement and despite there being greater awareness.'[91]

Luke Fehily was elected Auditor for the 250th session, with much of the focus of the year on the series of events planned for March 2020 to mark the historic anniversary. The artist Mick O'Dea was commissioned to do a number of paintings of distinguished former members: Mary Harney, Conor Cruise O'Brien, Owen Sheehy Skeffington, Frederick Boland and Jaja Wachuku. These paintings will be part of the legacy of Hist250, and will be on display in the newly refurbished Conversation Room. A week long series of events will take place in March 2020, beginning with the final of the Edmund Burke International Debate. The Hist250 group also worked with Mary Robinson on an event about Development and Climate Change, with former Auditor Jamie Walsh on an event on the Future of Capitalism, and with former Auditor, David O'Sullivan, on an event about the Future of Europe, with many national and international figures agreeing to come to the Society. An exhibition will also take place in the Long Room, paying tribute to the Society's role within national life over the previous 250 years.

The quality of debates remained high, and were available to a global audience, thanks to the innovation introduced in 2009 of live-streaming most of the meetings and then putting them on YouTube. Notable meetings in the 250th session included one involving former medalists of the Society debating 'This House Supports Violent Protest in Hong Kong' (2 October 2019), 'This House supports a Sex Strike' (9 October 2019), and the Oxford Corresponding Debate on the motion 'This House Would Elect Politicians by Lottery' (20 November 2019). Fehily's inaugural paper was presented on 30 October 2019 on 'Leadership in Crisis' and was a sophisticated analysis of the challenges facing Ireland and the world in the new century, and was ably responded to by former figures from the Society's past, including Adrian Langan and Rory Montgomery.

On 6 December 2019 Mary Harney was awarded an honourary doctorate by the University of Dublin, and it was presented by the

91 https://www.oireachtas.ie/en/debates/debate/seanad/2019-02-14/10.

new Chancellor, Mary McAleese, in her first official function since her election. The citation, delivered brilliantly by the Public Orator for the University of Dublin, Professor Anna Chahoud, paid tribute to Harney's considerable contribution to political life, as well as to education, including her role in the foundation of Science Foundation Ireland. The centrality of the Hist in the citation was notable. It recognized that the Society 'will soon celebrate 250 years of fearless promotion of new ideas, of respectful debate about crucial social issues, of strenuous advocacy for a democratic society'.[92] Harney's 'message to the new generations' was quoted. She had once said that 'whatever our profession, we must be aware of our responsibility: never be complacent about what is right and wrong. The country needs people who question and challenge the status quo, who are prepared to pursue causes, whether popular or unpopular.' This inspiring message, the Public Orator, said, was 'a founding principle of the Hist'. Quoting 'one of our notable historians', she noted that it has always been 'an instrument for the Enlightenment in Ireland'. The Society was also praised as being 'at the forefront of intellectual thought in the country'. The recognition of the contribution to public life of the first female Auditor of the Hist, in the 250th anniversary of the foundation of the Society, was an appropriate tribute to both.

Now 250 years from its foundation the Society is in a strong place. The turmoil of previous years has largely disappeared, with the Hist more certain of itself and its place within Trinity and within Irish society. The truth is that every session of the Society over its long history had its challenges as well as its triumphs, and it was how the members responded to the problems it faced that defined it in each new generation, as well as shaping those who were involved with it. Always informative, often entertaining, even if at times contradictory and infuriating, the Society continues to challenge old thinking while providing a safe forum for intellectual debate and a diversity of ideas. Over 250 years it has embraced change while protecting the best of its own traditions. To some, it represents something elitist and out-dated in a modern university. To those who recognise what it represents, it is an integral part of what a

92 My thanks to the Public Orator, Professor Anna Chahoud.

university is all about. With the rise of populism, and examples around the world of the truth being distorted and public debate coarsened, there needs to be places where students are inspired to be fearless in the search for the truth. The College Historical Society continues to promote oratory and encourage debate in defence of the democratic principle and in the service of society. In the twenty-first century these are things that are needed in the world now more than ever.

BIBLIOGRAPHY

PRIMARY SOURCES

Manuscript Sources.
Trinity College Dublin

MUN/SOC/HIST 1-112. Records of the College Historical Society, 1770-1999 and the Records of Edmund Burke's Club, 1747.

MUN/SOC/HIST Uncatalogued Papers. Records of the College Historical Society, 1901-2020. [Includes correspondence and materials collected by the author].

National Archives (London)

War Office 339/13046. British Expeditionary Force, 1919.

PRINTED AND ONLINE SOURCES

Parliamentary Records and Debates

Goold, Thomas. *Speech of Thomas Goold on* 14 *February* 1800. Dublin, 1800.

Hansard [https://hansard.parliament.uk].
Oireachtas Debates [www.oireachtas.ie].
Parliamentary Register of Ireland (Dublin, 1793).
Speeches of the Taoiseach and Ministers. [www.meerrionstreet.ie]
Speeches of the Irish President. [www.president.ie]

II. NEWSPAPERS AND PERIODICALS

Belfast Telegraph
Bentley's Miscellany
The Contemporary Review
Cork Examiner
Daily Express [Dublin]
The Dublin Inquisitor
Dublin Historical Record
Dublin University Magazine

Evening Herald
Freeman's Journal,
Frontline
The Guardian
History Ireland
Irish Examiner
Irish Independent
The Irish Law Times and Solicitors' Journal
The Irish Times
Life
London and Dublin Magazine
Morning Chronicle,
Nation
New Commonwealth
The New York Times
The New Yorker
The Niger Times
Northern Irish Legal Quarterly
Oxford Magazine
Oxford Review
St Stephen's
The Strand Magazine
Sunday Business Post
The Sunday Independent
Sunday Times
Tait's Edinburgh Magazine
TCD Miscellany.
Time
The Times
Trinity News,
Trinity Today
The Wall Street Journal,
United Irishmen
University Times

III. DIARIES, MEMOIRS, NOVELS AND CORRESPONDENCE

Anyoku, Emeka, *The Missing Headlines: Selected Speeches.* Liverpool, 1997.

Croker, John Wilson. *Crokeriana, or Familiar Epistles.* Dublin, 1818.

Ewald, Alexander Charles (ed.). *The Life and Letters of the Right Honourable Sir Joseph Napier, Baronet.* London, 1892.

Graves, Robert Perceval. *Life of Sir William Rowan Hamilton.* 3 vols, Dublin, 1882-89.

Hardy, Francis. *Memoirs of the Political and Private Life of James Caulfield, Earl of Charlemont.* 2 vols, London, 1810.

Houston, Arthur (ed.). *Daniel O'Connell: his Early Life, and Journal, 1795-1802.* London, 1906.

[Lecky, Elisabeth]. *A Memoir of the Right Hon. William Edward Hartpole Lecky, by his Wife.* London, 1903.

Le Fanu, Joseph Sheridan. *A Debt of Honour.* London, 2012.

MacDonell, John Cotter (ed.). *The Life and Correspondence of William Connor Magee Archbishop of York Bishop of Peterborough.* 2 vols, London, 1896.

O'Donnell, W.H. and Archibald, D.N. (eds). *The Collected Works of W.B. Yeats. Vol. 3. Autobiographies.* New York 1999.

[O'Sullivan, Samuel]. *College Recollections.* Dublin, 1825.

Plunket, David (ed.). *Life, Letters and Speeches of Lord Plunket.* 2 vols, London, 1867. Reeve, Henry (ed.). *The Greville Memoirs.* 3 vols, London, 1875.

Rooney, Sally, *Normal People.* London, 2018.

Samuels, A.P.I (ed.). *The Early Life, Correspondence and Writings of Edmund Burke : With a Transcript of the Minute Book of the Debating "Club" founded by him in Trinity College Dublin.* Cambridge, 1923.

Tone, William Theobald Wolfe (ed.). *Memoirs of Theobald Wolfe Tone.* London, 1827.

IV. CONTEMPORARY AND NEAR-CONTEMPORARY WORKS AND DESCRIPTIONS

Anderson, Robert. *Sidelights on the Home Rule Movement.* New York, 1906.

——*The Lighter Side of My Official Life.* London, 1910.

Budd, Declan and Hinds, Ross. *The Hist, and Edmund Burke's Club.* Dublin, 1997.

Burke, Oliver J. *Anecdotes of the Connaught Circuit.* Dublin, 1885.

Butt, Isaac. *An Address Delivered before the College Historical Society on the Evening of Monday 24 June 1833.* Dublin, 1833.

Curry, William. *The Picture of Dublin, or Stranger's Guide to the Irish metropolis.* Dublin, 1843.

Caball, Marc and Ford, David F. (eds). *Musics of Belonging: The Poetry of Michael O'Siadhail.* Dublin, 2007.

Campbell, Richard S.D. *'Ireland's Mission'.* Dublin, 1875.

Churchill, Winston. *Lord Randolph Churchill.* 2 vols, London, 1906.

Cochrane, John. *An Address delivered before the College Historical Society on 24 June 1836.* Dublin, 1836.

Gilfillan, Kathy (ed.). *Trinity Tales: Trinity College Dublin in the Seventies.* Dublin, 2011.

Heron, Denis Caulfield. *An Address Delivered Before the College Historical Society in the Dining Hall, Trinity College, on the First Night of the Fourth Session, 4 November 1846.* Dublin, 1846.

Lunn, H.S. *Chapters from My Life.* London, 1918.

Mackey, Herbert (ed.). *The Crime against Europe: the Writings and Poetry of Roger Casement.* Dublin, 1958.

Madden, R.R. *The United Irishmen: their Lives and Times.* 2nd series, 2 vols, London, 1843.

McGuinness, Katy (ed.). *Trinity Tales: Trinity College Dublin in the Eighties.* Dublin, 2014.

Napier, Joseph. *Address Delivered before the Dublin Historical and Literary Society on the Evening of the 21st of June 1828.* Dublin, 1828.

—— *Address Delivered at the Close of the Proceedings of the College Historical Society, 29 November 1855.* Dublin, 1855.

—— *The Lectures, Essays and Letters.* Dublin, 1888.

Norris, David. *A Kick against the Pricks: the Autobiography.* Dublin, 2013.

O'Brien, Conor Cruise. *Memoir: my Life and Themes.* Dublin, 1999.

O'Siadhail, Micheal. 'Facing each other'. In Greggs, Tom, Muers, Rachel and Zahl, Simeon (eds). *The Vocation of Theology Today: A Festschrift for David Ford*. Eugene, OR, 2013.

Phillips, Charles. *Specimens of Irish Eloquence*. London, 1819.

—— *Curran and his Contemporaries*. London, 1850.

Revington, Joe. 'Irish Life and Lore Oral History'. (www.irishlifeandlore.com).

Roche, Cecil. *Federalism: the Suppressed Address to the College Historical Society*. Dublin, 1873.

Rooney, Sally. 'Even if you beat me', *Dublin Review* (September 2015). https://thedublinreview.com/article/even-if-you-beat-me/

Savage, M. W. (ed.). *Sketches, Legal and Political by the late Right Honourable Richard Lalor Sheil*. 2 vols, London, 1855.

Taylor, W.B.S. *History of the University of Dublin*. Dublin, 1819.

Wachuku, Jaja et al. *Africa: the Political Pattern*. Toronto, 1961.

Walsh, John Edward. *Sketches of Ireland Sixty Years Ago*. Dublin, 1847.

Walsh, Robert. *Address Delivered in the Dining Hall of Trinity College on the 9 November 1864*. Dublin, 1864.

White, Terence de Vere. *A Fretful Midge*. London, 1957.

Yeats, Michael B. *Cast a Cold Eye: Memories of a Poet's Son and Politician*. Dublin, 1998.

SECONDARY SOURCES

Aldous, Richard (ed.). *Great Irish Speeches*. London, 2007.

Alayande, Lanre. *Our Rainmaker*. New York, 2010.

Atkinson, N.D. 'Sir Laurence Parsons, 2nd Earl of Rosse, 1758–1841'. Unpublished Ph.D. thesis, University of Dublin, 1961.

Auchmuty, James J. *Sir Thomas Wyse, 1791-1862: the Life and Career of an Educator*. London, 1939.

Baldwin, Neil. *Henry Ford and the Jews: The Mass Production of Hate*. New York, 2001.

Barnard, Toby. *A New Anatomy of Ireland: the Irish Protestants, 1649–1770*. New Haven, 2003.

Bartlett, Thomas. *The Fall and Rise of the Irish nation: the Catholic Question 1690–1830*. Dublin, 1992.

—— *Ireland : a History*. Cambridge, 2011.

Bartlett, Thomas, Kelly, James, Ohlmeyer, Jane, and Smith, Brendan (eds). *The Cambridge History of Ireland*. 4 vols. Cambridge, 2018.

Bew, John. *Clement Attlee: the Man who Made Modern Britain*. New York, 2017.

Bew, Paul. *Ireland, the Politics of Enmity, 1789-2006*. Oxford, 2013.

Blackwell, Leslie. *Of Judges and Justice*. Cape Town, 1965.

Bailey, K.C. *A History of Trinity College Dublin, 1892-1945*. Dublin, 1947.

Blamires, Harry. *The New Bloomsday book: a Guide through Ulysses*. London, 1996.

Bourke, Richard and McBride, Ian (eds). *The Princeton History of Modern Ireland*. Princeton, 2017.

Bourke, Richard. *Empire & Revolution : the Political Life of Edmund Burke*. Princeton, 2018.

Bowen, Zach. *Ulysses as a Comic Novel*. Syracuse, 1989.

Boyle, Peter. *Trinity College Dublin: The Provosts, 1592-1927*. Dublin, 2015.

Broun, K. S. *Saving Nelson Mandela*. Oxford, 2012.

Brown, Terence. *Ireland: Social and Cultural History, 1922-2002*. London, 2004.

Dagg, T.S.C. *College Historical Society: A History (1770-1920)*. Tralee, 1969.

Daly, Dominic. *The Young Douglas Hyde*. Ottawa, 1974.

Davison, Neil R. *James Joyce, Ulysses and the Construction of Jewish Identity*. Cambridge, 1998.

Diemont, Marius. *Brushes with the Law*. Cape Town, 1995.

Dunleavy, J.E. and Dunleavy, G.W. *Douglas Hyde: a Maker of Modern Ireland*. Los Angeles, 1981.

Dunne, Tom. *The Writer as Witness: Literature as Historical Evidence*. Cork, 1987.

Dutton, K.R., *Auchmuty: The life of James Johnston Auchmuty*. Brisbane, 2000.

Elliott, Marianne, *Robert Emmet: the Making of a Legend*. London, 2003.

—— *Wolfe Tone*, 2nd edition. Liverpool, 2012.

El Mahmud-Okereke, N. Enuma. *OUA, Time to Admit South Africa*. Abuja, 1983.

English, Richard. *Irish Freedom: a History of Nationalism in Ireland*. London, 2007.

Escott, T.H.S. *Social Transformations in the Victorian Age*. London, 1897.

Erzgraber, Willi. *James Joyce: Oral and Written Discourse as Mirrored in Experimental Narrative Art*. London, 2002.

Fahlbusch, Michael and Haar, Ingo (eds). *German Scholars and Ethnic Cleansing, 1919-1945*. New York, 2005.

Ferriter, Diarmaid. *The Transformation of Ireland, 1900-2000*. London, 2004.

—— *Occasions of Sin : Sex and Society in Modern Ireland*. London, 2012.

—— *Ambiguous Republic : Ireland in the 1970s*. London, 2013.

Fitzpatrick, David. *The Two Irelands, 1912-1939*. Oxford, 1998.

Foster, R.F. *Lord Randolph Churchill: A Political Life*. Oxford, 1981.

—— *Modern Ireland 1600–1972*. 2nd edn., London, 1989.

—— *W.B. Yeats*. 2 vols, Oxford 1997-98.

—— 'The Cruiser: Conor Cruise O'Brien (1917-2008): A Tribute to Ireland's Greatest Modern Public Intellectual', *Standpoint* (February 2009).

Garvin, John. *James Joyce's Disunited Kingdom and the Irish Dimension*. Dublin, 1976.

Gaughan, J. Anthony. *Alfred O'Rahilly*. Dublin, 1992.

Geoghegan, P.M. *Robert Emmet: a Life*. 2nd edition, Dublin, 2003.

—— *King Dan: the Rise of Daniel O'Connell*. Dublin, 2008.

Gifford, Don and Seidman, R.J. *Ulysses Annotated*. London, 1974.

Howard, T.L. et al. *Society Ties : a history of the Jefferson Society and Student Life at the University of Virginia*. Virginia, 2017.

Hughes, William. *Beyond Dracula: Bram Stoker's fiction and its Cultural Context*. New York, 2000.

Hyde, H.M. *Carson: the Life of Sir Edward Carson*. London, 1953.

Irish, Tomás. *Trinity in War and Revolution, 1912-1923.* Dublin, 2015.

Jackson, Alvin. *Ireland 1798-1998: Politics and War.* London, 1999.

—— *Sir Edward Carson.* Dublin, 2010.

Jackson, Alvin (ed.). *Oxford Handbook of Modern Irish History.* Oxford, 2017.

Kenny, Kevin (ed.). *Ireland and the British Empire*. Oxford, 2004.

Knowlson, James. *Damned to Fame: the Life of Samuel Beckett*. London, 2014.

Lee, J.J. *Ireland,* 1912-1984. Cambridge, 1987.

Lawrence, Jean St Leger. *Coming Home to Roost.* Cape Town, 1986.

Lock, F.P. *Edmund Burke: Volume 1, 1730-1784.* Oxford, 1999.

Lyons, F.S.L. *Culture and Anarchy in Ireland, 1890-1930.* Oxford, 1979.

Martin, F.X. *The Scholar Revolutionary: Eoin MacNeill, 1867-1945, and the Making of the New Ireland.* Dublin, 1973.

McBride, Ian. *Eighteenth-Century Ireland : the Isle of Slaves*. Dublin, 2014.

McCormack, W.J. *Blood Kindred: W.B. Yeats, the Life, the Death, the Politics.* London, 2005.

McDowell, R.B. *Irish Public Opinion 1750–1800.* London, 1943.

McDowell, R.B. and Webb, D.A.. *Trinity College Dublin, 1592-1952: an Academic History.* Cambridge, 1982.

McGing, Brian. *Polybius' Histories.* Oxford, 2010.

McMahon, Bryan. *Ascend or Die: Richard Crosbie, Pioneer of Balloon Flight.* Dublin, 2010.

Meisel, J.S. *Public Speech and the Culture of Public Life in the Age of Gladstone*. New York, 2001.

Moody, T.W. and Vaughan, W.E. (eds.). *A New History of Ireland,* vol. IV: *Eighteenth-Century Ireland, 1691–1800.* Oxford, 1986.

Mulvey, Helen. *Thomas Davis and Ireland: a Biographical Study.* Washington D.C., 2003.

Murphy, Brian, O'Rourke, Mary and Whelan, Noel (eds). *Brian Lenihan: in Calm and Crisis*. Dublin, 2014.

Nwadinigwe, Patrick J.O. *Umu-Nshi Royal Stool from 558 BC to Date.* Awka, 2000.

Brendan Ó Caothair, *John Blake Dillon: Young Irelander* (Dublin, 1990).

O'Connor, T.P. *The Home Rule Movement.* New York, 1891.

Onose, So. 'A Great Future Behind Him: John F. Taylor's Speech in "Aeolus" Revisited'. In *A Long the Kommerun: Selected Papers from the Utrecht James Joyce Symposium.* London, 2016.

Osteen, Mark. *The Economy of Ulysses: Making Both Ends Meet.* Syracuse, 1995.

Parkinson, Stephen. *Arena of Ambition : a History of the Cambridge Union.* Thriplow, 2009.

Pearse, Edward. *Golden Talking Shop: the Oxford Union Debates, Empire, World War, Revolution, and Women.* Oxford, 2018.

Paterson, Henry. *Ireland since* 1939. London, 2006.

Rafferty, Oliver (ed.). *Irish Catholic Identities.* Manchester, 2013.

Sheehy Skeffington, Andrée. *Skeff: A Life of Owen Sheehy Skeffington 1909-1970.* Dublin, 1991.

Sommerville, Edith and Ross, Martin. *An Incorruptible Irishman: Being an Account of Chief Justice Charles Kendal Bushe and his Wife, Nancy Crampton, and their Times, 1767-1843.* London, 1932.

Sterling, Claire. *The Masaryk Case.* New York, 1969.

Story, N.R. *The Dracula Secrets: Jack the Ripper and the Darkest Sources of Bram Stoker.* Stroud, 2010.

Quinn, James. *Young Ireland and the Writing of History.* Dublin, 2015.

Vaughan, W.E. (ed.). *A New History of Ireland, vol.* V*: Ireland under the Union, I, 1801–70.* Oxford, 1989.

—— *A New History of Ireland, vol.* VI*: Ireland under the Union, II, 1870–1921.* Oxford, 1996.

White, Terence de Vere. *The Road of Excess.* Dublin 1946.

—— 'Social Life in Ireland, 1927-1937'. In *Studies* (1965), vol. 54.

Whitelaw, Nancy. *Bram Stoker: Author of Dracula.* Greensboro, 1998.

Wicht, Wolfgang. *Utopianism in James Joyce's Ulysses.* Heidelberg, 2000).

Winks, R.W. et (eds). *The Oxford History of the British Empire.* 5 vols., Oxford, 2001.

BIOGRAPHICAL DICTIONARIES AND REFERENCE WORKS

Uwechue, Raph. *Africa's Who's Who.* London, 1991.

Biographical Legacy and Research Foundation. *Who's Who in Nigeria.* https://blerf.org.

Johnston-Liik, Edith Mary (ed.). *History of the Irish Parliament, 1692-1800.* 6 vols, Belfast, 2002.

Matthew, Colin and Harrison, Brian (eds). *Oxford Dictionary of National Biography.* 60 volumes. Oxford, 2004. www.oxforddnb.com.

McGuire, James and Quinn, James (eds). *Dictionary of Irish Biography.* 11 volumes. Cambridge, 2009-2019. dib.cambridge.org.

De Kock, W.J. (ed.). *Dictionary of South African Biography.* Pretoria, 1968-1987.

INDEX

MARY HARNEY
by Mick O'Dea RHA